REPASO

A Complete Review Workbook for Grammar, Communication, and Culture

Printed on recyclable paper

National Textbook Company
a division of NTC/Contemporary Publishing Company
Lincolnwood, Illinois USA

Photo credits:

UPPER LEFT AND SPINE: **Juan Kattán-Ibarra,** *Colonia de San Ángel; México, D.F.*

BOTTOM RIGHT: **Carl Purcell,** *Plaza Mayor; Madrid, España*

Published by National Textbook Company, a division of NTC/Contemporary Publishing Company.

Manufactured in the United States of America.

7 8 9 0 VL 9 8 7 6 5 4

PREFACE

Repaso—A Complete Review Workbook for Grammar, Communication, and Culture is designed to provide intermediate through advanced learners of Spanish with a powerful tool for review and progress in Spanish. *Repaso* presents clear, concise, and well-organized **grammar explanations** with examples that reflect everyday usage, most often in the format of conversational exchanges. These presentations of structure are easy to understand and the examples encourage readers to see the study of grammar as a stepping stone to communication. Learners are helped in their study by the straightforward format of *Repaso,* by the ample space provided to write answers, and by the side-of-page referencing of the chapter topic.

The **exercises** of *Repaso* provide practice with all the grammar topics that learners of Spanish at this level should know. These engaging **exercises** are contextualized and the instructions in Spanish help set the scene and prepare the student for the task at hand. **Vocabulary boxes** provide a review of the vocabulary common to most first- and second-year Spanish textbooks, as well as additional vocabulary that enhances the students' ability to express themselves on a variety of topics. Vocabulary presentations are grouped by topic and are integrated with the exercises. Many self-expression exercises are also included to encourage users to use the grammar and vocabulary presented to express their own ideas. A comprehensive **final examination** of grammar topics is presented so users can assess their progress and prepare for examinations and competitions. *Repaso* also contains verb charts and an end-vocabulary list containing all the words and expressions used in the exercises and the culture chapters.

Most lessons of *Repaso* have an **Ejercicio oral,** which gives an alternative opportunity for communicative expression. This oral exercise is followed in most chapters by a section called **Estructuras en acción,** a comprehension exercise based on the reading of authentic documents reproduced in the book, containing examples of the grammar topic of the chapter in an authentic context. Users of *Repaso* will greatly increase their oral and written mastery of structure and vocabulary as they work through these delightful and informative authentic Spanish language materials taken from a variety of Spanish-language newspapers, periodicals, and advertisements. To further learner progress, *Repaso* contains a chapter of ***Idioms, Expressions, & Proverbs*** (Chapter 26) and a chapter that aims at helping eliminate some of the most common errors made by English-speaking learners of Spanish, ***¡Ojo! Common Errors & Pitfalls*** (Chapter 28).

Repaso features **Notas culturales** in all lessons. These cultural notes enhance the effectiveness of the grammar exercises by allowing practice to be situated in an authentic Hispanic context and by providing a communicative motivation to work toward mastery of Spanish.

Repaso is organized into twenty-eight grammar chapters and seven culture chapters. The culture chapters furnish connected prose readings about the Spanish language and the geography, history, and literature of Spain and Spanish America. These chapters include the latest developments and information in each area and are written clearly and engagingly in order to encourage students to read Spanish for comprehension. Each culture chapter is followed by a self-test.

Repaso bridges grammar practice and communication by emphasizing culture and authentic language use along with structural exercises. It is a uniquely integrated and engaging review book that will provide learners with the solid knowledge needed to increase their confidence in using Spanish to express their own thoughts, to comprehend those of Spanish-speakers, and to communicate in both speaking and writing in a wide variety of contexts.

CONTENTS

Part One: Verbs—Forms and Uses

Part Five: Hispanic Culture

PART ONE

Verbs—Forms and Uses

CHAPTER 1

THE PRESENT TENSE

A *The present tense of regular* -ar, -er, *and* -ir *verbs*

- All Spanish verbs belong to one of three different classes, or conjugations, according to the ending of the infinitive, the verb form ending in **-ar, -er,** or **-ir**:
  - first conjugation (**-ar**) verbs like **hablar** (*to speak*)
  - second conjugation (**-er**) verbs like **aprender** (*to learn*)
  - third conjugation (**-ir**) verbs like **escribir** (*to write*)
- Each conjugation has its own set of endings that are added to the stem for the different persons of the verb. Verbs conjugated according to the patterns below are called *regular* verbs.
- Verbs of the first conjugation (**-ar** verbs) are conjugated like **hablar** (*to speak*):

	singular	*plural*
first person	**yo** hablo	**nosotros** habl**amos**
second person	**tú** hablas	**vosotros** habláis
third person	**él** **ella** **Ud.** } habla	**ellos** **ellas** **Uds.** } hablan

- Verbs of the second conjugation (**-er** verbs) are conjugated like **aprender** (*to learn*):

	singular	*plural*
first person	**yo** aprendo	**nosotros** aprend**emos**
second person	**tú** aprendes	**vosotros** aprendéis
third person	**él** **ella** **Ud.** } aprende	**ellos** **ellas** **Uds.** } aprenden

- Verbs of the third conjugation (**-ir** verbs) are conjugated like **escribir** (*to write*):

	singular	*plural*
first person	**yo** escribo	**nosotros** escrib**imos**
second person	**tú** escribes	**vosotros** escribís
third person	**él** **ella** **Ud.** } escribe	**ellos** **ellas** **Uds.** } escriben

Notes:

1. Verbs of the first conjugation (**-ar**) and the second conjugation (**-er**) are conjugated alike with the difference that **-ar** verbs have **-a-** in all endings except the *yo* form and **-er** verbs have **-e-** in all endings except the *yo* form.
2. Verbs of the third conjugation (**-ir**) have **-i-** in the endings for *nosotros* and *vosotros*. The other persons are the same as the second conjugation (**-er**).

B *Uses of the present tense*

- The present tense forms of Spanish verbs express both the English simple present (*I walk*) and the English present progressive (*I'm walking*):

Tocas el piano.	***You play** the piano.* ***You're playing** the piano.*
¿**Comen** Uds. torta?	***Do you eat** cake?* ***Are you eating** cake?*

- Questions can be formed in Spanish by inverting the subject and the verb or by changing intonation:

¿**Trabajan** Uds. aquí? ¿Uds. **trabajan** aquí?	*Do you work here?*

- The present tense can be used to ask for instructions:

¿**Hablamos** del tema ahora?	***Shall we talk** about the topic now?*
¿**Entrego** el informe?	***Shall I hand in** the report?*

- The present tense can refer to the future if another element of the sentence expresses future time. English often uses the present progressive to indicate future time:

Mando la carta mañana.	***I'll send** the letter tomorrow.*
Vera **cena** conmigo el viernes.	*Vera's **having dinner** with me on Friday.*

- The construction **hace** + *expression of time* + **que** + *verb in the present tense* is used to designate actions that began in the past but that continue into the present. The question form of this construction is **¿Cuánto tiempo hace que ...?** The word **tiempo** is optional:

—**¿Cuánto (tiempo) hace que viven** en esta casa?	***How long have you been living** in this house?*
—**Hace ocho años que vivimos** aquí.	***We've been living** here **for eight years.***

- **Hace** + *expression of time* may also appear at the end of the sentence; **que** is omitted in this case:

Vivimos aquí **hace ocho años.**	*We've been living here **for eight years.***

- Another construction used to designate actions that began in the past and continue into the present is *verb in present tense* + **desde hace** + *expression of time.* To form a question, **¿Desde cuándo ...?** is used:

—**¿Desde cuándo** buscas trabajo?	***How long** have you been looking for a job?*
—Busco trabajo **desde hace un mes.**	*I've been looking for a job **for a month.***

Some common **-ar** verbs:

aceptar *to accept*
acompañar *to go with, accompany*
aconsejar *to advise*
ahorrar *to save*
alquilar *to rent*
apagar *to turn off, shut off*
arreglar *to arrange, fix up*
aumentar *to increase*
averiguar *to find out*
ayudar *to help*
bailar *to dance*
bajar *to go down, lower, turn down*
besar *to kiss*
borrar *to erase*
buscar *to look for*
cambiar *to change*
caminar *to walk*
cantar *to sing*
celebrar *to celebrate*
cenar *to have dinner*
cocinar *to cook*
colocar *to put, place*
comprar *to buy*
contestar *to answer*
cortar *to cut*
cruzar *to cross*
dejar *to let, leave*
desear *to want*
dibujar *to draw*
disfrutar *to enjoy*
doblar *to turn (change direction)*
durar *to last*
echar *to throw*
empujar *to push*
entrar *to go/come in, enter*
entregar *to hand in/over*
escuchar *to listen (to)*
esperar *to wait, hope, expect*
esquiar *to ski*
estacionar *to park*
estudiar *to study*
explicar *to explain*
felicitar *to congratulate*
firmar *to sign*
ganar *to earn, win*
gastar *to spend, waste*
grabar *to record*
gritar *to shout*
hablar *to speak*
invitar *to invite*
llamar *to call*
llegar *to arrive*
llevar *to carry, wear*
llorar *to cry*
mandar *to send, order*
manejar *to drive*
marcar *to dial, mark*
mirar *to look at*
nadar *to swim*
necesitar *to need*
pagar *to pay*
parar *to stop*
pasar *to spend (time), pass*
patinar *to skate*
pintar *to paint*
practicar *to practice*
preguntar *to ask (a question)*
preparar *to prepare*
presentar *to present, introduce*
quitar *to take away*
regresar *to come back, return*
repasar *to review*
sacar *to take out*
saludar *to greet*
tardar *to be late*
terminar *to finish, end*
tirar *to throw*
tocar *to play a musical instrument, touch*
tomar *to take, drink*
trabajar *to work*
trotar *to jog*
usar *to use, wear*
viajar *to travel*

Some common **-er** verbs:

aprender *to learn*
beber *to drink*
comer *to eat*
comprender *to understand*
correr *to run*
deber *ought, must, to be supposed to*
leer *to read*
meter *to put in*
prender *to turn on*
romper *to break*
toser *to cough*
vender *to sell*

Some common **-ir** verbs:

abrir *to open*
añadir *to add*
asistir *to attend*
describir *to describe*
discutir *to discuss, argue*
escribir *to write*
interrumpir *to interrupt*
ocurrir *to happen*
recibir *to receive*
subir *to go up, raise*
sufrir *to suffer*
vivir *to live*

A. En la clase de español. Escriba lo que pasa en la clase de español del profesor Sierra. Construya oraciones en presente siguiendo el modelo.

MODELO los estudiantes / hablar español
➔ Los estudiantes hablan español.

En la clase de español

levantar la mano	to raise one's hand	**el modismo**	idiom
el libro de texto	textbook	**tomar apuntes**	to take notes

1. Daniel / pronunciar muy bien

___

2. nosotros / abrir el libro de texto

___

3. tú / levantar la mano

___

4. los chicos / comprender la lección

___

5. Ud. / tomar apuntes

___

6. yo / leer el diálogo

___

7. Isabel y tú / aprender los modismos

___

8. vosotros / escribir un ejercicio

___

Nota cultural

- En los países hispánicos, los estudiantes de los colegios particulares generalmente tienen que comprar sus libros. En la mayor parte de los colegios públicos los estudiantes tienen que comprarlos también. Los estudiantes reciben una lista de los libros que necesitan para cada clase.

- En Hispanoamérica la escuela secundaria se llama **colegio, liceo** o **instituto.** En los colegios de estos países y en España, las notas se calculan a base de diez como nota máxima.

B. ¿En esta clase? ¡Qué va! Use el presente para escribir las cosas que *nunca* pasan en la clase de la profesora Reyes. Siga el modelo.

MODELO ¿los estudiantes? / ¿gritar?
➔ Los estudiantes nunca gritan.

Lo que no se hace en la clase

empujar *to push*
faltar *to be absent*
gritar *to shout, scream*
mascar chicle *to chew gum*
saltar *to jump*
tardar en llegar *to take long to arrive*

1. ¿Uds.? / ¿correr?

____

2. ¿nosotros? / ¿faltar?

____

3. ¿Juan Carlos? / ¿mascar chicle?

____

4. ¿yo? / ¿saltar?

____

5. ¿Laura y Carmen? / ¿empujar?

____

6. ¿tú? / ¿interrumpir?

____

7. ¿las chicas? / ¿beber refrescos?

____

8. ¿Ud. y yo? / ¿tardar en llegar?

____

C. ¿Qué hacen sus profesores? Diga lo que sus profesores hacen o no hacen en la sala de clase escogiendo frases de la columna B para completar las frases de la columna A. Siga el modelo.

MODELO Mi profesor de inglés ... hablar en voz alta fumar
→ Mi profesor de inglés **habla en voz alta.**
→ Mi profesor de inglés **no fuma.**

A

1. Mi profesor de historia ...
2. Nuestra profesora de química ...
3. Nuestros maestros de matemáticas ...
4. Las profesoras de francés ...
5. Los maestros de gimnasia ...

B

a. enseñar bien
b. arreglar sus papeles
c. preparar exámenes
d. esperar mucho de nosotros
e. escribir en la pizarra
f. pasar lista
g. colocar sus libros en el escritorio
h. calcular las notas todos los días
i. hablar de muchos temas
j. saltar
k. trotar

D. **¡Las quince primaveras!** Cecilia celebra su cumpleaños con una fiesta en su casa. Para saber cómo es, llene los espacios en blanco con la forma correcta del presente de los verbos que aparecen entre paréntesis.

Los padres y los hermanos de Cecilia ____________ (1. planear) la fiesta. La mamá ____________ (2. cocinar) los platos favoritos de Cecilia y ____________ (3. comprar) una torta de chocolate. El padre y los hermanos de Cecilia ____________ (4. colocar) globos y una piñata en la sala. Cecilia ____________ (5. invitar) a todos sus amigos. ____________ (6. Llegar) la hora de la fiesta. Paula, la mejor amiga de Cecilia, ____________ (7. vivir) al lado y ____________ (8. llegar) primero. Durante la fiesta, todos ____________ (9. comer), ____________ (10. beber) y ____________ (11. bailar). Juan Pedro ____________ (12. tocar) el piano y los otros amigos ____________ (13. cantar). Mientras Cecilia ____________ (14. abrir) los regalos que ____________ (15. recibir), su padre ____________ (16. sacar) fotos. Los invitados ____________ (17. felicitar) a la cumpleañera y ____________ (18. brindar) por ella.

Nota cultural

Las chicas que viven en los países hispánicos suelen celebrar los quince años igual que las norteamericanas celebran los dieciséis. El cumpleaños de **las quince primaveras** es como el cumpleaños dieciséis que se llama *sweet sixteen* en los Estados Unidos.

E. **¡Un lío telefónico!** Mario necesita llamar a su novia para decirle que no puede llegar a su casa a las siete. Para saber lo que pasa, escoja los verbos correctos de la lista y escríbalos en la forma correcta del presente en los espacios en blanco.

marcar	contestar	meter	creer	dejar
deber	buscar	quedar	funcionar	tardar
decidir	esperar	desear	comunicar	

1. Mario ______________ llamar a su novia Isabel
2. para decirle que ______________ para su cita.
3. Él ______________ una cabina telefónica.
4. ______________ una en la esquina.
5. Mario ______________ una moneda
6. y ______________ el número de teléfono.
7. (Ellos) no ______________ en casa de Isabel.
8. Mario ______________ que
9. ______________ dejar un recado
10. y ______________ escuchar la contestadora.
11. Pero la contestadora no ______________.
12. Mario ______________ otra moneda.
13. Esta vez parece que (ellos) ______________
14. o ______________ descolgado.
15. ¡Por fin, Mario ______________ correr a casa de Isabel!

C *The present tense of irregular verbs*

- The following verbs have an irregular first person singular (*yo*) form in the present tense. All other forms are regular.
- **-G-** verbs, that is, verbs that have an unexpected **-g-** in the *yo* form:

infinitive	***yo** form*	*other forms of the present tense*
caer *to fall*	caigo	caes, cae, caemos, caéis, caen
hacer *to make, do*	hago	haces, hace, hacemos, hacéis, hacen
poner *to put*	pongo	pones, pone, ponemos, ponéis, ponen
salir *to go out*	salgo	sales, sale, salimos, salís, salen
traer *to bring*	traigo	traes, trae, traemos, traéis, traen
valer *to be worth*	valgo	vales, vale, valemos, valéis, valen

Notes:

1. Verbs conjugated like **poner: componer** (*to compose*), **disponer** (*to dispose*), **imponer** (*to impose*), **proponer** (*to propose*), **reponerse** (*to get well*), **suponer** (*to suppose*), etc.
2. Verbs conjugated like **traer: atraer** (*to attract*), **contraer** (*to contract*), **distraer** (*to distract*), etc.

- The following **-g-** verbs are irregular in other persons also:

decir *to say, tell*	
digo	decimos
dices	decís
dice	dicen

oír *to hear*	
oigo	oímos
oyes	oís
oye	oyen

tener *to have*	
tengo	tenemos
tienes	tenéis
tiene	tienen

venir *to come*	
vengo	venimos
vienes	venís
viene	vienen

Note: Verbs conjugated like **tener: contener** (*to contain*), **detener** (*to stop, detain*), **mantener** (*to maintain*), **obtener** (*to obtain*), **retener** (*to retain*), etc.

- **Ir** (*to go*) is conjugated like an **-ar** verb. The *yo* form ends in **-oy**: **voy**. The stem of the verb is the letter **v**. Note that the *vosotros* form has no accent because it has only one syllable: **vais**.

ir *to go*	
voy	vamos
vas	vais
va	van

- **Ir** + **a** + *infinitive* is used to refer to future time as is *to be going to* in English.

  —Aquí está el cine. **Voy a estacionar** el coche. *Here's the movie theater. **I'm going to park** the car.*
  —Y **yo voy a comprar** las entradas. *And **I'm going to buy** the tickets.*

- **Dar** (*to give*), like **ir**, is conjugated like an **-ar** verb. The *yo* form ends in **-oy**: **doy**. **Ver** (*to see*) is a regular **-er** verb except for the *yo* form: **veo**. The *vosotros* form has no accent because it has only one syllable: **veis**.
- **Saber** (*to know*) and **caber** (*to fit*) are irregular in the first person only.

infinitive	*yo form*	*other forms of the present tense*
saber *to know*	**sé**	sabes, sabe, sabemos, sabéis, saben
caber *to fit*	**quepo**	cabes, cabe, cabemos, cabéis, caben

- In most verbs that end in a vowel + **-cer** or **-cir**, **c** changes to **zc** before **o** and **a**. In the present tense, the change occurs only in the first-person singular (*yo* form).

conocer *to know*	
cono**zc**o	conocemos
conoces	conocéis
conoce	conocen

Note: Verbs conjugated like **conocer: reconocer** (*to recognize*), **desconocer** (*to be ignorant of*)

- Most verbs with infinitives in **-ecer** have **-zco** in the *yo* form like **conozco**. The other persons of the present tense are regular:

  agradecer (agradezco) *to thank,* **aparecer** (aparezco) *to appear,* **crecer** (crezco) *to grow,* **desaparecer** (desaparezco) *to disappear,* **establecer** (establezco) *to establish,* **merecer** (merezco) *to deserve,* **obedecer** (obedezco) *to obey,* **ofrecer** (ofrezco) *to offer,* **parecer** (parezco) *to seem,* **permanecer** (permanezco) *to remain,* **pertenecer** (pertenezco) *to belong,* etc.

- Verbs in **-ucir** also have **-zco** in the *yo* form, but are regular in the other persons: **conducir** (conduzco) *to drive,* **lucir** (luzco) *to shine/show off,* **producir** (produzco) *to produce,* **reducir** (reduzco) *to reduce,* **traducir** (traduzco) *to translate.*

F. **Un viaje de negocios.** Usted es jefe de una gran compañía internacional. Su secretario le hace unas preguntas sobre su viaje de negocios a Europa. Conteste sus preguntas según el modelo.

MODELO —¿Hace Ud. un viaje en noviembre?
—Sí, hago un viaje en noviembre.

1. ¿Sale Ud. la semana próxima?

____

2. ¿Viene Ud. a la oficina el viernes?

____

3. ¿Va Ud. a Francia y España?

____

4. ¿Conoce Ud. Italia?

____

5. ¿Hace Ud. las maletas mañana?

____

6. ¿Sabe Ud. cuándo regresa?

____

G. **¡Cuánto trabajo tenemos!** Los chicos reciben una invitación pero no saben si tienen tiempo para ir. Escriba lo que dicen, según el modelo.

MODELO Juan → **Viene** si **tiene** tiempo.

1. las chicas

____

2. Ud.

____

3. tú y yo

____

4. Sara

____

5. Uds.

____

6. yo

____

H. **¿Oyes lo que dicen?** ¡Aunque se habla en voz baja todo se oye! Escriba en español que todos oyen lo que dicen otras personas, según el modelo.

MODELO Anita / Gustavo ➔ Anita **oye** lo que Gustavo **dice**.

1. yo / Uds.
2. tú / nosotros
3. Guillermo / Teresa
4. Rosa y yo / Ud.
5. Ud. y su primo / yo
6. Carmen y Paco / tú

I. **¡Lo hago yo!** Escriba que Ud. es quien hace las siguientes cosas. Siga el modelo.

MODELO —¿Quién hace una pregunta?
—Yo hago una pregunta.

1. ¿Quién pone la mesa?
2. ¿Quién trae las flores?
3. ¿Quién da un paseo?
4. ¿Quién ve televisión?
5. ¿Quién traduce el libro?

J. **¿Hablan en serio?** ¡Sus amigos tienen ideas geniales! ¿O es que le toman el pelo? Escriba lo que dicen.

MODELO —Carlota, ¿qué propones? (un plan brillante)
—Propongo un plan brillante.

1. Luz, ¿qué mereces? (recibir el premio Nobel)

2. Juan Diego, ¿qué compones? (una obra maestra mozartiana)

____

3. Chicos, ¿qué obtienen? (una beca de dos millones de dólares)

____

4. Eugenia, ¿qué traduces? (novelas del vasco al sánscrito)

____

5. José Luis, ¿qué conduces? (la limosina presidencial)

____

6. Norberto, ¿qué supones? (que yo tengo razón siempre)

____

K. ¿Cuánto tiempo hace? Ud. le pregunta a su amigo cuánto tiempo hace que sus amigos se dedican a sus aficiones. Escriba cada pregunta dos veces usando las construcciones del modelo.

MODELO María / escribir cuentos
➔ **¿Cuánto tiempo hace que** María **escribe** cuentos?
➔ **¿Desde cuándo escribe** María cuentos?

1. Uds. / cocinar a la francesa

____

____

2. Mario y Federico / nadar

____

____

3. Consuelo / tocar el violín

____

____

4. tú / hacer carpintería

____

____

5. Esteban / bailar flamenco

____

____

6. sus hermanos / coleccionar monedas

____

____

L. **Hace mucho tiempo que ...** Su amigo le contesta las preguntas del ejercicio K de dos modos, como en el modelo.

MODELO María / escribir cuentos / seis meses
→ **Hace** *seis meses* **que** María **escribe** cuentos.
→ María **escribe** cuentos **desde hace** *seis meses.*

1. Uds. / cocinar a la francesa / un año

2. Mario y Federico / nadar / tres años

3. Consuelo / tocar el violín / seis años

4. tú / hacer carpintería / siete semanas

5. Esteban / bailar flamenco / ocho meses

6. sus hermanos / coleccionar monedas / dos años y medio

M. **¿Cómo son?** Nadie conoce a esta gente. Use el verbo **conocer** para decir eso, según el modelo. Recuerde que debe usar el **a** personal. (Si necesita repasar el **a** personal, vea el capítulo 19, sección C.)

MODELO —¿Sabe Juan si Paula es argentina?
—No, él no conoce a Paula.

1. ¿Sabes si esos muchachos son simpáticos?

2. ¿Saben tus padres si los señores Gorostiza son ricos?

3. ¿Saben Uds. si la profesora de economía es famosa?

4. ¿Sabemos tú y yo si aquel médico es competente?

5. ¿Sabe Ud. si Alfredo Parra es inteligente?

____

6. ¿Sabe Marta si Agustín es de Puerto Rico?

____

N. **¡Qué vanidad!** José Antonio es muy presumido. ¿Qué dice de su trabajo? Siga el modelo para saberlo.

MODELO conocer a todo el mundo
➔ Conozco a todo el mundo.

1. pertenecer a los círculos literarios de la ciudad

____

2. producir obras importantes

____

3. traducir poesía del inglés al español

____

4. dar muchas conferencias

____

5. siempre ofrecer ideas nuevas

____

6. merecer los aplausos de los oyentes

____

O. **¡Todos ayudamos!** En mi casa todo el mundo ayuda. Use **ir a** + el infinitivo dado para expresar lo que cada uno de nosotros va a hacer.

MODELO tú / poner en orden la sala
➔ Tú vas a poner en orden la sala.

Arreglando la casa

barrer el suelo *to sweep the floor*
cortar el césped *to mow the lawn*
hacer la cama *to make the bed*
hacer la compra *to do the shopping*
lavar la ropa *to do the laundry*
lavar los platos *to wash the dishes*
limpiar la alfombra *to clean the carpet*
pasar la aspiradora *to vacuum*
poner en orden *to straighten up*
sacar la basura *to take out the garbage*

1. mi hermano y yo / cortar el césped

____

2. mi abuela / lavar la ropa

____

3. yo / barrer el suelo

____

4. mamá / hacer la compra

____

5. mis hermanas / lavar los platos

____

6. mi abuelo / sacar la basura

____

7. Uds. / hacer las camas

____

8. papá / pasar la aspiradora

____

9. tú / limpiar la alfombra

____

Nota cultural

En los países hispánicos, tradicionalmente, los abuelos vivían con sus hijos y nietos. Muy a menudo un tío o una tía vivía también con la familia. Los abuelos y los tíos tenían casi la misma autoridad en la disciplina de los hijos como los padres mismos. Cuando los hijos se casaban solían vivir muy cerca de sus padres. Hoy en día se nota más el fenómeno de la familia nuclear como en los Estados Unidos y una tendencia de parte de los ancianos de ir a vivir a un asilo de ancianos (*old age home*) en vez de ir a vivir con sus hijos.

P. **La vida diaria.** Exprese en español algunas de las cosas que Paco, sus amigos y sus familiares hacen todos los días.

1. I drive the car.

____

2. Mom and Dad sign papers.

____

3. My brother jogs.

____

4. You (*Ud.*) turn on the computer.

____

5. Federico and I attend lectures.

____

6. You (*tú*) read the newspaper.

____

7. David and Mateo swim in the pool.

____

8. My aunt and uncle receive their bills.

____

9. All the students discuss the topics.

____

10. You (*Uds.*) cook rice.

____

11. Jaime and I cross the street.

____

12. María Elena and Martín read until 1:00 A.M.

____

Q. Ejercicio oral. Haga una encuesta. Pregúnteles a sus compañeros de clase lo que les gusta hacer los fines de semana y en las vacaciones. Por ejemplo:

- ir al cine / a los conciertos / al teatro
- salir al campo / a las montañas
- acampar
- hacer turismo
- visitar los museos
- bailar
- pintar
- jugar al tenis / al béisbol / al fútbol
- tocar un instrumento musical
- ir de compras

Luego, calcule cuántos hacen cada cosa y presente los resultados a la clase.

R. Estructuras en acción. Lea este anuncio de un servicio de plancha a domicilio. Después, resuma su contenido combinando elementos de la columna A con los de la columna B. Escriba oraciones completas como en el modelo.

DON PLANCHÓN

Cuando Juan Marín descubrió que la tarea más ingrata para la mayoría de las mujeres es la plancha, decidió crear un servicio de plancha a domicilio. Recogen la ropa y la devuelven planchada el mismo día. Una camisa, dependiendo del tejido, cuesta entre 200 y 300 pesetas. Y el único requisito es que el pedido supere las mil pesetas. Funcionan en Madrid con un horario de 9.00 a 14.00 y de 15.00 a 19.30. El negocio se abrió en febrero de 1994 y próximamente se ampliará a Barcelona, Mallorca, Pontevedra y Valencia. **Madrid: (91) 445 73 28**

Modelo la gente odiar la plancha de ropa
➔ La gente odia la plancha de ropa.

A	B
1. Juan Marín	a. ... costar entre 200 y 300 pesetas
2. los empleados de Don Planchón	b. ... funcionar desde febrero de 1994
3. una camisa	c. ... ofrecer un servicio de plancha a domicilio
4. el pedido	d. ... tener que superar las mil pesetas
5. el negocio	e. ... recoger la ropa y devolverla planchada el mismo día

1. ______________________________
2. ______________________________
3. ______________________________
4. ______________________________
5. ______________________________

CHAPTER 2

SER & ESTAR

A The uses of **ser**

- Spanish has two verbs that are equivalent to the English *to be:* **ser** and **estar**. Both verbs are irregular in the present tense. Both have **-oy** in the *yo* form, like **ir** (**voy**) and **dar** (**doy**).

ser	
soy	somos
eres	sois
es	son

estar	
estoy	estamos
estás	estáis
está	están

- **Ser** is used before most phrases beginning with **de**; for example, in expressing origin:

  Soy de los Estados Unidos. — ***I'm from** the United States.*

  and possession:

  La cartera **es de Felipe.** — *The wallet **is Phillip's.***

  and what material something is made of:

  La blusa **es de seda.** — *The blouse **is (made of) silk.***

- **Ser** is used before adjectives to indicate that the condition expressed by the adjectives does not result from a change. Thus, these adjectives express inherent qualities and characteristics such as nationality, age, physical and moral attributes, personality, religion, and color:

  Mis amigas **son** españolas. — *My friends are Spanish.*
  El presidente **es** joven. — *The president is young.*
  Carlos **es** alto y rubio. — *Carlos is tall and blond.*
  Nora **es** inteligente. — *Nora is intelligent.*
  Mis primos **son** graciosos. — *My cousins are witty.*
  Esos señores **son** protestantes/judíos/católicos. — *Those men and women are Protestant/Jewish/Catholic.*
  Nuestro coche **es** azul. — *Our car is blue.*

- **Ser** is used to link two nouns or pronouns or a noun and a pronoun. Both nouns and pronouns may appear in the sentence or merely be understood. Unlike English, Spanish omits the indefinite article **un/una** with a profession:

  El señor Lara **es arquitecto**. — *Mr. Lara **is an architect**.*
  Pilar Suárez **es médica**. — *Pilar Suárez **is a doctor**.*
  Somos ingenieros. — ***We're engineers**.*

- **Ser** is used to express time, dates, days of the week, and where an event takes place:

—¿Qué hora **es**? —**Son** las ocho.	*What time is it?* *It's eight o'clock.*
—¿Cuál **es** la fecha de hoy? —**Es** el seis de octubre.	*What's today's date?* *It's October 6th.*
—¿Qué día **es** hoy? —**Es** miércoles.	*What day is today?* *It's Wednesday.*
—¿El baile **es** en la universidad? —No, **es** en el Hotel Palacio.	*Is the dance at the university?* *No, it's at the Palacio Hotel.*

B *The uses of* ***estar***

- **Estar** is used to express location or position, whether it is permanent or temporary:

Santiago **está** en Chile.	*Santiago is in Chile.*
El perro **está** al lado del gato.	*The dog is next to the cat.*
La papelería **está** en frente de la pastelería.	*The stationery store is opposite the pastry shop.*

- **Estar** is used before adjectives to indicate that the condition expressed by the adjective results from a change. The condition may be a phase of health, happiness, etc.; a temporary state of being tired, seated, etc.; or the result of an action such as a window being closed. **Estar** also may indicate that the adjective is the subjective impression of the speaker. **Estar** is therefore more common with adjectives that describe mental or physical states:

—¿Cómo **está** Inés? —La pobre **está** enferma.	*How's Inés?* *The poor girl is (has gotten) sick.*
—¿**Están** levantados los niños? —No, **están** acostados todavía.	*Are the children up?* *No, they're still in bed.*
—¿**Están** abiertas las ventanas? —No, **están** cerradas.	*Are the windows open?* *No, they are closed.*
—¿No reconoces a Luis? —Apenas. **Está** muy gordo.	*Don't you recognize Luis?* *Hardly. He's so fat. (He's gotten very fat./He looks so fat to me.)*

- **Estar** is used in the formation of the progressive tenses: **estar** + the gerund. The gerund or **-ndo** form is equivalent to the *-ing* form in English:

Están esperando.	*They're waiting.*
Estaba viviendo en París.	*He was living in Paris.*

- **Ser** and **estar** are used with the past participle of the verb. **Ser** + the past participle is passive; it can have an agent phrase introduced by **por**. **Estar** + the past participle expresses the result of an action:

La puerta **fue abierta por** la chica. La puerta **está abierta.**	*The door was opened by the girl.* *The door is open.*
El trabajo **fue hecho por** él. El trabajo **estaba hecho.**	*The work was done by him.* *The work was done.*

- The choice of **ser** or **estar** in a sentence is crucial to the meaning. A change in the verb will change the meaning:

Lola **es** delgada.	*Lola is thin. (Lola is a thin person.)*
Lola **está** delgada.	*Lola is thin. (Lola has gotten thin./ Lola looks thin to me.)*
Mario **es** nervioso.	*Mario is nervous. (He is a nervous person.)*
Mario **está** nervioso.	*Mario is feeling nervous. (Mario has gotten nervous/seems nervous to me.)*
Esos profesores **son** aburridos.	*Those professors are boring.*
Esos profesores **están** aburridos.	*Those professors are bored.*
Fernando **es** listo.	*Fernando is clever.*
Fernando **está** listo.	*Fernando is ready.*
La actriz **es** vieja.	*The actress is old.*
La actriz **está** vieja.	*The actress looks old.*
Los hombres **son** vivos.	*The men are sharp/quick.*
Los hombres **están** vivos.	*The men are alive.*
Beatriz **es** pálida.	*Beatriz is pale-complexioned.*
Beatriz **está** pálida.	*Beatriz is pale.*
Es seguro.	*It's safe.*
Está seguro.	*He's sure.*
Paquito **es** bueno.	*Paquito is good (a good boy).*
La torta **está** buena.	*The cake is (tastes) good.*

- Note the difference in meaning between **ser** and **estar** when referring to food:

La carne **es** rica (mala).	*Meat is delicious (awful).* (in general)
La carne **está** rica (mala).	*The meat is/tastes delicious (awful).* (specific dish)

Note: Adjectives used with **ser** and **estar** must agree with the subject in number and gender:

- Commonly used expressions with **ser**:

  ¿Cómo es Ud.? *What are you like?, What do you look like?*
  ¿Cuál es la fecha de hoy? *What's today's date?*
  ¿Cuál es su nacionalidad? *What is your nationality?*
  ¿De dónde es Ud.? *Where are you from?*
  ¿De qué color es ...? *What color is ...?*
  ¿De qué origen es Ud.? *What is your background?*
  es importante/necesario/posible *it's important/necessary/possible*
  es que *the fact is that*
  ¿Qué hora es? *What time is it?*

- Commonly used expressions with **estar**:

  ¿Cómo está Ud.? *How are you?*
  estar a punto de + *infinitive* *to be about to*
  estar conforme *to be in agreement*
  estar de acuerdo (con) *to agree (with)*
  estar de vacaciones *to be on vacation*
  estar de vuelta *to be back*
  estar para + *infinitive* *to be about to*
  estar por *to be in favor of*
  estar por + *infinitive* *to be inclined to*

A. Soy yo. Escriba en español quién llama a la puerta. Siga el modelo empleando la forma correcta del verbo **ser**.

MODELO —¿Quién es? (yo)
—Soy yo.

1. ¿Quién es? (ella)

____

2. ¿Quién es? (Uds.)

____

3. ¿Quién es? (nosotros)

____

4. ¿Quién es? (yo)

____

5. ¿Quién es? (tú)

____

6. ¿Quién es? (él)

____

7. ¿Quién es? (ellas)

____

B. ¿De dónde son? ¿De qué origen son? Escriba de dónde son y de qué origen son los amigos del Club Internacional. Siga el modelo.

MODELO Tomás / Inglaterra / alemán
➔ Tomás es de Inglaterra pero es de origen alemán.

1. Pablo / la Argentina / inglés

____

2. los gemelos / Francia / ruso

____

3. la licenciada / el Canadá / japonés

____

4. Ud. / los Estados Unidos / irlandés

____

5. Ramón y Virginia / Puerto Rico / polaco

____

6. tú / España / portugués

____

7. Ud. y Raquel / México / griego

____

8. yo / Venezuela / italiano

____

C. Una encuesta. Ud. prepara una encuesta y necesita hacerles unas preguntas a sus amigos hispanos. Exprese en español las preguntas que va a hacerles. Se usa el verbo **ser** en todas las oraciones.

1. Who are you?

____

2. Where are you from?

____

3. What is your nationality?

____

4. What is your background?

____

5. What are you like? / What do you look like?

____

6. What color are your eyes?

____

D. Están de vacaciones. Escriba dónde y cómo están las siguientes personas, empleando el verbo **estar** como en el modelo.

Modelo Alicia / Los Ángeles / ocupada
➔ Alicia está en Los Ángeles y está ocupada.

1. Patricio / Madrid / contento

____

2. nosotros / Chile / cansados

____

3. los tíos / Tejas / nerviosos

____

4. Consuelo y su hermana / Suecia / aburridas

____

5. tú / Londres / enfermo

____

6. yo / París / feliz

____

E. ¿Cuál fue la pregunta? A continuación lea Ud. lo que escribió una persona al contestar las preguntas de un formulario. Luego escriba Ud. las preguntas. Para cada pregunta use el verbo **ser**.

1. Roberto Iglesias.

   ____

2. Canadiense.

   ____

3. Programador de computadoras.

   ____

4. Soltero. *(estado civil)*

   ____

5. El quince de febrero de 1970. *(fecha de nacimiento)*

   ____

6. Alto, moreno, de ojos castaños.

   ____

F. Biografías. Escriba en los espacios en blanco la forma correcta del verbo **ser** o **estar** para terminar los textos biográficos de las siguientes personas.

A. Baltasar Estévez (1) ____________ director de cine. Él (2) ____________ célebre por sus comedias. Sus películas (3) ____________ realmente muy cómicas. Estévez (4) ____________ muy gracioso. (5) ____________ mexicano pero (6) ____________ en Barcelona este año porque filma una comedia allí. Todos sus aficionados (7) ____________ entusiasmados con esa nueva película.

B. Camila de la Renta (1) ____________ diseñadora de ropa para mujeres. Su ropa (2) ____________ de alta costura y (3) ____________ muy cara. Este año los vestidos y los trajes que diseña (4) ____________ de seda y lana. (5) ____________ blancos, negros y de otros colores claros. La empresa de de la Renta (6) ____________ en París, que (7) ____________ la capital de la moda.

G. El museo de arte. Ud. es guía en un museo de arte y lleva a unos turistas a conocer el museo. Complete la descripción de la visita escribiendo las formas correctas de **ser** o **estar**.

Buenas tardes, señoras y señores. Aquí (nosotros) (1) ________________ en la entrada principal. A la derecha (2) ________________ la librería. (3) ________________ nueva y moderna. Y en frente de la librería (4) ________________ la sala de conferencias y conciertos. Esta noche precisamente hay una conferencia. Va a hablar Francisco Velázquez que (5) ________________ profesor de arte en la universidad. (6) ________________ especialista en la pintura renacentista y (7) ________________ muy inteligente. La conferencia (8) ________________ a las ocho. Va a (9) ________________ muy interesante. Ahora, vamos a subir la escalera. Aquí a la derecha (10) ________________ la sala de pintura impresionista. Esta exposición (11) ________________ muy importante. Muchos de los cuadros que (12) ________________ colgados aquí (13) ________________ de otros museos europeos. Uds. (14) ________________ viendo unas obras maestras que nunca habían salido de su país sino hasta ahora. Bueno, ya (15) ________________ las tres y me parece que (16) ________________ hora de terminar nuestra visita. Yo (17) ________________ muy contenta de haber podido enseñarles el museo. Uds. que (18) ________________ aficionados al arte deben volver a menudo. El museo (19) ________________ abierto de martes a domingo. (20) ________________ cerrado los lunes.

Nota cultural

El Museo del Prado, que se encuentra en Madrid, es una de las pinacotecas (*art museums*) más importantes del mundo. El Prado tiene la colección más completa de pintura española. Llaman la atención los cuadros de Velázquez, Goya, El Greco, Ribera, Zurbarán y Murillo. El museo tiene naturalmente obras de otros pintores célebres como Rembrandt, Bosco (*Bosch*), Brueghel, Rubens, Tiziano (*Titian*), Caravaggio, Gainsborough, etcétera. El edificio de estilo neoclásico fue construido por Juan de Villanueva por orden del rey español Carlos III (1716–88) que reinó a partir del año 1759.

H. Un semestre en el extranjero. Ud. está pasando un semestre en Madrid para perfeccionar su español. Toma clases en la universidad y vive en casa de una familia española. Ud. les escribe una carta a sus padres en la cual describe cómo es su vida en Madrid. En la página siguiente, complete cada oración con la forma correcta de **ser** o **estar**.

Queridos padres:

Ya hace dos meses que (1) ____________ en Madrid y (2) ____________ muy contento. (3) ____________ una ciudad vieja y también moderna. Voy al Museo del Prado, al Parque del Retiro, a la Plaza Mayor y a muchos lugares turísticos. Hay cafés, restaurantes, teatros, cines y la vida nocturna (4) ____________ impresionante. ¡Claro que asisto a mis clases también! La clase de literatura española (5) ____________ un poco difícil a veces porque el profesor habla muy rápido. Mi clase de historia (6) ____________ muy buena. Los dos profesores (7) ____________ inteligentes y simpáticos. Por desgracia, la profesora de lengua (8) ____________ aburrida. La casa donde vivo (9) ____________ en la calle Serrano. En frente de la casa (10) ____________ el Museo Arqueológico. Algunas tiendas (11) ____________ al lado de la casa también. Y la parada de autobuses (12) ____________ delante de la casa. Así (13) ____________ muy fácil viajar por la ciudad. La casa de la familia Ruiz (14) ____________ grande y bonita y mi cuarto (15) ____________ muy cómodo. Los señores Ruiz tienen cuatro hijos. (16) ____________ siete personas en total porque la abuela vive con ellos también. Esteban, el hijo mayor, (17) ____________ un buen amigo mío. (18) ____________ pequeño y moreno. (19) ____________ listo y simpático. Estela, la hija mayor, (20) ____________ encantadora y muy guapa. Tiene novio. ¡(21) ____________ una pena porque creo que (22) ____________ enamorado de ella! (23) (¡____________ una broma!)

¿Cómo (24) ____________ Uds.? Papá, (25) ¿____________ muy ocupado en la empresa? Mamá, ¿cómo (26) ____________ la nueva computadora? ¿Y mis hermanos? Todos (27) ____________ muy bien, espero. Claudia debe (28) ____________ contenta en el nuevo colegio, ¿verdad? ¿Cómo (29) ____________ los abuelos y los tíos? ¿La tía (30) ____________ enferma todavía? ¿Los tíos (31) ____________ de vuelta de Lisboa? ¿Y cómo (32) ____________ el nuevo coche que compraron? Espero recibir muchas noticias de Uds. Bueno, ya (33) ____________ las cinco y media. Dos amigos que toman clases conmigo van a pasar por mí a las seis. Jaime (34) ____________ de Nueva York y Carlos

(35) ____________________ de Nuevo México. Vamos a ir al cine. Faltan dos meses y voy a (36) ____________________ de vuelta en casa con Uds. Hasta pronto.

Un abrazo muy fuerte de

Miguel

Nota cultural

Madrid, capital de España, se encuentra en una extensa llanura (*plain*) aproximadamente en el centro de la Península. La ciudad, a orillas del río Manzanares, fue llamada Magerit por los árabes. Éstos se apoderaron de la Península en 711 y se quedaron hasta 1492 cuando fueron derrotados definitivamente en Granada por los Reyes Católicos. El rey Alfonso VI tomó Madrid definitivamente en 1084 y en 1561 Felipe II trasladó la Corte a Madrid. En 1600, Felipe III llevó la Corte a Valladolid (ciudad al noroeste de Madrid) pero volvió a llevarla a Madrid en 1605. Los reyes borbones (*Bourbons*), especialmente Carlos III, hicieron construir muchos monumentos y edificios y convirtieron la ciudad en el centro intelectual y artístico de España. Madrid no es solamente la capital de España, sino también uno de los centros culturales de la Unión Europea.

I. ¿Qué preguntó? A continuación hay unas respuestas que dio su amigo. Pero Ud. no oyó las preguntas que le hizo otro amigo. ¿Puede imaginarse cuáles son las preguntas? Escoja entre **ser** y **estar** en formular cada pregunta.

1. ¿La papelería? Enfrente del correo.

   ____

2. ¿Gloria? Rubia, alta y delgada.

   ____

3. ¿Los hermanos García? Brasileños.

   ____

4. ¿Juanito y Raúl? Preocupados y nerviosos.

   ____

5. ¿La familia Méndez? De origen español.

   ____

6. ¿Las primas de Paco? Encantadoras.

   ____

7. ¿El profesor Mora? En Costa Rica.

   ____

8. ¿El vestido? De algodón.

   ____

9. ¿La camisa y la corbata? Azules.

   ____

10. ¿Yo? Muy ocupado y cansado.

11. ¿Aquella casa? De los abuelos de Sara.

12. ¿Micaela? De Inglaterra.

J. Unos nuevos estudiantes extranjeros. Exprese en español una conversación entre dos amigas sobre los nuevos estudiantes extranjeros en su colegio.

1. Who are the new foreign students? Do you know where they're from?
2. I know María del Mar. She's in my math class. She's from Argentina.
3. Yes, and her background is Italian. She's very nice and smart.
4. But she's sad because she wants to go back to Buenos Aires.
5. Lorenzo Tomé is French, but his grandparents are of Spanish origin.
6. The family has been living in France for many years.
7. Lorenzo is studying biology and chemistry this year.
8. Yes. He says he wants to be a doctor.

K. Ejercicio oral. La familia. Pregúnteles a sus compañeros de clase cómo están los miembros de su familia y cómo son. Pregúnteles también dónde están sus familiares ahora.

L. Estructuras en acción. Lea este anuncio que explica las ventajas de la tarjeta de abono a los transportes públicos de Madrid. Luego, copie las frases u oraciones donde aparecen formas de los verbos **ser** y **estar** y tradúzcalas al inglés.

Vocabulario

el abono *(here)* subway and bus pass
la Comunidad de Madrid city of Madrid and environs
el consorcio consortium, association
constar de to consist of
la tercera edad old age

ABONO ANUAL
ABONO JOVEN
ABONO TERCERA EDAD
ABONO TRANSPORTES
B1
MAY 90
ESTOS SON TUS ABONOS
El Abono Transportes es la forma más práctica, cómoda y económica de disfrutar de las ventajas del transporte público.
Consta de **una tarjeta de Abono** personal y de carácter permanente, con tu foto, datos de identificación y número de abonado **más un cupón** que puede ser mensual o anual.
Con él podrás viajar por toda la Comunidad de Madrid o por la zona elegida, sin límite de viajes o combinaciones. Metro, tren, autobús y todos los transportes públicos están a tu disposición para moverte mejor.

1. ______________________________

2. ______________________________

3. ______________________________

4. ______________________________

CHAPTER 3 STEM-CHANGING VERBS & VERBS WITH SPELLING CHANGES

A Stem-changing verbs ending in -ar and -er

- Stem-changing verbs that end in **-ar** or **-er** change the stem vowel in the present tense in two possible ways: **e** > **ie** and **o** > **ue** in all forms except *nosotros* and *vosotros:*

querer *to want, love*	
quiero	queremos
quieres	queréis
quiere	quieren

volver *to return*	
vuelvo	volvemos
vuelves	volvéis
vuelve	vuelven

pensar *to think*	
pienso	pensamos
piensas	pensáis
piensa	piensan

poder *can, to be able to*	
puedo	podemos
puedes	podéis
puede	pueden

*Remember that **pensar** + *infinitive* means *to intend to.*

Some common verbs that pattern like **querer** and **pensar** (**e** > **ie**):

acertar *to be on target, guess right*
apretar *to be tight, squeeze*
ascender *to go up, promote*
atravesar *to cross*
cerrar *to close*
comenzar *to begin*
confesar *to confess*
defender *to defend*
descender *to go down*
despertar(se) *to wake up*
empezar *to begin*
encender *to light*
encerrar *to lock in, contain*
entender *to understand*
gobernar *to govern*
helar* *to freeze*
nevar* *to snow*
perder *to lose*
quebrar *to break*
recomendar *to recommend*
sentar(se) *to seat, sit down*

Some common verbs that pattern like **volver** and **poder** (**o** > **ue**):

acordarse *to remember*
acostar(se) *to put to bed, go to bed*
almorzar *to eat lunch*
conmover *to move (emotionally)*
contar *to count, tell*
costar *to cost*
demostrar *to show*
devolver *to return, give back*
doler *to hurt, ache*
encontrar *to find*
envolver *to wrap up*
jugar (u > ue) *to play*
llover* *to rain*
mostrar *to show*
oler (o > hue) *to smell*
probar(se) *to try, taste, try on*
recordar *to remember*
resolver *to solve*
soler *to be accustomed to*
tronar* *to thunder*
volar *to fly*

Note that **jugar** has the stem change **u** > **ue** and that **oler** has the change **o** > **hue**: **Huele bien.** *It smells good.*

*Impersonal verbs; conjugated only in the third-person singular.

A. **¿A qué juegan Uds.?** Escriba el deporte al que juega cada persona.

MODELO Roberto / el fútbol
→ Roberto **juega** al fútbol.

1. yo / el tenis

2. Daniel y Felipe / el béisbol

3. Carlota / el vólibol

4. tú / el baloncesto

5. Jorge y yo / el fútbol americano

6. Uds. / el jai alai

Nota cultural

- **El fútbol** es el deporte más popular en los países hispánicos. Los resultados de los partidos de fútbol ocupan varias páginas, muchas veces con fotos grandes en colores, en los principales periódicos de estos países.

- **El béisbol** es ahora muy popular en México, Venezuela, Centroamérica y el Caribe gracias a la influencia estadounidense. Los periódicos de estos países hispánicos dan noticias de los equipos nacionales tanto como de los norteamericanos. Varios jugadores de béisbol venezolanos y de otros países hispánicos juegan en equipos estadounidenses. Muchas palabras que tienen que ver con este deporte norteamericano han pasado al español de los países donde se juega: **el jonrón, el fildeo.**

- **El jai alai** es un juego de pelota de origen vasco (*Basque*). El País Vasco o las provincias de Vascongadas quedan al norte de España; allí se habla el vascuence a más del español. Los jugadores lanzan la pelota con una pala (*bat or paddle*), cesta (*basket*) o las manos contra un frontón (*wall*).

B. **¿A qué hora almuerzan?** Escriba a qué hora almuerzan estas personas.

MODELO yo / a las dos
→ Yo **almuerzo** a las dos.

1. Uds. / a la una

2. Eva / a las doce y media

3. nosotros / a las tres

4. Mauricio y Beatriz / a la una y cuarto

5. tú / a las once y media

6. yo / a las dos y media

Nota cultural

El almuerzo se toma generalmente en los países hispanoamericanos a eso de la una o las dos de la tarde. En España, donde se llama **la comida,** se tomaba tradicionalmente entre las dos y las tres. Los españoles tenían la costumbre de volver a casa para comer, pero con los cambios en la sociedad en cuanto al horario, el tránsito, etcétera, ya no se hace mucho. En general, ya no se come tan fuerte a esa hora ni se duerme la siesta después. **La cena** en los países hispanoamericanos se toma a eso de las ocho, a veces algo más temprano o algo más tarde, pero casi nunca llega a la hora española—entre las diez y las once de la noche. Claro que los niños pequeños generalmente siguen un horario más conveniente. **El desayuno,** generalmente ligero, se toma en los países hispanos a más o menos la misma hora que en los Estados Unidos.

C. **¡No puedo!** Escriba que nadie puede hacer nada hoy.

MODELO ¿Vas de compras hoy?
→ No, **no puedo**.

1. ¿Vienen Uds. conmigo hoy?

2. ¿Escribe Elena cartas hoy?

3. ¿Trabajan Josefa y Leonardo hoy?

4. ¿Toma Ud. el examen hoy?

5. ¿Voy a tu casa hoy?

6. ¿Visitamos el museo hoy?

D. En un almacén. Margarita va a un almacén para comprar ropa. Termine la conversación que tiene con la dependienta escribiendo la forma correcta de los verbos que aparecen entre paréntesis.

MODELO Yo ____________ (pensar) ir al almacén Princesa.
➔ Yo **pienso** ir al almacén Princesa.

1. Dependienta —Señorita, ¿en qué ____________ (poder) servirle?
2. Margarita —Es que yo no ____________ (encontrar) los trajes.
3. Dependienta —Aquí están a la derecha. ¿Qué color ____________ (querer) Ud.?
4. Margarita —____________ (Pensar) que el café o el azul marino.
5. Dependienta —Le ____________ (mostrar) dos. Este azul es muy bonito, ¿verdad?
6. Margarita —Ah sí. ¿____________ (Poder) mostrarme el otro?
7. Dependienta —Cómo no. Aquí tiene el café. Yo ____________ (encontrar) el estilo muy elegante.
8. Margarita —Los dos son hermosos. ¿Cuánto ____________ (costar)?
9. Dependienta —El azul ____________ (costar) ciento noventa dólares
10. y el café ____________ (costar) doscientos cinco dólares.
11. Margarita —De veras no sé. Creo que me ____________ (probar) los dos. *(Margarita termina de probarse los trajes.)*
12. Margarita —Me llevo los dos trajes. ¿Ud. me los ____________ (envolver), por favor?
13. Dependienta —Con gusto. ¿Ud. sabe que ____________ (poder) pagar con tarjeta de crédito?
14. Margarita —Ah sí. Yo ____________ (soler) pagar con mi tarjeta.
15. Dependienta —Bien. Yo ____________ (volver) en unos minutos.

Nota cultural

Todos los países hispánicos tienen **almacenes.** También hay sucursales (*branches*) de algunos almacenes estadounidenses, como Sears, en muchos países. Tradicionalmente se cerraban las tiendas en España unas horas por la tarde. Coincidía con las horas de la comida y del calor máximo. Actualmente, se sigue el horario corrido, es decir, el almacén se mantiene abierto todo el día. Tradicionalmente, a muchas personas de las sociedades hispánicas les gusta la atención personal que encuentran en las tiendas pequeñas. Tienen la costumbre de este contacto personal, pero también les llama la atención lo grande y variado del almacén. Les son muy atractivos también los nuevos centros comerciales que se construyen por todas partes.

E. Sinónimos. Consulte la lista de verbos que tienen cambios radicales en la página 30 y escoja sinónimos para los verbos que aparecen en las siguientes oraciones. Escriba cada oración empleando la forma correcta del nuevo verbo.

MODELO El diccionario *vale* treinta dólares.
→ El diccionario **cuesta** treinta dólares.

1. Uds. *solucionan* los problemas de álgebra.

____

2. Los niños *cruzan* la calle con cuidado.

____

3. El concierto *empieza* a las ocho.

____

4. *Bajamos* al primer piso en ascensor.

____

5. Yo no *comprendo* su idea.

____

6. ¿*Regresas* el sábado o el domingo?

____

7. Pedro nos *enseña* el apartamento.

____

8. Los Salcedo *desean* salir esta noche.

____

9. Yo *prendo* la luz.

____

F. Un día típico. Escriba lo que hacen estas personas en un día típico.

MODELO Juana / cerrar las ventanas
→ Juana **cierra** las ventanas.

1. mi papá / despertar a todos nosotros
2. mi mamá / contar lo que pasa
3. Uds. / almorzar en el centro
4. tú / devolver los libros a la biblioteca
5. los chicos / volver del colegio a las tres
6. Ana y yo / comenzar a estudiar a las cuatro
7. yo / jugar ajedrez
8. Federico / acostar a sus hermanitos

G. Hoy sí, mañana no. Escriba oraciones conjugando el segundo verbo de la construcción *verbo conjugado + infinitivo* para indicar que la acción ocurre hoy.

MODELO Mis tíos van a volver mañana.
→ Mis tíos **vuelven** hoy.

1. Vas a recordar la fecha mañana.
2. Pablo y Lorenzo van a jugar fútbol mañana.
3. Vamos a probar el nuevo plato mañana.
4. Alicia va a encontrar su secador mañana.
5. Yo voy a devolver el paraguas mañana.
6. Ud. va a almorzar con Raquel mañana.

H. **¿Qué tiempo hace?** Exprese en español el tiempo que hace hoy en varias ciudades.

¿Qué tiempo hace?

Hace sol/viento.	*It's sunny/windy.*	**nevar (e > ie)**	*to snow*
Hace calor/frío.	*It's warm/cold.*	**tronar (o > ue)**	*to thunder*
Hace buen/mal tiempo.	*The weather's good/bad.*	**el relámpago**	*lightning*
		escampar, despejar	*to clear up*
Está nublado/despejado.	*It's cloudy/clear.*	**helar (e > ie)**	*to freeze*
llover (o > ue)	*to rain*	**granizar**	*to hail*

1. It's raining in London.

____

2. It's snowing in Montreal.

____

3. It's thundering in Santa Fe.

____

4. The rain is beginning to freeze in Nome.

____

5. It's beginning to snow in Moscow.

____

6. It's beginning to rain in Barcelona.

____

7. It's clear in Patagonia.

____

8. It's hailing in New York.

____

Nota cultural

- **Sevilla,** a orillas del río Guadalquivir, es la capital de la Comunidad Autónoma de Andalucía. Es una típica ciudad andaluza con su barrio antiguo (Santa Cruz) de hermosos patios y calles estrechas. Sus muchos monumentos llaman la atención: la Catedral, de arquitectura gótica, la Giralda, el Alcázar, el Archivo de Indias, la Biblioteca Colombina (de Cristóbal Colón), el museo de pintura, etcétera. Hay muchísimo turismo durante Semana Santa y las ferias de abril.
- **Santa Fe,** capital del estado de Nuevo México, fue nombrada por la ciudad española que se encuentra en la provincia de Granada. Fue en esa ciudad española donde Colón y los Reyes Católicos firmaron los convenios (*agreements*) en 1492.
- **Barcelona,** segunda ciudad de España, es la capital de la Comunidad Autónoma de Cataluña. Va desde las orillas del Mediterráneo hasta el monte Tibidabo. Es un puerto muy importante y tiene la industria más importante del país. La ciudad está dividida en dos partes por las Ramblas, una hermosa avenida que baja hasta el puerto. Allí hay un monumento de Colón que conmemora su regreso triunfal de América en 1493; fue recibido en Barcelona por los Reyes Católicos. Barcelona atrae a muchos turistas por su Catedral, iglesias, paseos, parques, plazas de toros, teatros, etcétera. Se habla catalán en Cataluña.
- **Patagonia** es una región de América del Sur, en la parte sur de la Argentina y Chile. Se extiende hasta el estrecho de Magallanes.

B *Stem-changing verbs ending in* ***-ir***

- Stem-changing verbs that end in **-ir** have three types of possible changes in the vowel of the stem: **e** > **ie, o** > **ue, e** > **i.** These **-ir** verbs have the changes in the vowel of the stem in all persons of the present tense except *nosotros* and *vosotros*. Note that **morir(se)** is conjugated like **dormir.**

sentir *to regret*	
siento	sentimos
sientes	sentís
siente	**sienten**

dormir *to sleep*	
duermo	dormimos
duermes	dormís
duerme	**duermen**

pedir *to ask for, request*	
pido	pedimos
pides	pedís
pide	piden

Verbs like **sentir (e > ie)**:

advertir *to notify, warn*
convertir *to convert*
divertirse *to have a good time*
hervir *to boil*
mentir *to lie*
preferir *to prefer*
referirse (a) *to refer (to)*
sentir(se) *to regret, feel*

Verbs like **pedir (e > i)**:

despedir *to fire*
despedirse (de) *to say good-bye*
gemir *to groan, moan*
impedir *to prevent*
medir *to measure*
reír(se) *to laugh*
reñir *to quarrel, scold*
repetir *to repeat; have a second helping*
seguir *to follow, continue*
servir *to serve*
sonreír(se) *to smile*
vestir(se) *to dress*

Note that **reír** and **sonreír** have **í** as the stem vowel in the singular and third-person plural: **(son)río, (son)ríes, (son)ríe, (son)reímos, (son)reís, (son)ríen.**

I. En el restaurante. Escriba lo que piden estas personas que salen a comer.

MODELO Francisco / carne ➔ Francisco pide carne.

1. Ud. y José María / piña

____

2. la familia Herrera / paella

____

3. Pili y yo / ensalada

____

4. tú / flan

____

5. los chicos / pollo

____

6. yo / arroz

____

J. ¿Quién sirve? Escriba quién sirve cada bebida.

MODELO Uds. / vino ➔ Uds. sirven vino.

1. yo / limonada

____

2. Susana / refrescos

____

3. nosotros / cerveza

____

4. Eduardo y Dolores / jugo

____

5. tú / agua mineral

____

6. Ud. y Pepe / soda

____

Nota cultural

- **La paella** es un plato de arroz con carne, pollo, mariscos (*shellfish*) y pescado, guisantes, etcétera que se come en España. Es de origen valenciano, región conocida por su producción de arroz. Se usa el azafrán (*saffron*) para condimentar la paella y para darle al arroz su color amarillo.
- **El flan** es un plato dulce hecho con las yemas de huevo, leche y azúcar. Este postre español es parecido al dulce de leche hispanoamericano.
- España es un país vinícola (*wine-producing*). Hay **vinos** que se producen para exportación que son excelentes. Hasta los sencillos vinos de mesa que se sirven con la comida pueden ser buenísimos. El vino español más conocido en todo el mundo es el jerez (*sherry*) que se produce en la región de Jerez de la Frontera. Esta ciudad queda en la provincia de Cádiz, al sudoeste de Sevilla.
- **El agua mineral** se bebe corrientemente con la comida o en casa o en los restaurantes. Se puede pedir con gas (*carbonated*) o sin gas. Hay algunas regiones del país que tienen manantiales (*springs, sources*) conocidos por la calidad de su agua.

K. ¿Qué prefiere Ud. hacer? Escriba lo que prefiere hacer cada persona.

MODELO Isabel / estudiar → Isabel prefiere estudiar.

1. los primos / salir al campo

____

2. Julia / leer novelas

____

3. mis hermanos y yo / ir a un concierto

____

4. Uds. / ver televisión

____

5. yo / jugar a las damas

____

6. tú / viajar

____

L. Todos duermen la siesta. Escriba cuándo duermen la siesta estas personas.

MODELO tú / los viernes. ➔ Duermes la siesta los viernes.

1. el abuelo / todos los días

____

2. yo / los fines de semana

____

3. Uds. / una vez a la semana

____

4. nosotros / los lunes

____

5. los sobrinos / todas las tardes

____

6. Ud. / los días feriados

____

M. En otras palabras. Escriba lo que ocurre en las siguientes situaciones. Use la forma correcta de uno de los verbos que aparecen a continuación.

divertir	sentir	despedir	hervir
repetir	advertir	mentir	reír
sonreír	vestir	dormir	

MODELO Todos tienen hambre. Tú **sirves** la comida.

1. La abuela baña y _______________ a sus nietos antes de llevarlos al parque.
2. Va a llegar una tempestad del norte. El locutor de radio _______________ al público.
3. Las chicas dejan caer los vasos. Dicen que lo _______________.
4. Ya _______________ el agua. Ahora podemos meter las legumbres.
5. Ud. juega al tenis toda la mañana y siente un cansancio tremendo. Ud. _______________ toda la tarde.
6. Ramona exagera mucho. En realidad, ella _______________.
7. Diana _______________ a sus amigos con sus cuentos graciosos. Sin embargo, hay algunos de ellos que no _______________, ¡ni siquiera _______________!
8. Hace dos años que la fábrica pierde dinero. Los dueños _______________ a muchos obreros.
9. ¿Te gustó la torta? ¿Por qué no _______________?

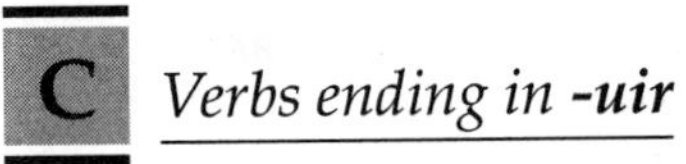

C Verbs ending in -uir

- Verbs ending in **-uir** (not including those ending in **-guir**) add **y** after the **u** in all forms except *nosotros* and *vosotros:*

construir *to build*	
constru**y**o	construimos
constru**y**es	construís
constru**y**e	constru**y**en

Verbs that pattern like **construir**:

atribuir *to attribute*
concluir *to conclude*
contribuir *to contribute*
destruir *to destroy*
distribuir *to distribute*
huir *to flee*
incluir *to include*
influir *to influence*
sustituir *to substitute*

N. Vamos a contribuir. Hubo un terremoto que destruyó muchas casas en la Ciudad de México. Ud. y sus amigos deciden recaudar dinero para mandar medicinas a los mexicanos afectados. Escriba con cuánto dinero contribuyen estas personas.

MODELO Vera / diez dólares
→ Vera contribuye con diez dólares.

1. los padres de Vera / treinta dólares
____
2. mis hermanos y yo / quince dólares
____
3. el director del colegio / veinte dólares
____
4. Ud. / doce dólares
____
5. la tía Adriana / veinticinco dólares
____
6. los ciudadanos del pueblo / mil quinientos dólares
____

O. **¡Qué desastre!** Hay un huracán en la Florida. Hay mucha gente sin casa. Escriba adónde huye la gente para escapar del peligro.

MODELO la familia Rivas / al norte
➔ La familia Rivas huye al norte.

1. tú / a la estación de tren

2. Uds. / al oeste

3. Fernando / a casa de sus abuelos

4. nosotros / a la capital

5. la familia Ortega / a un hotel

6. yo / al interior del estado

P. **Un proyecto.** Unos amigos colaboran en realizar un proyecto para la clase de biología. Escriba lo que propone incluir cada persona del grupo.

MODELO yo / una bibliografía
➔ Yo incluyo una bibliografía.

1. Roberto / investigaciones científicas

2. Uds. / fotos

3. Laura y yo / estadísticas

4. Ud. / buenas explicaciones

5. tú / un resumen

6. David y Ricardo / una introducción

D *Verbs ending in* ***-iar*** *and* ***-uar***

- Some verbs that end in **-iar** or **-uar** stress the **i** or the **u** (**í, ú**) in all forms except *nosotros* and *vosotros* in the present tense.

guiar *to guide*	
guío	guiamos
guías	guiáis
guía	guían

continuar *to continue*	
continúo	continuamos
continúas	continuáis
continúa	continúan

Verbs that pattern like **guiar**:

confiar (en) *to rely (on), confide (in)*
enviar *to send*
espiar *to spy*
fiarse (de) *to trust*
resfriarse *to catch cold*
variar *to vary*

Verbs that pattern like **continuar**:

actuar *to act*
graduarse *to graduate*

Q. **¿Cuándo se resfrían Uds.?** Las personas tienen ideas diferentes sobre cómo y cuándo se resfrían. Escriba lo que creen las siguientes personas.

MODELO Ud. / en diciembre → Ud. se resfría en diciembre.

1. Tomás / todos los inviernos

____

2. Uds. / cuando duermen poco

____

3. Lidia y Miguel / tres veces al año

____

4. Ud. / cuando come mal

____

5. yo / cuando me mojo

____

R. ¿Cuándo es su graduación? Escriba cuándo se gradúan sus amigos del colegio y de la universidad.

MODELO Daniela / en junio → Daniela se gradúa en junio.

1. Micaela y Jorge / el año próximo
   ____
2. Ud. / dentro de dos años
   ____
3. Timoteo / en enero
   ____
4. Uds. / para el noventa y ocho
   ____
5. Anita / este mes
   ____

S. Los espías. Complete esta narración breve sobre el espionaje. Escriba la forma correcta de cada verbo que aparece entre paréntesis.

MODELO El espía **guía** (guiar) a sus colegas por el laberinto.

1. Los espías no ______________ (fiarse) de nadie.
2. Todos los espías ______________ (enviar) mensajes secretos.
3. El espía X ______________ (confiar) solamente en el espía Y.
4. El espía Z ______________ (continuar) su trabajo con los códigos.
5. El espía 003 ______________ (resfriarse) trabajando bajo la lluvia.

T. ¿Qué dice Ud.? Conteste las siguientes preguntas personales.

1. ¿A Ud. le gustan las películas de espionaje y misterio? Describa lo que hacen los espías.
   ____
2. ¿A quiénes les envía cartas?
   ____
3. ¿Se fía Ud. en los anuncios de televisión? Explique.
   ____
4. ¿Qué hace y toma cuando se resfría?
   ____
5. ¿En quiénes confía Ud.?
   ____
6. ¿Cuándo se gradúa Ud.?
   ____

E *Verbs with spelling changes in the present tense*

- For verbs that end in **-ger** and **-gir**, **g** changes to **j** before **o** and **a.** In the present tense, the change occurs only in the first-person singular (*yo* form).

escoger *to choose*	
escojo	escogemos
escoges	escogéis
escoge	escogen

Verbs that pattern like **escoger**:

afligir *to afflict*
coger *to grab, catch*
corregir (e > i) *to correct*
dirigir *to direct, conduct*
elegir (e > i) *to choose, elect*
encoger *to shrink*
exigir *to demand*
fingir *to pretend*
proteger *to protect*
recoger *to gather, pick up*

- For verbs that end in **-guir**, **gu** changes to **g** before **o** and **a**. In the present tense, the change occurs only in the first-person singular (*yo* form).

distinguir *to distinguish*	
distingo	distinguimos
distingues	distinguís
distingue	distinguen

Extinguir (*to extinguish*) is conjugated like **distinguir**.

- **Seguir** (*to follow, continue*) patterns like **distinguir** and also has the stem change **e > i.** This applies to related verbs ending in **-seguir**: **conseguir** (*to get, acquire*), **perseguir** (*to pursue, persecute*), **proseguir** (*to proceed*):

seguir *to follow*	
sigo	seguimos
sigues	seguís
sigue	siguen

- For most verbs that end in **-cer** or **-cir**, **c** changes to **z** before **o** and **a**. In the present tense, the change occurs only in the first-person singular (*yo* form):

convencer *to convince*	
convenzo	convencemos
convences	convencéis
convence	convencen

- **Mecer** (*to rock*), **ejercer** (*to exercise*) and **vencer** (*to conquer, overcome*) pattern like **convencer**. **Cocer** (*to cook*) and **torcer** (*to twist*) also follow this pattern and in addition have the stem change **o** > **ue**:

torcer *to twist*	
tuerzo	torcemos
tuerces	torcéis
tuerce	**tuercen**

cocer *to cook*	
cuezo	cocemos
cueces	cocéis
cuece	**cuecen**

Verbs are marked with their spelling changes in the vocabulary list at the end of the book. See for example: **coger** (**g** > **j/o, a**). When the verb has a stem change and a spelling change, it is marked: **torcer** (**o** > **ue, c** > **z/o,a**).

U. **¿Qué escoge Ud.?** Nuestros tíos van a celebrar su 25.º aniversario el sábado. Por eso vamos al almacén para comprarles unos regalos. Escriba qué regalos escogemos.

MODELO Ud. / un florero
→ Ud. **escoge** un florero.

1. yo / una caja de bombones
____
2. mis padres / una bandeja de plata
____
3. nosotros / un perrito
____
4. tú / dos relojes
____
5. Uds. / un televisor
____
6. la abuela / un juego *(set)* de toallas
____

V. **¿Qué elige Ud.?** Ahora escriba las oraciones del ejercicio U sustituyendo **elegir** por **escoger**.

1. _______________
2. _______________
3. _______________
4. _______________
5. _______________
6. _______________

W. **¿Cuál es su trabajo?** Las siguientes personas hacen cierto trabajo. Escriba lo que hace cada persona escogiendo el verbo correcto de la lista abajo.

dirigir extinguir recoger corregir perseguir cocer

1. Soy campesino. Yo ______________________ manzanas y tomates.
2. Soy policía. Yo ______________________ a los ladrones.
3. Soy bombero. Yo ______________________ incendios.
4. Soy cocinero. Yo ______________________ platos muy sabrosos.
5. Soy director de orquesta. Yo ______________________ una orquesta sinfónica.
6. Soy profesor. Yo ______________________ exámenes y composiciones.

X. **Un misterio.** Describa el terror que experimenta el narrador escribiendo la forma correcta de los verbos que aparecen entre paréntesis.

Es la una de la mañana. Yo ______________________ (1. seguir) por las calles vacías y desoladas de la ciudad. Yo me ______________________ (2. dirigir) al hotel. De repente oigo pasos. Tengo miedo. Me ______________________ (3. encoger) de hombros (*shrug*). Vuelvo la cabeza para ver quién camina detrás de mí, quizás en pos de mí (*after me*). Yo ______________________ (4. distinguir) una sombra de persona. No la ______________________ (5. reconocer). La persona deja de caminar y ______________________ (6. fingir) no verme. Yo ______________________ (7. conseguir) ver que la persona ______________________ (8. lucir) un vestido blanco que brilla a la luz de la luna. Yo ______________________ (9. proseguir) mi camino al hotel pero ahora camino más rápido. La situación me ______________________ (10. producir) mucha angustia pero yo ______________________ (11. fingir) no estar nervioso. Yo ______________________ (12. distinguir) un paquete que está a mis pies. Lo ______________________ (13. recoger). ¡Me da un escalofrío ver que yo soy el destinatario (*addressee*)! Trato de persuadirme que esto es una pesadilla. Por desgracia, no me ______________________ (14. convencer). ¡Aunque yo ______________________ (15. desconocer) el camino voy corriendo por las calles como un loco!

Y. Consiguen hacer algunas cosas. Escriba lo que consiguen hacer Ud. y sus amigos el sábado.

MODELO Rosa y Margarita / terminar su tarea
→ Rosa y Margarita **consiguen** terminar su tarea.

1. Víctor / salir al centro comercial

2. Pablo y yo / reparar el coche

3. Ud. / ver la nueva exposición

4. yo / pasar la aspiradora

5. Uds. / arreglar los armarios

6. Teodoro y tú / colgar los cuadros

Z. Sinónimos. Escoja el sinónimo del verbo en cada oración de la lista abajo. Escriba la forma correcta del verbo en la nueva oración.

cocer	exigir	desconocer	elegir	conseguir
coger	producir	seguir	fingir	distinguir

1. *Continúa* con sus clases de pintura.

2. *Agarro* las monedas una por una.

3. *Ignoro* el motivo de los directores.

4. *Disimulo* tener interés en el proyecto.

5. *Cocinan* arroz para servir con el pollo.

6. No *diferencio* entre el mar y el cielo en el cuadro.

7. *Pido* más esfuerzos de parte de los estudiantes.

8. ¿*Seleccionas* tus clases para el próximo semestre?

9. No *logro* hablar con mis cuñados hoy.

10. *Cultivo* maíz y trigo en la finca.

AA. Las noticias. Exprese en español los titulares del periódico que Ud. lee. Trate de usar los verbos comprendidos en esta sección.

1. Leopoldo Soto is conducting the New York Philharmonic this week.
2. The firemen put out thirty fires each day.
3. The citizens are demanding better schools.
4. Senator Alonso is following the advice of his colleagues in the Senate.
5. The Americans elect a new president this year.
6. Young couple succeeds in winning the lottery!
7. A new recipe: chef cooks soup with ice cream!
8. News from abroad: the army of A vanquishes the army of B.
9. The campaign against illiteracy proceeds.
10. The governors are ignorant of many problems in their cities.

BB. Ejercicio oral: ¿Qué piensan hacer Uds.? Pregúnteles a sus compañeros lo que piensan hacer y adónde quieren ir este fin de semana. Que digan también cómo se modificarán sus planes si llueve o nieva. Use verbos con cambios radicales donde sea posible, tales como **pensar, querer, preferir, volver, poder,** etc.

CC. Estructuras en acción. Lea estos dos anuncios para programas de televisión del canal *Antena 3* de España e indique en la tabla a cuál de los dos programas se refieren las características dadas.

	Manuel Campo Vidal	Farmacia de Guardia
Noticias		
Comedia		
Cambio de ideas		
Hace pensar		
Ya tiene muchos televidentes		
Anuncio usa el estilo de la receta médica		
Programa digno de confianza		

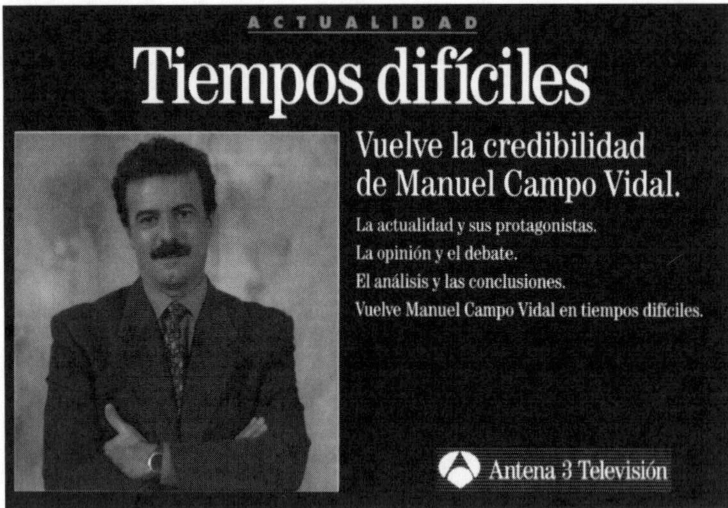

ACTUALIDAD
Tiempos difíciles
Vuelve la credibilidad de Manuel Campo Vidal.
La actualidad y sus protagonistas.
La opinión y el debate.
El análisis y las conclusiones.
Vuelve Manuel Campo Vidal en tiempos difíciles.
Antena 3 Televisión

TELECOMEDIAS
Los jueves, la química del éxito.
Según Antonio Mercero, no tiene contraindicaciones.
Efectos secundarios: Puede producir sonrisas múltiples.
FARMACIA DE GUARDIA
FARMACIA
PRODUCTOS QUIMICOS
AGUAS MINERALES
FARMACIA
GRAN EXITO DE AUDIENCIA
Antena 3 Televisión

CHAPTER 4

THE PRETERIT TENSE

A Regular verbs

- The preterit tense is used to express events that were completed in the past. Preterit-tense endings are added to the stem of regular **-ar, -er,** and **-ir** verbs.

tomar *to take; drink*	
tom**é**	tom**amos**
tom**aste**	tom**asteis**
tom**ó**	tom**aron**

comer *to eat*	
com**í**	com**imos**
com**iste**	com**isteis**
com**ió**	com**ieron**

vivir *to live*	
viv**í**	viv**imos**
viv**iste**	viv**isteis**
viv**ió**	viv**ieron**

Notes:

1. All preterit forms are stressed on the endings rather than on the stem.
2. For **-ar** verbs:
    - the first-person singular *(yo* form) in the present tense and the third-person singular *(él, ella, Ud.* form) are distinguished only by the stress: tom**o** / tom**ó**.
    - the first-person plural *(nosotros* form) is the same in the present tense and the preterit tense: **tomamos**. The meaning is clarified by context.
3. The preterit endings are the same for both **-er** and **-ir** verbs.
4. For **-ir** verbs:
    - the first-person plural *(nosotros* form) is the same in the present tense and the preterit tense: **vivimos**. The meaning is clarified by context.
5. For **-er** verbs:
    - the present and preterit of the *nosotros* forms are different: com**emos** / com**imos**.
6. **-Ar** and **-er** verbs that have changes in the vowel of the stem *(***e** > **ie** or **o** > **ue***)* in the present tense, do not have these changes in any of the preterit forms. For example: p**ie**nso / pens**é**, v**ue**lven / v**o**lvieron.
7. **-Ir** verbs that have a change in the vowel of the stem in the present tense also have a stem change in the preterit tense. In the preterit the vowel changes from **e** > **i** or from **o** > **u** in the third-person singular and plural.

pedir *to ask for*	
pedí	pedimos
pediste	pedisteis
pidió	pidieron

dormir *to sleep*	
dormí	dormimos
dormiste	dormisteis
durmió	durmieron

8. Some verbs that pattern like **servir**: **pedir** (*to ask for*), **divertirse** (*to have a good time*), **repetir** (*to repeat*), **medir** (*to measure*), **advertir** (*to point out, warn*), **mentir** (*to lie*), **convertir** (*to convert*). Like **dormir**: **morir** (*to die*).
9. The verbs **reír** and **sonreír** have a written accent mark on the **i** of the endings of the *yo, tú, nosotros,* and *vosotros* forms in the preterit: (son)reí, (son)reíste, (son)rió, (son)reímos, (son)reísteis, (son)rieron.
10. **-Ir** verbs that have **ñ** directly before the ending drop the **i** of the ending in the third-person singular and plural: **gruñir** (*to grunt*): **gruñó / gruñeron; reñir** (*to scold*): **riñó / riñeron**.

Verbs with spelling changes in the preterit

- **-Ar** verbs whose stems end in the letters **c, g,** and **z** have spelling changes in the *yo* form of the preterit. While these verbs are regular in speech, the rules of Spanish spelling require that the sounds /k/, /g/, and /s/ (written **z**) be written differently before **e** and **i**:

/k/	ca, **que, qui,** co, cu
/g/	ga, **gue, gui,** go, gu
/s/ (written **z**)	za, **ce, ci,** zo, zu

- Compare the spelling of the *yo* form of the present and preterit of the verbs **buscar, llegar,** and **comenzar**: busco / **busqué**, llego / **llegué**, comienzo / **comencé**.

Some verbs like **buscar**:

acercarse *to approach*
arrancar *to pull/root out; start up (vehicle)*
colocar *to put, place*
dedicarse *to devote oneself*
embarcarse *to embark, go on board*
equivocarse *to be mistaken*
explicar *to explain*
fabricar *to make, manufacture*
indicar *to indicate*
marcar *to dial; mark*
mascar *to chew*
masticar *to chew*
pescar *to fish*
publicar *to publish*
sacar *to take out*
tocar *to touch; play a musical instrument*

Some verbs like **llegar**:

agregar *to add*
ahogarse *to drown*
apagar *to put out, extinguish*
cargar *to load*
castigar *to punish*
colgar (o > ue) *to hang*
encargar *to put in charge, entrust, to order*
entregar *to hand in/over*
jugar (u > ue) *to play*
madrugar *to get up early*
negar (e > ie) *to deny*
pagar *to pay*
pegar *to stick/beat*
rogar (o > ue) *to beg, ask*
tragar *to swallow*

Verbs like **comenzar**:

abrazar *to hug, embrace*
alcanzar *to reach, overtake*
almorzar (o > ue) *to have lunch*
amenazar *to threaten*
cruzar *to cross*
deslizarse *to slip*
empezar (e > ie) *to begin*
gozar *to enjoy*
lanzar *to throw*
realizar *to fulfill*
rezar *to pray*
tranquilizarse *to calm down*
tropezar (e > ie) *to trip, stumble*

C *-Er and -ir verbs with stems ending in a vowel*

- **-Er** and **-ir verbs** that have a vowel immediately preceding the preterit ending, change **-ió** to **-yó** in the third-person singular and **-ieron** to **-yeron** in the third-person plural in the preterit. These verbs also add a written accent to the **i** of the *tú*, *nosotros*, and *vosotros* endings:

leer *to read*	
leí	leímos
leíste	leísteis
le**yó**	le**yeron**

oír *to hear*	
oí	oímos
oíste	oísteis
o**yó**	o**yeron**

- Verbs that end in **-uir** also pattern this way; however, there is no written accent on the *tú*, *nosotros*, and *vosotros* forms of the verbs:

construir *to build*	
construí	construimos
construiste	construisteis
constru**yó**	constru**yeron**

- **Traer**, which has an irregular preterit, verbs with prefixes added to **traer**, and verbs that end in **-guir** are exceptions to the above pattern.

Some verbs like **leer** and **oír**:

caer *to fall*
creer *to think, believe*
poseer *to have, possess*

Some verbs like **construir**:

concluir *to conclude*
contribuir *to contribute*
distribuir *to distribute*
huir *to flee*
incluir *to include*
intuir *to have a sense of, feel*

A. **¡Tanta tarea!** Escriba las cosas que Ud. y sus compañeros de clase hicieron ayer.

MODELO Bárbara / practicar el ruso en el laboratorio
➔ Bárbara practicó el ruso en el laboratorio.

1. Esteban / estudiar la historia de la Edad Media

____

2. Rosa y Elena / solucionar problemas de cálculo

____

3. tú / escribir poemas

____

4. nosotros / trabajar en la librería

____

5. yo / visitar el museo de historia natural

____

6. Uds. / contestar preguntas de filosofía

____

7. Miguel / usar la computadora

____

8. Ud. / aprender fechas de historia de memoria

____

B. **¡Vaya un día de examen!** Escriba las formas correctas del pretérito de los verbos que aparecen entre paréntesis. Así describe lo que le pasó el día del examen.

MODELO Mamá me **despertó** (despertar) a las siete.

En seguida yo me ____________ (1. levantar) y me ____________ (2. arreglar). ____________ (3. Bajar) a la cocina donde ____________ (4. saludar) a mis padres y a mi hermano. Mamá me ____________ (5. preparar) cereal y pan tostado. Yo ____________ (6. tomar) jugo y ____________ (7. empezar) a repasar mi libro de química. Mi amigo Carlos ____________ (8. pasar) por mí y ____________ (9. desayunar) con nosotros. Él y yo ____________ (10. terminar) el desayuno y yo ____________ (11. coger) mi mochila de la sala. Carlos y yo ____________ (12. salir) corriendo para la parada de autobuses. El número once ____________ (13. llegar) casi inmediatamente. Los dos ____________ (14. subir) y ____________ (15. viajar) quince minutos hasta llegar al colegio. Nosotros ____________ (16. bajar) casi en la puerta principal. Tan pronto como el autobús ____________ (17. arrancar) yo ____________ (18. buscar) mi mochila. No la ____________ (19. encontrar). ¡Y con mis apuntes adentro! ¡Qué susto! "Yo ____________ (20. colocar) la mochila en el asiento y no ____________ (21. recordar) cogerla al bajar!", yo ____________ (22. pensar). Carlos me ____________ (23. mirar) con mi cara de angustia y ____________ (24. hablar). "Chico, no te preocupes. Aquí la tienes", me ____________________ (25. explicar). Mi mejor amigo me ____________________ (26. entregar) la mochila y así me ____________________ (27. salvar) la vida.

C. Salimos a cenar. Escriba qué tal lo pasó Ud. cuando salió a cenar con sus amigos.

MODELO mis amigos y yo / salir a cenar / anoche
➔ Mis amigos y yo salimos a cenar anoche.

1. Felipe / escoger / el Café Valencia
____
2. nosotros / llegar / al restaurante a las siete
____
3. nosotros / mirar / la carta
____
4. el mozo/ recomendar / la paella
____
5. Lorenzo / pedir / ternera y sopa
____
6. Eva y Diana / pedir / pescado y ensalada
____
7. yo / preferir / el arroz con pollo
____
8. tú / comer / torta de postre
____
9. todos / tomar/ vino
____
10. nadie / beber / café
____
11. Felipe / pagar / la cuenta
____
12. Jaime / dejar / la propina
____
13. todos nosotros / cenar / muy bien
____
14. yo / gozar / mucho
____
15. todos los amigos / divertirse
____

Nota cultural

El arroz con pollo es un plato que se sirve en casi todos los países del mundo hispánico. Varía de un país a otro o de una región a otra en cuanto a los otros ingredientes y los condimentos.

D. **¡Todo hecho ya!** Su amigo le pregunta si va a hacer ciertas cosas hoy. Para responderle, escriba que ya las hizo.

MODELO ¿Vas a apagar las luces?
➔ Ya apagué las luces.

1. ¿Vas a sacar libros de la biblioteca?
______
2. ¿Vas a jugar al ajedrez?
______
3. ¿Vas a tocar la flauta?
______
4. ¿Vas a colocar los documentos en el archivo?
______
5. ¿Vas a arrancar la mala hierba del jardín?
______
6. ¿Vas a explicar lo que sucedió?
______
7. ¿Vas a colgar los cuadros?
______
8. ¿Vas a almorzar con Victoria?
______
9. ¿Vas a entregar el informe?
______
10. ¿Vas a empezar la novela inglesa?
______

E. **Pasaron los años.** Hace ocho años que Ud. no ve a unas personas. Ahora tiene noticias de ellas. Escriba lo que les pasó a lo largo de los años.

MODELO Jacinta / caer / enferma ➔ Jacinta cayó enferma.

1. los hermanos Serrat / construir / muchas casas
______

2. el profesor Burgos / influir / mucho en la política

____

3. Francisca / leer / libros para una casa editora

____

4. Marco e Isabel / huir / a otro pueblo por una tempestad

____

5. doña Elvira / contribuir / mucho dinero a las caridades

____

6. Leonardo / concluir / los trámites de la empresa

____

F. **¡Qué mala suerte!** Ayer todo le salió mal. Escriba lo que le pasó.

MODELO Yo me **caí** (caer) en la escalera.

1. Yo me _______________ (equivocar) de número de teléfono
2. y _______________ (marcar) mal cuatro veces.
3. Luego _______________ (tropezar) con la pared
4. y me _______________ (pegar) en el hueso de la alegría (*funny bone*).
5. Luego me _______________ (deslizar) en una cáscara de plátano.
6. En la cena _______________ (mascar) la carne demasiado rápido
7. y _______________ (tragar) mal.
8. Para tranquilizarme, me _______________ (bañar).
9. Casi me _______________ (ahogar) en la bañera.
10. ¡Claro que no me _______________ (tranquilizar)!

G. **Yo no hice eso.** Escriba las formas correctas de los verbos que aparecen entre paréntesis para describir lo que hicieron otras personas y lo que hizo o no hizo Ud.

MODELO Alicia **encargó** unos vestidos. (encargar)
Yo no **encargué** nada.

1. Jorge _______________ la pelota en el partido. (lanzar)
   Yo no _______________ la pelota.
2. Álvaro _______________ unos cuentos. (publicar)
   Yo no _______________ cuentos sino una novela.
3. Tú te _______________ a la pintura. (dedicar)
   Yo me _______________ a la música.
4. Uds. _______________ todos los cajones. (cargar)
   Yo no _______________ ninguno.

5. Los Sierra ________________ un viaje a Bruselas. (realizar)

   Yo ________________ un viaje a Estocolmo, capital de Suecia.

6. Ud. se ________________ para Córcega (*Corsica*). (embarcar)

   Yo me ________________ para las islas de Grecia.

H. **Una entrevista.** Ud. acaba de volver de Puerto Rico donde pasó tres semanas con sus amigos. Ahora un periodista del periódico del colegio le hace unas preguntas sobre el viaje. Contéstelas.

MODELO ¿Qué día llegó a Puerto Rico? (el 20 de diciembre)
→ Llegué el 20 de diciembre.

Turismo

el aeropuerto *airport*
almorzar *to have lunch*
aterrizar *to land*
la estancia *stay*
la fortaleza *fortress*
gozar (de) *to enjoy*
la iglesia *church*
el lugar turístico *tourist attraction*
el mar *sea, ocean*
el museo *museum*
pescar *to fish*
la playa *beach*
rezar *to pray*
la sinagoga *synagogue*
visitar *to visit*

1. ¿Dónde aterrizaron Uds.? (el aeropuerto de San Juan)

   ____

2. ¿Qué lugares turísticos visitó? (fortalezas, museos e iglesias)

   ____

3. ¿Rezó Ud. en una iglesia? (yo en la iglesia de San Juan y Sara en una sinagoga)

   ____

4. ¿Almorzó Ud. en la playa? (en varias playas de la isla)

   ____

5. ¿Jugaron Uds. al tenis? (y al fútbol también)

   ____

6. ¿Pescó Ud. en el mar? (y en los ríos también)

   ____

7. ¿Avanzaron Uds. en su dominio del español? (mucho)

   ____

8. ¿Qué tal el viaje que realizaron? (maravilloso)

   ____

9. ¿Gozó de su estancia en Puerto Rico? (muchísimo)

   ____

Nota cultural

El **Estado Libre Asociado de Puerto Rico** es un país que tiene el océano Atlántico al norte y el mar Caribe al sur. Es la isla más oriental de las Antillas Mayores cuyas otras islas más grandes son La Española (la República Dominicana y Haití), Jamaica y Cuba. La isla fue llamada Borinquen por los indígenas (arawacos y caribes). Cristóbal Colón desembarcó en la isla en su segundo viaje en 1493. A los turistas les llaman la atención el Viejo San Juan, la fortaleza de El Morro, el museo de arte de Ponce, el Yunque (bosque), la Casa Blanca de Ponce de León, explorador de Puerto Rico y fundador de San Juan (1508), etcétera. Hay también muchos festivales por toda la isla como el Festival Casals de música clásica que tiene lugar a mediados de junio. El festival lleva el nombre del célebre violonchelista puertorriqueño Pablo Casals, nacido en España, de madre puertorriqueña y padre catalán. Casals murió en Puerto Rico después de vivir allí casi veinte años. Los puertorriqueños llaman a Puerto Rico «la Isla».

I. ¿Cómo reaccionó la gente? Exprese en español cómo reaccionaron estas personas a una situación o a una noticia.

Modelo Laura denied it. → Laura lo negó.

1. You (*tú*) smiled.
____
2. The boys had a second helping. (repetir)
____
3. Patricio grunted.
____
4. We laughed.
____
5. You (*Uds.*) fell asleep. (dormirse)
____
6. Mrs. Gil served the soup.
____
7. Chelo scolded the children.
____
8. The thieves lied.
____
9. Our friends warned us.
____
10. Paquita had a good time.
____
11. They were sorry.
____

D Irregular verbs in the preterit

Many Spanish verbs have an irregular stem plus a special set of endings in the preterit. The endings for these verbs are: **-e, -iste, -o, -imos, -isteis, -ieron.** Note that the *yo* and *él* forms are stressed on the stem, not on the ending:

decir *to say, tell*	
dije	dijimos
dijiste	dijisteis
dijo	dijeron

estar *to be*	
estuve	estuvimos
estuviste	estuvisteis
estuvo	estuvieron

hacer *to do, make*	
hice	hicimos
hiciste	hicisteis
hizo	hicieron

poder *to be able, can*	
pude	pudimos
pudiste	pudisteis
pudo	pudieron

poner *to put*	
puse	pusimos
pusiste	pusisteis
puso	pusieron

querer *to want, love*	
quise	quisimos
quisiste	quisisteis
quiso	quisieron

saber *to know*	
supe	supimos
supiste	supisteis
supo	supieron

tener *to have*	
tuve	tuvimos
tuviste	tuvisteis
tuvo	tuvieron

traer *to bring*	
traje	trajimos
trajiste	trajisteis
trajo	trajeron

venir *to come*	
vine	vinimos
viniste	vinisteis
vino	vinieron

andar *to walk*	
anduve	anduvimos
anduviste	anduvisteis
anduvo	anduvieron

caber *to fit*	
cupe	cupimos
cupiste	cupisteis
cupo	cupieron

producir *to produce*	
produje	produjimos
produjiste	produjisteis
produjo	produjeron

Notes:

1. For the third-person singular of **hacer** in the preterit, the stem is spelled **hiz-** (**hizo**). The spelling change **c** > **z** before **o** retains the /s/.
2. Irregular preterits whose stem ends in **-j**, such as **dij-** (**decir**) and **traj-** (**traer**), have **-eron** and not **-ieron** in the third-person plural form: **dijeron, trajeron, produjeron.** Other verbs, ending in **-ducir,** are conjugated like **producir** in the preterit: **tradujeron** (**traducir** *to translate*), **condujeron** (**conducir** *to drive*), etc.

3. Compound forms of the verbs **hacer** (*rehacer, satisfacer,* etc.), **poner** (*proponer, reponerse,* etc.), **tener** (*mantener, sostener,* etc.), **traer** (*atraer, distraer,* etc.), **venir** (*convenir, prevenir*) are conjugated the same way as the main verb.
4. The preterit form of **hay** (*there is, there are*) is **hubo**.
5. **Dar** takes the endings of regular **-er** and **-ir** verbs in the preterit. Note that the first- and third-person singular forms are written without an accent mark. **Ver**, regular in the preterit, has no written accent marks, like **dar**.

dar *to give*	
di diste dio	dimos disteis dieron

ver *to see*	
vi viste vio	vimos visteis vieron

- **Ser** (*to be*) and **ir** (*to go*) have the same conjugation in the preterit tense. Although isolated sentences may be ambiguous (for example, **fue** means both *he was* and *he went*), context usually clarifies which verb is meant.

ser/ir	
fui fuiste fue	fuimos fuisteis fueron

- Some verbs take on a different meaning when they are used in the preterit. The distinction in meaning will be especially important when you study the difference between the preterit tense and the imperfect tense, which are two aspects or ways of looking at past time. In the case of these verbs used in the preterit, they focus on the beginning or completion of an action. For example, **conocí** means *I began to know,* that is, *I met.*

Verb	*Spanish*	*English*
saber *to know*	Supe la fecha hoy.	*I found out the date today.*
conocer *to know*	Conocimos a Carmen ayer.	*We met Carmen yesterday.*
tener *to have*	Tuvo una idea.	*He got an idea.*
poder *to be able to*	No pudieron salir.	*They didn't manage to go out.*
querer *to want*	No quisiste trotar.	*You refused to jog.*

J. El pronóstico meteorológico. Su amiga está leyendo el periódico y comenta sobre el tiempo que hace en varios lugares. Escriba que no ha cambiado desde ayer.

MODELO —Hace buen tiempo en Quito.
—Hizo buen tiempo ayer también.

1. Está nublado en Bilbao.

____

2. Hace frío en Estocolmo.

____

3. Llueve en Montevideo.

____

4. Hace sol en Guadalajara.

____

5. Está despejado en Jerusalén.

____

6. Nieva en los Andes.

____

7. Hace ochenta grados en Miami.

____

8. Hace fresco en Roma.

____

9. Truena en Marruecos.

____

10. Hay mucho viento en Chicago.

____

Nota cultural

- **Quito,** capital de Ecuador, queda a algunos 25 kilómetros de la línea ecuatorial, pero tiene los días calurosos y las noches frescas porque tiene una altitud de 2.850 metros.

- **Bilbao** es una ciudad que queda al norte de España. En Bilbao suele haber cielos nublados y mucha lluvia.

- **Montevideo** es la capital de Uruguay, el país más pequeño de América del Sur. Es una estación veraniega (*summer resort*) y el punto de partida para llegar a los balnearios (*beach resort*) de la costa uruguaya.

- **Guadalajara** es la segunda ciudad de México en población y la capital del estado de Jalisco. El clima es templado (*mild*), seco y despejado todo el año aunque las noches pueden ser tormentosas.

- **Los Andes,** cordillera (*mountain range*) de América del Sur que se extiende desde el mar de las Antillas o el Caribe hasta la Antártida. Va por la costa del Pacífico, y con sus 7.500 kilómetros de largo, es la mayor cadena (*chain*) del mundo, formando parte del paisaje de Argentina, Chile, Perú, Bolivia, Ecuador, Colombia y Venezuela. El clima varía de una parte de la cordillera a otra: lluvia en el sur, clima tropical y zonas de desierto en el centro, clima cálido y húmedo y nieves perpetuas a partir de los 4.000 metros en el norte. Hay mucha actividad volcánica también.

- **Marruecos** es un reino de África del Norte, que tiene el Mediterráneo al norte, el Atlántico al oeste y el Sáhara al sur y al sureste. Su capital es Rabat.

K. **Escenas breves.** Escriba las formas correctas en el pretérito de los verbos que aparecen entre paréntesis para saber lo que se dice en los diálogos breves.

1. —¿Qué ____________ Ud. entonces? (decir)
   —Pues, no ____________ nada.
2. —¿A qué hora ____________ Uds. al cine? (ir)
   —____________ a las nueve.
3. —¿Dónde (tú) ____________ el sábado? (estar)
   —____________ en el centro comercial.
4. —¿Las mozas les ____________ los platos principales? (traer)
   —No, una moza ____________ el pan y nada más.
5. —¿Uds. ____________ en coche? (venir)
   —Yo ____________ en coche pero Teri ____________ en tren.
6. —Yo ____________ con Catalina anteayer. (dar)
   —¿Ah sí? ¿Dónde la (Ud.) ____________? (ver)
7. —¿Clara ____________ lo que pasó? (oír)
   —Sí, lo ____________ la semana pasada. (saber)
8. —Tú ____________ la comida, ¿verdad? (hacer)
   —Claro. Y ____________ la mesa también. (poner)
9. —¿José ____________ el informe? (leer)
   —No, no ____________. (querer)
10. —¿Quién ____________ el postre? (hacer)
    —¡____________ yo! (ser)

L. **¿Y qué pasó después?** Para cada situación descrita abajo hay una reacción. Para saber cuál es, escoja la expresión de la lista y conjugue el verbo en el pretérito.

hacerse daño	decir que sí	poner la mesa	poder distinguir
tener frío	ir tras ella	estar feliz	hacerse médico

Modelo Yo invité a Marta a mi casa. (venir a verme)
→ Marta **vino a verme**.

1. Matilde ganó la lotería.
   Ella ____________________________.
2. Juan Carlos se graduó en la facultad de medicina.
   Él ____________________________.
3. Bajó mucho la temperatura entre las cinco y las seis de la tarde.
   Los niños ____________________________.
4. Preparamos una cena para veinte invitados.
   Nosotros ____________________________.

5. El pintor se cayó de la escalera.

   Él ______________________________.

6. Fue un día de mucha niebla.

   Yo ni ______________________________ la carretera.

7. Uds. le pidieron prestado el coche a Rodrigo.

   Rodrigo ______________________________.

8. Tu novia salió de la conferencia.

   Y tú ______________________________.

M. **Ayer, al contrario ...** Generalmente Ud. hace cosas de cierta manera. Ayer, sin embargo, no fue así. Escriba cómo salieron sus actividades empleando la información que se encuentra entre paréntesis.

MODELO Generalmente me acuesto a las diez. (las once)
→ Pero ayer me acosté a las once.

1. Generalmente me despierto a las ocho. (las siete)

   ____

2. Generalmente almuerzo en el Café Bélgica. (el Café Atenas)

   ____

3. Generalmente voy de compras por la tarde. (por la mañana)

   ____

4. Generalmente hago un plato de pollo. (un plato de pescado)

   ____

5. Generalmente juego al tenis con Roberto. (con Ricardo)

   ____

6. Generalmente sigo por la calle Toledo. (la calle Atocha)

   ____

7. Generalmente empiezo a trabajar después del desayuno. (antes del desayuno)

   ____

8. Generalmente vengo en tren. (en taxi)

   ____

N. **Una merienda en el campo.** Unos amigos recuerdan lo bien que lo pasaron ese domingo en julio cuando fueron a merendar en el campo. Escriba lo que dicen escogiendo los verbos correctos. Escriba los verbos en pretérito.

tener	oír	ver	comenzar	estar
hacer	conducir	poder	divertirse	
recoger	traer	ir	dar	

1. ¡Todos _______________ tanto ese día!
2. Todos nosotros _______________ en carro.
3. Antonio y Francisco _______________ los carros.
4. Por desgracia Pedro no _______________ acompañarnos.
5. _______________ muy buen tiempo.
6. Diego _______________ un paseo con los niños.
7. Lila y Berta _______________ margaritas.
8. Yo _______________ sándwiches y fruta.
9. Leticia y Manuel _______________ ensaladas y jugo.
10. Los chicos _______________ vacas y caballos
11. y _______________ cantar los pájaros.
12. A las cinco de la tarde _______________ a llover y
13. nosotros _______________ que volver a la ciudad.
14. ¡Nosotros _______________ muy contentos ese día!

O. ¡Qué suspenso! Ud. es escritor(a) de cuentos de misterio. Escriba un cuento de misterio expresando en español las siguientes frases.

1. The monster came to the city.
____
2. It smashed (*hacer pedazos*) cars and destroyed buildings.
____
3. When the people saw the monster they shouted (*dar gritos*).
____
4. I got (*ponerse*) pale.
____
5. My friend Lorenzo got a headache.
____
6. My friend Marisol got a stomachache.
____
7. We all started (*echarse a*) to run.
____
8. Some people didn't manage (*poder*) to escape.
____
9. The suspense became (*hacerse*) unbearable!
____

P. ¿Qué dice Ud.? Conteste las siguientes preguntas personales.

1. ¿Adónde fuiste el fin de semana?
____
2. ¿Qué hiciste el sábado (el domingo)?
____
3. ¿Adónde fuiste cuando saliste a comer?
____
4. ¿Con quiénes fuiste?
____
5. ¿Qué pidieron Uds.?
____
6. ¿Qué tal estuvo la comida?
____
7. ¿Qué tal sirvieron los mozos?
____
8. ¿Quién pagó la cuenta?
____
9. ¿Quién dejó la propina?
____
10. ¿Dónde pasó Ud. las vacaciones de verano (invierno)?
____
11. ¿Con quiénes fue?
____
12. ¿Qué hicieron Uds. allí?
____

Q. Ejercicio oral. Diálogos: El horario. Con un(a) compañero(a) compare su horario diario. Diga las cosas que hizo ayer y a qué hora las hizo. Hable de las comidas y cuándo se despertó, se acostó, tuvo clases, fue al cine, etcétera. Luego describa lo que hizo el fin de semana.

R. Estructuras en acción. Lea el siguiente artículo sobre una exposición de violines robados. Fíjese en las formas del pretérito y conteste las preguntas que siguen.

1. Jean-Baptiste Vuillaume y Jacobus Steiner son __________.
   a. visitantes de la exposición
   b. policías parisienses
   c. marcas de violín

2. Vinieron a la exposición __________.
   a. personas a quienes les robaron el violín o el violoncelo
   b. varios parientes del rey de Francia
   c. ladrones de instrumentos musicales

3. __________ personas recuperaron su instrumento musical.
   a. Dos mil
   b. Unas cien
   c. Todas las

4. La primera mujer que entró en la exposición __________.
   a. vio que el violín número uno era el suyo
   b. no pudo evitar las risas
   c. fue Adelaida, hija del rey de Francia

5. La policía francesa organizó la exposición __________.
   a. para atrapar a los ladrones de violines
   b. para fomentar entusiasmo para la música
   c. para que los dueños de los instrumentos robados los recuperaran

¿Dónde está mi violín?

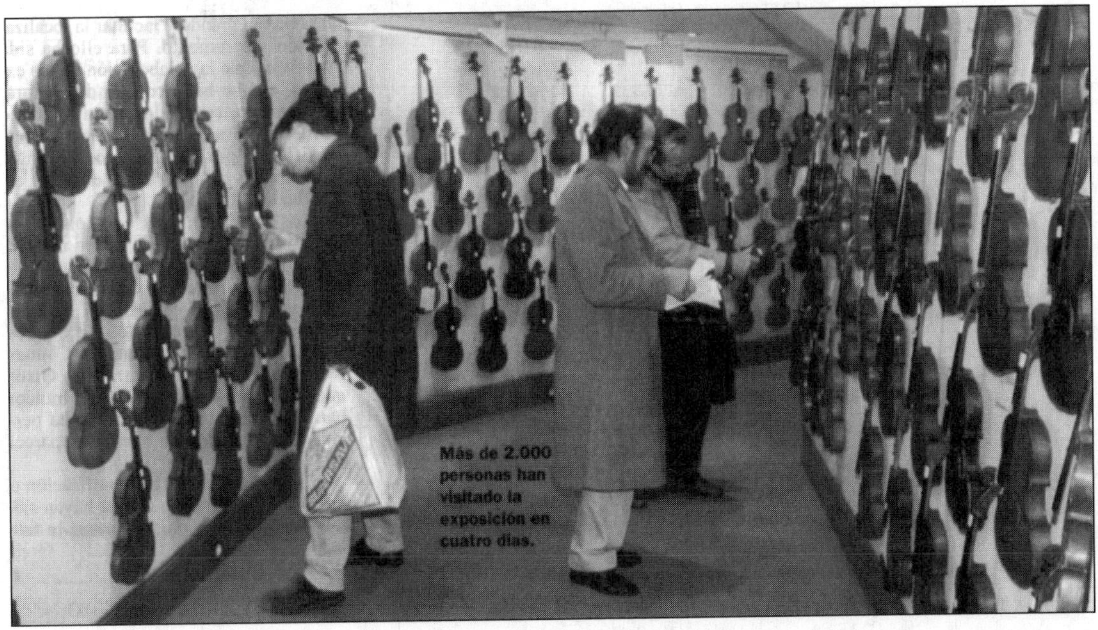

Más de 2.000 personas han visitado la exposición en cuatro días.

La policía de París organizó una exposición de mil violines y violoncelos robados para que sus dueños los identificaran. En los cuatro días que duró la exposición, cien personas recuperaron el suyo.

Algunos visitantes de la exposición estaban convencidos de que no encontrarían su violín, pero no renunciaron a intentarlo. Es el caso de André Miesch, de 73 años, que buscaba su violín Jean-Baptiste Vuillaume. Miesch aseguró que su violín, que fue robado hace 15 años, perteneció a la princesa Adelaida, hija del rey de Francia Luis XV. Otros tuvieron más suerte, como un músico de 70 años que encontró su Jacobus Steiner 1659 o como la primera mujer que entró en la exposición, quien inmediatamente señaló con el dedo el violín marcado con el número uno. Los expertos y policías presentes no pudieron evitar las risas, pensando que era un error fruto del entusiasmo, pero no. Era su violín.

No ha sido el caso de la mayoría. De las más de 2.000 personas que visitaron la exposición, sólo un centenar encontró su violín.

CHAPTER 5

THE IMPERFECT TENSE

Formation of the imperfect

- The endings of the imperfect tense for **-ar** verbs have **-aba-** in all forms. The endings for **-er** and **-ir** verbs are formed by placing **-ía** in all forms:

viajar *to travel*	
viaj**aba**	viaj**ábamos**
viaj**abas**	viaj**abais**
viaj**aba**	viaj**aban**

correr *to run*	
corr**ía**	corr**íamos**
corr**ías**	corr**íais**
corr**ía**	corr**ían**

salir *to go out*	
sal**ía**	sal**íamos**
sal**ías**	sal**íais**
sal**ía**	sal**ían**

Notes:

1. The first- and third-person singular forms are identical for all verbs in the imperfect: (*yo / él, ella, Ud.*) **viajaba, corría, salía.**
2. For **-ar** verbs, the *nosotros* form is the only one with a written accent.
3. For **-er** and **-ir** verbs, all forms have a written accent over the **í**.
4. The imperfect of **hay** is **había** (*there was, there were*).

- All verbs are regular in the imperfect tense with the exception of **ir, ser,** and **ver**.

ir *to go*	
iba	íbamos
ibas	ibais
iba	iban

ser *to be*	
era	éramos
eras	erais
era	eran

ver *to see*	
veía	veíamos
veías	veíais
veía	veían

B Basic uses of the imperfect

- The imperfect tense is used to express an event or action going on in the past without any reference to its beginning or end. Because the imperfect is not concerned with the beginning or completion of an action, it is the tense used for expressing repeated actions in past time. Adverbs and adverbial phrases such as **todos los días**, **siempre**, and **muchas veces** are often clues for the selection of the imperfect rather than the preterit. The imperfect is therefore also the tense used for description and expressing background in the past. Common English equivalents for the Spanish imperfect are *used to do, was doing*:

—¿**Eras** estudiante entonces?	***Were you** a student then?*
—No, yo **era** ingeniero ya.	*No, **I was** already an engineer.*
—**Querían** tocar en la orquesta.	***They wanted** to play in the orchestra.*
—¿No **querían** cantar en el coro?	***Didn't they want** to sing in the choir?*
—¿Dónde **estaban** anoche?	*Where **were you** last night?*
—**Estábamos** en el teatro.	***We were** at the theater.*
—**Leía** el periódico todos los días, ¿no?	***You used to read** the newspaper every day, didn't you?*
—Sólo cuando **tenía** tiempo.	*Only when **I had** time.*
—¿Qué tiempo **hacía**?	*What **was** the weather like?*
—**Hacía** frío y **llovía**.	***It was** cold and **it rained.***

- The imperfect tense is used to tell what time it was in the past. The preterit is *never* used:

—¿Qué hora **era**?	What time ***was** it?*
—**Era** la una en punto.	***It was** exactly one o'clock.*

- The imperfect tense is used in *indirect discourse* (in other words, to report what someone said) after the preterit form of verbs such as **decir**, **escribir**, **avisar**, **anunciar**, etc.:

¿Qué te dijo Loli?	*What did Loli tell you?*
Me **dijo** que **venía**.	***She told** me **she was coming**.*
¿Les escribiste?	*Did you write to them?*
Sí, les **escribí** que **viajaba**.	*Yes, I **wrote** them that **I was traveling.***
Paco nos **anunció** que **se casaba.**	*Paco **announced** to us **he was getting married.***
¡Y a mí me **informó** que **pensaba** romper con su novia!	*And **he informed** me that **he intended** to break off with his fiancée!*

A. Cuando yo era niño(a) … Ud. tiene nostalgia por esos años tan inolvidables de su niñez. Escriba sus recuerdos en su diario usando el imperfecto de los verbos que aparecen entre paréntesis.

MODELO Yo __________ (visitar) a mis amigos.
→ Yo visitaba a mis amigos.

El campo

al atardecer *at the end of the day*
el bosque *woods*
el campo *field*
la casa de campo *country house*
cultivar *to grow, raise*
la flor *flower*
fresco *fresh*
el lago *lake*
merendar (e > ie) *to picnic*
el monte *mountain*
nadar *to swim*
la sierra *mountains, mountain range*

Yo __________ (1. vivir) en Madrid con mis padres y mis hermanos Jaime y Marisol. Jaime __________ (2. ser) el mayor de los tres. Yo __________ (3. ir) al colegio y __________ (4. hacer) todas las cosas que __________ (5. soler) hacer los niños. Mis hermanos, mis amigos y yo __________ (6. ir) al cine, a los partidos de fútbol y a las fiestas. Lo que más me __________ (7. gustar) de aquellos años __________ (8. ser) la estancia en la casa de campo. Allí en la sierra de Guadarrama mis padres, mis hermanos y yo __________ (9. pasar) el mes de agosto . El aire __________ (10. ser) tan fresco y puro y no __________ (11. hacer) tanto calor como en Madrid. __________ (12. Haber) un campo detrás de la casa donde mis hermanos y yo __________ (13. jugar) al fútbol. Mi mamá __________ (14. cultivar) rosas y buganvillas en el jardín. ¡Qué hermosas __________ (15. ser)! Toda la casa __________ (16. oler) divinamente a flores. Nosotros __________ (17. salir) a merendar en el bosque todas las tardes. (Nosotros) __________ (18. Subir) en el monte hasta llegar a un lugar desde donde se __________ (19. ver) todo el valle. Mamá nos __________ (20. servir) los bocadillos más sabrosos del mundo. A veces papá nos __________ (21. leer) un cuento. Nosotros siempre __________ (22. ir) a nadar en uno de los lagos cristalinos de la sierra. Al atardecer (nosotros) __________ (23. estar) muy cansados. Mis hermanos __________ (24. volver) caminando a la casa pero papá me __________ (25. llevar) a mí en brazos porque yo __________ (26. ser) el bebé de la familia. ¡Qué felices recuerdos!

Nota cultural

- **La sierra de Guadarrama** es una cadena de montañas que queda en el centro de España, entre Madrid y Segovia. El pico más alto de la sierra es el de Peñalara, a 2.405 metros de alto. Muchos madrileños pasan sus vacaciones de verano o de invierno en la sierra. Casi todos los españoles, como casi todos los europeos, salen de vacaciones durante el mes de agosto.

- **El metro** equivale a 3.281 pies.

B. Reunión de la clase del año X. Ud. y sus compañeros de secundaria se reúnen después de no verse por muchos años. Se hacen preguntas para ponerse al tanto *(catch up on the news)*. Escriba lo que contestan empleando el imperfecto, como en el modelo.

MODELO Oye, Clara, ¿todavía estudias arte?
→ Antes estudiaba arte, pero ya no.

1. Oye, Manolo, ¿todavía escribes para *El tiempo?*

 ____

2. Oye, Dora, ¿todavía vas de vacaciones a Málaga?

 ____

3. Oye, Pepe, ¿todavía sales con Lola?

 ____

4. Oye, Jorge, ¿todavía te gusta la cocina tailandesa?

 ____

5. Oye, Ana María, ¿todavía cuidas a tu prima?

 ____

6. Oye, Paco, ¿todavía juegas en un equipo de fútbol?

 ____

7. Oye, Carmen, ¿todavía vienen al pueblo en invierno tú y tu marido?

 ____

8. Oye, Paula, ¿todavía almuerzas con tus padres los sábados?

 ____

9. Oye, Mario, ¿todavía eres socio del Club Atlántico?

 ____

10. Oye, Sofía, ¿todavía tocan la trompeta tus hijos?

 ____

11. Oye, Juan, ¿todavía le mandas bombones a Elena?

 ____

12. Oye, Laura, ¿todavía prefieres vivir en el centro?

 ____

13. Oye, Ramón, ¿todavía ves a los profesores?

____

14. Oye, Maribel, ¿todavía te despiertas a las cinco de la mañana?

____

C. Un vuelo. Ud. acaba de aterrizar en el aeropuerto donde lo (la) espera su familia. Mientras van a buscar su equipaje, Ud. les habla de los viajeros que conoció en el vuelo. Escriba qué eran y adónde iban. Use las formas del imperfecto de los verbos irregulares **ser** e **ir**.

MODELO Conocí al señor Torres. (abogado / Chicago)
→ El señor Torres era abogado. Iba a Chicago.

1. Conocí a la señorita Fajardo. (gerente de fábrica / Miami)

____

2. Conocí a unos señores italianos. (dueños de una pastelería / Uruguay)

____

3. Conocí a un señor. (profesor de economía / Irlanda)

____

4. Conocí a la señora Montoya. (banquera / Suiza)

____

5. Conocí a don Pedro Domínguez. (candidato a senador / Monterrey)

____

6. Conocí a Lorena Iglesias. (ama de casa / Costa Rica)

____

7. Conocí a los hermanos Machado. (músicos / Nueva York)

____

8. Conocí al señor Rubio. (cirujano / la India)

____

Nota cultural

- **Monterrey** queda al este de México, cerca de la frontera con Tejas. Es la capital del estado de Nuevo León y la tercera ciudad de México. Es un gran centro industrial y comercial.

- **Costa Rica,** país centroamericano, queda entre Nicaragua y Panamá con una costa en el Pacífico y otra en el Caribe. El país se destaca por su tradición democrática; en noviembre de 1989 celebró su centenario de la democracia. Costa Rica ha tenido más adelantos económicos y sociales que ningún otro país centroamericano y goza del nivel de vida más alto de toda esa región.

D. **¿Qué tal se veía?** La gente no podía ver ciertas cosas muy bien desde el lugar donde estaba. Escriba las formas correctas del imperfecto del verbo irregular **ver** al describir la situación de esas personas.

MODELO Pepe / el edificio suyo / la calle Mercado
→ Pepe no veía el edificio suyo desde la calle Mercado.

1. Carolina y Ramón / el mar Caribe / el avión

____

2. nosotros / la cara de los actores / el paraíso (*highest balcony*) del teatro

____

3. doña Federica / el embotellamiento / la ventana del dormitorio

____

4. Uds. / toda la cancha de fútbol / la tribuna (*stand*) del estadio

____

5. yo / la cumbre de la montaña / el valle

____

6. Daniel / la discoteca / la esquina

____

7. tú / al público / la parte derecha de la escena

____

C *The imperfect and the preterit: two aspects of past time*

- The imperfect and preterit tenses express different ways of looking at past actions and events. The imperfect tense designates an action as going on in the past without any reference to its beginning or end. The preterit tense designates an action as completed in the past. Spanish speakers must select one of these two aspects—imperfect or preterit—for every past action they refer to. The differences between the tenses can be expressed in English, but it is not obligatory:

Cuando estaba en la universidad, **estudiaba** chino.	*When I was at the university,* ***I studied*** *Chinese.* (or ***I used to study*** *Chinese.*)
Ayer **estudié** chino.	*Yesterday* ***I studied*** *Chinese.*

- Sometimes English uses entirely different verbs to express the difference between the imperfect and the preterit of some Spanish verbs. For example, **tenía** means *I was in the process of having* or *I had;* **tuve** means *I began to have* or *I got, received*:

Sabía el precio.	***I knew*** *the price.*
Supe el precio.	***I found out*** *the price.*
Conocían a Sergio.	***They knew*** *Sergio.*
Conocieron a Sergio.	***They met*** *Sergio.*
No podíamos llegar para las cuatro.	***We couldn't*** *arrive by four o'clock. (Doesn't say whether we arrived by four or not.)*
No **pudimos** llegar para las cuatro.	***We couldn't*** *arrive by four o'clock. (We didn't arrive by four.)*

Laura **no quería** ir en metro. — *Laura **didn't want** to take the subway.*
Laura **no quiso** ir en metro. — *Laura **refused to** (didn't want to and didn't) take the subway.*

- The imperfect and the preterit can be used in two different clauses in the same sentence. The imperfect expresses the background, a continuing action, or an ongoing state, against which a completed action or event takes place:

Mientras **trabajábamos**, Julia **durmió** la siesta. — *While **we were working**, Julia **took** a nap.*

- It is possible to have sentences with all verbs in the imperfect if the speaker sees the past actions or events as ongoing processes:

Pilar **leía** mientras Marta **jugaba** al tenis. — *Pilar **was reading** while Marta **was playing** tennis.*

- It is possible to have sentences with all verbs in the preterit if the speaker views the actions mentioned as a series of completed events:

Cené, **me arreglé** y **fui** al teatro. — ***I ate dinner, got ready,** and **went** to the theater.*

E. **¿Qué tiempo hacía ...?** Sus amigos quieren saber qué tiempo hacía cuando sucedieron ciertas cosas. Use el imperfecto para hablar del tiempo y el pretérito para hablar de los sucesos en escribir los siguientes diálogos.

MODELO Ud. / salir / hacer buen tiempo
→ Hacía buen tiempo cuando Ud. salió.

1. Beatriz y tú / volver / llover

___

2. los Sorolla / levantarse / hacer frío

___

3. tú / ir a la biblioteca / estar despejado

___

4. José Antonio / venir a la casa / hacer viento

___

5. nosotros / terminar el trabajo / nevar

___

6. Ud. / entrar en el cine / tronar

___

7. yo / llegar a la universidad / hacer sol

___

F. **¿Qué hora era cuando ...?** Su amigo quiere saber a qué hora pasaron ciertas actividades. Use el imperfecto para hablar de la hora y el pretérito para hablar de las actividades.

MODELO Carmen y Víctor / llamar / las ocho
→ Eran las ocho cuando Carmen y Víctor llamaron.

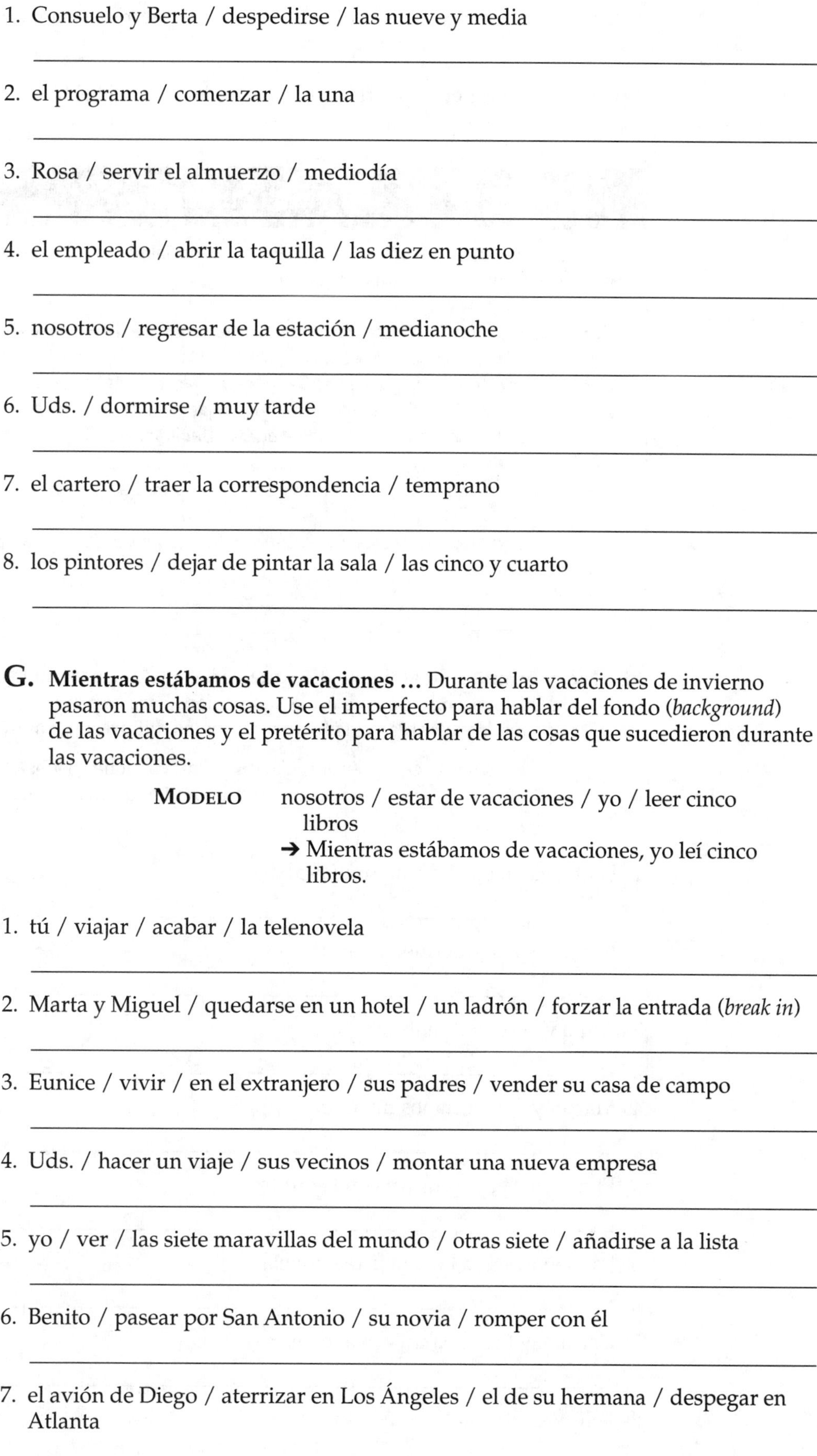

1. Consuelo y Berta / despedirse / las nueve y media

2. el programa / comenzar / la una

3. Rosa / servir el almuerzo / mediodía

4. el empleado / abrir la taquilla / las diez en punto

5. nosotros / regresar de la estación / medianoche

6. Uds. / dormirse / muy tarde

7. el cartero / traer la correspondencia / temprano

8. los pintores / dejar de pintar la sala / las cinco y cuarto

G. Mientras estábamos de vacaciones ... Durante las vacaciones de invierno pasaron muchas cosas. Use el imperfecto para hablar del fondo (*background*) de las vacaciones y el pretérito para hablar de las cosas que sucedieron durante las vacaciones.

MODELO nosotros / estar de vacaciones / yo / leer cinco libros
→ Mientras estábamos de vacaciones, yo leí cinco libros.

1. tú / viajar / acabar / la telenovela

2. Marta y Miguel / quedarse en un hotel / un ladrón / forzar la entrada (*break in*)

3. Eunice / vivir / en el extranjero / sus padres / vender su casa de campo

4. Uds. / hacer un viaje / sus vecinos / montar una nueva empresa

5. yo / ver / las siete maravillas del mundo / otras siete / añadirse a la lista

6. Benito / pasear por San Antonio / su novia / romper con él

7. el avión de Diego / aterrizar en Los Ángeles / el de su hermana / despegar en Atlanta

8. los turistas / conocer los Estados Unidos / la guerra / estallar en su país

____

9. nosotros / estar en el puerto / haber / un incendio en el barco

____

Nota cultural

Los españoles pusieron nombres españoles, y especialmente nombres de los santos, a muchos lugares de América, por ejemplo:

San Antonio, ciudad de Tejas, es donde ocurrió la batalla del Álamo en 1836. Cuando Tejas proclamó su derecho de separarse de México en 1835, Sam Houston asumió el mando del ejército tejano. En 1836 el general Santa Anna atacó el Álamo y mató a todos los soldados (23 febrero–6 marzo). Tejas declaró su independencia. Houston y los tejanos vencieron a los mexicanos en **San Jacinto.**

Donde hubo colonización española hay nombres españoles: *California, Tejas, la Florida.* Y en todo el sudoeste de los Estados Unidos: *Los Ángeles, Las Vegas, Santa Fe, San Francisco, San Diego, Santa Ana, San Antonio, El Paso, Alamogordo, Las Cruces, etcétera.*

H. Me sorprende. Su amiga le dice que varias personas ya no hacen ciertas cosas. A Ud. le sorprende porque antes las hacían. Para expresar esta idea Ud. dirá *Me sorprende* y cambiará las formas verbales del presente al imperfecto.

MODELO —Juan Carlos ya no escucha discos.
—Me sorprende. Antes escuchaba discos todos los días.

1. Felipe ya no corre quince millas al día.

____

2. Los tíos ya no duermen la siesta.

____

3. Anita ya no va al centro.

____

4. Martín ya no visita los museos.

____

5. El director ya no ensaya con la orquesta.

____

6. Las señoritas ya no ven la telenovela.

____

7. Carmen y Pablo ya no van al cine.

____

8. Felipe ya no conduce su coche.

____

I. Y al mismo tiempo ... Escriba las cosas que hacían las personas al mismo tiempo. Use el imperfecto para hablar de estas actividades. Escoja las actividades de la siguiente lista o invente otras.

trabajar en	ir de compras	jugar	divertirse
comer	bañarse	cocina	tocar
estudiar	esperar el tren	salir para	practicar
leer	ver una película	ensayar	arreglarse
escribir	caminar	dibujar	tomar algo

MODELO Sara escribía cartas mientras Teresa dibujaba.

1. ______________________________
2. ______________________________
3. ______________________________
4. ______________________________
5. ______________________________
6. ______________________________
7. ______________________________
8. ______________________________
9. ______________________________
10. ______________________________

J. Perspectivas. Las siguientes personas hablan de sus experiencias. Escoja el verbo en imperfecto o el verbo en pretérito para saber cómo estas personas ven el pasado.

El teatro

el/la acomodador(a) *usher*
el/la aficionado/a a la ópera *opera fan*
apagar las luces *to put out the lights*
el/la cantante *singer*
el decorado *scenery*
hacer el papel de *to play the role of*
la obra *work, piece*
la ópera *opera*
el programa *playbill, program*
sube el telón *the curtain goes up*

A. Cuando yo (1. tenía / tuve) once años, mis padres me (2. llevaban / llevaron) por primera vez a ver una ópera. La acomodadora nos (3. sentaba / sentó) y nos (4. dio / daba) el programa. Mientras (5. leíamos / leímos) las notas sobre la obra, las luces (6. se apagaban / se apagaron). Luego (7. subía / subió) el telón y (8. veíamos / vimos) la escena. (9. Había / Hubo) un decorado de palacio. Una cantante que (10. hizo / hacía) el papel de la reina (11. estaba / estuvo) sentada en el trono. Ella (12. llevó / llevaba) una corona *(crown)* de oro y (13. vestía / vistió) una capa de terciopelo *(velvet)* verde con armiño *(ermine)*. El cantante que (14. hacía / hizo) el papel del rey (15. salió / salía) a la escena y

(16. se ponía / se puso) a cantar. Yo (17. quedaba / quedé) tan impresionada con lo que vi y oí que (18. me hice / me hacía) aficionada a la ópera para siempre.

Nota cultural

El Teatro Colón, lugar conocido de Buenos Aires, es uno de los teatros de ópera más grandes del mundo. En este sitio todo dorado y de terciopelo (*velvet*) rojo, ponen ópera, conciertos de la Orquesta Filarmónica de Buenos Aires, recitales y obras de ballet. La temporada es de abril a primeros días de diciembre; está cerrado en enero y febrero. Recuerde que las estaciones están al revés en el hemisferio austral (sur).

B. Hace ocho años (1. me gradué / me graduaba) de la universidad. (2. Saqué / Sacaba) mi título en periodismo. (3. Esperaba / Esperé) encontrar trabajo en uno de los periódicos grandes de la ciudad donde (4. nacía / nací). (5. Quería / Quise) quedarme en Tejas porque mis padres y mis hermanos vivían allí. Por desgracia, no (6. hubo / había) empleo en ningún periódico del estado. Por lo tanto, yo (7. mandé / mandaba) mi currículum vitae a varios periódicos por todo el país. (8. Tenía / Tuve) suerte. (9. Encontré / Encontraba) trabajo de reportero en un periódico que (10. se publicaba / se publicó) en Maine. Al principio la vida en Maine me (11. fue / era) muy difícil. Yo no (12. conocí / conocía) a nadie donde (13. viví / vivía) y no (14. estaba / estuve) acostumbrado al clima. ¡(15. Hacía / Hizo) un frío horrible en invierno! Pero un día yo (16. conocía / conocí) a Marta quien (17. trabajó / trabajaba) en el periódico también. Ella (18. fue / era) editora. ¡Y (19. era / fue) un flechazo para nosotros (*love at first sight*)! En fin, Marta y yo (20. nos casamos / nos casábamos). Yo (21. llegaba / llegué) a ser jefe de redacción (*editor-in-chief*) del periódico. Marta y yo (22. tuvimos / teníamos) dos hijos. ¡Y todos (23. vivimos / vivíamos) muy felices (*we all lived happily ever after*)!

K. Contrastes. Exprese las siguientes ideas en español. Los contrastes surgen de la diferencia entre el imperfecto y el pretérito.

1. Bárbara thought Tomás knew her sister Luz.

   ____

   Actually, he met Luz last night at dinner.

   ____

2. The businessmen wanted to discuss the issues, but their lawyers refused to.

   ____

3. The bride (*la novia*) didn't have any gifts.

   ____

Then she got twenty gifts this morning.

____

4. We didn't know who had the documents.

____

We found out yesterday.

____

5. I wasn't able to assemble (*armar*) the toy.

____

Javier (tried but) couldn't assemble it either.

____

L. **¡Castillos de España!** Para describir una visita a un castillo español escoja el imperfecto o el pretérito de los verbos que aparecen entre paréntesis.

El turismo

el alcázar *citadel, fortress*
el billete de avión *plane ticket*
el castillo *castle*
la gira *tour, excursion*
hacer la reservación *to book*
hacer un viaje *to take a trip*
el lugar histórico *historic site*
el palacio *palace*
el parador *government-owned hotel (Spain)*
patrocinado por *sponsored by*

Yo siempre ____________ (1. querer) visitar un castillo en España. Por eso cuando mi esposo y yo ____________ (2. ir) a hacer un viaje en mayo, yo le ____________ (3. decir) a Rolando que me ____________ (4. interesar) visitar un castillo español. A Rolando le ____________ (5. gustar) la idea porque no ____________ (6. conocer) España. Rolando ____________ (7. comprar) los billetes de avión y también ____________ (8. hacer) la reservación para el hotel. Nosotros ____________ (9. pensar) hacer una gira de tres semanas con visitas a Madrid, Toledo, Sevilla, Segovia y Santiago de Compostela. Nosotros ____________ (10. tomar) el avión y ____________ (11. llegar) a Madrid el tres de mayo. Durante las tres semanas nosotros ____________ (12. visitar) varios lugares históricos y naturalmente ____________ (13. conocer) el Palacio Real en Madrid, el Alcázar de Sevilla, Segovia y Toledo y otros castillos y palacios. Al llegar a Santiago de Compostela yo ____________ (14. tener) una gran sorpresa. En vez de simplemente visitar un castillo, nosotros ____________ (15. poder) quedarnos en uno por tres días. Es que el famoso castillo ____________

(16. ser) un parador. Los paradores, es decir, hoteles patrocinados por el gobierno español, ____________________ (17. estar) por todas partes del país. ¡Por fin yo ____________________ (18. realizar) mi sueño de visitar un castillo en España!

Nota cultural

- **El Alcázar,** palabra de origen árabe, significa fortaleza, castillo o palacio real.
- **Sevilla,** a orillas del río Guadalquivir, es la capital de la Comunidad Autónoma de Andalucía. La construcción del **Alcázar de Sevilla** comenzó bajo los almohades, una dinastía árabe, en el siglo XII. Se siguió construyendo en época cristiana durante los reinos de Pedro I el Cruel, rey de Castilla y León (1334–69), Juan II, rey de Castilla (1405–54), los Reyes Católicos (Fernando II de Aragón 1452–1516 e Isabel I de Castilla 1451–1504), Carlos V, rey de España y emperador de Alemania (1500–58) y Felipe II, rey de España (1527–98). Se puede visitar los apartamentos reales, el palacio de Pedro el Cruel, los jardines, etcétera.
- **El Alcázar de Segovia** fue construido en el siglo XIV por Alfonso XI, rey de Castilla y León (1312–50). Fue transformado en el siglo XV. En las salas hay exposición de armas, cuadros y muebles de época medieval. Se dice que el Alcázar de Segovia sirvió de modelo para el castillo de Disneylandia.
- **El Alcázar de Toledo** fue construido por Alfonso VI, rey de Castilla y León (1030–1109) cuando reconquistó la ciudad de los moros en 1085. El Cid fue su primer gobernador. En el siglo XIII fue reformado y embellecido. Carlos I (1500–58) confió la restauración del Alcázar al arquitecto español Covarrubias (1488–1570). Este arquitecto fue uno de los introductores del Renacimiento en España.
- **Juan de Herrera** (1530–97), otro gran arquitecto español, continuó con la restauración. Hubo otras restauraciones durante los siglos XVIII, XIX y XX por los destrozos de las guerras. La última restauración fue necesaria por la destrucción del Alcázar a principios de la Guerra Civil española (1936) cuando el coronel Moscardó se negó a rendirles el Alcázar a los republicanos. Ante la negativa de Moscardó, el Alcázar fue destruido y su propio hijo fue ejecutado.
- **Santiago de Compostela,** capital de la Comunidad Autónoma de Galicia, queda al noroeste de España. En la Edad Media fue un importante lugar de peregrinación (*pilgrimage*), especialmente a partir del siglo XI. El sepulcro del Apóstol Santiago se encuentra aquí. La magnífica catedral fue construida entre los siglos XI y XIII.

M. **Del diario de un detective.** Aquí tiene Ud. una página de la libreta de apuntes del famoso detective privado Samuel Espada. Para poder leer los apuntes e intentar desenredar el misterio, llene los espacios en blanco con el imperfecto o el pretérito de los verbos que aparecen entre paréntesis.

El crimen

la cita *appointment*
el/la chantajista *blackmailer*
el detective privado *private detective*
el ladrón *thief*
maltés *Maltese*
la pandilla *gang*
la policía *police*
seguir la pista *to follow the lead*
sobresaltado *startled*

__________ (1. Ser) las diez de la mañana cuando __________ (2. sonar) el teléfono en mi oficina. Yo __________ (3. estar) despierto desde la noche anterior. (Yo) __________ (4. descolgar) y __________ (5. oír) la voz sobresaltada de una mujer. La mujer me __________ (6. decir) que una pandilla de ladrones le __________ (7. robar) su estatuilla (*figurine*) del halcón (*falcon*) maltés y que ahora le __________ (8. pedir) un rescate por el halcón. Además, la señorita me __________ (9. explicar) que __________ (10. tener) miedo de ir a la policía por razones especiales. Ella y yo __________ (11. quedar) en vernos en el vestíbulo del Hotel Casablanca. Ya __________ (12. ser) las siete de la tarde cuando yo __________ (13. llegar) al hotel. Toda la tarde yo __________ (14. seguir) la pista de los chantajistas hasta que __________ (15. llegar) la hora de la cita. En el vestíbulo yo __________ (16. ver) a una señorita guapísima que __________ (17. estar) sentada en un sofá. Ella __________ (18. tener) el pelo castaño y largo, los ojos verdes como dos esmeraldas y __________ (19. llevar) una gardenia en la chaqueta. Ella __________ (20. fumar) un cigarrillo igual que yo (¡porque todos los personajes de los años cuarenta fuman cigarrillos!). Yo me __________ (21. acercar) y me __________ (22. sentar) a su lado. Ella __________ (23. oler) a un perfume exótico. Yo le __________ (24. hablar) primero. "¿Es Ud. la señorita María Aster?", le __________ (25. preguntar). Ella se __________ (26. poner) a llorar y me __________ (27. decir) sollozando (*sobbing*): "Samuel, es que tú no comprendes ...". Pero sí, yo __________ (28. comprender) muy bien. ¡Esto __________ (29. ir) a ser otro dramón (*sob story*)!

- Remember that the Spanish construction **hace** + *expression of time* + **que** + *verb in the present tense* is used to label an action that began in the past and is continuing in the present. Similarly, the construction **hacía** + *expression of time* + **que** + *verb in the imperfect tense* is used to label an action that was continuing in the past when something else happened. The corresponding question is **¿Cuánto tiempo hacía ...?** The word *tiempo* may be omitted:

—**¿Cuánto (tiempo) hacía que esperabas** cuando llegó el tren?	***How long had you been waiting*** *when the train arrived?*
—**Hacía más de una hora** que **esperaba**.	***I had been waiting more than an hour.***

- A *verb in the imperfect tense* + **desde hacía** + *expression of time* is also used to label an action that was continuing in the past when something else happened:

—**¿Desde cuándo rodaban** la película cuando **hubo** un terremoto?	***How long had they been shooting*** *the film when* ***there was*** *an earthquake?*
—**Rodaban** la película **desde hacía siete semanas** cuando **hubo** un terremoto.	***They had been shooting*** *the film* ***for seven weeks*** *when* ***there was*** *an earthquake.*

N. **¿Cuánto tiempo hacía ...?** Pregunte y explique qué eran las cosas usando la construcción **hacía** + *expresión de tiempo* + **que** + *verbo en imperfecto* y **¿Cuánto (tiempo) hacía que ...?**

Modelo Leonor / estudiar inglés / salir para Inglaterra (dos años)
—¿Cuánto tiempo hacía que Leonor estudiaba inglés cuando salió para Inglaterra?
—Hacía dos años que estudiaba inglés.

1. Montserrat Pujol / cantar ópera / firmar un contrato con la Metropolitana (ocho años)

____

____

2. los señores Salazar / estar casados / su hija / nacer (cuatro años)

____

____

3. tú / vivir en París / tus padres / mudarse a Londres (once meses)

____

____

4. Susana y Lía / ser amigas / Susana / quitarle el novio a Lía (doce años)

____

____

5. Ud. / comprar billetes de lotería / ganar el premio (quince años)

____

____

6. Patricio y Ud. / tocar el violonchelo / el conservatorio / darles una beca (nueve años)

____

____

O. Cambios políticos y económicos. Pasaban unas cosas desde hacía tiempo cuando ocurrieron otras cosas en la vida política y económica del país. Use la construcción *verbo en imperfecto* + **desde hacía** + *expresión de tiempo* para describir los cambios. Junte las dos frases con *hasta que*.

MODELO el gobierno / prometer muchas cosas / dos años / los ciudadanos / empezar a reclamar
→ El gobierno prometía muchas cosas desde hacía dos años hasta que los ciudadanos empezaron a reclamar.

Política y economía

controlar la inflación *to control inflation*
establecer la democracia *to establish democracy*
explotar el petróleo *to exploit, develop oil*
intentar *to try, attempt*
privatizar la industria *to privatize industry*
reclamar *to demand*
los bienes *goods*
la década *decade*
el dictador *dictator*
el gobierno *government*
el golpe de estado *coup d'état*
el/la economista *economist*
la libertad *liberty*
el libre mercado *free market*
el obrero *worker*
la prensa *press*
el presidente *president*
el pueblo *the people*
el sindicato *union*
el sueldo *salary*

1. el gobierno / explotar el petróleo / treinta años / el presidente / privatizar la industria

____

____

2. la gente / sufrir por la inflación / cinco años / los economistas / intentar controlarla

____

____

3. la prensa / no ser libre / cincuenta años / haber / un golpe de estado

____

____

4. los obreros / no recibir un sueldo decente / cinco décadas / formarse los sindicatos

5. el país / no producir los bienes necesarios / varios años / el país establecer el mercado libre

6. el pueblo / no tener ninguna libertad / cuarenta y cinco años / morir el dictador y establecerse la democracia

P. ¿Qué dice Ud.? Conteste las siguientes preguntas personales.

1. ¿Cuántos años tenía cuando se vestía solo(a)?
2. ¿Cuántos años tenía cuando empezó a estudiar en el colegio?
3. Cuando era niño(a), ¿adónde iba de vacaciones?
4. ¿Qué le gustaba hacer cuando era niño(a)?
5. ¿Cómo era de niño(a)?
6. Hable de las cosas que solía hacer todos los días cuando asistía al colegio.
7. ¿Qué sueños quería realizar en la vida?
8. ¿Pudo realizar algunos ya?

Q. Un viaje a México. Exprese esta historia en español. Escoja entre el pretérito y el imperfecto para hablar del pasado.

1. The first day Beatriz and I spent in Mexico City we went to Chapultepec Park.
2. The weather was beautiful. It was sunny and warm.
3. There were many people in the park.

4. Little children were playing on the slides (*los resbalines*) and riding their bicycles.

____

5. As we walked through the park we saw Moctezuma's Tree and the Chapultepec Castle.

____

6. We arrived at the National Museum of Anthropology and went in.

____

7. We walked from room to room and saw the exhibit of pre-Columbian (*precolombino*) art.

____

8. We spent two hours in the museum.

____

9. Then we went to the bookstore where I bought a book about the Aztecs and the Mayans.

____

10. We had lunch in the museum cafeteria.

____

Nota cultural

- **El Bosque de Chapultepec** queda al final del Paseo de la Reforma en plena capital mexicana. El hermoso parque tiene miles de ahuehuetes (árboles coníferos), laberintos de caminos, lagos, un jardín botánico, un zoológico y varios museos.
- **El Castillo de Chapultepec,** situado en una colina, da hermosas vistas del valle de México desde sus balcones. La gran atracción del parque es el **Museo Nacional de Antropología** que presenta una espléndida exposición de las culturas mexicanas precolombinas, es decir, de los aztecas, los mayas y otros grupos que vivían allí antes de la llegada de Cristóbal Colón al Nuevo Mundo.
- Moctezuma II era el emperador azteca (1466–1520) cuando llegó Cortés a México en 1519. Fue hecho prisionero por los conquistadores españoles poco después de su llegada. **El Árbol de Moctezuma,** un poco más abajo del Castillo, era inmenso— de algunos 60 metros de alto. "El Sargento", como se le llama, se ha cortado hasta medir diez metros.

R. Ejercicio oral: Una encuesta. Prepare una lista de algunas actividades que Ud. hacía cuando era niño(a). Luego pregúnteles a sus compañeros de clase si ellos también hacían esas actividades. Algunas posibilidades:

1. Jugaba al fútbol.
2. Pintaba cuadros al aire libre.
3. Pasaba los veranos en un campamento.
4. Cocinaba con mi mamá o papá.

5. Tocaba un instrumento musical.
6. Montaba en bicicleta.
7. Buceaba (*dive under water*) en el mar.
8. Iba de compras en el centro comercial.

S. **Estructuras en acción.** Lea el artículo sobre las catedrales españolas fijándose especialmente en los verbos en tiempo imperfecto. Luego haga el ejercicio.

Vocabulario

el abad *abbot*
el animal de tiro *draft animal*
atar *to tie*
la cal *limestone*
el cantero *stonemason*
el carro *cart*
el cura *priest*
diferencia: a diferencia de *in contrast to*
la fachada *facade*
fiel *faithful*
girar en torno a *to revolve around*
impregnar *to fill, pervade*
el maestro de obras *foreman (construction)*
mediados: a mediados de *around the middle of*
el orfebre *goldsmith*
el sacerdote *priest*
semejante *similar*
el tallista de madera *wood carver*

1. El factor dominante en los siglos cuando se construyeron las catedrales era ___________.
   a. la riqueza
   b. la religión
   c. el trabajo
2. La tarea central de una ciudad era ___________.
   a. el transporte de vino
   b. la busca de curas competentes
   c. la construcción de su catedral
3. En la construcción de una catedral participaban ___________.
   a. gente de todas las clases sociales
   b. varios dioses y sacerdotes paganos
   c. los obreros solamente
4. El interior de las catedrales era inmenso para ___________.
   a. rivalizar con los templos paganos
   b. guardar la cal, la piedra y la madera
   c. recibir a todos los fieles que querían entrar
5. Hasta los nobles, hombres y mujeres, tiraban carros para ___________.
   a. quitarles trabajo a los obreros
   b. transportar materiales de construcción
   c. llevar a los curas a la iglesia

PIEDRA SANTA

LAS CATEDRALES ESPAÑOLAS—CONSTRUCCIONES RELIGIOSAS Y COMUNITARIAS

En aquellos tiempos —el siglo XII, el XIII, inclusive el XIV— cuando se construyeron las grandes catedrales españolas, la religiosidad lo llenaba todo, y la vida entera de una ciudad giraba en torno a esa manifestación suprema de la religión que era el interminable y exaltante trabajo de la construcción de la catedral. A diferencia de los templos paganos, reservados a los dioses y a sus sacerdotes, las iglesias cristianas estaban construidas para recibir la comunión de los fieles: por eso no eran meras fachadas, sino grandes cavernas en donde cabían todos. Y se construían entre todos, ricos y pobres, curas y reyes, canteros y orfebres, y durante generaciones trabajaban en ellas de padres a hijos los escultores y los maestros de obra, los arquitectos y los tallistas de madera. Decía a mediados del siglo XII el abad de Saint Pierre sur Dive: «¿Quién vio u oyó alguna vez algo semejante, que grandes señores y príncipes de este mundo que tenían riquezas y de honores, que aún damas nobles inclinaron su orgullosa cabeza y se ataran a los carros como animales de tiro para transportar vino, aceite, cal, piedras y madera a los obreros que construían una iglesia?»

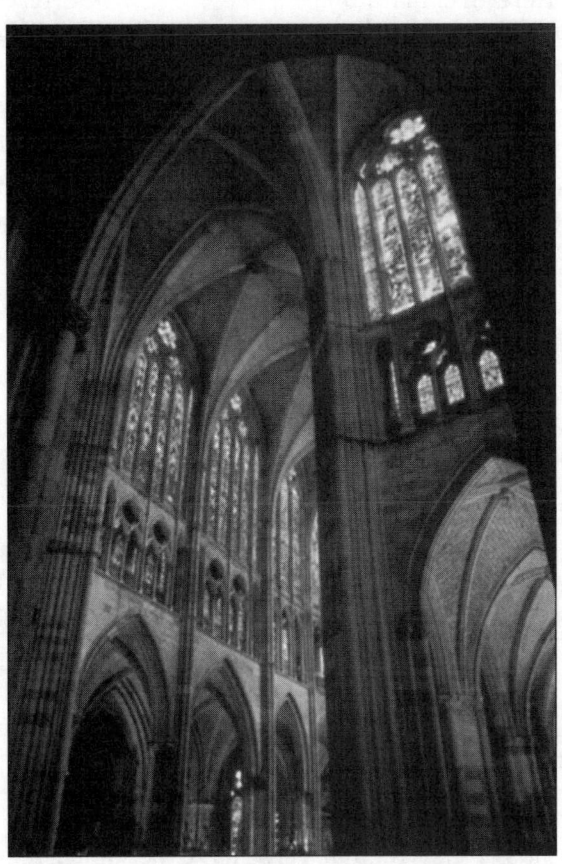

La catedral de León—Siglos xii–xv

CHAPTER 6

THE FUTURE & CONDITIONAL TENSES

A *Formation of the future tense*

- The future tense is formed in Spanish by adding a special set of endings to the infinitive. The endings are the same for **-ar**, **-er,** and **-ir** verbs.

firmar el documento *to sign the paper*	
Firmar**é** el documento. Firmar**ás** el documento. Firmar**á** el documento.	Firmar**emos** el documento. Firmar**éis** el documento. Firmar**án** el documento.

correr en el maratón *to run in the marathon*	
Correr**é** en el maratón. Correr**ás** en el maratón. Correr**á** en el maratón.	Correr**emos** en el maratón. Correr**éis** en el maratón. Correr**án** en el maratón.

asistir al concierto *to attend the concert*	
Asistir**é** al concierto. Asistir**ás** al concierto. Asistir**á** al concierto.	Asistir**emos** al concierto. Asistir**éis** al concierto. Asistir**án** al concierto.

- For some Spanish verbs the future tense endings are added on to modified versions of the infinitive. Some verbs have **-d-** in place of the infinitive vowel *-e-* or *-i-:*

  poner > **pondré** tener > **tendré** venir > **vendré**
  salir > **saldré** valer > **valdré**

- Some verbs lose the infinitive vowel *-e-:*

  caber > **cabré** querer > **querré**
  poder > **podré** saber > **sabré**

- Some verbs shorten the infinitive:

  decir > **diré** hacer > **haré**

- **-Ir** verbs that have an accent mark in the infinitive—**oír**, **reír**, **sonreír**—lose the accent mark in the future: **oiré**, **reiré**, **sonreiré**.
- The future of **hay** is **habrá** (*there will be*).
- Compounds of the irregular verbs have the same irregularities: componer (**compondré**), retener (**retendré**), prevenir (**prevendré**), contradecir (**contradiré**), satisfacer (**satisfaré**), etc.

B Uses of the future tense

- The future tense is used in Spanish and English to express future time:

  ¿A qué hora **llegarán** Uds.? — *At what time **will you arrive**?*
  Estaremos para las tres. — ***We'll be** there by three o'clock.*

- The future tense in Spanish is often replaced by the **ir a** + *infinitive* construction. This commonly used construction refers to the immediate future whereas the future tense refers to both the immediate and the remote future:

  Esquiaré en los Pirineos. — ***I'll ski** in the Pyrenees.*
  Voy a esquiar en los Pirineos. — ***I'm going to ski** in the Pyrenees.*

- The future tense is often replaced by the simple present tense when there is another element of the sentence that indicates future time:

  Llamo **el jueves**. — *I'll call **on Thursday**.*

- The future tense can be replaced by the present tense when asking for instructions; English *shall, should:*

  ¿**Doblo** aquí? — ***Shall (Should) I turn** here?*

- The future tense is commonly used in the main clause of a conditional sentence when the **si**-clause (*if-clause*) has the verb in the present tense:

  Si Juana **va**, yo **iré** también. — *If Juana **goes**, **I'll go** too.*

- The order of the clauses can be reversed with the **si**-clause following the main clause: Yo **iré si va** Juana.

A. Mis planes para el futuro. Cambie los verbos del tiempo presente al futuro en la siguiente narración para saber lo que piensa hacer su amigo Daniel después de graduarse.

MODELO Trabajo en una oficina.
➔ Trabajaré en una oficina.

1. Me gradúo en junio.
   ____
2. Mis amigos y yo celebramos con una fiesta.
   ____
3. Nuestros padres están muy contentos.
   ____
4. Yo hago un viaje a Europa en el verano.
   ____
5. Miguel me acompaña.
   ____
6. Nos encanta viajar.
   ____
7. Vamos a los países de la Europa oriental.
   ____

8. Andrés y Manuel quieren ir también.

9. Salimos para Polonia a mediados de junio.

10. Pasamos dos meses viajando.

11. Andrés vuelve antes porque

12. tiene que buscar empleo.

13. Al regresar yo empiezo a trabajar en una compañía internacional.

14. Miguel puede trabajar en la empresa de sus padres.

15. Manuel sigue con sus clases en la facultad de ingeniería.

16. ¡Tenemos tiempo de vernos, espero!

B. **¡Qué reacciones!** Ud. sabe cómo reaccionarán ciertas personas al oír unas noticias. Describa sus reacciones escribiendo los verbos en futuro.

MODELO Luisa / sonreír
➔ Luisa sonreirá.

1. Mari Carmen / llorar

2. las tías / decir "¡ay de mí!" gimiendo (*groaning*)

3. Ramón / tener vergüenza

4. tú / volverse loco

5. Juan y Alicia / poner el grito en el cielo (*scream bloody murder*)

6. Uds. / enfadarse

7. Margarita / reírse a carcajadas

____

8. Ud. / ponerse de buen humor

____

9. nosotros / estar contento

____

C. **¡Qué día!** Mañana será un día sumamante ajetreado (*hectic*), con muchas ocupaciones para Ud. Diga lo que pasará, escribiendo los verbos en futuro.

MODELO Estudiamos todo el día.
→ Estudiaremos todo el día.

1. ¡Mañana es un ajetreo continuo (*hustle and bustle*)!

____

2. ¡Tenemos un día lleno de frenética actividad!

____

3. Hay clases todo el día

____

4. y tomamos exámenes también.

____

5. Además, yo voy al almacén.

____

6. Le compro un regalo a mi hermana.

____

7. Sarita cumple diecisiete años pasado mañana.

____

8. Mamá hace una comida y una torta.

____

9. Papá y yo salimos para comprar vino.

____

10. También quiero ir a la biblioteca.

____

11. Mis amigos y yo trabajamos hasta muy tarde.

____

12. ¡Trasnochamos (*We'll go to bed very late*) porque tenemos exámenes pasado mañana también!

____

D. Actividad y descanso. Ud. y sus amigos se dedicarán a ciertas cosas durante las vacaciones de invierno. Diga lo que piensan hacer, escribiendo los verbos en futuro.

MODELO Felipe / escuchar discos todo el día
→ Felipe escuchará discos todo el día.

1. Yolanda y Ana / patinar

____

2. tú / cocinar yacu-chupe y un sancochado

____

3. Julio / bailar en la discoteca toda la noche

____

4. Consuelo / acostarse tarde

____

5. yo / pasear al perro

____

6. Uds. / jugar baloncesto

____

7. Magdalena / escribir cartas

____

8. nosotros / hacer una fiesta de disfraces (*costume party*)

____

9. Guillermo y Rodolfo / poder viajar al Canadá

____

10. Ud. / dormir la siesta todas las tardes

____

Nota cultural

La cocina peruana tiene muchos platos indígenas que les son exóticos a los extranjeros. **Yacu-chupe** es una sopa verde hecha a base de papas con queso, ajo, hojas de cilantro (*coriander*), perejil (*parsley*), pimentones, huevos, cebollas y menta. **El sancochado** es un guiso de carne y toda clase de legumbres y condimentado con ajo molido (*ground*).

E. Todo depende. ¡Ciertas cosas pasarán a condición de que pasen otras cosas! Para expresar esta idea escriba oraciones que tienen una cláusula con **si** con el verbo en presente y otra cláusula principal con el verbo en futuro.

MODELO tú / estudiar en la biblioteca: yo / trabajar allí también
→ **Si** tú **estudias** en la biblioteca, yo **trabajaré** allí también.

1. María / querer salir : nosotros / salir con ella
____
2. ellos / ir : Ud. / poder verlos
____
3. yo / hacer la comida : tú / venir a almorzar
____
4. Uds. / trabajar mucho : Uds. / tener éxito
____
5. tú / no saber qué pasó : yo / decirte
____
6. nosotros / no comprar harina : no haber tortillas esta noche
____
7. hacer calor : Carlos y Pedro / ir a la playa
____
8. hacer fresco : Celeste / querer ir al cine
____

C *The future tense used to express probability or conjecture*

- The future tense in Spanish is also used to express probability or conjecture in present time. The English equivalents of the future of probability (*I wonder, it's probably, it might,* etc.) are usually very unlike the Spanish structures.

—¿Qué hora es?	*What time is it?*
—**Serán** las ocho.	***It's probably** eight o'clock.*
—¿**Quién tendrá** las llaves?	***I wonder who has** the keys.*
—Las **tendrá** Mario.	*Mario **probably has** them.*

- Context will determine whether a verb in the future tense refers to the future or to probability in present time. For example: **¿Quién llamará?** means *Who will call?* as well as *I wonder who's calling.*
- **Deber de** + *infinitive* is also used to express probability in the present: **Deben de ser las diez. = Serán las diez.**

F. **¿Qué será?** Su amiga no está segura de varias cosas. Ud. tampoco está seguro(a) y por cada cosa expresa probabilidad o conjetura. Escriba los verbos en tiempo futuro. Quite la palabra o las palabras que indican probabilidad.

MODELO *Probablemente* los Hidalgo están en casa.
→ Los Hidalgo estarán en casa.

1. *Probablemente* son las seis.

____

2. *Me imagino que* Teodoro tiene catorce años.

____

3. *Supongo que* el reloj vale mucho.

____

4. *Probablemente* hay problemas entre los socios.

____

5. *Supongo que* Teresa sabe la hora de la conferencia.

____

6. *Me imagino que* Esteban quiere ir a la reunión.

____

7. *Supongo que* las muchachas vuelven pronto.

____

G. **¿Qué habrá en esa caja?** Ud. y sus amigos han visto a Juan Pedro que llevaba una caja enorme. Todos se mueren por saber lo que hay adentro. Uds. hacen conjeturas sobre el contenido usando el futuro de probabilidad.

MODELO *It's probably big.* *I wonder if it's beautiful.*
Será grande. ¿Será hermoso?

1. I wonder if it's green (blue, red, yellow).

____

2. It probably has batteries.

____

3. I wonder if there are many parts.

____

4. Do you think it's made of wood (metal, plastic)?

____

5. Could it cost a lot?

____

6. It probably makes a noise.

____

7. It must be bigger than a breadbox (*una caja para el pan*).

____

8. Could everybody have one?

____

9. I wonder if it's alive.

____

10. It probably fits in your hand.

____

D *Formation of the conditional tense*

- The conditional tense (English *would*) is formed in Spanish by adding the endings of the imperfect tense of **-er** and **-ir** verbs to the infinitive. These endings are the same for the conditional of **-ar**, **-er**, and **-ir** verbs:

cobrar el cheque *to cash the check*	
Cobrar**ía** el cheque.	*I'd cash the check.*
Cobrar**ías** el cheque.	*You'd cash the check.*
Cobrar**ía** el cheque.	*He'd/ She'd/You'd cash the check.*
Cobrar**íamos** el cheque.	*We'd cash the check.*
Cobrar**íais** el cheque.	*You'd cash the check.*
Cobrar**ían** el cheque.	*They'd/You'd cash the check.*

entender *to understand*	
Entender**ía.**	*I'd understand.*
Entender**ías.**	*You'd understand.*
Entender**ía.**	*He'd/She'd/You'd understand.*
Entender**íamos**.	*We'd understand.*
Entender**íais.**	*You'd understand.*
Entender**ían**.	*They'd/You'd understand.*

recibir cartas *to receive, get letters*	
Recibir**ía** cartas.	*I'd receive letters.*
Recibir**ías** cartas.	*You'd receive letters.*
Recibir**ía** cartas.	*He'd/She'd/You'd receive letters.*
Recibir**íamos** cartas.	*We'd receive letters.*
Recibir**íais** cartas.	*You'd receive letters.*
Recibir**ían** cartas.	*They'd/You'd receive letters.*

- Note that when *would* means *used to*, the imperfect tense rather than the conditional is used:

Cuando yo era niño, mi familia y yo **íbamos** al campo todos los veranos. — *When I was a child, my family and I* ***would go*** *to the country every summer.*

- The verbs that have modified infinitives in the future tense have the same changes in the conditional tense:

caber ➔ **cabría**	poner ➔ **pondría**	tener ➔ **tendría**
decir ➔ **diría**	querer ➔ **querría**	valer ➔ **valdría**
hacer ➔ **haría**	saber ➔ **sabría**	venir ➔ **vendría**
poder ➔ **podría**	salir ➔ **saldría**	

- The conditional of **hay** is **habría** (*there would be*).
- Compounds of the irregular verbs have the same irregularities: componer (**compondría**), retener (**retendría**), prevenir (**prevendría**), contradecir **contradiría**), satisfacer (**satisfaría**), etc.

E *Uses of the conditional tense*

- The conditional is used commonly in subordinate (dependent) clauses after main verbs of communication (e.g., *decir*) and knowledge or belief (*saber, creer*) when the main verb is in one of the past tenses. Observe a similar correspondence of tenses in Spanish and English: *present / future* and *past / conditional:*

Juan **dice** que **irá**.	*Juan **says he'll go.***
Juan **dijo** que **iría**.	*Juan **said he'd go.***
Sé que **llamarán.**	***I know they'll call.***
Sabía que **llamarían.**	***I knew they'd call.***

- The conditional is commonly used in the main clause of a sentence that has the imperfect subjunctive in the **si**-clause (*if*-clause), that is, the subordinate or dependent clause. The condition expressed here is called *contrary-to-fact.* This pattern is practiced in greater depth in Chapter 12.

Si Elena **saliera**, yo **saldría** también.	***If** Elena **were to leave, I'd leave** too.*

- The conditional tense in Spanish is also used to express probability or conjecture in past time. The verbs most commonly used to express probability with the conditional are **estar**, **haber**, **ser**, and **tener**:

Sería la una.	***It was probably** one o'clock.*
Habría algunas dificultades.	***There were probably** some difficulties.*
El niño **tendría** nueve años.	*The boy **was probably** nine years old.*
El coche **costaría** un dineral.	*The car **probably cost** a fortune.*

- Context will determine whether a verb in the conditional tense refers to the conditional or to probability in past time. For example: **Serían las tres** = *It would be three o'clock (by the time we got there)* and *It was probably three o'clock.*
- **Deber de** in the imperfect + *infinitive* may be used to express probability in past time. **Debían de ser las diez** = **Serían las diez.**

H. Y Ud., ¿qué haría? ¿Qué harían ciertas personas en cada una de las siguientes situaciones? Escriba los verbos en tiempo condicional.

MODELO Estás en la clase de historia. El profesor hace preguntas. ¿Qué harías?

a. contestar ➔ **Yo contestaría.**
b. cambiar el tema ➔ **Yo cambiaría el tema.**

1. Ud. está en un almacén. Busca los abrigos y no puede encontrarlos. ¿Qué haría?
   a. buscar a la dependienta
   ___
   b. salir del almacén
   ___
2. Carolina cena en casa de los Cela. Le encanta el arroz con pollo. ¿Qué haría?
   a. repetir
   ___
   b. pedir la receta
   ___
3. Estamos en el metro. Un pasajero grita "¡fuego!". ¿Qué haríamos?
   a. salir muy rápido
   ___
   b. llamar a los bomberos
   ___
4. Osvaldo está en el teatro. Mientras busca su asiento le pisa el pie a una señora. ¿Qué haría?
   a. disculparse con la señora
   ___
   b. sentarse en su regazo (*lap*)
   ___
5. La madre quiere bañar a sus hijos pero no hay agua caliente. ¿Qué haría?
   a. acostarlos sin bañarlos
   ___
   b. llamar al fontanero
   ___
6. Pepe y Paco ven que hay diez pulgadas (*inches*) de nieve en la calle y hace buen tiempo. ¿Qué harían?
   a. hacer una figura de nieve
   ___
   b. lanzar (*throw*) bolas de nieve
   ___
7. Hay un choque de coches no muy serio. Ud. es testigo del accidente. ¿Qué haría?
   a. decirle al policía lo que pasó
   ___
   b. ponerles vendas a los heridos
   ___

I. ¡Qué bonanza! Ud. y sus amigos acaban de comprar un billete para la lotería que esta semana llegó a tres millones de dólares. ¿Qué harían Uds. con tres millones de dólares? Escriba algunas ideas empleando el tiempo condicional.

Modelo yo / comprar un chalet (*villa*) en el campo
➔ Yo compraría un chalet en el campo.

1. Elena / pagar la matrícula en la universidad
   ____
2. mi primo Federico / venir a visitarnos
   ____
3. Uds. / hacer un viaje a China
   ____
4. Juan Pablo y Ana María / poner la plata en el banco
   ____
5. tú / no tener deudas (*debts*)
   ____
6. mi hermano y yo / querer darles dinero a los huérfanos (*orphans*)
   ____
7. nosotros / jugar a la Bolsa (*stock market*)
   ____

Nota cultural

La lotería es un juego público en el que se premian billetes que llevan ciertos números. A diferencia de los Estados Unidos donde las loterías son estatales, es decir, las dirigen los estados, España y los países latinoamericanos tienen loterías nacionales.

J. ¿Qué dijeron? Escriba lo que la gente dijo y preguntó sobre los planes para una fiesta. Use el condicional en las cláusulas subordinadas.

Modelo Pedro me dijo que **llamaría** (llamar).

1. Victoria nos dijo que le ______________ (gustar) tener una fiesta en su casa.
2. Pablo le preguntó a Victoria si ella ______________ (querer) planearla para el sábado.
3. Victoria nos aseguró que no ______________ (haber) problema con esa fecha.
4. Isabel quería saber lo que nosotros ______________ (poder) traer.
5. Victoria nos dejó saber que su mamá se ______________ (ocupar) de la comida.
6. José y yo le dijimos que ______________ (hacer) galletas y pasteles para la fiesta.

7. Marta y Carlos dijeron que __________________ (poner) la mesa antes de la fiesta.
8. Todos le prometimos a Victoria que __________________ (venir) muy temprano para ayudarla con los preparativos.

K. Probabilidad en el pasado. Exprese probabilidad o conjetura en el pasado al contestar las preguntas de su amiga. Use el condicional al contestar.

MODELO ¿Cuántos años tenía el primo de Fernando? (15 años)
→ Tendría quince años.

1. ¿Qué hora era cuando Uds. volvieron a casa? (las once)

____

2. ¿Cuántos invitados había en la fiesta? (60)

____

3. ¿Cómo estaban tus padres después del viaje? (cansados)

____

4. ¿Cuánto costó el carro de Felipe? (quince mil dólares)

____

L. Al contrario. Si ciertas personas fueran *(were going)* a la fiesta, algunas cosas pasarían. Para saber qué pasaría, escriba los verbos de la cláusula principal que aparecen entre paréntesis en el tiempo condicional.

MODELO **Si fuera Matilde a la fiesta,** Guillermo … también. (ir)
Si fuera Matilde a la fiesta, Guillermo **iría** también.
If Matilde were going to the party, Guillermo would go too.

1. Si fueran los Bello, nosotros __________________ (estar) contentos.
2. Si fueran Uds., yo __________________ (poder) llevarlos.
3. Si fuera Catalina, Tomás __________________ (querer) bailar con ella.
4. Si fuéramos todos nosotros, los Herrera no __________________ (caber) en el coche.
5. Si fuera Ud., __________________ (venir) conmigo.
6. Si fueras, te __________________ (poner) un esmoquin (*tuxedo*).
7. Si fueran todos los invitados, no __________________ (haber) lugar en la pista de baile (*dance floor*).

M. Gustos e intereses. Use el tiempo condicional para expresar lo que le gustaría hacer y lo que a otros les gustaría hacer. Use estos verbos: **gustar, encantar, interesar, preferir, querer.**

1. I'd like to …

   ____

2. My parents would prefer to …

   ____

3. My sister would want to …

   ____

4. My friend ______________ would love to …

   ____

5. My friend ______________ would be interested in …

   ____

6. My brother would like to …

   ____

7. I'd love to …

   ____

8. Our teachers would prefer to …

   ____

9. My classmates would be interested in …

   ____

10. My family would want to …

    ____

N. Ejercicio oral. Con un(a) compañero(a) de clase, haga un diálogo que tiene lugar en una oficina de la compañía donde trabajan. Uno de Uds. es el jefe y el otro es director de la empresa. El director le hace preguntas al jefe sobre el viaje de negocios que va a hacer. El jefe contesta sus preguntas. Use el tiempo futuro y el condicional lo más posible. Por ejemplo:

Director: ¿Adónde *iré* primero? *Me gustaría* hacer los preparativos para el viaje lo antes posible.
Jefe: Bueno, primero *visitarás* la oficina en Madrid. Luego *harás* el viaje a Barcelona.
Director: *Tendré* que comprar cheques de viajero. ¿Cuánto *valdrá* el viaje?
Jefe: ¿Sabes, Manuel? Te lo *podrían* calcular en contabilidad. Ahora, en cuanto al itinerario …

O. Estructuras en acción. Lea el siguiente artículo sobre la boda de la infanta Elena de España fijándose especialmente en los verbos en futuro. Luego haga el ejercicio que le sigue.

Matrimonio—Sí Quiero Pero Menos

El día 18 de marzo, a las 12.30, Sevilla y millones de españoles serán testigos de un "Sí, quiero" real. En ese momento, Elena de Borbón y Jaime de Marichalar entrarán a formar parte de las estadísticas. Serán una más de las 220.000 parejas que se calcula que este año contraerán matrimonio y como el 80 por ciento de ellas lo harán por la Iglesia, que en su caso es una Catedral.

El Rey paga

La tradición deja bien claro quién paga qué en una boda y don Juan Carlos I ha decidido ser fiel a ella en el enlace de su hija la Infanta Elena. Los padres de la novia deben costear las invitaciones, las fotografías y la ceremonia. Además del ajuar y el ágape para 1.500 invitados que se celebrará en los Reales Alcázares. Se calcula que el banquete nupcial costará 22 millones de pesetas.

La casa real también se hará cargo de cien entradas para que sus allegados disfruten del espectáculo ecuestre que tendrá lugar en la Maestranza el día anterior; y de los costos de la cena con que, esa noche, agasajará a las familias de los novios y la realeza en el Palacio de Villamanrique. Cerca de 500 comensales a 9.000 pesetas el cubierto.

El Rey correrá con los gastos de los adornos florales de la Catedral y el ramo de la novia, además de la factura del hotel Alfonso XIII de sus familiares cercanos. En total, Juan Carlos I tendrá que pagar 50 millones. El dinero saldrá de los 916 millones de pesetas de su asignación anual. La familia Marichalar, como también manda la tradición, costeará el traje de la Infanta Elena valorado en un millón de pesetas.

Vocabulario

el ágape *banquet*
agasajar *to receive warmly*
el ajuar *trousseau*
los allegados *entourage*
la asignación *allowance*
los comensales *guests at a meal*
contraer matrimonio *to get married*
correr con los gastos *to foot the bill*
costear *to pay for*
el cubierto *place setting*
ecuestre *equestrian*
el enlace *marriage*
las estadísticas *statistics*
la factura *bill*
hacerse cargo de *to be responsible for*
la infanta *princess*
los invitados *guests*
los novios *bride and groom (before the ceremony); newlyweds*
la pareja *couple*
el ramo *bouquet*
la realeza *royalty*
sí quiero *(marriage vow) I do*
tener lugar *to take place*
el testigo *witness*

Escoja la oración de la columna B que complete correctamente la frase de la columna A.

A	B
______ 1. El Rey Juan Carlos I ...	a. serán testigos de la boda real.
______ 2. 220.000 parejas ...	b. será costeado por la familia Marichalar.
______ 3. El banquete ...	c. contraerán matrimonio en la catedral de Sevilla.
______ 4. El traje de la Infanta ...	d. tendrá lugar el día anterior a la boda.
______ 5. Millones de españoles ...	e. tendrá que pagar 50 millones de pesetas por la boda.
______ 6. El espectáculo ecuestre ...	f. se quedarán en el hotel Alfonso XIII.
______ 7. La Infanta Elena y Jaime de Marichalar ...	g. costará 22 millones de pesetas.
______ 8. Los parientes del Rey ...	h. se casarán en España este año.

CHAPTER 7

REFLEXIVE VERBS

A Reflexive verbs—introduction and conjugation

- Spanish has a large class of verbs called *reflexive verbs*. These verbs always have a reflexive pronoun that refers to the same person or thing as the subject. Most Spanish reflexive verbs correspond to English verbs that don't have a direct object (intransitive verbs) or English verb phrases consisting of *to be* or *to get* + an adjective or past participle. Reflexive verbs appear in vocabulary lists with the reflexive pronoun **se** attached to the infinitive: **acostarse** (*to go to bed*), **lavarse** (*to wash up*), **sentarse** (*to sit down*), **vestirse** (*to get dressed*).
- Observe that the reflexive pronoun precedes the conjugated verb:

acostarse (o > ue) *to go to bed* *(present tense)*	
me acuesto	**nos acostamos**
te acuestas	**os acostáis**
se acuesta	**se acuestan**

vestirse (e > i) *to dress, get dressed* *(preterit)*	
me vestí	**nos vestimos**
te vestiste	**os vestisteis**
se vistió	**se vistieron**

bañarse *to bathe, take a bath* *(imperfect)*	
me bañaba	**nos bañábamos**
te bañabas	**os bañabais**
se bañaba	**se bañaban**

- For most reflexive verbs there is a corresponding transitive verb in which the subject and direct object refer to different things or people:

  Lavo el carro. *I wash the car. (I = subject; car = direct object)*
  Me lavo. *I wash (up). (subject and direct object refer to* **yo***)*

  Acuestas a los niños. *You put the children to bed.*
  (you = subject; children = direct object)
  Te acuestas. *You go to bed. (subject and direct object refer to* **tú***)*

- The **se** of the infinitive must change to agree with the subject of the verb + infinitive construction. The reflexive pronoun may be placed either before the conjugated verb or after the infinitive. When placed after the infinitive, it is attached to it in writing:

quedarse *to stay, remain*	
Me quiero **quedar.**	Quiero **quedarme.**
Te quieres **quedar.**	Quieres **quedarte.**
Se quiere **quedar.**	Quiere **quedarse.**
Nos queremos **quedar.**	Queremos **quedarnos.**
Os queréis **quedar.**	Queréis **quedaros.**
Se quieren **quedar.**	Quieren **quedarse.**

B The reflexive pronoun as indirect object

- With some verbs the reflexive pronoun is an indirect object rather than a direct object. These verbs, such as **ponerse** + article of clothing (*to put on an article of clothing*), have a direct object (the article of clothing) in addition to the reflexive pronoun:

Los niños se ponen **el abrigo.**	*The children put on* ***their coats.***
Y se ponen **las botas** también.	*And they put on* ***their boots*** *also.*
Marta se lavó **las manos.**	*Marta washed* ***her hands.***
Nos lavamos **la cara.**	*We washed* ***our faces.***

- Spanish uses a singular noun for articles of clothing and parts of the body, even with plural subjects. It is assumed that each person has one item. Only if each person has more than one item does Spanish use a plural noun.

  Here are some common reflexive verbs and expressions that are used in this pattern:

ponerse + *article of clothing*	*to put on*
quitarse + *article of clothing*	*to take off*
romperse + *article of clothing*	*to tear*
lavarse + *part of the body*	*to wash*
quebrarse (e > ie) + *part of the body*	*to break*
quemarse + *part of the body*	*to burn*
romperse + *part of the body*	*to break*

abrocharse los cordones *to tie one's shoelaces*
amarrarse los cordones *to tie one's shoelaces*
atarse los cordones *to tie one's shoelaces*
cepillarse los dientes *to brush one's teeth*
cortarse el pelo *to get a haircut*
desabrocharse los cordones *to untie one's shoelaces*
desamarrarse los cordones *to untie one's shoelaces*
desatarse los cordones *to untie one's shoelaces*
lastimarse el dedo *to hurt one's finger*
lavarse la cabeza *to wash one's hair*
limarse las uñas *to file one's nails*
limpiarse los dientes *to brush one's teeth*
maquillarse la cara *to put makeup on*
pintarse los labios *to put lipstick on*
torcerse el tobillo (o > ue) *to twist one's ankle*

A. ¿Reflexivo o no? Complete las siguientes oraciones escogiendo la forma transitiva o reflexiva del verbo que aparece entre paréntesis. Use el tiempo verbal indicado.

MODELO Rosita **bañó** a los niños y después ella **se bañó.** (bañar—*preterit*)

1. Mañana yo ________________ a las siete y ________________ a mi hermana a las siete y cuarto. (despertar—*present*)

2. Aunque el profesor Vélez ____________________ a sus estudiantes, Miguel y Carlota no ____________________. (aburrir—*imperfect*)
3. Los novios ____________________ en la catedral de Burgos. El cura de la novia los ____________________. (casar—*preterit*)
4. Al jugar al escondite (*hide-and-seek*) nosotros ____________________ a los niñitos y luego nosotros ____________________. (esconder—*future*)
5. ¿Tú ____________________ ahora mismo o ____________________ primero a Luisita? (vestir—*present*)
6. Nosotros ya ____________________ y ____________________ al perro también. (pasear—*preterit*)
7. La carta que Carmen recibió ayer no la ____________________. Sin embargo al leerla Martín ____________________. (tranquilizar—*preterit*)
8. Yo ____________________ durante el primer acto de la obra pero los otros dos actos no me ____________________. (divertir—*preterit*)
9. Pepe me hacía tantas preguntas que francamente yo ____________________. ¡Ese chico ____________________ a todo el mundo! (marear—*imperfect*)
10. Daniel no tiene ganas de hacer nada. A ver si nosotros lo ____________________. Vamos a invitarlo a jugar al tenis. A ver si él ____________________. (animar—*present*)
11. Cuando Pablo y Laura eran niños ____________________ al ver las películas de terror. Las películas con fantasmas (*ghosts*) los ____________________ más que nada. (asustar—*imperfect*)
12. Uds. ____________________ por cualquier cosa. Menos mal que no ____________________ a otras personas. (ofender—*present*)

B. Todavía no, abuelita. La abuela llama desde Buenos Aires para hablar con sus nietos gemelos en Filadelfia. Ella les pregunta si pueden hacer ciertas cosas solos (*by themselves*). Los niños le dicen a su abuela que no pueden hacerlas solos todavía, que se las hace su mamá. Practique los verbos como verbos transitivos y reflexivos.

MODELO **(bañarse)**
abuelita: ¿Ustedes ya **se bañan** solos?
nietos: No, abuelita. **Nos baña** mamá.

1. **(despertarse)**
abuelita: ____
nietos: ____
2. **(lavarse la cabeza)**
abuelita: ____
nietos: ____

3. **(peinarse)**

abuelita: ______________________________

nietos: ______________________________

4. **(quitarse los zapatos)**

abuelita: ______________________________

nietos: ______________________________

5. **(prepararse el desayuno)**

abuelita: ______________________________

nietos: ______________________________

6. **(acostarse)**

abuelita: ______________________________

nietos: ______________________________

Nota cultural

Buenos Aires figura en un huso horario (*time zone*) internacional una hora más tarde que el huso horario de Filadelfia. La ciudad de México está en otro huso horario, una hora más temprano que Filadelfia. Madrid está en otro, seis horas más tarde que Filadelfia.

C. Una excursión al campo. Ud. y sus amigos pasaron un día en el campo. Escriba lo que cada persona llevó ese día. Practique el uso del verbo reflexivo **ponerse** en pretérito.

MODELO tú / los zapatos de tenis
➔ Te pusiste los zapatos de tenis.

La ropa

el abrigo *overcoat*
la blusa *blouse*
las botas *boots*
la bufanda *scarf*
los calcetines *socks (Spain)*
la camisa *shirt*
la camiseta *T-shirt*
el cinturón *belt*
la corbata *tie*
la chaqueta *jacket*
el gorro *cap*
los guantes *gloves*
el impermeable *raincoat*
los jeans, el pantalón vaquero *jeans*
las medias *socks (Latin America); stockings (Spain)*
los pantalones *pants*
el saco *jacket*
las sandalias *sandals*
el smoking *tuxedo (also,* **el esmoquin***)*
el sombrero *hat*
el suéter *sweater*
el traje *suit*
el traje de baño *bathing suit*
el vestido *dress*
los zapatos *shoes*
 de tacón alto *high-heeled shoes*
 de tenis *tennis shoes*

¿De qué es?: Las telas

el algodón *cotton*
el cuero *leather*
el charol *patent leather*
la lana *wool*
el nailon *nylon*
el poliéster *polyester*
la seda *silk*
el terciopelo *velvet*

1. Marina y yo / los jeans

___

2. Arturo / un traje de baño

___

3. Uds. / un impermeable

___

4. yo / un suéter de lana

___

5. Víctor y Paco / un gorro

___

6. todos nosotros / una camiseta

___

D. **¿Qué se llevará para ir al trabajo?** Escriba lo que llevarán ciertas personas para ir al trabajo. Practique el uso del verbo reflexivo **ponerse** en futuro.

MODELO Alberto / un saco
➔ Alberto se pondrá un saco.

1. yo / un vestido

___

2. Alicia / una blusa

___

3. nosotros / zapatos de cuero

___

4. Uds. / una camisa de algodón

___

5. los jefes / un traje de lana

___

6. tú / una corbata

___

E. **¡Ya llega el baile de gala (*prom*)!** Ud. y sus amigos están emocionados porque el baile de gala es el sábado. Todos Uds. necesitan probarse la ropa que van a llevar. Practique el uso del verbo reflexivo **probarse** en presente.

MODELO nosotros / los zapatos de charol
→ Nos probamos los zapatos de charol.

1. Pilar y Luz / el traje largo

____

2. yo / el abrigo de terciopelo

____

3. Lorenzo / el smoking

____

4. Uds. / los zapatos de tacón alto

____

5. tú / la blusa de seda

____

6. Antonio y Esteban / la corbata

____

F. **¡Qué malas noticias!** Un amigo que acaba de volver de México pregunta por sus amigos. ¡Le toca a Ud. darle las malas noticias! Escriba los verbos reflexivos en pretérito.

MODELO Alfonso / caerse / cruzando la calle
→ Alfonso se cayó cruzando la calle.

1. Miguel / romperse la pierna / montando a caballo

____

2. Ana / quemarse la mano / cocinando

____

3. el perro de Bernardo / perderse / en las afueras

____

4. Eunice / torcerse el tobillo / patinando sobre el hielo

____

5. todos nosotros / enfermarse / comiendo hamburguesas poco cocidas

____

6. yo / hacerse daño / cortando el césped

____

7. los hermanos de Pedro / quebrarse el dedo / jugando al básquetbol

____

G. Estimados televidentes ... Ud. es locutor(a) en la tele. Por desgracia las noticias de hoy son todas malas. Expréselas en oraciones completas usando los verbos reflexivos en pretérito y los otros elementos propuestos.

MODELO dos panaderos / quemarse las manos / cuando hubo una explosión en el horno
→ Dos panaderos se quemaron las manos cuando hubo una explosión en el horno.

1. la actriz Ramona Taylor / lastimarse / en el rodaje (*filming*) de su nueva película

 ____

2. el futbolista Diego Suárez / romperse el pie / en el partido de hoy

 ____

3. unos turistas norteamericanos / caerse / en la escalera mecánica del metro

 ____

4. un carpintero / cortarse la mano / aserruchando (*sawing*) madera

 ____

5. diez arqueólogos / hacerse daño / en una excavación en las pirámides

 ____

6. un bombero / quemarse / apagando un incendio

 ____

7. los bailarines / divorciarse / después de cuarenta años de bailar juntos

 ____

H. El aseo personal (*personal hygiene*). Escriba oraciones explicando cuándo y cómo algunas personas hacen su aseo personal. Practique el uso de los verbos reflexivos en presente.

MODELO Guillermo / limpiarse los dientes / dos veces al día
→ Guillermo se limpia los dientes dos veces al día.

El aseo personal

afeitarse *to shave*
arreglarse *to get ready to go out*
bañarse *to take a bath*
cepillarse el pelo/los dientes *to brush one's hair/teeth*
cortarse el pelo/las uñas *to cut one's hair/nails*
ducharse *to take a shower*
lavarse *to wash up*
limarse las uñas *to file one's nails*
lavarse los dientes *to brush one's teeth*
maquillarse *to put makeup on*
peinarse *to comb one's hair*
pintarse *to put makeup on*
vestirse *to get dressed*

1. Felisa / lavarse la cabeza / todos los días

2. yo / vestirse / rápidamente por la mañana

3. nuestros padres / ducharse / por la noche

4. Carlos / afeitarse / con una maquinilla de afeitar

5. Laura y Teresa / limarse las uñas / antes de ponerse el esmalte de uñas (*nail polish*)

6. tú / peinarse / con cuidado

7. Benjamín y yo / arreglarse / en el dormitorio

8. Ud. / cepillarse el pelo / después de maquillarse

I. Hay que hacerlo. Escriba oraciones en las cuales se expresa que las personas **quieren, van a, acaban de** (u otra expresión) hacer ciertas cosas. Practique la construcción del verbo conjugado con el verbo reflexivo en infinitivo. Escriba las oraciones de dos maneras.

MODELO Guillermo se afeita todos los días. (necesitar)
➔ Guillermo **necesita afeitarse** todos los días.
➔ Guillermo **se necesita afeitar** todos los días.

1. Samuel se coloca en una sucursal de la empresa. (querer)

2. Nosotros nos desayunamos antes de las ocho. (deber)

3. Los amigos se reúnen en casa de Felipe esta noche. (pensar)

4. Teresa se pesa todas las semanas. (necesitar)

5. Yo me voy de vacaciones en julio. (ir a)

____

____

6. Las señoras se aprovechan de las liquidaciones. (acabar de)

____

____

7. ¿Te sientas en esta fila? (querer)

____

____

8. Uds. se secan el pelo. (tener que)

____

____

C *The imperative of reflexive verbs*

- Reflexive pronouns precede negative command forms but follow affirmative commands and are attached to them in writing. Observe that a written accent mark is added to affirmative command forms of more than one syllable when the reflexive pronoun is added:

Acuéstense ahora, chicos.	***Go to bed** now, kids.*
No se levanten hasta las ocho.	***Don't get up** until eight.*

- Here are some common reflexive verbs that refer to the daily routine. Their nonreflexive forms, usually transitive verbs, and meanings are also given:

acostar (o > ue) *to put (someone) to bed*	**acostarse (o > ue)** *to go to bed*
afeitar *to shave (someone)*	**afeitarse** *to shave*
arreglar *to arrange, fix*	**arreglarse** *to get ready (fix hair, clothing, etc.)*
bañar *to bathe (someone)*	**bañarse** *to bathe, take a bath*
cansar *to tire (someone)*	**cansarse** *to get tired*
colocar *to place, put*	**colocarse** *to get a job*
cortar *to cut*	**cortarse** *to cut oneself*
despedir (e > i) *to fire, dismiss*	**despedirse de (e > i)** *to say goodbye to*
despertar (e > ie) *to wake someone up*	**despertarse (e > ie)** *to wake up*
dormir (o > ue) *to sleep*	**dormirse (o > ue)** *to fall asleep*
enfermar *to make ill*	**enfermarse** *to get sick*
lastimar *to hurt*	**lastimarse** *to hurt oneself*
lavar *to wash someone, something*	**lavarse** *to wash up*
levantar *to raise, pick up*	**levantarse** *to get up*
maquillar *to put makeup on someone*	**maquillarse** *to put on makeup*
peinar *to comb someone's hair*	**peinarse** *to comb one's hair*
reunir *to join, gather*	**reunirse (con)** *to get together (with)*
vestir (e > i) *to dress (someone)*	**vestirse (e > i)** *to dress, get dressed*

- Here are some common reflexive verbs expressing feelings and emotions. Corresponding nonreflexive verbs are usually transitive:

aburrir *to bore someone*
alegrar *to make someone happy*
animar *to cheer someone up, encourage someone*
asustar *to frighten someone*
calmar *to calm someone down*
decidir *to decide*
divertir (e > ie) *to amuse*
enfadar *to make (someone) angry*
enojar *to make (someone) angry*
entusiasmar *to excite, thrill, stir*
exasperar *to exasperate, make (someone) lose his/her patience*
interesar *to interest*
marear *to make (someone) dizzy*
molestar *to annoy, bother*
ofender *to offend, insult, hurt someone*
preocupar *to worry someone*
probar (o > ue) *to try, taste*
sorprender *to surprise someone*
tranquilizar *to calm someone down, reassure*

aburrirse *to get, be bored*
alegrarse *to be glad, happy*
animarse *to cheer up, take heart, feel like doing something*
asustarse *to get scared*
calmarse *to calm down*
decidirse a *to make up one's mind*
divertirse (e > ie) *to have a good time*
enfadarse *to get angry*
enojarse *to get angry*
entusiasmarse *to get excited, feel thrilled*
exasperarse *to get exasperated, lose one's patience*
interesarse en *to be interested in*
marearse *to get, feel dizzy*
molestarse *to get annoyed*
ofenderse *to get offended, insulted; feel hurt*
preocuparse *to worry*
probarse (o > ue) *to try on*
sorprenderse *to be surprised*
tranquilizarse *to calm down, stop worrying*

J. Dando consejos. Lea las siguientes situaciones y luego dé algunos consejos empleando los verbos entre paréntesis con la forma formal e informal singular del mandato.

MODELO Tengo calor. (quitarse el suéter)
➔ Quítese el suéter. / Quítate el suéter.

1. Me gustan los dos trajes. (probarse los dos)

____

____

2. Tengo muchísimo sueño. (acostarse temprano)

____

____

3. ¡Tengo cita a las tres y ya son las tres menos cuarto! (darse prisa)

____

____

4. Empieza a llover. (ponerse el impermeable)

____

____

5. Voy a ver la nueva película española esta noche. (divertirse mucho)

6. ¡Me encanta París! (quedarse otra semana entonces)

7. Tengo que recoger a mis padres en el aeropuerto. (irse ahora mismo)

K. **¡No lo haga!** Déle a la persona un mandato negativo empleando el verbo entre paréntesis con la forma formal e informal singular.

MODELO Me gusta el pelo largo. (no cortarse el pelo entonces)
➔ No se corte el pelo entonces.
➔ No te cortes el pelo entonces.

1. Tengo fiebre. (no levantarse todavía)

2. Tengo los pies mojados por la lluvia. (no enfermarse)

3. A Roberta se le rompió mi reloj. (no enfadarse con ella)

4. Voy a coger el tren de las ocho. (no despertarse tarde)

5. Necesito estudiar para un examen de biología. (no dormirse)

6. Yo no tengo la menor idea de lo que pasó. (no hacerse el desentendido)

7. Me como varios dulces todos los días. (no ponerse gorda)

L. **¡Niños, hagan esto!** Empleando la forma del mandato de los verbos entre paréntesis, déles mandatos a los niños. Dígales las cosas que deben hacer.

MODELO bañarse ahora ➔ Niños, báñense ahora.

1. vestirse para salir

2. cepillarse los dientes

3. atarse los cordones

4. ponerse serios

5. lavarse las manos

M. **¡Niños, pórtense bien!** Empleando la forma del mandato de los verbos entre paréntesis, déles mandatos a los niños. ¡Esta vez, dígales las cosas que *no* deben hacer!

MODELO no quitarse los guantes
➔ Niños, no se quiten los guantes.

1. no ensuciarse la cara

2. no hacerse los sordos

3. no caerse patinando

4. no olvidarse de guardar sus juguetes

5. no irse del jardín

6. no pintarse los labios

7. no quejarse tanto

D The position of reflexive pronouns with the present participle

- In the progressive tenses, the reflexive pronouns may either precede the forms of **estar** or follow the present participle (gerund). When they follow, they are attached in writing and a written accent is added to the vowel before the **-ndo** of the gerund.

Me estoy vistiendo. — *I'm getting dressed.*
Ana **está arreglándose.** — *Ana is getting ready.*

- Here are some commonly used reflexive verbs that refer to motion or to a change in position. In most cases, the corresponding nonreflexive verb is transitive:

acercar *to bring something closer, over*
alejar *to move something away*
caer *to fall (usually figurative)*
correr *to move (an object)*
detener *to stop, bring to a halt*
instalar *to install*
ir *to go*
levantar *to lift*
mover (o > ue) *to move (put in motion)*
parar *to stop*
pasear *to take for a walk, to walk*
perder (e > ie) *to lose*
quedar *to remain, be left*
tirar *to throw*
volcar (o > ue) *to knock over*

acercarse (a) *to come closer, approach*
alejarse (de) *to move away from*
caerse *to fall down*
correrse *to move over, make room for*
detenerse *to stop, come to a halt*
instalarse *to move in*
irse *to go away*
levantarse *to get up, rise*
moverse (o > ue) *to move, stir, budge*
pararse *to stand up (especially Span. America)*
pasearse *to stroll*
perderse (e > ie) *to get lost*
quedarse *to stay, remain*
tirarse *to jump, throw oneself; to lie down*
volcarse (o > ue) *to get knocked over*

- The following verbs of motion or change of position are used primarily as reflexives:

apresurarse de *to hurry*
echarse *to lie down*
escaparse *to escape*
inclinarse *to bend over*
mudarse *to move (change residence)*
ponerse de pie *to stand up (esp. Spain)*
recostarse (o > ue) *to lie down*

- Here are some verbs that are used primarily or exclusively as reflexives in Spanish, at least in the meanings given. Verbs marked with an asterisk exist only as reflexives:

acordarse (o > ue) (de) *to remember*
apoderarse (de) *to take possession (of)*
aprovecharse (de) *to take advantage (of)*
apuntarse a/para *to register, sign up for*
arrepentirse de (e > ie) *to regret, repent*
***atreverse a** *to dare to do something*
ausentarse *to be out, away*
burlarse de *to laugh at, make fun of*
casarse (con) *to get married (to)*
comprometerse *to get engaged*
***desmayarse** *to faint*
***divorciarse** *to get divorced*
empeñarse (en) *to insist (on), persist (in)*
enamorarse (de) *to fall in love (with)*
enterarse (de) *to find out (about)*
fiarse de *to trust*
figurarse *to imagine*
fijarse (en) *to notice*
***jactarse de** *to boast about*
negarse a (e > ie) *to refuse to*
ocuparse de *to take care of*
olvidarse (de) *to forget*
oponerse a *to oppose, be against*
parecerse a *to resemble*
portarse bien/mal *to behave well/badly*
***quejarse de** *to complain about*
reírse de *to laugh at*
sentirse (e > ie) *to feel*
***suicidarse** *to commit suicide*

Note: **Olvidar** is followed by a direct object; **olvidarse** by the preposition **de. Olvidaron el número.** = **Se olvidaron del número**. *They forgot the number.* **Olvidarse** is also used with the indirect object pronoun: **Se les olvidó el número**. = *They forgot the number.* (See Chapter 19 on unplanned occurrences.)

N. **¡Haciendo diabluras (*Making mischief*)!** En una reunión dominical (*Sunday*), los niños están haciendo sus diabluras como siempre. ¡Y los adultos están reaccionando como siempre! Escriba oraciones con los verbos en presente progresivo para describir la escena. Escriba cada oración de dos maneras.

MODELO Sarita / mojarse con la sopa
➔ **Sarita está mojándose con la sopa.**
➔ **Sarita se está mojando con la sopa.**

la hermana de Sarita / quejarse
➔ **La hermana de Sarita está quejándose.**
➔ **La hermana de Sarita se está quejando.**

1. Luisito / portarse mal

____

____

2. los abuelos de Luisito / ponerse rojos

____

____

3. Adrianita / reírse como una loca

____

____

4. la tía de Adrianita / desmayarse

5. Fernandito / esconderse en un armario

6. el tío de Fernandito / asustarse

7. los gemelos (*twins*) / escaparse de su padre

8. el padre de los gemelos / enojarse

9. Pedrito / burlarse de sus primos

10. los primos de Pedrito / exasperarse

11. Mari Carmen / ensuciarse con el guacamole

12. la madre de Mari Carmen / avergonzarse

Nota cultural

El *guacamole* *es* una ensalada hecha con aguacate (*avocado*), tomate, cebolla y condimentos. *Se come en* México, América Central y Cuba.

O. Están en movimiento. Hay mucha actividad en el barrio hoy. Use el presente progresivo para decir lo que está haciendo cada persona.

MODELO ¿Dónde está Juan Pedro? (levantarse de la mesa)
→ Se está levantando de la mesa. /
Está levantándose de la mesa.

1. ¿Qué hace tu mamá? (apresurarse para salir)

____

____

2. ¿Qué hacen los Pereira? (mudarse a otro barrio)

____

____

3. ¿Dónde están los niños? (acercarse a la escuela)

____

____

4. ¿Qué hacen tus abuelos? (pasearse por el centro)

____

____

5. ¿Qué haces tú? (instalarse en un nuevo apartamento)

____

____

6. ¿Qué hacen Uds.? (irse al campo)

____

____

7. ¿Dónde está Elena? (quedarse en casa)

____

____

8. ¿Qué hace el señor Peña? (tirarse a la piscina)

____

____

E *Reflexive verbs with reciprocal meaning*

- The plural forms of reflexive verbs are used to express *reciprocal action* which corresponds to the English phrase "each other." Because **se ven** means either *they see each other* or *they see themselves* (e.g., in the mirror), the meaning must be clarified by the context:

—Jacinto y Laura **se quieren** mucho.	*Jacinto and Laura* ***love each other*** *very much.*
—**Se ven** todos los días.	***They see each other*** *every day.*
—¿Dónde **se conocieron** Uds.?	*Where* ***did you meet each other****?*
—**Nos conocimos** en una conferencia.	***We met*** *at a lecture.*

- Spanish uses the phrase **el uno al otro** (or **uno a otro**) to focus on or to clarify the meaning "each other." This phrase agrees with the gender and number of the people referred to: **el uno al otro / la una a la otra / los unos a los otros / las unas a las otras**:

Mis hermanos se ayudan **el uno al otro**.	*My brothers help **each other.***
Las chicas se miran **la una a la otra**.	*The girls look at **each other.***

- The reflexive pronoun is not used to express "each other" with prepositions other than **a**:

Diana y Felisa no pueden ir de compras **la una sin la otra.**	*Diana and Felisa can't shop without **each other.***

P. Mi mejor amigo(a) y yo. Escriba oraciones en las cuales describe cómo es la relación entre Ud. y su mejor amigo(a). Practique el uso del reflexivo con el significado *each other.* Use el tiempo presente del verbo.

MODELO Pablo y yo / conocer muy bien
➔ Pablo y yo nos conocemos muy bien.

1. Marisol y yo / hablar por teléfono cuatro veces al día
____
2. Jorge y yo / entender perfectamente
____
3. José María y yo / ver todos los días
____
4. Consuelo y yo / escribir mucho durante las vacaciones
____
5. Felipe y yo / ayudar con la tarea
____
6. Victoria y yo / prestar ropa
____

Q. Un gran amor. ¿Cómo llegaron Alejandra y Claudio a comprometerse? Escriba oraciones en pretérito con la forma recíproca del reflexivo para explicarlo.

MODELO ver por primera vez hace un año
➔ Se vieron por primera vez hace un año.

1. conocer en una fiesta
____
2. llamar a menudo
____
3. ver todos los días
____

4. hablar constantemente

____

5. comprar regalos

____

6. decir muchas cosas importantes

____

7. hacer promesas

____

8. llegar a querer

____

Nota cultural

En las sociedades tradicionales de los países hispánicos, las familias arreglaban el **matrimonio** para sus hijos. Los padres y abuelos sólo dejaban que la hija saliera con un joven bien educado y de ciertos medios económicos. Y cuando salía con el joven iban acompañados de una chaperona o dueña. Después de varios años de noviazgo (*courtship and engagement*), entre cinco y diez quizás, los novios se casaban. En las últimas décadas las cosas fueron cambiando, aunque todavía era necesario que la pareja esperara hasta que el esposo se ganara la vida para poder comprar un apartamento. Hoy en día los jóvenes se conocen, se enamoran y escogen un cónyuge (*mate*) sin tanta intervención de la familia. Y claro que ahora las mujeres trabajan también. Pero con todos estos cambios, la opinión de los familiares y su influencia en el matrimonio de los jóvenes sigue siendo más fuerte en el mundo hispánico que en los Estados Unidos.

R. Travesuras (*Mischief*) en el parque. Dos niños estaban en el parque ayer. Complete el siguiente relato con el pretérito de los verbos entre paréntesis para saber lo que les pasó. Ud. practicará el uso del reflexivo con el significado de *each other.*

1. (conocerse) Luisito y Juanito ______________________ en el parque ayer.
2. (Ponerse) ______________________ a jugar. Pronto, Luisito le quitó el camión a Juanito.
3. (Enojarse) ______________________ tanto que
4. (pegarse) ______________________.
5. (acercarse) Las dos mamás ______________________ y trataron de calmar a sus hijos.
6. (tranquilizarse) Los niños ______________________ y
7. (abrazarse) ______________________ y
8. (darse) ______________________ un beso.

How to say "become" in Spanish

- The English verb *to become* has several different translations in Spanish. When *to become* is followed by an adjective, the most common Spanish expression is **ponerse** + *adjective.* It is used for physical or emotional changes, where no effort is implied:

Esteban **se puso bravo** al leer la carta.	*Esteban **got angry** when he read the letter.*
Lidia y María **se pusieron pálidas** del susto.	*Lidia and María **turned pale** from fright.*
Juanita **se pone roja** porque es tímida.	*Juanita **blushes (gets red)** because she's shy.*

- **Volverse** + *adjective* is used to express a sudden, involuntary change, most commonly in the expression **volverse loco** *to go crazy, mad.* Changes indicated by **ponerse** may be superficial, while those indicated by **volverse** are more profound:

El psicólogo **se volvió loco.**	*The psychologist **went mad.***
Los políticos **se volvieron muy arrogantes.**	*The politicians **got very arrogant.***
¡Ese niño **se ha vuelto imposible!**	*That kid **has become impossible!***

- **Hacerse** and **llegar a ser** also mean *to become* and are used with nouns expressing profession or adjectives expressing social status. They imply effort on the part of the subject. **Pasar a ser**, stressing the process of change, is also used:

Sarita **se hizo abogada.** Lola **llegó a ser abogada** también.	*Sarita **became a lawyer.*** *Lola **became a lawyer** also.*
Pedro y yo **nos hicimos amigos.** Pedro y Tomás nunca **llegaron a ser amigos.**	*Pedro and I **became friends.*** *Pedro and Tomás never **got to be friends.***
Laura **pasó a ser directora ejecutiva** de la compañía. Y **se hizo rica** también.	*Laura **got to be executive director** of the company.* *And **she got rich** too.*

- The idioms **convertirse en (e > ie)** and **transformarse en** also express ideas related to the verb *to become*:

Atlanta **se convirtió en** una ciudad importante.	*Atlanta **became** an important city.*
El vino **se transformó en** vinagre.	*The wine **turned to** vinegar.*

- Very often the idea of *become* or *get* is expressed by a reflexive verb in Spanish. For example: **cansarse** (*to get tired*), **enojarse** (*to get angry*), **emocionarse** (*to get excited*). Some ideas can be expressed both with a verb meaning *to become* followed by an adjective and with a reflexive verb; the latter is more literary. Some examples: **hacerse rico** / **enriquecerse** (*to become rich*), **ponerse furioso** / **enfurecerse** (*to become furious*), **volverse orgulloso** / **enorgullecerse** (*to become haughty*).

- There are some verbs in Spanish that express a change of state similar to **cansarse** and **enojarse** that are *not reflexive.* These verbs have alternate constructions consisting of one of the verbs for *to become* followed by an adjective: **adelgazar / quedarse delgado** (*to get thin*), **enflaquecer / ponerse flaco** (*to get* *thin*), **engordar / ponerse gordo** (*to get fat*), **enloquecer / volverse loco** (*to go mad*), **enmudecer / volverse mudo** (*to become mute*), **ensordecer / volverse sordo** (*to go deaf*), **envejecer / ponerse viejo** (*to grow old*), **palidecer / ponerse pálido** (*to turn pale*).

S. Cómo se dice *to become* en español. Indique cuál de las expresiones que significan *to become* corresponde en cada oración.

1. Los chicos __________ contentísimos al ver su nueva bicicleta.

   a. se pusieron   b. se hicieron

2. Después de unas campañas políticas muy duras, Jorge Cuevas __________ senador.

   a. se volvió   b. llegó a ser

3. ¡__________ locos por la cantidad de trabajo!

   a. Nos volvemos   b. Nos hacemos

4. Rita __________ brava cuando el taxi chocó con su coche.

   a. se hizo   b. se puso

5. Este pueblo está __________ en un centro turístico.

   a. poniéndose   b. convirtiéndose

T. *To become* y *to get*. Exprese las siguientes oraciones en español escogiendo la expresión correcta para *become* or *get* en cada caso.

1. Ricardo became a millionaire.

   ____

2. The archaeologists got excited when they saw the ruins.

   ____

3. Magdalena often blushes (gets red) because she's very shy.

   ____

4. Daniel is marrying Tere because he wants to become an American citizen.

   ____

5. Carlitos has become impossible!

   ____

6. Felisa is getting very fat because of the cake and ice cream she eats every day!

   ____

7. The valley became an important technological center.

   ____

Nota cultural

Los **inmigrantes indocumentados** (*illegal aliens*) vienen a los Estados Unidos generalmente por razones económicas y políticas. Por no tener los documentos necesarios, tienen que aceptar trabajos que pagan mal y que no les dan ni beneficios ni seguridad. Les conviene solicitar la tarjeta verde (*Alien Registration Card*) porque con ella tienen todos los derechos de un ciudadano estadounidense salvo el de votar. Una manera de legalizar su estado de inmigrante indocumentado es casarse con un ciudadano de los Estados Unidos.

G *Other reflexive verbs*

- There are cases of reflexive verbs that do not fit exactly into the categories given above and that require special attention:
- **Equivocarse** has a basic meaning of *to be mistaken, be wrong:*

Si crees que Paula te va a devolver el dinero, **te equivocas.**	*If you think Paula is going to return the money to you,* ***you're mistaken.***

- Note that **equivocarse** means to be wrong only when the subject is a person. **Estar equivocado** means *to be wrong* both for persons and things:

El físico **se equivocó.**	*The physicist* ***was wrong.***
El físico **estuvo equivocado.**	*The physicist* ***was wrong.***
La respuesta **está equivocada.**	*The answer* ***is wrong.***

The expression **equivocarse de** can translate other uses of English *wrong:*

Ud. **se ha equivocado** de casa.	*You've come to the* ***wrong*** *house.*
Nos equivocamos de carretera.	*We took the* ***wrong*** *highway.*

- **Quedarse** has a basic meaning of *to remain, stay:*

Quédate en casa si no te sientes bien.	***Stay at home*** *if you don't feel well.*
Pensamos quedarnos en un parador en Segovia.	***We intend to stay*** *at an inn in Segovia.*

- **Quedarse** can express *to become* to indicate a new state, either physical or emotional:

Todos **se quedaron atónitos.**	*Everyone* ***was astonished.***
Dos víctimas del terremoto **se quedaron ciegas y sordas.**	*Two victims of the earthquake* ***went blind and deaf.***

- Nonreflexive **quedar** is used to mean different things:

El cuarto **queda bien / mal** con las nuevas cortinas.	*The room* ***looks good / bad*** *with the new curtains.*
Tu corbata roja **queda bien** con tu camisa azul.	*Your red tie* ***goes well*** *with your blue shirt.*
Paco **quedó bien** regalándole flores a su suegra.	*Paco* ***made a good impression*** *giving flowers to his mother-in-law.*
El director de la orquesta **quedó mal** con los músicos.	*The conductor* ***made a bad impression*** *on the musicians.*

- **Hacerse**, when followed by the definite article and an adjective, means *to pretend to be, to act like*:

  El ladrón **se hizo el desentendido** al ser encontrado por la policía. — *The thief* ***played dumb (pretended not to understand)*** *when he was found by the police.*

  Lola **se hizo la sorda** cuando su hermana le pidió prestado el coche. — *Lola* ***pretended to be deaf (turned a deaf ear)*** *when her sister asked to borrow the car.*

  Berta **se hizo la dormida** para no tener que hacer las labores domésticas. — *Berta* ***pretended to be asleep*** *so that she wouldn't have to do the household chores.*

  Nicolás **se hacía el tonto** en la fiesta. — *Nicolás* ***was acting silly (playing the fool)*** *at the party.*

- Both **acordarse de** and **recordar** mean *to remember*:

  Si no **me acuerdo** mal. — *If* ***I remember*** *correctly.*
  Si no **recuerdo** mal. — *If* ***I remember*** *correctly.*

- **Recordar** also means *to remind*:

  Les recuerdo que mañana tenemos ensayo. — ***I'm reminding them*** *that we have a rehearsal tomorrow.*

  Me recuerdas a tu mamá. — ***You remind me*** *of your mother.*

Some expressions with reflexive verbs:

darse cuenta (de) *to realize*
darse prisa *to hurry*
echarse a + *infinitive* *to begin to*
hacerse daño *to hurt oneself*
hacerse tarde *to get late*
ponerse a + *infinitive* *to begin to*
ponerse de acuerdo *to come to an agreement*
quedarse con *to keep, hold onto*
tratarse de *to be about, be a question of*

- Certain verbs are made reflexive to stress participation by the subject or to convey an intensification of the action:

  Compré un coche. — ***I bought*** *a car.*
  Me compré un coche. — ***I bought (myself)*** *a car.*
  Leo **comió** los pasteles. — *Leo* ***ate*** *the pastries.*
  Leo **se comió** los pasteles. — *Leo* ***gobbled up*** *the pastries.*

U. Preposiciones con verbos reflexivos. Complete las siguientes oraciones escribiendo las preposiciones correctas que faltan.

1. Este niño malcriado (*spoiled*) no se lleva bien __________ nadie.
2. Los turistas se fijaron __________ la arquitectura de los castillos.
3. No debemos aprovecharnos __________ las demás personas.
4. Jorge se arrepiente __________ haberles mentido a sus padres.
5. Yo me intereso mucho __________ la historia europea.
6. Los Cela se negaron __________ hacer cola en la taquilla.

7. ¿No te fías __________ tu abogado?
8. El vecino se ofreció __________ cortarnos el césped.
9. Los abuelos siempre se jactan (*brag*) __________ sus nietos.
10. Ud. se olvidó __________ desenchufar los aparatos eléctricos.
11. Daniel se casará __________ Luz en mayo.
12. No nos atrevemos __________ viajar de noche sin linterna.

V. En otras palabras. Vuelva a escribir las siguientes oraciones usando un sinónimo de los verbos o expresiones que aparecen en letra cursiva.

1. *Si me acuerdo bien,* los Aranda se mudaron a Los Ángeles.

   ____

2. Ud. *no tiene razón.* Lima es la capital del Perú, no de Ecuador.

   ____

3. Dos personas *perdieron la vista* a causa del accidente.

   ____

4. *Parece que* la niña *está dormida, pero no lo está.*

   ____

5. Juan Carlos *ha bajado mucho de peso.*

   ____

6. Creíamos que íbamos a *volvernos locos* por el desorden de la casa.

   ____

7. Todos los habitantes *están enfureciéndose* por el número de robos en el barrio.

   ____

8. Diego *se ponía pálido* corriendo la última milla de la carrera.

   ____

W. Ejercicio oral. Mi día. Con sus compañeros de clase describa su día típico. Hable de sus actividades diarias y a qué hora las hace. Por ejemplo: *despertarse, levantarse, vestirse, peinarse, ducharse, bañarse, desayunarse, acostarse.*

X. Estructuras en acción. Lea el siguiente artículo sobre la contaminación del ambiente en la Ciudad de México, fijándose especialmente en los verbos reflexivos. Luego haga el ejercicio que lo sigue.

MÉXICO SE ASFIXIA

En la Ciudad de México ya no saben qué hacer para combatir la contaminación. Un estudio de la Organización Mundial de la Salud—OMS—afirma que respirar un día el aire de la Ciudad de México equivale a fumarse 40 cigarrillos. Otros especialistas aseguran que el ozono que deja la contaminación provoca el envejecimiento de los pulmones, lo que se traduce en aumento de infartos cardíacos.

En estos días, la temperatura aumentó a 30 grados, lo que junto a los escasos vientos, el intenso sol y la emisión diaria de 12.000 toneladas de gases, está convirtiéndose en un peligroso coctel para los 20 millones de habitantes.

En los últimos cuatro años el gobierno mejoró la calidad de los combustibles, obligó a las fábricas a filtrar sus gases y aplicó programas para restringir el tránsito de vehículos. Pero estas medidas no han logrado mejorar la situación.

La razón es que las políticas adoptadas por las autoridades poco se cumplen por la corrupción de las áreas de vigilancia y control, según ha denunciado el Centro de Ecología y Desarrollo de México.

Vocabulario

aplicar *to put into effect*
asegurar *to assure*
asfixiarse *to suffocate*
el aumento *increase*
el combustible *fuel*
cumplir *to do, accomplish*
denunciar *to report*
el desarrollo *development*
el envejecimiento *aging*
equivaler a *to be the equivalent of, amount to*
fumarse *to smoke*
el infarto cardíaco *heart attack*
la medida *measure, step*
obligar *to force*
peligroso *dangerous*
la política *policy*
provocar *to cause*
el pulmón *lung*
respirar *to breathe*
la vigilancia *vigilance, watchfulness*
restringir *to restrict, limit*
la tonelada *ton*
traducirse *to result in, bring about*

Escoja la respuesta correcta para completar cada oración.

1. La población de la Ciudad de México es de __________ millones de habitantes.
   a. treinta　　b. veinte
2. Los pulmones envejecidos por la contaminación causan más __________.
   a. ataques al corazón　　b. enfermedades digestivas
3. Se afirma que respirar un día el aire de la Ciudad de México es equivalente a __________.
   a. tomarse un peligroso coctel　　b. fumarse cuarenta cigarrillos
4. __________ hace peligrar la salud de los habitantes de la capital.
   a. La emisión de doce mil toneladas de gases cada día
   b. La filtración de los gases emitidos por las fábricas

5. El gobierno mexicano __________ en los últimos cuatro años.

   a. ha eliminado la corrupción en los sectores de vigilancia y control
   b. ha mejorado la calidad de los combustibles

6. Aún la aplicación de programas para __________ no ha logrado reducir la contaminación del ambiente.

   a. limitar el tránsito de vehículos   b. estudiar el ozono

7. Los gases emitidos en el aire son más dañinos cuando __________.

   a. las fábricas están obligadas a filtrar sus gases
   b. hace mucho calor y sol y poco viento

CHAPTER 8

PASSIVE CONSTRUCTIONS

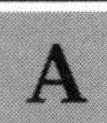

A The passive voice—use and formation

- The passive voice in Spanish consists of a form of **ser** + the past participle. This is often followed by the agent phrase introduced by the preposition **por**. The past participle agrees in number and gender with the subject of the sentence:

La cena fue servida ***por Margarita.***	*Dinner was served by Margarita.*
Los paquetes serán entregados ***por el cartero.***	*The packages will be delivered by the mailman.*
El coche ha sido reparado ***por los mecánicos.***	*The car has been repaired by the mechanics.*

- The passive voice is used in Spanish when the speaker wishes to deemphasize the performer of the action. In the passive construction, the speaker can focus on the direct object by making it the subject of the passive sentence:

(active voice)	Los obreros construirán el rascacielos.
(passive voice)	El rascacielos será construido por los obreros.

Note that the direct object of the active sentence, **el rascacielos,** becomes the subject of the passive sentence. The subject of the active sentence, the performer of the action, **los obreros**, appears in the "agent phrase" introduced by **por**. In the rephrasing of the active sentence into a passive sentence, the speaker focuses on **el rascacielos** and on its building rather than on the performer of the action, **los obreros.**

A. En la oficina. Vuelva a escribir las siguientes oraciones, cambiándolas de construcción activa a construcción pasiva para describir las actividades que ocurren en la oficina. Mantenga el tiempo verbal de la oración en voz activa.

MODELO El secretario arregló los papeles.
→ Los papeles fueron arreglados por el secretario.

1. La recepcionista encontró el número de teléfono.

____

2. Los empleados llenarán los formularios.

____

3. El bibliotecario ha preparado el folleto.

____

4. La cajera cobra los cheques.

____

5. Las secretarias escribirán las cartas y las tarjetas postales.

____

6. Los agentes de viajes tradujeron los documentos.

____

7. El programador reparó la pantalla de la computadora.

____

8. Los mensajeros han puesto los recados en los escritorios.

____

B. **Día de mudanza.** Escriba oraciones con verbos en voz pasiva y en pretérito para describir lo que pasó en casa de los Pidal el día de su mudanza de San Salvador a Nueva York.

MODELO los muebles / llevar / cargadores (*movers*)
➔ Los muebles fueron llevados por los cargadores.

1. las camas / subir a los dormitorios / tres hombres

____

2. la alfombra de la sala / correr / la señora Pidal

____

3. los cuadros / colgar en las paredes / Benito y Ramona

____

4. la secadora / bajar al sótano / un cargador

____

5. el sillón azul / colocar al lado de la ventana / el señor Pidal

____

6. las lámparas / poner en las mesas / la abuela

____

Nota cultural

- Hay mucha **emigración** de ciertos países hispánicos a los Estados Unidos por razones económicas, políticas y personales. Los inmigrantes hispanos más numerosos son de México, la República Dominicana, El Salvador, Colombia, Perú, Ecuador y Cuba.
- Muchos inmigrantes necesitan los servicios de las empresas de mudanza internacional. Por eso se ven tantos anuncios para las mudanzas en los periódicos hispánicos que se publican en los Estados Unidos; por ejemplo, en *El Diario/ La Prensa* de Nueva York o *El Tiempo Latino* de Washington, D.C.
- El Salvador es el país centroamericano más pequeño y más densamente poblado. Muchos salvadoreños han emigrado a los Estados Unidos como resultado de los doce años de guerra civil que ha desgarrado (*torn apart*) El Salvador.

B *Se constructions with passive meaning*

- Spanish uses the construction **se** + verb in third-person singular or plural to deemphasize the subject. The agent phrase is not used in this construction. Notice that in English this **se**-construction (**se** + verb) can be translated in many different ways. The verb in this construction is either third-person singular or third-person plural depending on whether the grammatical subject is singular or plural:

El locutor **dio** los premios.	*The announcer* ***gave out (awarded)*** *the prizes.*
Los premios **fueron dados** por el locutor.	*The prizes* ***were given out (awarded)*** *by the announcer.*
Se dieron los premios.	*The prizes* ***were given out (awarded).***
Se sabe el motivo.	*The reason* ***is known. / You (They, People) know*** *the reason. /* ***One knows*** *the reason.*
Se entregó el informe.	*The report* ***was handed in.***
Se entregaron los informes.	*The reports* ***were handed in.***

- For intransitive verbs, that is, those that do not take a direct object, the verb is always in third-person singular:

Se sale por aquí.	***You go out*** *this way. / This* ***is the way out.***
Se vive bien en este país.	***People live*** *well in this country.*
Se trabaja con entusiasmo.	***We (You, They) work*** *enthusiastically.*

- Note that reflexive verbs such as **divertirse** and **despertarse** can only show an unidentified or deemphasized subject with the addition of **uno** (or **una** if the reference is feminine) to a third-person singular verb:

Uno se divierte mucho en el tiovivo.	***You*** *have a lot of fun on the merry-go-round.*
Uno se despierta más tarde los domingos.	***People*** *wake up later on Sundays.*

- Spanish also uses **la gente** with a third-person singular verb to label an indefinite subject. Compare this usage to English *people.* This Spanish construction is less common than its English equivalent:

Para divertirse, **la gente** va a un concierto.	*To have a good time,* ***people*** *go to a concert.*

- Spanish also uses the third-person plural of the verb to label an indefinite subject. In this case, the subject pronouns **ellos/ellas** cannot be used.

Dicen que va a llover.	***They say*** *it's going to rain.*
Me **van** a invitar a la boda.	***They're going*** *to invite me to the wedding. (I'm going to be invited to the wedding.)*
Lo **entrevistaron** la semana pasada.	***They interviewed*** *him last week. (He was interviewed last week.)*

C. **¡Se están instalando todavía!** A los Pidal les quedan muchas cosas que hacer en instalarse. Diga qué son estas cosas formando oraciones con la construcción con **se** y el verbo en futuro. Fíjese que esta vez no hay agente en las oraciones.

> **Modelo** correr / las cortinas
> → Se correrán las cortinas.

1. enchufar / la nevera

____

2. encender / las lámparas

____

3. guardar / las cajas

____

4. poner / el sofá / en la sala

____

5. colocar / el lavaplatos / en la cocina

____

6. meter / las sábanas / en el armario

____

7. poner / las sillas / con la mesa del comedor

____

D. **Titulares y anuncios del periódico.** Escriba oraciones usando la construcción con el sujeto indefinido **se** + la tercera persona singular o plural del verbo. Use el mismo tiempo verbal que en la oración original.

> **Modelo** Los políticos estudian los problemas económicos.
> → Se estudian los problemas económicos.

1. La empresa busca programadores de computadoras.

____

2. La ley prohíbe el fumar en los restaurantes.

____

3. Los contadores (*accountants*) calculaban los impuestos.

____

4. Los inquilinos (*tenants*) alquilaron el apartamento en la playa.

____

5. El Café Alicante entrega comida a la casa hasta la una de la mañana.

____

6. Los clientes pagan con cheque o tarjeta de crédito.

____

7. Esta sucursal del Banco de Barcelona solicitará gerentes.

____

8. La compañía necesita secretarios bilingües.

____

Nota cultural

Otro servicio de conveniencia que recién empieza a tener un gran impacto en la sociedad de ciertos países hispánicos es **el servicio a domicilio.** Cada día hay más repartidores (*delivery people*) que, llamados por sus clientes, llegan a la casa de éstos en su furgoneta de reparto (*delivery van*). Actualmente en Madrid no sólo se entrega comida—paella, mariscos, pizza, bocadillos, comida china, comida congelada y vinos—sino también hay servicio de recoger y planchar ropa el mismo día, y de llevar a casa todo tipo de productos que venden las farmacias de guardia (*24-hour drugstores*). Se le envía al cliente cualquier cosa que necesite, que sea un fontanero (*plumber*), un chófer, reservas de billetes para espectáculos, etcétera. Hay empresas de servicio a domicilio en Barcelona, Valencia, (la isla de) Mallorca y otras ciudades españolas, tanto como en las ciudades grandes de los países hispanoamericanos.

E. Una excursión al zoológico. Escriba oraciones con el sujeto definido para describir una excursión al zoológico. Use los sujetos que aparecen entre paréntesis.

MODELO Se visita el zoológico. (nosotros)
→ Visitamos el zoológico.

1. Se va de excursión al zoológico. (mis amigos y yo)

____

2. Para llegar al zoológico, se toma el autobús en la calle Azorín. (nosotros)

____

3. Se ven leones, tigres, leopardos y panteras. (yo)

____

4. Se da de comer a los animales. (los guardianes)

____

5. Se entra en las jaulas para limpiarlas. (unos trabajadores)

____

6. Se comen las hojas de los árboles. (las jirafas)

____

7. Se tiran cacahuates a los elefantes. (tú)

____

8. Se juega tirando plátanos. (un mono)

____

9. Se grita en voz alta. (los loros)

____

10. Uno se baña en la piscina de la jaula. (los hipopótamos)

____

11. Se cura la pata de un jaguar. (una guardiana)

____

12. Se compran palomitas y refrescos. (Pilar y Arturo)

____

Nota cultural

Los grandes **zoológicos** que se encuentran en los Estados Unidos, como los de San Diego, Nueva York, Chicago o Washington, D.C., tienen sus equivalentes en algunos países hispánicos. Se destacan los zoológicos de la ciudad de México y de Madrid.

El jaguar es un félido (*gato*) grande, una especie de pantera de América.

C *Ser and **estar** with the past participle*

- Both **ser** and **estar** are used with the past participle of the verb. Passive sentences have **ser** + the past participle and usually have the agent phrase introduced by **por.** Sentences that have **estar** + the past participle express the result of an action. They do not have an agent phrase introduced by **por.**

La torta **fue hecha** por el cocinero.	*The cake **was made** by the chef.*
La torta **estaba hecha**.	*The cake **was made** (done, completed, finished).*

F. Todo estaba hecho. Cuando Ud. llegó todo estaba hecho ya. Dígaselo a su amigo siguiendo el modelo.

Modelo ¿Quién abrió las ventanas?
→ No sé. Cuando yo llegué, las ventanas ya estaban abiertas.

1. ¿Quién arregló el cuarto?

____

2. ¿Quién preparó el almuerzo?

____

3. ¿Quién cerró la puerta?

____

4. ¿Quién apagó el microondas?

____

5. ¿Quién puso la mesa?

____

6. ¿Quién lavó los vasos?

7. ¿Quién planchó el mantel?

8. ¿Quién prendió las luces?

G. ¿Qué significa? Su amigo español está pasando las vacaciones de verano en su casa. Mientras Uds. se pasean por la ciudad, su amigo le pregunta qué quieren decir los letreros que ve. Explíquele lo que dicen en español usando la construcción con **se.**

1. Newspapers and magazines are sold here.
2. You park here.
3. You eat well.
4. One turns right.
5. You enter this way.
6. French is spoken here.
7. Travelers checks cashed.
8. The department store opens at ten.

H. ¿Qué dice Ud.? Un nuevo estudiante en su colegio le hace unas preguntas sobre la vida escolar y la de la calle. Conteste sus preguntas usando la construcción con **se.**

1. ¿Qué materias toman en el colegio?
2. ¿A qué hora almuerzan en el colegio?
3. ¿Cómo llegan al colegio?

4. ¿Dónde compran sus libros de texto?

____

5. ¿Cómo pueden sacar buenas notas?

____

6. ¿Qué hacen para divertirse los fines de semana?

____

7. ¿En qué restaurantes comen?

____

8. ¿Qué deportes juegan?

____

I. **Ejercicio oral. Adivinanza (*guessing game*).** En este juego de adivinanza Ud. y sus compañeros de clase intentan adivinar quién escribió una famosa obra literaria. Uno de Uds. dice el título de la obra, por ejemplo, *Don Quijote*, y los otros estudiantes tienen que decir lo más rápido posible quién la escribió. Se contesta así: *Fue escrito por Cervantes.* Hay que contestar empleando la voz pasiva.

J. **Estructuras en acción.** Lea los siguientes anuncios de un periódico argentino sobre los cursos y conferencias que se dan. Luego haga el ejercicio.

Cursos y conferencias

Historia del arte. La Alianza Francesa de Mendoza organizó un curso de historia del arte "Desde Constantino el Grande hasta el fin de la Guerra de los Cien Años. El arte del occidente medieval". Estará a cargo del profesor Horacio Rosa y se desarrollará el 5, 12, 19 y 26, de 18.30 a 20.30. Mayores informes se ofrecen en la sede de la Alianza, Chile 1754.

Oratoria. Un curso sobre "Oratoria y comunicación oral" será ofrecido por el profesor Luis Osvaldo Perrotin y la licenciada Ana Gloria Ortega de Sevilla, en el Centro Cultural Matesis, Belgrano 29000, de Godoy Cruz, teléfonos 221864 y 240033.

Alemán. El Instituto Goethe anunció que hoy iniciará un ciclo de cursos de alemán. El primer año intensivo se desarrollará los lunes y miércoles de 16.30 a 19.45, mientras que de 15.15 a 17 tendrá lugar el de introducción a las técnicas de traducción simultánea. Para mayor información llamar al teléfono 340323.

Universidades

Facultad de Artes. La Escuela de Teatro informó sobre los seminarios internacionales que se ofrecerán este mes: del 12 al 14, Guillermo Heras (España), dictará uno sobre "Experiencia de montaje"; el 22 y 23, Alberto Isola (Perú) se referirá a "El training del actor" y Ramón Griffero (Chile) hablará sobre "Dramaturgia desde el espacio".

Se indicó que estos cursos se efectuarán en cooperación con el Teatro General San Martín, de Buenos Aires, y son coordinados por el Centro de Estudios e Investigación Teatral de la Escuela de Teatro. Las inscripciones se reciben de 15 a 20.

Vocabulario

la alianza *alliance*
a cargo de uno *to be in one's charge*
el ciclo *cycle*
desarrollar *to develop*
dictar un seminario *to give a seminar*
la dramaturgia *dramatic art*
efectuarse *to take place*
el espacio *space*
la investigación *research*
la inscripción *registration*
la licenciada *lawyer*
mayores informes *more information*
el montaje *staging*
la oratoria *oratory, oratorical art*
referirse *to refer to, speak about*
la sede *headquarters*
la traducción *translation*

Escriba los ejemplos de construcción pasiva que se encuentran en los anuncios y tradúzcalos al inglés.

Historia del arte

1. ______________________________

traducción ______________________________

Oratoria

2. ______________________________

traducción ______________________________

Facultad de artes

3. ______________________________

traducción ______________________________

4. ______________________________

traducción ______________________________

5. ______________________________

traducción ______________________________

6. ______________________________

traducción ______________________________

CHAPTER 9

THE PERFECT TENSES

A The formation of the present perfect

- The perfect tenses in Spanish are similar to their English equivalents. They consist of a conjugated form of the auxiliary verb **haber** (*to have*) + the past participle, which is the form of the verb ending in **-do**. The past participle of regular verbs is formed by dropping the infinitive ending and adding **-ado** to **-ar** verbs and **-ido** to **-er** and **-ir** verbs:

mandar	**mandado**	*sent*
comprender	**comprendido**	*understood*
servir	**servido**	*served*

- The following verbs have irregular past participles:

abrir	**abierto**	hacer	**hecho**	ver	**visto**
cubrir	**cubierto**	morir	**muerto**	volver	**vuelto**
decir	**dicho**	poner	**puesto**		
escribir	**escrito**	romper	**roto**		

- When a prefix is added to any of the above verbs, the past participle shows the same irregularities:

describir	**descrito**	devolver	**devuelto**	predecir	**predicho**
descubrir	**descubierto**	imponer	**impuesto**	prever	**previsto**
deshacer	**deshecho**	posponer	**pospuesto**	revolver	**revuelto**

- **-Er** and **-ir** verbs that have stems ending in a vowel have an accent mark over the **-í-** in the past participle:

caer	**caído**	leer	**leído**	traer	**traído**
creer	**creído**	oír	**oído**		

- The past participle forms of **ser** and **ir** are **sido** and **ido** respectively.
- In the perfect tenses, object pronouns precede the forms of **haber** and are not attached to the *past participle.* In questions, subject pronouns follow the *past participle.* They are not placed between the auxiliary verb and the past participle as they are in English:

¿**Lo** has leído?	*Have you read **it**? (object pronoun)*
¿Qué han visto **Uds.**?	*What have **you** seen?*
¿Todavía no se ha levantado **Ud.**?	*Haven't **you** gotten up yet?*

- The present perfect consists of a conjugated form of the auxiliary verb **haber** + the past participle. The past participle does not change to show gender or number in compound tenses where the auxiliary verb is **haber**. The present perfect is used in Spanish, as in English, to mark or describe past events that have an influence on the present or that continue into the present.

ganar, comprender, salir	
(yo) **he** ganado, comprendido, salido (tú) **has** ganado, comprendido, salido (él/ella/Ud.) **ha** ganado, comprendido, salido	(nosotros) **hemos** ganado, comprendido, salido (vosotros) **habéis** ganado, comprendido, salido (ellos/ellas/Uds.) **han** ganado, comprendido, salido

A. **¿Listos para viajar?** Ud. y su familia se van de vacaciones. Antes de salir de la casa tienen que hacer ciertas cosas. Use el pretérito perfecto (*present perfect*) para escribir oraciones que explican quién hizo cada cosa.

MODELO papá / comprar / el mapa
→ Papá ha comprado el mapa.

Preparándose para un viaje

el baúl *trunk (car)*
el cheque de viajero *traveler's check*
desenchufar los aparatos eléctricos *to unplug the appliances*
el equipaje *luggage*
hacer las maletas *to pack*
la linterna *flashlight*
llenar el tanque del coche *to fill the tank*
el mapa *map*
la pila *battery (flashlight)*
prepararse *to get ready*
la ventanilla *car window*

1. Pedro / apagar / las luces

___

2. Cecilia y Pilar / hacer / las maletas

___

3. papá / llenar / el tanque del coche

___

4. Berta / desenchufar / los aparatos eléctricos

___

5. David y Juan Carlos / meter / el equipaje en el baúl

___

6. yo / decirles / a los vecinos / que nos vamos

___

7. mamá / poner / las pilas en la linterna

___

8. Paco y yo / comprar / los cheques de viajero

___

9. tú / limpiar / las ventanillas del coche

___

B. Una receta de cocina (*recipe*). Ud. y unos amigos están preparando un plato especial para servir en la cena. Use el pretérito perfecto para describir paso a paso lo que han hecho.

MODELO Vera / comprar / mariscos
➔ Vera ha comprado mariscos.

Una receta de cocina

el aguacate *avocado*
añadir *to add*
la cacerola *saucepan*
el camarón *shrimp*
la cebolla *onion*
cortar *to cut*
cubrir *to cover*
encender el fuego *to turn on the flame*
la ensalada *salad*
los espárragos *asparagus*
freído *past participle* **freír**
(**frito**—*more commonly used*)
freír *to fry*
la mayonesa *mayonnaise*
picar *to chop*
la pimienta picante *hot pepper*
el pollo *chicken*
poner al horno *to put in the oven*
quemar *to burn*
la sal *salt*
la salchicha *sausage*
la sartén *frying pan*

1. nosotros / leer / la receta
____
2. Jorge / encender / el fuego
____
3. yo / hacer / la mayonesa
____
4. Alicia y Juan Diego / picar / las pimientas picantes
____
5. Ud. / freír / las cebollas
____
6. Estrella y yo / cortar / la salchicha
____
7. tú / lavar / los espárragos y los aguacates
____
8. Marianela / añadir / sal
____
9. Uds. / poner / el pollo al horno
____
10. yo / mezclar / la ensalada de camarones
____

11. Martín / cubrir / la cacerola

___

12. Lupe y Julio / quemar / las sartenes

___

C. Vuelva a escribir las oraciones del *ejercicio B* cambiando los sustantivos que son complementos directos de los verbos a pronombres.

Modelo Vera ha comprado **mariscos**.
➔ Vera **los** ha comprado.

1. ___
2. ___
3. ___
4. ___
5. ___
6. ___
7. ___
8. ___
9. ___
10. ___
11. ___
12. ___

D. **¡Nos aburrimos como una ostra (*oyster*)! (*We're dying of boredom!*)** Ud. y sus amigos quieren escaparse de una fiesta muy aburrida. Describa lo que han hecho todos Uds. cambiando los verbos del tiempo presente al pretérito perfecto.

Modelo Pablo trata de huir.
➔ Pablo ha tratado de huir.

1. María Dolores se duerme.

___

2. Ud. bosteza.

___

3. Yo me pongo el abrigo.

___

4. Carlos y Beatriz se despiden de la anfitriona (*hostess*).

___

5. ¡Nos matan de aburrimiento!

___

6. Tú te quejas que la comida te cayó mal.

7. Ud. y Clara dan excusas.

8. Ramón dice que se enferma.

E. Preguntas personales. Conteste las siguientes preguntas usando el pretérito perfecto.

1. ¿Qué materias ha tomado Ud. este año?
2. ¿Qué notas ha sacado en estas materias?
3. ¿Se ha hecho Ud. socio (*Have you joined*) de un club? ¿Del cuál?
4. ¿A qué países han viajado Ud. y sus padres?
5. ¿Qué planes han hecho Ud. y sus amigos para el verano?
6. ¿Ha decidido Ud. lo que va a estudiar en la universidad?
7. ¿Qué películas ha visto Ud. este año? ¿Cuál le ha gustado más?
8. ¿Cómo ha celebrado Ud. su último cumpleaños?
9. ¿Qué regalos ha recibido? ¿Quién le ha dado cada regalo?
10. ¿Qué cosas han hecho sus amigos y Ud. hoy?

F. ¡Hecho consumado! (*¡Cosa hecha!*) Conteste las siguientes preguntas empleando el pretérito perfecto del verbo reflexivo en la oración original para explicar que las cosas ya están hechas.

MODELO ¿Cuándo van Uds. a mudarse?
→ Nos hemos mudado ya.

1. ¿Cuándo va Cristóbal a matricularse?

2. ¿Cuándo van Uds. a apoderarse de la finca?

___

3. ¿Cuándo vas a instalarte en la nueva casa?

___

4. ¿Cuándo van Irene y Jaime a comprometerse?

___

5. ¿Cuándo va Nora a enterarse de los líos de la familia?

___

6. ¿Cuándo vas a apuntarte en la lista de voluntarios?

___

7. ¿Cuándo van los Roldán a ausentarse de la ciudad?

___

B *The past perfect*

- The past perfect consists of the imperfect of the auxiliary verb **haber** + past participle. The English equivalent of the past perfect is *had done something*.

llegar, comer, subir	
(yo) **había** llegado, comido, subido (tú) **habías** llegado, comido, subido (él/ella/Ud.) **había** llegado, comido, subido	(nosotros) **habíamos** llegado, comido, subido (vosotros) **habíais** llegado, comido, subido (ellos/ellas/Uds.) **habían** llegado, comido, subido

- The past perfect or pluperfect tense designates an event that happened prior to another past event that is further removed in the past:

Yo ya me había despertado cuando sonó el despertador.	***I had already awakened*** *when the alarm clock went off.*
María ya había ido al teatro cuando Pedro la llamó.	***María had already gone to the theater*** *when Pedro called her.*
Nosotros habíamos vuelto a casa cuando empezó a nevar.	***We had gotten back home*** *when it began to snow.*

G. No, fue antes. Escriba oraciones en las cuales explica que las cosas mencionadas no pasaron ayer sino antes. Ud. practicará el uso del pretérito pluscuamperfecto (*past perfect*).

MODELO ¿Llegó Lorenzo ayer? (la semana pasada)
→ No, **había llegado** la semana pasada.

1. ¿Fueron Uds. a ver la exposición en el museo ayer? (hace unos meses)

___

2. ¿Se cortó Amelia el pelo anteayer? (el sábado)

___

3. ¿Se casaron Ricardo y Leonor en abril? (dos meses antes)

4. ¿Hiciste el asado el cuatro de julio? (el primero de julio)

5. ¿Celebró Pepita su santo hace quince días? (hace un mes)

6. ¿Cambió Ud. de idea hace unos días? (hace mucho tiempo)

7. ¿Pusieron Uds. los papeles en orden este año? (el año pasado)

8. ¿Te devolvió Javier los libros esta semana? (la semana pasada)

9. ¿Escribimos los informes en febrero? (noviembre)

10. ¿Se rompió Ud. el codo hace seis meses? (hace casi un año)

Nota cultural

En los países hispánicos las personas celebran su **santo**, es decir, el día de su santo. El santo que se celebra depende del nombre de pila (*given name*) de la persona. El calendario hispánico incluye el santoral en el cual nombran a los santos de cada día del año. En ciertos países hispánicos no sólo se celebra el santo sino el cumpleaños también. El cumpleaños ha cobrado más importancia en algunos países por la influencia de los Estados Unidos.

H. Tomás, el holgazán (*loafer*). Es que los amigos de Tomás no pueden contar con él porque no le gusta trabajar y siempre llega tarde. Ya cuando Tomás llega, todo está hecho. ¡Los amigos lo habían hecho todo! Escriba oraciones en las cuales explica lo que ya habían hecho los amigos cuando llegó Tomás por fin.

MODELO Cuando Tomás llegó por fin … (los amigos / lavar el carro)
➔ Cuando Tomás llegó por fin, los amigos ya habían lavado el carro.

1. Cuando Tomás llegó por fin … (Raúl/ barrer el piso)

2. Cuando Tomás llegó por fin … (Uds. / poner la mesa)

3. Cuando Tomás llegó por fin … (Diana y Judit / recoger las manzanas)

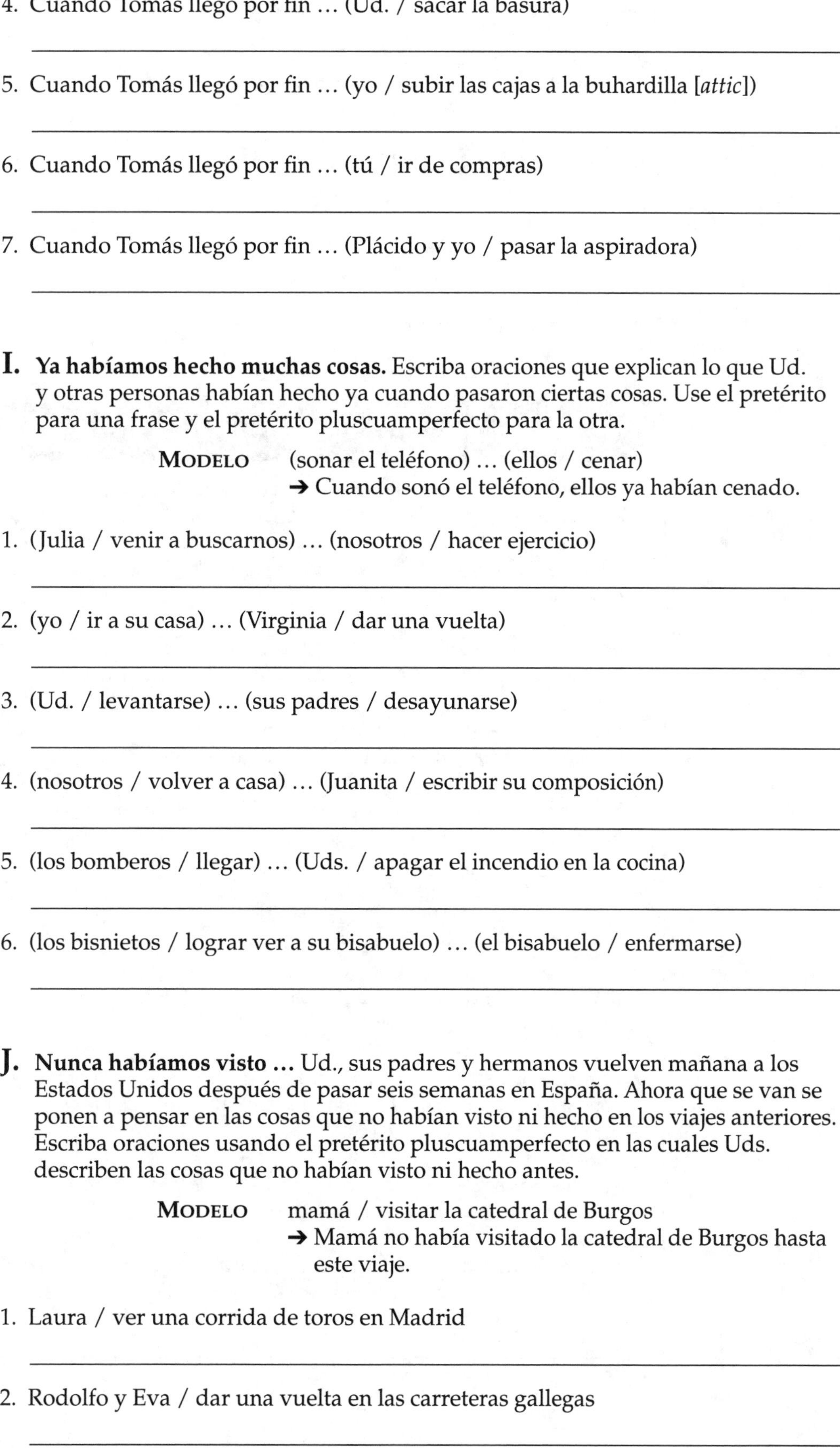

4. Cuando Tomás llegó por fin ... (Ud. / sacar la basura)

5. Cuando Tomás llegó por fin ... (yo / subir las cajas a la buhardilla [*attic*])

6. Cuando Tomás llegó por fin ... (tú / ir de compras)

7. Cuando Tomás llegó por fin ... (Plácido y yo / pasar la aspiradora)

I. **Ya habíamos hecho muchas cosas.** Escriba oraciones que explican lo que Ud. y otras personas habían hecho ya cuando pasaron ciertas cosas. Use el pretérito para una frase y el pretérito pluscuamperfecto para la otra.

MODELO (sonar el teléfono) ... (ellos / cenar)
➔ Cuando sonó el teléfono, ellos ya habían cenado.

1. (Julia / venir a buscarnos) ... (nosotros / hacer ejercicio)

2. (yo / ir a su casa) ... (Virginia / dar una vuelta)

3. (Ud. / levantarse) ... (sus padres / desayunarse)

4. (nosotros / volver a casa) ... (Juanita / escribir su composición)

5. (los bomberos / llegar) ... (Uds. / apagar el incendio en la cocina)

6. (los bisnietos / lograr ver a su bisabuelo) ... (el bisabuelo / enfermarse)

J. **Nunca habíamos visto ...** Ud., sus padres y hermanos vuelven mañana a los Estados Unidos después de pasar seis semanas en España. Ahora que se van se ponen a pensar en las cosas que no habían visto ni hecho en los viajes anteriores. Escriba oraciones usando el pretérito pluscuamperfecto en las cuales Uds. describen las cosas que no habían visto ni hecho antes.

MODELO mamá / visitar la catedral de Burgos
➔ Mamá no había visitado la catedral de Burgos hasta este viaje.

1. Laura / ver una corrida de toros en Madrid

2. Rodolfo y Eva / dar una vuelta en las carreteras gallegas

3. yo / hacer una excursión a El Escorial

____

4. tú y Susana / pasearse por el barrio de Santa Cruz

____

5. mamá, papá y yo / subir al monte Tibidabo

____

6. Jaime / conocer la Alhambra

____

7. tú / pasar Semana Santa en Sevilla

____

Nota cultural

- **La catedral de Burgos**—la ciudad de Burgos, capital de la provincia de Burgos, queda en Castilla la Vieja, al norte céntrico del país. Queda a las orillas del río Arlanzón. Su catedral, por sus dimensiones la tercera catedral española después de las de Sevilla y Toledo, se destaca por su estilo gótico. La construcción de la catedral empezó en el siglo XIII.

- **La corrida de toros** es el espectáculo nacional español. Las plazas de toros más importantes de España son las de Madrid, Sevilla y Barcelona.

- **Las carreteras gallegas**, es decir, de la región de Galicia al noroeste de España. Comprende las provincias de La Coruña, Lugo, Orense y Pontevedra.

- **El Escorial** es el monasterio y palacio construido por el rey español Felipe II en 1563. El plan del edificio fue supervisado por Felipe II al igual que la creación de un gran monumento para honrar la memoria de su padre, Carlos V. Se encuentra aquí el panteón de los reyes españoles donde están enterrados todos los reyes españoles salvo tres. El majestuoso edificio queda en la sierra de Guadarrama en la villa de San Lorenzo de El Escorial, a poca distancia al norte de Madrid.

- **El barrio de Santa Cruz**, que era el barrio judío en la Edad Media, es hoy el barrio más típico y pintoresco de Sevilla.

- **El monte Tibidabo** queda al noroeste de Barcelona. Desde la cima hay un hermoso panorama de Barcelona y el Mediterráneo. Hay un funicular (*cable car*) que lleva a la gente a lo alto del monte.

- **La Alhambra** es el hermoso palacio y fortaleza de los reyes moros en Granada. Se construyó en su mayor parte durante el siglo XIV.

- **La Semana Santa** es el período que precede al domingo de Resurrección. Las procesiones religiosas sevillanas son célebres. Muchos españoles van de vacaciones durante esta semana.

C *The future perfect*

- The future perfect consists of the future tense of the auxiliary verb **haber** + the past participle.

llegar, comer, subir	
(yo) **habré** llegado, comido, subido (tú) **habrás** llegado, comido, subido (él/ella/Ud.) **habrá** llegado, comido, subido	(nosotros) **habremos** llegado, comido, subido (vosotros) **habréis** llegado, comido, subido (ellos/ellas/Uds.) **habrán** llegado, comido, subido

- In Spanish, as in English, the future perfect tense designates an event that will be completed in the future before another event occurs or before some point in time in the future:

Habrán vuelto para finales del mes. — *They'll have returned by the end of the month.*

Lo habré terminado todo antes de irme. — *I'll have finished everything before I leave.*

- The future perfect is also used to express probability in past time. The future perfect of probability corresponds to the preterit or the present perfect:

Habrá pasado algo.
Probablemente pasó algo.
Probablemente ha pasado algo. } *Something probably happened.*

- **Deber de** + perfect infinitive, which is the infinitive **haber** + the past participle, can be used instead of the future perfect to express probability in past time: **Marta debe de haber llamado.** *Marta must have (probably) called.*

K. **¿Qué habrá ocurrido?** Escriba oraciones con el verbo en futuro perfecto para explicar para cuándo ciertas cosas habrán ocurrido.

MODELO nosotros / almorzar / para las dos
➔ Habremos almorzado para las dos.

1. Elena / graduarse / para el año próximo

____

2. Alfredo y Armando / mejorarse / antes de regresar al colegio

____

3. nosotros / ahorrar dinero / antes de las vacaciones de invierno

____

4. yo / darte tu regalo / antes de tu fiesta de cumpleaños

____

5. Ud. y Laura / mudarse / para mediados del mes

____

6. tú / sacar un pasaporte / para julio

____

L. Conjeturas (*Conjectures*). Exprese sus conjeturas sobre lo que pasó usando el futuro perfecto para expresar probabilidad en el pasado.

MODELO *Probablemente* llegó el cartero.
→ **Habrá llegado** el cartero.

1. Su coche probablemente le costó un ojo de la cara.
____
2. Clara escribió la carta, probablemente.
____
3. Felipe y Eduardo probablemente ganaron la regata.
____
4. Uds. probablemente tomaron la merienda.
____
5. Martín y yo probablemente no entendimos el motivo.
____
6. Ud. probablemente no hizo cola por mucho tiempo.
____

D *The conditional perfect*

- The conditional perfect consists of the conditional tense of the auxiliary verb **haber** + the past participle. It corresponds to English *would have done something*.

llegar, comer, subir	
(yo) **habría** llegado, comido, subido (tú) **habrías** llegado, comido, subido (él/ella/Ud.) **habría** llegado, comido, subido	(nosotros) **habríamos** llegado, comido, subido (vosotros) **habríais** llegado, comido, subido (ellos/ellas/Uds.) **habrían** llegado, comido, subido

- The conditional perfect is used to designate an action or event that would have been completed in the past or when there is a real or implied condition:

Yo no lo **habría dicho**. — *I **wouldn't have said** it.*

Nosotros **nos habríamos quedado** más tiempo. — *We **probably would have stayed** longer.*

- The conditional perfect is also used to express probability in past time. It corresponds to the past perfect + *probably:*

Ya **se habría ido**, me imagino. — ***He had probably left,** I imagine.*

- The perfect infinitive consists of the infinitive **haber** + the past participle. It is used after prepositions and as the complement of some verbs:

Lorenzo ha sacado excelentes notas **por haber estudiado** tanto. — *Lorenzo has gotten excellent grades **for having studied** so much (because he studied so much).*

No recuerdo **haberlo visto**. — *I don't remember **having seen him.***

M. No lo habríamos hecho. Escriba oraciones que expresan que Ud. y otras personas no habrían hecho las cosas que hicieron algunas personas.

MODELO Gregorio pidió el plato de langosta con salsa de chocolate. (yo)
➔ Yo no lo habría pedido.

1. Diego y Jaime salieron a la calle durante la tormenta. (Patricia y yo)

____

2. Tere rompió su compromiso con su novio. (Sofía)

____

3. Uds. hicieron el viaje a California en autobús. (los turistas venezolanos)

____

4. Ariana se cortó el pelo en la peluquería Melenas. (tú)

____

5. Nosotros creímos lo que nos dijo Baltasar. (Ud.)

____

6. Te reíste cuando se te cayeron los vasos. (yo)

____

N. ¡Felicidades! Ud. es el maestro de ceremonias del programa de los Óscar. Les presenta la estatuilla del Óscar a los ganadores de las diferentes categorías artísticas de las películas del año. Practique el uso del infinitivo compuesto (*perfect infinitive*) tras (*after*) **por**.

MODELO Maribel Sánchez / trabajar en "Alma y corazón"
➔ A Maribel Sánchez **por haber trabajado** en "Alma y corazón".

1. Lope Cernuda / dirigir "Plátanos y cerezas"

____

2. Ernesto del Olmo / componer la música de "Mosquitos mágicos"

____

3. Ela Pantoja y Roberto Campillo / escribir el guión de "Agua hervida"

____

4. Agustín Domingo / cantar en "Después de haber bailado"

____

5. Beatriz Perales / ser primera actriz en "Salchichas al sol"

____

6. Mateo de León y Diana Duque / producir "Grapadora en la mesa"

____

7. Silvia Siles / hacer la escenografía de "Narices al aire"

____

8. Memo Morado / actuar en "Langostas en el cielo"

____

9. Edit Revueltas / diseñar el vestuario de "Tijeras de poliéster"

____

10. Pepe del Oeste / maquillar a los actores de "Tamales quemados"

____

O. Allá en el rancho grande. Exprese en español sus conjeturas sobre el rancho o la estancia que tenía su familia hace muchos años. Escriba oraciones de probabilidad con el potencial compuesto (*conditional perfect*).

1. The ranch had probably been very big.

____

2. The farmers probably had had hens in a henhouse.

____

3. The farm workers probably had picked cherries and strawberries.

____

4. The landscape of the countryside probably had been beautiful.

____

5. My great-grandfather probably had gone fishing in the lake that was nearby.

____

6. My great-grandmother probably had cooked fresh fruits and vegetables from the harvest.

____

7. There probably had been horses and cows on the ranch.

____

8. The farmers had probably sowed seeds in the vegetable garden.

____

9. We probably would have loved life on the ranch.

____

P. Ejercicio oral. Diálogos. Trabaje con un(a) compañero(a) para discutir las cosas que Uds. *han hecho* este año y las cosas que *habrían hecho* este año. Por ejemplo, Ud. dice: *Yo he estudiado latín este año.* Su compañero responde: *Yo habría estudiado griego.* Se puede hablar de las materias, los deportes, los amigos, los pasatiempos, las vacaciones, etcétera.

Q. Estructuras en acción. Lea este artículo sobre el turismo español en Portugal fijándose especialmente en los verbos en tiempos compuestos. Luego haga el ejercicio que sigue. (Se recomienda que el/la estudiante consulte un mapa de la península Ibérica para aprovechar al máximo el contenido cultural del artículo.)

La crisis no perdona: Portugal espera menos turistas españoles

Lisboa. José María Moreiro

Las vacaciones de Semana Santa han sido siempre una de las épocas en que Portugal ha registrado una mayor afluencia de turistas españoles. Somos el primer cliente de este país, lo que en cifras viene a equivaler al 50 por ciento del turismo procedente de los restantes países. Sin embargo, durante la semana de Pascua de este año las perspectivas son menos halagüeñas y se teme aquí un notable descenso con respecto al largo medio millón de años anteriores, hecho que puede repetirse también durante el verano.

Las causas esenciales son dos: por un lado, la crisis económica, que lleva consigo un menor poder adquisitivo de los españoles; por otro, la última depreciación de nuestra moneda que, acompañada de la del escudo varios puntos por debajo, está aproximando la paridad, con el consiguiente encarecimiento.

A esto ha de sumarse el notabilísimo aumento del precio de los servicios en algunos casos, como es el de la vivienda, muy superior en Lisboa con respecto a ciudades como Madrid. Portugal, aunque dotado de los mismos encantos y de la ventaja de la proximidad para disfrutar de unas cortas vacaciones como las que se avecinan, ha dejado de ser el país de turismo barato que fue, esencialmente hasta 1986, año de su adhesión a la Unión Europea.

De todas formas, las previsiones señalan un mantenimiento del turismo que llega de Galicia a la región norte, con Viana do Castelo, Braga y Oporto como principales centros receptivos.

El área de la Gran Lisboa—Estoril, Cascaes, Sintra y playa de Caparica, y el litoral de la zona centro—Peniche, Nazaré, Figueira da Fozson los destinos turísticos preferidos donde gozar del incipiente verano con que esta primavera nos regala.

Por lo que se refiere al Algarve, el mayor contingente de turistas hispanos siguen siendo los vecinos andaluces.

La entrada en vigor de un rigurosísimo código de circulación hacen indispensables dos esenciales consejos si los automovilistas no se quieren ver desagradablemente sorprendidos: el pago de las multas *ipso facto* y un moderadísimo consumo de alcohol, ya que la detección de 1,2 miligramos de alcoholemia está penado con prisión inmediata.

Vocabulario

la adhesión *membership*
la afluencia *crowd, flow*
la alcoholemia *presence of alcohol in the blood*
aproximar *to near*
el aumento *increase*
avecinarse *to approach*
la cifra *figure*
el código de circulación *highway code*
consigo *with it*
consiguiente *resulting*
el consumo *consumption*
el descenso *decline*
el destino *destination*
dotado de *endowed with*
el encanto *charm*
el encarecimiento *rise, increase in price*
la entrada en vigor *taking effect*
equivaler *to be equivalent, mean*
el escudo *Portuguese unit of currency*
ha de sumarse *it has to be added*
halagüeño *promising, flattering*
el hecho *fact*
el largo medio millón *good half a million*
el litoral *coast*
el mantenimiento *maintenance*
la moneda *currency*
la multa *fine, ticket*
notabilísimo *very considerable*
la paridad *parity (of currency)*
la Pascua *Easter*
penar *to punish*
las perspectivas halagüeñas *promising prospects*
el poder adquisitivo *purchasing power*
Por lo que se refiere al Algarve, ... *As for Algarve ..., As regards Algarve ...*
la previsión *forecast*
la prisión *imprisonment*
la proximidad *proximity, closeness*
regalar *to treat well, royally*
registrar *to note, notice*
restante *remaining, rest*
señalar *to point to*
sumarse *to add*
la ventaja *advantage*
la vivienda *housing*

1. Muchos turistas españoles pasan sus vacaciones de __________ en Portugal.
   a. Navidad
   b. Semana Santa
   c. Año Nuevo
2. Hay menos turismo español en Portugal por __________.
   a. los precios tan bajos
   b. el código de circulación
   c. la depreciación de la peseta
3. La mayor parte de los turistas españoles que van al Algarve son de __________.
   a. Galicia
   b. Andalucía
   c. la Gran Lisboa
4. Los turistas gallegos suelen hacer turismo en __________.
   a. Braga y Oporto
   b. Peniche y Nazaré
   c. Estoril y Sintra
5. La moneda portuguesa es __________.
   a. el escudo
   b. la peseta
   c. el franco
6. Según el artículo, Lisboa __________.
   a. no se encuentra en el área de la Gran Lisboa
   b. recibe más turismo que el litoral de la zona centro
   c. tiene mejor vivienda que Madrid
7. Se ofrecen consejos a los automovilistas en cuanto al pago de las multas y __________.
   a. a la adhesión a la Unión Europea
   b. al consumo de alcohol
   c. al poder adquisitivo de los españoles
8. Un 50 por ciento del turismo del Portugal __________.
   a. tiene 1,2 miligramos de alcoholemia
   b. goza de una disminución del precio de los servicios
   c. es procedente de España

CHAPTER 10 THE GERUND & THE PROGRESSIVE TENSES

 A *The formation of the gerund (present participle)*

- The gerund or **-ndo** form in Spanish corresponds to the *-ing* form in English. For **-ar** verbs, the ending of the gerund is **-ando**; for **-er** and **-ir** verbs, the ending is **-iendo**:

tomar	tom**ando**	aprender	aprend**iendo**	escribir	escrib**iendo**
ensayar	ensay**ando**	comer	com**iendo**	abrir	abr**iendo**

- **-Er** and **-ir** verbs whose stem ends in a vowel use **-yendo** and not **-iendo** to form the gerund:

caer	ca**yendo**	leer	le**yendo**	traer	tra**yendo**
creer	cre**yendo**	oír	o**yendo**		

- **-Ir** verbs that have a change in the vowel of the stem in the third-person singular of the preterit, have the same change in the gerund:

infinitive	*preterit*	*gerund*
decir	dijo	**diciendo**
dormir	durmió	**durmiendo**
morir	murió	**muriendo**
pedir	pidió	**pidiendo**
repetir	repitió	**repitiendo**
sentir	sintió	**sintiendo**
servir	sirvió	**sirviendo**
venir	vino	**viniendo**

- **Poder** and **ir** have irregular gerunds:

poder	**pudiendo**
ir	**yendo**

- Object pronouns are attached to the present participle in writing and an accent mark is written over the **a** or **e** of the gerund ending:

esperándolo **dándomelos** **viéndolas** **levantándose**

- The gerund in Spanish is usually equivalent to an English clause or gerund phrase beginning with *by, while, if, when,* or *because:*

Se aprende mucho **estudiando** con el profesor Padilla.	*You learn a lot* ***studying (when you study)*** *with Professor Padilla.*
Viajando en marzo, Nicolás ahorró mucho dinero.	***By traveling*** *in March, Nicolás saved a lot of money.*

- With verbs of perception, such as **ver, mirar, oír,** and **escuchar**, either the infinitive or the gerund can be used, as in English:

Los oímos cantar. Los oímos cantando.	*We heard them sing/singing.*

A. **¡La vecina entremetida (*busybody*)!** ¡Su vecina se mete en todo! Ahora quiere saber lo que Ud. y otras personas hicieron hoy porque no los vio en todo el día. Contéstele usando **pasar** + el gerundio.

MODELO —¿Trabajó Ud. en la oficina hoy?
—Sí, **pasé** el día **trabajando** en la oficina.

1. ¿Llamó Ud. por teléfono hoy?

____

2. ¿Estudiaron Carlos y Celeste en la biblioteca hoy?

____

3. ¿Durmió hoy el señor Marqués?

____

4. ¿Leyeron hoy Ud. y su hermano?

____

5. ¿Oíste las noticias hoy?

____

6. ¿Se bañó hoy la señora Pelayo?

____

B. **¡Cómo va volando el tiempo! (*How time flies!*)** Ud. piensa en las cosas que hizo ayer y en cuánto tiempo le llevó cada cosa. ¡Qué rápido se te fue el día! Escriba oraciones usando **pasar** + el gerundio para describir su horario de ayer.

MODELO yo / desayunar (media hora)
➔ **Pasé** media hora **desayunando.**

1. yo / arreglarse (cuarenta y cinco minutos)

____

2. Estrella y yo / montar en bicicleta (hora y media)

____

3. yo / escribir un informe (dos horas)

____

4. Fernando, Chelo y yo / comprar cosas en el centro comercial (un par de horas)

____

5. mis amigos y yo / vestirse (una hora y cuarto)

____

6. yo / ver un documental (una hora)

____

B The progressive tenses

- The progressive tenses consist of the present, past, future, or conditional forms of the verb **estar** followed by the gerund:

Estoy oyendo música. *present progressive*	*I'm listening to music.*
Estaba oyendo música. *imperfect progressive*	*I was listening to music.*
Estuve oyendo música hasta que salimos. *preterit progressive*	*I was listening to music until we went out.*
Estaré oyendo música toda la tarde. *future progressive*	*I'll be listening to music all afternoon.*
Estaría oyendo música. *conditional progressive*	*I'd be listening to music.*

- The gerunds of **estar, ir,** and **venir** are not commonly used.
- The present, imperfect, and future progressive are different from the corresponding simple tenses in that they emphasize that the action is or was in progress. They may also suggest that the action is temporary, not habitual, or represents a change from the usual pattern:

Miguel juega al fútbol.	*Miguel plays soccer.* (habitual action)
Miguel está jugando al fútbol.	*Miguel's playing soccer.* (He's playing soccer right now *or* He's begun to play soccer.)

- The preterit progressive is used to show an action that was in progress in the past but is now completed:

  Estuvimos estudiando latín hasta que Óscar vino a buscarnos.
  We were studying Latin until Oscar came to pick us up.

- The present progressive in Spanish can never refer to the future as the present progressive in English does. To express future time, Spanish uses the simple present, the **ir a** + infinitive construction, or the future tense:

Sacamos los boletos mañana. **Vamos a sacar** los boletos mañana. **Sacaremos** los boletos mañana.	***We're buying** the tickets tomorrow.*

- In the progressive tenses, object pronouns may either precede the form of **estar** or be attached to the gerund in writing, in which case a written accent is added:

Isabel y Juan están paseándo**se**. Isabel y Juan **se** están paseando.	*Isabel and Juan are strolling.*

- The verb **seguir** is used with the gerund to mean *to be still doing something, to keep on doing something:*

Marta **sigue despertándose** antes de las seis.	*Marta **is still waking up** before six o'clock.*
Sigan buscando la llave.	***Keep on looking for** the key.*

- **Ir** is commonly used with the gerund as well. It is used to convey the idea of *gradually* or *little by little:*

La empresa **va prosperando.**	*The company* ***is gradually prospering.***
Las flores **se fueron secando** poco a poco.	*The flowers* ***withered away*** *little by little.*

C. En el campamento (*camp, campground*) de verano. Escriba lo que están haciendo los niños en un día típico en el campamento. Use el verbo en presente progresivo.

MODELO Eva y Ángela trabajan en un campamento.
→ Eva y Ángela están trabajando en un campamento.

En el campamento

acampar *to camp*
apagar el fuego *to put out the fire*
la araña *spider*
asar *to roast*
atrapar *to catch*
desenvolver *to unroll*
encender el fuego *to light the fire*
la hormiga *ant*
el hormiguero *anthill*
ir de camping *to go camping*
el lago *lake*
la linterna *flashlight*
la mariposa *butterfly*
la mochila *backpack, knapsack*
el mosquito *mosquito*
nadar *to swim*
el perro caliente *hot dog*
la picadura *bite*
la pila *battery*
el saco (la bolsa) de dormir *sleeping bag*
la serpiente *snake*
la sierra *mountains*
la tienda de campaña *tent*

1. Los niños acampan en la sierra.

 ____

2. Ricardo nada en el lago.

 ____

3. Lupe y yo llenamos la mochila.

 ____

4. Ester desenvuelve el saco de dormir.

 ____

5. Ud. y Andrés atrapan mariposas para su colección.

 ____

6. Pablo se acuesta en el saco de dormir.

 ____

7. Yo observo las hormigas en el hormiguero.

 ____

8. Tú enciendes el fuego para asar los perros calientes.

____

9. Pepe y Lucía meten las pilas en la linterna.

____

10. Todos nosotros nos quejamos de las picaduras de los mosquitos.

____

11. Ud. se asusta al ver las arañas en la tienda de campaña.

____

12. Consuelo grita al ver una serpiente.

____

D. Escriba oraciones con los verbos en presente, imperfecto o futuro progresivo. Cambie los sustantivos que son complementos directos a pronombres. Haga todos los cambios necesarios.

Modelo Carlos practica el ruso.
➔ Carlos **está practicándolo.**
➔ Carlos **lo está practicando.**

1. Leíamos los periódicos.

____

____

2. Uds. harán las maletas.

____

____

3. Me pongo el traje.

____

____

4. Ud. se lavaba la cabeza.

____

____

5. Nos dirás los planes.

____

____

6. Rita se viste en el dormitorio.

____

____

E. ¡Cuando estalló (*broke out*) el fuego, …! Cuando estalló el fuego en la cocina del Hotel Dos Reyes en Cartagena, los huéspedes y los empleados del hotel estaban haciendo ciertas cosas. Escriba oraciones con el verbo en imperfecto progresivo que describen lo que estaban haciendo estas personas. Escriba cada oración de dos maneras cuando sea posible.

Modelo el señor Escudero / bañarse
→ El señor Escudero estaba bañándose.
→ El señor Escudero se estaba bañando.

En el hotel

el aire acondicionado *air conditioning*
el ascensor *elevator*
el botones *bellhop*
la camarera *chambermaid*
el equipaje *luggage*
el gerente *manager*
el huésped *guest (in hotel)*
el juego de toallas *set of towels*
el lavado *wash*
la lavandera *laundress*
el mozo *waiter*
el noveno piso *ninth floor*
la recepción *check-in desk*
registrarse *to check in*
tocar el timbre *to ring the bell*

1. los señores Sotomayor / registrarse

2. la señorita Serrano / pedir un juego de toallas

3. el botones / subirles el equipaje a unos huéspedes

4. las camareras / arreglar los cuartos

5. los mozos / servirles la cena a los clientes

6. el gerente / prender el aire acondicionado

7. el doctor López / afeitarse

8. la lavandera / devolverle el lavado a la señora Casona

9. los huéspedes del noveno piso / bajar en el ascensor

10. los turistas ingleses / tocar el timbre en la recepción

11. los cocineros / ¡jactarse de los plátanos flameados que habían preparado!

Nota cultural

La ciudad colombiana de **Cartagena** queda al noroeste del país en el mar Caribe. Fue fundada por Pedro de Heredia en 1533. Es un puerto importante que fue una de las bases principales en la colonización. Cartagena servía de almacén para las mercancías y riquezas que España recogía en sus colonias americanas destinadas a España y para mercancías enviadas a las colonias de España Se construyeron murallas y fortalezas alrededor de la ciudad para protegerla de ataques por piratas.

F. ¡Qué va! Siguen haciéndolo. Su amiga acaba de volver de Bogotá donde pasó un semestre estudiando español. Ella supone que ha habido muchos cambios mientras estaba en el extranjero. Ud. le dice que *¡qué va!*, que todo sigue siendo igual. Escriba oraciones usando formas de **seguir** + el gerundio. Cambie los sustantivos que son complementos directos a pronombres.

MODELO Ya no estudias química, ¿verdad?
➔ ¡Qué va! **Sigo estudiándola.**

1. Elena ya no dice chismes (*gossip*), ¿verdad?

2. Ya no construyen la autopista, ¿verdad?

3. Ya no lees ciencia-ficción, ¿verdad?

4. Tus padres ya no duermen la siesta, ¿verdad?

5. Ud. ya no asiste a los conciertos de jazz, ¿verdad?

6. Nosotros, los Gatos Azules, ya no jugamos al fútbol en el estadio, ¿verdad?

Nota cultural

Bogotá, capital de Colombia, se encuentra en un altiplano a 2.650 metros de alto. Santa Fe de Bogotá, su nombre original, fue fundada por Gonzalo Jiménez de Quesada en 1538. La ciudad siempre ha sido el centro principal del país desde la conquista. Lo más interesante de la ciudad es el centro histórico llamado La Candelaria. En este barrio se encuentra la Plaza Bolívar con una estatua del Libertador, Simón Bolívar (1783–1830), el general y estadista venezolano que fue responsable por la independencia de Colombia, Venezuela y otros países hispanoamericanos de España.

G. **¡Nosotros, los trasnochadores (*night owls*)!** A Ud. y a sus amigos les gusta trasnochar (*stay up late*). Escriba oraciones en futuro progresivo describiendo lo que Uds. estarán haciendo a esas horas.

MODELO yo / hablar por teléfono / a la una de la mañana
→ Yo **estaré hablando** por teléfono a la una de la mañana.

1. Luisa / ver televisión / a las dos y media
____
2. Ud. / ducharse / a medianoche
____
3. mis amigos y yo / morirnos de sueño / a las cuatro
____
4. Pablo y Ramón / jugar al ajedrez / a las doce y media
____
5. yo / oír música / a la una y media
____
6. tú / comerse unos bocadillos / a las tres
____

C *The progressive tenses with **llevar** to express "have been doing"*

- In addition to **hace** + expression of time + **que** + verb in the present tense, Spanish expresses actions that begin in the past and that continue into the present with the present tense of **llevar** + the gerund:

Llevo tres años **estudiando** español. Hace tres años que estudio español. Estudio español desde hace tres años.	*I've been studying Spanish for three years.*

- The gerund of **estar** is not used in the **llevar** + gerund construction. **Llevar** is used by itself:

Llevo dos horas aquí. *I've been here for two hours.*

H. Una entrevista. Un periodista le entrevista al famoso pintor-escultor peruano Pablo de Lima. Las preguntas se hacen con la construcción **hace** + expresión de tiempo y se contestan usando **llevar** + el gerundio.

MODELO ¿Cuánto tiempo hace que Ud. hace esculturas? (quince años)
→ **Llevo** quince años **haciendo** esculturas.

La pintura

abstracto *abstract*
la cerámica *ceramics*
el cuadro *painting*
dibujar *to draw*
el dibujo *drawing*
el escultor/la escultora *sculptor*
la escultura *sculpture*
el fondo *background*
la galería *gallery*
el/la modelo *model*
el mural *mural*
el paisaje *landscape*
el pincel *paintbrush*
pintar *to paint*
el pintor/la pintora *painter*
la pintura *painting; paint*
el retrato *portrait*

1. ¿Cuánto tiempo hace que Ud. pinta retratos? (doce años)

____

2. ¿Cuánto tiempo hace que Ud. usa estos pinceles? (unos meses)

____

3. ¿Cuánto tiempo hace que Ud. dibuja con modelos? (varios años)

____

4. ¿Cuánto tiempo hace que Ud. se dedica a la pintura? (toda la vida)

____

5. ¿Cuánto tiempo hace que Ud. cuelga sus cuadros de paisajes en la galería Olmo? (un año)

____

6. ¿Cuánto tiempo hace que Ud. se interesa en los murales? (poco tiempo)

____

7. ¿Cuánto tiempo hace que Ud. trabaja en cerámica? (nueve años)

____

8. ¿Cuánto tiempo hace que Ud. vive en París? (cinco años)

____

Nota cultural

Lima, capital del Perú, queda a orillas del río Rimac, no muy lejos del océano Pacífico. La ciudad fue fundada como "La ciudad de los Reyes" por Francisco Pizarro, conquistador español, en 1535. Lima tuvo una enorme importancia durante la época de la colonia hasta que se independizó Perú de España en 1821. Hay mucho que ver en Lima incluso la Universidad Nacional Mayor de San Marcos (fundada en 1551); la Catedral e iglesias; edificios públicos y casas históricas; varios museos de las culturas precolombinas e historia desde la conquista—el Museo Nacional de Antropología y Arqueología, el Museo de la Nación, el Museo de Oro, el Museo Nacional de Historia, el Museo del Tribunal de la Santa Inquisición, etcétera, y de arte—el Museo de Arte, el Museo de Arte Italiano, la Colección Pedro de Osma y la Pinacoteca (*galería, museo de arte*) Municipal donde hay una exposición grande de artistas peruanos, como Ignacio Merino (1817–76).

I. Un partido de fútbol. Un locutor de televisión describe un partido de fútbol empleando el presente progresivo de los verbos entre paréntesis.

1. Los aficionados ____________ ____________ sus equipos. (animar [*to cheer*])
2. Redondo ____________ ____________ el balón (*ball*). (robar)
3. Nosotros ____________ ____________ un partido emocionante. (ver)
4. Manrique ____________ ____________ un gol. (marcar [*to score*])
5. Los entrenadores (*trainers*) ____________ ____________ al campo de fútbol. (salir)
6. Cuéllar ____________ ____________ el balón. (regatear [*to dribble*])
7. Los técnicos (*managers*) ____________ ____________ un gran esfuerzo a los jugadores. (pedirles)
8. Los aficionados ____________ ____________. (entusiasmarse)
9. Uds., los televidentes, ____________ ____________ los gritos de los aficionados. (oír)
10. Este partido de campeonato ____________ ____________ mucha atención. (atraer)

J. Exprese en español las siguientes oraciones empleando el progresivo.

1. We're having a wonderful time!

____

2. You (*Ud.*) were jogging until it began to rain. (*use preterit progressive*)

____

3. They're still serving dinner at the Palacio Hotel.

____

4. I'm getting to know Madrid little by little.

____

5. Mateo and Victoria will be playing tennis all afternoon.

____

6. Pedro and I kept on reading.

____

K. Ejercicio oral. ¿Qué están haciendo los compañeros de clase? Trabaje con un(a) compañero(a) de clase en describir lo que están haciendo los amigos durante su hora libre en el colegio.

L. Estructuras en acción. Lea el siguiente anuncio sobre el aprendizaje de idiomas y haga los ejercicios.

Vocabulario

el dominio *command, mastery*
gratuito *free*
la jornada *working day*
lectivo (adj.) *school*
la plaza *place, seat*

¡BASTA YA DE PERDER AÑOS ESTUDIANDO IDIOMAS...!

En SEA hablará INGLÉS - Francés o Alemán en 4 semanas

Aprendiendo 2.000 palabras y toda la gramática básica.

USTED TIENE LA LIBERTAD DE ELEGIR

Pero... ¿Para qué estudiar durante años? Si puedes comunicarte en un idioma en 4 semanas o conseguir un cómodo dominio de él en 50 días lectivos

¡RESERVE SU PLAZA ANTES DEL 30/04/95!

✓ PARKING GRATUITO ✓ RESULTADOS GARANTIZADOS

¡¡LLÁMENOS!!... O VENGA A NUESTRAS JORNADAS INFORMATIVAS

al ☎ 308 36 69
en C/FERNANDO EL SANTO, 11

SEA

1. La idea principal del anuncio es __________.

   a. Hace falta aprender no más de 2.000 palabras de una lengua extranjera.
   b. El aprendizaje de una lengua extranjera debe ser rápido.
   c. Los idiomas extranjeros más importantes son el inglés, el francés y el alemán.

2. Según el anuncio, una persona puede entender y hacerse entendido en un idioma extranjero en __________.

   a. un año lectivo
   b. varios años
   c. cuatro semanas

3. Se pide información sobre los cursos __________.

   a. asistiendo a una sesión informativa
   b. reservando una plaza
   c. llamando a SEA solamente

4. *La libertad de elegir* se refiere a __________.

   a. optar entre francés e inglés
   b. llevar mucho o poco tiempo estudiando un idioma
   c. aprender gramática o vocabulario

5. En 50 días lectivos se puede __________.

   a. lograr un dominio de la lengua extranjera
   b. conseguir una plaza de parking
   c. escoger alemán u otro idioma

6. Fernando el Santo es __________.

   a. un profesor de inglés
   b. el telefonista
   c. la calle donde queda SEA

7. Escriba los dos gerundios que se encuentran en el anuncio.

   a. ____________________
   b. ____________________

8. Escriba la forma del gerundio de los verbos que se encuentran en el anuncio. El infinitivo de los verbos: **perder, hablar, elegir, poder, comunicarse, conseguir, reservar, llamarnos, venir.**

   a. ____________________
   b. ____________________
   c. ____________________
   d. ____________________
   e. ____________________
   f. ____________________
   g. ____________________
   h. ____________________
   i. ____________________

9. Escriba su propio anuncio cambiando el texto del anuncio que acaba de leer. Por ejemplo, los idiomas pueden cambiarse al chino, al hebreo, al italiano, al japonés, etcétera.

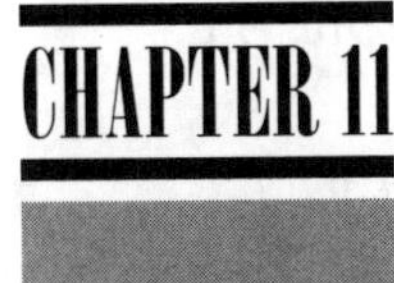

CHAPTER 11 THE SUBJUNCTIVE IN NOUN CLAUSES: PRESENT & PRESENT PERFECT SUBJUNCTIVE

A *Forms of the present subjunctive: regular verbs*

- The present subjunctive is formed by changing the vowel **-a-** of the present indicative to **-e-** in **-ar** verbs and the vowels **-e-** and **-i-** of the present indicative to **-a-** in **-er** and **-ir** verbs. Regular **-er** and **-ir** verbs have identical endings in all persons of the subjunctive.

estudiar		
Quiere que	estudi**e** idiomas.	*He wants me to study languages.*
	estudi**es**	*He wants you to study languages.*
	estudi**e**	*He wants her to study languages.*
	estudi**emos**	*He wants us to study languages.*
	estudi**éis**	*He wants you to study languages.*
	estudi**en**	*He wants them to study languages.*

comprender		
Espera que	comprend**a**.	*She hopes I'll understand.*
	comprend**as**.	*She hopes you'll understand.*
	comprend**a**.	*She hopes he'll understand.*
	comprend**amos**.	*She hopes we'll understand.*
	comprend**áis**.	*She hopes you'll understand.*
	comprend**an**.	*She hopes they'll understand.*

vivir		
Prefieren que	viv**a** aquí.	*They prefer me to live here.*
	viv**as**	*They prefer you to live here.*
	viv**a**	*They prefer her to live here.*
	viv**amos**	*They prefer us to live here.*
	viv**áis**	*They prefer you to live here.*
	viv**an**	*They prefer them to live here.*

- In the present subjunctive the *yo* form and the *él* form are identical.

- **-Ar** and **-er** verbs that have changes in the vowel of the stem in the present indicative have these same changes in the present subjunctive:

Le aconsejan que p**ie**nse más.	*They advise her to think more.*
Nos aconsejan que pensemos más.	*They advise us to think more.*
Espera que yo enc**ue**ntre las llaves.	*He hopes that I find the keys.*
Espera que encontremos las llaves.	*He hopes that we find the keys.*

- **-Ir** verbs that have the change **e** > **ie** or **e** > **i** in the present indicative also have these changes in the present subjunctive. These verbs also have **i** in the stem of the *nosotros* and *vosotros* forms in the present subjunctive. **Dormir** and **morir** have the **o** > **ue** change in the present subjunctive and **u** in the stem of the *nosotros* and *vosotros* forms.

sentir	
sienta	sintamos
sientas	sintáis
sienta	sientan

seguir	
siga	sigamos
sigas	sigáis
siga	sigan

dormir	
duerma	durmamos
duermas	durmáis
duerma	duerman

- Some verbs that end in **-iar** or **-uar** have an accent mark on the **í** or the **ú** in all forms except *nosotros* and *vosotros*. For example: **enviar:** envíe, envíes, envíe, enviemos, enviéis, envíen; **continuar:** continúe, continúes, continúe, continuemos, continuéis, continúen.

A. **¡Pero yo sí quiero!** Un amigo suyo le menciona varias cosas que no están sucediendo. Ud. le dice que sí quiere que pasen. Use el presente del modo (*mood*) subjuntivo.

MODELO Alicia no estudia química.
➔ Pero yo quiero que estudie química.

1. Marcos no trabaja.

____

2. Yo no consigo empleo.

____

3. Federico y Paula no nos escriben.

____

4. Juanita no sigue nuestros consejos.

____

5. Nosotros no comemos fuera hoy.

____

6. Yo no vuelvo temprano.

____

7. Los niños no duermen por la tarde.

____

8. Tú y yo no pedimos taxi.

____

9. Mis tíos no abren la tienda hoy.

____

10. Juan no entiende.

____

11. Amalia no piensa en nosotros.

____

12. La oficina no envía el paquete.

____

13. Yo no cierro las ventanas.

____

14. Tú y yo no nos divertimos.

____

15. Tú y yo no repetimos el vocabulario.

____

B *Forms of the present subjunctive: irregular verbs*

- Verbs that have an irregularity such as **-g-** or **-zc-** in the *yo* form of the present indicative have that irregularity in all persons of the present subjunctive. These irregularities occur only in **-er** and **-ir** verbs, and therefore all the present subjunctive endings have the vowel **-a-.**
- Here is a table of **-g-** verbs:

infinitive	*present indicative* (*yo form*)	*present subjunctive*
caer	**caig**o	caiga, caigas, caiga, caigamos, caigáis, caigan
decir	**dig**o	diga, digas, diga, digamos, digáis, digan
hacer	**hag**o	haga, hagas, haga, hagamos, hagáis, hagan
oír	**oig**o	oiga, oigas, oiga, oigamos, oigáis, oigan
poner	**pong**o	ponga, pongas, ponga, pongamos, pongáis, pongan
salir	**salg**o	salga, salgas, salga, salgamos, salgáis, salgan
tener	**teng**o	tenga, tengas, tenga, tengamos, tengáis, tengan
traer	**traig**o	traiga, traigas, traiga, traigamos, traigáis, traigan
venir	**veng**o	venga, vengas, venga, vengamos, vengáis, vengan

- Here is a table of the present subjunctive of other verbs that are irregular in the *yo* form:

infinitive	*present indicative (**yo** form)*	*present subjunctive*
caber	**quep**o	quepa, quepas, quepa, quepamos, quepáis, quepan
conocer	**conozc**o	conozca, conozcas, conozca, conozcamos, conozcáis, conozcan
nacer	**nazc**o	nazca, nazcas, nazca, nazcamos, nazcáis, nazcan
parecer	**parezc**o	parezca, parezcas, parezca, parezcamos, parezcáis, parezcan
construir	**construy**o	construya, construyas, construya, construyamos, construyáis, construyan
destruir	**destruy**o	destruya, destruyas, destruya, destruyamos, destruyáis, destruyan
ver	**ve**o	vea, veas, vea, veamos, veáis, vean

- **Dar** and **estar** are regular in the present subjunctive except for the accent marks. The first- and third-person singular forms of **dar** have the written accent (**dé**) and all of the present subjunctive forms of **estar** have the written accent, except the first-person plural form **estemos**:

dar	
dé	demos
des	deis
dé	den

estar	
esté	estemos
estés	**estéis**
esté	**estén**

- **Haber, ir, saber,** and **ser** have irregular stems in the present subjunctive. However, their endings are regular:

infinitive	*subjunctive stem*	*present subjunctive*
haber	**hay-**	haya, hayas, haya, hayamos, hayáis, hayan
ir	**vay-**	vaya, vayas, vaya, vayamos, vayáis, vayan
saber	**sep-**	sepa, sepas, sepa, sepamos, sepáis, sepan
ser	**se-**	sea, seas, sea, seamos, seáis, sean

B. **Le parece muy bien.** Su amiga María se alegra de muchas cosas. Dígalo usando el presente del subjuntivo.

MODELO ¿Sabe María que viene Juan Carlos?
➔ Sí. Se alegra de que venga.

1. ¿Sabe María que conoces a Pedro?

____

2. ¿Sabe María que tenemos un día libre?

____

3. ¿Sabe María que Alfredo le trae flores?

____

4. ¿Sabe María que yo no veo más películas de terror?

____

5. ¿Sabe María que los Ibáñez construyen una casa?

____

6. ¿Sabe María que Marcos y Julia salen juntos?

____

7. ¿Sabe María que tú y yo oímos mucha música clásica?

____

8. ¿Sabe María que su hermanito obedece a su profesor?

____

9. ¿Sabe María que Raquel compone música?

____

10. ¿Sabe María que la fiesta es mañana?

____

11. ¿Sabe María que hay reunión la semana que viene?

____

12. ¿Sabe María que sus primos van a España?

____

C *Spelling changes in the present subjunctive*

1. **-Ar** verbs whose stem ends in **c, g,** or **z** change those letters as follows in the present subjunctive:

   c → qu
   g → gu
   z → c

   Lle**g**an el lunes. → Espero que lle**gu**en el lunes.
   Bus**c**amos casa. → Es necesario que bus**qu**emos casa.
   Almor**z**amos aquí. → Prefiero que almor**c**emos aquí.

2. **-Er** and **-ir** verbs whose stems end in **g, gu,** or **c** change those letters as follows in the present subjunctive:

   g → j
   gu → g
   c → z

   Esco**g**es otro plato. → Queremos que esco**j**as otro plato.
   Si**gu**en andando. → Es posible que si**g**an andando.
   Te conven**c**e. → Espero que te conven**z**a.

3. -**Ar** verbs whose stem ends in **j** do not change **j** to **g** before **e**:

   Traba**j**o los domingos. → Quieren que traba**j**e los domingos.

4. Irregular verbs such as **hacer** and **conocer** don't follow the spelling change in the second rule above, but show the irregularities of the *yo* form of the present indicative:

   Haces la cena. ➔ Quiero que ha**g**as la cena.
   Conocen a Marta. ➔ No creo que cono**z**can a Marta.

C. Ortografía (*Spelling*). Escriba en presente de subjuntivo los verbos que aparecen entre paréntesis recordando el cambio ortográfico.

1. Espero que tú ______________________ (realizar) tus planes.
2. Es necesario que Uds. ______________________ (acercarse) más.
3. ¡Qué lástima que ______________________ (comenzar) a llover!
4. Se alegran que yo ______________________ (dirigir) la orquesta.
5. Es probable que los chicos ______________________ (sacar) muy buenas notas.
6. Nos piden que ______________________ (recoger) las manzanas.
7. Es importante que Ud. ______________________ (dedicarse) a los negocios.
8. Me extraña que Vera no ______________________ (explicar) lo que pasó.
9. Te aconsejamos que ______________________ (entregar) el informe mañana.
10. Ojalá que Daniel ______________________ (conseguir) el puesto.
11. Tal vez Uds. ______________________ (organizar) la reunión.
12. No creo que Bárbara ______________________ (almorzar) antes de las dos.
13. Es difícil que yo los ______________________ (convencer).
14. Insisten en que nosotros ______________________ (apagar) las luces.
15. Tenemos miedo de que los soldados no ______________________ (vencer) a sus enemigos.

D *Use of the present subjunctive in noun clauses*

- A noun clause is a clause that functions as a noun, that is, it can serve as either the subject or the object of a verb. Noun clauses that are incorporated into a longer sentence are called dependent or subordinate clauses and are introduced in Spanish by the conjunction **que.**
- All the Spanish tenses studied so far belong to the *indicative mood*. Verbs in the *indicative mood* express events or states that are considered factual, definite, or part of the speaker's experienced reality. The following examples have dependent noun clauses in the indicative. They show events perceived as part of reality because they are the objects of verbs such as **saber, parecer, oír, ver**:

Sabes **que lo hizo Sandra.**	*You know* ***that Sandra did it.***
Nos parece **que está lloviendo.**	*We think* ***it's raining.***
He oído **que hay una buena noticia.**	*I've heard* ***there's good news.***
Verán **que Juan no entiende.**	*You'll see* ***that Juan doesn't understand.***

- The *present subjunctive* in Spanish is used in dependent noun clauses that mark events or states that the speaker considers not part of reality or of his/her experience. These dependent noun clauses follow main clauses that express, as in the examples below, (1) expectation, skepticism, doubt, uncertainty; (2) demands, wants, needs, insistence, advice, impositions of will; (3) negated facts. The verbs in the main clauses are in the present, present perfect, future, or imperative:

(1) **Dudo** que Uds. **lleguen** para las tres.	***I doubt*** *you'll* ***arrive*** *by three o'clock.*
(2) Paula **quiere** que la **visites.**	*Paula* ***wants*** *you* ***to visit*** *her.*
(3) **No es cierto** que **nos quedemos**.	***It's not certain*** *that* ***we'll stay.***

- Verbs such as **desear** (*to want*), **esperar** (*to hope*), **insistir en** (*to insist*), **necesitar** (*to need*), **preferir** (*to prefer*), **querer** (*to want*) are followed by a dependent noun clause in the subjunctive and not by an infinitive *unless the subjects of both clauses are the same*:

Verb in main clause + dependent noun clause in subjunctive (two clauses: two different subjects)

Espero que Roberto **vaya.**	*I hope Roberto goes.*
Quieren que **salgamos.**	*They want us to go out.*
Insistimos en que Uds. **se queden.**	*We insist that you stay.*

Verb in main clause + infinitive (the same subject in both parts of the sentence)

Espero ir.	*I hope to go.*
Quieren salir.	*They want to go out.*
Insistimos en quedarnos.	*We insist on staying.*

- The verbs **decir** (*to tell someone to do something*) and **pedir** (*to ask someone to do something*) are followed by a subjunctive clause. They may occur with an indirect object:

Le dicen a Felipe que **tenga** cuidado.	*They tell Felipe to be careful.*
Susana **nos pide** que **traigamos** el periódico.	*Susana asks us to bring the newspaper.*

- **Decir** is followed by a dependent clause in the *indicative* when the dependent clause reports what someone said. For example, **José les dice: "Leo mucho"** or **"Leí mucho."** Contrast the use of the indicative and subjunctive after **decir**:

José les dice que **lee** mucho.	*José tells them he reads a lot.*
José les dijo que **leyó** mucho.	*José told them he read a lot.*
José les dice que **lean** mucho.	*José tells them to read a lot.*
José les dijo que **leyeran** mucho.	*José told them to read a lot.*

- Some verbs can be followed either by a noun clause in the subjunctive or by an infinitive without a change in meaning. An indirect object pronoun is optional if these verbs are followed by a subjunctive clause, but is obligatory when these verbs are followed by the infinitive. These verbs include: **aconsejar** (*to advise*), **exigir** (*to demand*), **impedir** (*to prevent*), **mandar** (*to order*), **permitir** (*to permit*), **prohibir** (*to forbid*), **recomendar** (*to recommend*), **rogar** (*to request, beg*), **sugerir** (*to suggest*):

(Les) aconsejo que **tomen** el tren. **Les aconsejo tomar** el tren.	*I advise you to take the train.*

(Le) exigimos a Beatriz que **regrese.**
Le exigimos a Beatriz **regresar.** } *We demand that Beatriz return.*

- The verb **dejar** (*to let, allow*) can also be followed by a noun clause in the subjunctive or by an infinitive without a change in meaning. **Dejar** takes a direct object pronoun before a subjunctive clause:

(Los) **dejan** que **entren.**
Los **dejan entrar.** } *They let them come in.*

- Some verbs that express an emotional state, an attitude, or a bias are followed by dependent noun clauses in the subjunctive. These verbs include: **alegrarse (de)** (*to be glad, happy*), **extrañar** (*to surprise*), **gustar** (*to like*), **sentir** (*to regret*), **sorprender** (*to surprise*), **temer** (*to fear*), **tener miedo (de)** (*to be afraid [of]*).

Me alegro (de) que Uds. **visiten** Lima.	*I'm glad that you're visiting Lima.*
¿No **te extraña** que Claudia no **llame**?	*Aren't you surprised that Claudia doesn't call?*
Los Ayala **temen** que sus hijos no **saquen** buenas notas.	*Mr. and Mrs. Ayala are afraid their children aren't getting good grades.*

- **Gustar, extrañar,** and **sorprender** are usually used with an indirect object pronoun. (See Chapter 19 on the indirect object.)

D. **¿Indicativo o subjuntivo?** Escoja entre el presente del indicativo y el presente del subjuntivo de los verbos que aparecen entre paréntesis para completar las siguientes oraciones.

MODELO Creo que Fernando ____________ el miércoles. (llegar)
➔ Creo que Fernando **llega** el miércoles.

Prefiero que Fernando ____________ el miércoles. (llegar)
➔ Prefiero que Fernando **llegue** el miércoles.

1. Daniel quiere que nosotros le ____________ lo que pasó. (decir)
2. Vemos que estos chicos ____________ muchas fechas de memoria. (aprender)
3. Siento que Javier no ____________ este año. (graduarse)
4. Nos extraña que Uds. no ____________ el trabajo. (comenzar)
5. Piensan que tú ____________ de todo. (quejarse)
6. Mis padres insisten en que yo ____________ lo antes posible. (matricularse)
7. Me alegro de que Juan y Diana ____________ a casarse. (ir)
8. Parece que Ud. no ____________ hasta más tarde. (salir)
9. ¿Sabes que Raquel ____________ razón? (tener)
10. Isabel comprende que nosotros no ____________ ayudarla. (poder)

11. Le aconsejamos a Diego que ____________________ más responsable. (ser)
12. Les gusta que ya no ____________________ problemas con la casa. (haber)
13. Todo el mundo entiende que Uds. ____________________ ocupadísimos. (estar)
14. Yo exijo que tú me ____________________ caso. (hacer)
15. Pedro cree que yo lo ____________________ todo. (saber)
16. Debes darte cuenta que ya no se ____________________ ese libro. (conseguir)

E. **¡Viva México!** Ud. y sus amigos están emocionados pensando en el viaje que van a hacer a México durante el verano. Escriba oraciones que expresen lo que quieren hacer en México. El sujeto de la cláusula principal y el de la subordinada (dependiente) deben ser el mismo; incluya el verbo conjugado + infinitivo.

MODELO yo / querer / ver las pirámides de San Juan de Teotihuacán
➔ Yo quiero ver las pirámides de San Juan de Teotihuacán.

1. Laura / esperar / perfeccionar su español

____

2. Ricardo y Beti / preferir / visitar la catedral del Zócalo

____

3. Ud. / deber / conocer Taxco

____

4. Pablo y yo / desear / ir a Puebla

____

5. tú / preferir / hacer una excursión a la Ciudad Universitaria

____

6. yo / sentir / no poder quedarme más tiempo en el Bosque de Chapultepec

____

7. Uds. / insistir en / escaparse un par de días a Mérida

____

8. todos nosotros / alegrarse de / estar en Oaxaca

____

Nota cultural

- **El Bosque de Chapultepec.** Este gran parque, hermoso con sus muchos ahuehuetes (árboles coníferos), queda al final del Paseo de la Reforma en la ciudad de México. Hay bellas vistas del Valle de México desde los balcones del Castillo de Chapultepec y también hay algunos museos interesantes. El más importante de éstos es el Museo Nacional de Antropología con su magnífica exposición de culturas precolombinas.

- **La catedral en el Zócalo.** El Zócalo, la Plaza Mayor de la parte más antigua de la ciudad de México, fue el sitio del gran templo azteca Teocalli. En ese mismo lugar los españoles construyeron la catedral más vieja y más grande de Latinoamérica. Fue concebida por Herrera, el arquitecto de El Escorial en España y de la catedral de Puebla. La construcción de la catedral empezó en 1525.

- **La Ciudad Universitaria.** De fama mundial, la Ciudad Universitaria queda a 18 kilómetros del centro de la capital. Se destaca la biblioteca de diez pisos con sus paredes de mosaicos en las cuales se narra la historia del saber científico. La Universidad de México fue fundada en 1551.

- **Mérida.** Capital del estado mexicano de Yucatán en la península de Yucatán, Mérida fue fundada en 1542 en el sitio de la ciudad maya de Tihoo. Esta península de la América Central, que queda entre el golfo de México y el mar Caribe, es un centro de turismo por su arqueología maya y sus playas.

- **Oaxaca.** Esta pintoresca ciudad de arquitectura del siglo XVII y mercados indígenas queda a 531 kilómetros al sureste de la ciudad de México.

- **Puebla (de los Ángeles).** "La ciudad de los Ángeles", una de las ciudades más antiguas y más famosas de México, queda al sur de la ciudad de México. Es una ciudad colonial muy atractiva por su catedral, las vistas de los volcanes y sus 60 iglesias, muchas de las cuales tienen tejas que brillan a la luz del sol. Por desgracia, la contaminación del ambiente, los embotellamientos y otros problemas causados por el desarrollo industrial, van destruyendo el hermoso aspecto colonial de la ciudad.

- **San Juan de Teotihuacán.** Las pirámides de San Juan de Teotihuacán quedan a unos 45 kilómetros al noreste de la ciudad de México. Estas enormes pirámides fueron construidas por los toltecas, quienes formaron una de las civilizaciones precolombinas del Valle de México. La Pirámide del Sol se construyó a fines del siglo primero y la Pirámide de la Luna se terminó alrededor del siglo dos. Teotihuacán fue un importante centro religioso y cultural. La civilización tolteca estaba ya en decadencia a principios del siglo XIII cuando llegaron los aztecas al Valle de México. Los aztecas fundaron su imperio en 1325 con su capital en Tenochtitlán, actualmente la ciudad de México.

- **Taxco.** Esta ciudad colonial muy pintoresca queda al sur de la ciudad de México. El primer envío (cargamento) de plata enviado a España desde el Nuevo Mundo fue de las minas de Taxco. Muchos turistas van a Taxco por los monumentos, las vistas y las platerías (*silversmiths*).

F. ¡Con la palomilla (*group of friends* [*México*]) en México! Ahora exprese lo que Ud. quiere que hagan los otros amigos en México. El sujeto de la cláusula principal es diferente del de la subordinada; por eso se usa el subjuntivo.

MODELO yo : querer / Paco y Mari : ver las pirámides de San Juan de Teotihuacán
→ Yo quiero que Paco y Mari vean las pirámides de San Juan de Teotihuacán.

1. Laura : esperar / nosotros : perfeccionar nuestro español

____

2. Ricardo y Beti : preferir / Ud. : visitar la Catedral del Zócalo

____

3. Ud. : necesitar / Leo : conocer Taxco

____

4. Pablo y yo : desear / Uds. : ir a Puebla

____

5. a ti : gustar / yo : hacer una excursión a la Ciudad Universitaria

____

6. yo : sentir / nosotros : no poder quedarse más tiempo en el Bosque de Chapultepec

____

7. Uds. : insistir en / los cuates (*pals* [*México*]) : escaparse un par de días a Mérida

____

8. todos nosotros : alegrarse de / tú : estar en Oaxaca

____

G. Una familia unida (*close*). Los miembros de la familia Ayala son muy unidos. Todos se quieren mucho y comparten sus pensamientos y sentimientos. Escriba oraciones que expresen lo que quieren para los demás miembros de la familia. Use el subjuntivo.

Lazos familiares (*family ties*)

la ahijada *goddaughter*
el ahijado *godson*
los ahijados *godchildren*
la bisabuela *great-grandmother*
el bisabuelo *great-grandfather*
los bisabuelos *great-grandparents*
la cuñada *sister-in-law*
el cuñado *brother-in-law*
los familiares *relatives*
la nieta *granddaughter*
el nieto *grandson*
los nietos *grandchildren*
la novia *bride, fiancée*
el novio *groom, fiancé*
los novios *bride and groom*
la madrina *godmother*
el padrino *godfather*
los padrinos *godparents*
la suegra *mother-in-law*
el suegro *father-in-law*

MODELO el abuelo : desear / su familia : vivir bien
➔ El abuelo desea que su familia viva bien.

1. Elena : esperar / sus cuñados : tener éxito

____

2. el señor Ayala : pedirles / sus suegros : venir a verlos los domingos

____

3. la madrina : alegrarse / su ahijado : sacar buenas notas en el colegio

____

4. los padres : querer / sus hijos : ganarse la vida (*to earn a living*)

____

5. a la señora Ayala : gustarle / los bisabuelos : ser felices en la tercera edad (*old age*)

____

6. yo : aconsejarle / la nieta : hacerse arquitecta

____

7. Terencio : prohibirles / las ahijadas : ir solas al extranjero

____

8. tú : sentir / el cuñado : no estar contento con el nuevo empleo

____

9. la suegra : preferir / los novios : mudarse con ella

____

10. Uds. : rogarles / los padrinos : aceptar su regalo

____

11. Ricardo y yo : necesitar / los nietos : darnos muchos besos y abrazos

___

12. los hijos : no dejar / sus padres : trabajar demasiado manteniéndolos

___

H. **Una carta.** Ana María Vázquez vive en Bogotá, Colombia. Le escribe una carta a su amiga Isabel García que vive en Los Ángeles. Para enterarse de lo que Ana María dice, llene los espacios en blanco con el presente del subjuntivo o el presente del indicativo del verbo entre paréntesis.

Querida Isabel:

Espero que tú ___ (1. encontrarse) bien. Mis papás, hermanos y yo ___ (2. estar) perfectamente. Recibí tu carta ayer. Me alegro que tú ___ (3. poder) venir a verme durante las vacaciones. Creo que yo ___ (4. ir) a ir a la playa con mi familia todo el mes de julio. Por eso es mejor que tú ___ (5. llegar) a principios de agosto. Mis padres quieren que tus papás y hermanos ___ (6. pasar) el mes con nosotros también. Les recomiendo que ___ (7. comprar) los boletos de avión lo antes posible. Les aconsejo también que ___ (8. traer) ropa un poco gruesa (heavy), *un impermeable y un paraguas porque ___ (9. hacer) fresco, ___ (10. estar) nublado y ___ (11. llover). Tú ___ (12. deber) recordar que Bogotá queda en las montañas. Yo ___ (13. saber) que tú no ___ (14. ir) a aburrirte en Bogotá. Tú ___ (15. ir) a ver que ___ (16. haber) tantas cosas que ver y hacer aquí. Voy a insistir en que Uds. ___ (17. despertarse) muy temprano todos los días aunque vamos a trasnochar* (stay up late) *oyendo música. Así yo ___ (18. poder) enseñarles las muchas cosas que hay en la ciudad y las afueras. Bueno, querida amiga, yo ___ (19. tener) muchas ganas de volver a verte. ¡Ojalá que tú me ___ (20. escribir) con la buena noticia de que ___ (21. venir) tu familia también!*

Cariños de Ana María

Nota cultural

- Además de sus excelentes museos, edificios históricos y paisajes, **Bogotá** tiene también mucha vida nocturna. Hay clubes, discotecas y bares en la Zona Rosa, la región Carrera 15, C 82 en el plano. Este sistema de la carrera que cruza la calle a un ángulo cuadrado se usa por toda Colombia. Las avenidas, bulevares anchos e importantes, pueden ser calles o carreras.

- Colombia se conoce por su variedad de música **folklórica** debido a sus cuatro regiones musicales que van de los Andes al Caribe: montañas, costa del Pacífico, costa del Caribe y los llanos (*plains*) orientales. El instrumento nacional es **el tiple,** una pequeña guitarra de 12 cuerdas. El baile nacional es **el bambuco.** La música del Caribe, recién integrada en el repertorio de **la salsa,** es buena para bailar **la cumbia**, baile típico de esta región.

E *The present subjunctive in noun clauses after impersonal expressions*

- Impersonal expressions (expressions with no specific subject) require the subjunctive in dependent noun clauses if they suggest that the event or state mentioned in the dependent clause is not part of perceived reality. For example: **es necesario que** (*it's necessary that*), **es importante que** (*it's important that*), **es imposible que** (*it's impossible that*), **es improbable que** (*it's improbable that*), **es posible que** (*it's possible that*), **es preciso que** (*it's necessary that*), **es probable que** (*it's probable that*), **Ojalá (que)** (*I hope [that]*).

—**Es necesario que discutamos** el asunto.	***It's necessary that we discuss*** *the matter.*
—**Es posible que yo no tenga** tiempo hoy.	***It's possible I won't have*** *time today.*
—**Pero es importante que resolvamos** algo.	***But it's important that we resolve*** *something.*
—De acuerdo. **Es probable que podamos** discutirlo mañana.	*Agreed.* ***It's probable we can*** *discuss it tomorrow.*
—**Ojalá que tengas** razón.	***I hope you're*** *right.*

- Impersonal expressions that show the speaker's emotional attitude or bias toward the event or state of the dependent clause also require the subjunctive: **es bueno que** (*it's good that*), **es inútil que** (*it's useless that*), **es malo que** (*it's bad that*), **es mejor que** (*it's better that*), **es peor que** (*it's worse that*), **es triste que** (*it's sad that*), **es útil que** (*it's useful that*), **más vale que** (*it's better that*). **Es una lástima que** (*It's a pity that*) and **¡qué lástima que!** (*what a pity that!*) are impersonal expressions that may be followed by the subjunctive or the indicative in the dependent clause:

—**Es triste** que José Luis **tenga** tantos problemas.	***It's sad*** *that José Luis* ***has*** *so many problems.*
—**Es inútil** que **tratemos** de ayudarlo, ¿verdad?	***It's useless*** *for* ***us to try*** *to help him, isn't it?*
—**Es una lástima** que no **haya** solución.	***It's a pity there's*** *no solution.*

- When the speaker does not identify a specific subject in the dependent clause, the impersonal expression is followed by an infinitive. Study the following pairs of sentences:

Es preciso saber la fecha.	***It's necessary to know*** *the date.*
Es preciso que sepamos la fecha.	***It's necessary that we know*** *the date.*
Es útil hacer investigaciones.	***It's useful to do*** *research.*
Es útil que hagas investigaciones.	***It's useful for you to do*** *research.*

- There are certain verbs and expressions in Spanish that require the subjunctive in the dependent clause *only when they are negative,* that is, when they suggest that the event or state in the dependent clause is a negated fact. For example: **no es cierto que, no es evidente que, no es obvio que, no es que, no es/está seguro, no es verdad que, no creer que, no pensar que**. When they are not negative they are followed by the indicative.

  Note: The negative constructions of **creer** and **pensar** (**no creer que** and **no pensar que**), as well as **tal vez** (*perhaps*), may be followed by the indicative as well as the subjunctive. The choice of the indicative by the speaker suggests he/she thinks the event in the dependent clause is closer to reality while the use of the subjunctive suggests that the speaker is less certain about the event:

Creo que Lola y Paco **van** al cine.	*I think Lola and Paco are going to the movies.*
No creo que Lola y Paco **vayan** al cine.	*I don't think Lola and Paco are going to the movies. (Speaker isn't sure whether Lola and Paco are going to the movies—it's quite possible they're going.)*
No creo que Lola y Paco **van** al cine.	*I don't think Lola and Paco are going to the movies. (Speaker thinks Lola and Paco are probably not going to the movies.)*
Es verdad que Jaime **está** preocupado.	*It's true Jaime is worried.*
No es verdad que Jaime **esté** preocupado.	*It's not true Jaime is worried.*
Tal vez se enfadan.	*Perhaps they'll get angry.*
Tal vez se enfaden.	*Perhaps they might get angry. (Speaker is less certain.)*

- When they are used in the affirmative, **dudar** (*to doubt*) and **es dudoso** (*it's doubtful*), require the use of the subjunctive in the dependent clause. Conversely, when **dudar** and **es dudoso** appear in the negative, the verb in the dependent clause is in the indicative:

Dudamos que Andrés **vuelva** hoy.	*We doubt Andrés is coming back today.*
Es dudoso que Andrés **vuelva** hoy.	*It's doubtful Andrés is coming back today.*
No dudamos que Andrés **vuelve** hoy.	*We don't doubt Andrés is coming back today.*
No es dudoso que Andrés **vuelve** hoy.	*It's not doubtful Andrés is coming back today.*

I. ¡Qué desorden! ¡Y viene mamá! Ud. vive en un apartamento con tres compañeros(as) de cuarto. Este fin de semana vienen los padres a visitar a sus hijos en la universidad. Uds. están contentos(as) de ver a sus padres. ¡Están también un poco preocupados(as) porque mamá va a ver que el apartamento es una pocilga (*pigsty*)! Use las expresiones impersonales con el subjuntivo para describir la situación.

Haciendo la limpieza

barrer el piso *to sweep the floor*
el cristal de ventana *windowpane*
el desorden *mess*
encerar el piso *to wax the floor*
la estantería *bookcase*
fregar las cacerolas *to scour the pans*
guardar *to put away*
meterse en *to get involved in*
ordenar *to clean up*
el producto para la limpieza *cleaning product*
sacudir el polvo *to dust*
la telaraña *cobweb, spiderweb*
el trapo *cleaning rag*

Modelo Vienen mis papás. (es bueno)
➔ Es bueno que vengan mis papás.

1. Las mamás ven el desorden. (es malo)
___
2. Hacemos la limpieza del apartamento. (es necesario)
___
3. Lupe friega las cacerolas. (es importante)
___
4. Juan y Antonio barren los pisos. (es útil)
___
5. Uds. enceran los pisos. (es probable)
___
6. Las mamás traen trapos y productos para la limpieza. (más vale que)
___
7. Los papás no se meten en todo esto. (es dudoso)
___
8. Yo sacudo el polvo. (es preciso)
___
9. Leonor guarda los libros en las estanterías. (ojalá)
___
10. Mario y Griselda lavan los cristales de las ventanas. (es posible)
___

11. Tú quitas las telarañas del techo. (es mejor)

____

12. No nos relajamos en todo el día. (¡qué lástima que!)

____

J. Reacciones. Ud. reacciona a unas afirmaciones. Al reaccionar, tiene que escoger entre el presente del subjuntivo y el presente del indicativo.

MODELO Manuela trabaja de moza. (es verdad) / (no es verdad)
→ **Es verdad** que Manuela **trabaja** de moza.
→ **No es verdad** que Manuela **trabaje** de moza.

1. Lorenzo sigue enfermo. (no estoy seguro)

____

2. Teresa y Jesús se quieren mucho. (es obvio)

____

3. Uds. tienen problemas con el coche. (no es cierto)

____

4. Julia llega el sábado. (es que)

____

5. Alejandro es de origen ruso. (no es seguro)

____

6. Los niños están aburridos. (no es evidente)

____

7. Carmen lo sabe todo. (no es que)

____

8. Martín renuncia a su puesto. (es cierto)

____

K. Pereza del fin de año. Ahora que termina el año escolar y hace tan buen tiempo, sus amigos prefieren jugar al béisbol en vez de estudiar. ¡Le toca a Ud. convencerlos que deben trabajar más! Use el presente del subjuntivo.

MODELO Pedro: No quiero asistir a la clase de química hoy. (es necesario)
Ud.: Oye, Pedro, es necesario que asistas a la clase de química.

1. Anita: No voy a estudiar para los exámenes finales. (insisto en que)

____

2. Miguel: No deseo trabajar en la librería. (me sorprende)

____

3. Rebeca: No pienso escribir el informe para sociología. (más vale que)

____

4. Tomás: No me gusta practicar ruso en el laboratorio de lenguas. (es útil)

____

5. Graciela: No me interesa tomar apuntes en historia. (es importante)

____

6. Alfredo: Prefiero no hacer la tarea. (te ruego)

____

7. Carolina: No me importa sacar buenas notas. (espero)

____

8. Joaquín: Voy a jugar al béisbol todo el día. (te prohíbo)

____

L. En un coloquio (*discussion*). Use el presente del subjuntivo cuando sea necesario para expresar las ideas de los participantes de un coloquio sobre el mundo a fines del siglo veinte.

1. It's good there are so many technological advances (*adelantos*).

____

2. We prefer to use nuclear energy even more.

____

3. Everyone's happy to have the computer.

____

4. It's a pity that wars continue to break out (*estallar*).

____

5. We regret that the cities have so much crime.

____

6. I'm afraid new illnesses are killing many people.

____

7. It's probable that environmental pollution isn't doing so much harm.

____

8. It's obvious that the free market economy is best.

____

9. It's necessary to control inflation and unemployment.

____

10. We advise the political leaders to spend money more accountably (*con más responsabilidad*).

____

11. I hope (*Ojalá*) there will be free elections in every country.

12. Nobody doubts that the 21st century is going to bring many changes.

F *The present perfect subjunctive*

- The present perfect subjunctive is used in the same kinds of dependent clauses as the present subjunctive. It is used to indicate that the action of the dependent clause happens before the action of the main clause.

Me alegro de que Uds. **vayan.**	*I'm glad you **are going.*** *(two actions in the present)*
Me alegro de que **hayan venido.**	*I'm glad you **came.*** *(dependent clause action happens prior to action of main clause)*

- The present perfect subjunctive consists of the present subjunctive of **haber** + the past participle.

Esperan que lo	**haya visto.**	*They hope I saw him.*
	hayas visto.	*They hope you saw him.*
	haya visto.	*They hope he saw him.*
	hayamos visto.	*They hope we saw him.*
	hayáis visto.	*They hope you saw him.*
	hayan visto.	*They hope they saw him.*

M. Escriba oraciones empleando la frase que aparece entre paréntesis en la cláusula principal y cambiando el verbo del pretérito al perfecto del subjuntivo.

Modelo Los Fernández llegaron. (es bueno)
➔ Es bueno que los Fernández hayan llegado.

1. Uds. no vieron la exposición de arte. (Clara siente)

2. Patricia escribió las cartas. (dudamos)

3. Carlos se hizo ciudadano. (me alegro)

4. Viste la nueva película policíaca. (esperan)

5. Murió el bisabuelo de Paco. (es una lástima)

6. Las chicas no dijeron nada. (es mejor)

7. Hubo un incendio en el metro. (nos sorprende)

8. Luz se puso brava. (no piensan)

9. Me encantó el concierto. (se alegran)

N. Exprese las siguientes oraciones en español.

1. I'm glad Julia and Paco got married.

2. It's good that a bookstore opened in this neighborhood.

3. They doubt that the Tigers won the soccer championship.

4. We hope Fernando got rich.

5. Are you (*Ud.*) surprised that the Núñez family moved?

6. Ana doesn't think the boys broke the window.

O. Ejercicio oral. ¿Qué mandan que haga? Con un compañero de clase hable de las cosas que le mandan hacer y que Ud. manda que hagan los demás. Diga en cada caso quién manda y lo que le dice a Ud. que haga. ¿A su compañero le mandan hacer las mismas cosas que a Ud.?

CHAPTER 12 THE IMPERFECT SUBJUNCTIVE & PAST PERFECT SUBJUNCTIVE; CONDITIONAL SENTENCES

Forms of the imperfect subjunctive

- The forms of the imperfect subjunctive are derived from the third-person plural form of the preterit. Any irregularity or vowel change in the stem of the third-person plural of the preterit occurs in all persons of the imperfect subjunctive: **hablaron** ➔ que yo **hablara, comieron** ➔ que yo **comiera, escribieron** ➔ que yo **escribiera, pidieron** ➔ que yo **pidiera, hicieron** ➔ que yo **hiciera, fueron** ➔ que yo **fuera, durmieron** ➔ que yo **durmiera, trajeron** ➔ que yo **trajera.** The preterit ending **-ron** is replaced by the following endings in all verbs:

-ra	Querían que	**hablara**	**comiera**	**escribiera**
-ras		**hablaras**	**comieras**	**escribieras**
-ra		**hablara**	**comiera**	**escribiera**
-ramos		**habláramos**	**comiéramos**	**escribiéramos**
-rais		**hablarais**	**comierais**	**escribierais**
-ran		**hablaran**	**comieran**	**escribieran**

Meaning: *They wanted me/you/him/her/us/them to speak/eat/write.*

- The *yo* and *él* forms are identical in the imperfect subjunctive, and the *nosotros* form has a written accent mark on the vowel before the **-r: habláramos, comiéramos, escribiéramos.**
- There is an alternate form of the imperfect subjunctive that has endings in **-se.** The **-ra** and **-se** forms are largely interchangeable, but the **-se** forms are less common in colloquial speech:

-se	Querían que	**hablase**	**comiese**	**escribiese**
-ses		**hablases**	**comieses**	**escribieses**
-se		**hablase**	**comiese**	**escribiese**
-semos		**hablásemos**	**comiésemos**	**escribiésemos**
-seis		**hablaseis**	**comieseis**	**escribieseis**
-sen		**hablasen**	**comiesen**	**escribiesen**

A. Escriba los verbos que aparecen entre paréntesis en imperfecto del subjuntivo. Escriba cada verbo con las dos desinencias (*endings*) **-ra** y **-se.**

1. Yo esperaba que Manolo ____________ / ____________ cuenta. (darse)
2. Nos alegramos que Lorna ____________ / ____________ su collar de perlas. (encontrar)

3. Rita insistió en que los niños ____________ / ____________ las botas. (ponerse)
4. No era cierto que nosotros lo ____________ / ____________. (saber)
5. Ojalá que ____________ / ____________ pescado en la carta. (haber)
6. Te aconsejaron que ____________ / ____________ derecho. (seguir)
7. Dudaban que Ud. ____________ / ____________ la siesta. (dormir)
8. No fue posible que yo los ____________ / ____________ sino hasta el jueves. (ver)
9. Habíamos querido que Uds. ____________ / ____________ con nosotros. (reunirse)
10. Le gustaría que nosotros ____________ / ____________ esta sinfonía. (oír)
11. Preferiríamos que Elena nos lo ____________ / ____________. (decir)
12. No creían que los turistas ____________ / ____________ de Inglaterra. (ser)
13. Era preciso que se ____________ / ____________ nuevas casas en las afueras. (construir)
14. Yo querría que tú ____________ / ____________ los documentos. (traer)
15. Le dijeron a Mateo que no ____________ / ____________. (irse)

B *The imperfect subjunctive in noun clauses; the sequence of tenses*

- The imperfect subjunctive is used in dependent noun clauses instead of the present subjunctive when the verb in the main clause is in the imperfect, preterit, past perfect, or conditional:

Queríamos que lo **hicieras**. *(imperfect)*	*We wanted you to do it.*
Quisimos que lo **hicieras**. *(preterit)*	*We wanted you to do it.*
Habíamos querido que lo **hicieras**. *(past perfect)*	*We had wanted you to do it.*
Querríamos que lo **hicieras**. *(conditional)*	*We would want you to do it.*

- The present subjunctive is used when the verb in the main clause is in the present, present perfect, future, or imperative:

Queremos que lo **hagas**.	*We want you to do it.*
Hemos querido que lo **hagas**.	*We've wanted you to do it.*
Querremos que lo **hagas**.	*We'll want you to do it.*

- The English equivalents of many noun clauses in Spanish are in the infinitive so they do not show the tense distinctions seen in Spanish:

Queremos que lo **hagas**.	*We want you* ***to do*** *it.*
Queríamos que lo **hicieras**.	*We wanted you* ***to do*** *it.*

- Remember that in Spanish, if the subjects of the main clause and the dependent clause are the same, the infinitive is used, not the present or imperfect subjunctive:

Queremos **hacerlo**.	*We want* ***to do it.***
Queríamos **hacerlo**.	*We wanted* ***to do it.***

- **Ojalá** used with the present subjunctive means *I hope*. **Ojalá** used with the imperfect subjunctive means *I wish*:

Ojalá que **saquen** boletos.	*I hope they'll get tickets.*
Ojalá que **sacaran** boletos.	*I wish they'd get tickets.*

- Spanish uses the imperfect subjunctive, as well as the conditional, to soften a request or suggestion. The imperfect, used only with **querer, poder**, and **deber,** is more courteous than the conditional, which is used with any verb. In English, *would* is also used to soften a request: ¿Me lo **explicarías?** ***Would you*** *explain it to me?:*

Quisiera hablar con Ud.	***I'd like*** *to speak with you.*
¿Pudiera prestármelo?	***Could you*** *lend it to me?*
Uds. debieran volver a casa.	***You ought*** *to return home.*

B. Un caso de celos. Narre la historia de dos chicos que quieren a Angélica. Cambie los verbos de la cláusula independiente según los verbos que aparecen entre paréntesis, y los verbos de las cláusulas dependientes de presente del subjuntivo a imperfecto del subjuntivo.

MODELO Felipe les **dice** a sus amigos que **salgan**. (dijo)
➔ Felipe les **dijo** a sus amigos que **salieran**.

1. Felipe les sugiere que vayan a una discoteca. (sugirió)

____

2. Felipe espera que Angélica baile con él toda la tarde. (esperaba)

____

3. Teodoro también desea que Angélica pase la tarde con él. (deseaba)

____

4. Angélica teme que los chicos tengan celos. (temía)

____

5. Es posible que Felipe y Teodoro se peleen por Angélica. (Era)

____

6. Felipe no cree que sea una buena idea ir a la discoteca. (no creía)

____

7. Felipe le propone a Angélica que vean una película. (propuso)

____

8. A Angélica le agrada que Felipe y Teodoro la quieran (agradaba), ¡pero ella estaba enamorada de Julio!

____

C. Expectativas. Cuando Timoteo fue a pasar un semestre en la Ciudad de Guatemala para estudiar español, tenía ciertas expectativas y preocupaciones sobre cómo iba a ser su experiencia. Lea lo que pensaba y escriba los verbos que aparecen entre paréntesis en imperfecto del subjuntivo.

MODELO Timoteo deseaba que la casa donde iba a vivir **quedara** (quedar) cerca de la universidad.

1. Timoteo esperaba que ____________ (haber) un chico de su edad en la familia.
2. Sentía que su mejor amigo no ____________ (ir) a la Ciudad de Guatemala también.
3. Temía que nadie ____________ (poder) comprender su español.
4. Era posible que Timoteo no ____________ (llevarse) bien con sus compañeros de clase.
5. Tenía miedo que la comida le ____________ (caer) mal.
6. Dudaba que sus profesores le ____________ (aprobar) en todas las materias.
7. Era probable que Timoteo ____________ (querer) mudarse a un hotel.

Nota cultural

Ciudad de Guatemala, *capital de Guatemala, queda a 1.500 metros sobre el nivel del mar en una meseta de la Sierra Madre. La capital fue fundada por decreto (decree) de Carlos III de España en 1776 después que un terremoto acabó con la capital anterior, Guatemala Antigua, en 1773.* ***Antigua,*** *fundada en 1543, fue una de las ciudades más atractivas de Centroamérica con una población de 60.000, varias iglesias grandes, una universidad (1680), una imprenta (1660) y famosos pintores, escultores, escritores y artesanos. Ciudad de Guatemala es actualmente uno de los lugares más populares de Hispanoamérica para aprender español y muchos estudiantes norteamericanos y canadienses pasan el verano o el año académico allí estudiando el idioma.*

D. ¿Qué tal le fue a Timoteo? Para saberlo, escriba los verbos que aparecen entre paréntesis en imperfecto del subjuntivo.

MODELO Los señores de la casa insistían en que Timoteo **se quedara** (quedarse) con ellos un mes más.

1. Era bueno que sus clases ____________ (ser) tan interesantes.

2. Timoteo se alegró que sus profesores no lo ____________________ (colgar [*to fail*]).
3. Los señores permitían que Timoteo ____________________ (salir) con su hija Aurora.
4. La madre le pidió a Timoteo que los ____________________ (acompañar) a la sierra.
5. Los hijos de la familia le rogaron a Timoteo que ____________________ (jugar) al fútbol con ellos.
6. A Timoteo le sorprendió que todos lo ____________________ (tratar) tan bien.
7. El señor dejó que Timoteo ____________________ (conducir) el coche.

E. **Vida de familia.** Describa lo que los padres esperaban que sus hijos hicieran escribiendo los verbos de las oraciones en imperfecto del subjuntivo.

MODELO Mis papás querían que nosotros **estudiáramos** mucho. (estudiar)

1. Papá esperaba que yo ____________________ ingeniero. (hacerse)
2. Mamá insistía en que nosotros ____________________ sus tradiciones. (seguir)
3. Nuestros papás nos aconsejaban que ____________________ valores tradicionales. (tener)
4. Papá prefería que Pepe ____________________ con él en la empresa. (trabajar)
5. Nuestros padres deseaban que mis hermanos y yo ____________________. (casarse)
6. A nuestros papás les era importante que nosotros ____________________ responsables, honrados y trabajadores. (ser)
7. Mamá nos pedía que ____________________ a nuestra familia. (dedicarse)
8. Papá nos decía que ____________________ los unos a los otros. (ayudarse)
9. A nuestros padres les era necesario que mis hermanas ____________________ cerca. (vivir)

F. **¡Me sobra tiempo! (*I have plenty of time!*)** Sus padres le pidieron que hiciera unas cosas para ayudarlos. Ud. creía que le sobraba tiempo para hacerlas y fue a jugar al béisbol con sus amigos. Al llegar a casa, sus padres ven que todo ha quedado sin hacer. Complete las oraciones empleando el imperfecto del subjuntivo del verbo que aparece entre paréntesis.

MODELO Hijo/Hija, yo quería que **buscaras** el correo. (buscar)

1. Hijo/Hija, te pedí que ____________________ el césped. (cortar)
2. Hijo/Hija, ¿no te dijimos que ____________________ la carne? (descongelar)
3. Hijo/Hija, te exigí que ____________________ los arbustos (*bushes*). (regar [*to water*])
4. Hijo/Hija, esperábamos que ____________________ la compra. (hacer)
5. Hijo/Hija, yo quería que ____________________ al perro. (bañar)

6. Hijo/Hija, te rogamos que ____________________ el garaje en orden. (poner)
7. Hijo/Hija, yo deseaba que ____________________ las herramientas (*tools*). (guardar)
8. Hijo/Hija, insistíamos en que ____________________ la basura. (sacar)
9. Hijo/Hija, tu hermanito necesitaba que le ____________________ su bicicleta. (reparar)

G. **¡Josefina, la muy pesada!** A Josefina no le queda ni un solo amigo porque se porta mal con todo el mundo. Para saber lo que pasó con sus amigos, escriba el imperfecto del subjuntivo de cada verbo que aparece entre paréntesis.

MODELO Josefina le pidió al novio de Lola que la **llevara** al baile. (llevar)

1. Javier le dijo a Josefina que ____________________ con Arturo. (salir)
2. A los amigos no les gustaba que Josefina les ____________________. (mentir)
3. Josefina le aconsejó a Paquita que ____________________ con su novio. (romper)
4. Sus amigos sentían que Josefina ____________________ mala lengua (*vicious tongue*). (tener)
5. Josefina exigió que Pedro ____________________ la tarea de cálculo por ella. (hacer)
6. Josefina insistió en que los chicos la ____________________ a todas sus reuniones. (invitar)
7. Los amigos no querían que Josefina les ____________________ el pelo. (tomar)
8. Josefina les impidió a los amigos que ____________________ al cine sin ella. (ir)
9. A nadie le gustaba que Josefina ____________________ a los amigos en un lío. (meter)

H. **¡Ojalá!** Ud. quiere que sucedan ciertas cosas pero duda que sea posible. Exprese lo que son esas cosas empleando el imperfecto del subjuntivo.

MODELO los primos / venir a visitarme
➔ Ojalá que los primos vinieran a visitarme.

1. yo / encontrar / las llaves del coche

____

2. Uds. / recibir / el cheque

____

3. Diana / no quejarse / de todo

____

4. servirse / la cena / antes de las diez de la noche

____

5. Bernardo y Marta / no discutir / tanto

____

6. Lorenzo / vestirse / más rápido

7. tú y yo / ocuparse / del congreso (*conference*)

8. Timoteo / mantener / a sus padres

C *The past perfect (or pluperfect) subjunctive*

- The past perfect subjunctive consists of the imperfect subjunctive of **haber** + the past participle. The most important use of the past perfect subjunctive is in conditional sentences. The past perfect subjunctive is also used to express a contrary-to-fact wish in the past after **ojalá (que).**

Ojalá (que)	hubiera sabido.	*I wish I had known.*
	hubieras sabido.	*I wish you had known.*
	hubiera sabido.	*I wish she had known.*
	hubiéramos sabido.	*I wish we had known.*
	hubierais sabido.	*I wish you had known.*
	hubieran sabido.	*I wish they had known.*

- The past perfect subjunctive is used instead of the present perfect subjunctive to indicate that the action of the dependent clause happens before the action of the main clause when the main clause is in the preterit, imperfect, or conditional.

I. Escriba oraciones empleando la frase que aparece entre paréntesis en la cláusula principal y el verbo de la cláusula dependiente en pluscuamperfecto del subjuntivo.

MODELO Néstor había ganado la lotería. (esperábamos)
→ **Esperábamos** que Néstor **hubiera ganado** la lotería.

1. Jorge había llegado a ser arquitecto. (era bueno)

2. Las hermanas Cela habían hecho un viaje a Santo Domingo. (nos gustó)

3. Uds. se habían quedado tanto tiempo. (me extrañó)

4. Tú habías comprado una pulsera de oro. (esperaban)

5. Yo había asistido a la conferencia en Roma. (era importante)

6. Juan y yo nos habíamos comprometido. (todos se alegraron)

Nota cultural

Santo Domingo, capital de la República Dominicana, es la más antigua de las ciudades americanas fundadas por los conquistadores. Fue fundada en 1496 por Bartolomé Colón, un hermano de Cristóbal Colón. La ciudad fue modernizada después que un huracán la dejó casi totalmente destruida, pero conserva cierto carácter colonial con sus muchos edificios y monumentos de interés histórico.

J. Expresé las siguientes oraciones en español.

1. You (*tú*) were hoping that they had been successful.

____

2. They were afraid that someone had told me.

____

3. We were sorry that you (*Ud.*) hadn't heard what happened.

____

4. Sarita doubted that we had come back from the country.

____

5. I was glad that it had been warm and sunny.

____

6. I wish you (*Uds.*) had told us as soon as possible.

____

D *Conditional sentences*

- In Spanish and English, conditional sentences include two clauses: a **si-**clause (*if-*clause) and a main clause. Both languages use similar tenses for the two clauses. The **si-**clause may come before or after the main clause.
- Possible conditions are expressed in both languages by using the present in the **si-**clause and the future in the main clause:

***si**-clause*	*main clause*	
Si vas, *(present)*	**yo iré** también. *(future)*	*If you go, I'll go too.*

- To express a condition that is contrary to a fact or situation in present time, Spanish uses the imperfect subjunctive in the **si-**clause and the conditional in the main clause:

***si**-clause*	*main clause*	
Si fueras, *(imperfect subjunctive)*	**yo iría** también. *(conditional)*	*If you were going, I'd go too.*

The sentence **Si fueras, yo iría también** expresses a condition that is *contrary-to-fact*. The fact is that *tú no vas* and the result is that *yo no voy*. The meaning is **(Pero) si fueras** (*But if you were going, which you're not*), **yo iría** también (*I'd go too*).

- Spanish expresses a condition that is contrary to a fact or situation in past time by using the past perfect subjunctive in the **si**-clause and the conditional perfect *or* the past perfect subjunctive in the main clause:

***si**-clause*	*main clause*	
Si hubieras ido, **Si hubieras ido,**	**yo habría ido** también. **yo hubiera ido** también.	*If you had gone, I would have gone too.*

K. Todo está pendiente (*up in the air*). Complete las siguientes oraciones llenando los espacios en blanco con la forma correcta del verbo que aparece entre paréntesis. El verbo de la cláusula que empieza con **si** está en el presente de indicativo.

MODELO Si Uds. **van** (ir), yo los **veré** (ver).

1. Si yo ____________________ (poder), los ____________________ (visitar).
2. Si ellos le ____________________ (ofrecer) el puesto a Daniel, lo ____________________ (aceptar).
3. Pepita y yo ____________________ (salir) si ____________________ tiempo. (tener)
4. Si Mario me ____________________ (llamar), yo se lo ____________________ (decir).
5. Si tú ____________________ (poner) la mesa , Isabel y Leo ____________________ (hacer) la cena.
6. ____________________ (Haber) mucha gente en la playa si ____________________ (hacer) un gran calor.
7. Tú ____________________ (tener) hambre si no ____________________ (comer) algo ahora.
8. Si Uds. no le ____________________ (preguntar) a Carlos, no lo ____________________ (saber).
9. Todos nosotros ____________________ (venir) en taxi si no ____________________ (haber) lugar en el coche de Manuel.

L. Si fuera posible ... Complete las siguientes oraciones llenando los espacios en blanco con la forma correcta del verbo que aparece entre paréntesis. El verbo de la cláusula que empieza con **si** está en imperfecto del subjuntivo.

MODELO Si **fuera** (ser) posible, nosotros **iríamos** (ir).

1. Si yo ____________________ (tener) tiempo, ____________________ (hacer) un viaje a todos los países del mundo.
2. Los Madariaga ____________________ (venir) a visitarnos si nosotros los ____________________ (invitar).
3. Laura ____________________ (ver) esa obra de teatro si ____________________ (haber) entradas.

4. Si Diego ____________________ (ganar) la lotería, ____________________ (comprarse) un coche deportivo.
5. Si ____________________ (hacer) mucho viento, nosotros ____________________ (salir) con la cometa (*kite*).
6. Daniel ____________________ (dormir) la siesta si ____________________ (sentirse) cansado.
7. Si tú ____________________ (poder), ____________________ (resolver) el problema.
8. Uds. ____________________ (salir) más temprano si ____________________ (ser) posible, ¿no?
9. Si Ana María y Esteban ____________________ (saber) los motivos, se los ____________________ (decir) a Uds.

M. **Cuentos de hadas.** Recuerde lo que pasa en estos cuentos de hadas (*fairy tales*) llenando los espacios en blanco con la forma correcta del verbo que aparece entre paréntesis. El verbo de la cláusula que empieza con **si** emplea el imperfecto del subjuntivo.

MODELO Si Ricitos de Oro no **se durmiera** (dormirse) en la cama del osito, los tres osos no la **verían** (ver).

1. «Si yo ____________________ (encontrar) a la señorita que perdió la zapatilla de cristal, ____________________ (casarse) con ella», pensó el príncipe.
2. «Si una princesa me ____________________ (besar), yo ____________________ (dejar) de ser sapo (*toad*) y ____________________ (convertirse) en príncipe».
3. «Si ____________________ (haber) un guisante debajo de mi colchón, yo lo ____________________ (notar)», se dijo la princesa.
4. «Si Hansel y Gretel ____________________ (venir) a mi casa, yo me los ____________________ (comer)», pensó la bruja.
5. «Si yo no ____________________ (mentir), no se me ____________________ (crecer) la nariz», se dijo Pinocho.
6. «Si yo le ____________________ (dar) un beso a la bella durmiente, ella ____________________ (despertarse)», se dijo el príncipe.
7. «Si la reina no ____________________ (tener) celos de mí, no ____________________ (tener) que vivir con los siete enanos», pensó Blancanieves.
8. «Si yo ____________________ (soplar) fuerte, ____________________ (derrumbar) la casa de los tres cerditos», pensó el lobo.

N. **¡Viajes soñados!** El verbo de la cláusula que empieza con **si** está en imperfecto del subjuntivo y la cláusula principal en condicional.

1. Si yo ____________________ (ir) a Costa Rica, me ____________________ (gustar) entrar en los bosques nacionales.
2. Si Graciela y Miguel ____________________ (hacer) un viaje al Brasil, ____________________ (ir) para el Carnaval.
3. Si Uds. ____________________ (poder) visitar Uruguay ____________________ (quedarse) en Montevideo.
4. Si nosotros ____________________ (pasar) las vacaciones en Puerto Rico, ____________________ (tomar) el sol en la playa de Dorado.
5. Si tú ____________________ (visitar) Venezuela, ____________________ (probar) sancocho, arepas y cachapas.
6. Si Felipe ____________________ (querer) viajar al Ecuador, ____________________ (conocer) Quito.

Nota cultural

- Hay mucho ecoturismo en **Costa Rica** gracias a su red de bosques nacionales. En el de Monteverde, por ejemplo, hay más de 400 especies de aves (incluso el quetzal), monos, jaguares, pumas, reptiles y otros animales, 2.500 especies de plantas y más de 6.000 especies de insectos.

- **El Carnaval** es el período de diversiones que empieza el día de los Reyes y termina el martes anterior al miércoles de Ceniza (*Ash Wednesday*). Se celebra por toda Latinoamérica. El de Río de Janeiro es el más célebre.

- **Montevideo**, capital del Uruguay, es la única ciudad grande del país. Fue fundada por los españoles en 1726 como fortaleza contra los portugueses. Queda a orillas del río de la Plata, frente a Buenos Aires.

- **Dorado** es una hermosa playa de Puerto Rico. Queda en el océano Atlántico cerca de San Juan.

- El sancocho, las arepas y las cachapas son platos típicos de Venezuela. El **sancocho** es un guisado de yuca y legumbres con carne, pollo o pescado. Las **arepas** son un pan de maíz blanco y las **cachapas** son tortillas blandas de maíz. Las dos se llenan de un queso blanco u otras cosas.

- **Quito,** capital de Ecuador, queda a 25 kilómetros de la línea ecuatorial. Sin embargo, esta cuidad colonial, la segunda capital más alta de Latinoamérica, goza de días calurosos y noches frescas por su altitud. Quito era una ciudad del Imperio Inca cuando fue tomado en 1534 por los tenientes de Pizarro.

O. **Si hubiera sido posible ...** Complete las siguientes oraciones llenando los espacios en blanco con la forma correcta del verbo que aparece entre paréntesis. El verbo de la cláusula que empieza con **si** está en pluscuamperfecto del subjuntivo. El verbo de la cláusula principal aparece en potencial compuesto (*conditional perfect*) o en pluscuamperfecto del subjuntivo.

MODELO Si **hubiera sido** (ser) posible, nosotros **habríamos ido** (ir).
Si **hubiera sido** (ser) posible, nosotros **hubiéramos ido** (ir).

1. Si Uds. nos ____________ (preguntar), les ____________ / ____________ (decir).
2. Yo te ____________ / ____________ (devolver) la cartera si te ____________ (ver).
3. Si Jaime ____________ (hacerse) médico, ____________ / ____________ (estar) más contento.
4. Eva y yo ____________ / ____________ (llamar) en seguida si lo ____________ (saber).
5. Si yo ____________ (jugar) béisbol en el parque, no ____________ / ____________ (romper) la ventana de la casa.

P. **¿Campo o ciudad?** Pablo se crió en el campo, su primo Gregorio en la ciudad. Hablan de las maneras en las cuales hubiera sido diferente su vida si Pablo se hubiera criado en la ciudad y Gregorio en el campo. El verbo de la cláusula que empieza con **si** está en pluscuamperfecto del subjuntivo. El verbo de la cláusula principal aparece en potencial compuesto (*conditional perfect*) o en pluscuamperfecto del subjuntivo.

MODELO Pablo: estudiar en un colegio grande / criarse en la ciudad
➔ Pablo **habría/hubiera estudiado** en un colegio grande si **se hubiera criado** en la ciudad.

1. Pablo: asistir al teatro / vivir en la ciudad

____

2. Gregorio: ordeñar (*to milk*) las vacas / nacer en una finca

____

3. Pablo: ponerse más nervioso / oír tanto ruido todos los días

____

4. Gregorio: respirar aire no contaminado / vivir en el campo

____

5. Pablo: tomar el metro y los taxis / trabajar en la ciudad

____

6. Gregorio: aprender a montar a caballo / viajar por el campo

____

7. Pablo: comprar comida en el supermercado / ir de compras en la ciudad

____

8. Gregorio: comer frutas y legumbres muy frescas / criarse en el campo

____

9. Pablo: llevar un traje, camisa y corbata / ganarse la vida en una empresa

____

10. Gregorio: usar un sombrero de paja (*straw*) / cultivar la tierra

____

Q. **¡Julio el tardón (*slow poke*)!** A Julio le lleva tanto tiempo hacer cosas que siempre llega tarde a sus citas. Acaba de llegar a la fiesta de sus amigos. En vez de ver una fiesta, despierta a su amigo Memo que le explica que la fiesta terminó a las dos de la mañana. Julio piensa en cómo le habría salido si hubiera llegado antes. El verbo de la cláusula que empieza con **si** está en pluscuamperfecto del subjuntivo y el de la cláusula principal está en potencial compuesto (*conditional perfect*) o en pluscuamperfecto del subjuntivo.

MODELO Si yo **hubiera llegado** (llegar) antes, **habría/hubiera visto** (ver) a mis amigos.

1. Si yo ____________ (terminar) mi trabajo para las diez, ____________ (poder) llegar a tiempo.
2. Si yo ____________ (planear) mejor mi horario, no me ____________ (perder) la fiesta.
3. Si yo ____________ (hacer) mi trabajo más eficazmente, ____________ (bailar) con Julieta, la mujer de mis sueños.
4. Si yo no ____________ (gastar) tanto tiempo echándome agua de colonia, ____________ (disfrutar) de una comida rica.
5. Si yo ____________ (manejar) más rápido, no ____________ (atrasarse).
6. Si mis amigos ____________ (divertirse) más, ellos ____________ (quedarse) hasta las tres de la mañana.
7. Si Memo no ____________ (acostarse) de inmediato, yo no ____________ (tener) que tocar el timbre cien veces.

R. Exprese las siguientes oraciones en español.

1. If Victoria had had the key she would have opened the suitcase.

____

2. If you (*Ud.*) were to take a trip this summer, where would you go?

____

3. If they had been more careful, they wouldn't have lost their traveler's checks.

____

4. If you (*Uds.*) turn right at the corner, you'll see the museum.

____

5. I would pay attention to Roberto if he gave good advice.

____

S. Ejercicio oral. Converse con otros estudiantes sobre lo que harían en cada caso. Pregúnteles, por ejemplo: ¿Qué harías si tuvieras un millón de dólares? Si tuvieras un año de vacaciones, ¿adónde irías?, etcétera.

T. Estructuras en acción. Lea los comentarios sobre los exámenes finales en España y luego haga el ejercicio.

Vocabulario

agobiarse *to get tired*
el agobio *exhaustion, worry*
el aliado *ally*
el aprobado *passing grade*
aprobar (o > ue) *to pass an exam*
la autoconfianza *self-confidence*
la chuleta *(slang) cheating on exam*
dar de sí *to do one's best*
dar palo al agua *(here) to study, work*
el dominio *mastery, good knowledge*
el enemigo *enemy*
el esquema *outline*
lo hecho, hecho está *what's done is done*
insoportable *unbearable*
la materia *subject*
la pesadilla *nightmare*
procurar *to try*
reñir *to scold*
la selectividad *selective course taken before technical studies in university*
sobresaliente *excellent grade*
suspender *to fail*
el tema *question (on an exam)*
el temario *exam questions*
tumbado *lying down*
vago *lazy*

Exámenes: La prueba final

El curso se acaba y estudiantes y padres sufren los agobios de los exámenes finales. El mejor aliado para aprobar es la autoconfianza, además del dominio de la materia. El peor enemigo son los nervios.

Hablan los estudiantes:

"No me gusta memorizar" (*Silvia Rivero, 17 años*)

"Intento comprender los temas, no me gusta memorizar. Me hago esquemas, leo, procuro entender y escribo los temas porque así se te quedan mejor. Pongo en común los temas con la gente de clase y, si no entendemos algo, nos llamamos por teléfono. Mi madre me dice que me tranquilice y que 'lo hecho, hecho está'. Me pongo insoportable, no hay quien me hable".

"La selectividad es lo más difícil del mundo" (*Carlos Gustavo García, 18 años*)

"Soy tranquilo para los exámenes, pero con la selectividad me pongo muy nervioso: es lo más difícil que hay. Tengo miedo de que me pregunten cosas que no han entrado en el temario. Las *chuletas* no ayudan".

"Tengo pesadillas" (*Silvia Heredia, 15 años*)

"Ante los exámenes me pongo muy nerviosa, muy nerviosa. Tomo mucho café y tengo pesadillas: sueño con los exámenes. Para estudiar copio los temas en un papel y luego me lo voy preguntando o le pido a mi madre que me lo pregunte ella. Estudio de todas las formas posibles: tumbada, de pie, andando ... Pero siempre estudio sola, porque hablo mucho y si no, me distraigo".

Hablan los padres:

"No hay quien le hable" (*Josefa Sánchez*)

"Tengo dos hijos estudiando. Beatriz está muy nerviosa y se agobia mucho. Hasta que no acabe los exámenes no hay quien le hable. Mi marido es psicólogo y les dice a nuestros hijos que se tranquilicen y que no se agobien".

"No me gusta que estudie tanto" (*Germana Baile*)

"Mi hijo José Jorge está en segundo curso de Telecomunicaciones. Estudia demasiadas horas y hay que reñirle para que salga. La verdad, no me gusta que estudie tanto".

"Sólo les exijo lo que puedan dar de sí" (*Benito de Lucas*)

"Sólo les exijo lo que puedan dar de sí. Me da igual que saquen sobresalientes o aprobados. Si suspenden tampoco pasa nada. Lo que quiero es que trabajen, porque los buenos resultados vienen solos".

"Son un poco vagos" (*Carmen Martín*)

"Está claro que los que se ponen nerviosos es porque no han estudiado. Los que no han dado palo al agua en todo el curso es imposible que puedan aprobar, aunque se tomen cosas de la farmacia como hacen algunos. Yo les digo a mis hijos que no se preocupen porque otros saquen un 10 y ellos no. Pero la verdad es que son un poco vagos y podrían sacar más".

Empareje las cláusulas subordinadas (dependientes) con sus cláusulas independientes como ocurren en los comentarios. Use el subjuntivo, el indicativo o el infinitivo según sean necesarios.

A

1. Yo les digo a mis hijos __________
2. Le pido a mi madre __________
3. Me da igual __________
4. Tengo miedo de __________
5. Procuro __________
6. Lo que quiero __________
7. No me gusta __________
8. Es imposible __________
9. Mi madre me dice __________
10. Intento __________
11. Les dice a nuestros hijos __________
12. Les exijo __________
13. Hay que reñirle __________
14. La verdad es __________

B

a. que no se agobien
b. lo que puedan dar de sí
c. comprender los temas
d. memorizar
e. que no se preocupen porque otros saquen un 10
f. para que salga
g. que puedan aprobar
h. que saquen sobresalientes o aprobados
i. entender
j. que me lo pregunte ella
k. es que trabajen
l. que me tranquilice
m. que son un poco vagos
n. que me pregunten cosas que no han entrado en el temario

CHAPTER 13 THE SUBJUNCTIVE: ADVERB & ADJECTIVE CLAUSES

A Adverb clauses that require the subjunctive

- A clause that modifies a verb the way an adverb does is called an adverb clause. Compare the use of adverbs and adverb clauses in the following pairs of sentences:

Salimos **temprano**.	*We went out **early**.*
Salimos **cuando terminamos**.	*We went out **when we finished**.*
Cantaron **bien**.	*They sang **well**.*
Cantaron **como les habían enseñado**.	*They sang **as they had been taught**.*

- Adverb clauses are introduced by conjunctions, such as **cuando** and **como** in the above examples. The following conjunctions introduce adverb clauses in which the verb must be in the subjunctive: **a fin de que** (*in order that, so that*), **a menos que** (*unless*), **antes (de) que** (*before*), **con tal (de) que** (*provided that*), **en caso de que** (*in case*), **para que** (*so that*), **sin que,** (*without*). The same sequence-of-tense rules apply in adverb clauses as in noun clauses:

Saldré **antes de que** vuelvan.	*I'll leave before they get back.*
Salí **antes de que** volvieran.	*I left before they got back.*
Tito va a comprar huevos **para que** hagamos la torta.	*Tito's going to buy eggs so we can make the cake.*
Tito compró los huevos **para que** hiciéramos la torta.	*Tito bought eggs so that we might make the cake.*
Escondemos el regalo **sin que** Olga sepa dónde.	*We're hiding the gift without Olga knowing where.*
Escondimos el regalo **sin que** Olga supiera dónde.	*We hid the gift without Olga knowing where.*

- **A menos que** and **con tal (de) que** are followed by the present subjunctive if the action of the dependent (subordinate) clause occurs *at the same time* as the action of the main clause. They are followed by the present perfect subjunctive if the action of the dependent clause occurs *before* the action of the main clause:

Estudiará matemáticas con tal que le **devuelvas** su libro.	*He'll study math provided that you return his book to him.*
Estudiará matemáticas con tal que le **hayas devuelto** su libro.	*He'll study math provided that you've returned his book to him.*

B Adverb clauses with indicative or subjunctive

- Certain conjunctions are followed by the indicative when the action of the dependent or subordinate clause is considered a known or established fact. They are followed by the subjunctive when the action of the dependent clause is considered uncertain or indefinite. In these dependent clauses with subjunctive, the conjunction often has the English equivalent of *ever* attached to it, as in *whenever, however, wherever.* These conjunctions include: **como** (*how*), **aunque** (*although, even though*), **según** (*according to*), **donde** (*where*), **mientras** (*while*), **de manera que** (*so that*), **de modo que** (*so that*):

Iremos **donde** tú **quieres**.	*We'll go* ***where*** *you want. (We know where you want to go.)*
Iremos **donde** tú **quieras**.	*We'll go* ***wherever*** *you want to go. (We don't know yet where you want to go.)*
Hágalo **como** ellos **dicen**.	*Do it* ***how (the way)*** *they say. (I know the way they say.)*
Hágalo **como** ellos **digan**.	*Do it* ***however*** *they say. (I don't know the way they say.)*
Aunque va Elena, yo no voy.	***Even though Elena is going,*** *I'm not going. (I know Elena is going.)*
Aunque vaya Elena, yo no voy.	***Even though Elena may go,*** *I'm not going.*

- Adverb clauses introduced by conjunctions of time such as **después (de) que** (*after*), **cuando** (*when*), **hasta que** (*until*), **tan pronto (como)** (*as soon as*), **en cuanto** (*as soon as*), **luego que** (*as soon as*), and **así que** (*as soon as*), are followed by the subjunctive when the main clause refers to the future or is a command:

Me quedaré **hasta que terminemos**.	*I'll stay until we finish.*
Díselo **cuando lleguen**.	*Tell it to them when they arrive.*

- If the action of the dependent clause is considered to be a habitual occurrence, the indicative, not the subjunctive, is used:

Se lo das **cuando llegan**.	*You (usually) give it to them when they arrive.*
Me quedo **hasta que terminamos**.	*I (usually) stay until we finish.*

- When the sentence relates a past action, the indicative is used after the conjunction of time as the event in the adverbial clause is considered to be part of reality:

Se lo dijiste **cuando llegaron**.	*You told it to them when they arrived.*
Me quedé **hasta que terminamos**.	*I stayed until we finished.*

- The conjunction of time **antes (de) que** is an exception because it is *always* followed by the subjunctive even when the verb of the main clause is in a past tense:

Nora **mandó** la carta **antes que** Pablo la **llamara**.	*Nora sent the letter before Pablo called her.*

- If the subject of the main clause and the dependent clause is the same, the clause is replaced by an infinitive:

Estudien ***hasta que Beti lo entienda.***	*Study until Beti understands it.*
Estudien ***hasta entenderlo.***	*Study until you understand it.*
Voy a leer *antes que juguemos* **tenis.**	*I'm going to read before we play tennis.*
Voy a leer *antes de jugar* **tenis.**	*I'm going to read before (playing) I play tennis.*
Salimos ***sin que Uds. almorzaran.***	*We went out without your having lunch.*
Salimos ***sin almorzar.***	*We went out without having lunch.*

A. No se sabe todavía. Diga que Ud. no sabe cómo son las cosas mencionadas completando las oraciones con las palabras que faltan en las cláusulas adverbiales. Se debe usar el presente del subjuntivo de los verbos.

1. Lo haré según Uds. ______________________. (mandar)
2. Viviremos donde Pepita ______________________. (aconsejar)
3. Aunque ______________________ habrá un partido de fútbol. (llover)
4. Guillermo quiere pintar los cuadros donde ______________________ mucha luz. (haber)
5. Realizarán el proyecto como tú ______________________. (querer)
6. Voy a leer el informe aunque no ______________________ muy interesante. (ser)
7. Vicente comerá donde Ud. ______________________. (preferir)
8. Prepara el plato según nosotros ______________________. (decir)
9. Van al cine aunque yo no ______________________. (ir)

B. Haciendo las diligencias (*Running errands*). Explique que algunas personas hicieron ciertas cosas **antes de que** otras personas hicieran otras. Use el pretérito para el verbo de la cláusula principal y el imperfecto del subjuntivo para la cláusula adverbial.

Las tiendas

la carnicería *butcher shop*
la cita *appointment, date*
el correo *post office*
la droguería *drugstore*
los frenos *brakes*
la gasolinera *gas station*
la joyería *jewelry store*
el lavado *wash*
la lavandería *laundry*
la librería *bookstore*
el mecánico *mechanic*
la pastelería *pastry shop*
la peluquería *beauty salon, barber shop*
reparar *to repair*
el sello *stamp*
la tintorería *dry cleaner's*
la zapatería *shoe store*

MODELO Marta / ir a la pastelería : yo / ir a la carnicería
→ Marta fue a la pastelería **antes de que yo fuera** a la carnicería.

1. Elena y Mario / salir de la gasolinera : nosotros / entrar en la zapatería

____

____

2. Ud. / llevar el lavado a la lavandería : yo / volver a la droguería

____

____

3. Uds. / comprar los sellos : Consuelo / poder ir al correo

____

____

4. Fernando y yo / no hablar con el mecánico : él / repararnos los frenos

____

____

5. yo / sacar la ropa de la tintorería : Juana / tener su cita en la peluquería

____

____

6. tú / ir a la joyería : Arturo y Paco / buscar una librería

____

____

Nota cultural

- En el centro de las ciudades de habla hispana, se hace **la compra** tradicionalmente en las tiendas especializadas. La panadería, la carnicería, la pastelería, la tienda de comestibles, la lechería, la frutería son lugares frecuentados en los barrios antiguos. Todo el mundo conoce a los dueños de estas tiendas y a sus empleados. Sin embargo, el nuevo sistema de supermercados e hipermercados hace competencia con las tiendas tradicionales y poco a poco las va reemplazando. Ya en pleno centro se encuentran supermercados donde se vende todo.

- Hoy día hay mucha construcción de nuevas urbanizaciones y **centros comerciales** fuera de las ciudades. Estos centros de múltiples comercios, restaurantes y cines son muy atractivos y ya que todos tienen coche, es probable que mucha gente abandone las tiendas céntricas por el centro comercial.

- En las zonas rurales de Hispanoamérica, **el mercado campesino** que se realiza en los pueblos los domingos por la tarde es el centro para la compra de comida y también una institución social de mucha importancia.

C. Complete las siguientes oraciones llenando los espacios en blanco con la forma correcta del verbo que aparece entre paréntesis. Escoja entre el indicativo y el subjuntivo (en presente o imperfecto).

MODELO No queremos ir al museo sin que tú **vayas.** (ir)

1. Llamaré a Julio para que él ____________________ lo que está pasando. (saber)
2. Se quedaron hasta que Federico ____________________. (venir)
3. Iremos al centro comercial a menos que Uds. nos ____________________. (necesitar)
4. Le presté el dinero a Marisol para que ____________________ comprarse el vestido. (poder)

5. Tú puedes venir a la casa sin que nosotros te ____________________. (invitar)
6. Los vimos tan pronto como nosotros ____________________ en la librería. (entrar)
7. No pensaban salir sin que mamá les ____________________ de comer. (dar)
8. Carmen se puso de pie en cuanto ____________________ la conferencia. (terminar)
9. Hazme saber cuando ____________________ los paquetes. (llegar)
10. Los muchachos iban al cine a menos que Clarita no ____________________ ganas de ver la película. (tener)
11. Hice el desayuno después que (yo) ____________________. (ducharse)
12. Uds. jugarán al béisbol así que ____________________ la tarea. (hacer)

D. Exprese las siguientes oraciones en español.

1. I'll call them when I get to the airport.

____

2. We'll watch the soccer match until it begins to rain.

____

3. Consuelo set the table an hour before her friends arrived.

____

4. They stood in line at the box office after they had lunch.

____

5. You (*Ud.*) didn't want to go shopping without our going too.

____

6. Do it (*Uds.*) whichever way they want.

____

7. Even though it's cold out, we should take a walk.

____

8. I'll lend you (*tú*) the book so that you won't have to take it out of the library.

____

9. Carlos is going to study for his exam before playing tennis.

____

C Adjective clauses that require the subjunctive

- An adjective clause modifies a noun the way an adjective does. All relative clauses are adjective clauses. In the example, **una obra que se titula *Don Quijote*, "que se titula *Don Quijote*"** modifies **obra** the way that **maravillosa** does in **una obra maravillosa.** The noun modified by an adjective clause is called the antecedent. Thus, **obra** is the antecedent of the **que**-clause.
- In Spanish, there are two types of antecedents—those considered part of reality, definite or existent, and those that are not part of reality, indefinite or nonexistent. In the sentence **Tenemos un profesor que habla chino**, the antecedent, **un profesor,** is a definite person who can be identified by name. Therefore, the indicative **habla** is used.
- For adjective clauses that modify antecedents that are not part of reality or the speaker's experience, the subjunctive is used. These include indefinite, undetermined, and negative antecedents:

Buscamos un profesor que **hable** chino.	*We're looking for a professor who speaks Chinese.*
Queremos un profesor que **hable** chino.	*We want a professor who speaks Chinese.*
Necesitamos un profesor que **hable** chino.	*We need a professor who speaks Chinese.*
No conozco a nadie que **hable** vasco.	*I don't know anyone who speaks Basque.*
No hay revista que le **guste**.	*There's no magazine he likes.*

- Note that **buscar, querer, necesitar,** and other such verbs may also have direct objects that are definite and identifiable. In this case, adjective clauses that modify these objects are in the *indicative*. In the example below, the professor being sought is known to the speakers:

Buscamos al profesor que **habla** chino.	*We're looking for the professor who speaks Chinese.*
Necesitamos al profesor que **habla** chino.	*We need the professor who speaks Chinese.*

- The sequence-of-tense rules apply in adjective clauses also:

Quiero una novela que **tenga** un buen argumento.	***I want** a novel that **has** a good plot.*
Quería una novela que **tuviera** un buen argumento.	***I wanted** a novel that **had** a good plot.*
No hay casa que les **guste.**	***There's no** house they **like.***
No había casa que les **gustara.**	***There was no** house they **liked.***

- In addition to **que,** other relative words such as **donde** and **quien** can introduce adjective clauses:

Buscan una florería **donde vendan** tulipanes.	*They're looking for a florist **where they sell** tulips.*
Tere quería un amigo **con quien pudiera** jugar tenis.	*Tere wanted a friend **with whom she could** play tennis.*

E. Se busca apartamento. Escriba oraciones que describan el apartamento que Ud. y sus amigos esperan encontrar. Use el presente de subjuntivo en la cláusula adjetival y el presente de indicativo en la cláusula principal.

MODELO nosotros / buscar un apartamento / tener cuatro dormitorios
→ Nosotros buscamos un apartamento que tenga cuatro dormitorios.

1. tú / querer un apartamento / tener dos baños

____

2. Mateo / necesitar un apartamento / donde / haber aire acondicionado

____

3. Javier y yo / buscar un apartamento / estar cerca de la universidad

____

4. Uds. / necesitar un apartamento / no costar un ojo de la cara (*not cost an arm and a leg*)

____

5. yo / querer un apartamento / no necesitar renovación

____

6. Pepe y Leo / desear un apartamento / ser moderno y fácil de limpiar

____

7. Octavio / buscar un apartamento / dar a una calle poco transitada (*a street with little traffic*)

____

8. Ud. / necesitar un apartamento / donde / caber todos los fiesteros (*party-lovers*)

____

F. ¡Mi novia ideal! Para saber lo que Esteban le cuenta a su amigo Felipe sobre la mujer ideal que busca, complete las cláusulas adjetivales de las oraciones con el presente del subjuntivo del verbo que aparece entre paréntesis.

1. Busco una novia que _______________ ser una buena amiga. (saber)
2. Quiero una chica con quien _______________ hablar fácilmente. (poder)
3. Me hace falta una mujer que me _______________. (comprender)
4. Quiero tener una novia con quien yo _______________. (divertirse)
5. Necesito una chica que _______________ inteligente. (ser)
6. Estoy buscando una novia que _______________ un buen sentido del humor. (tener)

G. **¡No hay candidatas al puesto! (*There are no candidates for the job!*)** Por desgracia, Felipe no puede ayudar a Esteban porque no tiene amigas que tengan todas estas cualidades. Complete las cláusulas adjetivales de las oraciones con el presente de subjuntivo del verbo que aparece entre paréntesis.

1. No conozco a ninguna chica que ____________________ todas estas características. (reunir)
2. No hay nadie que ____________________ tan perfecta. (ser)
3. No conozco a ninguna mujer con quien tú ____________________ salir. (querer)
4. No hay ninguna que te ____________________ a interesar mucho. (ir)
5. No conozco a ninguna muchacha que ____________________ un cociente intelectual (*I.Q.*) tan alto. (tener)
6. ¡No hay ninguna chica que ____________________ de ti en cuanto te vea! (enamorarse)

H. **¡En la cumbre! (*At the top of the ladder!*)** Hacía varios años que Manuel trepaba en los peldaños del éxito hasta llegar a la cumbre. Ahora es presidente de su propia empresa internacional y conoce el éxito y la prosperidad. A veces Manuel se pone a pensar en el pasado. Complete las cláusulas adjetivales con el imperfecto del subjuntivo del verbo que aparece entre paréntesis para saber cómo eran las cosas.

Los negocios

compartir *to share*
confiar en *to trust*
la cumbre *the top*
el dineral *fortune, a lot of money*
la empresa *firm, company*
esforzarse por *to strive to, try hard to*
el éxito *success*
la fama *name, reputation*
el horario de trabajo *work schedule*
invertir *to invest*
los peldaños del éxito *ladder of success*
la prosperidad *prosperity*
realizar *to achieve*
trepar *to climb*

1. Yo buscaba una profesión que me ____________________ un dineral, fama y felicidad. (dar)
2. No había nadie que ____________________ más que yo por conseguir el éxito. (esforzarse)
3. Yo quería tener un horario de trabajo que me ____________________ pasar mucho tiempo con mi familia. (permitir)
4. Yo necesitaba una esposa que ____________________ mis ideas y opiniones sobre la vida. (compartir)
5. No conocía a nadie que ____________________ más plata en su compañía que yo. (invertir)
6. No había ninguna persona que ____________________ de vacaciones menos que yo. (ir)
7. Me hacían falta unos empleados en quienes ____________________ confiar. (poder)

8. ¡Mi esposa y yo buscábamos una casa donde ____________ mucho lugar para mi oficina y para los niños! (haber)
9. Yo quería tener una empresa donde se ____________ mis ambiciones. (realizar)

Nota cultural

En muchos países hispánicos las letras **S.A.** aparecen tras el nombre de una empresa. S.A. es la abreviatura de **Sociedad Anónima,** el equivalente en español de *Inc.*

D *Adjective clauses with indicative or subjunctive*

- In Spanish, a noun may be followed by a relative clause beginning with **que** that has a verb either in the indicative or the subjunctive. If the indicative is used, it suggests that the antecedent has already been identified. If the relative clause is in the subjunctive, it suggests that the antecedent has not been identified:

Traigo la torta que **quieres.** *(Yo sé cuál de las tortas te gustó.)*	*I'll bring the cake you want. (I know which of the cakes you liked.)*
Escoge la torta que **quieras.** *(Yo no conozco tus gustos.)*	*Choose the cake you want. (I don't know your tastes.)*

- The meaning of the subjunctive in these adjective clauses can be conveyed in English by words ending in *-ever:*

Iremos a la hora que tú **digas.**	*We'll go at* ***whatever*** *time you say.*
Ceno en el restaurante que ellos **quieran.**	*I'll have dinner in* ***whichever*** *restaurant they want.*

I. Exprese las siguientes oraciones en español.

1. Mario and Carmen are looking for a house that has nine rooms.

____

2. There's no food that he likes!

____

3. I wanted a friend who would go to museums with me.

____

4. Don't you (*Ud.*) know anyone who's arriving before three o'clock?

____

5. Rosa will prepare whatever dish we choose.

____

6. They needed a secretary who worked on Saturdays.

____

7. We'll take the class with whichever professor teaches best.

____

J. Ejercicio oral. Con tres o cuatro compañeros de clase, complete oraciones con cláusulas adjetivales como: Busco unos(as) profesores(as) que ..., Quiero un novio (una novia) que ..., Necesito unos amigos que ..., etcétera.

K. Estructuras en acción. Lea los anuncios y haga el ejercicio que les sigue.

Costa Cruceros

Navegamos para divertirte.

Éstas pueden ser las vacaciones más divertidas de tu vida, o las más aburridas. Depende de si vienes o no.

Depende de las ganas que tengas de divertirte en Grecia. Porque hay muchas formas de conocerla. Pero ninguna tan mágica y diferente como a bordo del Costa Classica o del Costa Riviera. Dos hoteles flotantes de lujo con los que podrás descubrir lo mejor de las costas griegas. Y todo de una forma que jamás imaginaste. Este verano lo más fácil es pasárselo bien. Ven a Grecia con nosotros.

Tele ABC

Siempre junto a su televisor Tele ABC

Toda la información de todas las televisiones para que usted elija cómodamente su programación. Novedades, entrevistas y reportajes en TELEABC, cada fin de semana, sin aumento de precio, con *ABC* y *Blanco y Negro.*

SEAT

En la vida hay oportunidades que no puedes dejar escapar.

Este mes, el Seat Ibiza que tú quieras por sólo 9.900 Ptas. al mes, durante el primer año.

Olivetti

Le damos 50.000 ptas. por su viejo ordenador para que se compre un nuevo Olivetti.

Paradores

Haga realidad sus sueños por menos de lo que imagina

Porque Paradores le ofrece, a usted y a su acompañante, un 35% de descuento en sus estancias en régimen de habitación y desayuno. Para que disfruten, desde 3.250 pesetas, de lugares de ensueño.

En una hoja de papel, escriba las oraciones de los anuncios que tengan cláusulas adverbiales o adjetivales y tradúzcalas al inglés.

CHAPTER 14

COMMANDS

A Command forms for Ud. and Uds.

- The command forms of a verb are used to tell someone to do or not to do something. The formal command forms for **Ud.** and **Uds.** are the same as the corresponding present subjunctive forms:

Escuche el ruido.	*Listen to the noise.*
Lea el libro.	*Read the book.*
Escriban el informe.	*Write the report.*
Traigan el periódico.	*Bring the newspaper.*

- Negative commands are formed by the addition of **no** before the affirmative command:

No escuche el ruido.	*Don't listen to the noise.*
No escriban el informe.	*Don't write the report.*

- A polite tone can be given to the command to soften it by the addition of **Ud.** or **Uds.** much as the addition of *please* does in English commands:

Espere.	*Wait.*
Espere Ud.	*Please wait.*
No griten.	*Don't shout.*
No griten Uds.	*Please don't shout.*

A. Una receta: La tortilla española. Póngase el gorro de cocinero y aprenda a preparar este plato español típico cambiando el infinitivo de los verbos al imperativo formal. ¡Trabajando paso a paso, Ud. llegará a ser un cocinero/una cocinera de primera (*first rate*)!

La cocina

el aceite de oliva *olive oil*
a fuego lento *low heat, slowly*
añadir *to add*
batir *to beat*
calentar (e > ie) *to heat*
la cebolla *onion*
cocinar *to cook*
dorar *to brown*
espolvorear *to sprinkle*
freír (e > i) *to fry*
la fuente *serving dish*
el gorro de cocinero *chef's hat*
la patata (Spain) *potato*
pegar *to stick*
pelar *to peel*
picar *to chop*
la pimienta *pepper*
rehogar (Spain) *to brown*
remover (o > ue) *to stir*
la sal *salt*
salpimentar *to season*
la (or el) sartén *frying pan*

MODELO Calentar el aceite de oliva en una sartén.
➔ Caliente el aceite de oliva en una sartén.

1. Añadir las patatas y cebollas peladas y picadas.
añada
2. Cocinar a fuego lento.
cocine
3. No rehogar las patatas y las cebollas.
no rehogue
4. Espolvorear con sal.
espolvore ?
5. Batir los huevos.
bata
6. Poner los huevos en la sartén.
ponga
7. Hacer dorar los huevos.
haga
8. No dejar que se pegue la tortilla.
no deje
9. Servir en una fuente.
sirva

B. **Una formación profesional (*Professional training*).** Unos jóvenes ingenieros comienzan un programa de formación profesional con la empresa que acaba de contratarlos. Como jefe del programa, Ud. les dice lo que tienen que hacer usando el imperativo.

MODELO Llegar a las nueve menos cuarto todos los días
➔ **Lleguen** a las nueve menos cuarto todos los días.

1. Encontrarse en la oficina del señor Aguilar.
encuentrense
2. Traer la calculadora.
traigan
3. Hacer preguntas.
hagan
4. Usar la computadora.
usen
5. Seguir los consejos del gerente.
sigan

6. Estudiar informática (*data processing*).

estudien

7. Leer el manual de telecomunicaciones.

lean

8. Tener cuidado con la entrada y salida de datos (*data input and output*).

tengan

C. Trámites de banco (*Bank procedures*). Ud. está de vacaciones en Santiago de Chile. Mientras cambia unos cheques de viajero en el banco, oye algunas conversaciones. Escriba los verbos que aparecen en las preguntas en imperativo. Cambie los sustantivos complementos directos a pronombres. (See page 219 to review the position of object pronouns with command forms.)

En el banco

calcular *to compute*
la cuenta *(bank) account*
cuenta corriente *checking account*
el cheque de viajero *traveler's check*
firmar *to sign*
el formulario *form (paper)*
el interés *interest*
llenar *to fill out*
el peso *monetary unit of Chile and other Latin American countries*
la planilla de retiro *withdrawal form, slip*
la plata *money*
el préstamo *loan*
retirar *to withdraw*
la ventanilla *teller's window (station)*

MODELO —¿Debo abrir la cuenta?
—Sí, **ábrala.**
—No, **no la abra.**

1. ¿Debo retirar dinero?

2. ¿Puedo acercarme a la ventanilla?

3. ¿Tengo que firmar la planilla de retiro?

4. ¿Debo llenar el formulario?

5. ¿Le doy la plata en pesos?

6. ¿Puedo pedirles a Uds. un préstamo?

____

____

7. ¿Le calculo los intereses?

____

____

8. ¿Cierro la cuenta corriente?

____

____

9. ¿Le cobro los cheques de viajero?

____

____

Nota cultural

- **Santiago,** capital de Chile, queda a las orillas del río Mapocho. Tiene hermosos jardines públicos y se puede ver los picos de los Andes desde la ciudad. Fundada por Pedro de Valdivia en 1541, Santiago tiene una universidad del Estado, una universidad Católica y numerosas instituciones culturales, científicas y artísticas a más de una pintoresca zona antigua.

- **El peso** es la moneda de Chile. El peso chileno está a 373 al dólar americano. Los otros países latinoamericanos que tienen el peso como moneda son Argentina, México, Colombia, Uruguay, Bolivia, la República Dominicana y Cuba.

B *Command forms for* **nosotros** *(let's, let's not)*

- The present subjunctive forms for **nosotros** are used as commands:

Tomemos el tren.	*Let's take the train.*
No hagamos nada.	*Let's not do anything.*

- The affirmative **nosotros** command is often replaced by **vamos a** + infinitive. **Vamos a estudiar** may mean either *We're going to study* or *Let's study.* **No vamos a estudiar** can only mean *We're not going to study.*

Vamos a salir esta noche. **Salgamos** esta noche.	*Let's go out tonight.*

- **Vamos** is used instead of **vayamos** for *let's go.* The regular present subjunctive form is used for the negative: **no vayamos.**

Vamos al centro.	*Let's go downtown.*
No vayamos al cine.	*Let's not go to the movies.*

- In affirmative **nosotros** commands the final **-s** of the verb ending is dropped when the reflexive pronoun **nos** or the indirect object pronoun **se** is added. An accent mark is written over the stressed syllable. For example: **Lavémonos (Lavemos + nos)** *Let's wash up* or **Prestémoselo (Prestemos + se + lo)** *Let's lend it to her.*

(quedarse)	**Quedémonos.**	*Let's stay.*
(sentarse)	**Sentémonos.**	*Let's sit down.*
(irse)	**Vámonos.**	*Let's go.*
(enseñarse)	**Enseñémosela.**	*Let's show it to them.*
(hacerse)	**Hagámoselos.**	*Let's make them for him.*

D. **¡Veámoslo todo en Perú!** Ud. y sus amigos están pasando las vacaciones en el Perú. Recién llegados a Lima, Uds. hablan de sus planes. Escriba oraciones empleando la primera persona del plural del imperativo.

MODELO viajar a Nasca
Viajemos a Nasca.
Vamos a viajar a Nasca.

1. dar un paseo por la zona de la Plaza de Armas

____

____

2. ir de compras en el Jirón de la Unión

____

____

3. conocer la Universidad de San Marcos

____

____

4. hacer una excursión a Machu Picchu

____

____

5. visitar la catedral y unas iglesias de Cuzco

____

____

6. quedarse en Miraflores

____

____

7. tomar un colectivo (*small van*) a una playa limeña

____

____

8. sentarse en el Malecón

____

____

Nota cultural

- **Lima**, capital del Perú, fue fundada por los españoles en 1535. Fue una ciudad rica e importante hasta que fue destruida por un terremoto en 1746. El casco antiguo (*old part*) de la ciudad conserva la arquitectura de la época colonial. Aquí se puede ver la Plaza de Armas alrededor de la cual se encuentran el Palacio de Gobierno, la Catedral y otros lugares históricos. Esta zona ha sido declarada patrimonio internacional por la UNESCO. Las nuevas zonas de Lima se encuentran en la Plaza San Martín, al sur del Jirón (calle larga) de la Unión, la principal calle comercial. Lima es también una ciudad moderna con rascacielos, contaminación del ambiente y "pueblos jóvenes" (*shanty settlements*).

- **La Universidad de San Marcos** fue fundada en 1551.

- **Machu Picchu,** una ciudad inca, queda en el departamento de Cuzco al sudeste de Lima. Las ruinas de la ciudad sagrada, que consiste en una fortaleza, terrazas, escaleras, templos, palacios, torres, fuentes y un reloj de sol, fueron descubiertas en 1911.

- La ciudad de **Cuzco** fue fundada en el siglo XI por Manco Cápac y era capital del Imperio Incaico hasta que los conquistadores españoles se apoderaron de la ciudad en 1533, nombrándola ciudad española en 1534. Hay varias iglesias incluso las de La Merced, San Francisco y Belén de los Reyes y una catedral de estilo barroco que data del siglo XVII.

- **Miraflores** es el suburbio más grande y más importante de la capital peruana. Con sus muchos comercios, excelentes restaurantes y hoteles, Miraflores, con San Isidro, constituyen ahora el centro social de Lima. Desde la Avenida Diagonal hay una magnífica vista del litoral (*coastline*) de Lima. El malecón (*jetty*) pasa por todas estas estaciones balnearias (*seaside resorts*).

- **Nasca** es una ciudad que queda al sudeste de Lima. A unos 22 kilómetros al norte de Nasca se pueden ver las famosas líneas nascas que son líneas paralelas, formas geométricas y las figuras de un perro, un mono, aves, una araña, un árbol y otras cosas. Se cree que fueron grabadas en las arenas de la Pampa Colorada por tres pueblos indígenas diferentes a partir de 900 antes de Jesucristo.

E. ¡Cómo no! Sus amigos le dicen que quieren hacer ciertas cosas hoy. Ud. les dice que está conforme expresando el imperativo para *nosotros* de dos maneras.

MODELO Quiero comprarle un regalo a Elisa.
Cómo no. **Comprémoselo.**
Cómo no. **Vamos a comprárselo.**

1. Quiero darle a Maximiliano la mochila.

____

____

2. Quiero sacar entradas para el concierto de la Sinfónica.

____

____

3. Me gustaría ir al museo por la tarde.

4. Sería agradable caminar por el parque.

5. Quiero inscribirme en la clase de computación.

6. Me gustaría jugar al tenis.

7. Quiero decirles a los chicos el motivo del disgusto (*argument*).

8. Sería lindo tumbarse (*to lie down*) en la playa.

C *Command forms for **tú** and **vosotros***

- Negative informal commands for **tú** and **vosotros** are derived from the present subjunctive:

tú	**No compres** más.	*Don't buy more.*
	No comas tanto.	*Don't eat so much.*
	No pidas cerveza.	*Don't order beer.*
	No digas eso.	*Don't say that.*
vosotros	**No compréis** más.	*Don't buy more.*
	No comáis tanto.	*Don't eat so much.*
	No pidáis cerveza.	*Don't order beer.*
	No digáis eso.	*Don't say that.*

- Affirmative informal commands for **tú** and **vosotros** have their own endings. The affirmative informal commands are derived from the present indicative **tú** form minus the person ending **-s**:

present indicative		*command*	
Contestas el teléfono.	➔	**Contesta** el teléfono.	*Answer the telephone.*
Vendes el coche.	➔	**Vende** el coche.	*Sell the car.*
Abres la ventana.	➔	**Abre** la ventana.	*Open the window.*
Sirves la cena.	➔	**Sirve** la cena.	*Serve dinner.*

- Affirmative **vosotros** commands are formed by replacing the **-r** of the infinitive by **-d.** They lose their final **-d** when the reflexive pronoun **os** is attached: **Acordaos** (*Remember*). The one exception to this rule is **idos** (*go away*).

(contestar)	➔ Contesta**d** el teléfono.	*Answer the telephone.*
(vender)	➔ Vende**d** el coche.	*Sell the car.*
(abrir)	➔ Abri**d** la ventana.	*Open the window.*
(servir)	➔ Servi**d** la cena.	*Serve dinner.*
(arregla**rse**)	➔ Arregl**aos.**	*Get ready.*

F. **¡Venid a la fiesta!** Vosotros estáis en España donde estáis organizando una fiesta para esta noche. Decid lo que los demás tienen que hacer usando la segunda persona del plural (*vosotros*) del imperativo.

MODELO preparar las ensaladas / no cocinar la carne todavía
➔ **Preparad** las ensaladas, pero **no cocinéis** la carne todavía.

1. hacer la torta / no ponerle el glaseado (*icing*) todavía

____

2. abrir las botellas de sangría / no cortar las rebanadas (*slices*) de naranja todavía

____

3. sacar los platitos para las tapas / no preparar el chorizo y el pulpo todavía

____

4. poner la mesa / no colocar los claveles todavía

____

5. salir a comprar aceitunas / no ir todavía

____

6. destapar (*uncork*) el vino / no servirlo en un jarro todavía

____

7. colgar los globos / no dejarlos en la entrada

____

8. escoger los discos compactos / no poner música con palabrotas (*bad words*)

____

Nota cultural

- **La sangría** es una bebida española hecha con vino tinto, agua y azúcar a la cual se puede añadir rebanadas de naranja, durazno y otras frutas.
- **Las tapas** son bocados (*snacks*) que acompañan las bebidas en España. Algunas tapas que se sirven comúnmente son las aceitunas (*olives*), la tortilla española, el salchichón (*seasoned pork sausage*), el chorizo (*sausage seasoned with red peppers*), el pulpo en su tinta (*octopus in its ink*).
- **El clavel** (*carnation*) es una flor muy apreciada por los españoles. Hay una canción española tradicional titulada *Clavelitos*.

G. Exprese en español los siguientes mandatos usando la segunda persona del plural del imperativo (*vosotros*).

1. Be patient.
2. Go away.
3. Tell the truth.
4. Be charming.
5. Take a bath.
6. Write a short story.
7. Attend the lecture.
8. Play the piano.
9. Go to bed early.

- The following verbs have irregular affirmative **tú** commands. Note that the negative **tú** commands of these verbs are regular: they are derived from the present subjunctive forms: **no digas, no hagas, no vayas,** etc.

decir	➔ di	salir	➔ sal
hacer	➔ haz	ser	➔ sé
ir	➔ ve	tener	➔ ten
poner	➔ pon	venir	➔ ven

Note: The affirmative **tú** commands for **ir** and **ver** are the same: **ve.**

H. **¡Tengo los nervios de punta! (*I'm all on edge!*)** Manuela está nerviosísima estos días por los exámenes y el trabajo, y se peleó con su novio. Dígale lo que debe hacer para calmarse usando el imperativo.

Modelo salir a divertirse
➔ **Sal** a divertirte.

1. dar un paseo todos los días
2. hacer ejercicio

3. tomar una infusión de manzanilla (*chamomile tea*)

4. tranquilizarse escuchando música

5. no beber mucha cafeína

6. dormir la siesta todas las tardes

7. reunirse con los amigos

8. no preocuparse por tonterías

9. buscarse otro novio

Nota cultural

La infusión de manzanilla se toma mucho en España para curar toda clase de problemas digestivos. Se conoce como calmante natural.

I. ¡Paquito, deja de poner el grito en el cielo! (*Paquito, stop kicking up a fuss!*) Ud. está cuidando a un niño malcriado (*spoiled*) que hace diabluras (*is up to mischief*). Emplee el imperativo para decirle que haga o no haga ciertas cosas.

MODELO limpiar la mancha del jugo
→ **Limpia** la mancha del jugo.

1. portarse bien

2. no hacer payasadas (*to clown around*)

3. no ser terco

4. dejar al perro en paz (*to leave alone*)

5. recoger las migas de las galletas

6. no derramar el perfume de tu mamá

7. hacerme caso

____

8. no encerrarse en el baño

____

9. venir acá inmediatamente

____

J. **¡Tito el desgraciado (*unlucky guy*)!** Todo le pasa a Tito porque tiene mala suerte. Ayúdele a hacer o no hacer ciertas cosas con consejos escritos en imperativo.

MODELO Tito, **mira.** (mirar)
Tito, **no corras.** (no correr)

1. Tito, _______________. (darse prisa)
2. Tito, _______________. (no lastimarse)
3. Tito, _______________. (no cortarse el dedo)
4. Tito, _______________. (tener cuidado)
5. Tito, _______________. (no romperse el pie)
6. Tito, _______________. (no encender los fósforos)
7. Tito, _______________. (conducir más lentamente)
8. Tito, _______________. (ponerse una armadura [*suit of armor*])

K. **El médico aconseja ...** Carlitos se quebró el tobillo jugando al fútbol. Su mamá lo lleva al consultorio donde el médico les da consejos a Carlitos y a su mamá. Escriba el verbo en imperativo para expresar lo que dice el médico a la señora y a Carlitos.

MODELO Señora, **póngale** esta crema. (ponerle)
Carlitos, **anda** con cuidado. (andar)

Las fracturas

la quebradura *fracture, break*
escayolado *in a plaster cast*
la muleta *crutch*
quebrarse (e > ie) *to break*
el tobillo *ankle*
el vendaje *dressing*

1. Señora, _______________ ir al colegio. (dejarlo)
2. Carlitos, no _______________ la pierna escayolada. (mojarse)
3. Señora, _______________ estas pastillas si le duele el tobillo. (darle)
4. Carlitos, no _______________ deportes por ahora. (jugar)
5. Señora, _______________ la receta. (hacerle)
6. Carlitos, no _______________ el vendaje. (quitarse)

7. Señora, ________________________ al consultorio la semana próxima. (traerlo)
8. Carlitos, ________________________ a verme el miércoles o el jueves. (venir)
9. Carlitos, ________________________ a la calle con muletas. (salir)

D *The position of object pronouns with command forms*

- Object pronouns (direct, indirect, reflexive) are placed in their usual position *before* the verb in *negative* commands.

No **lo** hagas.	*Don't do it.*
No **se lo** digas.	*Don't tell it to him.*
No **me la** traiga.	*Don't bring it to me.*
No **se** preocupen Uds.	*Please don't worry.*
No **nos** sentemos.	*Let's not sit down.*
No **te los** pongas. (los = guantes)	*Don't put them on.*

- Object pronouns *follow* affirmative commands and are attached to them. When attached, an accent mark is placed over the stressed syllable, except when a single object pronoun is added to a one-syllable command form: **dime** (*tell me*); **dímelo** (*tell me it*). However, **dé, esté,** and **está** may keep their accent marks when a single object pronoun is added: **deme** or **déme.**

Hazlo.	*Do it.*
Díselo.	*Tell it to him.*
Tráigamela.	*Bring it to me.*
Quédense Uds.	*Please stay.*
Sentémonos.	*Let's sit down.*
Póntelos. (los = guantes)	*Put them on.*

L. Sí, hágalo. Conteste las preguntas con la forma adecuada del imperativo—*Ud., tú, Uds.* Cambie los sustantivos que son complementos directos a pronombres y haga todos los cambios necesarios.

MODELO ¿Quieres que yo te traiga las revistas?
→ Sí, **tráemelas.**

1. ¿Quieres que yo les dé los informes a los jefes?

____

2. ¿Uds. quieren que yo les mande las cartas (a Uds.)?

____

3. ¿Ud. necesita que le entreguemos la tarea (a Ud.)?

____

4. ¿Quieres que te ponga el abrigo?

____

5. ¿Uds. necesitan que yo les prepare los bocadillos?

____

6. ¿Uds. quieren que les sirvamos el postre?

____

7. ¿Prefieres que te explique la idea?

____

8. ¿A Ud. le interesa que le diga los motivos?

____

9. ¿Debemos enseñarle los cuadros a Pedro?

____

M. **No, no lo haga.** Ahora, conteste las preguntas del *ejercicio L* con imperativos negativos.

MODELO ¿Quieres que yo te traiga las revistas?
→ No, **no me las traigas.**

1. ¿Quieres que yo les dé los informes a los jefes?

____

2. ¿Uds. quieren que yo les mande las cartas (a Uds.)?

____

3. ¿Ud. necesita que le entreguemos la tarea (a Ud.)?

____

4. ¿Quieres que te ponga el abrigo?

____

5. ¿Uds. necesitan que yo les prepare los bocadillos?

____

6. ¿Uds. quieren que les sirvamos el postre?

____

7. ¿Prefieres que te explique la idea?

____

8. ¿A Ud. le interesa que le diga los motivos?

____

9. ¿Debemos enseñarle los cuadros a Pedro?

____

E *Indirect commands*

- Indirect commands in Spanish consist of **que** + present subjunctive. Object and reflexive pronouns are placed before the verb. English equivalents are *Let* or *Have him/her/it/them do something*. Sometimes *I hope* is suggested in these sentences:

Que pase.	*Have him come in.*
Que espere.	*Let her wait.*
Que me llamen.	*Have them call me.*
Que se matriculen.	*Let them register.*
Que no se lo dé.	*Don't let him give it to them.*

- Subject pronouns are added to indirect commands for emphasis: Que lo haga **él.** (*Let **him** do it.*)
- Indirect commands of **se** constructions with indirect object pronouns (see Chapter 19—Unplanned occurrences) are usually the equivalents of regular commands in English. For example: **Que no se te olvide** el carnet (*Don't forget your driver's license*) or **Que no se les acaben** los cheques de viajero (*I hope you don't run out of traveler's checks*).

N. **¡Que lo hagan los otros!** Rosario se niega a colaborar con sus compañeros de clase en el proyecto de ciencias. Incluso manda que los amigos se ocupen de todo. Explique lo que Rosario no quiere hacer y propone, usando el imperativo indirecto, que los otros hagan estas cosas.

Modelo No quiero participar en el proyecto. (los demás)
➔ **Que participen** los demás.

1. No voy a leer los libros de consulta (*reference books*). (Manolo)
____
2. No me interesa dibujar tablas (*charts*). (Terencio y Elena)
____
3. No quiero observar los experimentos en el laboratorio. (Paulina)
____
4. Me niego a hacer los gráficos (*plot graphs*). (los otros)
____
5. No tengo ganas de investigar estas teorías. (Samuel)
____
6. No quiero dedicarme a las ciencias. (mis amigos)
____
7. No pienso escribir un informe. (Federico)
____

O. Exprese los siguientes mandatos indirectos en español.

1. Have her give it to you. (it = *el cheque*, to you = *a Ud.*)
____
2. Let them go away.
____
3. Have him send them to her. (them = *las tarjetas*)
____
4. I hope you don't lose your wallet. (use **se** construction with indirect object pronoun, you = *tú*)
____

5. Let them come back in the afternoon.

____

6. I hope you don't run out of soft drinks. (use **se** construction with indirect object pronoun; you = *Uds.*)

____

F *Other ways of giving commands*

- Often in newspaper ads for employment, recipes, notices, instructions, etc., the infinitive of the verb is used as an imperative rather than the command form:

Interesados **mandar** curriculum vitae.	*Interested persons,* ***send*** *your curriculum vitae.*
Enviar historial con fotografía a …	***Send*** *résumé with photograph to …*
Interesados **llamar** al teléfono …	*Interested persons,* ***call*** *…*
Secar las berenjenas, **pasarlas** por harina y **freírlas** en aceite hirviendo.	***Dry*** *the eggplants,* ***dip them*** *into flour and* ***fry them*** *in boiling oil.*

- The infinitive rather than the command form is used with the following expressions that convey formality and politeness. They are the English equivalent of asking something with *please:*

Favor de llamarme mañana.	***Please call me*** *tomorrow.*
Favor de esperar.	***Please wait.***
Tenga la bondad de sentarse.	***Please sit down.***
Haga el favor de firmar el documento.	***Please sign*** *the paper.*
Hágame el favor de enviar el cheque.	***Please send*** *the check.*

P. Libro de cocina. Escriba los siguientes verbos en imperativo como infinitivos.

MODELO Limpie el pollo.
→ **Limpiar** el pollo.

1. Córtelos a tiritas (*in strips*).

____

2. Añada el vino.

____

3. Déjelo evaporar.

____

4. Pártalos en trozos.

____

5. Tape las patatas.

____

6. Seque los tomates.

7. Añádalas a la salsa.

8. Remuévalo (*stir*).

9. Póngala en una fuente (*serving dish*).

Q. **El primer día de clase.** El profesor de español les dice a sus estudiantes que hagan unas cosas. Escriba los verbos en imperativo como infinitivos usando las expresiones que aparecen entre paréntesis.

MODELO Estudien el primer capítulo. (favor de)
➔ **Favor de estudiar** el primer capítulo.

1. Vayan al laboratorio de lenguas. (hagan el favor de)

2. Aprendan los diálogos de memoria. (tengan la bondad de)

3. Traigan el diccionario. (favor de)

4. Matricúlense si no lo han hecho. (tengan la bondad de)

5. Compren el libro de texto y el cuaderno de trabajo. (háganme el favor de)

6. Apúntense en esta lista. (favor de)

7. Hagan hincapié (*emphasize*) en los ejercicios de fonética todos los días. (hagan el favor de)

8. No actúen mucho en grupo. (tengan la bondad de)

9. Vean películas y lean periódicos en español. (favor de)

R. Busque empleo. Complete los siguientes anuncios de periódico para empleos con los mandatos que faltan. Use el infinitivo en cada caso. Elija entre: **enviar, dirigirse, llamar, mandar, concertar, remitir, escribir, ponerse en contacto, adjuntar, presentarse.**

MODELO Interesados **enviar** curriculum vitae. (*send*)

1. Interesados ______________________ lunes día 3 al teléfono 91-742-42-63. (*call*)
2. ______________________ historial y fotografía al Apto. (apartado = *box*) 36492, 28080 Madrid. (*Send*)
3. Interesados ______________________ a: ARA Publicidad, 08008 Barcelona. (*write*)
4. Interesados ______________________, lunes 3 de 9,30 a 14 horas y de 15,30 a 17,30 horas, en C/Alcalá, 54, Srta. Núñez. (*apply*)
5. Interesados ______________________ a: PAR-7. Avda. del Mediterráneo, 22, 28007 Madrid. (*go to*)
6. Interesados ______________________ fotografía reciente al apartado de Correos número 2.059 de Madrid. (*attach*)
7. Los interesados deben ______________________ con Ignacio Doncel llamando de 9 a 14 horas y de 16 a 18 horas al teléfono (91) 585-83-64. (*get in touch*)
8. Las personas interesadas, ______________________ entrevista en el teléfono (91) 653-95-00. (*arrange*)

S. Ejercicio oral. Escenas de teatro. Dos o tres estudiantes crean escenas en las cuales los personajes emplean el imperativo. Por ejemplo: en el consultorio, el médico aconseja a sus pacientes sobre sus problemas de salud; los padres les dicen a sus hijos que arreglen su cuarto; un profesor de computación enseña a sus estudiantes cómo hacer funcionar la computadora; jugar *Simple Simon,* juego en el cual un(a) estudiante da mandatos a los demás.

T. Estructuras en acción. Lea los siguientes anuncios de periódicos y haga el ejercicio.

A.

No permitas que dejen sin bosques a tu hijo. Por sólo 3.000 Ptas., hazle socio del Club del Árbol. Plantaremos un árbol en su nombre, en la Comunidad de Madrid. Planta un árbol para tu hijo. Llámanos al (91) 308 23 09 para más información. Regálale un árbol.

B.

BELLSOUTH CELULAR (CHILE)

Aproveche los precios de otoño. No se pierda esta oportunidad. Compre ahora su celular y pague el equipo en julio a precio contado. Exija su casilla (*box*) de mensajes gratis. Llame hoy mismo al 339-5050.

C.

Acer ¡No se la pierda!

¡Nuestra experiencia de 15 años es su garantía! Surtimos (*we supply*) a toda la República.

Llame primero a: Asesoría en Cómputo, S.A.

Visítenos en el stand 104 de la Feria de la ciudad de México 12:00 a 9:00 P.M., 16 de abril.

D.

AMERICAN LANGUAGE COMMUNICATION CENTER

APRENDA INGLÉS de una manera rápida, fácil y divertida. ¡Mejore sus oportunidades y obtenga una vida mejor en Nueva York! Certificado por el departamento de educación del estado de Nueva York.

¡Matricúlese ahora y reciba una semana gratis!

¡Llame hoy! Pregunte por María. (212) 736-2373

En una hoja de papel, escriba las formas del imperativo que aparecen en los anuncios y tradúzcalas al inglés.

CHAPTER 15

THE INFINITIVE

The conjugated verb + infinitive

- In Spanish, an important function of the infinitive of the verb is to serve as a complement or completion form in verb + infinitive constructions. The conjugated verb can be followed directly by an infinitive:

Debe cursar durante el verano.	***He should take courses*** *during the summer.*
Necesitamos tomar una decisión.	***We had to make*** *a decision.*
Querían salir a cenar.	***They wanted to go out*** *to have dinner.*
¿Has podido encontrarlos?	***Have you been able to find*** *them?*
Prefiero ir al concierto.	***I prefer to go*** *to the concert.*
Procure llegar para las siete.	***Try to arrive*** *by seven o'clock.*
Creo poder tenerlo listo para mañana.	***I think I can*** *have it ready for tomorrow.*

These verbs may be followed directly by an infinitive:

conseguir *to succeed in, manage to*
creer *to think, believe*
deber *should, ought to*
decidir *to decide*
dejar *to let, allow*
desear *to want*
esperar *to hope, expect, wait*
hacer *to make*
impedir *to prevent from*
intentar *to try to*
lograr *to succeed in*
mandar *to order to*
merecer *to deserve to*
necesitar *to need, have to*
ofrecer *to offer*
oír *to hear*
olvidar *to forget*
ordenar *to order*
parecer *to seem to*
pensar (e > ie) *to intend*
permitir *to allow*
poder (o > ue) *can, to be able to*
preferir (e > ie) *to prefer*
pretender *to try to*
procurar *to try to*
prohibir *to prohibit*
prometer *to promise to*
recordar (o > ue) *to remember to*
resolver (o > ue) *to resolve to*
querer (e > ie) *to want*
saber *to know how to*
sentir (e > ie) *to regret, be sorry*
soler (o > ue) *to be used to, accustomed to*
temer *to be afraid to*
ver *to see*

A. Fiestas y celebraciones. Practique la construcción del verbo conjugado + infinitivo. Desarrolle unas nuevas oraciones añadiendo a las oraciones originales los verbos que aparecen entre paréntesis. Guarde el tiempo verbal de la oración original.

MODELO Los Arriaga pasan la Nochebuena en casa. (preferir)
→ Los Arriaga **prefieren pasar** la Nochebuena en casa.

1. Los españoles celebraron el santo del Rey Juan Carlos el 24 de junio. (querer)

____

2. Uds. siempre iban de vacaciones en Semana Santa. (procurar)

____

3. Paco no salió con su novia el Día de los Enamorados. (poder)

____

4. Comes una uva por cada campanada (*bell ringing*) el 31 de diciembre. (soler)

____

5. Raúl y Pepita no asistieron a la Misa del Gallo este año. (conseguir)

____

6. Los niñitos recibían muchos regalos lindos el Día de Reyes. (esperar)

____

7. No gastas bromas el Día de los Inocentes. (resolver)

____

8. Hay unas fiestas grandes el Día de la Raza. (deber)

____

9. Les traje flores y bombones a los tíos por el Año Nuevo. (decidir)

____

Nota cultural

- **La Nochebuena,** es decir, el 24 de diciembre, se celebra en todos los países hispánicos. Las familias suelen festejarla con una cena tradicional. Muchas personas van a la **Misa del Gallo** a las doce de la noche.
- Para el 31 de diciembre, **el Fin de Año,** cuando se oyen las campanadas a las doce de la noche, la gente come una uva por cada campanada. ¡Así asegura la buena suerte para el año nuevo!
- El 6 de enero es la Epifanía o **el Día de Reyes.** Este día, cuando los Reyes Magos (*Magi*) les traen regalos a los niños, señala el fin de las fiestas de Navidad.
- **Semana Santa** es el período de la Pascua Florida (*Easter*) cuando mucha gente toma sus vacaciones.
- **El Día de la Raza (**o **el Día de la Hispanidad)** se celebra el 12 de octubre en el mundo hispánico y coincide con el Día de Cristóbal Colón en los Estados Unidos.
- Para muchas personas hispánicas **el santo** es más importante que el cumpleaños. Hay gente que celebra las dos cosas. En España, el 24 de junio es el día de San Juan y también se celebra el santo del Rey Juan Carlos.
- **El Día de los Enamorados** se celebra en el mundo hispánico el 14 de febrero tanto como el Día de San Valentín en los Estados Unidos.
- **El Día de los Inocentes** se celebra en los Estados Unidos como *April Fool's Day.*

B. Expansión de oraciones. Practique la construcción del verbo conjugado + infinitivo. Desarrolle unas nuevas oraciones añadiendo a las oraciones originales los verbos que aparecen entre paréntesis. Guarde el tiempo verbal de la oración original.

MODELO Sirvió la comida. (mandar)
→ **Mandó servir** la comida.

1. Nadaban muy bien. (saber)

 ____

2. Ud. ganó más plata. (merecer)

 ____

3. Terminé el proyecto. (lograr)

 ____

4. Felipe está solo en la casa. (temer)

 ____

5. Se sale por esa puerta. (prohibir)

 ____

6. Han tocado un vals. (ofrecer)

 ____

7. Limpiábamos la casa. (hacer)

 ____

8. No escuchaste los discos compactos. (dejar)

 ____

B *The conjugated verb + preposition + infinitive*

- Some verbs require a preposition before an infinitive. The most common prepositions are **a** and **de**, but some verbs require **en** or **por**:

Van a pedir paella.	*They're going to order paella.*
Comenzó a llover hace media hora.	*It began to rain half an hour ago.*
Yo me encargué de hacer las investigaciones.	*I took charge of doing the research.*
No insistas en sentarte en la primera fila.	*Don't insist on sitting in the first row.*
¿Uds. no se interesaban por coleccionar sellos?	*Weren't you interested in collecting stamps?*

The following verbs take **a** before an infinitive:

acercarse a *to approach*
acostumbrarse a *to be accustomed to*
animar a *to encourage to*
aprender a *to learn to*
atreverse a *to dare to*
ayudar a *to help*
bajar a *to go down to*
comenzar a (e > ie) *to begin to*
cuidar a/de *to take care of*
decidirse a *to decide to*
dedicarse a *to devote oneself to*
disponerse a *to get ready to*
echar(se) a *to begin to*
empezar a (e > ie) *to begin to*
enseñar a *to show how, teach to*
invitar a *to invite to*
ir a *to be going to*
llegar a *to get to, succeed in*
llevar a *to lead to*
meterse a *to start to*
negarse a (e > ie) *to refuse to*
obligar a *to force, compel to*
persuadir a *to persuade*
ponerse a *to begin to*
prepararse a *to get ready to*
renunciar a *to renounce*
volver a (o > ue) *to do (something) again*

Some examples:

—¿Te decidiste **a** seguir trabajando en esta oficina?	*Did you make up your mind to continue working in this office?*
—Sí. Ya me he acostumbrado **a** trabajar aquí.	*Yes. I've already gotten used to working here.*
—Mañana empiezo **a** estudiar en serio.	*Tomorrow I'll start studying seriously.*
—Yo también debo ponerme **a** trabajar.	*I also ought to begin working.*
—¿Volvieron **a** pedirte dinero?	*Did they ask you for money again?*
—No. No se atrevieron **a** pedirme nada.	*No. They didn't dare ask me for anything.*

- After verbs of motion **a** indicates the purpose of the action:

Bajo/Subo **a** ayudarte.	*I'm coming downstairs/upstairs (in order) to help you.*

The following verbs take **de** before an infinitive:

acabar de *to have just (done something)*
acordarse de (o > ue) *to remember*
arrepentirse de (e > ie) *to regret*
avergonzarse de (o > üe) *to be ashamed of*
cuidar de/a *to take care of*
dejar de *to stop*
encargarse de *to take charge of*
jactarse de *to boast of*
olvidarse de *to forget*
presumir de *to boast about*
terminar de *to stop*
tratar de *to try to*

—No te olvides **de** venir a cenar el jueves.	*Don't forget to come have dinner on Thursday.*
—No te preocupes. Acabo **de** anotar el día y la hora.	*Don't worry. I've just written down the day and the hour.*

The following verbs take **en** before an infinitive:

consentir en (e > ie) *to consent, agree to*
consistir en *to consist of*
dudar en *to hesitate over*
empeñarse en *to insist on, be determined to*
insistir en *to insist on*
interesarse en/por *to be interested in*
quedar en *to agree to*
tardar en *to delay in, be long in*
vacilar en *to hesitate over*

—Carlos se interesa mucho **en** hablarme.	*Carlos is very interested in talking to me.*
—¿Consentiste **en** verlo?	*Did you consent to see him?*
—Sí. Quedamos **en** vernos mañana.	*Yes. We agreed to see each other tomorrow.*

The following verbs take **con** before an infinitive:

amenazar con *to threaten to*
contar con (o > ue) *to count on, rely on*
soñar con (o > ue) *to dream of, about*

—En vez de trabajar, Juanita sueña todo el día **con** hacerse actriz.	*Instead of working, Juanita dreams all day of becoming an actress.*
—Por eso el jefe amenazó **con** despedirla.	*That's why the boss threatened to fire her.*

- The verb **tener** is followed by **que** before an infinitive. **Tener que** means *to have to do something:*

Teníamos que estacionar el coche.	***We had to** park the car.*

- Many of the above verbs take the same preposition before a noun object as well:

—¿Se dedica la señora Gómez **a su familia**?	*Does Mrs. Gómez devote herself to her family?*
—Sí, se encarga **de la casa** y **de sus hijos**.	*Yes, she's in charge of the house and her children.*

C. **¿Qué hacen los estudiantes?** Practique el uso de las preposiciones. Llene los espacios en blanco con las preposiciones correctas que faltan.

MODELO Empiezan **a** estudiar francés.

1. Ricardo se prepara ___________ tomar los exámenes.
2. Carolina y Miguel quedaron ___________ verse en la clase de física.
3. Jorge se empeña ___________ sacar buenas notas este semestre.
4. Isabel se ha dedicado ___________ hacer investigaciones.
5. Marco presume ___________ saberlo todo.
6. Fernanda volverá ___________ cursar biología.
7. Uds. se interesan ___________ leer literatura inglesa.
8. Tú y yo nos encargaremos ___________ organizar los archivos.
9. Pablo sueña ___________ graduarse el año que viene.

10. Teresa se decidió __________ matricularse en la escuela de verano.
11. Yo trato __________ ir a la biblioteca todas las tardes.
12. Pancho cuenta __________ terminar la carrera (*course of study*) este año.
13. Julia y Lorenzo acaban __________ completar sus requisitos (*requirements*).
14. Nosotros tendríamos __________ buscar otras optativas (*electives*).

D. Exprese las siguientes oraciones en español.

1. We were accustomed to having dinner at 9:00 P.M.

____

2. Why did they take so long in calling us?

____

3. Esteban refused to lend Diego money.

____

4. Try to pay with a credit card. (you = *Ud.*)

____

5. Sing that song again. (you = *Uds.*)

____

6. I'm going to attend the lecture.

____

7. Silvia threatened to leave immediately.

____

8. They dream about becoming millionaires!

____

E. **Sinónimos.** Escoja un sinónimo de las listas de verbos con y sin preposiciones para cada expresión escrita en bastardilla (*italics*).

MODELO Los miembros del comité *acuerdan* reunirse el martes.
➔ Los miembros del comité **convienen en** reunirse el martes.

1. Pedro *logró* hacerse presidente de la empresa.

____

2. Consuelo *se jacta de* ser la mejor futbolista del equipo.

____

3. Los Arcos *se prepararán a* recibir a sus tíos.

____

4. El profesor *mandó* cerrar los libros.

____

5. Uds. *sintieron* perderse la boda.

6. Yo no *recordé* recoger los pasteles.

7. ¿Cómo es que *te pusiste a* hacer la tarea a las dos de la mañana?

8. No se *dejaba* entrar en las salas de escultura.

9. Están *dudando en* invertir dinero en la compañía.

C *The infinitive after prepositions*

- The infinitive can be used after many prepositions, such as: **a, al, antes de, a pesar de, con el objeto de, con tal de, después de, en caso de, en lugar de, en vez de, hasta, para, por, sin.**

Almorcemos **después de montar** en bicicleta.	*Let's have lunch after we go for a bicycle ride.*
Estudie más **para aprender** más.	*Study more (in order) to learn more.*
Me alegré **al oír** la buena noticia.	*I became happy when I heard the good news.*
Mario irá **con tal de ver** a Susana.	*Mario will go provided that he sees Susana.*
Llenen el formulario **antes de firmarlo.**	*Fill out the form before you sign it.*
¿Entraste **sin vernos?**	*Did you come in without seeing us?*

F. Exprese las siguientes oraciones en español. Practique usando el infinitivo después de ciertas preposiciones.

1. We'll call you before we go out. (*tú*)

2. They traveled to Ponce by car without stopping.

3. Children, go to bed after you brush your teeth. (*Uds.*)

4. Bernardo should read a book instead of watching television.

5. I'll be in the library until I come home.

6. Elena will skate provided that Daniel skates too.

7. Invite them in case you see them. (*Ud.*)

8. When we got to the party we started to dance.

Nota cultural

Ponce, ciudad de Puerto Rico, es un puerto en el Caribe. Es un centro de las industrias petrolera, agrícola, textil y del cemento. Ponce tiene una universidad y un museo de arte.

D *The infinitive after verbs of perception*

- The infinitive is used after verbs of perception such as **ver** and **oír** to signal a completed action. The gerund rather than the infinitive is used to show an incomplete or in-progress action:

Los **oí cantar.**	*I heard them sing.*
¿Uds. no nos **vieron entrar**?	*Didn't you see us come in?*

G. ¿Qué oyó? Lorenzo tiene problema del oído y va con un audioprotesista (*hearing aid specialist*) porque necesita un aparato. El especialista le pregunta lo que oyó.

MODELO ¿Oyó Ud. el ruido de los coches? (frenar [*to brake*])
→ Sí, los oí frenar.

1. ¿Oyó Ud. el trueno? (retumbar [*to thunder*])

2. ¿Oyó Ud. el maullido del gato? (maullar [*to meow*])

3. ¿Oyó Ud. el despegue y el aterrizaje de los aviones? (despegar [*to take off*] y aterrizar [*to land*])

4. ¿Oyó Ud. el susurro de las hojas? (susurrar [*to whisper*])

5. ¿Oyó Ud. los gritos de sus hijos? (gritar)

6. ¿Oyó Ud. los ronquidos de su mujer? (roncar [*to snore*])

H. **¿Qué vieron Uds.?** Forme oraciones usando **ver,** un verbo de percepción.

MODELO María / bailar
→ La vimos bailar.

1. José y Pablo / trotar

____

2. Anita y Rosita / hacer los bocadillos

____

3. Roberto / entrar en la discoteca

____

4. la señorita Barba / dictar una conferencia

____

E *The infinitive preceded by* ***que***

- The infinitive is often preceded by **que.** However, the **que** + infinitive construction cannot be used with verbs of searching, needing, and requesting:

Me queda mucho **que hacer.**	*I have a lot left to do.*
Nos han dado tantas cosas **que/para hacer.**	*They've given us so many things to do.*
Compra algo **que/para leer.**	*Buy something to read.*
Pidió algo **para aplacar** su sed.	*He ordered something to slake his thirst.*
Queríamos algo **para comer.**	*We wanted something to eat.*

I. Complete las siguientes oraciones escogiendo **que** o **para** antes del infinitivo como sea necesario.

1. Teníamos mucho ____________ hacer.
2. Están buscando algo ____________ comer.
3. Compraré algo ____________ leer.
4. Hay muchas cosas ____________ ver.

F *Adjective +* ***de*** *+ infinitive*

- The construction adjective + **de** + infinitive is used when the infinitive of a transitive verb is not followed by an object or a clause. The **de** is omitted when an object or a clause appears:

El vasco es muy difícil **de** aprender. Es muy difícil aprender vasco.	*Basque is very difficult to learn.* *It's very difficult to learn Basque.*
Su teoría es imposible **de** comprobar. Es imposible comprobar su teoría.	*His theory is impossible to prove.* *It's impossible to prove his theory.*

J. Complete las siguientes oraciones escribiendo **de** antes del infinitivo como sea necesario.

1. No es posible ____________ comprenderlo.
2. Eso es fácil ____________ ver.
3. Es triste ____________ pensar que ya no vuelven.
4. El japonés no es difícil ____________ aprender.

K. **Ejercicio oral: juego de expansión de oraciones.** Se juega entre dos equipos de estudiantes. Uno de los equipos da una oración y un verbo para expandirla al otro equipo como en el *ejercicio B* de este capítulo. Cada respuesta correcta vale un punto. Se juega hasta que uno de los equipos tenga 20 puntos.

PART TWO

Nouns and Their Modifiers; Pronouns

CHAPTER 16

NOUNS & ARTICLES

A *Gender of nouns*

- In Spanish, all nouns are either masculine or feminine. There are some clues to the gender of nouns.
- Most nouns that end in **-o** or that refer to males are masculine:

el libro	el hijo	el hombre
el banco	el señor	el duque
el laboratorio	el profesor	el toro
el padre	el doctor	el piano

- Most nouns that end in **-a** or that refer to females are feminine:

la revista	la hija	la duquesa
la librería	la señora	la vaca
la oficina	la profesora	la cartera
la madre	la mujer	la flauta

- There are many nouns that end in **-a** and **-ma** that are masculine and some nouns that end in **-o** that are feminine. The gender of these words must be memorized:

masculine

el día	el mediodía	el problema
el mapa	el idioma	el programa
el tranvía	el planeta	el sistema
el panda	el clima	el poema

feminine

la mano
la radio
la foto (*abbreviation of* la fotografía)
la moto (*abbreviation of* la motocicleta)

- The gender of most nouns that end in **-e** or a consonant cannot be predicted and must therefore be memorized:

masculine

el lápiz	el examen	el jarabe (*syrup*)
el papel	el buzón (*mailbox*)	el desván (*attic*)
el arroz (*rice*)	el cobre (*copper*)	el alfiler (*pin*)
el aceite (*oil*)	el disfraz (*disguise*)	el cine

feminine

la clase	la llave	la piel (*skin*)
la gente	la torre (*tower*)	la luz

- Nouns that have endings in **-dad, -tad, -tud, -umbre, -ión, -ie, -cia, -ez, -eza, -nza, -sis,** and **-itis** are usually feminine:

la ciudad	la serie (*series*)
la verdad	la superficie (*surface*)
la felicidad (*happiness*)	la presencia (*presence*)
la libertad	la diferencia
la fraternidad	la sencillez (*simplicity*)
la juventud (*youth*)	la pereza (*laziness*)
la multitud	la esperanza (*hope*)
la cumbre ([*mountain*] *top*)	la tesis (*thesis*)
la certidumbre (*certainty*)	la crisis
la nación	la faringitis (*pharyngitis*)
la reunión (*meeting*)	

- Nouns that refer to people (and some animals) that end in **-or, -és -ón,** and **-ín** are usually masculine and add **-a** to make the feminine form. The accent mark of the masculine form is dropped in the feminine:

masculine	*feminine*
el doctor	la doctora
el profesor	la profesora
el francés	la francesa
el anfitrión (*host*)	la anfitriona (*hostess*)
el campeón (*champion*)	la campeona
el león (*lion*)	la leona (*lioness*)
el bailarín (*dancer*)	la bailarina (*dancer*)

- Nouns that end in **-aje, -ambre, -or, -án,** or a stressed vowel are usually masculine:

el equipaje (*luggage*)	el amor
el paisaje (*landscape*)	el refrán (*proverb*)
el calambre (*cramp*)	el champú (*shampoo*)
el enjambre (*swarm* [*of bees, etc.*])	el rubí (*ruby*)
el valor (*value*)	

- In forming the feminine, some nouns that refer to people (or some animals) change only their article but not their form. Many of these nouns end in **-e, -a, -ista, -nte**, or a consonant:

el/la joven (*young man/woman*)	el/la artista
el/la líder (*leader*)	el/la turista
el/la intérprete (*interpreter*)	el/la agente
el/la atleta (*athlete*)	el/la cantante
el/la mártir (*martyr*)	el/la dependiente
el/la tigre (*tiger* [*also, tigresa*])	el/la estudiante
el/la dentista	

A feminine form ending in **-nta** is common: **la dependienta, la estudianta.**

- The days of the week are masculine:

Iremos a la sierra **el jueves** y volveremos **el lunes.**	*We'll go to the mountains on Thursday and we'll come back on Monday.*

- The months of the year are masculine:

el enero más frío	*the coldest January*
el agosto más caluroso	*the hottest August*

- The names of languages are masculine:

El español se habla en veinte países.	*Spanish is spoken in twenty countries.*
El inglés es la lengua de muchos países también.	*English is the language of many countries also.*

- Compound nouns that consist of a verb and a noun are masculine:

el paraguas *umbrella*
el lavaplatos *dishwasher*
el salvavidas *lifeguard, life preserver*
el parachoques *bumper*
el limpiacristales *window cleaner*
el tocadiscos *record player*
el sacacorchos *corkscrew*

- Numbers (*el número*) are masculine:

El veintisiete de enero es el cumpleaños de Mozart.	*January 27 is Mozart's birthday.*
Mi número de suerte es **el 15**.	*My lucky number is 15.*

- Colors are masculine when used as nouns:

Me gusta **el azul** más que **el marrón.**	*I like blue more than brown.*

- Many names of trees are masculine while their fruit is feminine:

el árbol	*la fruta*
el almendro *almond tree*	la almendra
el castaño *chestnut tree*	la castaña
el cerezo *cherry tree*	la cereza
el manzano *apple tree*	la manzana
el naranjo *orange tree*	la naranja
el peral *pear tree*	la pera

- All infinitives used as nouns are masculine:

El fumar hace daño.	***Smoking*** *is harmful.*

- Nouns that begin with stressed **a** or **ha** are feminine but take the masculine article in the singular, but **las** in the plural:

el agua *water*
el águila *eagle*
el ave *bird*
el hambre *hunger*
el hacha *hatchet*

el agua fría del lago	*the cold water of the lake*
las aguas tibias del Caribe	*the warm waters of the Caribbean*

- The names of rivers, seas, and oceans are masculine:

Los Estados Unidos tiene costa en **el (océano) Atlántico** y **el Pacífico.**	*The United States has coasts on the Atlantic Ocean and on the Pacific.*
El (río) Amazonas atraviesa el Brasil.	*The Amazon River passes through Brazil.*

- Some Spanish nouns have both a masculine and feminine gender, but with a difference in meaning:

masculine	*feminine*
el capital *money*	la capital *capital city*
el mañana *tomorrow*	la mañana *morning*
el frente *front (weather, military)*	la frente *forehead*
el orden *order (tidiness)*	la orden *order (command)*
el policía *policeman*	la policía *policewoman, police force*

- The word **arte** is masculine in the singular but feminine in the plural:

  el arte español — *Spanish art*
  las bellas artes — *fine arts*

- Foreign words that enter Spanish, usually from English, are almost always masculine. Some words remain feminine when borrowed into Spanish:

  el jazz
  el marketing
  el (e)spray *aerosol*
  el campus
  el/la cassette *cassette player/cassette tape*

- Some nouns do not vary in gender and are applied to males and females, in some cases with a change in article:

  el ángel
  el bebé
  la persona
  el personaje *character (in a book, play)*
  la víctima
  el/la testigo *witness*
  el/la modelo

  Thus you say **Juan fue *la* víctima más joven del accidente** but **Marta es *la* testigo más importante**.

- Sometimes an inanimate feminine noun can be applied to a male person with a change in meaning. In this case, the new noun is masculine:

  la cámara *camera* — **el** cámara *cameraman*
  la trompeta *trumpet* — **el** trompeta *trumpet player*
  las medias *socks* — **los** Medias Rojas *the Red Sox*

A. **¿Masculino o femenino?** Escriba la forma masculina o femenina del artículo definido para cada sustantivo de la lista.

1. __________ concierto
2. __________ sistema
3. __________ escritor
4. __________ tierra
5. __________ drama
6. __________ mano
7. __________ natación
8. __________ día
9. __________ natalidad (*birthrate*)
10. __________ parque
11. __________ legumbre
12. __________ guión (*script*)
13. __________ capital (*capital city*)
14. __________ pararrayos (*lightning rod*)
15. __________ computadora
16. __________ seguridad (*security*)
17. __________ rompecabezas (*riddle*)
18. __________ idioma
19. __________ dirección (*address*)
20. __________ escocés
21. __________ banano
22. __________ verde
23. __________ frente (*forehead*)
24. __________ ascensor
25. __________ parabrisas (*windshield*)

B. Por parejas. Escriba quién es la pareja femenina (*counterpart*) de cada hombre. Practique usando la forma femenina de los sustantivos. Escriba el artículo también.

1. el profesor / ________________
2. el rey / ________________
3. el artista / ________________
4. el abogado / ________________
5. el príncipe / ________________
6. el gobernador / ________________
7. el representante / ________________
8. el policía / ________________
9. el emperador / ________________
10. el actor / ________________
11. el estadista (*statesman*) / ________________
12. el holandés (*Dutchman*) / ________________
13. el cliente / ________________
14. el atleta / ________________
15. el programador / ________________

C. Exprese las siguientes oraciones en español.

1. Mr. Galíndez is leaving on a business trip on Tuesday and will return on Thursday.

   ____

2. Don't put the frying pan in the dishwasher. (*Ud.*)

   ____

3. English and French are the official languages of Canada.

   ____

4. Beethoven was born on December 16, 1770.

   ____

5. My favorite colors are green and blue.

   ____

6. Let's pick apples from that (apple) tree.

   ____

7. The official bird of the United States is the eagle.

   ____

8. Did they like the cruise (*crucero*) in the Mediterranean or the Caribbean better?

   ____

9. Reading is so pleasant.

10. A tropical front will arrive tomorrow.

11. We'll invest our capital in an international company.

12. What are the names of the characters in the novel?

13. The cameraman lost his camera.

14. In the film we saw, the angels saved the baby.

15. The witnesses talked to the victim of the accident.

B *Number of nouns*

- In Spanish, nouns that end in a vowel form the plural by adding **-s**:

singular	*plural*
el hermano	los hermanos
el espejo *mirror*	los espejos
la carretera *highway*	las carreteras
la placa *license plate*	las placas
el clarinete	los clarinetes
el café	los cafés

- Nouns that end in a consonant, including **y**, form the plural by adding **-es**:

el titular *headline*	los titulares
la ley *law*	las leyes
el huracán *hurricane*	los huracanes
el peatón *pedestrian*	los peatones
el limón	los limones
la opinión	las opiniones
el inglés	los ingleses
el mes	los meses
el país	los países
el pez *fish*	los peces
la voz *voice*	las voces
el lápiz	los lápices
el examen	los exámenes
el origen	los orígenes

Notes on the formation of the plural:

Nouns stressed on the last syllable in the singular lose their accent mark in the plural: **limón → limones, inglés → ingleses, autobús → autobuses**. Exception: **país → países**.

Lápices and all nouns that have a written accent on the next to the last syllable in the singular retain that accent in the plural: **azúcar ➔ azúcares.**

Examen and **origen** add an accent mark in the plural: **exámenes, orígenes.**

A few common nouns shift their stress in the plural: **el carácter ➔ los caracteres, el régimen ➔ los regímenes, el espécimen ➔ los especímenes.**

When **-es** is added to final **z** , the **z** is changed to **c: pez ➔ peces, voz ➔ voces, lápiz ➔ lápices**.

Nouns that end in a stressed **-í** or **-ú** add **-es** to form the plural: **el rubí ➔ los rubíes, el tabú ➔ los tabúes.**

Nouns of more than one syllable ending in an unstressed vowel plus **s** do not add a plural ending:

el viernes		➔	los viernes
el miércoles		➔	los miércoles
la crisis		➔	las crisis
el atlas		➔	los atlas
el paraguas		➔	los paraguas
el abrelatas	*can opener*	➔	los abrelatas

- The masculine plural of nouns referring to people includes both males and females:

  los hijos *children, sons and daughters*
  los hermanos *brothers and sisters*
  los Reyes de España *The King and Queen of Spain*

- If a proper name refers to a family, it has no plural form. If a group of individuals happen to have the same name, a plural form is used. Names that end in **-z** are usually invariable:

Los Prado viven en esta calle.	*The Prado family lives on this street.*
La guía telefónica tiene tantos **Morelos** y **Blancos.**	*The telephone book has so many Morelos and Blancos (people named Morelo and Blanco).*
¿No conoces a **los Fernández**?	*Don't you know the Fernándezes?*

- Some nouns are always plural in Spanish as they are in English:

  los anteojos *eyeglasses*
  las gafas *eyeglasses*
  los gemelos *twins, binoculars, cuff links*
  las tijeras *scissors*
  los auriculares *earphones*

- Some nouns are usually plural in Spanish. Many of them appear in set expressions, for example: **hacerle cosquillas a alguien** *to tickle someone.*

  las vacaciones *vacation*
  los bienes *goods*
  las afueras *outskirts*
  los alrededores *surroundings*
  las cosquillas *tickling*
  las ganas *urge, desire*

  Note that **las ganas** appears in singular in **No me da la gana** *I don't feel like it.*

- The Spanish equivalent of *They washed their heads* is **Se lavaron la cabeza.** Notice that Spanish uses the singular noun **la cabeza** implying there is one for each person.

Se cortaron **la rodilla.**	*They cut their knees.*
Se pusieron **la chaqueta.**	*They put on their jackets.*
¿Tienen Uds. **novia**?	*Do you have girlfriends?*

D. En plural. Escriba la forma en plural de estos sustantivos y de su artículo.

1. el guante ________________
2. el lavaplatos ________________
3. la religión ________________
4. el origen ________________
5. el pizarrón ________________
6. el color ________________
7. la amistad ________________
8. el rey ________________
9. la tos ________________
10. el martes ________________
11. el irlandés ________________
12. el paréntesis ________________
13. el señor Sánchez ________________
14. la luz ________________
15. el té ________________

E. El arca de Noé. ¡No se olvide que hay dos animales de cada especie que suben al arca de Noé! Practique usando el plural de los sustantivos.

Modelo caballo **caballos**

1. vaca ________________
2. orangután ________________
3. elefante ________________
4. avestruz (*ostrich*) ________________
5. león ________________
6. castor (*beaver*) ________________
7. loro (*parrot*) ________________
8. cóndor ________________
9. delfín (*dolphin*) ________________
10. gorrión (*sparrow*) ________________
11. faisán (*pheasant*) ________________

12. pantera (*panther*) ______________________
13. tigre ______________________
14. oveja ______________________
15. mono (*monkey*) ______________________

F. Sobre gustos no hay nada escrito. (***Everyone to his/her own taste.***) Escriba oraciones en las cuales Ud. explica lo que le gusta comer a cada persona. Cambie el sustantivo (la comida) al plural.

MODELO Carlos / comer / haba (beans)
➔ Carlos come **habas.**

1. Lucía / pedir / guisante (*peas*)

____

2. yo / preferir / el espárrago (*asparagus*)

____

3. tú / ordenar / papa frita

____

4. Claudia y Jesús / querer / macarrón (*macaroni*)

____

5. nosotros / tener ganas de comer / espinaca

____

6. Ud. y Lourdes / pedir / frijol

____

7. Ud. / querer / palomita de maíz

____

Nota cultural

Los frijoles (*kidney beans*), alimento básico de la dieta mexicana, es la misma planta que cultivaron los indios precolombinos de México. Los frijoles se comen en muchos platos en todos los países hispanoamericanos. En España se llaman judías o alubias. La papa (la patata en España), indígena de América, fue llevada a España y Europa por los conquistadores en el siglo XVI. La palabra es de origen quechua, el idioma hablado por los incas del Perú.

G. ¡Que toque la orquesta! Vuelva a escribir estos instrumentos en el plural con el artículo definido.

1. piano ______________________
2. flauta ______________________
3. viola ______________________
4. clarinete ______________________

5. violonchelo ______________________________
6. violín ______________________________
7. trompeta ______________________________
8. trombón ______________________________
9. arpa ______________________________
10. oboe ______________________________
11. tambor ______________________________
12. tuba ______________________________

The definite article: forms, uses

- In Spanish, the definite article, English *the,* changes its form to agree with the noun in gender (masculine/feminine) and number (singular/plural):

	masculine	*feminine*
sing.	**el**	**la**
pl.	**los**	**las**

el cuerpo — **la** cabeza
los cuerpos — **las** cabezas

- In Spanish, unlike English, the definite article is used before a noun to refer to something in a general way (mass or uncountable nouns) or to refer to all the members of its class. Colors, like abstract nouns, also require the article:

La democracia es el mejor sistema de gobierno. — *Democracy is the best system of government.*
El agua mineral es buena para la digestión. — *Mineral water is good for digestion.*
El verde es el color que más me gusta. — *Green is the color I like best.*
No le gustan **las espinacas.** — *She doesn't like spinach.*

Note that the sentence **No le gustan las espinacas** is ambiguous out of context because it can mean she doesn't like all spinach, that is, spinach in general, or she doesn't like a particular spinach already mentioned in the conversation.

- The definite article **el** is used before the names of languages except directly after **hablar** and after the prepositions **de** and **en**. It is also commonly omitted directly after the verbs **aprender, enseñar, estudiar, leer, practicar,** and **saber.**

Hablamos español. — *We speak Spanish.*
Hablamos bien **el** español. — *We speak Spanish well.*
Escribió la carta **en** francés. — *He wrote the letter in French.*
Te presto el diccionario **de** chino. — *I'll lend you the Chinese dictionary.*
Saben hebreo y estudian japonés. — *They know Hebrew and they're studying Japanese.*

- The definite article is used before titles except when the person is being addressed directly. It is not used before **don / doña** and **Santo / San / Santa**:

El señor Lerma está bien.	*Mr. Lerma is well.*
Señor Lerma, ¿cómo está Ud.?	*Mr. Lerma, how are you?*
Don Juan nació el día de **San** Juan.	*Juan was born on St. John's day.*

- The definite article is used to express the time of day:

Son **las cuatro** y media.	*It's four thirty.*
Se acostaron a **la una** de la mañana.	*They went to bed at one A.M.*

- The definite article is used with the days of the week except after the verb **ser** when expressing dates:

El concierto fue **el sábado.**	*The concert was on Saturday.*
Los lunes el museo está cerrado.	*On Mondays the museum is closed.*
Hoy **es miércoles.**	*Today is Wednesday.*

- The definite article is used with the names of the seasons. It can be omitted after the preposition **en** when it is suggested that the event mentioned occurs in that season every year:

Me encanta **el verano.**	*I love summer.*
Alano va a Madrid **en el otoño.**	*Alano is going to Madrid in the fall.*
Gonzalo viaja a Barcelona **en invierno.**	*Gonzalo travels to Barcelona in winter.*

- Spanish uses the definite article rather than the possessive adjective that English prefers with parts of the body and articles of clothing, especially with reflexive verbs:

Sofi se puso **los jeans.**	*Sofi put on her jeans.*
Mauricio está cepillándose **los dientes.**	*Mauricio is brushing his teeth.*

- The definite article is used before infinitives that function as nouns. The article is often omitted when the infinitive is the subject of the sentence:

(El) robar es malo.	*Stealing is bad.*
El estafar es también un vicio.	*Cheating is also a vice.*

- The definite article is used with the names of rivers, oceans, and mountains:

El Sena pasa por París y **el Támesis** por Londres.	*The Seine flows through Paris and the Thames through London.*
Los Pirineos quedan entre España y Francia.	*The Pyrenees are between Spain and France.*

- The definite article is traditionally used before the names of some countries, although it tends to be omitted more and more in the modern language. The definite article *must* be used before the name of a country, city, or continent that is modified:

en (**los**) Estados Unidos	*in the United States*
a través de (**del**) Canadá	*through Canada*
por (**la**) Argentina	*through Argentina*
hacia (**el**) Perú	*toward Peru*
sobre (**el**) Japón	*about Japan*
la Europa central	*Central Europe*
la España medieval	*Medieval Spain*

- The definite article is used before nouns of measurement:

un dólar **la libra**	*a dollar a/the pound*
cincuenta centavos **el kilo**	*fifty centavos a/the kilo*

- In Spanish, many set phrases that require the definite article do not have it in their English equivalents:

a/en/de **la** iglesia	*to/in/from church*
en **la** televisión	*on television*
en **el** mar	*at sea, on/in the sea*

H. El artículo definido. Complete la siguiente tabla llenando los espacios en blanco con la forma correcta del artículo definido en singular y plural de los sustantivos.

	artículo definido singular	artículo definido plural	plural del sustantivo
1. aceituna			
2. ensayo			
3. agua			
4. árbol			
5. dulce			
6. demora			
7. sal			
8. pasaporte			
9. volcán			
10. actividad			
11. salvavidas			
12. origen			
13. foto			
14. mes			
15. serpiente			
16. sillón			
17. miel			
18. lápiz			
19. francés			
20. vez			
21. tenedor			
22. pirámide			
23. raíz			
24. sacapuntas			
25. pensión			
26. pintor			

	artículo definido singular	artículo definido plural	plural del sustantivo
27. jardín			
28. jugador			
29. esquí			
30. pan			

I. ¡Retrato de la heroína romántica! Armando, un pintor romántico, pinta el retrato de la mujer ideal. ¿Cómo es? Para saberlo, llene los espacios en blanco con la forma correcta del artículo definido y el sustantivo.

MODELO La mujer ideal tiene: **los pies** pequeños (*feet*)

1. ________________________ azules (*eyes*)
2. ________________________ rosadas (*cheeks* [mejillas])
3. ________________________ suaves (*hands*)
4. ________________________ largos (*fingers*)
5. ________________________ como cerezas (*lips*)
6. ________________________ como perlas (*teeth*)
7. ________________________ como el oro (*hair*)
8. ________________________ como cisne (*swan*) (*neck*)
9. ________________________ bien formadas (*ears*)

J. **¿Artículo definido o no?** Llene los espacios en blanco con la forma correcta del artículo definido donde sea necesario.

1. Bogotá, __________ capital de Colombia, se encuentra en las montañas.
2. Nos interesa __________ cine.
3. Laura y Encarnación saben perfectamente __________ ruso.
4. Hay multa por __________ ensuciar las calles.
5. ¿Adónde va Ud., __________ señorita Maldonado?
6. Volvimos a casa a __________ diez y cuarto.
7. Estas revistas están escritas en __________ catalán.
8. La comida fue __________ miércoles.
9. __________ legumbres son buenas para __________ salud.
10. __________ verano es la estación más agradable del año.
11. Hoy es __________ domingo.
12. Hicimos investigaciones sobre __________ España contemporánea.
13. __________ duraznos se venden a 79 centavos __________ libra en verano.
14. ¿Habrá algo interesante en __________ televisión?
15. __________ señorita Suárez llega de __________ iglesia.

Nota cultural

El catalán se habla en Cataluña, la región al noreste de España. El español y el catalán son oficiales en Cataluña. El catalán también se habla en Valencia (el dialecto se llama valenciano) y en las islas Baleares (el dialecto es el mallorquín).

K. Exprese las siguientes oraciones en español.

1. The Sánchez family is going to Florida in the spring.

____

2. Florencia put on her socks.

____

3. Give (*Ud.*) us the Latin books.

____

4. Juli and Nicolás love swimming.

____

5. What did the tourists do at sea?

____

6. The twins washed their faces.

____

7. Elías knows Portuguese, speaks Italian, reads Russian, and is learning German.

____

8. The masked ball was on Saturday. It began at 9:30 P.M.

____

9. The novel was written in Polish and translated into Greek.

____

D *The definite article: omissions*

- The definite article is omitted before mass or count nouns which do not refer to the whole of their class, but only to some of it or a part of it (an unspecified quantity):

Guadalupe tiene paciencia.	*Guadalupe is patient.*
Toman aspirinas.	*They're taking aspirin.*
Amparo compró carne.	*Amparo bought meat.*

- Spanish usually omits the definite article after **haber:**

Hay gente en el comedor.	*There are people in the dining room.*

- When two nouns are joined by **de** to form a compound noun, the definite article is omitted before the *second* noun:

la carne de res	*beef*
el dolor de cabeza	*headache*
libros de historia	*history books*

- The definite article is usually omitted in apposition:

Caracas, capital de Venezuela	*Caracas, the capital of Venezuela*
Santa Fe, capital de Nuevo México	*Santa Fe, the capital of New Mexico*
Simón Bolívar, libertador de Sudamérica	*Simón Bolívar, the liberator of South America*
Mario Vargas Llosa, novelista	*Mario Vargas Llosa, the novelist*

- The definite article is omitted before ordinal numbers with kings and other rulers:

Alfonso X (décimo)	*Alfonso the Tenth*
Carlos V (quinto)	*Charles the Fifth*

- In Spanish, there are many set adverbial phrases that do not take the definite article whereas their English equivalents usually do:

en nombre de	*in the name of*
a corto/largo plazo	*in the short/long run*
en camino	*on the way*

L. **¿Falta el artículo definido?** Llene los espacios en blanco con el artículo definido donde sea necesario.

1. Plácido Domingo, __________ tenor, y Montserrat Caballé, __________ soprano, son españoles.
2. Juan Carlos __________ I (primero) subió al trono español en 1975.
3. ¡Alfonsito tiene dolor de __________ estómago y Luisito tiene dolor de __________ muelas por los bombones que se comieron!
4. Los chicos compraron __________ refrescos más naturales para la fiesta.
5. Aurelia no está en casa porque ya está en __________ camino.
6. No hay __________ sillones en la sala todavía.
7. Tomamos __________ vitaminas para tener __________ energía.

Nota cultural

Hay varios artistas hispanos que tienen una fama internacional en la música clásica. Plácido Domingo y José Carreras, dos de "los tres tenores" (con Pavarotti), son españoles. Montserrat Caballé y Victoria de los Ángeles, sopranos, son españolas. Alicia de Larrocha, pianista española. Pablo Casals, violonchelista español. Rafael Frühbeck de Burgos, director español. Claudio Arrau, pianista chileno. Jaime Laredo, violinista, nació en Bolivia. José Gutiérrez, pianista, nació en Cuba. El director de orquesta Eduardo Mata nació en México.

E The neuter article lo

- Spanish has a neuter article **lo** which is placed before an adjective used as a noun to express an abstract idea or a certain quality. The form **lo** is invariable and is used with masculine and feminine and singular and plural adjectives + **que** to express *how*. **Lo** is also used with adverbs and adverbial phrases:

lo bueno	*the good part, what's good*
lo fácil	*the easy part, what's easy*
Lo importante es que nosotros pensamos **lo mismo**.	*The important thing is that we think the same.*
Vi **lo listo/lista** que es.	*I saw how clever he/she is.*
Oí **lo graciosos/graciosas** que son.	*I heard how witty they are.*
Pensaban en **lo bien** que lo iban a pasar.	*They were thinking about the good time they were going to have.*

- **Lo** is used before a **de** phrase which means *the matter concerning:*

lo del ingeniero	*the matter concerning the engineer*
lo de tus documentos	*the business about, situation of your papers*

Lo is used in the phrases **lo más/menos posible** *as much as possible/as little as possible* and **lo antes posible** *as soon as possible.*

M. **¡Artículos en el museo!** Cuando Ud. fue al museo con su amiga vieron muchas cosas interesantes. Llene los espacios en blanco con la forma correcta del artículo que falta. Escoja entre el artículo neutro **lo**, el definido y el indefinido. No se olvide de escribir las contracciones **al** y **del** cuando sean necesarias. ¡Tenga en cuenta que es posible que no falte el artículo!

_______________ (1) viernes yo fui con Edita a _______________ (2) museo de _______________ (3) arte. Todo _______________ (4) de _______________ (5) arte nos interesa mucho. _______________ (6) bello de _______________ (7) museo son _______________ (8) salas de _______________ (9) escultura. Hay tantos *artículos* y piezas de _______________ (10) gran valor. No pudimos ver _______________ (11) esculturas porque _______________ (12) mes pasado hubo _______________ (13) robo en _______________ (14) museo. Parece que _______________ (15) ladrones entraron a _______________ (16) museo a _______________ (17) tres de _______________ (18) mañana. Se llevaron _______________ (19) estatuas preciosas. _______________ (20) guardia muy simpático nos dijo que _______________ (21) de _______________ (22) seguridad en _______________ (23) museo es _______________ (24) problema.

F The indefinite article: forms, uses, and omissions

- The Spanish indefinite article (English *a, an*) appears as **un** before a masculine noun and as **una** before a feminine noun.

	masculine	*feminine*
sing.	**un**	**una**
pl.	**unos**	**unas**

- The plural indefinite articles **unos/unas** are the equivalent of English *some, a few, a couple of*.
- **El** and **un** are always used before feminine nouns that begin with a stressed **a-** or **ha-**. The plural of these nouns always uses **las** and **unas**. This rule does not apply where the first vowel is not stressed: **la alfombra, la ambición**. Also, the name of letter **a** is **la a** and the letter **h** is **la hache**:

el/un agua	**las/unas** aguas
el/un águila *eagle*	**las/unas** águilas
el/un alma *soul*	**las/unas** almas
el/un arca *ark*	**las/unas** arcas
el/un área	**las/unas** áreas
el/un arma *arm, weapon*	**las/unas** armas
el/un arpa *harp*	**las/unas** arpas
el/un haba *bean*	**las/unas** habas
el/un habla *language*	**las/unas** hablas
el/un hambre *hunger*	**las/unas** hambres

- The indefinite article is omitted before predicate nouns that denote profession, occupation, nationality, religion, social status, gender, etc. If, however, the noun is modified by a phrase or an adjective, the indefinite article is expressed:

Amparo es violinista.	*Amparo is a violinist.*
Es una violinista brillante.	*She's a brilliant violinist.*
Francisco es carpintero.	*Francisco is a carpenter.*
Esos chicos son argentinos.	*Those kids are Argentine.*
Ester es judía/católica/protestante.	*Ester is Jewish/Catholic/Protestant.*

- The indefinite article is usually omitted after the verbs **tener**, **llevar** (*to wear*), **usar, comprar, buscar, sacar**:

Asunción tiene jardín.	*Asunción has a garden.*
Nieves y Julián usan anteojos.	*Nieves and Julián wear glasses.*
Compra pasteles.	*Buy pastries.*

- The indefinite article is in phrases with **¡qué ...!** (*what a ...!*) and before **otro** (*another*), **cierto** (*a certain*), **tal** (*such a*), **medio** (*half a*), **ciento** (*a hundred*), and **mil** (*a thousand*). The English equivalents of these words have the indefinite article:

¡Qué día!	*What a day!*
otro color y otro estilo	*another color and another style*
cierta persona	*a certain person*
tal problema	*such a problem*
medio kilo	*half a kilo*
cien/mil dólares	*a hundred/a thousand dollars*

N. El artículo indefinido. Ahora llene los espacios en blanco con la forma correcta del artículo indefinido en singular y plural de los sustantivos.

	artículo indefinido singular	artículo indefinido plural	plural del sustantivo
1. mar			
2. optimista			
3. orden			
4. parador			
5. olor			
6. oboe			
7. área			
8. mochila			
9. joven			
10. nadador			
11. papel			
12. volibol			
13. menú			
14. cereal			
15. buzón			
16. irlandés			
17. alma			
18. paraguas			
19. camarón			
20. garaje			
21. voz			
22. desfile			
23. nación			
24. lavaplatos			
25. lema			
26. sucursal			
27. ascensor			
28. habla			
29. postal			
30. agua			

O. En el taller. El pintor Dionisio está pintando en su taller donde se encuentran las siguientes cosas. Escriba la forma correcta del artículo indefinido al lado del sustantivo.

1. __________ cuadro
2. __________ artista (*masc.*)
3. __________ pinceles
4. __________ mural
5. __________ modelos (*fem.*)
6. __________ colección
7. __________ paisajes
8. __________ escultura
9. __________ retratos

P. ¿Artículo indefinido o no? Llene los espacios en blanco con la forma correcta del artículo indefinido donde sea necesario.

1. Sergio es __________ ingeniero.
2. Es __________ día muy caluroso.
3. Gabriel es __________ judío y Carmen es __________ católica.
4. Verónica tiene entre __________ cien y __________ mil sellos en su colección.
5. ¿Puede Ud. enseñarme __________ otro estilo de abrigo, por favor?
6. Simón Colón es __________ pianista muy talentoso.
7. La nueva vecina es __________ mexicana.
8. Todos los niños de esa familia usan __________ gafas.
9. No se puede encontrar __________ paraguas grande.

G *Contractions **del** and **al***

- There are two contractions in Spanish. The masculine article **el** combines with the preposition **de** to form **del** *of the* and with **a** to form **al** *to the*. These prepositions do not contract with the other forms of the definite article **la, los, las.** The contractions are not used if the definite article is part of a proper name:

Mateo es el gerente **del** hotel.	*Mateo is the manager of the hotel.*
Álvaro fue **al museo.**	*Álvaro went to the museum.*
Sol fue **a El Prado.**	*Sol went to El Prado.*

Q. ¿Dónde están todos? Diga que las personas no están porque fueron a distintos lugares. Use la contracción **al** cuando sea necesario.

MODELO Nieves / teatro → Nieves fue al teatro.

1. Concepción y Simón / puesto de periódicos

____

2. yo / ayuntamiento (*town hall*)

____

3. Domingo y Brígida / supermercado

____

4. Ud. / parque de atracciones

____

5. Lourdes / iglesia

____

6. mi hermano / la bolsa (*stock exchange*)

____

7. nosotros / estación de tren

____

8. tú / centro comercial

____

H *Possession*

- In Spanish, possession is expressed by the use of a prepositional phrase with **de.** Spanish titles such as **señor** and **profesora** must be preceded by the definite article when referring to the specific person. (When directly addressing a person with a title, the definite article is not used.)

Leí el informe **de Jacobo.**	*I read Jacobo's report.*
Leí todos los capítulos **del libro.**	*I read all the chapters of the book.*
Hoy es el día **del** examen final.	*Today is the day of the final exam.*
Cenaron en el restaurante **del** hotel.	*They had dinner in the hotel restaurant.*
¿Conoces el comercio **del** señor Bermúdez?	*Are you familiar with Mr. Bermúdez' store?*

- In Spanish, **¿De quién?** followed by **ser** is equivalent to English *Whose?*

¿De quién es el cinturón?	*Whose belt is it?*
¿De quién son estos pendientes?	*Whose earrings are these?*
¿De quién(es) es el barco?	*Whose boat is it?*
¿De quién son estas postales?	*Whose postcards are these?*

A form **¿De quiénes?** also exists to refer to a plural possessor but is not common in the spoken language.

R. **¿De quién es?** Escriba preguntas y respuestas que demuestran posesión.

Modelo los libros de texto / el profesor
→ ¿De quién son los libros de texto?
→ Son del profesor.

1. el almacén / el señor Acosta

____

____

2. los peines / Adela y Matilde

3. el equipaje / las turistas

4. los discos compactos / el pianista

5. este llavero / la empleada

6. las sartenes / el cocinero

7. las raquetas / estas tenistas

8. el reloj / el doctor Villanueva

S. Exprese las siguientes frases en español.

1. Mr. Valle's florist shop

2. the (*masc.*) president's office

3. the programmer's disks

4. the shop's windows

5. the nuclear plant's energy

6. the students' notebooks

7. Professor (*fem.*) Salas' lectures

T. Ejercicio oral. Un programa de concursos (*Quiz show*). El presentador del programa lee sustantivos a los dos equipos que luego tienen que ponerles el artículo definido o indefinido correcto. Se puede variar con frases de posesión, las contracciones **al** y **del**, etc. ¡Al final se calculan los puntos ganados por cada equipo para saber quiénes sacaron el premio gordo (*grand prize*)!

U. Estructuras en acción. Lea el siguiente anuncio sobre una velada literaria con Carlos Fuentes, el célebre escritor mexicano. El anuncio aparece sin algunos artículos. Luego coloque los artículos con su forma correcta donde sean necesarios.

Vocabulario

a partir de *from*
el círculo *circle*
con motivo de *because of, on the occasion of*
correr a cargo de *to be the responsibility of, in the hands of*
la charla *informal talk*
el encuentro *meeting*
intervenir *to participate, take part*
el lector *reader*
los medios *media*
recoger *to pick up*
la velada literaria *literary evening*

Círculo de Lectores organiza __________ (1) encuentro con Carlos Fuentes, con __________ (2) motivo de __________ (3) presentación de __________ (4) Biblioteca Carlos Fuentes y de __________ (5) biografía ilustrada *Retrato de Carlos Fuentes*, escrita por Julio Ortega.

__________ (6) presentación correrá a __________ (7) cargo de Julio Ortega, __________ (8) profesor de __________ (9) literatura latinoamericana en __________ (10) Universidad de Brown, __________ (11) Estados Unidos.

Carlos Fuentes intervendrá con __________ (12) charla titulada *Vida de* __________ (13) *obra, obra de* __________ (14) *vida.*

La velada tendrá __________ (15) lugar en __________ (16) Centro Cultural de Círculo de Lectores en Madrid, calle de O'Donnell, 10.

__________ (17) invitaciones pueden recogerse en __________ (18) mismo Centro Cultural a partir de __________ (19) 10 de __________ (20) mañana del lunes 3 de __________ (21) julio. Teléfono: (91) 435 37 40. Información a los medios, teléfono: (91) 435 83 44.

Veladas Literarias

Carlos Fuentes en Círculo de Lectores

Jueves 6 de julio de 1995, a las 8 de la tarde.

Círculo de Lectores organiza un encuentro con **Carlos Fuentes,** con motivo de la presentación de la **Biblioteca Carlos Fuentes** y de la biografía illustrada ***Retrato de Carlos Fuentes,*** escrita por Julio Ortega.

La presentación correrá a cargo de **Julio Ortega,** profesor de literatura latinoamericana en la Universidad de Brown, Estados Unidos.

Carlos Fuentes intervendrá con una charla titulada *Vida de la obra, obra de la vida.*

La velada tendrá lugar en el Centro Cultural de Círculo de Lectores en Madrid, calle de O'Donnell, 10.

Las invitaciones pueden recogerse en el mismo Centro Cultural a partir de las 10 de la mañana del lunes 3 de julio. Teléfono: (91) 435 37 40
Información a los medios, teléfono: (91) 435 83 44

CÍRCULO DE LECTORES

CHAPTER 17

ADJECTIVES

A *Agreement of adjectives*

- Spanish adjectives agree in gender and number with the nouns they modify. Adjectives that have a masculine singular form ending in **-o** have four forms:

bonito		
	masculine	*feminine*
sing.	bonit**o**	bonit**a**
pl.	bonit**os**	bonit**as**

maravilloso		
	masculine	*feminine*
sing.	maravillos**o**	maravillos**a**
pl.	maravillos**os**	maravillos**as**

- Adjectives that have a masculine singular ending in a consonant or in **-e** have only two forms, a singular and a plural. They do not change for gender:

difícil	
	masculine & feminine
sing.	difícil
pl.	difícil**es**

triste	
	masculine & feminine
sing.	triste
pl.	triste**s**

- A small number of adjectives of nationality end in **-a** or in stressed **-í** or **-ú**. These also have only two forms:

belga *Belgian*	
	masculine & feminine
sing.	belga
pl.	belga**s**

israelí *Israeli*	
	masculine & feminine
sing.	israelí
pl.	israelí**es**

hindú *Hindu*	
	masculine & feminine
sing.	hindú
pl.	hindú**es**

Other similar adjectives: **azteca** (*Aztec*), **marroquí** (*Moroccan*), **iraní** (*Iranian*), **pakistaní** (*Pakistani*), **bantú** (*Bantu*). There are also adjectives ending in **-ista, -sta,** and **-ita** that follow the above pattern: **realista, entusiasta, nacionalista, cosmopolita.**

- Adjectives ending in the suffixes **-dor, -ón,** and **-án** add **-a** to form the feminine, and therefore have four forms like adjectives ending in **-o**. These adjectives form their masculine plural by adding **-es** and their feminine plural by adding **-as**. The accented suffixes lose their accent when an ending is added.

hablador *talkative*		
	masculine	*feminine*
sing.	hablador	hablador**a**
pl.	hablador**es**	hablador**as**

preguntón *inquisitive*		
	masculine	*feminine*
sing.	preguntón	pregunton**a**
pl.	pregunton**es**	pregunton**as**

- Spanish adjectives usually follow the nouns they modify:

—En esa tienda de ropa venden cosas **maravillosas**. *In that clothing store they sell wonderful things.*
—Sí. Veo que te has comprado unos vestidos muy **bonitos**. *Yes. I see that you've bought yourself some very pretty dresses.*

A. ¿Cómo están? Su amigo le pregunta cómo están ciertas personas. Contéstele usando los adjetivos que aparecen entre paréntesis haciendo la concordancia necesaria.

MODELO ¿Cómo está tu hermana? (ocupado)
➔ Está ocupada.

1. ¿Cómo están tus padres? (feliz)

______

2. ¿Cómo estás? (contento)

______

3. ¿Cómo se encuentra Raquel? (nervioso)

______

4. ¿Cómo se siente Claudio? (deprimido)

______

5. ¿Cómo se encuentran las hermanas de Augusto? (triste)

______

6. ¿Cómo están Uds.? (cansado)

______

7. ¿Cómo se sienten los primos de Paco? (enfermo)

______

8. ¿Cómo está Matilde? (preocupado)

______

9. ¿Cómo está tu tía? (aburrido)

______

B. **¡Don de gentes!** Jacobo y su hermana Luisa son estudiantes de intercambio que llegaron de Tegucigalpa, capital de Honduras el año pasado. Viven con una familia norteamericana y se llevan muy bien con todo el mundo. ¿Qué creen las personas de los hermanos hondureños? Para saberlo, escriba oraciones usando los adjetivos que aparecen entre paréntesis. Haga las concordancias necesarias.

MODELO Elena cree / Luisa / honesto
→ Elena cree que Luisa es honesta.

Carácter y personalidad

buena gente *nice (person/people)*
cortés *courteous*
el don de gentes *charm, getting on well with people*
encantador *charming*
generoso *generous*
gracioso *witty*
honesto *honest*
independiente *independent*
inteligente *intelligent*
listo *clever*
responsable *reliable*
serio *serious*
simpático *nice, pleasant*
sincero *sincere*
tener personalidad *to have personality or character*
trabajador *hard-working*

1. Paco cree / Jacobo / listo

____

2. la señora Alvarado piensa / Luisa / encantador

____

3. el profesor de cálculo encuentra / a los hermanos / inteligente y trabajador

____

4. Nieves cree / Jacobo / sincero

____

5. el señor Alvarado dice / Luisa / gracioso y generoso

____

6. las profesoras de literatura europea encuentran a Jacobo / serio y responsable

____

7. los hijos de los Alvarado creen / Luisa / independiente y simpático

____

8. todo el mundo dice / Jacobo y Luisa / buena gente y cortés

____

Nota cultural

Tegucigalpa, capital de Honduras, fue fundada como campamento de minas en 1578. Los españoles empezaron a poblar la ciudad en este año aunque los indígenas ya llamaban la ciudad Tisingal. Tegucigalpa quiere decir "montaña de plata" en el idioma indígena original. La ciudad se convirtió en capital en 1880. A diferencia de la ciudad de Guatemala que fue casi totalmente destruida por terremotos, Tegucigalpa conserva mucha de su arquitectura original porque no queda en una falla (*fault*) geológica. La ciudad tiene plazas grandes, hermosos jardines, una universidad nacional, un paraninfo (salón) universitario donde tienen lugar muchos eventos culturales, una catedral del siglo XVIII tardío, el Teatro Nacional Manuel Bonilla, etcétera.

C. ¿Qué se piensa de ellos? Juan y Teresa no le caen bien a nadie. ¿Qué piensa la gente de ellos? Escriba oraciones usando los adjetivos que aparecen entre paréntesis. Haga las concordancias necesarias.

MODELO Laura dice: No soporto a Juan porque es **antipático.**

Más carácter y personalidad

aguantar *to stand*
antipático *unpleasant*
desleal *disloyal*
engañoso *deceitful*
Me cae mal. *I don't like her.*
mentiroso *lying*
molesto *annoying*
No los puedo ver. *I can't stand them.*
odiar *to hate*
soportar *to stand*
tonto *silly, stupid*

1. Ramón dice: Creo que Teresa es muy ________________. (arrogante)
2. Patricio dice: No aguanto a Juan porque es ________________. (molesto)
3. Matilde dice: Los encuentro ________________. (tacaño)
4. Ana dice: No los puedo ver porque son ________________. (tonto)
5. Luisa dice: Teresa me cae mal porque es ________________. (mentiroso)
6. Joaquín dice: Yo odio a los dos porque son ________________. (desleal)
7. Adela dice: Yo encuentro a los dos ________________. (engañoso)

D. Pintura mexicana. Los estudiantes de «Pintura mexicana del siglo XX» están viendo unas diapositivas (*slides*). Comentan sobre los colores del cuadro titulado *Campamento Zapatista*. Escriba adjetivos de color haciendo las concordancias necesarias.

1. Es impresionante la capa ______________________ (*blue*) de la Virgen de Guadalupe.
2. Salta a la vista (*stands out*) el sombrero ______________________ (*yellow*).
3. Es bonita la piel ______________________ (*brown*) de los campesinos.
4. Me encanta la camisa ______________________ (*pink*).
5. Los pantalones ______________________ (*white*) tienen pliegues (*folds*) ______________________ (*blue*).
6. Los ojos ______________________ (*black*) de los campesinos son muy sensibles.
7. El campesino tiene en la mano un fusil (*rifle*) ______________________ (*brown*).
8. Llama la atención la jarra (*jug*) ______________________ (*red*).
9. Se nota la piña ______________________ (*green*) y ______________________ (*brown*).

Nota cultural

- **Campamento Zapatista** fue pintado por el pintor mexicano Fernando Leal en 1922. Leal, que nació en 1900 y murió en 1964, fue uno de los primeros pintores en usar temas indigenistas para los murales grandes. Otros grandes muralistas mexicanos fueron Orozco, Rivera y Siqueiros. El campamento zapatista se refiere a Emiliano Zapata, político y revolucionario mexicano (1883–1919), que reclamó tierras para los campesinos.

- **La Virgen de Guadalupe** fue símbolo de los zapatistas. La Virgen apareció al indio Juan Diego y su imagen quedó grabada (*imprinted*) en su manta (poncho). Desde 1910, año que empezó la Revolución Mexicana, la Virgen de Guadalupe es patrona (*patron saint*) de Hispanoamérica.

E. ¡El Príncipe Azul (*Prince Charming*)! El Príncipe Azul estudia su ropa. Escriba lo que tiene en su armario empleando los adjetivos de color. ¡Fíjese bien si tiene ropa apropiada para pescar una princesa (*to catch a princess*)!

Para montar a caballo:

1. una chaqueta ______________________ (rojo)
2. unos pantalones ______________________ (amarillo)

3. unas botas ________________________ (marrón)
4. unos guantes ________________________ (negro) o
________________________ (rojo)
5. un sombrero con plumas ________________________ (amarillo)
________________________ (anaranjado)
y ________________________ (verde)

Para ir a un baile de etiqueta (*dress ball*):

6. un esmoquin (*tuxedo*) ________________________ (negro)
7. un sombrero de copa (*top hat*) ________________________ (negro)
8. una faja (*cummerbund*) ________________________ (morado)
9. unos calcetines ________________________ (morado) y
________________________ (gris)

B *Position of adjectives; shortened forms of adjectives*

- Although descriptive adjectives in Spanish usually follow the noun they modify, descriptive and other adjectives can also appear before nouns in certain cases:

1. When they express an inherent characteristic of the noun that is known to all and does not add any new information about the noun:

la **blanca** nieve	*white snow*
el **tímido** cordero	*the timid lamb*
una **olorosa** rosa	*a fragrant rose*

2. When they express a subjective judgment of the speaker. **Bueno, malo,** and their comparatives **mejor** and **peor** fall into this category:

Vivimos en una **pequeña** ciudad.	*We live in a small city.*
Tenemos que leer una **larga** novela.	*We have to read a long novel.*
Sobrevolaron la **enorme** selva.	*They flew over the huge jungle.*
Es el **peor** libro que leímos.	*It's the worst book that we read.*
Prepararon una **buena** comida.	*They prepared a good meal.*

3. Adjectives that express quantity precede the noun: **mucho, poco, bastante, suficiente, cuánto, alguno, ninguno, ambos** (*both*), **varios** (*several*):

Alberto siempre tiene **muchas** ideas.	*Alberto always has a lot of ideas.*
¿Hay **alguna** farmacia por aquí?	*Is there a (any) drugstore around here?*
No ganan **suficiente** dinero.	*They don't earn enough money.*

4. After exclamations with **¡Qué!:**

¡Qué **mala** suerte!	*What bad luck!*
¡Qué **hermosa** plaza!	*What a beautiful square!*

When an adverb such as **más, tan, muy,** etc. modifies the adjective, the adjective usually follows the noun:

¡Qué plaza **más hermosa**! — *What a beautiful square!*

Prepararon una comida **muy buena**. — *They prepared a very good meal.*

Fue una clase **especialmente interesante**. — *It was an especially interesting class.*

- The adjectives **bueno, malo, primero, tercero, uno, alguno,** and **ninguno** lose their final **-o** before a masculine singular noun. **Alguno** and **ninguno** add an accent mark when shortened: **algún, ningún**:

—¿No conoces a **ningún** estudiante? — *Don't you know any students?*
—No conozco a nadie todavía. Es mi **primer** día aquí. — *I don't know anyone yet. It's my first day here.*
—¿Hay **algún** consejo que te puedo dar? — *Is there any advice that I can give you?*
—No, he tenido **un mal** día, nada más. — *No, I've had a bad day, that's all.*

- The adjectives **grande** and **cualquiera** (*any*) shorten to **gran** and **cualquier**, respectively, before any singular noun:

Cualquier restaurante por aquí es un **gran** restaurante. — *Any restaurant around here is a great restaurant.*

- The adjective **Santo** shortens to **San** before all masculine saints' names except those that begin with **To-** and **Do-** as in **Santo Tomás** and **Santo Domingo**.

Some adjectives have different English equivalents depending on whether they precede or follow the nouns they modify:

nuestro **antiguo** jefe *our former boss*	una ciudad **antigua** *an old, ancient city*
cierto país *a certain country, some countries*	una cosa **cierta** *a sure thing, a true thing*
una **nueva** casa *another house*	una casa **nueva** *a new house*
el **mismo** profesor *the same teacher*	el profesor **mismo** *the teacher himself*
un **pobre** hombre *a poor man (unfortunate)*	un hombre **pobre** *a poor man (penniless)*
un **gran** presidente *a great president*	un hombre **grande** *a big man*
diferentes libros *various books*	libros **diferentes** *different books*
Paco es **medio** español. *Paco is half Spanish.*	el español **medio** *the average Spaniard*
Este café es **pura** agua. *This coffee is nothing but water.*	Prefiero beber agua **pura**. *I prefer to drink pure water.*
Juan es un **simple** camarero. *Juan is just a waiter.*	Juan es un muchacho **simple**. *Juan is a simple boy.*
Me interesa **cualquier** película española. *I'm interested in any Spanish film.*	Vamos a alquilar una película **cualquiera**. *Let's rent any old film.*
María es la **única** mexicana aquí. *María is the only Mexican here.*	María es una chica **única**. *María is a unique girl.*

F. Adjetivos pre- y pospuestos. Ponga el adjetivo o antes o después del sustantivo. Haga los cambios necesarios.

1. ¡Éste es el ______________ día ______________ de mi vida! (mejor)
2. Hay ______________ discos compactos ______________ en el escritorio. (alguno)
3. Ha habido ______________ días ______________ de lluvia este año. (mucho)
4. Los estudiantes leyeron unos ______________ poemas ______________. (renacentista)
5. Los franceses usan mucho la ______________ energía ______________. (nuclear)
6. El profesor dará el examen a ______________ clases ______________ el miércoles. (ambos)
7. Pili tiene los ______________ ojos ______________. (castaño)
8. No retiraron ______________ plata ______________ de su cuenta de ahorros. (suficiente)
9. Nos encanta el ______________ vino ______________. (tinto)
10. No se sabe ______________ horas ______________ de trabajo quedan. (cuánto)
11. Pedro tomó la ______________ decisión ______________ posible. (peor)
12. Miguel y Víctor se dedican al análisis de ______________ teorías ______________. (político)

G. ¡Qué exclamación! Amplíe cada exclamación con la forma correcta del adjetivo que aparece entre paréntesis. Haga los cambios necesarios.

MODELO ¡Qué casa! (lindo) → ¡Qué linda casa!

1. ¡Qué situación! (absurdo)
____
2. ¡Qué clima! (tan perfecto)
____
3. ¡Qué partido! (más emocionante)
____
4. ¡Qué paella! (tan rico)
____

5. ¡Qué zapatos! (hermoso)

____

6. ¡Qué ideas! (más estupendo)

____

7. ¡Qué problemas! (más complicado)

____

8. ¡Qué legumbres! (fresco)

____

9. ¡Qué niños! (cariñoso)

____

10. ¡Qué reunión! (tan animado)

____

H. Adjetivos: ¿forma apócope (*shortened*) o no? Complete las siguientes oraciones llenando los espacios en blanco con la forma correcta del adjetivo que aparece entre paréntesis.

1. El cinco de septiembre es el _______________ día del semestre. (primero)
2. No es _______________ idea llevar el paraguas hoy. (malo)
3. Estos estadistas son _______________ hombres. (grande)
4. Unas canicas (*marbles*) son un _______________ juguete para Paquito. (bueno)
5. Ya es la _______________ vez que me han invitado a salir. (tercero)
6. Esperamos que vengan a vernos _______________ día. (alguno)
7. No hemos hecho _______________ plan hasta ahora. (ninguno)
8. Yo nací el día de _______________ Juan. (santo)
9. Sánchez dictó una serie de _______________ conferencias. (bueno)
10. Albéniz fue un _______________ compositor español. (grande)
11. No les gustó _______________ bicicleta. (ninguno)
12. Pruebe _______________ recetas de este libro de cocina italiana. (alguno)
13. _______________ librería tendrá el libro que buscas. (Cualquiera)
14. ¿No celebras tu santo el día de _______________ Rosa? (santo)
15. Jesús y Pepe fueron los _______________ jugadores en llegar al estadio. (primero)
16. Carlos es el _______________ rey de la dinastía. (tercero)
17. ¡No des _______________ ejemplo para los niños! (malo)

I. Adjetivos: antes o después del sustantivo. Exprese en español el adjetivo que aparece entre paréntesis poniéndolo antes o después del sustantivo.

1. Beti y yo vamos al ________________ dentista ________________. (*same*)
2. Atenas es una ________________ ciudad ________________. (*ancient*)
3. La fecha de su boda es una ________________ cosa ________________. (*sure*)
4. Tino es ________________ portugués ________________ y ________________ mexicano ________________. (*half/half*)
5. Bolívar fue un ________________ soldado ________________. (*great*)
6. Habla con un ________________ funcionario ________________. (*any old*)
7. ¡El ________________ dramaturgo ________________ no aguanta su obra! (*himself*)
8. La sopa que pedí es ________________ agua ________________. (*nothing but*)
9. Ricardo es una ________________ persona ________________. (*unique*)
10. ________________ empresa ________________ sigue perdiendo dinero. (*A certain*)
11. Los hermanos Ayala son ________________ hombres ________________ desde que su compañía quebró (*went bankrupt*). (*poor*)
12. La ________________ casa ________________ de Daniela y Pablo quedaba en las afueras de la ciudad. (*former*)
13. Mi biblioteca tiene ________________ libros ________________ sobre el ________________ tema ________________. (*several/same*)
14. A Leonor le va a encantar ________________ regalo ________________ que le demos. (*any*)
15. Agustín y Patricia son los ________________ pianistas ________________ que tocan con la orquesta. (*only*)
16. Le dimos el pésame (*we offered our sympathy*) a la ________________ señora ________________. (*poor [sad, in mourning]*)

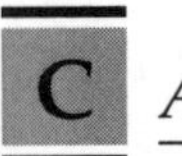

Adjectives of nationality

- Adjectives of nationality that end in **-o** in the masculine singular have the regular four forms:

chileno *Chilean*		
	masculine	*feminine*
sing.	chilen**o**	chilen**a**
pl.	chilen**os**	chilen**as**

mexicano *Mexican*		
	masculine	*feminine*
sing.	mexican**o**	mexican**a**
pl.	mexican**os**	mexican**as**

- Adjectives of nationality that end in a consonant also have four forms. An **-a** is added to form the feminine. The masculine plural ends in **-es**, not **-os**. Adjectives of nationality that have an accent mark on the last syllable of the masculine singular lose that accent mark when an ending is added:

español *Spanish*		
	masculine	*feminine*
sing.	español	español**a**
pl.	español**es**	español**as**

inglés *English*		
	masculine	*feminine*
sing.	inglés	ingles**a**
pl.	ingles**es**	ingles**as**

alemán *German*		
	masculine	*feminine*
sing.	alemán	aleman**a**
pl.	aleman**es**	aleman**as**

andaluz *Andalusian*		
	masculine	*feminine*
sing.	andaluz	andaluz**a**
pl.	andalu**ces**	andaluz**as**

- Adjectives of nationality that end in a vowel other than **-o** have only two forms. Many of these have the suffix **-ense** such as **canadiense** (*Canadian*), **bonaerense** (from Buenos Aires). *See also section **A** of this chapter.*

Adjetivos de nacionalidad (gentilicios)

continente

África — africano
la Antártida — antártico
el Ártico — ártico
Asia — asiático
Australia — australiano
Europa — europeo
Norteamérica — norteamericano (= estadounidense)
Sudamérica — sudamericano

islas

las Antillas — antillano
las Bahamas — bahamiano
las Baleares — balear
Mallorca — mallorquín
las Canarias — canario
las Filipinas — filipino

	país	gentilicio		país	gentilicio
	Alemania	alemán		Israel	israelí
	Arabia Saudita	saudí/saudita		Jamaica	jamaicano
	Argelia	argelino		Jordania	jordano
(la)	Argentina	argentino	(el)	Japón	japonés
	Australia	australiano		Kuwait/Kuweit	kuwaití
	Austria	austríaco		Líbano	libanés
	Bélgica	belga		Luxemburgo	luxemburgués
	Bolivia	boliviano		Madagascar (República Malgache)	malgache
(el)	Brasil	brasileño		Marruecos	marroquí
	Camboya	camboyano		México	mexicano
(el)	Canadá	canadiense		Nicaragua	nicaragüense
	Chile	chileno		Noruega	noruego
	China	chino		Nueva Zelanda	neocelandés
	Colombia	colombiano	los	Países Bajos	holandés
	Corea	coreano	(el)	Panamá	panameño
	Costa Rica	costarricense	(el)	Paraguay	paraguayo
	Cuba	cubano	(el)	Perú	peruano
	Dinamarca	danés		Polonia	polaco
(el)	Ecuador	ecuatoriano		Portugal	portugués
	Egipto	egipcio		Puerto Rico	puertorriqueño
	Escocia	escocés	(la)	República Dominicana	dominicano
	España	español		Rusia	ruso
(los)	Estados Unidos	norteamericano, estadounidense	El	Salvador	salvadoreño
	Finlandia	finlandés		Siria	sirio
	Francia	francés		Sudán	sudanés
	Grecia	griego		Suecia	sueco
	Guatemala	guatemalteco	(la)	Suiza	suizo
	Haití	haitiano		Tailandia	tailandés
	Holanda	holandés		Taiwán	taiwanés
	Honduras	hondureño		Túnez	tunecino
	Hungría	húngaro		Turquía	turco
(la)	India	indio, hindú	(el)	Uruguay	uruguayo
	Inglaterra	inglés		Venezuela	venezolano
	Irak/Iraq	iraquí		Vietnám	vietnamita
	Irán	iraní		Yemen	yemení
	Irlanda	irlandés			

ciudad	gentilicio	ciudad	gentilicio
Bogotá	bogotano	Málaga	malagueño
Buenos Aires	bonaerense/porteño	Nueva York	neoyorquino
Caracas	caraqueño	París	parisiense/parisino
Florencia	florentino	Quito	quiteño
Lima	limeño	Roma	romano
Londres	londinense	Sevilla	sevillano
Madrid	madrileño	Toledo	toledano

J. **¿De dónde son?** Ud. y su amigo están preparando una lista de los estudiantes extranjeros de la facultad de ingeniería (*school of engineering*). Su amigo le pregunta si son de cierto país y Ud. lo confirma con el adjetivo de nacionalidad.

MODELO Catalina es de Italia, ¿verdad?
➔ Sí, es italiana.

1. Abrahán es de Rusia, ¿verdad?
____

2. Rosalinda y Arturo son del Canadá, ¿verdad?
____

3. David es de Israel, ¿verdad?
____

4. Mercedes es de Costa Rica, ¿verdad?
____

5. Hugo es de Guatemala, ¿verdad?
____

6. Xavier y Paula son de Bélgica, ¿verdad?
____

7. Alano es del Japón, ¿verdad?
____

8. Bárbara es de la India, ¿verdad?
____

9. Isabel y Lucía son de Egipto, ¿verdad?
____

10. Margarita es de Inglaterra, ¿verdad?
____

11. Gerardo es de Corea, ¿verdad?
____

12. Cristina y Oliverio son de Francia, ¿verdad?
____

K. **¡De muchos uno solo!** Estados Unidos es un país de habitantes de miles de orígenes distintos. ¡Sin embargo, son todos *americanos!* Escriba oraciones que dicen de qué origen son estos habitantes usando el adjetivo del nombre del país.

MODELO Josefa e Ignacio / Panamá
Josefa e Ignacio son de origen panameño.

1. yo / Nueva Zelanda
____

2. Teodoro e Irene / El Salvador

3. Uds. / Líbano

4. Gabriel / Vietnám

5. Adela y Rosa / Irán

6. Estanislao y Sofía / Grecia

7. tú / Marruecos

8. Ud. y yo / Taiwán

9. Gualterio / Hungría

Nota cultural

Panamá tiene al norte el océano Atlántico o mar Caribe, al este Colombia, al sur el océano Pacífico y al oeste Costa Rica. El Canal de Panamá es una gran encrucijada (*crossroad*) estratégica del mundo que hace comunicar los dos mares. El Canal, construido por los Estados Unidos, fue abierto en 1914. Estados Unidos controlaba la Zona del Canal hasta 1978 cuando Estados Unidos y Panamá ratificaron un nuevo tratado (*treaty*) cambiando el nombre de la Zona al Área del Canal y dando soberanía (*sovereignty*) sobre el Canal a Panamá. Estados Unidos mantiene bases militares en el área. A partir del año 2000 el Canal será propiedad de Panamá.

D *More on the agreement of adjectives*

- Adjectives modifying two plural nouns of the same gender are in the plural of that gender:

libros y periódicos argentin**os**	*Argentine books and newspapers*
ciudades y provincias argentin**as**	*Argentine cities and provinces*

- If two nouns of different genders, whether singular or plural, are modified by a single adjective, the adjective is masculine plural:

pantalones y chaquetas barat**os**	*inexpensive pants and jackets*
un colegio y una universidad antigu**os**	*an ancient school and university*

- When a noun is used as an adjective, it usually does not agree in gender and number with the noun it modifies:

una visita **relámpago** (relámpago *lightning*)	*a quick visit*
la luz **piloto** (piloto *pilot*)	*pilot light* (*stove*)
apartamentos **piloto**	*model apartments*

- Some of these nouns eventually become adjectives and show agreements. This is especially true of some nouns used as adjectives of color:

zapatos **marrón/marrones**	*brown shoes*
medias **café/cafés**	*light brown stockings*

L. Sustantivos en plural. Escriba la forma correcta del adjetivo en plural.

1. Hay ____________ almacenes y restaurantes en el centro comercial. (bueno)
2. Conocimos varios pueblos y aldeas ____________. (español)
3. Queremos manzanas y cerezas recién ____________. (recogido)
4. Tengo mapas y guías ____________. (inglés)
5. En la sala hay un sofá y dos sillones ____________. (blanco)
6. Compre pan y torta ____________. (fresco)
7. Laura necesita una blusa y unas medias ____________. (rojo)
8. Busquen un lavaplatos y una máquina de lavar ____________. (rebajado)
9. No se vende ni agua ni sales ____________. (mineral)
10. El resultado del choque fueron un parachoques y una puerta ____________. (nuevo)
11. Hay ofertas y liquidaciones ____________ toda esta semana. (magnífico)
12. Clara tiene el pelo y las pestañas ____________. (negro)

E *Two or more adjectives modifying a noun*

- Typically, if two adjectives modify a noun, they both follow it and are joined by **y**:

una chica inteligente **y** simpática	*a nice, intelligent girl*
un día caluroso **y** agradable	*a warm, pleasant day*

- If **y** is left out, the adjective that the speaker wishes to emphasize comes last:

artistas europeos **modernos**	***modern*** *European artists (out of all European artists, the modern ones)*
artistas modernos **europeos**	*modern* ***European*** *artists (out of all modern artists, the European ones)*

- However, if one of the two adjectives usually precedes the noun, it is placed there:

cierto país europeo	***a certain*** *European country*
el único estudiante español	***the only*** *Spanish student*
diferentes libros científicos	***various*** *scientific books*
otra ciudad moderna	***another*** *modern city*
ese **pobre** hombre enfermo	*that* ***poor*** *sick man*

M. El rodaje de una película. (*The shooting of a film.*) Para comentar sobre el rodaje de una película por el director de cine Federico Felino, ponga los elementos de cada grupo en su orden correcto. Cada grupo consiste en un sustantivo, un adjetivo descriptivo y un adjetivo que aparece antes del sustantivo. Escriba la oración completa.

1. Federico Felino es director de cine / mejor / joven

 ____

2. Es su film / primero / doblado (*dubbed*)

 ____

3. Será una película / grande / extranjero

 ____

4. Tiene escenas / alguno / romántico

 ____

5. Se oye diálogo / uno / bueno

 ____

6. Hay efectos / alguno / especial

 ____

7. Escribieron guión (*script*) / uno / inteligente

 ____

8. Trabajaron en el film intérpretes (*masc. and fem.*) / principal (*star, lead*) / alguno

 ____

9. Hay subtítulos / alguno / bien traducido

 ____

10. La película tiene argumento (*plot*) / interesante / uno

 ____

11. La película ganará un premio / importante / cinematográfico

 ____

F *The past participle as an adjective*

- The past participle of most verbs can function as an adjective:

El ladrón entró por la ventana **abierta**.	*The thief got in through the open window.*
Quiero dominar la lengua **escrita** y la lengua **hablada**.	*I want to master the written language and the spoken language.*
Encontré los documentos **perdidos**.	*I found the lost documents.*

- The Spanish past participle is used to describe positions of people and objects where the present participle is used in English:

Todos están **sentados** en el comedor.	*Everyone is **sitting** in the dining room.*
A estas horas hay mucha gente **parada** en el metro.	*At this hour there are a lot of people **standing** in the subway.*

N. Diálogos. Termine los siguientes diálogos llenando los espacios en blanco con la forma correcta del adjetivo del modismo. Todos los adjetivos son participios pasados. El adjetivo se encuentra en el modismo o se deriva del verbo del modismo.

MODELO **estar loco de contento** *to be wild with joy*

Felipe —¿Sabes? Gané la lotería. ¡Estoy *loco* de contento!

Isabel —¡Enhorabuena, chico! Si yo la ganara estaría *loca* de contento también.

1. **estar frito** *to be all washed up*

   Diana: ¡Qué mala nota saqué en el examen! ¡Estoy ____________________!

   Mateo: Yo también. ¡Los dos estamos ____________________!

2. **estar hecho una sopa** *to be soaking wet*

   Raúl: Está lloviendo a cántaros. (*It's raining cats and dogs.*) Estoy ____________________ una sopa.

   Sara: ¡Yo estoy ____________________ una sopa también!

3. **morirse de risa** *to die laughing*

   Roberto: Mira a Clara e Inés. Están ____________________ de risa.

   Dorotea: Fíjate que Pepe y Esteban también están ____________________ de risa.

4. **comerse de envidia** *to be eaten up with envy*

   Julia: ¿Sabes que Aurelia está ____________________ de envidia porque yo salgo con Matías?

   Anita: ¡No sólo Aurelia sino todas las chicas están ____________________ de envidia!

5. **meterse en lo que no le importa** *to butt in*

   Lola: Como siempre, Raúl está ____________________ en lo que no le importa.

   Paco: Así son sus hermanos también, siempre ____________________ en lo que no les importa.

6. **estar muy pagado de sí mismo** *to have a high opinion of oneself*

   Alfredo: Chico, ya no salgo con Brígida porque está muy ____________________ de sí misma.

   Nicolás: Haces muy bien. ¡Yo rompí con Tere, Eva y Paloma porque están muy ____________________ de sí mismas!

7. **dormirse en los laureles** *to rest on one's laurels*

   Tito: Veo que no te esfuerzas porque estás ____________________ en los laureles.

   José: Cuando logres algo como yo, ¡tú también estarás ____________________ en los laureles!

8. **estar hecho una lástima** *to be a sorry sight, in a sad state*

   Leonor: ¿Qué les pasa a Paula y Dora? Están ____________________ una lástima.

   Alicia: A lo mejor tienen lo que tiene Mari que también está ____________________ una lástima.

O. **¿Qué están haciendo?** Use adjetivos que terminan en **-do** para explicar la posición de ciertas personas. Termine las oraciones llenando los espacios en blanco con la forma correcta del adjetivo que termina en **-do** y del verbo **estar.**

MODELO Mario **está levantado** (levantar) ya.

1. Rosario ______________________ (acostar) durmiendo la siesta.
2. Clemente ______________________ (parar [*to stand*]) en la puerta de la casa esperando a su novia.
3. Los García ______________________ (sentar) a la mesa todavía por la sobremesa.
4. Pili ______________________ (asomar [*to lean out*]) en la ventana.
5. Los niños ______________________ (arrodillar) en el suelo jugando con sus cochecitos.
6. Adolfo y Javier ______________________ (tirar) en el suelo por los puñetazos que se dieron.
7. Paloma ______________________ (inclinar [*to bow*]) mientras el público aplaude.

Nota cultural

La sobremesa se refiere a la conversación alrededor de la mesa después de comer. Es una costumbre española tradicional.

P. **¡Preparados! ¡Listos! ¡Ya!** (*Ready! Set! Go!*) Su amiga le pregunta cuándo Ud. y otras personas van a hacer ciertas cosas porque tiene prisa por salir. Escriba oraciones que dicen que Uds. están listos porque esas cosas ya están hechas. Practique usando adjetivos que terminan en **-do.**

Modelo ¿Cuándo van Uds. a arreglarse?
→ Ya estamos arreglados(as).

1. ¿Cuándo va Gerardo a bañarse?

___

2. ¿Cuándo van Elías e Isaac a afeitarse?

___

3. ¿Cuándo va Juliana a maquillarse?

___

4. ¿Cuándo van Uds. a vestirse?

___

5. ¿Cuándo va Ud. a peinarse?

___

6. ¿Cuándo van Simón y Martín a ducharse?

___

7. ¿Cuándo vas a pintarte?

___

Q. **¡A comer pues!** Ya es hora de comer. Su mamá les dice a Ud. y a los otros miembros de su familia que hagan ciertas cosas. Pero parece que todo está ya. Explique eso derivando el adjetivo del verbo en el mandato.

Modelo Polo, prende el horno, por favor.
→ Ya está prendido.

1. Margara, pon los cubiertos (*place settings*), por favor.

___

2. Benjamín, sirve el agua, por favor.

___

3. Abuela, prepara el dulce de leche, por favor.

___

4. Pancho, rompe los huevos, por favor.

___

5. Pepe y Nano, corten el pan, por favor.

___

6. Trini, haz la ensalada, por favor.

___

7. Tía, bate las natillas, por favor.

8. Toni, pela unos dientes de ajo, por favor.

Nota cultural

Natillas, un postre español, es un dulce que contiene huevo, leche y azúcar.

G *Adjectives used as nouns (nominalization of adjectives)*

- Spanish adjectives can be used as nouns when the noun they modify is deleted:

—Las camisas verdes son más caras que **las rojas.**	*The green shirts are more expensive than* ***the red ones.***
—De acuerdo. Pero prefiero **las verdes.**	*OK. But I prefer* ***the green ones.***
—La casa vieja es más grande que **la moderna.**	*The old house is bigger than* ***the modern one.***
—Por eso vamos a comprar **la vieja.**	*That's why we're going to buy* ***the old one.***

R. Opciones y preferencias. Sus amigos le preguntan qué cosas prefiere. Conteste sus preguntas escribiendo una de las dos posibilidades primero y luego la otra. ¡Es que, en realidad, le gustan ambas cosas! Use los adjetivos como sustantivos.

MODELO ¿Cuál prefieres, la novela histórica o la novela fantástica?
➔ Prefiero la histórica. *and* Prefiero la fantástica.

1. ¿Cúal te gusta más, la música instrumental o la música vocal?

2. ¿Cuáles prefieres, los programas serios o los programas cómicos?

3. ¿Dónde prefieres comer, en un restaurante chino o en un restaurante francés?

4. ¿Cuáles te gustan más, los trajes azules o los trajes marrones?

5. ¿Prefieres un apartamento moderno o un apartamento viejo?

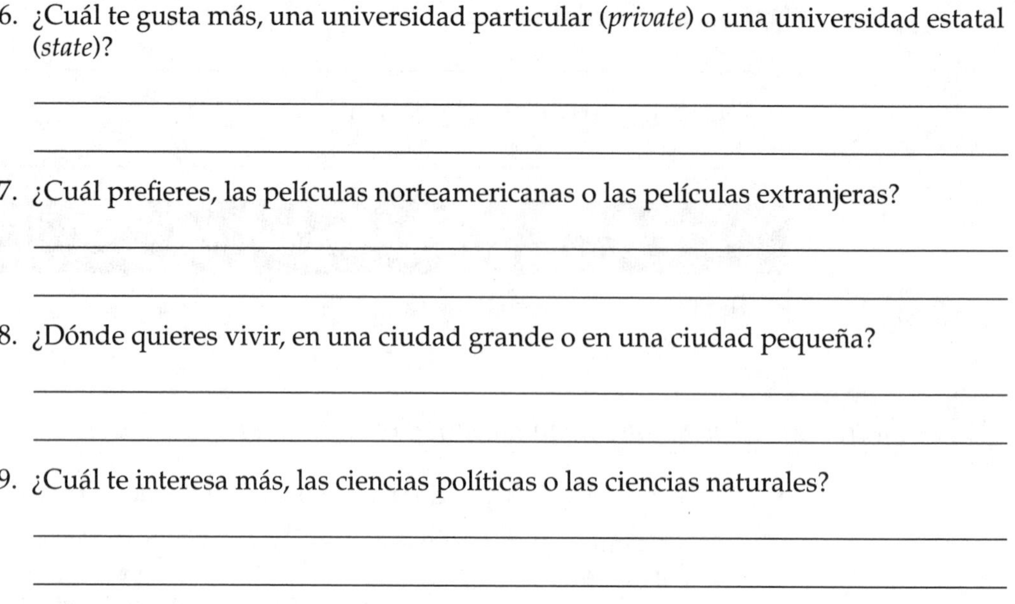

6. ¿Cuál te gusta más, una universidad particular (*private*) o una universidad estatal (*state*)?

7. ¿Cuál prefieres, las películas norteamericanas o las películas extranjeras?

8. ¿Dónde quieres vivir, en una ciudad grande o en una ciudad pequeña?

9. ¿Cuál te interesa más, las ciencias políticas o las ciencias naturales?

H *Comparative of adjectives*

- One object or person may be seen as having more, less, or the same amount of a characteristic as another. To express this, Spanish and English use the comparative construction:

  Comparison of superiority (**más** + adjetivo + **que**):

La avenida es **más ancha que** nuestra calle.	*The avenue is **wider than** our street.*

  Comparison of inferiority (**menos** + adjetivo + **que**):

Pero la avenida es **menos ancha que** la autopista.	*But the avenue is **less wide than** the superhighway.*

  Note that in English the comparison of inferiority is usually expressed as *not as:* The avenue is *not as wide as* the superhighway.

  Comparison of equality (**tan** + adjetivo + **como**):

La avenida es **tan ancha como** el Paseo de Miraflores.	*The avenue is as wide as Miraflores Boulevard.*

- The adjectives **bueno** and **malo** have irregular comparative forms:

  bueno ➔ **mejor**   malo ➔ **peor**

Este restaurante es **mejor** que el otro.	*This restaurant is better than the other one.*
El ruido aquí es **peor** que en el barrio mío.	*The noise is worse here than in my neighborhood.*

  Más bueno and **más malo** are used to refer to moral qualities.

- **Grande** and **pequeño** have irregular comparative forms when they refer to age:

  grande ➔ **mayor** *older*   pequeño ➔ **menor** *younger*

Mi hermano **menor** es más alto que mi hermana **mayor**.	*My younger brother is taller than my older sister.*

- Adverbs are compared in the same way as adjectives:

Ella contesta **más cortésmente que** él.	*She answers **more politely than** he does.*
Ella contesta **menos cortésmente que** él.	*She answers **less politely than** he does.*
Ella contesta **tan cortésmente como** él.	*She answers **as politely as** he does.*

- In comparing verbs and nouns, **tan** changes to **tanto**. **Tanto** is invariable with verbs, but agrees with nouns that follow it:

Comparing verbs:

Yo trabajo **más que** tú.	*I work **more than** you do.*
Yo trabajo **menos que** tú.	*I work **less than** you do.*
Yo trabajo **tanto como** tú.	*I work **as much as** you do.*

Comparing nouns:

—Creo que tú tienes **menos exámenes que** Amalia.	*I think you have **fewer exams than** Amalia.*
—Te equivocas. Tengo **tantos exámenes como** ella, y **más trabajos** escritos.	*You're mistaken. I have **as many exams as** she has, and **more papers**.*

- **Que** (*than*) is followed by *subject pronouns* unless the pronoun is the direct or indirect object of the verb. In that case, **que** is followed by **a** + stressed pronoun:

Yo estudio más **que tú**.	*I study more **than you do.***
A mí me gusta más **que a ti**.	*I like it more **than you do**.*

- **Que** is followed by **nada** and **nadie** where English uses *anything, anyone:*

El curso es difícil, más **que nada.**	*The course is hard, more **than anything.***
Luis Alberto baila mejor **que nadie.**	*Luis Alberto dances better **than anyone.***

- **Que** is replaced by **de** before a numeral:

Ganan más **de** ochocientos dólares por semana.	*They earn more than eight hundred dollars a week.*

- **Que** is replaced by **de lo que** before a clause implying a standard for comparison:

—Este libro es más difícil **de lo que** cree el profesor.	*This book is more difficult than the teacher thinks.*
—Y menos interesante **de lo que** yo me imaginaba.	*And less interesting than I imagined.*

How difficult the teacher thought the book was or *how interesting I imagined the book was* is the basis for comparison.

- **Que** is replaced by **de** before **el que, la que, los que, las que**. The article represents a deleted noun:

Necesito más plata **de la que** me prestaste. (*la que = la plata que*)	*I need more money than (the money) you lent me.*
Encontramos menos problemas **de los que** esperábamos. (*los que = los problemas que*)	*We found fewer problems than (the problems) we expected.*

S. En comparación. Combine las dos oraciones de cada grupo en una sola que expresa una comparación. Escriba dos oraciones de comparación para cada grupo.

MODELO Loren es listo./Julio es más listo.
→ Julio es **más** listo que Loren.
→ Loren es **menos** listo que Julio.

1. Ana es astuta./Luisa es más astuta.

____

____

2. El museo de arte es bueno./El museo de historia natural es mejor.

____

____

3. Mi novio (Mi novia) es inteligente./Yo soy más inteligente.

____

____

4. El cuarto de Elena es hermoso./Tu cuarto es más hermoso.

____

____

5. La película inglesa es aburrida./La película francesa es más aburrida.

____

____

6. Los bailarines son talentosos./Los cantantes son más talentosos.

____

____

7. Las blusas de algodón son elegantes./Las blusas de seda son más elegantes.

____

____

8. Tu hermano es grande./Tu hermana es mayor.

____

____

T. Comparación de adverbios. Escriba una comparación de adverbios de tres maneras: **más, menos** e **igual**.

MODELO Él corrió **más** rápidamente **que** ella.
Ella corrió **menos** rápidamente **que** él.
Él corrió **tan** rápidamente **como** ella.

1. José habló ____________ francamente ____________ Consuelo.
   Consuelo habló ____________ francamente ____________ José.
   José habló ____________ francamente ____________ Consuelo.
2. Los enfermeros trabajaron ____________ cuidadosamente ____________ los médicos.
   Los médicos trabajaron ____________ cuidadosamente ____________ los enfermeros.
   Los enfermeros trabajaron ____________ cuidadosamente ____________ los médicos.
3. Virginia resolvió los problemas ____________ fácilmente ____________ Cristina.
   Cristina resolvió los problemas ____________ fácilmente ____________ Virginia.
   Virginia resolvió los problemas ____________ fácilmente ____________ Cristina.

U. Adjetivos: igualdad. Escriba oraciones que demuestran la comparación de igualdad de los dos sustantivos.

MODELO Eduardo/diligente/Memo
→ Eduardo es tan diligente como Memo.

1. la obra de teatro/divertida/la película
   ____
2. las clases de física/fáciles/las clases de cálculo
   ____
3. los documentales/artísticos/los reportajes
   ____
4. los platos griegos/sabrosos/los platos húngaros
   ____
5. esta actriz/célebre/ese actor
   ____
6. el arroz/bueno/el maíz
   ____
7. el príncipe/valiente/el rey
   ____

8. Francisca/aburrida/su hermana María

____

9. la inflación/baja/la inflación de hace tres años

____

I *Superlative of adjectives; absolute superlative*

- Spanish has no special superlative form. Usually, the definite article (or possessive adjective) is used with the noun that the adjective modifies to imply a superlative. Compare the following comparative and superlative sentences:

—Quiero ver una película **más emocionante**. (*comparative*)	*I want to see a **more exciting** film.*
—Ésta es **la película más emocionante** que alquilé. (*superlative*)	*This is **the most exciting film** that I rented.*

- After a superlative, *in* is translated by **de**:

—Estamos en la ciudad más importante **del** país.	*We're in the most important city **in** the country.*
—Y ésta es la calle más elegante **de** la ciudad.	*And this is the most elegant street **in** the city.*

- Spanish has a suffix **-ísimo,** called the absolute superlative, that is added to adjectives. This suffix adds the idea of *very* to the adjective. Note that **c** and **g** change to **qu** and **gu,** and **z** changes to **c** when **-ísimo** is added. Adjectives in **-ísimo** are four-form adjectives:

lindo ➔ lindísimo	feo ➔ feísimo	largo ➔ larguísimo
fácil ➔ facilísimo	rico ➔ riquísimo	feliz ➔ felicísimo

V. Nuestra clase. Use los signos aritméticos para formar superlativos que describan a los estudiantes de la clase.

Modelo Carlos / − atento
➔ Carlos es el estudiante menos atento.

1. Juan Pablo / + aplicado

____

2. Fermín y Cosme / − obediente

____

3. Silvia / + simpático

____

4. Irene y María / − trabajador

____

5. Verónica / + inteligente

____

6. Íñigo y Esteban / + hablador

____

7. Sergio / + encantador

____

8. Rosa y Jacinto / − preparado

____

W. ¡Qué parque más precioso! Confirme las observaciones de su amigo respecto al parque que están visitando con el superlativo absoluto del adjectivo.

MODELO El parque es lindo.
→ Sí. Es **lindísimo.**

1. La vegetación es interesante.

____

2. Ese árbol es viejo.

____

3. Esas flores son hermosas.

____

4. El zoológico del parque es grande.

____

5. Ese león parece feroz.

____

6. Los monos son simpáticos.

____

7. Las veredas (*paths*) son largas.

____

8. El lago es bello.

____

X. Visitando la ciudad. Raquel les enseña su ciudad a sus amigos. Les explica todo lo que ven con superlativos. Escriba lo que les dice a los amigos.

MODELO aquí está/biblioteca/importante/ciudad
→ Aquí está la biblioteca más importante de la ciudad.

1. allí se encuentra/plaza/imponente/ciudad

____

2. aquí ven/catedral/antigua/estado

____

3. en frente hay/universidad/conocido/país

____

4. ésta es/calle/largo/ciudad

____

5. en esta calle hay / tiendas / hermoso / zona

___

6. allí está / tienda de comestibles / estimado / barrio

___

7. delante de nosotros hay / hotel / internacional / país

___

8. en este barrio se encuentran / restaurantes / concurrido (*busy, much frequented*) / ciudad

___

9. aquí ven / casa / viejo / ciudad

___

10. pronto veremos / estadio / grande / región

___

Y. La clase de literatura. El profesor y los estudiantes describen las obras que estudian con superlativos. Escriba lo que dicen.

MODELO novela / interesante / siglo
→ Es la novela más interesante del siglo.

1. poema / conocido / literatura europea

___

2. obra de teatro / presentado / año

___

3. comedia / aplaudido / teatro nacional

___

4. novela / vendido / literatura moderna

___

5. tragedia / estimado / nuestro teatro

___

6. poeta / respetado / su siglo

___

7. novelista / leído / mundo

___

8. dramaturgo / apreciado / nuestra época

___

Z. Exprese las siguientes ideas en español.

1. I read more than you (*Ud.*) do.

2. They know less than we do.

3. Ignacio complains as much as his wife does.

4. I have more compact discs than Federico.

5. Eva sees fewer films than Margarita.

6. We take as many trips as they do.

7. We have more than ten thousand books in our library.

8. The soccer game was more exciting than they expected.

9. I want more jewels than you gave me!

10. This is the most expensive coat that I've bought.

11. Ruiz is the best programmer in the company.

12. This is the most beautiful beach in the country.

AA. **Ejercicio oral.** Converse con un(a) compañero(a) en describir a sus parientes y a sus amigos. Describa cómo son (carácter, personalidad, lo físico), cómo están, de dónde son, de qué origen son, etcétera.

BB. Estructuras en acción. Lea el pronóstico meteorológico de un periódico español fijándose mucho en los adjetivos. Luego haga los ejercicios. Pero antes de hacerlos, unos consejos:

- repase el vocabulario sobre el tiempo y los puntos cardinales (*directions*)
- relacione adjetivos con sus sustantivos correspondientes (piense en la familia lingüística)
- consulte un mapa en el cual figuran España, las islas españolas y el norte de África (Marruecos)

El tiempo

a lo largo del día *throughout the day*
a última hora *at the end of the day*
el carácter *kind, nature*
costero *coastal*
cubierto *overcast*
el chubasco *downpour, shower*
el descenso *decline*
despejado *clear*
disperso *scattered*
flojo *light*
la granizada *hailstorm*
ligero *light*
el litoral *coast*
matinal *morning*
la mitad sur *the southern half*
la niebla *mist, fog*
la nube *cloud*
nuboso *cloudy*
occidental *western*
parcialmente *partially*
el predominio *prevalence, predominance*
el pronóstico (meteorológico) *(weather) forecast*
el riesgo *risk*
salvo *except*
soleado *sunny*
el tercio norte *the northern third*
el tiempo *weather*
la tormenta *storm*
tormentoso *stormy*

Términos geográficos

Andalucía región del sur de España
Asturias región del norte de España
Baleares islas españolas del Mediterráneo (Mallorca, Menorca, Ibiza, etcétera)
las Canarias islas españolas del Atlántico (cerca de Marruecos [*Morocco*])
Castilla y León Castilla la Vieja, región del centro de España
Cataluña región del nordeste de España
Ceuta plaza de soberanía (*city enclave*) española en Marruecos
la Comunidad Valenciana Comunidad Autónoma y provincia de España en el Mediterráneo
Extremadura Comunidad Autónoma y región que queda al oeste de España
Galicia Comunidad Autónoma y región que queda al noroeste de España
Murcia Comunidad Autónoma y región que queda al sudeste de España
Navarra Comunidad Autónoma y región que queda al norte de España
Madrid capital de España y de la provincia de Madrid; Comunidad Autónoma
Melilla plaza de soberanía (*city enclave*) española en Marruecos
los Pirineos cadena de montañas entre España y Francia

EL TIEMPO
Tormentas, más irregulares en el tercio norte

El cielo estará casi despejado en Canarias y parcialmente nuboso en Ceuta, Melilla y litoral andaluz. Predominio del cielo nuboso en el resto de la mitad sur de la Península con intervalos muy nubosos. Podrán producirse granizadas muy locales. Nieblas matinales y temperaturas en ligero descenso.

Área de Madrid: Núcleos nubosos que irán aumentando a lo largo del día, con algunos chubascos tormentosos a última hora. Vientos flojos.
Andalucía: Nubes dispersas, con cielos más despejados por la mitad occidental.
Asturias: Cielos muy nubosos o cubiertos, con algunos chubascos de carácter débil a moderado.
Baleares: Nuboso, especialmente en la isla de Menorca, donde habrá alguna precipitación.
Canarias: Ambiente soleado, aunque con núcleos nubosos por la zona norte.
Castilla y León: Cielos muy nubosos, con algunas precipitaciones, que pueden ser de origen tormentoso.
Cataluña: Cielos muy nubosos, sobre todo en el Pirineo, donde hay riesgo de tormentas.
Comunidad Valenciana: Soleado en la mayor parte de la Comunidad.
Extremadura: Soleado, excepto en la parte norte, donde se formarán núcleos nubosos.
Galicia: Cielos nubosos, con precipitaciones de carácter débil.
Murcia: Predominio de los cielos poco nubosos o despejado, salvo nubes dispersas por la zona costera.
Navarra: Muy nuboso, con tormentas, más abundantes por la tarde.

1. Escriba adjetivos que aparecen en el pronóstico que están relacionados con las siguientes palabras.

1. sol ________
2. tormenta ________
3. costa ________
4. occidente ________
5. cubrir ________
6. nube ________
7. Andalucía ________
8. abundancia ________
9. despejar ________
10. mañana ________
11. debilidad ________
12. ligereza ________
13. dispersar ________
14. flojera ________

El Tiempo
Sale
EL SOL
6.23 Barcelona 21.26
6.49 Madrid 21.48
6.59 La Coruña 22.16
8.08 Las Palmas 22.01
Se pone
Fase de la Luna
MENGUANTE
Sale
LA LUNA
10.41 Barcelona 23.50
11.06 Madrid
11.22 La Coruña 0.06
12.04 Las Palmas 0.03
Se pone
Previsión para hoy
LA CORUÑA 19/14
OVIEDO 18/14
BILBAO 24/18
LEÓN 20/13
BURGOS 23/13
GIRONA 30/18
VALLADOLID 22/15
BARCELONA 27/19
ZARAGOZA 28/19
SALAMANCA 20/14
MADRID 28/18
CASTELLÓN 28/19
CÁCERES 25/14
ALBACETE 26/16
VALENCIA 29/18
PALMA DE MALLORCA 31/18
CIUDAD REAL 28/19
ALICANTE 29/22
CÓRDOBA 28/18
JAÉN 27/15
MURCIA 34/22
SEVILLA 27/18
ALMERÍA 28/21
GRANADA 28/15
HUELVA 25/16
MÁLAGA 28/21
CÁDIZ 26/20
SANTA CRUZ 27/22
LAS PALMAS 26/21
CEUTA 22/20
MELILLA 24/20
DESPEJADO
NUB./CLAR.
CUBIERTO
LLUVIA
CHUBASCOS
NIEBLA
TORMENTA
HELADAS
NIEVE
VIENTO
MAREJADA
MAR GRUESA

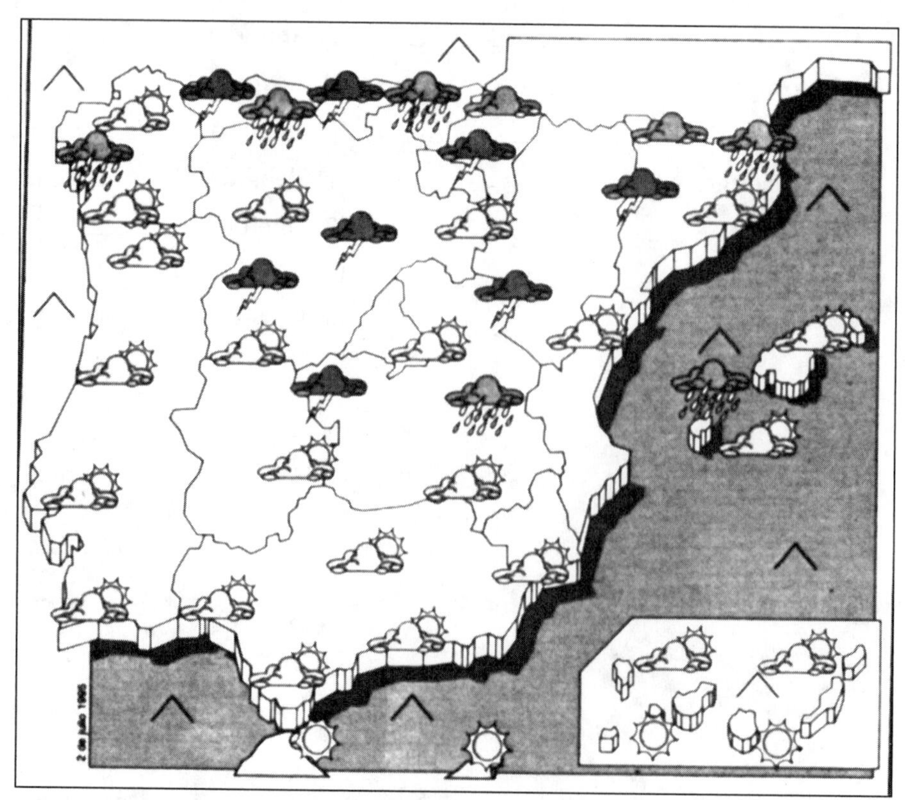

2. Escriba frases que describan el tiempo que hace en ciertas regiones de España. Haga una paráfrasis de lo que está escrito en el pronóstico. Por ejemplo, en Cataluña, **está muy nublado, es posible que haya tempestades.**

1. En Castilla y León ______________________________
2. En la Comunidad Valenciana______________________________
3. En el área de Madrid ______________________________
4. En Asturias ______________________________
5. En las Baleares ______________________________
6. En Ceuta y Melilla ______________________________
7. En Galicia ______________________________
8. En Murcia ______________________________

CHAPTER 18

DEMONSTRATIVES & POSSESSIVES

A *Demonstrative adjectives*

- Spanish has three demonstrative adjectives: **este** *this* (*near the speaker*), **ese** *that* (*near the person spoken to*), and **aquel** *that* (*removed from both the speaker and the person spoken to*). The demonstrative adjectives agree in gender and number with the noun they modify:

	masculine	*feminine*
sing.	**este**	**esta**
pl.	**estos**	**estas**

	masculine	*feminine*
sing.	**ese**	**esa**
pl.	**esos**	**esas**

	masculine	*feminine*
sing.	**aquel**	**aquella**
pl.	**aquellos**	**aquellas**

Este apartamento tiene más habitaciones que **aquellas** casas. — *This apartment has more rooms than those houses (over there).*

Préstame **ese** bolígrafo que tienes. **Este** bolígrafo que tengo ya no escribe. — *Lend me **that** ballpoint pen that you have. **This** ballpoint that I have doesn't write any more.*

Note that the three demonstratives correspond to the three place words for *here* and *there*:

este ~ **aquí**	
ese ~ **ahí**	
aquel ~ **allí**	

- The demonstrative **ese** can be placed after the noun to convey a note of contemptuousness:

No sé por qué una muchacha tan inteligente como Margarita saldría con el chico **ese**. — *I don't know why a girl as intelligent as Margarita would go out with a guy like that.*

A. Útiles de escuela. Cambie el artículo definido o indefinido a la forma correcta del adjetivo demostrativo para hablar de sus útiles de escuela. Escriba cada oración de tres maneras.

Útiles de escuela

el átlas *atlas*
el bolígrafo *ballpoint pen*
el compás *compass*
el diccionario *dictionary*
la enciclopedia *encyclopedia*
la goma de borrar *eraser*
el libro de texto *textbook*
el papel cuadriculado *graph paper*
la regla *ruler*
el sacapuntas *pencil sharpener*

MODELO Necesito un cuaderno.
→ Necesito **este** cuaderno.
→ Necesito **ese** cuaderno.
→ Necesito **aquel** cuaderno.

1. Los libros de texto están bien escritos.

____

____

____

2. Compré el compás anteayer.

____

____

____

3. Consultaré el atlas.

____

____

____

4. Prefiero el papel cuadriculado.

____

____

____

5. La marca de sacapuntas es conocida.

____

____

____

6. Me gusta el diccionario de español.

____

____

____

7. Los bolígrafos no sirven.

____

____

____

8. Encontré las reglas en la papelería.

____

____

____

9. Las enciclopedias no tienen información sobre el tema.

____

____

____

B. De compras en El Corte Inglés. Complete los siguientes diálogos entre unos amigos que van de compras. Llene los espacios en blanco con la forma correcta del adjetivo demostrativo.

En la sección de ropa para mujeres

1. Irene —Oye, Trini, ¿qué te parece _______________ (*this*) traje?
2. Trini —¿Cuál? ¿_______________ (*That*) traje azul?
3. Irene —Sí. ¿Verdad que _______________ (*this*) color es muy bonito?
4. Trini —Francamente me gusta más _______________ (*that, over there*) traje verde.
5. Pero me gustan _______________ (*these*) blusas y no hacen juego con el traje verde.
6. Trini —Bueno chica, llévate _______________ (*that*) traje azul y _______________ (*those*) blusas entonces. Y si te queda dinero todavía, cómprate el traje verde con _______________ (*that, over there*) blusa negra. ¡El conjunto (*outfit*) te quedará fenómeno!

En la sección de ropa para hombres

7. Lupe —Bueno, Tito, ayúdame. ¿Qué le regalo a Mateo por su cumpleaños? ¿_______________ (*This*) corbata roja o _______________ (*that*) cinturón negro?
8. Tito —Querida hermana, no me gustan ni _______________ (*these*) corbatas ni _______________ (*those*) cinturones. Mateo es un gran chico. _______________ (*This*) novio tuyo se merece algo más interesante e importante. Mira _______________ (*this*) sección de deportes …

_____ (*that*) bate, o _____ (*that, over there*) guante para jugar béisbol ... o quizás _____ (*that*) raqueta de tenis, o ...

9. Lupe —Tito, yo comprendo lo que estás haciendo. ¡Quieres que Mateo te preste su nuevo bate o guante o raqueta! _____ (*This*) no puede ser. ¡Es mejor que escoja el regalo yo!

Nota cultural

El Corte Inglés es uno de los grandes almacenes españoles con sucursales por todo el país. Se vende de todo en el almacén—ropa, muebles, aparatos electrodomésticos (*appliances*), etcétera. Tiene hasta un supermercado completo también.

B *Demonstrative pronouns*

- Demonstrative pronouns in Spanish have the same form as demonstrative adjectives. The noun is deleted and an accent mark is added over the stressed vowel of the demonstrative:

—Estas tortas son más ricas que **aquéllas**.	*These cakes are more delicious than **those (over there)**.*
—Pero aquellas galletas no son tan buenas como **éstas**.	*But those cookies (over there) aren't as good as **these**.*
—¿Qué camisa prefiere Ud.? ¿**Ésta** o **ésa**?	*Which shirt do you prefer? **This one** or **that one?***
—Creo que me gusta más **aquélla** que está en el otro mostrador.	*I think that I like **that one** on the other counter best.*
—Aquellos anteojos son más bonitos que **ésos**.	*Those eyeglasses (over there) are prettier than **those**.*
—Puede ser, pero **éstos** tienen la montura que más me gusta.	*That may be, but **these** have the frame I like best.*
—¿Quiénes son los dos muchachos que figuran en la foto?	*Who are the two boys in the photograph?*
—**Éste** es mi primo Carlos y **ése** es su amigo.	***This one** is my cousin Carlos and **that one** is his friend.*

Note: In modern usage, the written accent is sometimes left off demonstrative pronouns.

- Spanish has three neuter demonstrative pronouns ending in **-o: esto, eso, aquello**. These never have a written accent. They refer to situations or ideas, not to specific nouns:

—Dicen que Pedro toma y que después maneja.	*They say that Pedro drinks and then drives.*
—No hay nada más peligroso que **eso**.	*There's nothing more dangerous than **that**. (**eso** = drinking and driving)*

—El tío Marcos tenía antes una tienda de ropa en el centro.	*Uncle Marcos used to have a clothing store downtown.*
—**Aquello** fue hace muchos años, ¿verdad?	***That** was many years ago, wasn't it?* (***aquello** = that he had a clothing store downtown*)

- The neuter demonstratives can be followed by **de** to express *this/that situation regarding* or *this/that matter of/about:*

Esto de trabajar demasiado no te hace ningún bien.	***This situation of (your) working too much** is not doing you any good.*
Aquello de tu hermano Íñigo me puso triste.	***That business about your brother Iñigo** made me sad.*

C. Un crítico de restaurantes. Ud. es crítico de restaurantes. Alguien le hace una entrevista sobre ciertas comidas que probó. Contéstele usando los pronombres demostrativos en su respuesta.

MODELO ¿Qué queso le gustó más? ¿Este queso o ese queso?
→ Me gustó **éste** más que **ése.**
or Me gustó **ése** más que **éste.**

1. ¿Qué salsa de champiñones (*mushrooms*) le gustó más? ¿Esa salsa o aquella salsa?
____
2. ¿Qué fideos le gustaron más? ¿Aquellos fideos o estos fideos?
____
3. ¿Qué bizcocho le gustó más? ¿Este bizcocho o ese bizcocho?
____
4. ¿Qué salchichas le gustaron más? ¿Esas salchichas o aquellas salchichas?
____
5. ¿Qué guisado (*stew*) le gustó más? ¿Este guisado o ese guisado?
____
6. ¿Qué panes le gustaron más? ¿Estos panes o aquellos panes?
____
7. ¿Qué sopa de legumbres le gustó más? ¿Esta sopa de legumbres o esa sopa de legumbres?
____

C *Possessive adjectives*

- Possessive adjectives in Spanish agree with the noun they modify. Possessive adjectives referring to the singular pronouns and to the third-person plural have only two forms: a singular and a plural. The possessives **nuestro** and **vuestro** are four-form adjectives. On the next page is a chart of the short-form or unstressed possessive adjectives in Spanish.

(yo) **mi/mis**	(nosotros) **nuestro/-a/-os/-as**
(tú) **tu/tus**	(vosotros) **vuestro/-a/-os/-as**
(él/ella/Ud.) **su/sus**	(ellos/ellas/Uds.) **su/sus**

- The possessive adjective **su/sus** means *his, her, its, your, their*. To clarify who is referred to, a phrase consisting of **de** + pronoun may be added:

—¡Qué bueno! Allí están Sergio y Marisa. Necesito su libro.	*Great! There are Sergio and Marisa. I need (his/her/their) book.*
—¿El libro **de él** o el libro **de ella**?	*His book or her book?*
—¿Qué cinta te gustó más?	*Which tape did you like best?*
—La cinta **de Uds.** La cinta **de ellos** no me gustó tanto.	*Your tape. I didn't like their tape so much.*

- Spanish has a set of long-form or stressed possessive adjectives that can be used to contrast one possessor with another (*It's **my** book, not **your** book.*). These are all four-form adjectives and follow the noun they modify:

el libro **mío** **los** libros **míos**	**la** cinta **mía** **las** cintas **mías**	**el** libro **nuestro** **los** libros **nuestros**	**la** cinta **nuestra** **las** cintas **nuestras**
el libro **tuyo** **los** libros **tuyos**	**la** cinta **tuya** **las** cintas **tuyas**	**el** libro **vuestro** **los** libros **vuestros**	**la** cinta **vuestra** **las** cintas **vuestras**
el libro **suyo** **los** libros **suyos**	**la** cinta **suya** **las** cintas **suyas**	**el** libro **suyo** **los** libros **suyos**	**la** cinta **suya** **las** cintas **suyas**

The phrases consisting of **de** + pronoun clarify the person **suyo** refers to:

—Rogelio y Paula escribieron muchos artículos.	*Rogelio and Paula wrote a lot of articles.*
—**Los** artículos **de él** se publicaron en España y **los** artículos **de ella** en México.	*His articles were published in Spain and her articles in Mexico.*
—**La** pluma **mía** no tiene tinta. ¿Me prestas **la** pluma **tuya**?	*My pen doesn't have any ink. Can you lend me your pen?*
—Lo siento. **La** pluma **mía** no funciona tampoco.	*I'm sorry. My pen doesn't work either.*

- The long-form possessive adjectives can also occur with the indefinite article:

unos amigos **míos**	*some friends of mine*
una idea **tuya**	*an idea of yours*

D. **¡En el depósito de artículos perdidos** (*lost and found*)! ¿Adónde van a parar las cosas perdidas? Ud. y su amigo buscan esos artículos en el depósito donde suelen acabar. Dígale a su amigo que las cosas pertenecen a otra persona de la que creía. Use un adjetivo posesivo en su respuesta.

MODELO Esta bufanda será de Paco, ¿no? (Jorge)
→ No, no es suya. Será de Jorge.

1. Este guante será de Rebeca, ¿no? (Martina)

____

2. Estas llaves serán de Carlos y Pepe, ¿no? (nosotros)

____

3. Este cepillo para el pelo será de Amparo, ¿no? (Rosita)

____

4. Estos apuntes de historia serán del nuevo estudiante de intercambio, ¿no? (Uds.)

____

5. Estas calculadoras serán de Fernando y Graciela, ¿no? (tú)

____

6. Este pañuelo será de Anita, ¿no? (la profesora Márquez)

____

7. Esta agenda (*appointment book*) será de Uds., ¿no? (Eduardo)

____

E. Viajes. ¿Qué se lleva en un viaje? Escriba cada frase empleando un adjetivo posesivo de forma larga.

Modelo el paquete/(yo)
→ el paquete mío

Hacer un viaje

el billete de ida y vuelta *round-trip ticket*
la bolsa de viaje *travel bag*
el cheque de viajero *traveler's check*
el equipaje de mano *hand luggage*
la maleta *suitcase*
el maletín *small suitcase*
la mochila *backpack*
el paquete *package*
la visa *visa*

1. las maletas/(tú)

____

2. el equipaje de mano/(nosotros)

____

3. los cheques de viajero/(ellos)

____

4. la bolsa de viaje/(Ud.)

____

5. los maletines/(tú y yo)

____

6. la mochila/(Uds.)

____

7. el pasaporte/(yo)

____

8. las visas/(ellas)

____

9. los billetes de ida y vuelta/(tú)

____

D *Possessive pronouns*

- Spanish possessive pronouns consist of the definite article plus the long-form possessive adjective. The noun is deleted:

—Javier se compró un coche espléndido.	*Javier bought himself a terrific car.*
—Sí, **el suyo** costó mucho más que **el nuestro**.	*Yes, **his** cost much more than **ours** did.*
—Los estudiantes míos son muy buenos este semestre. ¿Y **los suyos**?	*My students are very good this semester. What about **yours**?*
—**Los míos** también son excelentes.	***Mine** are excellent too.*
—Mira mi computadora nueva.	*Look at my new computer.*
—Es fabulosa. Creo que **la tuya** tiene más memoria que **la mía**.	*It's fabulous. I think **yours** has more memory than **mine**.*

- The masculine plural of the possessive pronoun can refer to family members or to teams:

—¿Cómo están **los tuyos**?	*How's your family?*
—¿**Los míos**? Perfectamente, gracias.	*My family? Just fine, thanks.*
—Espero que ganen **los nuestros**.	*I hope our team wins.*
—Vamos a ver. Los otros son muy buenos también.	*Let's see. The others are very good too.*

- The neuter article **lo** + the masculine singular of the long-form possessives forms a neuter possessive pronoun meaning *whose part, whose task, etc.*:

—Denme **lo mío** y me voy.	*Give me **my share** and I'll leave.*
—**Lo tuyo** son veinte dólares.	***Your part** is twenty dollars.*
—No encontramos **lo nuestro**, señor.	*We can't find **our things**, sir.*
—**Lo suyo** está en la oficina.	***Your things** are in the office.*

F. **¡Fernando el fanfarrón** (*braggart*)! ¡Cada vez que alguien dice que tiene algo bueno, Fernando se jacta (*brags*) de tener algo mejor! Escriba lo que dice Fernando usando los pronombres posesivos.

Modelo Martín —Mi coche es muy lujoso.
Fernando —¡Pero el mío es más lujoso que el tuyo!

1. Lorenzo: Mi raqueta de tenis es muy moderna.

   Fernando: ____

2. Patricia: Mis discos compactos son nuevos.

   Fernando: ____

3. Ricardo: Mi novia es muy simpática.

   Fernando: ____

4. Dalia: Mi computadora funciona muy bien.
   Fernando: ______________________________

5. Carlos: Mis revistas de deportes son muy interesantes.
   Fernando: ______________________________

6. Clara: Mis notas son muy buenas.
   Fernando: ______________________________

7. Leo: Mi perro es sumamente inteligente.
   Fernando: ______________________________

G. **¿Dónde está?** Use pronombres posesivos para explicar dónde Ud. cree que están ciertas cosas.

MODELO ¿Dónde está el anillo de Virginia? (en el dormitorio)
→ El suyo estará en el dormitorio.

1. ¿Dónde están los manuales de José? (en el estante [*shelf*])
   ____

2. ¿Dónde está tu permiso de manejar? (en mi cartera)
   ____

3. ¿Dónde están las pulseras de Lola y Nieves? (en la cómoda)
   ____

4. ¿Dónde están los sellos de Uds.? (en la gaveta [*drawer*])
   ____

5. ¿Dónde está nuestra agenda? (en el escritorio)
   ____

6. ¿Dónde están vuestros frascos de agua de colonia? (en el baño)
   ____

7. ¿Dónde está su (de Ud.) guitarra? (encima del piano)
   ____

H. **¡Qué niño más repipí** (*precocious brat*)! Angelito siempre se sale con la suya (*gets his own way*). ¿Y estas otras personas? ¿Siempre se salen con la suya? Use el pronombre posesivo apropiado en contestar que sí o que no.

MODELO la hermanita de Angelito (sí)
→ Sí, se sale con la suya.

1. las hermanas mayores de Angelito (no)
   ____

2. Rafaelito (no)
   ____

3. Ud. (sí)

___

4. Bárbara (no)

___

5. Uds. (no)

___

6. tú (sí)

___

7. vosotros (sí)

___

I. Exprese las siguientes oraciones en español.

1. This business about the company is difficult to understand.

___

2. That situation regarding our trip has to be resolved.

___

3. We'll have to talk about that matter of buying a new car.

___

4. An old friend of mine is arriving on Saturday.

___

5. How's your (*tú*) family? (use a possessive pronoun)

___

6. We hope our team wins. (use a possessive pronoun)

___

7. Your part (task) is to bring the flowers. (*Ud.*)

___

8. My part is to make copies (*fotocopiar*).

___

J. **Ejercicio oral.** Practique usando los demostrativos y los posesivos. Pregúnteles a otros estudiantes a quiénes pertenecen ciertas cosas. Por ejemplo, Ud. pregunta «¿De quién es este libro de texto?» Un compañero contesta: «Es mío» o «Es suyo», señalando a otro compañero.

CHAPTER 19 PERSONAL PRONOUNS: SUBJECT, OBJECT, PREPOSITIONAL

A *Subject pronouns*

- The subject pronouns in Spanish are:

singular	*plural*
yo *I*	**nosotros, nosotras** *we*
tú *you (informal singular)*	**vosotros, vosotras** *you (informal plural, Spain only)*
él *he, it*	**ellos** *they, masculine*
ella *she, it*	**ellas** *they, feminine*
Ud. (**usted**) *you (formal singular)*	**Uds.** (**ustedes**) *you (formal and informal plural in Latin America, formal plural in Spain)*

- There are several important differences between the personal pronouns in English and Spanish:
  1. Spanish has four forms for *you* that show politeness and number. However, **vosotros/vosotras** is used only in Spain, giving Latin American Spanish three forms for *you*: two singular forms **tú** (informal) and **usted** (formal), and one plural form **ustedes** that can be used for any group of two or more people.
  2. Since all Spanish nouns are either masculine or feminine, **él** and **ella** refer to things as well as to people.
  3. **Ud.** and **Uds.** are often abbreviated **Vd.** and **Vds.** in Spain.
  4. Subject pronouns are less common in Spanish than in English because the verb endings show who is performing the action. They are used, however, to contrast or emphasize the subject of the verb.

—¿Qué haces mañana? *What are you doing tomorrow?*
—Trabajo. *I'm working.*

—¿Qué hacen (Uds.) mañana? *What are you doing tomorrow?*
—**Ella** tiene el día libre, pero **yo** trabajo. ***She** has the day off, but **I'm** working.*

- Note the following use of the subject pronouns with **ser** (colloquial English translations appear in parentheses):

Soy yo. *It is I. (It's me.)*	**Somos nosotros, Somos nosotras.** *It is we. (It's us.)*
Eres tú. *It is you.*	**Sois vosotros, Sois vosotras.** *It is you.*
Es él. *It is he. (It's him.)*	**Son ellos.** *It is they. (masculine) (It's them.)*
Es ella. *It is she. (It's her.)*	**Son ellas.** *It is they. (feminine) (It's them.)*
Es Ud. *It is you.*	**Son Uds.** *It is you.*

A. Identifique el sujeto de cada oración. Escriba el pronombre sujeto al lado de la oración. Si hay más de una posibilidad, escriba todos los pronombres posibles.

MODELO ¡Lees una cantidad de libros! **tú**

1. Estacionemos en esta calle. ____________________
2. Es español. ____________________
3. Sois simpáticas. ____________________
4. Buscaban casa. ____________________
5. Tengo razón. ____________________
6. Está contentísima. ____________________
7. Cenasteis a las nueve. ____________________
8. Lo verás. ____________________
9. Eran bellas. ____________________
10. Es inglesa. ____________________

B. Yo … pero tú … Practique usando el pronombre sujeto en combinar las dos oraciones en una.

MODELO Estudias español. Estudia (ella) francés.
→ *Tú* estudias español, pero *ella* estudia francés.

1. Trabajo de lunes a viernes. Trabajas los fines de semana.

 ____

2. Estudiamos en una universidad particular. Estudian (Uds.) en una universidad estatal.

 ____

 ____

3. Viven (ellas) en pleno centro. Vive (Ud.) en las afueras.

 ____

4. Vas de compras el sábado. Vamos de compras el jueves.

 ____

5. Es (él) abogado. Soy profesor.

 ____

6. Desayuna (Ud.) fuerte. Desayuna (ella) poco.

 ____

7. Escuchan (ellos) música clásica. Escucháis rock.

 ____

B Pronouns after prepositions (prepositional pronouns)

- After a preposition, Spanish uses the subject pronouns, except for **yo** and **tú:**

para **mí**	para **nosotros/nosotras**
para **ti**	para **vosotros/vosotras**
para **él**	para **ellos**
para **ella**	para **ellas**
para **Ud.**	para **Uds.**

Note that **mí** has a written accent but **ti** does not.

- Two irregular forms exist with the preposition **con**: **conmigo** (*with me*) and **contigo** (*with you*) (*informal singular*). There is also a form **consigo** (*with himself, with herself, with themselves*).

—¿Puedes ir conmigo? *Can you go with me?*
—Hoy no. Mañana voy contigo. *Not today. Tomorrow I'll go with you.*

—Alicia está enojada con nosotros. *Alicia is angry with us.*
—Debería estar enojada consigo misma. Ella tiene la culpa de todo. *She should be angry with herself. She's to blame for everything.*

- After the prepositions **como** (*like*), **según** (*according to*), **salvo** (*except*), **excepto** (*except*), **menos** (*except*), **entre** (*between, among*), subject pronouns are used even in the first- and second-persons singular: **entre tú y yo** (*between you and me*), **todos menos tú**, (*everyone except you*), **según yo** (*according to me*). **Yo** and **tú** replace **mí** and **ti** after **y** with other prepositions:

Lo dijo delante de Ud. y **yo**. *He said it in front of you and me.*

C. Pronombres preposicionales. Llene los espacios en blanco con la forma correcta de la preposición.

Modelo de **mí** (yo)

1. para ______________ (él)
2. con ______________ (tú)
3. según ______________ (tú)
4. por ______________ (nosotros)
5. salvo ______________ (yo)
6. sobre ______________ (Ud.)
7. con ______________ (yo)
8. de ______________ (vosotros)
9. para ______________ (ellas)
10. por ______________ (tú)
11. menos ______________ (tú)
12. como ______________ (yo)

13. en ____________________ (ella)

14. entre ____________________ y yo (tú)

D. Pronombres preposicionales. Conteste las siguientes preguntas usando los pronombres preposicionales correctos.

MODELO ¿Trajiste algo para Elenita?
→ Sí, traje algo para **ella.**

1. ¿Vive Ud. cerca de las tiendas?

____

2. ¿Trabajaba Timoteo en esa oficina?

____

3. ¿Lograron Uds. hablar sobre esos asuntos?

____

4. ¿Pagaste un dineral (*fortune*) por el estéreo?

____

5. ¿Salió Ud. con Isabel y Alfonso?

____

6. ¿Hay mucho trabajo para la clase de filosofía?

____

7. ¿Se casó María Elena con el pintor?

____

8. ¿Felicitaste a los jugadores por la victoria?

____

E. ¡Te equivocas! Su amigo cree que Ud. hizo algunas cosas con ciertas personas o para ellas. Dígale que no hizo las cosas ni con las personas que él cree ni para ellas. Use pronombres preposicionales en sus respuestas.

MODELO Saliste con Gabriela, ¿verdad?
→ No, con ella, no.

1. Almorzaste con Paquita y Laura, ¿verdad?

____

2. Fuiste al cine con Víctor, ¿verdad?

____

3. Hiciste el informe para la profesora Godoy, ¿verdad?

____

4. Trabajaste en la librería por tu hermana, ¿verdad?

____

5. Compraste un regalo para tus padres, ¿verdad?

___

6. Escribiste el trabajo por Daniel, ¿verdad?

___

7. Jugaste tenis con los Vilas, ¿verdad?

___

8. Preparaste el almuerzo para mí, ¿verdad?

___

C *Personal* ***a*** *and direct objects*

- A direct object noun in Spanish is joined to its verb directly, without a preposition, if it refers to a thing. Direct object nouns that refer to specific people are preceded by **a.** This use of **a** is called ***personal*** *a:*

—No veo **a tu abuela**.	*I don't see your grandmother.*
—Está en la cocina **ayudando a mi madre.**	*She's in the kitchen helping my mother.*
—¿Alquilaste **la película**?	*Did you rent the film?*
—Sí, y compré **palomitas de maíz**.	*Yes, and I bought popcorn.*

In the above examples, the nouns **abuela, madre, película, palomitas de maíz** are direct objects.

- Several verbs that take a direct object in Spanish have English equivalents that have prepositions:

aprovechar algo	*to take advantage of something*
buscar algo / a alguien	*to look for something/for someone*
escuchar algo / a alguien	*to listen to something/to someone*
esperar algo / a alguien	*to wait for something/for someone*
mirar algo / a alguien	*to look at something/at someone*
pagar algo	*to pay for something*
pedir algo	*to ask for something*

- Personal **a** is also used before **alguien** and **nadie**, and before **alguno, ninguno, cualquiera,** and any other pronoun or, optionally, a number that refers to people:

—¿**A quién** llamas?	*Whom are you calling?*
—No puedo llamar **a nadie**. El teléfono está descompuesto.	*I can't call anyone. The telephone is out of order.*
—¿Despidieron **a alguien?**	*Did they fire anyone?*
—No, no despidieron **a ningún empleado.**	*No, they didn't fire a single employee.*
—¿**A cuántos** invitaste a la fiesta?	*How many did you invite to the party?*
—Invité **(a) quince.**	*I invited fifteen.*
—Hoy llevo **a los míos** al centro.	*Today I'm taking my family downtown.*
—¿Puedo ir con Uds.? Me encantaría conocer **a los tuyos.**	*Can I go with you? I would love to meet your relatives.*

- Personal **a** is not used before nouns referring to people if they are not specific:

—Este restaurante busca **camareros.**	*This restaurant is looking for waiters.*
—También necesitan **un cajero.**	*They also need a cashier.*

- Personal **a** is usually not used with **tener**:

—¿Cuántos hijos tienen los Sánchez?	*How many children do the Sanchezes have?*
—Tres. Tienen dos muchachas y un muchacho.	*Three. They have two girls and a boy.*

F. El *a* personal. Escriba el **a** personal donde sea necesario para completar las siguientes oraciones. No se olvide de escribir la contracción **al** (**a** + **el**) cuando haga falta.

1. Yo buscaba ____________ los sobres.
2. Encontré ____________ los niños en el patio.
3. Busquen ____________ los documentos en el escritorio.
4. Encontraron ____________ el arquitecto en su oficina.
5. Paco conoció ____________ su novia hace seis meses.
6. ¿____________ quién viste en el teatro?
7. Llevamos ____________ nuestros amigos a la sierra.
8. ¿No comprendes ____________ el problema todavía?
9. Me gustaría conocer ____________ la ciudad.
10. Llévate ____________ el paquete.
11. Vamos a buscar ____________ Mari Carmen.
12. No he encontrado ____________ el número de teléfono.
13. Jesús y Tito llevan ____________ la camiseta de su equipo.
14. ¿Quién llamó ____________ el médico?
15. Ayuda ____________ tu hermano.
16. ¿Conoce Ud. ____________ ese centro comercial?
17. Voy a ver ____________ mis tíos mañana.
18. Nadie comprende ____________ el profesor Delgado.
19. ¿Es verdad que no pudiste encontrar ____________ el hotel?
20. ¿____________ quiénes llamaste?

G. ¡Un flechazo! (*Love at first sight!*) Simón le explica a su amigo cómo se enamoró en Palma de Mallorca. Llene los espacios en blanco con el **a** personal cuando sea necesario.

1. Pedro: Entonces, ¿ya conocías ____________ algunos estudiantes de la facultad de ciencias sociales?

2. Simón: Por desgracia, las primeras semanas no conocí ____________________ ninguno de los estudiantes.
3. Pedro: ¿Pero no viste ____________________ tantos chicos en la universidad?
4. Simón: Claro que los vi pero no me presenté ____________________ ellos porque no dominaba el español.

   Pedro: ¿Cómo es que cambió la situación entonces?
5. Simón: Bueno, después de un mes más o menos conocí ____________________ alguien de la facultad de ingeniería que me llevó a una fiesta.
6. Pedro: Allí conociste ____________________ mucha gente, ¿verdad?
7. Simón: ____________________ muchas personas, no, pero ____________________ una muy especial sí. Es que vi ____________________ tantas chicas muy lindas.
8. Pedro: Y querías sacar a bailar ____________________ todas, ¿no?

   Simón: Sí, al principio. ¡Hasta que me fijé en una que me dejó boquiabierto!
9. Pedro: ¡Un flechazo! Total, no invitaste ____________________ ninguna a salir ...
10. Simón: ¡Excepto ____________________ Josefa!

Nota cultural

Palma de Mallorca es la capital de la provincia de Baleares, las islas españolas en el Mediterráneo. Es también capital de la isla de Mallorca, la mayor de las Baleares. Por su hermoso paisaje y clima perfecto, Mallorca es un gran centro de turismo internacional. Un lugar de visita es la Cartuja de Valldemosa, un convento donde el compositor Federico Chopin (1810–49) y la escritora francesa la baronesa Dudevant, cuyo seudónimo era Jorge (George) Sand, pasaron el invierno de 1838.

H. **Verbos.** Exprese las siguientes oraciones en español. No se olvide que varios verbos en español que tienen complemento directo y no tienen preposición corresponden a verbos con preposición en inglés.

1. Ask for another bottle of wine. (*Ud.*)

   ____

2. Let's take advantage of this sale.

   ____

3. Look at the beautiful ocean. (*tú*)

   ____

4. I'll wait for them until three o'clock.

   ____

5. He's looking for his brother and sister.

____

6. Did their parents pay for the furniture?

____

7. Let's listen to the orchestra.

____

D *Direct object pronouns: forms and position*

- Direct object nouns can be replaced by direct object pronouns. The direct object pronouns in Spanish are:

me	**nos**
te	**os**
lo	**los**
la	**las**

Note the following:

1. **Lo, la, los, las** refer to both people and things.
2. **Lo, la, los, las** are also the direct object pronouns for **Ud.** and **Uds.**, so they mean *you* as well as *him, her, it, them.*
3. In Spain, **lo** is replaced by **le** when referring to people.

- Direct object pronouns precede the conjugated verb in Spanish (they follow in English):

—¿Dónde estarán los niños? Hace quince minutos que **los** busco y no **los** encuentro. — *Where can the children be? I've been looking for them for fifteen minutes and I can't find them.*
—**Los** vi en el parque. — *I saw them in the park.*

—¡Ay! No tengo el libro de química. **Lo** dejé en el colegio. — *Oh! I don't have the chemistry book. I left it at school.*
—Aquí tengo el mío. ¿**Lo** quieres? — *I have mine here. Do you want it?*

—**Me** avisará si hay un cambio en el horario de mañana. — *You'll inform me if there's a change in tomorrow's schedule.*
—Cómo no, señora. Cualquier cosa y **la** llamo en seguida. — *Of course, madam. If anything comes up I'll call you immediately.*

—¿Vas al centro ahora? ¿**Nos** llevas? — *Are you going downtown now? Will you take us?*
— Con mucho gusto. **Los** dejo delante del correo. ¿Está bien? — *Gladly. I'll leave you in front of the post office. Is that all right?*

- In compound tenses the direct object pronouns are placed before the auxiliary verb **haber**:

—Carlos, ¡qué milagro! No **te** hemos visto por tanto tiempo. — *Carlos, what a surprise! We haven't seen you for such a long time.*
—Es que **me** han contratado en una empresa de las afueras. — *That's because they've hired me at a firm in the suburbs.*

- In verb + infinitive constructions, the direct object pronoun may either precede the first verb or be attached to the infinitive:

—¿Has visto la nueva película española?	*Have you seen the new Spanish film?*
—No, pero **la** quiero ver. *or* No, pero quiero ver**la**.	*No, but I want to see it.*

- In the progressive tenses, the direct object pronoun can be placed either before the form of **estar** or be attached to the present participle. When the pronoun is attached to the present participle, an accent mark is added to the vowel before the **-ndo**:

—¿Has leído la nueva novela de Atienza?	*Have you read the new novel by Atienza?*
—**La** estoy leyendo ahora. *or* Estoy ley**é**ndo**la** ahora.	*I'm reading it now.*

- The direct object pronoun is also attached to affirmative command forms. An accent mark is added to the stressed vowel of the command form, except in the case of one-syllable commands:

—Ah, tienes el periódico. **Ponlo** en la mesa.	*Ah, you have the newspaper. Put it on the table.*
—No, **cógelo** tú y **llévalo** arriba.	*No, you get it and take it upstairs.*
—Éstas son las palabras nuevas, chicos. **Apréndanlas** de memoria.	*These are the new words, kids. Learn them by heart.*
—Por favor, **repáselas** con nosotros, profesor.	*Please, review them with us, sir.*

- To emphasize or contrast direct object pronouns referring to people, a phrase consisting of **a** + the corresponding stressed pronoun is added to the sentence:

—¿Reconociste a Laura y a Marcos?	*Did you recognize Laura and Marcos?*
—**La** reconocí **a ella**, pero no **lo** vi **a él**.	*I recognized **her**, but I didn't see **him**.*
—Parece que las secretarias son más simpáticas que el jefe.	*It seems that the secretaries are nicer than the boss.*
—Sí, **a ellas las** encuentro encantadoras, pero **a él** no **lo** aguanto.	*Yes, I find **them** delightful, but I can't stand **him**.*

- When a direct object noun *precedes* the verb, the direct object pronoun must be present. Compare Veo **a Juan** *with* **A Juan lo** veo. This is true even if the direct object is a thing. Compare: Dejé **los libros** en la mesa *with* **Los libros los** dejé en la mesa.

I. **¡A jugar pues!** Sus amigos quieren pasar la tarde jugando juegos en casa porque está lloviendo. Diga si quiere jugar los juegos que proponen. Escriba la respuesta de dos maneras usando un complemento directo.

Juegos

la batalla naval *battleship*
la charada *charades*
las damas *checkers*
los dardos *darts*
el dominó *dominoes*
la lotería *lotto*
el monopolio *monopoly*
las palabras cruzadas *crossword puzzle*
el rompecabezas *riddle*
el tres en raya *tic-tac-toe*

Modelo ¿Quieres jugar damas? (sí)
→ Sí, quiero jugar**las.** *or* Sí, **las** quiero jugar.

1. ¿Quieres jugar dominó? (sí)

___

2. ¿Prefieres jugar batalla naval? (sí)

___

3. ¿Quieres hacer un tres en raya? (no)

___

4. ¿Prefieres tirar dardos? (no)

___

5. ¿Quieres hacer la charada? (sí)

___

6. ¿Prefieres jugar lotería? (no)

___

7. ¿Quieres ver unas palabras cruzadas? (sí)

___

8. ¿Prefieres jugar monopolio? (no)

___

9. ¿Quieres hacer rompecabezas? (no)

___

Nota cultural

El **dominó** se juega mucho en los países hispánicos. Se usa la palabra **crucigrama** también para palabras cruzadas.

J. Mi coche. Conteste las siguientes preguntas sobre el cuidado de su coche cambiando el sustantivo a un pronombre complemento directo. Escriba dos oraciones para cada respuesta.

Modelo ¿Compraste la bomba de aire (*air pump*)?
→ No, no **la** compré. Voy a compra**rla.**

El coche

la caja de herramientas *toolbox*
el faro *headlight*
el gato *jack*
el parachoques *bumper*
las piezas de repuesto *spare parts*
la placa de matrícula *license plate*
el silenciador *muffler*
el volante *steering wheel*

1. ¿Cambiaste el aceite?

2. ¿Reparaste el parachoques?

3. ¿Pediste las placas de matrícula?

4. ¿Llevaste una caja de herramientas y piezas de repuesto?

5. ¿Usaste el gato?

6. ¿Pusiste otros faros?

7. ¿Arreglaste el volante?

8. ¿Instalaste el silenciador?

K. Bernardo y los coches. Bernardo acaba de sacar su licencia de conducir y piensa mucho en su coche. Escriba oraciones sobre la afición de Bernardo cambiando el sustantivo a un pronombre complemento directo. Escriba cada oración de dos maneras.

MODELO Bernardo quiere limpiar el baúl.
→ Bernardo quiere limpiarlo. / Bernardo lo quiere limpiar.

El *coche*

la avería *breakdown*
el baúl *trunk*
cargar la batería *to charge the battery*
el coche descapotable *convertible*
el coche todo terreno *jeep*
el pinchazo *blowout*
la señal de tráfico *road sign*

1. Piensa comprar el coche todo terreno.

2. Tiene que llenar el tanque de gasolina.

3. Trata de leer todas las señales de tráfico.

4. Prefiere conducir un coche descapotable.

5. Debe cargar la batería.

____

6. Teme tener un pinchazo.

____

7. Procura evitar las averías.

____

L. Lo significa *you*. El complemento directo **lo, la, los, las** también reemplaza *Ud.* y *Uds.* Conteste las preguntas empleando el complemento directo en su respuesta.

MODELO ¿Me conoce Ud.?
➔ Sí, señor, **lo conozco**.

1. ¿Me conoce Ud.?
   Sí, señorita, _______________.
2. ¿Nos comprende Ud.?
   Sí, señores, _______________.
3. ¿Me llama Ud.?
   No, señora, no _______________.
4. ¿Nos busca Ud.?
   No, señoras, no _______________.
5. ¿Me lleva Ud.?
   Sí, señor, _______________.
6. ¿Nos conoce Ud.?
   No, señoritas, no _______________.
7. ¿Me ayuda Ud.?
   Sí, profesor, _______________.
8. ¿Nos ve Ud.?
   No, señores, no _______________.

M. ¡Míralo! Dé mandatos a varias personas diciéndoles lo que deben hacer en ciertos deportes. Escriba mandatos afirmativos y negativos colocando el pronombre complemento directo en su posición correcta.

MODELO ver / Ud. / los Juegos Olímpicos
➔ Véalos. / No los vea.

1. marcar / Ud. /goles

____

2. llamar / tú / al árbitro (*umpire*)

____

3. jugar / Uds. / béisbol

4. saltar / Ud. / vallas (*hurdles*)

5. hacer / tú / gimnasia

6. mirar / Uds. / la cancha

7. lanzar / tú / la pelota

8. ser / Ud. / plusmarquista (*masc.*) (*record holder*)

9. levantar / Uds. / las pesas

N. ¿Lo ha visto Ud.? Unos amigos quieren saber si Ud. ha visto a ciertas personas y cosas hoy. Conteste usando el pronombre complemento directo.

MODELO ¿Ha visto a Paulina hoy? (sí / no)
→ Sí, la he visto.
→ No, no la he visto.

1. ¿Has visto al señor Domínguez hoy? (sí)

2. ¿Ha visto Ud. a los decanos de la universidad? (no)

3. ¿Han visto Uds. la cámara? (sí)

4. ¿Ha visto Ud. los alicates (*pliers*)? (no)

5. ¿Has visto a las hermanas Moya? (no)

6. ¿Han visto Uds. las tarjetas de crédito? (sí)

7. ¿Ha visto Ud. el recibo? (sí)

8. ¿Has visto a la ortodontista? (no)

O. La catedral de Sevilla. La catedral se remonta (*dates back*) al siglo XV cuando se empezó a construir. Ud. vive en la Edad Media y es testigo de la construcción. Describa las actividades que está viendo en oraciones que cambian el sustantivo al pronombre complemento directo. Escriba las oraciones de dos maneras.

La catedral de Sevilla: su construcción

el albañil *bricklayer*
los andamios *scaffolding*
la argamasa *mortar* (mezcla de arena y agua)
el dibujante *draftsman*
echar los cimientos *to lay the foundation*
el fraile *monk*
el maestro de obras *master builder*
la mezquita *mosque*
la monja *nun*
rezar las oraciones *to say prayers*

MODELO Yo estoy viendo la construcción.
→ Yo estoy viéndola.
→ Yo la estoy viendo.

1. Los arquitectos están empleando el estilo gótico.

 ____

 ____

2. Los constructores van destruyendo la mezquita.

 ____

 ____

3. Los dibujantes están dibujando las ventanas.

 ____

 ____

4. Los maestros de obras están echando los cimientos.

 ____

 ____

5. Los frailes y las monjas siguen rezando sus oraciones.

 ____

 ____

6. Los trabajadores siguen colocando los andamios.

 ____

 ____

7. Los albañiles van trayendo piedras.

 ____

 ____

8. Los obreros están poniendo argamasa.

 ____

 ____

Nota cultural

La catedral de Sevilla es por sus dimensiones la primera de España y la tercera del mundo cristiano después de San Pedro del Vaticano y San Pablo de Londres. Es una de las últimas catedrales góticas españolas y tiene algunas influencias renacentistas. La catedral fue comenzada en 1402 y terminada a principios del siglo XVI.

Hubo influencia árabe en España a partir de la batalla de Guadalete en 711 en la cual los árabes derrotaron a Don Rodrigo, el último rey visigodo, y se apoderaron de la península Ibérica. Duró la influencia árabe en España ocho siglos hasta que perdieron la campaña (*campaign*) de Granada en 1492. Sin embargo, la influencia árabe en España perdura en la onomástica (nombres de lugares), comida, lingüística y arquitectura. La catedral de Sevilla fue construida sobre las ruinas de una **mezquita.**

P. Una criada *muy* trabajadora. El señor Salas vuelve a su casa y quiere saber dónde están las cosas y la gente. Su criada Pepa le contesta con oraciones que tienen el complemento directo en primer lugar. ¿Qué le dice Pepa al señor Salas?

MODELO ¿Dónde está mi esposa? (ver salir hace una hora)
➔ A su esposa la vi salir hace una hora.

1. ¿Dónde está la revista? (poner en su mesa de trabajo)

____

2. ¿Dónde están los chicos? (llevar al cine)

____

3. ¿Dónde está el balón de fútbol? (dejar en el jardín)

____

4. ¿Dónde está el bebé? (acostar)

____

5. ¿Dónde están mis libros? (arreglar en su cuarto)

____

6. ¿Dónde están las cartas que escribí? (echar al correo)

____

7. ¿Dónde está mi camisa amarilla? (colgar en su armario)

____

8. ¿Dónde están las galletas que compré? (comer)

____

E *Indirect object pronouns: forms and position*

- Indirect objects are joined to the verb by the preposition **a**. Indirect objects most commonly refer to people.

- The indirect object pronouns in Spanish are:

me	**nos**
te	**os**
le	**les**

- Indirect object pronouns follow the same rules of position as direct object pronouns:

  Te dije la verdad.
  Le debo decir la verdad. *or* Debo decir**le** la verdad.
  Les estoy diciendo la verdad. *or* Estoy diciéndo**les** la verdad.
  Nos han dicho la verdad.
  Díga**me** la verdad.

- An indirect object noun in Spanish is usually accompanied by the corresponding indirect object pronoun (**le** or **les**, depending on whether the noun is singular or plural):

  —¿**Les** escribiste **a tus padres**? — *Did you write to your parents?*
  —Sí, y también **le** mandé una carta **a mi hermana**. — *Yes, and I also sent my sister a letter.*

Some verbs that take an indirect object in Spanish take a direct object in English:

contestarle a alguien	*to answer someone*
pedirle algo a alguien	*to ask someone for something*
preguntarle a alguien	*to ask someone*
recordarle a alguien	*to remind someone*

Many verbs take an indirect object of the person (**le ... a alguien**) and a direct object that is a thing (**algo**):

contarle algo a alguien	*to relate, recount something to someone*
darle algo a alguien	*to give something to someone*
decirle algo a alguien	*to tell, say something to someone*
devolverle algo a alguien	*to return something to someone*
enseñarle algo a alguien	*to show something to someone*
escribirle algo a alguien	*to write something to someone*
entregarle algo a alguien	*to hand over something to someone*
enviarle algo a alguien	*to send something to someone*
explicarle algo a alguien	*to explain something to someone*
mandarle algo a alguien	*to send something to someone*
mostrarle algo a alguien	*to show something to someone*
ofrecerle algo a alguien	*to offer something to someone*
pedirle algo a alguien	*to ask someone for something*
recordarle algo a alguien	*to remind someone of something*
regalarle algo a alguien	*to give something to someone as a gift*
traerle algo a alguien	*to bring something to someone*

The indirect object is the equivalent of English *from* with verbs meaning *take away, steal, remove,* etc.:

arrebatarle algo a alguien	*to snatch, grab something from someone*
comprarle algo a alguien	*to buy something from someone*
esconderle algo a alguien	*to hide something from someone*
exigirle algo a alguien	*to demand something of someone*
ganarle algo a alguien	*to win something from someone*
ocultarle algo a alguien	*to hide something from someone*
pedirle prestado algo a alguien	*to borrow something from someone*
quitarle algo a alguien	*to take something away from someone*
robarle algo a alguien	*to steal something from someone*
sacarle algo a alguien	*to get something out of someone*
solicitarle algo a alguien	*to ask, request something of someone*
suspenderle algo a alguien	*to revoke, cancel something of someone*

¿**A quién le** compraste el coche?	*Whom did you buy the car from?*
Me exigieron mis documentos de identidad.	*They demanded my identification papers (of/from me).*
Le solicité trabajo **al padre de Lucas**.	*I applied for work with/from Lucas's father.*
Al turista le quitaron el pasaporte.	*They took the tourist's passport from him.*

- To emphasize or contrast indirect object pronouns, a phrase consisting of **a** + the corresponding stressed pronoun is added to the sentence:

—¿Qué **les** pidieron los aduaneros **a ustedes?**	*What did the customs officers ask **you** for?*
—**A mí me** pidieron el pasaporte, pero **a él le** pidieron todos los documentos.	*They asked for **my** passport, but they asked for all of **his** documents.*
—¿**A ustedes les** regalaron algo?	*Did they give **you** anything as a gift?*
—**A nosotros nos** regalaron muchas cosas, pero **a ellos no les** dieron nada.	*They gave **us** many things, but they didn't give **them** anything.*

Q. El complemento indirecto. Cambie el pronombre del complemento indirecto en cada oración.

MODELO Yo le pedí unas revistas. (a ellos)
→ Yo les pedí unas revistas.

1. Les traje los refrescos. (a ti)

___

2. Me dieron flores. (a nosotros)

___

3. Le mandó una tarjeta postal. (a mí)

___

4. Nos dijeron los precios. (a Ud.)

____

5. Te ofrecimos el escritorio. (a él)

____

6. Les preguntó la hora. (a ella)

____

7. Le expliqué mis ideas. (a vosotros)

____

8. Me recordaron el cumpleaños de Leo. (a Uds.)

____

R. **Salir ganando o salir perdiendo.** Añada a cada oración una frase que consiste en **a** + el pronombre enfático para hacer énfasis en o contraste de los pronombres de complemento indirecto.

MODELO **A mí** me enviaron mucha plata, pero **a ella** (Roberta) no le enviaron nada.

1. ____________________ nos mostraron el castillo, pero ____________________ (Ud. y Felipe) les mostraron solamente el establo de caballos.
2. Marta me contó ____________________ la pura verdad, pero ____________________ te contó puras mentiras.
3. Yo le escribí una carta de amor ____________________ (Daniel), pero le escribí una carta de odio ____________________ (su novia).
4. ____________________ te dimos la llave de la casa, pero ____________________ (Catarina y Jorge) les dimos una carta de despedida.
5. ____________________ os regalaron unos discos compactos fabulosos, pero ____________________ nos regalaron unos discos rayados (*scratched*).
6. ____________________ (Elena y Margarita) les trajo unos bombones, pero ____________________ (Ud.) le trajo una caja vacía.

S. **Un mal día en el barrio.** Muchas cosas malas sucedieron hoy en el barrio. Miguel pasó todo el día en el barrio y cuenta los lamentables sucesos a los amigos que regresan de sus clases en la universidad. Haga oraciones con los elementos dados para completar la narración de Miguel. Debe haber un pronombre complemento indirecto en cada oración que Ud. escribe.

1. ¿Conocen a la señora de Pacheco?
un joven/arrebatar el bolso

____

2. ¿Conocen a los Caballero, los dueños de la bodega?
dos hombres enmascarados/robar treinta mil pesos

___

3. ¿Se acuerdan de que Martín vendió su estéreo?
los compradores/pagar con billetes falsos

___

4. Mi hermanito jugaba en el parque.
alguien/quitar la bicicleta

___

5. La señora de Parrondo está molesta.
su hijo de cuatro años/esconder las llaves del coche

___

6. Un policía pilló (*caught*) al hijo de Galván manejando borracho.
el juez/suspender el permiso de manejar

___

7. El señor Ribera está furioso con su hijo.
éste/ocultar sus salidas con Elvira Camacho

___

8. Matilde Peña está preocupada.
su sobrino/pedir prestado mucho dinero

___

F *Verbs usually appearing with an indirect object pronoun (e.g., **gustar**)*

- Certain verbs in Spanish are almost always used with an indirect object pronoun. This construction is different from the English equivalents of these verbs. The most common of these is **gustar**:

Me gusta la torta. *I like the cake.* **Me gustan** las galletas. *I like the cookies.*	**Nos gusta** la torta. *We like the cake.* **Nos gustan** las galletas. *We like the cookies.*
Te gusta la torta. *You like the cake.* **Te gustan** las galletas. *You like the cookies.*	**Os gusta** la torta. *You like the cake.* **Os gustan** las galletas. *You like the cookies.*
Le gusta la torta. *He, She likes/You like the cake.* **Le gustan** las galletas. *He, She likes/You like the cookies.*	**Les gusta** la torta. *They/You like the cake.* **Les gustan** las galletas. *They/You like the cookies.*

Note that the verb agrees with the subject of the Spanish sentence, **torta** or **galletas.**

- When the grammatical subject of a verb like **gustar** is an infinitive, the verb is always third-person singular:

—**Me encanta patinar** sobre el hielo. *I love to ice skate.*
—A mí **me gusta más esquiar**. *I like skiing better.*

Here are some other verbs that function like **gustar**:

convenirle a alguien	*to suit someone, be good for someone*
encantarle a alguien	*to love something*
entusiasmarle a alguien	*to be excited about something*
faltarle a alguien	*to be missing something, not to have something*
fascinarle a alguien	*to be fascinated*
hacerle falta a alguien	*to need something*
importarle a alguien	*to care about something, to mind*
interesarle a alguien	*to be interested in something*
quedarle a alguien	*to have something left*
sobrarle a alguien	*to have more than enough of something*
tocarle a alguien	*to be someone's turn*

—¿**Te importa** acompañarme a la exposición de arte? — *Would you mind accompanying me to the art show?*
—**Me encantaría**. **Me interesa** mucho la pintura. — *I'd love to. I'm very interested in painting.*

—Creo que **te convendría** salir un poco. — *I think it would be good for you to go out a little.*
—Sé que **me hace falta**, pero **me sobra** trabajo. — *I know I need to, but I have too much work.*

—Parece que no **te entusiasman** mucho estos juegos. — *It seems that you're not very excited about these games.*
—Cada vez que **me toca a mí**, pierdo. — *Every time it's my turn, I lose.*

- To emphasize or contrast the indirect object pronouns, a phrase consisting of **a** + the corresponding stressed pronoun is added to the sentence. This prepositional phrase is also used for "short responses":

—¿Cuánto dinero nos queda? — *How much money do we have left?*
—A mí me quedan doscientos pesos. **¿Y a ti?** — *I have two hundred pesos left. How about you?*

—Chicos, ¿a quién le gusta la torta de chocolate? — *Kids, who likes chocolate cake?*
—**¡A mí! ¡A mí! ¡A mí!** — *I do! I do! I do!*

The phrase **¿Y a ti?** is short for **Y a ti, ¿cuánto dinero te queda?** The phrase **¡A mí!** is short for **A mí me gusta la torta de chocolate**.

T. En plural. Cambie el sujeto de las siguientes oraciones al plural. Todos los verbos son del tipo **gustar.** No se olvide de hacer todos los cambios necesarios.

Modelo Me gusta ese suéter.
➔ Me gustan esos suéteres.

1. Le encanta su perfume.

____

2. Nos interesa esta novela.

____

3. Les queda un examen.

____

4. Te entusiasma la comedia.

____

5. Os importa la idea.

____

6. Me hace falta una guía.

____

7. Les fascina esta materia.

____

8. Le falta un cuaderno.

____

U. En el futuro. Añada la construcción **ir a** + infinitivo a las siguientes oraciones con verbos como **gustar.**

Modelo Me gusta esa película. ➔ Me va a gustar esa película.
Me gustan esas películas. ➔ Me van a gustar esas películas.

1. Nos importan sus problemas.

____

2. No les queda mucho dinero.

____

3. Le encanta visitar a sus abuelos.

____

4. No les sobra comida.

____

5. Os conviene viajar en tren.

____

6. Te fascinan esos cuadros.

____

7. Me entusiasman sus obras.

____

8. No le interesan esos programas.

____

V. Conteste cada pregunta escogiendo entre el pronombre sujeto y la frase con **a.**

Modelo ¿Quién estudia chino? (Yo./A mí.)
→ Yo.

1. ¿A quién le gusta jugar baloncesto? (Él./A él.) __________
2. ¿Quiénes vieron a los niños? (Ellos./A ellos.) __________
3. ¿A Juana le quedan cincuenta dólares? (Ella no./A ella no.) __________
4. ¿Conociste a Diana? (Yo no./A mí no.) __________
5. ¿Comprendieron al profesor? (A nosotros sí./Nosotros sí.) __________
6. ¿A quién le interesan estos poemas? (Ud./A Ud.) __________
7. ¿Te hace falta manejar? (A mí sí./Yo sí.) __________
8. ¿Devolvieron los libros a la biblioteca? (A mí sí./Yo sí.) __________

W. **Los Castellón planean un viaje.** Exprese en español la conversación que tienen los señores Castellón y sus tres hijos sobre el viaje que piensan hacer en el verano. Escriba oraciones usando en cada caso un verbo como **gustar.**

1. Alicia Castellón: I'd like to take a trip to Spain.

   ____

2. Rafael Castellón: I'd love to visit my relatives in Venezuela and Argentina.

   ____

3. Lorenzo: I'd be interested in going camping in New Mexico or Arizona.

   ____

4. Nora: And I'd be fascinated to see the new Italian fashions.

   ____

5. Carlos: I'd be very enthusiastic about following Miguel Induraín in *el Tour de Francia*.

   ____

6. Rafael Castellón: It's good for us (suits us) to make a decision as soon as possible.

   ____

7. Lorenzo: We have more than enough suggestions. Let's draw lots! (*echar suertes*)

   ____

8. Nora: It's my turn first!

   ____

G Other uses of the indirect object

- The indirect object in Spanish is often the equivalent of the English possessive with parts of the body and articles of clothing. This is also true of reflexive pronouns:

—¿**Te quito** el abrigo?	*Shall I help you off with your jacket?*
—No, gracias. Siempre **me haces daño** en el brazo cuando me lo quitas.	*No, thank you. You always hurt my arm when you help me off with it.*
—Ven, Carlitos. **Te lavo** las manos.	*Come, Carlitos. I'll wash your hands.*
—No, no. Yo mismo **me las lavo**.	*No, no. I'll wash them myself.*

- The indirect object tells for whose benefit or for whose disadvantage something is done:

—¿**Me haces** el almuerzo, mamá?	*Can you make my lunch for me, Mom?*
—Sí, si **me llevas** las bolsas de comida a la cocina.	*Yes, if you carry the bags of food to the kitchen for me.*
—Espero que no **nos** caiga otra vez la vecina con sus dos hijos.	*I hope the neighbor doesn't drop in on us again with her two children.*
—Sí, la última vez esos dos diablos casi **nos** destruyeron la casa.	*Yes, the last time those two rascals almost destroyed our house.*
—¡Y **nos** comieron todas las galletas que teníamos!	*And they ate up all the cookies that we had.*

- The indirect object pronouns can be added to certain impersonal expressions:

Es difícil caminar cuando nieva.	*It's hard to walk when it snows.*
Me es difícil caminar cuando nieva.	*It's hard for me to walk when it snows.*
Es necesario estudiar más.	*It's necessary to study more.*
Nos es necesario estudiar más.	*It's necessary for us to study more.*

- The indirect object pronoun can be added to a **se** construction with certain verbs to express *unplanned occurrences*. These constructions focus on the object affected rather than on the person involved:

acabársele a alguien	*to run out of*
caérsele a alguien	*to drop*
ocurrírsele a alguien	*to dawn on, get the idea of*
olvidársele a alguien	*to forget*
perdérsele a alguien	*to lose*
quedársele a alguien	*to leave something behind*
rompérsele a alguien	*to break*

—Veo que **se te rompieron** los anteojos.	*I see that you broke your glasses.*
—Sí, **se me cayeron** en la calle.	*Yes, I dropped them in the street.*
—¿Cómo **se les ocurrió** venir ayer?	*How did they get the idea to come yesterday?*
—**Se les había olvidado** que la reunión era mañana.	*They had forgotten that the meeting was tomorrow.*

—**Se nos está acabando** la gasolina. Tenemos que comprar. — *We're running out of gas. We have to buy some.*

—Pero **se me perdió** la tarjeta de crédito. — *But I lost my credit card.*

X. Sucesos inesperados. Llene los espacios en blanco con los elementos de la oración que faltan. Todas las oraciones expresan la idea de un suceso inesperado, es decir, complemento directo + construcción con **se.** Use el pretérito de los verbos entre paréntesis.

1. No pudimos hacer los sándwiches. (acabársele)

   ______________________________ el pan.
2. Plácido no pudo entrar en su casa. (perdérsele)

   ______________________________ las llaves.
3. No le mandé una tarjeta a Beatriz. (olvidársele)

   ______________________________ la fecha de su cumpleaños.
4. ¡Pero estáis mojadísimos! (quedársele)

   ¿______________________________ el paraguas en casa?
5. ¡Cuidado de no cortarte la mano! (rompérsele)

   ¿Cómo ______________________________ los vasos?
6. ¡Pasando por Madrid, Uds. no visitaron a los tíos! (ocurrírsele)

   ¿Ni ______________________________ llamarlos?
7. Los niños están recogiendo todos los papeles en el suelo. (caérsele)

   ¿Cómo ______________________________?

Y. Prevenir (*to warn*) **contra lo inesperado.** Escriba oraciones previniéndoles a unas personas contra ciertas cosas. Fíjese que el imperativo de los verbos como **acabársele** es un mandato indirecto.

Modelo tú/no caérsele/los platos → Que no se te caigan los platos.

1. Uds./no olvidársele/asistir a la conferencia

   ____
2. él/no perdérsele/los anteojos

   ____
3. Ud./no acabársele/la paciencia

   ____
4. vosotros/no quedársele/los cheques de viajero

   ____
5. ella/no rompérsele/las estatuillas de porcelana (*china figurines*)

   ____

6. tú/no ocurrírsele/tales cosas

____

7. ellos/no caérsele/la torta de chocolate

____

Z. Exprese los siguientes diálogos en español usando la construcción del suceso inesperado.

1. —Did you (*Ud.*) lose your wallet?
—No, I had left it at home.

____

____

2. —They're running out of pastries at the bake shop.
—Didn't it occur to you (*tú*) to buy them this morning?

____

____

3. —Be careful! You're (*Uds.*) going to drop the cups!
—We already broke two!

____

____

4. —I forgot to pick Tere and Leo up.
—Didn't it dawn on you (*tú*) that they were waiting all night?

____

____

H *Double object pronouns*

- In Spanish a direct object pronoun and an indirect object pronoun can appear together with a verb. The indirect object pronoun precedes the direct object pronoun:

—Necesito mil pesos. ¿**Me los** prestas?	*I need a thousand pesos. Will you lend them to me?*
—**Te los** presto con tal de que **me los** devuelvas la semana que viene.	*I'll lend them to you as long as you return them to me next week.*
—Nos interesa tu colección de sellos. ¿**Nos la** enseñas?	*We're interested in your stamp collection. Will you show it to us?*
—Claro. Ahora **se la** traigo.	*Of course. I'll bring it to you right now.*

- When a third-person indirect object pronoun (**le** or **les**) precedes a third-person direct object pronoun (**lo, la, los, las**), the indirect object pronoun changes to **se**.

le/les + lo ➔ se lo
le/les + la ➔ se la
le/les + los ➔ se los
le/les + las ➔ se las

- Double object pronouns cannot be separated from each other. Double object pronouns follow the same rules of position as single object pronouns. When double object pronouns are added to an infinitive, present participle, or affirmative command, an accent mark is always added, even to infinitives and command forms of one syllable: **Quiero dártelo, Dámelo**:

—¿Cuándo le va a entregar Ud. el informe al jefe? — *When are you going to submit the report to the boss?*
—Ya **se lo** he entregado. — *I've already submitted it to him.*

—Hay un problema que no comprendo. — *There's a problem that I don't understand.*
—Mu**é**stra**melo**. A ver si **te lo** puedo explicar. *or* A ver si puedo **explicártelo.** — *Show it to me. Let's see if I can explain it to you.*

—¿Dónde están nuestras maletas? — *Where are our suitcases?*
—El botones **nos las** está subiendo ahora. *or* El botones está subi**é**ndo**noslas** ahora. — *The bellhop is bringing them up for us now.*

- Sentences with **se** out of context can be ambiguous. Context or a phrase consisting of **a** + prepositional pronoun clarifies who **se** refers to:

—¿La niñita se puso los zapatos? — *Did the little girl put on her shoes?*
—Sí, **se los** puso. (**se** = reflexive pronoun referring to **la niña**) — *Yes, she put them on.*

—¿La niñita se puso los zapatos? — *Did the little girl put on her shoes?*
—No, **yo se los puse**. (**se** = indirect object pronoun referring to **la niña**) — *No, I put them on (for her).*

—¿El gerente y la directora tienen copias del informe? — *Do the manager and the director have copies of the report?*
—Sí, a él **se lo** mandé por correo y a ella **se lo** di personalmente. — *Yes, I sent it to him by mail and I gave it to her personally.*

AA. Dos pronombres complementos directo e indirecto. Escriba oraciones cambiando el sustantivo complemento directo a un pronombre y haga todos los cambios necesarios.

MODELO Les entregaré las cartas el martes.
➔ Se las entregaré el martes.

1. Me dijeron los motivos.

____

2. Le hemos puesto los zapatos.

____

3. Está explicándoles la idea.

____

4. Os muestro el paquete.

5. ¿Te darían una beca?

6. Les cuentas los chismes.

7. Nos ha hecho las chuletas de cordero.

8. Devuélvame el cortacésped (*lawnmower*).

9. Me estaban enseñando las fotos.

10. ¿A quién le vendiste tu velero?

11. Os había escrito una tarjeta postal.

12. ¿Nos prestarás unos disquetes?

13. Apréndanle las fechas de memoria.

14. ¿Estáis preguntándole el por qué?

15. Le pusieron una multa.

16. Les preparó arroz y maíz.

17. Estará bajándome el equipaje.

18. Vendámosles la casa.

19. Estuvimos trayéndole los periódicos ingleses.

20. Te apagaré la televisión.

BB. Algo pasará./Algo pasó. Añada la construcción **ir a** + infinitivo o **acabar de** + infinitivo a las siguientes oraciones. Haga los cambios necesarios respeto a los verbos y a los pronombres complementos directo e indirecto. Escriba cada oración de dos maneras.

MODELO	Se los doy.	**(ir a)**	**(acabar de)**
		Voy a dárselos.	Acabo de dárselos.
		Se los voy a dar.	Se los acabo de dar.

1. Me la traen. (ir a)
   ____
   ____
2. Te lo dice. (acabar de)
   ____
   ____
3. Se los hacemos. (ir a)
   ____
   ____
4. Os las pongo. (acabar de)
   ____
   ____
5. Se lo muestra. (ir a)
   ____
   ____
6. Nos la compráis. (acabar de)
   ____
   ____
7. Me los cuentas. (ir a)
   ____
   ____
8. Se las arreglo. (acabar de)
   ____
   ____
9. Te la suben. (ir a)
   ____
   ____
10. Os lo damos. (acabar de)
   ____
   ____

11. Se lo describimos. (ir a)

12. Se la pruebas. (acabar de)

13. Te los limpia. (ir a)

14. Se las encuentro. (acabar de)

15. Me la piden. (ir a)

16. Nos lo buscas. (acabar de)

17. Os los llevamos. (ir a)

18. Se las sirve. (acabar de)

19. Se lo devolvéis. (ir a)

20. Te la canto. (acabar de)

CC. **¡Mami, papi, cómprenmelo!** ¡Esta niña Rita vuelve locos a toda su familia! No deja de pedir cosas y por desgracia, sus familiares se lo conceden todo. Por eso es una niña mal criada (*spoiled brat*). Escriba diálogos entre Rita y sus familiares en los cuales Ud. emplea los pronombres complementos directo e indirecto con mandatos y verbos en tiempo presente.

Modelo Mami / comprarme / una bicicleta
→ Rita: Mami, cómpramela.
Mamá: Sí, hijita, te la compro.

1. Papi / darme / bombones

   Rita: Papi, ______

   Papá: Sí, hijita, ______

2. Rita: Mami / comprarme / canicas (*marbles*)

   Rita: Mami, ______

   Mamá: Sí, hijita, ______

3. Rita: Juan / prestarme / tu patineta (*scooter*)

   Rita: Juan, ______

   Juan: Sí, hermanita, ______

4. Rita: Amparo / comprarme / soldaditos de plomo (*tin soldiers*)

   Rita: Amparo, ______

   Amparo: Sí, hermanita, ______

5. Rita: Abuelo / regalarme / un billete de cien dólares

   Rita: Abuelo, ______

   Abuelo: Sí, hijita, ______

6. Rita: Elvira / servirme / todo el helado de chocolate

   Rita: Elvira, ______

   Elvira: Sí, hermanita, ______

7. Rita: Tía / ponerme / tus joyas de oro

   Rita: Tía, ______

   Tía: Sí, hijita, ______

DD. **¿Las cosas claras?** Exprese las siguientes oraciones en inglés aclarando a quién(es) se refiere el ambiguo **se.** Unas oraciones pueden tener más de una sola traducción.

1. a. Se la dio Fernando.

   ______

   b. Se la dio a Fernando.

   ______

2. a. Se lo dijeron los profesores.

   ______

   b. Se lo dijeron a los profesores.

   ______

3. a. Se las prestó el vecino.

   ______

   b. Se las prestó al vecino.

   ______

4. a. Se los pidieron mis colegas.

____

b. Se los pidieron a mis colegas.

____

5. a. Se la devolvió Laura.

____

b. Se la devolvió a Laura.

____

I *Special uses of the object pronouns*

- The object pronoun **lo** is used to replace a clause or an adjective or a predicate noun of both genders and numbers. This **lo** has no equivalent in English:

—Los Ochoa se mudaron a Ecuador.	*The Ochoas moved to Ecuador.*
—Sí, **lo sé**. (**lo** = que se mudaron a Ecuador)	*Yes, I know.*
—¿María Elena es simpática?	*Is María Elena nice?*
—Sí, **lo es**. (**lo** = simpática)	*Yes, she is.*
—¿Son profesoras Marta y Sara?	*Are Marta and Sara teachers?*
—**Lo** fueron. Ahora son abogadas. (**lo** = profesoras)	*They were. Now they're lawyers.*

- The object pronouns **la** and **las** appear in many idioms without any antecedent. They must be memorized as part of the idiom:

apañárselas	*to manage, get by*
arreglárselas	*to manage, get by*
componérselas	*to manage, get by*
echárselas de + adjective, noun	*to boast of being*
habérselas con	*to be up against, face, have to deal with*
tenérsela jurada a alguien	*to have it in for someone*
vérselas con	*to explain oneself to*

—Creo que el profesor Méndez **me la tiene jurada**.	*I think Professor Méndez has it in for me.*
—No te preocupes. **Te las arreglarás** bien en su clase.	*Don't worry. You'll manage fine in his class.*
—Oscar siempre **se las echa de rico**.	*Oscar always boasts of being rich.*
—Y no tiene dónde caerse muerto. No sé cómo **se las apaña**.	*And he doesn't have a penny. I don't know how he manages.*
—Este profesor tiene que **habérselas con una clase mediocre**.	*This teacher has to face a class of mediocre students.*
—Y si no hacen progresos, tiene que **vérselas con el director**.	*And if they don't do well, he has to explain why to the principal.*

EE. **¡En español, por favor!** Exprese estas oraciones en español.

1. —Do you (*tú*) know if the stores are open?
   —I couldn't (*sabría*) tell you.

2. I don't know how Raúl manages. He thinks that everyone has it in for him.

3. Any student who behaves badly will have to explain himself to me.

4. —Are Ramón and Sergio students?
   —No, they're not. They're programmers.
   —I think they're very intelligent.
   —Yes, they are.

5. Pedrito couldn't put on his coat so I helped him on with it.

6. —Should I ask Alicia and Pablo for their history notes?
   —Ask him for them. Don't ask her for them. (*tú*)

FF. **Ejercicio oral.** Hable de este año escolar con unos compañeros. Háganse preguntas sobre libros, exámenes, tareas, amigos, actividades, etcétera. Usen pronombres de complemento directo e indirecto en las respuestas.

GG. Estructuras en acción. Lea el siguiente anuncio sobre una inmobiliaria (*real estate company*) y haga los ejercicios.

I. Conteste las siguientes preguntas.

1. ¿Qué es lo que se vende en este anuncio?

____

2. ¿Cuál es el regalo que se le da al comprador?

____

3. ¿Cuál es el regalo que se le da al cliente por conocer el chalet piloto?

____

4. ¿Qué es Satafi?

____

II. Exprese las siguientes frases del artículo en inglés.

1. Sólo tendrá que ocuparse de cómo decorarla.

____

2. Huarte le hace un regalo de lujo.

____

3. o si Vd. lo prefiere

____

4. Visítenos o llámenos.

____

5. Le obsequiaremos con dos fantásticas noches en el Hotel Alcora de Sevilla.

____

CON UNA CASA ASÍ SÓLO TENDRÁ QUE OCUPARSE DE CÓMO DECORARLA

Y DE DÓNDE INSTALAR LA SAUNA.

Porque ahora, al comprar su casa en SATAFI, HUARTE le hace un regalo de lujo*. Una maravillosa sauna, totalmente equipada e instalada, para relajarse 365 días al año, o si Vd. lo prefiere, un descuento por importe equivalente.

*Promoción válida hasta el 30 de septiembre 1995.

Visítenos o llámenos, concertaremos hora de visita. **Y además le obsequiaremos con dos fantásticas noches en el Hotel Alcora de Sevilla,** sólo por conocer nuestro chalet piloto, decorado con estilo propio.

MADRID
SATAFI
GETAFE

10 a 14'30 h. y de 17 a 20'30 h. Tel. 682 49 30

CHAPTER 20

RELATIVE PRONOUNS

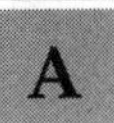 The relative pronoun *que*

- Relative pronouns are used to join two sentences into a single sentence. The clause introduced by the relative pronoun is the relative clause.
- The relative pronoun **que** can refer to animate or inanimate antecedents (persons or things) and can be either the subject or direct object of the verb of the relative clause it introduces. **Que** can refer to both singular and plural nouns and is the most common relative pronoun in everyday conversation:

el hombre **que** trabaja aquí (***que*** *refers to* ***hombre*** *and is the subject of its clause*)	*the man who works here*
los paquetes **que** están en la mesa (***que*** *refers to* ***paquetes*** *and is the subject of its clause*)	*the packages that are on the table*
los abogados **que** conozco (***que*** *refers to* ***abogados*** *and is the direct object of its clause*)	*the lawyers whom I know*
la casa **que** compré (***que*** *refers to* ***casa*** *and is the direct object of its clause*)	*the house that I bought*

- In English the relative pronoun can be omitted when it is the object of the verb: *the lawyers I know, the house I bought*. In Spanish, **que** is never omitted.
- **Nadie** and **alguien**, when antecedents, have **que** as the subject or direct object of a relative clause. **Todo** takes **lo que**:

—Si hay **alguien que** comprende, es él.	*If there's someone who understands, it is he.*
—No, él no comprende tampoco. No hay **nadie que** comprenda.	*No, he doesn't understand either. There's no one who understands.*
Esto es **todo lo que** tengo.	*This is all (everything) I have.*

A. Seamos precisos. Conteste las preguntas de su amigo con una cláusula relativa para que él sepa de qué objeto o persona se trata.

Modelo ¿Qué libro quieres? (El libro está en la estantería.)
→ Quiero el libro que está en la estantería.

¿Qué suéter lleva Paula? (Su novio le compró el suéter en Ecuador.)
→ Lleva el suéter que su novio le compró en Ecuador.

1. ¿A qué médico ves? (Tiene su consulta en aquel edificio.)

2. ¿Qué película quieres ver? (La película se rodó en Perú.)

3. ¿Qué revistas te gustan más? (Las revistas se publican en Asunción.)

4. ¿Qué restaurante prefieres? (El restaurante sirve comida del Caribe.)

5. ¿A qué peluquería vas? (La peluquería está en la calle del Conde.)

6. ¿Qué libros quieres comprar? (El profesor nos recomendó los libros.)

7. ¿Qué abrigo llevas? (Mis padres me regalaron el abrigo para Navidad.)

8. ¿Con qué secretaria hablaban Uds.? (Contratamos a esa secretaria la semana pasada.)

9. ¿Qué mecánico repara tu coche? (El vecino conoce al mecánico.)

10. ¿Qué carta estás leyendo? (Silvia me mandó esta carta ayer.)

Nota cultural

- **Asunción**, capital del Paraguay, fue fundada en 1537 por Juan de Salazar y Gonzalo de Mendoza. Fue una importante base de penetración de la Conquista española por la cuenca (*basin*) del río de la Plata. Es una ciudad colonial que tiene monumentos interesantes y jardines lindos. Muchas avenidas están bordeadas (*lined*) de árboles del caucho (*rubber*), naranjos y lapachos (árbol americano).

- Casi todos los paraguayos hablan no sólo el español sino también **el guaraní**, la lengua de los indígenas. El guaraní es el segundo idioma oficial después del español. Se enseña en los colegios particulares, se publican periódicos y revistas en guaraní y hay un teatro guaraní.

B. Más precisiones. La persona que habla usa cláusulas relativas para indicar exactamente a qué objeto o persona se refiere. Escriba sus precisiones según el modelo.

MODELO ¿Qué computadora?
(Olivia la usa.) → La computadora que usa Olivia.
(Tiene mucha memoria.) → La computadora que tiene mucha memoria.

1. ¿Qué profesora?

(Todos los estudiantes la admiran.)

___

(Enseña francés y español.)

___

(Acaba de casarse.)

___

(Mis padres la conocen.)

___

2. ¿Qué casa?

(Juana y Rafael la compraron.)

___

(Tiene patio y piscina.)

___

(La construyeron en 1975.)

___

(Es de ladrillos.)

___

3. ¿Qué regalo?

(Mis hermanos y yo lo recibimos hace dos días.)

___

(Mis tíos nos lo mandaron.)

___

(Te lo enseñé ayer.)

___

(Nos gustó tanto.)

___

4. ¿Qué restaurante?

(Nuestros amigos lo abrieron el año pasado.)

___

(Sirve comida española.)

___

(Tiene manteles rojos.)

___

(Muchos artistas lo frecuentan.)

___

5. ¿Qué senador?

   (El pueblo lo eligió el año pasado.)

   ____

   (Prometió combatir la inflación.)

   ____

   (Está casado con una extranjera.)

   ____

   (Los obreros lo apoyan.)

   ____

B *The relative pronoun* ***quien***

- When **que** is the direct object of the verb in its clause and it has an antecedent that is a person, it can be replaced by **a quien** or, if the antecedent is plural, **a quienes**:

El empleado **a quien** conocíamos ya no trabaja aquí.	*The employee (whom) we knew doesn't work here any longer.*
Busqué a los estudiantes **a quienes** vi ayer, pero no los encontré.	*I looked for the students (whom) I saw yesterday, but I couldn't find them.*

- **Quien** and **quienes** can also serve as the subject of a relative clause if that clause is set off by commas (nonrestrictive clause):

José Pedro fue a hablar con la profesora Umbral, **quien** siempre tiene tiempo para sus estudiantes.	*José Pedro went to speak with Professor Umbral, who always has time for her students.*

C. El profesor, quien ... Quien y **quienes** sirven también de sujeto de una cláusula relativa si esa cláusula está apartada con unas comas. Combine las siguientes oraciones con **quien / quienes** para describir a algunas personas que están en la universidad.

La universidad

aprobar *to pass*
los archivos *files*
el ayudante *assistant*
el congreso *conference*
el decano *dean*
dictar una conferencia *to deliver a lecture*
jubilarse *to retire*
el salón de actos *assembly hall, auditorium*
el secretario general *registrar*
el tribunal de exámenes *board of examiners*

MODELO Cajal, Toledano y Puche aprobaron sus exámenes./ Ellos son compañeros de cuarto en una residencia universitaria.
→ Cajal, Toledano y Puche, quienes son compañeros de cuarto en una residencia universitaria, aprobaron sus exámenes.

1. El señor Mora es secretario general de la universidad./Él se encarga de los archivos.

___

2. El profesor Uriarte enseña química./Él asistió a un congreso en la UNAM.

___

3. Los estudiantes tienen que entregar una tesis./Ellos se gradúan en junio.

___

4. La doctora Arrieta tiene dos ayudantes de laboratorio./Ella figura en el tribunal de exámenes.

___

5. Estos decanos trabajan en la facultad de ingeniería./Ellos planean el programa.

___

6. El rector de la universidad es abogado./Él dicta conferencias de ciencias políticas.

___

7. Algunos estudiantes de medicina fueron a hablar con el profesor Quijano./Él estaba ya en el salón de actos.

___

8. La profesora Arenas se jubila el año que viene./Ella hace investigaciones de biología.

___

Nota cultural

- La **UNAM** es la Universidad Nacional Autónoma de México. La universidad mexicana fue fundada en 1551. La primera universidad fundada en América fue la de Santo Domingo (1538). Las universidades hispanoamericanas fundadas después fueron las de San Marcos de Lima (1551), Córdoba (1621), Javierana de Bogotá (1622), Caracas (1721), La Habana (1728), Buenos Aires (1821).

- La **Ciudad Universitaria mexicana,** que queda a 18 kilómetros al sur de la ciudad de México, tiene una fama mundial por su arquitectura, obra del arquitecto mexicano Juan O'Gorman (1905–82). Se destaca la torre de la biblioteca cubierta por fuera de mosaicos que narran la historia del conocimiento científico desde la astronomía azteca hasta la teoría molecular. La Rectoría (edificio administrativo del presidente de la universidad) es notable por su mural de David Siqueiros y el estadio Olímpico por su pintura-escultura de Diego Rivera.

D. **... a quien/... a quienes. A quien** y **a quienes** se usan como complemento directo de un verbo cuando el antecedente es una persona. Combine las siguientes oraciones en una con **a quien** o **a quienes** para describir a ciertas personas.

MODELO Las chicas vinieron a vernos./Las conocimos en el teatro.
→ Las chicas a quienes conocimos en el teatro vinieron a vernos.

1. Mis primos están de vacaciones en Estados Unidos./Los vi en Caracas hace dos años.

___

2. La pintora sólo pinta acuarelas./La vieron en la exposición.

___

3. La muchacha me dio las gracias hoy./Yo le di un regalo ayer.

___

4. Los amigos no quisieron salir./Los llamamos a la una de la mañana.

___

5. Los vecinos se habían mudado./Los buscábamos.

___

6. La dependiente ya no trabaja en esta tienda./Ud. la conoció el año pasado.

___

7. El señor es mi profesor de cálculo./Lo encontraste en la calle.

___

Nota cultural

- **Caracas**, capital de Venezuela, queda a 25 kilómetros de La Guaira, que le sirve de puerto en el Caribe. Esta ciudad modernísima fue fundada en 1567 por Diego de Losada. La ciudad ha crecido enormemente en los últimos 50 años extendiéndose de su centro en la Plaza de Bolívar a los alrededores por hermosas avenidas. Hubo un boom económico causado por la nacionalización de la industria petrolera en 1976. La nacionalización fue llevada a cabo con compensación para los Estados Unidos y los otros países. Las grandes reservas de petróleo se encuentran en la región del lago Maracaibo en la parte occidental de Venezuela cerca de su frontera con Colombia. Venezuela sufrió una crisis económica durante los años ochenta porque el precio del petróleo bajó en el mercado internacional y Venezuela no había desarrollado una industria y tecnología nacionales. Por eso el gobierno ha tratado de reducir la dependencia del país en el petróleo. Venezuela ayudó a formar la OPEP (Organización de Países Exportadores de Petróleo) y es el tercer país en producción de petróleo de la OPEP. Desde 1959, Venezuela ha tenido gobiernos elegidos democráticamente.

- **Simón Bolívar,** *el Libertador*, nació en Caracas (1783–1830). Formado en las ideas de los escritores de la Ilustración europea (el Siglo de las Luces [*The Enlightenment*]), Bolívar fue el gran líder del movimiento independentista de los países sudamericanos.

- Caracas, como casi todas las ciudades hispánicas, ha nombrado sus grandes avenidas y calles por sus héroes nacionales. Por ejemplo, uno se pasea en **la avenida Bolívar** o en **la avenida Andrés Bello**. Bello fue un gran escritor, filólogo, poeta y político que nació en Caracas en 1781. Bello fundó y fue rector de la universidad de Chile y murió en Santiago en 1865. Naturalmente hay una avenida Andrés Bello en Santiago. En ciertas ciudades hispánicas también se conmemoran las fechas más importantes de la historia del país. La ciudad de México no sólo tiene muchas avenidas como la de Benito Juárez, nombrada por el gran político (1806–72), sino también muchas calles con fechas como la del 16 de septiembre, fecha en la que el cura Hidalgo pronunció el "Grito de Dolores" en 1810 comenzando así la guerra de la Independencia mexicana.

E. ¿Sujeto u objeto? Complete las siguientes oraciones escogiendo **quien(es)** si se refiere al sujeto de una cláusula relativa o **a quien(es)** si se refiere al complemento directo del verbo. Subraye su respuesta.

1. Te presento al señor quien/a quien conocimos ayer.
2. Llamemos a aquella señorita, quien/a quien siempre está dispuesta a ayudarnos.
3. Voy a la casa de los señores, a quienes/quienes compraron la casa de enfrente.
4. ¿Conoces a los chicos a quienes/quienes invité a la fiesta?
5. Esos arquitectos, a quienes/quienes trabajan en el rascacielos nuevo, son mis cuñados.
6. ¿Comprende Ud. a la locutora quien/a quien yo no comprendo bien?
7. Jorge llama a su novia a quien/quien quiere muchísimo.
8. La novia de Jorge está enamorada de Alfredo, quien/a quien es el mejor amigo de Jorge.

C *The relative pronouns* ***el que, el cual***

- The relative pronouns **el que** and **el cual** have four forms each: **el que, la que, los que, las que; el cual, la cual, los cuales, las cuales**. They can replace **que** or **a quien/a quienes** when the antecedent is animate and the relative pronoun is the object of the verb:

los españoles **a los que** he conocido	*the Spaniards (whom) I met*
el electricista **al que** he llamado	*the electrician (whom) I called*
la vecina **a la que** no soportamos	*the neighbor (whom) we can't stand*

- In nonrestrictive clauses (those set off by commas), **el que** and **el cual** can function as both subject and object and can refer to either people or things. Since **el que** and **el cual** show gender and number distinctions, they are used to avoid confusion when there is more than one possible antecedent for **que** or **quien**:

El amigo de mi prima, **el cual/el que** estudia física, llega mañana de Caracas.	*My (female) cousin's (male) friend, who (refers to the male friend) studies physics, is arriving from Caracas tomorrow.*
El amigo de mi prima, **la cual/la que** estudia física, llega mañana de Caracas.	*My (female) cousin's (male) friend, who (refers to the female cousin) studies physics, is arriving from Caracas tomorrow.*

- The neuter relative pronouns **lo que** and **lo cual** refer to a preceding clause or idea. They only occur in clauses set off by commas (nonrestrictive clauses):

Su hija le dijo que no quería seguir estudiando, **lo que/lo cual** no le gustó para nada al señor Lara.	*His daughter told him that she didn't want to continue with her studies, which Mr. Lara didn't like at all.*

F. **¿El que o lo que?** Escoja el pronombre **el que (la que, los que, las que)** o **lo que** para completar las siguientes oraciones.

1. Me cayeron muy bien los turistas a ____________________ conocimos en la excursión.
2. Los Merino nos invitaron a pasar el fin de semana en su barco, ____________________ nos agradó mucho.
3. La hermana de Federico, ____________________ vive en Bogotá, estudiará administración de empresas en Estados Unidos.
4. Nadie vio llegar a Isabel, ____________________ nos sorprendió.
5. ¡Por fin fuimos en la montaña rusa, ____________________ nos dejó medio muertos!
6. El amigo de mi primo, ____________________ trabaja en Barcelona, se casará en mayo.
7. Esas chicas tan antipáticas con ____________________ saliste son mis primas.

G. **¿El cual o lo cual?** Ahora reemplace los pronombres relativos del ejercicio anterior con **el cual (la cual, los cuales, las cuales)** o **lo cual.**

1. Me cayeron muy bien los turistas a ______________________ conocimos en la excursión.
2. Los Merino nos invitaron a pasar el fin de semana en su barco, ______________________ nos agradó mucho.
3. La hermana de Federico, ______________________ vive en Bogotá, estudiará administración de empresas en Estados Unidos.
4. Nadie vio llegar a Isabel, ______________________ nos sorprendió.
5. ¡Por fin fuimos en la montaña rusa, ______________________ nos dejó medio muertos!
6. El amigo de mi primo, ______________________ trabaja en Barcelona, se casará en mayo.
7. Esas chicas tan antipáticas con ______________________ saliste son mis primas.

D *Relative pronouns after prepositions*

- **Que** may be used after the prepositions **a, de,** and **con** when the antecedent is not a person:

Éste es el tema **a que** nos limitamos.	*This is the subject to which we will limit ourselves.*
¿Comprendes los problemas **de que** te hablé?	*Do you understand the problems that I spoke to you about?*
Mi abuelo me mostró el bastón **con que** camina.	*My grandfather showed me the cane he walks with.*

- **En que** is common after expressions of time and to express imprecise location:

el mes **en que** se fueron	*the month they went away*
un siglo **en que** la vida era muy difícil	*a century in which life was very difficult*
el edificio **en que** trabajamos	*the building we work in*
la materia **en que** se interesa	*the subject she's interested in*

- When **en** expresses physical location inside an object, **en el que/en la que/en los que/en las que** are used:

Abrió la gaveta **en la que** había metido las llaves.	*He opened the drawer in which he had put the keys.*

  Donde can replace these relatives with **en**: see *section E* of this chapter.

- **Quien/quienes** or **el que** are used after prepositions for human antecedents. Some speakers also use **el cual**:

el tío **a quien/al que** Pablito se parece	*the uncle (whom) Pablito looks like*
la chica **con quien/con la que** se casó mi hermano	*the girl (whom) my brother married*
los amigos **de quienes/de los que** me fío	*the friends (whom) I trust*

- After prepositions other than **a, de, con,** and **en**, the relative pronoun **que** is not used. **Quien/quienes** may be used for people, **el que** and **el cual** for both people and things. **El cual** is especially common after prepositions of more than one syllable (**para, según, hacia, desde, contra, mediante, durante, sobre**) and with compound prepositions (**a causa de, delante de, detrás de, encima de, debajo de, por medio de, en frente de, al frente de, antes de, después de,** etc.):

una guerra **durante la cual** cayeron muchos soldados	*a war during which many soldiers fell*
el edificio **delante del cual** la vi	*the building in front of which I saw her*
los problemas **a causa de los que** dejé de estudiar	*the problems because of which I stopped studying*
los señores **para quienes** (**para los que/para los cuales**) trabajo	*the men for whom I work*
las ancianas al lado **de quienes** (**al lado de las que/al lado de las cuales**) vivimos	*the old ladies next door to whom we live*

H. Te enseño mi ciudad. Ud. le enseña su ciudad a un amigo extranjero. Exprese la información dada con una cláusula relativa como en el modelo.

MODELO Hay un festival de teatro durante el verano.
El verano es la estación ...
➔ El verano es la estación durante la cual hay un festival de teatro.

1. Hay varias líneas de metro debajo de estas calles.
   Éstas son las calles ____________________
2. Vivimos cerca de la facultad.
   Allí ven la facultad ____________________
3. Hay un restaurante en frente de ese cine.
   Allí está el cine ____________________
4. Solemos pasar los domingos aquí.
   Ven y te presento a los muchachos ____________________
5. Hay una exposición de arte en medio de la plaza.
   Ésta es la plaza ____________________
6. Hay un mercado al aire libre detrás de aquellos edificios.
   Aquéllos son los edificios ____________________
7. Ahora caminamos hacia un barrio muy antiguo.
   El barrio ____________________
8. Unas tiendas elegantes se encuentran al otro lado de este río.
   Éste es el río ____________________

I. ***En* de varios significados.** Escoja el pronombre relativo correcto en cada caso. Recuerde que hay una diferencia entre el **en** concreto que significa *dentro de* y el **en** que expresa una relación abstracta.

1. los libros ______________ me intereso (en que/en los que)
2. el armario ______________ cuelgo mi ropa (en que/en el que)
3. la exactitud ______________ insiste el profesor (en que/en la que)
4. el arreglo ______________ quedaron (en que/en el que)
5. el bolsillo ______________ tengo mis llaves (en que/en el que)
6. los cuadernos ______________ escribo (en que/en los que)
7. los métodos ______________ creemos (en que/en los que)
8. las bolsas ______________ llevaban la comida (en que/en las que)

J. Exprese las siguientes oraciones en inglés.

1. El concierto benéfico fue un evento mediante el cual la universidad recibió mucho dinero.

   ____

2. Se ha construido un nuevo rascacielos desde el cual hay fabulosas vistas de la ciudad.

   ____

3. Éstos son los libros según los cuales el profesor Sorolla sacó sus conclusiones.

   ____

4. Siempre me acuerdo de las ruinas griegas entre las cuales caminamos.

   ____

5. Se abrió una librería al lado de la cual se abrirá una heladería.

   ____

6. Vamos a reunirnos en la confitería en frente de la cual nos conocimos.

   ____

7. ¡Allí está la fuente delante de la cual nos enamoramos!

   ____

8. ¿Cómo se llama la empresa para la cual Antonio trabaja?

   ____

9. ¿Sabe Ud. cuáles son las ideas sobre las cuales los investigadores formularon sus teorías?

   ____

E The relative pronoun **cuyo; donde** as a relative pronoun

- **Cuyo** means *whose*. It agrees in gender and number with the following noun:

La doctora Paredes es la profesora **cuyas clases** cursé con mucho provecho.	*Dr. Paredes is the teacher whose classes I took and benefited greatly from.*
Ése es el autor **cuyos libros** leemos en la clase de literatura.	*That's the author whose books we read in literature class.*
Él es un hombre sobre **cuya vida** se comenta mucho.	*He's a man about whose life people comment a lot.*

- **Donde** is used after prepositions to refer to a place. It can also replace **en el que** when the relative pronoun refers to a concrete place. As a relative pronoun, **donde** does not take a written accent.

la avenida **donde** hay muchos cafés	*the avenue on which/where there are many cafés*
la puerta **por donde** salieron	*the door through which they went out*
la playa **hacia donde** caminábamos	*the beach toward which we were walking*

K. Cuyo. Complete las siguientes oraciones escribiendo la forma correcta del pronombre relativo **cuyo.**

1. Éste es el nuevo cantante ____________________ canciones han ganado muchos premios.
2. Éstos son los señores ____________________ hijos asisten a la universidad con los nuestros.
3. Tengo que buscar a la persona ____________________ coche está estacionado delante de mi garaje.
4. Quieren conocer al compositor ____________________ sinfonía será estrenada el sábado.
5. Habla con tu vecino ____________________ perro ladra (*barks*) toda la noche.
6. Se habla mucho de la profesora de arqueología ____________________ clases son tan interesantes.
7. Es un país ____________________ historia no se estudia lo suficiente.
8. Ésos son los técnicos ____________________ equipos han llegado al campeonato.

L. Exprese las siguientes oraciones en inglés.

1. Ahora sabes la razón por la cual me enfadé.

2. Vivíamos en un barrio donde había muchas tiendas.

3. Allí a la derecha está la puerta por donde entran y salen los actores.

4. Yo no entiendo los motivos por los cuales el sindicato declaró la huelga.

5. Los muchachos no me dijeron para donde iban.

6. Son las horas durante las cuales Menchu hace su tarea.

7. Aquí está el kiosko detrás del cual Sergio y Sol quedaron en verse.

PART THREE

Other Elements of the Sentence

CHAPTER 21

ADVERBS

The formation of adverbs

- Spanish adverbs are formed by adding **-mente** to the feminine form of the adjective. Spanish **-mente** corresponds to the English adverbial suffix *-ly*:

histórico *historic* → históricamente *historically*
intenso *intense* → intensamente *intensely*
lento *slow* → lentamente *slowly*
loco *crazy* → locamente *crazily*
profundo *deep* → profundamente *deeply*
serio *serious* → seriamente *seriously*

- Adjectives that do not have a distinct feminine form add **-mente** to the masculine/feminine singular:

amable *kind* → amablemente *kindly*
fácil *easy* → fácilmente *easily*
feliz *happy* → felizmente *happily*
inteligente *intelligent* → inteligentemente *intelligently*
triste *sad* → tristemente *sadly*

- Several adverbs either have irregular forms or are identical to the corresponding adjectives:

bueno *good* → bien *well*
malo *bad* → mal *badly*
mejor *better* → mejor *better*
peor *worse* → peor *worse*

- Many adverbs of quantity have no suffix but are identical to the masculine singular of the adjective:

mucho demasiado más
poco tanto menos

- Adverbs referring to loudness and softness have no ending:

hablar alto/bajo *to speak loudly, softly*
hablar fuerte *to speak loudly*

A. Para describir acciones. Escriba el adverbio que corresponde a los adjetivos siguientes.

MODELO maravilloso ➔ maravillosamente

1. alegre ____________________
2. descuidado ____________________
3. cruel ____________________
4. artístico ____________________
5. normal ____________________
6. abierto ____________________
7. franco ____________________
8. nervioso ____________________
9. evidente ____________________
10. responsable ____________________
11. débil ____________________
12. verdadero ____________________
13. torpe ____________________
14. violento ____________________
15. perspicaz (*perceptive*) ____________________
16. burlón (*mocking*) ____________________
17. comercial ____________________
18. sagaz (*wise*) ____________________
19. honrado ____________________
20. humilde ____________________
21. difícil ____________________
22. admirable ____________________
23. estupendo ____________________
24. afectuoso ____________________
25. vulgar ____________________

B. ¿Cómo hablaron? Escriba oraciones que describan cómo algunas personas hablaron en ciertas situaciones. Se practica formando adverbios.

MODELO Marisol hablaba. ¿Fue sincera?
➔ Sí, habló sinceramente.

1. Hernán pidió un préstamo en el banco. ¿Estaba nervioso?

____

2. Matías pidió disculpas (*apologized*). ¿Fue honesto?

____

3. Anita y Bárbara contaron sus problemas. ¿Estaban tristes?

____

4. Ud. se enojó con un compañero de clase. ¿Estuvo furiosa?

____

5. La señorita Cortés se quejó. ¿Estaba malhumorada (*peevish*)?

____

6. A Uds. se les rompieron nueve vasos. ¿Estuvieron incómodos (*embarrassed*)?

____

7. Hablaste por teléfono. ¿Estabas distraído?

____

8. Gladis chocó con un árbol montando en bicicleta. ¿Estuvo incoherente?

____

B *The use of adverbs of manner; adverbs as intensifiers*

- Adverbs of manner (adverbs that tell *how* something is done), such as the ones presented in the previous section, come right after the verbs they modify, or as close to the verb as possible:

—Hiciste **mal** el trabajo.	*You did the work poorly.*
—¿Qué dices? Lo hice **bien**. De todas formas, lo hice **mejor** que tú.	*What are you talking about? I did it well. Anyway, I did it better than you did.*
—Mentira. Yo trabajé **cuidadosamente**.	*Not true. I worked carefully.*
—A mí me parece que no hiciste nada **sistemáticamente**.	*I think you didn't do anything systematically.*

- Adverbs cannot come between an auxiliary verb and the main verb, as they often do in English:

El huracán ha destruido el pueblo **totalmente**.	*The hurricane has* ***totally*** *destroyed the town.*
El enfermo está mejorando **rápidamente**.	*The patient is* ***rapidly*** *improving.*

- Direct objects, including negative and indefinite words such as **algo, nada, nadie,** and neuter demonstratives, often come between the verb and the adverb:

Leyó **el artículo** atentamente.	*He read the article attentively.*
No explicó **nada** claramente.	*He didn't explain anything clearly.*
Dijo **eso** torpemente.	*He said that awkwardly.*

- When two or more adverbs ending in **-mente** modify the same verb, the suffix **-mente** is dropped from all but the last adverb:

Nos habló **franca** y **abiertamente**.	*He spoke to us frankly and openly.*
Hay que explicar las cosas **clara** e **inteligentemente**.	*One has to explain things clearly and intelligently.*

- Adverbs ending in **-mente** can be replaced by **con** + the corresponding noun:

alegremente ➔ con alegría	elegantemente ➔ con elegancia
claramente ➔ con claridad	inteligentemente ➔ con inteligencia
cuidadosamente ➔ con cuidado	torpemente ➔ con torpeza

- Intensifiers, or adverbs that modify adjectives and other adverbs, precede the adjective or adverb they modify:

muy bonito	*very pretty*
extremadamente inteligente	*extremely intelligent*
totalmente ridículo	*totally ridiculous*
completamente inútil	*completely useless*
elegantemente vestido	*elegantly dressed*
sumamente bien	*extremely well*
muy rápidamente	*very quickly*

C. Cada adverbio en su lugar. Ordene los elementos para formar oraciones colocando los adverbios en su lugar debido *(right)*.

MODELO problema/claramente/el/explicó
➔ Explicó claramente el problema.

1. las/mal/frases/pronunciaron

____

2. responsablemente/trabajaron/muy

____

3. bien/cosas/las/andaban

____

4. hijos/que/felizmente/mis/quiero/vivan

____

5. su/interesante/última/fue/película/muy

____

6. padres/inocentemente/a/niño/miraba/el/sus

____

7. esos/sumamente/Patricia/difíciles/encontró/problemas

____

8. salgan/la/rápidamente/de/muy/casa

____

9. totalmente/proyecto/encontramos/ridículo/el

____

D. **En otras palabras.** Vuelva a escribir estas oraciones, utilizando el verbo que corresponda al sustantivo y el adverbio que se forma del adjetivo.

MODELO Juan es un hablador apasionado.
➔ Juan habla apasionadamente.

1. Martín y Fernando son unos trabajadores inteligentes.

___

2. Lola es una cantante maravillosa.

___

3. Carmen y Pilar son escritoras hábiles.

___

4. El señor Ibáñez es un conductor prudente.

___

5. Lucas es un estudiante diligente.

___

6. Marcos es un pintor divino.

___

7. Carla y Pedro son viajeros frecuentes.

___

8. Alfonso es un jugador enérgico.

___

E. ***Con*** **+ sustantivo = adverbio +** ***-mente.*** Cambie el adverbio que termina en **-mente** a una frase que consiste en la preposición **con** + sustantivo.

1. inteligentemente ___
2. armónicamente ___
3. elegantemente ___
4. diligentemente ___
5. delicadamente ___
6. cariñosamente ___
7. alegremente ___
8. ligeramente ___
9. lealmente ___
10. suavemente ___
11. fuertemente ___
12. felizmente ___
13. tristemente ___
14. calurosamente ___
15. claramente ___

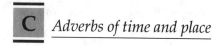

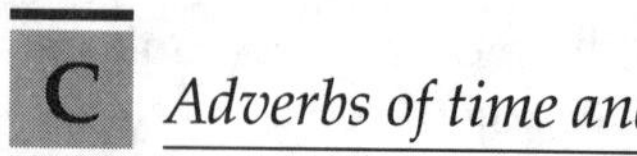

C Adverbs of time and place

- **Ya** means *already, now, right now.* **Ya no** means *no longer.*

—Tocan a la puerta.	*Someone's at the door.*
—**Ya** voy.	*I'll be right there.*
—¿**Ya** has visto la nueva película?	*Have you already seen the new film?*
—No, **ya** no voy al cine.	*No, I don't go to the movies anymore.*

- The adverb **recién** appears before past participles with the meaning *newly, just, recently.*

un niño **recién** nacido	*a newborn child*
los **recién** casados	*the recently married couple*
una casa **recién** construida	*a newly built house*

- Other common adverbs of time are **ahora** (*now*), **ahora mismo** (*right now*), **antes** (*before*), **mucho antes** (*a long time before*), **anteriormente** (*formerly*), **apenas** (*hardly, scarcely*), **posteriormente** (*subsequently*), **luego** (*then, afterwards*), **en seguida** (*right away*), **todavía** (*still*), **todavía no** (*not yet*), **siempre** (*always*), **aún** (*still, yet*), etc.

- The basic adverbs of place in Spanish are **aquí** (*here*), **ahí** (*there* [*near the person spoken to*]), and **allí** (*there* [*not near the speaker or the person spoken to*]). The adverbs **acá** and **allá** are used in the phrases **para acá** (*this way, in this direction*) and **para allá** (*that way, in that direction*). **Allá** means *way over there, somewhere over there.* In South America, **acá** often replaces **aquí** in speech:

—**Aquí** hay excelentes escuelas.	*There are excellent schools here.*
—**Allá** en mi país también.	*Back in my country also.*
—¿Qué veo **ahí** en tu mecedora?	*What do I see there on your rocking-chair?*
—Es mi gato.	*It's my cat.*

Other common adverbs of place:

arriba	*up, upstairs*
abajo	*down, downstairs*
en lo alto	*up, up there, up high*
(a)delante	*in front*
atrás	*in back*
cerca	*nearby*
lejos	*far off*
al fondo	*in back, at the bottom*
a la derecha/izquierda	*on the right/left*
al lado	*next door, next to it*
por algún sitio/lado	*somewhere*
por ningún sitio/lado	*nowhere, not anywhere*

- Adverbs of place combine with various prepositions and with each other:

por aquí	*around here*	hasta allí	*up to there*
por ahí	*around there*	hacia allá	*toward that place far away*
por allí	*around there*	allí arriba	*up there*
por allá	*around there (far away)*	aquí abajo	*down here*
desde aquí	*from here*	aquí cerca	*near here*

- Adverbs of place can also express time in certain phrases:

de aquel momento para acá	*from that time until now*
por allá por el año 1920	*around the year 1920*
de ayer acá	*from yesterday until now*
allá en mi juventud	*back then in my youth*

F. Exprese los siguientes diálogos en español. Tenga presente especialmente el uso de los adverbios.

1. —Did you (*Uds.*) go to the supermarket already?

   ____

   —Not yet.

   ____

2. —I'll be back right away.

   ____

   —Come here right now! (*tú*)

   ____

3. —Mariana can't find her cat anywhere.

   ____

   —Look (*Ud.*) up there! The cat's in the tree.

   ____

4. —Are the boys around here?

   ____

   —They're probably inside the house.

   ____

   —Do you (*tú*) know if they're upstairs or downstairs?

   ____

   —They're probably hiding behind some piece of furniture.

   ____

Nota cultural

En muchos países hispánicos, la planta baja se refiere al *ground floor* de un edificio. El primer piso de un edificio es generalmente lo que llamamos en inglés *the second floor.*

G. Un adverbio más otro. Escriba frases con dos adverbios para describir cómo se hicieron ciertas cosas. Cambie los adjetivos a la forma correcta del adverbio.

1. elegante y cuidadoso
____
2. lento y suave
____
3. cariñoso y caluroso
____
4. oportuno y apasionado
____
5. ligero y perezoso
____
6. fiel y leal
____
7. sabio y astuto
____
8. deprimido y triste
____

H. Ejercicio oral. Diálogos con adverbios. Un(a) estudiante le pregunta a otro(a) cómo se hicieron ciertas acciones. Por ejemplo: ¿Cómo hablaste con el profesor? Su compañero(a) le contesta usando un adverbio: *Hablé francamente.* Luego, los dos estudiantes cambian de papel para que los dos tengan la oportunidad de preguntar y contestar.

CHAPTER 22

PREPOSITIONS

A Basic prepositions: *a, de, en, con*

1. The preposition **a**:

☞ indicates motion toward a place:

ir a la ciudad *to go to the city*
llegar a la oficina *to arrive at the office*
regresar a casa *to return home*

☞ labels the animate, specific direct object (*personal **a***):

ver a Consuelo *to see Consuelo*
ayudar a los niños *to help the children*

☞ labels the indirect object, usually accompanied by the indirect object pronoun, especially in American Spanish:

Le di el paquete a Carla. *I gave Carla the package.*
Les compré helado a los chicos. *I bought the children ice cream.*

☞ connects verbs of motion to a following infinitive (*conveys the idea of purpose*):

salir a comer *to go out to eat*
venir a vernos *to come to see us*

☞ labels the rate or price:

¿A cuánto está el dólar hoy? *What's the exchange rate of the dollar today?*
a sesenta millas por hora *at sixty miles an hour*
Estos camiones se venden a veinte mil dólares. *These trucks sell at/for $20,000.00.*
dos veces al día, a la semana *twice a day, a week*

☞ labels the manner:

a pie *on foot*
a caballo *on horseback*
andar a gatas *to crawl on all fours*
a regañadientes *reluctantly*
a doble espacio *double-spaced*
escribir a lápiz *to write in pencil*
hecho a mano *made by hand*
a la española *Spanish-style*
a la americana, a lo americano *American-style*

☞ expresses location (instead of **en**) in certain fixed expressions of place and time:

estar sentados a la mesa *to be seated at the table*
tocar a la puerta *to knock at the door*
a la izquierda/derecha, a mano izquierda/derecha *on the left/right*
a la salida del pueblo *at the edge of town*
a la salida del trabajo *upon leaving work*
al final de la calle *at the end of the street*
Mi colegio está a dos kilómetros de aquí. *My school is two kilometers from here.*
a la vuelta de la esquina *around the corner*
a(l) mediodía/a medianoche *at noon/midnight*
a las dos de la tarde *at two in the afternoon*
a nuestra llegada *upon our arrival*
estar a dieta, a régimen *to be on a diet*

☞ is found in idiomatic expressions:

al mes de trabajar aquí *after working here for one month*
paso a paso *step by step*
uno a uno *one by one*
a veces *sometimes*
a escondidas *stealthily, behind someone's back*
a espaldas de uno *behind someone's back*
a mi juicio, a mi parecer *in my opinion*

A. **¿A o nada?** Complete cada oración añadiendo la preposición **a** donde sea necesaria.

1. Les envié unas tarjetas ____________ mis amigos.
2. ¿Conociste ____________ la Alhambra?
3. No pudimos ir ____________ verlos.
4. Leonardo habló con nosotros ____________ dos veces.
5. Llegué ____________ pueblo ____________ la una.
6. Ya han viajado ____________ cien millas.
7. ¿____________ cuánto está el peso hoy?
8. Ya son ____________ las ocho.
9. La parada queda ____________ seis cuadras de mi casa.

B. Exprese las siguientes oraciones en español.

1. I wrote the paper double-spaced.

____

2. Upon his arrival at midnight, he went to bed.

____

3. The baby crawls on all fours.

____

4. I love the clothing that's made by hand.

____

5. The children ate all the cookies behind our backs.

____

2. The preposition **de**:

☞ indicates motion from place:

El avión llega de Colombia. *The plane is arriving from Colombia.*
Vengo de la farmacia. *I'm coming from the drugstore.*
Salgo de casa a las ocho menos diez. *I leave home at ten to eight.*

☞ indicates origin and possession:

Son de Venezuela. *They're from Venezuela.*
el tren de Buenos Aires *the train from Buenos Aires*
la mochila de Pedrito *Pedrito's backpack*
la casa de mis tíos *my aunt and uncle's house*

☞ indicates the material of which something is made or the content of a container:

una casa de ladrillos *a brick house*
un reloj de oro *a gold watch*
una camisa de algodón *a cotton shirt*
una taza de café *a cup of coffee*
un vaso de agua *a glass of water*
una caja de juguetes *a box of toys*

☞ is often the equivalent of English *with* or *in* in descriptive expressions such as the following:

lleno de agua *filled with water (also: full of water)*
cubierto de nieve *covered with snow*
forrado de plumón *down lined, lined with down*
vestido de negro *dressed in black*
pintado de azul *painted (in) blue*

☞ forms noun phrases that are the equivalent of noun + noun or present participle + noun constructions in English:

una lección de música *a music lesson*
una exposición de arte *an art show*
la máquina de lavar *the washing machine*
la facultad de medicina *the medical school*
el cuarto de baño *the bathroom*
el libro de biología *the biology book*

☞ indicates a characteristic:

una persona de dinero *a wealthy person*
la mujer del sombrero rojo *the woman in the red hat*
una chica de talento *a talented girl*
un hombre de porte medio *a man of medium build*

☞ indicates a limitation or restriction on a verb or adjective:

Trabajo de programador. *I work as a programmer.*
ciego del ojo izquierdo *blind in one's left eye*
alto de estatura *tall*
ancho de espaldas *broad-shouldered*
un metro de largo, de ancho, de alto *a meter long, wide, high*

☞ indicates time in certain fixed expressions:

trabajar de día, de noche *to work days, nights*
Es de día, de noche. *It's daytime, nighttime.*
muy de mañana *very early in the morning*

☞ indicates the manner in which something is done:

ponerse de pie, de rodillas *to stand up, get on one's knees*
estar de luto *to be in mourning*
Se viste, se disfraza de policía. *He dresses as, disguises himself as a policeman.*
servir de intérprete *to serve as interpreter*
hacer algo de buena fe, de mala gana *to do something in good faith, unwillingly*
beber algo de un trago *to drink something in one gulp*

☞ connects nouns in humorous or mocking descriptions of people:

el loco de Pedro *crazy Pedro*
la muy tonta de Marta *silly Marta*
el pobre de mi cuñado *my poor brother-in-law*
aquel burro de recepcionista *that jerk of a receptionist*

☞ indicates the cause or reason:

saltar de alegría *to jump for joy*
gritar de dolor *to scream in pain, because of the pain*
morir de hambre *to starve to death*
estar loco de alegría *to be mad with joy*
no poder moverse de miedo *to be paralized with fear*

☞ indicates the topic (English *about*):

hablar de filosofía *to talk about philosophy*
saber poco de aquella familia *to know little about that family*

C. **¿De o nada?** Complete cada oración añadiendo la preposición **de** donde sea necesaria.

1. ¡Qué hermosa es tu blusa ______________ seda!
2. Esos turistas son ______________ chilenos.
3. Diana lleva un vestido ______________ azul.
4. Éstos son los documentos ______________ ingeniero.
5. La niñita saltó ______________ alegremente.
6. Salieron ______________ casa a las diez y cuarto.
7. Pedro tomará su lección ______________ piano el jueves.
8. Sírvame una taza ______________ té, por favor.

D. Exprese las siguientes oraciones en español.

1. They gave me (as a gift) a gold bracelet and silver earrings.

____

2. Bernardo is tall and broad-shouldered.

____

3. Do you (*tú*) want to work days or nights?

____

4. Her poor aunt is in mourning.

____

5. They got down on their knees.

____

3. The preposition **en**:

☞ indicates location (English *at, in, on*):

en el comedor *in the dining room*
en la mesa *on the table*
en el aeropuerto *at the airport*

☞ indicates extent of time:

Vuelvo en unos minutos. *I'll be back in a few minutes.*
Roma no se construyó en un día. *Rome wasn't built in a day.*

☞ is used in some expressions of manner:

en serio *seriously*
en broma *not seriously, as a joke*
estar en contra *to be against something, to be against it*

☞ labels the amount by which:

más alto que yo en una cabeza *a head taller than I*
Los precios han aumentado en un 20 por ciento. *Prices have gone up (by) 20%.*

☞ labels the price:

Te lo doy en diez dólares. *I'll give it to you for ten dollars.*

☞ labels the means by which:

Te reconocí en la voz, en el andar. *I recognized you by your voice, by your way of walking.*
ir en avión, en barco, en tren, en coche *to go by plane, by boat, by train, by car*

E. Exprese las siguientes oraciones en inglés.

1. La reconocí en la voz.

____

2. Me lo vendieron en dos mil dólares.

____

3. El valor ha subido en un quince por ciento.

___

4. Los obreros están en contra de la huelga.

___

F. Exprese las siguientes oraciones en español.

1. We plan to go by plane.

___

2. I'll pick you (*Uds.*) up at the airport.

___

3. Miguel is taller than Juan by a head.

___

4. Are you saying this seriously or as a joke?

___

4. The preposition **con**:

☞ expresses accompaniment:

salir con los amigos *to go out with friends*
llegar con un ramillete de flores *to arrive with a bouquet of flowers*
té con limón *tea with lemon*

☞ expresses attitude (sometimes **para con**):

Es muy amable conmigo. *He's very nice to me.*
generoso con uno *generous to someone*
insolente para con el maestro *fresh to the teacher*

☞ labels the means:

abrir la puerta con una llave *to open the door with a key*
atar el paquete con cuerda *to tie the package with string*

When preceding an infinitive, **con** labels the action as a means:

Con pulsar esta tecla, se guarda el archivo. *By pushing this key, you save the file.*

☞ labels the manner:

Nos recibió con una sonrisa. *He received us with a smile.*
Lo hice con mucho esfuerzo. *I did it with a great deal of effort.*

☞ expresses *in spite of* or *notwithstanding*:

Con todos sus problemas, se hizo abogado. *In spite of all his problems, he became a lawyer.*
Con tener tanto dinero de su tío, acabó sin un centavo. *In spite of all the money he had from his uncle, he wound up penniless.*

☞ can label the content of a container and is less ambiguous than **de**:

una cesta con ropa *a basket of clothing*
una bolsa con cebollas *a bag of onions*

G. **¿Con qué?** Complete las siguientes oraciones con una de las expresiones con **con.** Escoja entre *con caramelos / sonrisa / cuerda / llave / esfuerzo / leche.*

1. Tomó café ____________________.
2. Abrieron la puerta ____________________.
3. Se ató el paquete ____________________.
4. Nos saludó ____________________.
5. Búscame la bolsa ____________________.
6. Lo hacen todo ____________________.

H. **¿Qué falta?** Complete estas oraciones con la preposición que falta. Escoja entre **a, de, en** y **con**. No se olvide de escribir las contracciones **al** y **del** donde sean necesarias.

1. ¿Viste a la señora ________________ el vestido rojo?
2. ________________ todos sus defectos, José me parece una buena persona.
3. Vivo ________________ dos cuadras de la oficina.
4. ¿Hablas ________________ serio?
5. Tengo que terminar mi tesis ________________ una semana.
6. El señor Salas es muy generoso ________________ sus hijos.
7. Es una mujer ________________ estatura media.
8. El dólar está ________________ veintiocho pesos.
9. Las calles están cubiertas ________________ nieve.
10. Limpio el suelo ________________ un trapo.
11. ¿Me puedes dar agua ________________ hielo?
12. Hay un buen restaurante ________________ la estación de trenes.
13. Ahora me voy. Hablaremos ________________ mi regreso.
14. Vengan a sentarse ________________ la mesa.
15. La reconocí ________________ la voz.
16. El inocente ________________ mi hermano se compró un coche usado que no funciona.
17. Este jarro fue hecho ________________ máquina.
18. Hace frío. Ponte el gorro ________________ lana.
19. No comprendo ________________ ese profesor.
20. La sala es grande. Tiene cinco metros ________________ largo.
21. ________________ mes de trabajar en la empresa, Víctor renunció a su puesto.
22. ________________ principio, no nos gustaba la casa.

B Por and para

1. The preposition **para**:

☞ labels the destination, the time by which, or the figurative goal:

Tomaron el tren para Córdoba.	*They took the train for Cordoba. (destination)*
Los chicos salieron para el colegio.	*The kids left for school. (destination)*
Terminaré para el martes.	*I'll finish by Tuesday. (time by which)*
El regalo es para ti.	*The gift is for you. (figurative goal)*
Estudio para médico.	*I'm studying to be a doctor. (figurative goal)*
Es un honor para nosotros.	*It's an honor for us. (figurative goal)*
Leo para mejorar mi español.	*I read to improve my Spanish. (infinitive as figurative goal)*
Busqué otro empleo para ganar más plata.	*I looked for another job in order to earn more money. (infinitive as figurative goal)*

☞ labels the standard for comparison:

Para profesor tiene poca paciencia.	*For a teacher, he doesn't have much patience.*
Para médico sabe poco.	*For a doctor, he doesn't know much.*

☞ labels the information in the sentence as someone's opinion:

Para mí, la obra fue excelente.	*In my opinion, the play was excellent.*
Para ella, el precio es bueno.	*In her opinion, the price is good.*

☞ appears in some common expressions and idioms:

para entonces *by that time*
para otra vez *for another (later) occasion*
¿Para qué echar la soga tras el caldero? *Why throw good money after bad?*
para siempre *forever*
para variar *just for a change*
ser tal para cual *to be two of a kind*

2. The preposition **por**:

☞ expresses motion through a place or location somewhere in a place (imprecise location):

Salga por esa puerta.	*Go out through that door. (motion through)*
Hay varios restaurantes por este barrio.	*There are several restaurants in (around) this neighborhood. (imprecise location)*
por todas partes, por todos lados	*everywhere (imprecise location)*
No lo he visto por aquí.	*I haven't seen him around here. (imprecise location)*

☞ expresses duration of time or imprecise point in time:

Trabajó por muchos años.	*He worked for many years. (duration)*
Tuve que hacer cola por tres horas.	*I had to stand in line for three hours. (duration)*
Ayer por la tarde.	*Yesterday in the afternoon. (imprecise point in time)*
Nos veremos por Navidad.	*We'll see each other around Christmas. (imprecise point in time)*

☞ designates the cause or reason:

Se ofenden por cualquier cosa.	*They get insulted at/over any little thing.*
Te felicito por tus buenas notas.	*I congratulate you on your good grades.*
Lo pasé mal en Panamá por el calor.	*I had a bad time of it in Panama because of the heat.*

☞ designates the means:

Mándeme un mensaje por correo electrónico.	*Send me a message by e-mail.*

☞ designates the motivation or inducement, or the person for whose sake something is done:

Brindaron por el equipo vencedor.	*They toasted the winning team.*
Todo lo hice por mi familia.	*Everything I did was for my family.*
Me callé por ti.	*I kept quiet for your sake.*

☞ expresses exchange or substitution:

Pagamos mucho dinero por el coche.	*We paid a lot of money for the car.*
Enseñé la clase por el profesor.	*I taught the class for the teacher. (instead of him)*

☞ adds the idea of motion to prepositions of location:

El caballo saltó **por encima de** la valla.	*The horse jumped over the hurdle.*
El mozo pasó **por detrás de** las sillas.	*The waiter passed behind the chairs.*
El perro corrió **por debajo de** la mesa.	*The dog ran under the table.*

☞ **Por** labels the agent in passive constructions (see Chapter 8).

☞ **Por** appears in many common expressions:

por acá/ahí/allá/aquí *around here/there/there/here*
por ahora *for now*
por añadidura *in addition*
por aquel entonces *at that time*
por casualidad *by chance*
por cierto *certainly*
por completo *completely*
por lo común *usually*
por consecuencia *consequently*
por consiguiente *consequently*
por culpa de *the fault of*
por lo demás *furthermore*
por dentro y por fuera *inside and outside*
por desgracia *unfortunately*
por ejemplo *for example*
por esa época *around that time*
por escrito *in writing*
por eso *therefore, that's why*
por excelencia *par excellence*
por favor *please*
por fin *finally*
por lo general *generally*
por lo menos *at least*
por primera vez *for the first time*

por lo mismo *for that very reason*
por lo pronto *for the time being*
por lo que a mí me toca *as far as I'm concerned*
por lo tanto *therefore*
por lo visto *apparently*
por mi parte *as far as I'm concerned*
por poco *almost*
por si acaso *just in case*
por su cuenta *on one's own*
por su parte *as far as one is concerned*
por supuesto *of course*
por último *finally*
por un lado, por otro *on the one hand, on the other*

☞ **Por** appears in many useful idioms:

dar gato por liebre *to put something over on someone*
(de) una vez por todas *once and for all*
en un dos por tres *in a jiffy*
poner por las nubes *to praise to the skies*
por las buenas o por las malas *whether one likes it or not*
por los cuatro costados *on both sides*
escaparse por un pelo *to have a narrow escape, to escape by the skin of one's teeth*
Pasó el examen por los pelos. *He barely got through the exam.*
traído por los pelos *far-fetched*
por motivo de *on account of*
por si las moscas *just in case*
siete por dos son catorce *seven times two are fourteen*
trabajar por cuatro *to work like a slave*

☞ **Por** and **para** contrast with each other in certain contexts:

por esa época para esa época	*around that time* *by that time*
Por algo lo hizo. Para algo lo hizo.	*He did it for some reason or other.* *He did it for some purpose.*
¿Para quién trabaja Ud.? Trabajo para el señor Domínguez.	*For whom are you working?* *I'm working for Mr. Domínguez. (he's my boss)*
¿Por quién trabaja Ud.? Trabajo por el señor Domínguez.	*For whom are you working?* *I'm working for Mr. Domínguez. (in his place)*

I. **¡Pepita la preguntona** (*busybody*)! Pepita pregunta muchas cosas por ser curiosa. Conteste sus preguntas usando la preposición **por** en sus respuestas.

Modelo —¿Por qué se durmió Ud. tan temprano? (un tremendo sueño)
—Me dormí tan temprano por un tremendo sueño.

1. ¿Por qué fue Ud. al almacén? (un par de zapatos)

____

2. ¿Por qué felicitaron Uds. a Verónica? (su cumpleaños)

____

3. ¿Por qué te duele la espalda? (jugar tenis / cuatro horas)

____

4. ¿Por qué no terminó Javier el informe? (pereza)

____

5. ¿Cuándo veremos a Carlos y Elena? (la tarde)

____

6. ¿Cómo salieron los Salcedo de la ciudad? (el puente más céntrico)

____

7. ¿Por qué cosas irán Uds. a la bodega? (salchicha y queso)

____

8. ¿Cómo tendrás que hacer la tarea? (escrito)

____

9. ¿Por dónde darán un paseo los muchachos? (el bulevar Alameda)

____

10. ¿Por quiénes vas a pasar por la casa de los Granados? (Micaela y Angustias)

____

Nota cultural

Hay varios nombres que se usan para el *grocery store* norteamericano. Además de **bodega** en América se dice: **tienda de abarrotes, pulpería, colmado, almacén;** y en España: **mantequería, tienda de comestibles, tienda de ultramarinos.**

J. ¿Una película encantadora? A su amiga le gustó tanto la película *Mangos del Caribe* que la vio cinco veces. Ud. quiere saber por qué le gustó tanto porque Ud. la encontró francamente aburrida. Se contesta usando la preposición **por.**

MODELO ¿Por qué te gustó la película tanto? (los actores principales)
➔ Fue por los actores principales.

1. ¿Por qué la viste cinco veces? (la fotografía)

____

2. ¿Por qué te interesa tanto? (el argumento)

____

3. ¿Por qué quedaste tan impresionada? (la dirección)

____

4. ¿Por qué te llamó la atención? (el guión [*script*])

____

5. ¿Por qué estás loca por ella? (los decorados [*scenery*])

____

6. ¿Por qué la encontraste tan buena? (la banda sonora [*soundtrack*])

____

7. ¿Por qué le haces un relato entusiasta (*rave review*)? (los efectos especiales)

____

8. ¿Por qué estás tan entusiasmada por ella? (el diálogo)

____

Nota cultural

El centenario del **cine español** se celebra el 14 de mayo de 1996, fecha de la primera proyección en Madrid. Algunos directores españoles han logrado una fama internacional, entre ellos, Luis Buñuel, Luis García Berlanga, Victor Erice, Carlos Saura y Pedro Almodóvar.

K. **¿Para qué?** ¡Ud. es el hermano modelo para su hermanito! Por eso él tiene interés en saber todo lo que Ud. hace y por qué lo hace. Ud. le contesta dándole muy buenos consejos. Use la preposición **para** + infinitivo en su respuesta.

MODELO ¿Para qué estudias tanto? (sacar buenas notas)
→ Para sacar buenas notas.

1. ¿Para qué trabajas en la biblioteca? (ganar plata)

____

2. ¿Para qué lees tantos libros? (aprender mucho)

____

3. ¿Para qué te quedas en casa los sábados hasta las tres? (ayudar a mamá y a papá)

____

4. ¿Para qué le compras flores y bombones a tu novia? (demostrarle mi cariño)

____

5. ¿Para qué practicas español cuatro horas al día todos los días? (perfeccionarlo)

____

6. ¿Para qué votas en todas las elecciones? (ser buen ciudadano)

____

7. ¿Para qué hablas de los principios éticos? (llevar una vida moral y feliz)

____

L. **¡Una semana muy ocupada!** Hay tantas cosas que hacer y tan poco tiempo para hacerlas. Escriba para cuándo todas las cosas se tienen que hacer. Use **para** en su respuesta.

MODELO ¿Para cuándo te cortas el pelo? (el jueves)
→ Para el jueves.

1. ¿Para cuándo tienes que entregar el informe? (pasado mañana)

____

2. ¿Para cuándo arreglaste cita con el dentista? (la semana entrante)

____

3. ¿Para cuándo vas a entrevistarte para el empleo? (el martes)

____

4. ¿Para cuándo necesitas devolver los libros a la biblioteca? (finales del mes)

____

5. ¿Para cuándo precisas el regalo para el aniversario de tus papás? (el mes próximo)

____

6. ¿Para cuándo debes recoger la ropa en la tintorería? (las cinco de la tarde)

____

7. ¿Para cuándo vas a alquilar un coche? (el fin de semana)

____

M. **¿Por o para?** Complete los siguientes diálogos llenando los espacios en blanco con **por** o **para.**

1. —¿Cuándo sale el tren de Madrid ______________ Barcelona?
   —Sale ______________ la mañana pasando ______________ Zaragoza ______________ la tarde.
2. —¿Van tú y Mari Carmen al centro comercial ______________ ver los escaparates?
   —Ah, sí, una vez ______________ semana.
3. —______________ peluquera, Teresa no sabe cortar el pelo.
   —______________ eso ya no voy a esa peluquería.
4. —Hagamos una excursión ______________ la sierra ______________ mediados de julio.
   —______________ variar, viajemos ______________ las islas ______________ principios de agosto.
5. —¿______________ quién es este hermoso traje hecho a la medida?
   —Es ______________ mi hermana Rosa. Fue hecho ______________ Gabriela, la famosa modista.
6. —¿Le dijiste a Juan lo de Armando ______________ teléfono?
   —¡Qué va! ______________ darle esta noticia tengo que hacerlo ______________ escrito.
   —¿______________ cuándo va a recibir la carta?
   —¡Será ______________ el 30 de febrero del año 2000 ______________ el hecho de que no la he escrito todavía!

7. —¿Cuánto pagaste ____________ los boletos?

   —____________ mí, un precio especial—¡el doble del precio normal!

8. —Parece que el ladrón se escapó ____________ los pelos.

   —¿____________ dónde entró en la tienda?

   —____________ lo que leí en el periódico, entró ____________ una ventana del sótano.

9. —Rodrigo estuvo enfermo ____________ la leche estropeada que tomó.

   —Yo sé. Él me llamó para pedirme que fuera al trabajo ____________ él.

Nota cultural

- **Zaragoza** es la capital de la Comunidad Autónoma de Aragón, que queda a orillas del río Ebro en el noreste de España. Su monumento más importante es la basílica de Nuestra Señora del Pilar. Zaragoza fue una ciudad ibera (pueblo europeo antiguo), una colonia romana, fue conquistada por los árabes (714) y ganada por Alfonso I (1118). En 1808 y 1809 resistió con gran heroísmo el ataque de las tropas francesas.

- En España, una gran parte de **la ropa** fue tradicionalmente hecha a la medida (*made to order, tailor-made*) por modistos (*couturiers*). Luego llegó la industria ropera con ropa ya confeccionada en las fábricas. Los españoles empezaron a comprar sus prendas de vestir en los almacenes y tiendas pequeñas igual que en los países latinoamericanos. La ropa suele costar mucho dinero en España tanto como en Latinoamérica. Por eso, muchos hispanoamericanos viajan a menudo a Estados Unidos en busca de precios más módicos y gangas. Hoy en día España goza de mucha fama en la alta costura.

N. Exprese las siguientes oraciones en inglés. Fíjese especialmente en las preposiciones **por** y **para.**

1. Soy norteamericano por los cuatro costados.

   ____

2. Iremos con Uds. más temprano por si las moscas.

   ____

3. Ponen a la tía Natalia por las nubes.

   ____

4. Ricardo habrá llamado para algo.

   ____

5. Tres por ocho son veinticuatro.

   ____

6. Mortadelo y Filemón son tal para cual.

____

7. «Te querré para siempre» le dijo don Quijote a Dulcinea.

____

Nota cultural

- **Mortadelo y Filemón** son los espías tan populares de las historietas españolas. Su creador, Francisco Ibáñez, empezó a escribir y dibujar estas historias en forma de tiras cómicas (*comic strips*) en los tebeos, publicaciones infantiles ilustradas, hace casi 40 años.
- **Don Quijote** es el protagonista de la novela *El ingenioso hidalgo Don Quijote de la Mancha* que fue escrita por Miguel de Cervantes Saavedra. Cervantes escribió la novela para burlarse de las novelas de caballerías cuyos protagonistas eran los caballeros andantes (*knights errant*). Se publicó la primera parte del Quijote en Madrid en 1605 y la segunda en Madrid en 1615. Don Quijote trata de hacer justicia en el mundo en nombre de su dama Dulcinea.

O. **¡Vivan los fiesteros!** (*Hooray for the party lovers!*) Les toca a los estudiantes hacer una fiesta del fin de curso. Cada persona salió a comprar algo y ahora cuenta lo que compró y cuánto costó. Use la preposición **por** en las respuestas.

MODELO yo/ir/los manteles : pagar/doce dólares
➔ Yo fui por los manteles. Pagué doce dólares por ellos.

1. Beatriz/ir/panecillos : pagar/treinta dólares

____

2. Carlos y Leo/ir/refrescos : pagar/cincuenta y cinco dólares

____

3. Paula y yo/ir/servilletas : pagar/siete dólares

____

4. tú/ir/fiambres (*cold cuts*) : pagar/ciento setenta y nueve dólares

____

5. yo/ir/torta : pagar/dieciocho dólares

____

6. Uds./ir/vino : pagar/cuarenta y tres doláres

____

7. Ud./ir/fruta : pagar/veintidós dólares

____

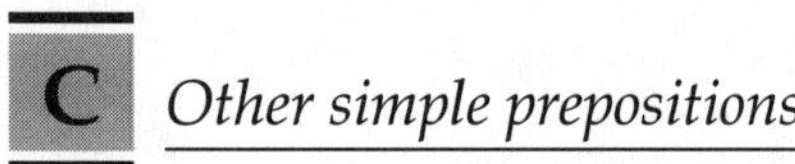

C Other simple prepositions

desde *from*	**menos** *except*
durante *during*	**salvo** *except*
entre *between, among*	**según** *according to*
excepto *except*	**sin** *without*
hacia *toward*	**sobre** *above, about*
hasta *until*	

- **Desde** is more specific than **de** in labeling the starting point:

Lo vi desde la ventana.	*I saw him from the window.*
Desde aquel día hemos sido buenos amigos.	*From that day on we have been good friends.*

- **Hacia** can refer to attitudes and feelings as well as direction:

Siente mucho cariño hacia sus sobrinos.	*He feels deep affection for his nieces and nephews.*

Note the following combinations of **hacia** + adverb:

hacia atrás *backward; toward the rear*
hacia adelante *toward the front*
hacia arriba *upward*
hacia abajo *downward*

- **Hasta** can mean *even* as well as *until*:

Hasta mis abuelos vinieron a la fiesta.	*Even my grandparents came to the party.*

- **Sin** + infinitive has a variety of English equivalents:

El trabajo quedó sin hacer.	*The work remained undone.*
Las calles están sin pavimentar.	*The streets are unpaved.*
Habla sin parar.	*He talks without a stop.*
Quedamos sin comer.	*We ended up not eating.*

- **Sobre** means *about* as well as *above, on top of*. It can also mean *about* in the sense of *approximately*:

un artículo sobre la industria mexicana	*an article on (about) Mexican industry*
Vamos a comer sobre las siete.	*We'll eat at about seven o'clock.*

P. En español, por favor. Exprese estas oraciones en español.

1. My homework is unfinished.

____

2. I put one book on top of the other.

____

3. I saw him go out toward the rear.

____

4. She lived for (= during) many years among the Indians.

____

5. It's hot even in the mountains.

___

6. The immigrants feel love for their new country.

___

7. They followed us from the door of the movie theater.

___

8. I'm reading a book about Puerto Rico.

___

D Sets of prepositions and compound prepositions

1. **Ante, antes de** (*before*), **delante de** (*in front of*)

   Antes de is used to mean *before* with time expressions; **ante** is figurative. **Delante de** expresses physical location:

antes de su llegada	*before your arrival*
antes de Navidad	*before Christmas*
antes de las ocho	*before eight o'clock*
comparecer ante el juez	*to appear before the judge*
ante todo	*first of all, above all*
No sé qué hacer ante tantas posibilidades.	*I don't know what to do faced with so many possibilities.*
Hay un jardín delante de la casa.	*There's a garden in front of the house.*

2. **Bajo** and **debajo de** (*under*)

   Bajo is mostly figurative; **debajo de** is usually literal:

bajo la administración de González	*under the Gonzalez government*
bajo Carlos V	*under Charles the Fifth*
bajo ningún concepto	*in no way*
diez grados bajo cero	*ten degrees below zero*
bajo llave	*under lock and key*
bajo juramento	*on oath, under oath*
debajo del puente	*under the bridge*

3. **Contra** and **en contra de** (*against*)

   En contra de usually expresses being against someone's ideas, policies, or political views. **Contra** means against in most other contexts:

apoyarse contra el árbol	*to lean against the tree*
pastillas contra la gripe	*pills for the flu*
luchar contra el enemigo	*to fight against the enemy*
escribir un artículo en contra de la guerra	*to write an article against (opposing) the war*
hablar en contra del proyecto	*to speak against the plan*
Los hechos van en contra de sus ideas.	*The facts run counter to your ideas.*

4. **Frente a** and **enfrente de** (*opposite, facing, across from*) are synonyms. Note that **delante de** should be used to mean *in front of*:

Hay una parada de autobuses enfrente de/frente a nuestra casa.	*There's a bus stop across from our house.*

5. **Tras** means *behind, after* in certain set expressions. Generally, **detrás de** means *behind* and **después de** means *after*:

año tras año	*year after year*
un artículo tras otro	*one article after another*
detrás de la casa	*behind the house*
después de la clase	*after class*

6. Other compound prepositions:

a causa de *because of*
acerca de *about (concerning)*
al lado de *next to*
a lo largo de *along*
a pesar de *in spite of*
a través de *through*
cerca de *near; about (approximately)*
dentro de *inside of*
encima de *on, upon, on top of (similar to* sobre, *but cannot mean "approximately")*
(a)fuera de *outside of*
junto a *close to, right next to*
lejos de *far from*
por medio de *by means of (a synonym of* mediante*)*
respecto a *about (concerning)*

Q. Ejercicio de conjunto. Escoja la preposición que complete correctamente las oraciones.

1. No pudieron lanzar el nuevo cohete ____________ mal tiempo que hacía.
   a. por medio del
   b. junto al
   c. a causa del
2. Todo lo que sé lo supe ____________ noticiero del Canal 7.
   a. encima del
   b. sobre el
   c. a través del
3. No puedo salir de la oficina a las cinco. Llegaré al restaurante ____________ las seis.
   a. a pesar de
   b. respecto a
   c. después de
4. El señor Aranda tuvo un ataque de nervios ____________ la perspectiva de perder su empleo.
   a. ante
   b. para
   c. al lado de

5. Ricardo mandó carta __________ carta y nunca recibió una respuesta.
   a. tras
   b. atrás
   c. detrás de
6. Si alquilas un apartamento tan __________ la oficina, tendrás que viajar por lo menos una hora para llegar al trabajo.
   a. junto a
   b. lejos de
   c. por medio de
7. En la radio están hablando constantemente __________ peligro de un ciclón.
   a. sobre el
   b. encima del
   c. cerca del
8. El coche resbaló, salió de la carretera, y fue __________ por la cuesta.
   a. afuera
   b. hacia abajo
   c. cerca
9. Miré por la ventana mientras mi avión volaba __________ Nueva York.
   a. entre
   b. por encima de
   c. antes de
10. Alfredo tiene gripe. __________ lo tanto, no viene hoy.
   a. Por
   b. En
   c. De
11. El tren de alta velocidad viaja __________ 270 kilómetros __________ hora.
   a. por/de
   b. en/para
   c. a/por
12. Bueno, eso es todo __________ ahora.
   a. para
   b. hacia
   c. por
13. __________ culpa de él, el proyecto quedó __________ terminar.
   a. Para/en
   b. Con/hasta
   c. Por/sin
14. A ese sobrino mío lo quiero __________ todo.
   a. a pesar de
   b. a lo largo de
   c. frente a
15. Los ciclistas tienen que pasar __________ los coches cuando hay mucho tráfico.
   a. por entre
   b. ante
   c. después de
16. Varios senadores se expresaron __________ Tratado de Libre Comercio con México.
   a. por medio del
   b. en contra del
   c. dentro del

17. Todos estos sarapes están hechos __________ mano.
    a. a
    b. con
    c. de

18. Pedro Camacho es el señor __________ traje gris.
    a. con el
    b. dentro del
    c. del

19. —¿No vino Zenaida?
    —No. Vinieron todos __________ ella.
    a. con
    b. después de
    c. menos

20. Este autor vivió __________ los Reyes Católicos.
    a. debajo de
    b. sin
    c. bajo

R. Ejercicio oral. Preposiciones: por, para y más. Dos o más equipos tratan de ganar puntos expresando en español o en inglés ciertas expresiones y oraciones presentadas por un presentador/mediador. Las expresiones y oraciones se deben sacar de las listas de este capítulo.

S. Estructuras en acción. Lea el siguiente anuncio fijándose especialmente en las preposiciones. Luego haga el ejercicio.

Vocabulario

ajustar *to fit*
asesorar *to advise*
el corredor *agent*
dar gato por liebre a uno *to take someone in, sell a pig in a poke*
los seguros *insurance*

Llene los espacios en blanco con la preposición que falta. Escoja entre las dos dadas, una de las cuales aparece en el texto del anuncio.

Un agente __________ (1. de/en) seguros nunca le dará gato __________ (2. para/por) liebre. Detrás __________ (3. a/de) un buen seguro siempre hay un buen agente o corredor __________ (4. de/para) seguros. Porque sólo ellos son los profesionales que más saben __________ (5. en/de) seguros. Porque sólo ellos son los que le asesorarán y aconsejarán __________ (6. sobre/hacia) el seguro que mejor se ajuste __________ (7. a/hasta) sus necesidades. Porque sólo ellos estarán allí donde usted lo necesite y __________ (8. con/en) el momento que lo precise, __________ (9. para/por) resolver sus problemas. Y porque sólo ellos saben,

__________ (10. a/en) todo momento, qué compañías son las que dan mejor servicio y cuáles son las más seguras.

Un agente de seguros nunca le dará gato por liebre.

Detrás de un buen seguro siempre hay un buen agente o corredor de seguros. Porque sólo ellos son los profesionales que más saben de seguros. Porque sólo ellos son los que le asesorarán y aconsejarán sobre el seguro que mejor se ajuste a sus necesidades. Porque sólo ellos estarán allí donde usted lo necesite y en el momento que lo precise, para resolver sus problemas. Y porque sólo ellos saben, en todo momento, qué compañías son las que dan mejor servicio y cuáles son las más seguras.

Es un mensaje de Winterthur, Schweiz y Equitativa.

Grupo Winterthur está formado por Winterthur, Schweiz, Equitativa e Hispasalud.

winterthur

Grupo Winterthur

CHAPTER 23

INTERROGATIVE WORDS & QUESTION FORMATION

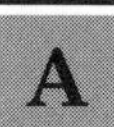

A Interrogative words in information questions

- Questions that begin with an interrogative word such as **¿Cuándo?** or **¿Quién?** ask for a piece of information (*When is the party?*, *Who is your teacher?*, *Which one do you want?*). They are called *information questions.*
- Interrogative words have a written accent. The most important interrogative words are:

¿cuál?, ¿cuáles? *which one(s)?*
¿cuándo? *when?*
¿cuánto? *how much?*
¿cuántos? *how many?*
¿cómo? *how?*
¿dónde? *where? (at what place?)*
¿adónde? *where? (to what place?)*
¿de dónde? *from where?*
¿qué? *what?, which?*
¿por qué? *why?*
¿para qué? *for what purpose?*
¿quién?, ¿quiénes? *who? (subject)*
¿a quién?, ¿a quiénes? *whom? (object)*
¿de quién?, ¿de quiénes? *whose?*

- Some of the interrogatives are not used exactly like their English equivalents:

☞ **¿Cómo?**

1. **¿Cómo?** is used to ask for repetition of something you didn't understand or to express surprise at something you have just heard (English uses *what* for this purpose):

—Hay examen de física hoy.	*There's a physics exam today.*
—¿Cómo?	*What?*

2. Unlike English *how* in questions such as *How heavy is the package?*, *How wide is the river?*, *How fast does he run?*, **¿cómo?** cannot precede adjectives or adverbs directly. Here are the ways Spanish asks for measurements:

¿Cuánto pesa el paquete? ¿Cómo es de pesado el paquete? ¿Cuánto es de pesado el paquete?	*How heavy is the package?*
¿Cómo es el río de ancho? ¿Cuánto es el río de ancho? ¿Cuánto tiene el río de ancho? ¿Qué anchura tiene el río? ¿Cuánto mide el río de ancho?	*How wide is the river?*
¿Con qué rapidez corre?	*How fast does he run?*

In Spanish America, a colloquial form **¿Qué tan ancho es el río?** exists.

3. **¿Cómo?** has different meanings depending on whether it is used with **ser** or **estar**:

¿Cómo está tu hermano?	*How is your brother? (asks about health or mental state)*
¿Cómo es tu hermano?	*What does your brother look like?* or *What is your brother like? (character, personality)*

☞ ¿Cuál?

1. **¿Cuál?** and **¿Cuáles?** are replaced by **¿Qué?** before a noun in standard Spanish:

¿Qué libros leíste?	*Which books did you read?*
¿Qué materias escogiste?	*Which subjects did you choose?*

In parts of Spanish America, such as Mexico and Cuba, sentences such as **¿Cuáles materias escogiste?** are acceptable.

2. **¿Cuál?** is used for English *what* when an identification is asked for:

¿Cuál es la diferencia?	*What's the difference?*
¿Cuál es la capital de Nicaragua?	*What's the capital of Nicaragua?*
¿Cuál es la fecha de hoy?	*What's today's date?*
¿Cuál fue el resultado?	*What was the result?*
¿Cuál fue el año de la crisis económica?	*What was the year of the crisis in the economy?*

Note that **¿qué?** before **ser** asks for a definition:

¿Qué es filosofía?	*What is philosophy?*
¿Qué es programación?	*What is programming?*

☞ ¿Dónde? *vs.* ¿Adónde?

1. **¿Dónde?** is used to ask about location. **¿Adónde?** asks direction and is used with verbs of motion:

¿Dónde trabaja Jimena?	*Where does Jimena work?*
¿Adónde va Jimena?	*Where is Jimena going?*

Many speakers use **¿dónde?** with both meanings.

2. Note also **¿para dónde?** and **¿hacia dónde?** *toward where?*

☞ ¿De quién(es)?

Questions beginning with **¿De quién(es)?** have a different word order than their English equivalents:

¿De quién es el libro?	*Whose book is this?*

☞ Prepositions always precede the interrogative word in Spanish:

¿Con cuántas personas llegó?	*How many people did he arrive with?*
¿Para quiénes es el regalo?	*Whom is the gift for?*
¿Sobre qué habló el profesor?	*What did the teacher talk about?*
¿En qué casa vive Nélida?	*Which house does Nélida live in?*

A. Los detalles, por favor. Cuando su amiga le habla de lo que hacen unas personas, Ud. le pide más detalles usando las palabras interrogativas con las preposiciones apropiadas.

MODELO Francisca se lamenta de todo.
→ ¿De qué se lamenta?

1. Monserrat se quejaba de todo.
____
2. Jorge y Maribel se interesan en todo.
____
3. Eduardo se jacta de todo.
____
4. Carlota se casó en mayo.
____
5. Cristóbal y Tere se metieron en todo.
____
6. Luz se fija en todo.
____
7. Hernán se ríe de todo.
____
8. Elvira se enamoró.
____
9. Pablo soñó con muchas personas.
____

B. ¿Quiénes son? Lea la información dada sobre cada persona y derive preguntas con palabras interrogativas de ella. Escriba más preguntas cuando sea posible.

MODELO Es venezolano.
→ ¿De dónde es? *or* ¿De qué nacionalidad es?

A. Leonardo Gustavo Sáenz
(1) Es argentino. (2) Es ingeniero. (3) Trabaja para una compañía argentina con sucursales en los Estados Unidos. (4) Vive en Nueva York. (5) Está casado con una norteamericana. (6) Tienen tres hijos.

1. ______________________________
2. ______________________________
3. ______________________________
4. ______________________________
5. ______________________________
6. ______________________________

B. Delmira Danielo

(7) Nació en Francia. (8) Sus abuelos son de España. (9) Se mudó al Canadá cuando tenía cuatro años. (10) Hace estudios posgraduados en química en una universidad canadiense. (11) Estudia para química. (12) Vive con sus padres y hermanos en las afueras de Montreal.

7. ______________________________
8. ______________________________
9. ______________________________
10. ______________________________
11. ______________________________
12. ______________________________

C. Claudio del Mundo

(13) Ganó la gran carrera de bicicletas. (14) Es un héroe nacional en España. (15) Fue condecorado por el rey español. (16) Tiene cuarenta y dos bicicletas. (17) Le gusta más su italiana amarilla. (18) Quiere descansar. (19) Irá de vacaciones al Caribe. (20) Llevará a su mujer y a sus dos hijas.

13. ______________________________
14. ______________________________
15. ______________________________
16. ______________________________
17. ______________________________
18. ______________________________
19. ______________________________
20. ______________________________

Nota cultural

__Miguel Induraín__ fue otra vez un héroe nacional de España cuando ganó el 82 Tour de Francia en julio de 1995. Induraín triunfó sobre algunos 188 ciclistas en esta famosa carrera de bicicleta, la del jersey amarillo—¡por quinta vez!

C. ¿Cómo? ¡Habla más fuerte! Su amiga llama para invitarlo/la a ir de compras con ella. Por desgracia, hay interferencias en la línea y Ud. le pregunta lo que dijo usando las palabras interrogativas apropiadas. Escriba más de una pregunta donde sea posible.

Modelo —Voy al centro comercial.
—¿Adónde?

1. —Pienso ir al centro comercial que queda en la carretera de Salamanca.

   —______________________________

2. —Hay ochenta y siete tiendas en el centro comercial.

   —______________________________

3. —Hay unos veintiséis restaurantes y cafés en el centro comercial.

   —____

4. —Voy a comprar dos pares de zapatos.

   —____

5. —Necesito comprarle un regalo a mi cuñada.

   —____

6. —Trataré de gastar menos de cincuenta dólares.

   —____

7. —Quizás le compre una blusa de seda.

   —____

8. —No sé si le guste más la azul o la verde.

   —____

9. —Pagaré con tarjeta de crédito o con cheque.

   —____

10. —Voy a llegar en coche.

    —____

11. —Saldré para el centro comercial a eso de las dos.

    —____

12. —Volveré a casa antes de la cena.

    —____

D. **Estudiantes.** Complete los siguientes diálogos llenando los espacios en blanco con las palabras interrogativas que faltan.

A.

1. Nati: ¿____________________ materias estás tomando este semestre?

   Sergio: Estoy tomando cuatro.

2. Nati: ¿____________________ son?

   Sergio: Historia de los Estados Unidos, literatura inglesa, física y español.

3. Nati: ¿____________________ enseña la clase de historia?

   Sergio: El profesor Durán.

4. Nati: ¿____________________ es la clase?

   Sergio: ¡Excelente, y fuerte! El profe es estupendo. No hay cosa que no sepa.

5. Nati: ¿____________________ estudiantes hay en la clase?

6. Sergio: Creo que somos veintidós. ¿____________________ te interesa tanto?

7. Nati: Es que soy aficionada a la historia norteamericana. Es posible que tome la clase de oyente (*auditor*). ¿____________________ se reúnen Uds.?

   Sergio: En el edificio de ciencias políticas, aula número 387.

8. Nati: ¿____________________ días?

   Sergio: Lunes, miércoles y jueves.

9. Nati: ¿____________________ hora?

   Sergio: De las diez y media hasta las doce.

B.

10. Diego: Oye, Paco, ¿____________________ es esta carpeta (*briefcase*)? ¿De Baltasar?

11. Paco: ¿____________________ dice adentro? ¿No tiene nombre ni papeles?

12. Diego: ¿____________________? (*Where?*) Yo no veo nada. Mira.

13. Paco: ¿____________________ color es la de Jaime? ¿No tiene él una así?

14. Diego: No me acuerdo. Vamos a llamarlo. ¿____________________ es su número de teléfono?

    Paco: No creo que lo encontremos en la casa porque lo vi hace poco por aquí.

15. Diego: ¿____________________ iba?

    Paco: No tengo la menor idea.

16. Diego: ¿Con ____________________ estaba?

    Paco: Ni te puedo decir porque yo hablaba con Aurelia.

17. Diego: ¿____________________? (*What?*) ¿____________________ dices? ¿Tú y Aurelia otra vez?

18. Paco: Ay, chico, ¿____________________ quieres que yo haga? La quiero mucho. ¿____________________ me hablas de esto ahora?

19. Diego: Bueno, es tema de otro día. Por ahora, ¿____________________ estará Jaime?

E. Un testigo. Ud. estaba paseándose por la calle cuando vio un choque de coches. Un policía acaba de llegar a la escena del accidente y quiere hacerle unas preguntas. Forme las preguntas escribiendo las palabras interrogativas que faltan.

1. ¿____________________ estaba Ud. cuando vio ocurrir el accidente?
2. ¿____________________ pasó? Déme todos los detalles.
3. ¿____________________ pasó? Dígame la hora exacta.
4. ¿____________________ de los dos coches fue responsable del accidente?
5. ¿____________________ pasó la luz roja sin parar?
6. ¿____________________ iba el conductor del coche blanco?
7. ¿____________________ venía el conductor del coche rojo?
8. ¿____________________ peatones (*passersby*) se acercaron a la escena?
9. ¿____________________ minutos transcurrieron (*elapsed*) entre el choque y la llegada de la policía?

F. Una conversación telefónica. Ud. está escuchando lo que dice su amigo mientras habla por teléfono. Porque no oye lo que dice la otra persona, Ud. tiene que imaginarse lo que ésta le pregunta a su amigo. Escriba las preguntas que habrá hecho.

MODELO **—¿Qué tiempo hace?**
—Hace calor.

1. —____
—De parte de Jaime Vega.
2. —____
—La casa queda en la calle Olmo.
3. —____
—El coche es de Roberto.
4. —____
—Es verde oscuro.
5. —____
—Voy a llevar a Ofelia.
6. —____
—Llegaremos a las nueve.
7. —____
—Tengo cincuenta y uno.
8. —____
—Pienso ver a Leo y a Matilde.
9. —____
—Será el sábado.
10. —____
—Llegan mis primos.
11. —____
—Gasté mucha plata.
12. —____
—Está lloviendo.
13. —____
—Tito y César se encuentran muy bien.
14. —____
—Me quedo hasta el domingo.
15. —____
—No quiero ninguno de los dos.
16. —____
—Jugaron tenis.

G. Vamos a comprar boletos. Exprese las siguientes oraciones en español. Preste mucha atención a las palabras interrogativas.

1. When are we going to buy the tickets for the play?

____

2. How about going tomorrow? Where's the box office?

____

3. On Pamplona Avenue. How many tickets do we need?

____

4. Six. How much do they cost?

____

5. Eighteen dollars each. Who's paying for them?

____

6. Each one will pay for his/her ticket. What day are we going?

____

7. Thursday. What time does the show start?

____

8. At eight o'clock. Whom are you inviting?

____

9. Nobody! The ticket is too expensive! How are we getting there?

____

10. By car or by train.

____

H. ¡Maravillas naturales de las Américas!: para expresar la magnitud. Con los elementos dados, forme preguntas acerca de la magnitud de estos lugares tan conocidos.

1. el río Iguazú / tener 1.320 kilómetros / largo

¿_______________?

2. el río Amazonas / tener 6.500 kilómetros / longitud

¿_______________?

3. el río Mississippi / medir 3.780 kilómetros / largo

¿_______________?

4. el lago Titicaca / ser 3.815 metros / altura

¿_______________?

5. el desierto de Atacama / tener 600 millas / largo

¿_______________?

6. el monte McKinley / tener 6.096 metros / altura

¿____?

7. la cumbre Aconcagua / medir 6.959 metros / alto

¿____?

Nota cultural

- **Un kilómetro** (1.000 metros) equivale aproximadamente a 5/8 de una milla. Un metro equivale a 39.37 pulgadas (*inches*).
- **El río Iguazú** se encuentra al sur del Brasil y desemboca en (*flows into*) el Paraná donde se unen Argentina, Brasil y Paraguay.
- **El río Amazonas** nace en los Andes de Perú y atraviesa (*crosses*) Brasil.
- **El río Mississippi** (en español **Misisipí**) desemboca en el golfo de México por un ancho delta.
- **El lago Titicaca** se encuentra en la altiplanicie (*high plateau*) andina de Perú y Bolivia.
- **El desierto de Atacama,** que queda al norte de Chile, es una región rica en cobre y nitrato (*saltpeter*).
- **El monte McKinley** es la cumbre (*peak*) más alta de las montañas Rocosas (*Rocky*). La sierra se extiende desde Alaska, donde se encuentra el monte McKinley, hasta México.
- **Aconcagua,** la cumbre más alta de América, se encuentra en los Andes argentinos.

I. Complete las siguientes oraciones llenando los espacios en blanco con las palabras interrogativas correctas. Escoja **¿cuál?, ¿cómo?** o **¿qué?**

1. ¿____________________ es la capital de Costa Rica?
2. ¿____________________ es computación?
3. ¿____________________ son tus hermanos?
4. ¿____________________ fue el problema?
5. ¿____________________ están por tu casa?
6. ¿____________________ es la fecha de hoy?
7. ¿____________________ es guacamole?

J. Escriba preguntas derivadas de las oraciones. Tenga presente que la preposición precede la palabra interrogativa.

Modelo Van *para el mar.*
➔ ¿Para dónde van?

1. Estas rosas son *para Susana.*

    ____

2. Los ingenieros hablaron *sobre el nuevo puente.*

    ____

3. Celeste trabaja *en aquella oficina.*

    ____

4. Alberto fue *con otras siete personas.*

    ____

5. Los disquetes son *de Uds.*

    ____

6. Caminabas *hacia el río.*

    ____

7. Jeremías entró *por aquí.*

    ____

8. Soñó *con su novia.*

    ____

9. Se metieron *en un lío.*

    ____

B *Yes/no questions*

- Questions that do not begin with a question word require either *yes* or *no* as an answer. In English, they are called *yes/no questions* (in Spanish, **preguntas generales**).
- To make a statement into a *yes/no question* in Spanish, the intonation changes from falling to rising at the end of the sentence without changing the word order:

¿Los chicos tienen juguetes?	*Do the children have toys?*
¿Alfonsina trabaja mañana?	*Is Alfonsina working tomorrow?*
¿Martín sacó las entradas?	*Did Martín buy the tickets?*

- Yes/no questions can also be formed from statements by inverting the subject and the verb:

¿Tienen los chicos juguetes?	*Do the children have toys?*
¿Trabaja Alfonsina mañana?	*Is Alfonsina working tomorrow?*
¿Sacó Martín las entradas?	*Did Martín buy the tickets?*

- The subject can also be placed at the end of the sentence to emphasize it:

¿Trabaja Alfonsina mañana?	*Is Alfonsina working* tomorrow? *(focus on* tomorrow*)*
¿Trabaja mañana Alfonsina?	*Is* Alfonsina *working tomorrow? (focus on* Alfonsina*)*

- In *yes/no questions* consisting of just a subject and verb, either the subject or the verb may come at the end, depending on which element is the focus of the question. Thus, the questions **¿Carlos se va?** and **¿Se va Carlos?** require different answers, since their focus is different:

—¿Carlos se va? —No, se queda.	*Is Carlos* leaving? *(focus on the verb)* *No, he's* staying.
—¿Se va Carlos?	*Is* Carlos *leaving? (focus on who's leaving)*
—No, Carlos no. Se va Raúl.	*No, not Carlos.* Raúl *is leaving.*

- Statements consisting of a subject, **ser** or **estar**, and an adjective are usually made into *yes/no questions* by placing the subject at the end of the sentence, not right after the verb as in English:

El coche es caro. ¿Es caro el coche?	*The car is expensive.* *Is the car expensive?*
Las tiendas están cerradas. ¿Están cerradas las tiendas?	*The stores are closed.* *Are the stores closed?*

- Spanish can add phrases such as **¿verdad?, ¿no es verdad?, ¿no es cierto?, ¿no?** to statements to turn them into questions. The added phrases are called *tags*. These *tag questions* signal that the speaker expects the answer *yes*. Note that if the statement is negative, only **¿verdad?** can be used as a tag.

Vienes con nosotros, ¿no es cierto?	*You're coming with us, aren't you?*
Te gustó la clase, ¿no?	*You liked the class, didn't you?*
No tienes hambre, ¿verdad?	*You're not hungry, are you?*

K. ¿Cuál es la pregunta? Derive preguntas generales de las oraciones enunciativas colocando el sujeto inmediatamente después del verbo.

MODELO Raúl estudia arquitectura.
→ ¿Estudia Raúl arquitectura?

1. Gustavo y Melinda aprenden francés.

 ____

2. Pepe trabaja en una tienda de videos.

 ____

3. Ud. toca piano.

 ____

4. Los niños se han vestido.

 ____

5. Cristóbal jugará tenis.

 ____

6. Elena se matriculó anteayer.

 ____

7. Uds. deben quedarse unos días más.

8. Ramona está a dieta.

L. ***¿Ser/estar* + adjetivo + sujeto?** Derive preguntas generales de las siguientes oraciones. Ponga el verbo **ser** o **estar** primero seguido del adjetivo y al final el sujeto.

MODELO El edificio es alto.
→ ¿Es alto el edificio?

1. Estos niños son traviesos.
2. Las margaritas (*daisies*) son bonitas.
3. El televisor estaba descompuesto.
4. El museo está abierto.
5. La revista es italiana.
6. Las joyas fueron robadas.
7. Los pantalones están rotos (*torn*).
8. Esta marca es buena.
9. El espectáculo fue impresionante.

M. **Para hacer un picnic.** Unos amigos quieren hacer un picnic y necesitan hacer ciertas cosas para que resulte bien. ¿Quién se ocupa de cada cosa? Para saberlo, conteste las siguientes preguntas generales usando el nombre o los nombres que aparece(n) entre paréntesis en su respuesta.

MODELO ¿Trae la carne Marianela? (Clarita)
→ No, Marianela no. La trae Clarita.

1. ¿Compra los panes Pedro? (Memo)
2. ¿Domingo y Toni nos llevan en coche? (Salvador y Bartolo)

3. ¿Dora va a preparar las ensaladas? (Leonor)

____

4. ¿Traerá Jorge el bate y la pelota? (Miguel)

____

5. ¿Piensa Carmen llevar los manteles? (Marcos)

____

6. ¿Harán Uds. los bocadillos? (Olivia y Nacho)

____

7. ¿Jesús y Marta invitarán a los amigos? (tú)

____

8. ¿Te ocupas tú de la fruta? (Mari)

____

C *Questions in indirect speech*

- When a question is not asked directly, but incorporated into a larger sentence as a dependent clause, it is called an indirect question. Compare the following examples. The first one has a question quoted directly, the second one has the same question reported indirectly by being incorporated into a larger sentence:

  She asked me, "Where is the post office?"
  She asked me where the post office was.

- Information questions are turned into indirect questions as subordinate clauses. The question word retains its accent mark.

Me preguntaron: —¿De dónde vienes?	*They asked me, "Where are you coming from?"*
Me preguntaron de dónde venía.	*They asked me where I was coming from.*
Te pregunté: —¿Cuándo regresarás?	*I asked you, "When will you return?"*
Te pregunté cuándo regresarías.	*I asked you when you would return.*
Siempre nos preguntan: —¿Qué quieren?	*They always ask us, "What do you want?"*
Siempre nos preguntan qué queremos.	*They always ask us what we want.*

- *Yes/no questions* are turned into indirect questions by means of **si** (*whether, if*).

Direct question: ¿Sales, Juan?	*Are you going out, Juan?*
Indirect: Le pregunté a Juan si salía.	*I asked Juan if he was going out.*

- If **preguntar** is in the present or future, then the tense of the original question is kept in the indirect questions:

Me pregunta para qué lo hago.	*He asks me why I do it.*
Nos pregunta cuándo vendrá Marta.	*He asks us when Marta will come.*
Me preguntará cuándo regresaron.	*He'll ask me when they returned.*

- The following table sums up the changes in tense in indirect questions.

If the verb of the main clause (**preguntar**) is in the preterit:

The tense of the original question	**changes to:**
present ¿Para qué lo haces?	➔ *imperfect* Me preguntó para qué lo hacía.
future ¿Cuándo vendrá Marta?	➔ *conditional* Me preguntó cuándo vendría Marta.
preterit ¿Por qué regresaron?	➔ *pluperfect* Me preguntó por qué habían regresado. or ➔ *preterit* Me preguntó por qué regresaron.

N. ¡Cuántas preguntas! ¡Unas personas le machacaron los oídos (*repeated over and over again*) con tantas preguntas hoy que Ud. se encuentra mareado(a) (*dizzy*)! Ahora Ud. le cuenta a otro amigo lo que le preguntaron usando la pregunta indirecta.

MODELO Anita me preguntó: —¿Adónde vas?
➔ Anita me preguntó adónde iba.

1. Felipe me preguntó: —¿Qué harás en la tarde?

____

2. Isabel me preguntó: —¿Con quiénes saliste?

____

3. Carlos me preguntó: —¿Por qué no quieres jugar baloncesto?

____

4. Sol me preguntó: —¿A qué hora volviste a casa?

____

5. Claudio me preguntó: —¿Para cuándo necesitas escribir el informe?

____

6. Mi hermanita me preguntó: —¿Cuándo me llevas a una discoteca?

____

7. Mis primos me preguntaron: —¿Por qué no nos invitas al parque de atracciones?

____

8. Mi mamá me preguntó: —¿Por qué tienes dolor de cabeza?

____

9. Yo me pregunté a mí mismo: —¿Por qué te levantaste de la cama?

____

O. Ejercicio oral: Una adivinanza. (*Guessing game.*) Uno de los estudiantes piensa en una persona, una cosa o un acontecimiento histórico. Los otros estudiantes tienen que hacerle preguntas hasta adivinar lo que es. Le toca al (a la) estudiante que lo adivina pensar en otra persona, cosa o acontecimiento.

P. Estructuras en acción. Lea el siguiente anuncio sobre una corrida de toros. Luego, escriba las preguntas con palabras interrogativas que se pueden hacer a base de la información dada en el anuncio. En algunos casos se pueden formar dos o más preguntas.

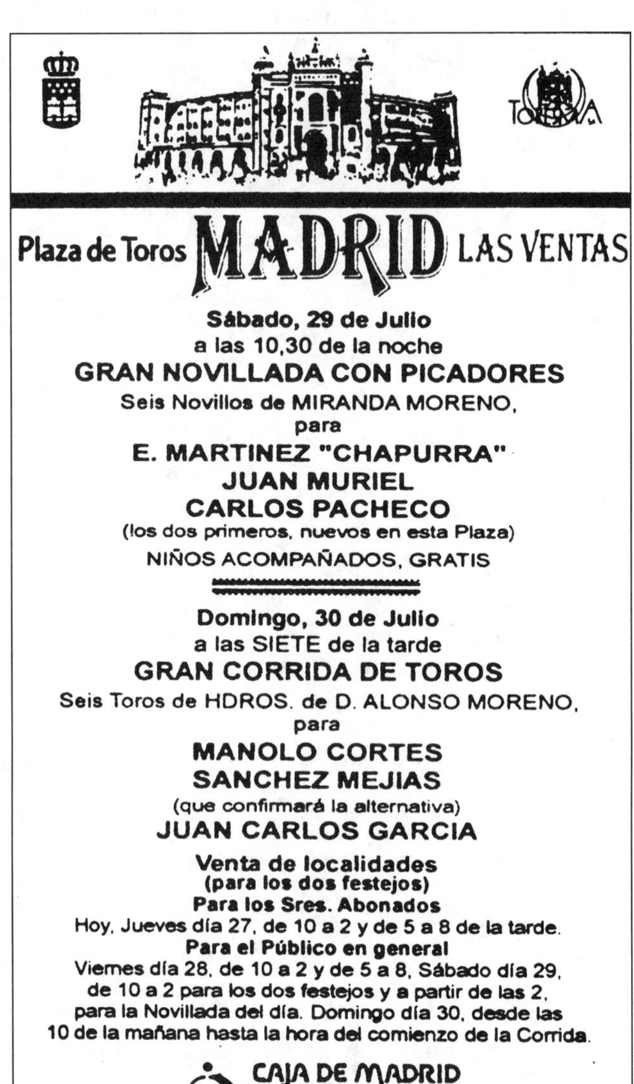

Plaza de Toros, Madrid Las Ventas

Gran novillada (corrida con toros jóvenes)
con picadores (toreros que montados a caballo hieren [*wound*] al toro con una pica para debilitarlo)

1. **Plaza de Toros—Las Ventas, Madrid**

   pregunta ______________________________

   pregunta ______________________________

2. **sábado, 29 de julio**
   pregunta ________________________________
   pregunta ________________________________
3. **a las 10,30 de la noche**
   pregunta ________________________________
4. **seis novillos**
   pregunta ________________________________
5. **novillo = toro joven**
   pregunta ________________________________
6. **toreros E. Martínez "Chapurra", Juan Muriel, Carlos Pacheco**
   pregunta ________________________________
   pregunta ________________________________
7. **niños acompañados, gratis**
   pregunta ________________________________
   pregunta ________________________________

Gran corrida de toros

8. **domingo, 30 de julio**
   pregunta ________________________________
   pregunta ________________________________
9. **a las siete de la tarde**
   pregunta ________________________________
10. **seis toros**
    pregunta ________________________________

Venta de localidades (se venden billetes en taquilla)

11. **para los dos festejos (fiestas)**
    pregunta ________________________________
12. **para el público en general**
    pregunta ________________________________
13. **viernes, día 28**
    pregunta ________________________________
14. **de 10 a 2 y de 5 a 8**
    pregunta ________________________________

CHAPTER 24

NEGATIVE & INDEFINITE WORDS

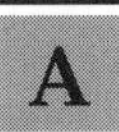

A Negative words and expressions

- Study the following list of Spanish negative words and expressions and their affirmative counterparts:

nunca, jamás *never*	**alguna vez** *sometime* **algunas veces** *sometimes* **a veces** *sometimes* **muchas veces, a menudo** *often* **siempre** *always*
nunca más *never again*	**otra vez** *again*
nada *nothing*	**algo** *something*
nadie *no one, nobody*	**alguien** *someone, somebody*
tampoco *neither, not either*	**también** *also*
ni, ni siquiera *not even*	**o** *or*
ni ... ni *neither ... nor*	**o ... o** *either ... or*
en/por ninguna parte *nowhere*	**en/por alguna parte** *somewhere*
en/por ningún lado / sitio / lugar *nowhere*	**en/por algún lado / sitio / lugar** *somewhere*
ya no *no longer*	**todavía** *still*
de ninguna manera, de ningún modo *in no way*	**de alguna manera, de algún modo** *somehow, in some way*

- Spanish also has negative and affirmative adjectives: **ninguno** (*no, not a*) and **alguno** (*some*). **Ninguno** and **alguno** are shortened to **ningún** and **algún** before a masculine singular noun:

Laura trabaja en **algún** edificio del centro.	*Laura works in some building downtown.*
Mercedes trabaja en **alguna** oficina.	*Mercedes works in some office.*
Hay **algunos** anuncios en el periódico.	*There are some ads in the newspaper.*
Conozco **algunas** tiendas elegantes por aquí.	*I know some elegant stores around here.*

- **Ninguno** is not used in the plural unless the noun it modifies is always used in the plural such as **anteojos, tijeras, vacaciones**, etc.:

No hay **ningún** hospital aquí.	*There is no hospital here. (There are no hospitals ...)*
No recibí **ninguna** respuesta.	*I didn't receive any answer.*
Este año no tenemos **ningunas** vacaciones.	*This year we don't have any vacation.*

- When negative words follow the verb, **no** precedes it:

No hice **nada** hoy.	*I didn't do anything today.*
Catalina **no** hizo **nada tampoco**.	*Catalina didn't do anything either.*
No vamos **nunca** a esquiar.	*We never go skiing.*

However, if a negative word precedes the verb, then **no** is not used:

—**Nunca** voy al cine.	*I never go to the movies.*
—Yo **tampoco** voy mucho.	*I don't go much either.*

- Personal **a** is used before **alguien** and **nadie** when they are direct objects and also before forms of **alguno** and **ninguno** when they refer to people and are direct objects:

—¿Viste **a alguien** en la plaza?	*Did you see anyone in the square?*
—No, no vi **a nadie**.	*No, I didn't see anyone.*
—¿Invitaste **a alguno** de los vecinos?	*Did you invite any of the neighbors?*
—No, no llamé **a ninguno**.	*No, I didn't call any (of them).*

- When words joined by **ni ... ni** or **o ... o** are the subject of a sentence, the verb can be either singular or plural:

—Debe venir **o Pepe o Rosa**.	*Either Pepe or Rosa should be coming.*
—¿Y si no vienen **ni él ni ella**?	*And what if neither he nor she comes?*

- A single **ni** means *not even*. **Ni siquiera** is a more emphatic form:

—¿Cuántos asistieron a la reunión?	*How many attended the meeting?*
—**Ni** uno./**Ni siquiera** uno.	*Not even one.*
—¿Te ofrecieron algo?	*Did they offer you anything?*
—**Ni** un vaso de agua.	*Not even a glass of water.*

A. **¡No!** Conteste las preguntas negativamente usando **no** y las palabras negativas que corresponden a las afirmativas.

MODELO —¿Quieres tomar *algo?*
—No, no quiero tomar **nada.**

1. ¿Fuiste *alguna vez* a la Isla de Pascua?

____

2. ¿Aprendieron Uds. chino *también?*

____

3. *¿Alguien* ha llamado esta tarde?

____

4. ¿Va Isabel a tomar álgebra *otra vez?*

____

5. ¿Leerás *o* la novela *o* el guión de la película?

____

6. *¿Algunos* jefes renunciaron al puesto?

____

7. ¿Conoció Osvaldo *a alguien* por fin?

____

8. ¿Quedan *algunos* duraznos?

9. ¿*Siempre* limpias la casa los sábados?

10. ¿Has visto *a alguna* de las empleadas?

Nota cultural

Isla de Pascua, que queda en el Pacífico, pertenece a Chile. La isla, que es de 180 kilómetros cuadrados, tiene un observatorio meteorológico. Se conoce por sus enormes estatuas de piedra que fueron construidas probablemente por gente primitiva de origen polinesio.

B. ¡Angustias, la aguafiestas (*the wet blanket*)**!** Angustias lo ve todo negro, es decir, es muy pesimista. Lea sus comentarios sobre una fiesta y cambie el orden de la palabra negativa.

MODELO **Nadie** se divierte.
→ **No** se divierte **nadie.**

1. Nada queda de la comida.
2. Tampoco hay refrescos.
3. Ni los chicos ni las chicas bailan.
4. Ninguno de los chicos se acerca para hablarme.
5. Ningún cantante canta bien.
6. Nadie tiene ganas de quedarse.
7. Nunca dan fiestas divertidas.

C. ¡Qué iluso (*dreamer*)**!** ¡Humberto pasa la vida soñando … pero son mirlos blancos (*impossible dreams* [mirlo *blackbird*]). Dígale que no puede ser empleando las palabras negativas apropiadas.

MODELO Siempre gano becas.
→ ¡Qué va! **Nunca/Jamás** ganas becas.

1. Alguien me regaló dos millones de dólares.

____

2. Algunas chicas dicen que soy un Adonis.

____

3. Muchas veces saco un diez en mis exámenes.

____

4. Yo nado y patino mejor que nadie.

____

5. Los reyes de España me mandaron algo.

____

6. Yo también voy a la luna.

____

7. Conchita va a salir conmigo otra vez.

____

8. Mis padres me van a regalar o un Jaguar o un Ferrari.

____

B *Further uses of negative words*

- Spanish, unlike English, allows two or more negative words in a sentence:

Nadie trae **nada nunca**.	*Nobody ever brings anything.*

- **Alguno** can have an emphatic *negative* meaning when placed after the noun:

No hay problema **alguno**.	*There is no problem at all.*
No recibimos carta **alguna**.	*We received no letter at all.*

- In Spanish, negatives are used in certain constructions where English uses indefinite words rather than negatives:

1. after **que** (*than*) in comparatives:

—La lluvia fue peor **que nada**.	*The rain was worse than anything.*
—Sí, y yo me mojé más **que nadie.**	*Yes, and I got wetter than anyone.*
—Lo que es la guerra lo sabe este país mejor **que ningún otro**.	*This country knows better than any other what war is.*
—Se ha sufrido más aquí **que en ningún otro lugar**.	*People have suffered more here than anywhere else.*
—Hoy habló el profesor mejor **que nunca**.	*Today the teacher spoke better than ever.*
—Y aprendimos más cosas **que en ningún otro momento**.	*And we learned more than at any other time.*

2. after **sin, antes de,** and **antes que**:

Lo hizo **sin** pedir **nada a nadie nunca**.	*He did it without ever asking anything of anyone.*
Antes de hacer **nada**, lee las instrucciones.	*Before doing anything, read the instructions.*
Has llegado **antes que nadie.**	*You've arrived before anyone else.*

3. after **imposible, poco probable, inútil**, expressions of doubt, and other similar words that imply negation:

Es **imposible** hacer **nada** aquí.	*It's impossible to do anything here.*
Es **inútil** pedirle **nada**.	*It's useless to ask him for anything.*
Dudo que venga **nadie**.	*I doubt that anyone will come.*

- The conjunction **pero** is replaced by **sino** after a negative clause:

No viene ella, **sino** él.	*Not she, but he, is coming.*

Note also **no solamente (sólo) ... sino también** *not only ... but also.*

D. Hay que ser negativo. Complete las siguientes oraciones llenando los espacios en blanco con las expresiones negativas o indefinidas apropiadas.

1. Es imposible decirle ____________________ a este chiquillo porque no le hace caso a ____________________.
2. ¡____________________ he oído tantas barbaridades!
3. El programa no fue ____________________ bueno pero los locutores sí fueron ____________________ interesantes.
4. ¿No probaste la sopa? Y salió mejor que ____________________.
5. No sólo visitamos Córdoba ____________________ nos quedamos ocho días en Granada.
6. Aunque Diego y yo nos conocimos hace un año es como si él no me conociera ____________________.
7. ¡Qué señora más distinguida! Será ____________________.
8. ¡Ay, sus cuentos tan largos y siempre con los mismos temas! Son los cuentos de ____________________.
9. Maribel es tan torpe; no sabe nada ____________________.
10. Mauricio es siempre el primero en llegar. Llega antes que ____________________.
11. —¿Vino Alicia Delgado?
    —Sí, y ____________________ ella, ____________________ su hermano Francisco.
12. Muchos dicen que Toledo es más interesante por su arte e historia que ____________________ otra ciudad española.

Nota cultural

- **Córdoba** es una pintoresca ciudad andaluza que queda a orillas del río Guadalquivir. Sus monumentos más importantes incluyen la catedral (que era mezquita [*mosque*]), el Alcázar (fortaleza, palacio real) y un puente romano sobre el Guadalquivir. Córdoba y Granada impresionan por su arquitectura y arte árabes.

- **Granada** es otra hermosa ciudad andaluza. Queda al pie de la Sierra Nevada. Algunos monumentos que destacan son la Alhambra (el palacio de los reyes moros), el palacio de Carlos V, la Catedral y el Generalife (el palacio y jardines de los reyes moros). Granada, la última defensa de los moros en España, fue conquistada por los Reyes Católicos en 1492.

- **Toledo,** una gran ciudad rica en historia y arte, queda al sur de Madrid en Castilla. A orillas del río Tajo, Toledo fue la capital visigoda (*Visigoth*) y residencia de la Corte española hasta 1560. Toledo se destaca como lugar turístico por su catedral gótica, la sinagoga del Tránsito, la iglesia de Santo Tomé, el puente romano de Alcántara y la casa de El Greco. Este famoso pintor que nació en Creta en 1541 (o 1542), vivió muchos años en Toledo y allí murió en 1614. La ciudad influyó mucho en su obra (véase *La vista de Toledo*). Se puede ver su obra maestra *El entierro del Conde de Orgaz* en la iglesia de Santo Tomé.

C *Negative words in conversation*

- Negative words frequently serve as one-word answers to questions:

—¿Vas a menudo al café estudiantil? —**Nunca.**	*Do you often go to the student café?* *Never.*
—¿Quién te ayudó con el trabajo? —**Nadie.**	*Who helped you with the work?* *Nobody.*

- Negative words, including **no**, often appear with subject pronouns or with phrases consisting of **a** + prepositional pronoun as short answers to questions:

—¿Cursan tú y Carla español? —Yo, sí. **Ella, no.**	*Are you and Carla taking Spanish?* *I am. She's not.*
—No voy a la fiesta hoy. ¿Y tú?	*I'm not going to the party today. What about you?*
—Yo tampoco.	*Neither am I.*
—A mí no me gusta este plato. **—A nosotros tampoco.**	*I don't like this dish.* *We don't either.*
—A mí siempre me escriben. **—A nosotros nunca.**	*People are always writing to me.* *Never to us.*

- Some non-negative expressions such as **en absoluto** and **en la vida** can function as negatives:

—**En la vida** he visto un espectáculo tan bueno. —Yo tampoco.	*I have never in my life seen such a good show.* *Neither have I.*
—¿Contrataría Ud. a ese señor? —**En absoluto**.	*Would you hire that man?* *Absolutely not.*

- **Algo** and **nada** can function as adverbs and modify adjectives and verbs:

—El discurso fue **algo** confuso.	*The speech was somewhat confusing.*
—Y no fue **nada** interesante.	*And it wasn't at all interesting.*
—Tomás trabaja **algo**.	*Tomás works a little.*
—Pero no se concentra **nada**.	*But he doesn't concentrate at all.*

Para nada is an emphatic replacement for **nada**: **No se concentra para nada**.

- **Algo de** and **nada de** are used before nouns:

—¿Quieres **algo de** chocolate?	*Do you want a little chocolate?*
—No, no debo comer **nada de** dulces.	*No, I'm not supposed to eat any sweets.*

Algo de is a synonym for **un poco de**.

Negative and indefinite words appear in many idiomatic expressions:

Expressions with negative words:

nunca *and* **jamás**
jamás de los jamases *never ever*
el cuento de nunca acabar *the never-ending story*
casi nunca *hardly ever*
¡Hasta nunca! *Good-bye forever!*
nunca jamás *never ever*
nunca más *never again, no more*

ni
ni hablar, ni modo *nothing doing*
No lo puedo ver ni en pintura. *I can't stand him at all.*
No tengo ni idea. *I haven't the slightest idea.*

nada
No por nada vendimos la casa. *We had good reason to sell the house.*
No por nada le llaman 'tonto'. *They don't call him 'dumb' for nothing.*
¡De eso nada, monada! (*slang*) *None of that!, No way!*
De nada. Por nada. *You're welcome./Don't mention it.*
¡Nada de salir antes de terminar la tarea! *Forget about going out before you finish your homework!*
No me conoce de nada. *He doesn't know me from Adam.*
antes de nada *first of all*
casi nada *hardly*
como si nada *as if it were nothing at all*
dentro de nada *in a moment*
más que nada *more than anything*
nada de eso *nothing of the sort*
nada de extraordinario *nothing unusual*
nada de nada *nothing at all*
nada más *that's all*
no servir para nada *to be useless*
no tener nada de + noun *to not have ___________ at all*
no tener nada de particular *to have nothing special about*
por nada del mundo *for nothing in the world*
quedarse en nada *to come to nothing*
tener en nada *to think very little of; take no notice of*

nadie
Es un don nadie. *He's a nobody.*

Expressions with indefinite words:

Algo es algo. Más vale algo que nada. *Something is better than nothing.*
Ya es algo. *That's something at least./It's a start.*
¡Por algo será! *There must be a reason.*
De algo lo conozco. *I know you from somewhere.*
algo así *something like that*
tener algo que ver con *to have something to do with*
ser alguien *to be somebody*
Nos vemos a la hora de siempre. *We'll see each other at the usual time.*
Es lo de siempre. *It's the same old story.*
Para siempre. *Forever.*

E. ¿Cómo se dice eso en inglés? Exprese las siguientes oraciones en inglés. Tenga en cuenta especialmente las expresiones con palabras negativas e indefinidas.

1. ¡No la puedo ver ni en pintura!

 ____

2. ¡De eso nada, monada!

 ____

3. Van a verse a la hora de siempre.

 ____

4. No por nada la llaman encantadora.

 ____

5. Guillermo dice que no tiene ni idea.

 ____

6. Todo el tiempo y todos los planes se quedaron en nada.

 ____

7. Al fin y al cabo todo el discutir no sirvió para nada.

 ____

8. Lo que dices no tiene nada que ver con la situación actual.

 ____

F. ¿Algo? ¿Nada? ¿Nunca? Exprese las siguientes ideas escogiendo una de las expresiones con **nunca/jamás, algo** o **nada.**

1. Eso es inútil.
   a. No sirve para nada. b. Por nada del mundo.
2. ¿Ir al cine? ¡Ni hablar!
   a. Algo es algo. b. ¡Nada de salir!
3. Es lo de siempre.
   a. Nunca jamás. b. Nada de extraordinario.

4. X está relacionado con Y.
   a. X tiene algo que ver con Y. b. X se queda en nada.
5. No volveremos a vernos.
   a. Nos veremos más que nunca. b. Nunca más nos veremos.
6. Se le acabó la paciencia.
   a. No tiene nada de paciencia. b. Más vale algo que nada.
7. Camilo tendrá algún motivo.
   a. Por algo será. b. Por nada.
8. Van poco a ese café.
   a. Como si nada. b. Casi nunca.
9. Olga vuelve muy pronto.
   a. Dentro de nada. b. Antes de nada.

D *Other indefinite words and constructions*

- The pronoun **cualquiera** means *anyone* or *any one* and can refer to people or things:

—¿Cuál de los dos pasteles quieres?	*Which of the two pastries do you want?*
—**Cualquiera** de los dos.	*Any one (either one) of the two.*
—**No cualquiera** podría hacer esto.	*Not just anyone would be able to do this.*
—Al contrario. **Cualquiera** lo habría hecho mucho mejor.	*On the contrary. Anyone would have done it much better.*

Note also the idiomatic use of **cualquiera** as a noun: **Él es un cualquiera.** *He's a nobody.*

- When used as an adjective, **cualquiera** becomes **cualquier**:

El tren puede llegar en **cualquier** momento.	*The train can arrive at any moment.*
La vida es más fácil en **cualquier** otro lugar.	*Life is easier anywhere else.*
Está contento con **cualquier** cosa.	*He's happy with anything.*

- Spanish also indicates "indefiniteness" by the subjunctive. English often uses *whatever, wherever,* etc. in these cases. Compare the following pairs of sentences:

Lee el libro que recomiendan.	*Read the book that they recommend. (indicative: speaker knows which book it is)*
Lee el libro que **recomienden**.	*Read whatever book they recommend. (subjunctive: speaker does not know which book it is)*
Haga lo que quiere.	*Do what you want. (indicative: we already know what you want to do)*
Haga lo que **quiera**.	*Do whatever you want. (subjunctive: we don't yet know what you want to do)*

- Note that **todo** is usually followed by the definite article and noun:

Por **todo el** país.	*Throughout the whole country.*
Toda la casa.	*The whole house.*
Todos los estudiantes.	*All the students.*
Todas las calles.	*Every street.*

- When **todo** is followed directly by a *singular* noun, it means *every* or *any:*

Todo jugo de fruta es bueno.	*Any fruit juice is good.*
Todo mexicano apoya el tratado.	*Every Mexican supports the treaty.*
Nos sirvieron **toda** clase de fruta.	*They served us every kind of fruit.*

- Note also the use of **todo** with place names:

Hay paradores por **toda España**.	*There are government inns all over Spain.*
En casi **todo Santiago** hay servicio de metro.	*The subway serves almost all of Santiago.*

- **Todo** can also be used as a pronoun or in pronominal phrases:

Todo es interesante en España.	*Everything is interesting in Spain. (**Todo** takes a singular verb.)*
Todos son amables.	*Everyone is nice. (**Todos** takes a plural verb.)*
Todo el mundo trata de ayudar.	*Everyone, everybody tries to help (**Todo el mundo** takes a singular verb.)*

G. **¡En español, por favor!** Exprese las siguientes oraciones en español. Tenga en cuenta especialmente las expresiones con palabras negativas o indefinidas.

1. He had good reason to quit his job.

 ____

2. They'll call at any moment.

 ____

3. We walked the whole day through the whole city.

 ____

4. Anyone could help us with the work.

 ____

5. Every avenue is blocked during rush hour.

 ____

6. There are Roman ruins all over Spain.

 ____

Nota cultural

Las ruinas romanas. Al comenzar los tiempos históricos, España estaba poblada por los iberos y los celtas que se fundieron entre sí creando los celtíberos. Luego los fenicios y los griegos fundaron colonias en España. Hacia el siglo VI antes de Jesucristo, llegaron los cartagineses. Los romanos vencieron a los cartagineses en España en 202 a. de J.C. A pesar de la heroica resistencia de las poblaciones indígenas, Roma logró someterlas a su poder unificador (*unifying*) a través de su lengua y su legislación. Los romanos construyeron acueductos, caminos, puentes, anfiteatros y arcos de triunfo, algunos de los cuales se han conservado espléndidamente en Segovia, Sagunto, Mérida, Toledo, etcétera.

H. ¡Finales dramáticos o "Lo que el viento se llevó"! Le toca a Ud. como guionista *(scriptwriter)* escribir las últimas palabras de unas películas. Escríbalas expresando las siguientes ideas en español. Tenga en cuenta las expresiones con palabras negativas e indefinidas.

1. Although I'll love you forever, I must say: "good-bye forever!"

____

2. Something is better than nothing.

____

3. Forget about going to Mars before you graduate! (use *tú*)

____

4. And here ends the never-ending story!

____

5. I know you from somewhere. You must be somebody. (use *Ud.*)

____

6. Do whatever you want! Go wherever you want! I shall never ever forget you! (use *tú*)

____

7. This ending? That ending? I'm happy with either one!

____

8. That's all. Tomorrow is another day!

____

I. Ejercicio oral. Un(a) estudiante de cada pareja afirma algo. El otro contesta haciendo negativa la afirmación. Luego, se hace al inverso: uno dice algo usando palabras o expresiones negativas y el otro contesta con una respuesta afirmativa.

J. Estructuras en acción. Lea el siguiente anuncio que salió en un periódico mexicano y haga los ejercicios que se encuentran a continuación.

¿Ha soñado alguna vez con estar en...?

Tierra Santa

Viaje por los Caminos de la Fe.

Salidas mensuales a Galilea, Tiberiades, Nazaret, Belén y Jerusalén.

Desde: 2,199[00] dólares.

Incluye transportación aérea, hoteles de primera, guía en español, desayunos y cenas en todo el recorrido. Seguro de gastos médicos y maletín de viaje. No incluye impuestos aéreos.

Extensión opcional:

Audiencia Papal, Roma, Asís y Florencia. Desde 600 dólares.

Consulte a su Agente de Viajes o llame al 564-5354, 564-5364, 564-6369.

M.R.T., S.A. de C.V. (Operador mayorista).

Exprese las siguientes frases en inglés.

1. ¿Ha soñado alguna vez con estar en ...?

____

2. Tierra Santa

____

3. Viaje por los Caminos de la Fe.

____

4. Galilea, Tiberíades, Nazaret, Belén, Jerusalén

____

5. Audiencia Papal, Roma, Asís, Florencia

____

Conteste las siguientes preguntas.

6. ¿Cuándo hay salidas a Jerusalén?

____

7. ¿Cómo son los hoteles incluidos?

____

8. ¿Qué idioma habla el/la guía?

____

9. ¿Qué comidas se sirven en todo el viaje?

____

10. ¿Qué cosa no se incluye?

____

11. ¿Cómo se llaman las dos líneas aéreas mencionadas en el anuncio? ¿De qué país es cada una?

____

CHAPTER 25

NUMBERS; DATES; TIME

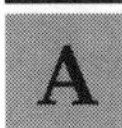

A Cardinal numbers

- Cardinal numbers are used for counting. The Spanish cardinal numbers from 1 to 99 are:

0 cero	10 diez	20 veinte
1 uno (una)	11 once	21 veintiuno (-una)
2 dos	12 doce	22 veintidós
3 tres	13 trece	23 veintitrés
4 cuatro	14 catorce	24 veinticuatro
5 cinco	15 quince	25 veinticinco
6 seis	16 dieciséis	26 veintiséis
7 siete	17 diecisiete	27 veintisiete
8 ocho	18 dieciocho	28 veintiocho
9 nueve	19 diecinueve	29 veintinueve
30 treinta	40 cuarenta	70 setenta
31 treinta y uno (una)	50 cincuenta	80 ochenta
32 treinta y dos	60 sesenta	90 noventa

- Numbers ending in *one* agree in gender with the following noun. **Uno** shortens to **un** before a masculine noun. The number **veintiún** has a written accent in the masculine:

  veintiún libros *21 books*
  veintiuna revistas *21 magazines*
  cincuenta y un estudiantes *51 students*
  cincuenta y una profesoras *51 female teachers*

- **Una** also shortens to **un** before a noun beginning with a stressed **a** sound:

  un águila *one eagle*
  veintiún aulas *21 lecture halls*
  cuarenta y un hachas *41 axes*

- Numbers ending in **uno** are used in counting and when no masculine noun follows directly:

  —¿Cuánto es? ¿Treinta y dos pesos? *How much is it? 32 pesos?*
  —No, treinta y uno. *No, 31.*

- The numbers from 16 to 19 and from 21 to 29 can be written as three words: **diez y seis, diez y siete, diez y ocho, diez y nueve, veinte y uno (una), veinte y dos, veinte y tres**, etc. No accent marks are used when these numbers are spelled as three words. Compare **veintis*é*is** and **veinte y seis**.

- The Spanish numbers from 100 to 999 are:

100	cien	400	cuatrocientos/cuatrocientas
101	ciento uno (una)	500	quinientos/quinientas
110	ciento diez	600	seiscientos/seiscientas
167	ciento sesenta y siete	700	setecientos/setecientas
200	doscientos/doscientas	800	ochocientos/ochocientas
300	trescientos/trescientas	900	novecientos/novecientas

Notes:

1. **Cien** becomes **ciento** before another number: **ciento sesenta** *160.*
2. Spanish does not use **y** to connect hundreds to the following number the way English may use *and*: *two hundred **and** forty* **doscientos cuarenta**.
3. The hundreds from 200 to 900 agree in gender with the noun they modify. This agreement takes place even when other numbers come between the hundreds and the noun.

doscient**os** edificios	*two hundred buildings*
doscient**as** casas	*two hundred houses*
doscient**as** treinta y cuatro casas	*two hundred thirty-four houses*

- Numbers above 1,000:

1.000	mil	100.000	cien mil
2.000	dos mil	250.000	doscientos cincuenta mil
6.572	seis mil quinientos setenta y dos	1.000.000	un millón
10.000	diez mil	2.000.000	dos millones

Notes:

1. Numerals ending in **-cientos** agree across the word **mil**: seiscient**as** cincuenta mil pesetas.
2. Spanish uses the period to separate thousands in writing numbers and the comma as a decimal point: $7.560 = **siete mil quinientos sesenta dólares;** $7,50 = **siete dólares cincuenta centavos**.
3. Spanish does not count by hundreds above 1,000. Thus, *seventeen hundred* must be rendered **mil setecientos**; *thirty-two hundred* as **tres mil doscientos.**
4. **Millón** is a noun and is followed by **de** before a noun unless another number comes between **millón** and the following noun: **un millón de pesos; dos millones de pesos; un millón doscientos mil pesos**.
5. *A billion* in Spanish is **mil millones. Un billón** means *a trillion.*
6. The word **o** *or* is written **ó** between figures to avoid confusion with zero: **5 ó 6.**

A. Para hacer un inventario. Ud. trabaja de empleado de tiempo parcial en una papelería. Hoy le toca hacer el inventario de las existencias (*stock*). Ponga en la lista la cantidad de cada cosa que encuentra, escribiendo el número en letras.

La papelería

la agenda de entrevistas *appointment book*
el bloc de papel *writing pad*
el bolígrafo *ballpoint pen*
la caja *box*
el calendario *calendar*
la etiqueta *label*
las existencias *stock*
la goma *rubber band*
la goma de borrar *eraser*
la grapa *staple*
la grapadora *stapler*
hacer un inventario *to take inventory*
el papel de escribir *stationery*
el pegamento *glue*
el rotulador *felt-tip pen*
el sobre *envelope*
los sujetalibros *bookends*
los sujetapapeles *paper clips*
el taco *writing pad (Spain)*
tiempo parcial *part-time*
tiempo completo *full-time*
el tubo *tube*

MODELO gomas de borrar/386
→ trescientas ochenta y seis gomas de borrar

1. grapadoras/100

____

2. tacos/1.821

____

3. rotuladores y bolígrafos/1.549

____

4. cajas de gomas, grapas y sujetapapeles/751

____

5. cajas de papel de escribir y sobres/467

____

6. agendas de entrevistas y calendarios/909

____

7. tubos de pegamento y etiquetas/1.000

____

8. los sujetalibros de metal y de plástico/1.381

____

Nota cultural

Hay palabras españolas cuyo significado varía mucho de un país a otro. Por ejemplo, en España, **el taco** es un bloc de papel o un librito de billetes de metro. Siendo una palabra de múltiples significados, también significa un pedazo de madera o comida, un bocado ligero, un trago de vino, un calendario trepado (*tear-off*), un lío, una palabrota, etcétera. En ciertos países de Hispanoamérica, **el taco** es una tortilla rellena o un tacón de zapato. En Chile, es una persona rechoncha (gruesa y baja). En Centroamérica significa una preocupación o un temor. A pesar de las diferencias de vocabulario, todos los hispanos de todos los países de habla española se entienden debido a la unidad fundamental del idioma.

B. El censo: población de países. Ud. se encarga de escribir el número de habitantes de los siguientes países hispánicos, según su último censo de 1990 ó 1992.

1. Argentina: 32.901.000

____

2. Colombia: 34.296.000

____

3. Chile: 13.528.000

____

4. Ecuador: 10.933.000

____

5. España: 39.118.000

____

6. México: 92.380.000

____

B *Ordinal numbers*

- Ordinal numbers are used for ranking (*first, second, etc.*). In conversation, usually only the ordinal numbers through *tenth* are used in Spanish. Spanish ordinal numbers are adjectives that agree with the noun they modify in gender and number:

primero *first*	sexto *sixth*
segundo *second*	séptimo *seventh*
tercero *third*	octavo *eighth*
cuarto *fourth*	noveno *ninth*
quinto *fifth*	décimo *tenth*

- Ordinal numbers usually precede the noun. **Primero** and **tercero** become **primer** and **tercer** before a masculine singular noun:

el **primer** día *the first day*	el **tercer** capítulo *the third chapter*
la **segunda** hija *the second daughter*	la **séptima** casa *the seventh house*

- Ordinals often follow nouns such as **siglo** and the names of kings and queens:

  el siglo segundo *the second century* Carlos Quinto *Charles the Fifth*

- Above *tenth,* Spanish generally uses the cardinal numbers after the noun instead of the ordinals. Sometimes the cardinal numbers are used even below *tenth*:

  Vive en el piso quince. *He lives on the fifteenth floor.*
  Vamos a leer el capítulo tres. *We're going to read the third chapter.*

- Ordinals are abbreviated in various ways in Spanish: 1er, 1^{era}, 1°, 2^{a}, 3ro, 5to, 7ma, 8°.

C. **¡Todos juntos en los Estados Unidos!** Alberto y un grupo de amigos chilenos están en los Estados Unidos para estudiar inglés durante el verano. Y todos viven en la misma residencia. Alberto les escribe a sus padres y les dice en qué piso está cada uno de los amigos.

Modelo Ramón/6
➔ Ramón vive en el sexto piso.

1. Silvia y Adela/12
____
2. Carlos/5
____
3. yo/1
____
4. Margarita/9
____
5. Ana María/10
____
6. Patricio/4
____
7. Lucía/3
____
8. Daniela/14
____

C *Days, dates, and years*

- The days of the week and the months of the year are not capitalized in Spanish. Note that the Hispanic week begins with Monday:

Days of the Week

lunes *Monday*
martes *Tuesday*
miércoles *Wednesday*
jueves *Thursday*
viernes *Friday*
sábado *Saturday*
domingo *Sunday*

Months of the Year

enero *January*	mayo *May*	septiembre *September*
febrero *February*	junio *June*	octubre *October*
marzo *March*	julio *July*	noviembre *November*
abril *April*	agosto *August*	diciembre *December*

Seasons

la primavera *spring*	el otoño *fall, autumn*
el verano *summer*	el invierno *winter*

- In Spanish there are several patterns for using the above words in expressions of time:

  1. The singular definite article **el** means *on* before the days of the week.

     Nos vamos **el** lunes. *We're leaving on Monday.*

  2. The plural definite article **los** indicates repeated action or regular occurrence.

     Van a la iglesia **los** domingos. *They go to church on Sundays.*

  3. The preposition **en** is used before months of the year and the names of the seasons: **en enero, en otoño**. The definite article is sometimes used after **en** with the names of the seasons: **en la primavera**.

- To express dates, Spanish uses cardinal numbers, except for **el primero** (some speakers say **el uno**). The definite article **el** precedes the date. The order is day-month-year and the preposition **de** is placed before the month and also the year, if it is given. Note that as with days of the week, no preposition is used for *on*.

  —Creía que tus primos llegaban el treinta de noviembre. *I thought your cousins were arriving on November thirtieth.*
  —No, vienen el primero de diciembre. *No, they're coming December first.*

Notes:

1. The definite article **el** in dates is usually left out after the day of the week: **martes, 5 de mayo**.
2. When abbreviating dates, the Spanish order day-month-year is used. Roman numerals are often used for the month: **25-VIII-44,** el veinticinco de agosto de mil novecientos cuarenta y cuatro.
3. As in English, the last two numbers are often used in speech to express the years of the present century. In this case the definite article **el** precedes the year:

   Llegamos en el setenta y dos. *We arrived in '72.*

Some useful expressions for talking about the days and dates or that use the days and months in idiomatic ways:

¿Cuál es la fecha de hoy?	*What's today's date?*
¿A cuánto estamos hoy?	*What's today's date?*
Es el primero de junio.	*It's June first.*
Estamos a diez de octubre.	*It's October tenth.*
¿Qué día es hoy?	*What day is today?*
Hoy es jueves.	*Today is Thursday.*
pasando un día, un día de por medio	*every other day*
a principios de marzo	*toward the beginning of March*
a mediados de julio	*toward the middle of July*
a finales de septiembre	*toward the end of September*
No es cosa del otro jueves.	*It's nothing special.*
martes trece	*Tuesday the 13th (equivalent of Friday the 13th)*

D. El premio Nobel. Diez escritores hispánicos han recibido el premio Nobel en literatura desde que el premio se comenzó a otorgar (*award*) en 1901. Aquí tiene Ud. una lista de cinco de los galardonados (*prize winners*) con el año del premio y las fechas de nacimiento y muerte. Escriba estos números en letras.

1. Octavio Paz (México)

   premio Nobel: 1990 ______________________________

   nacimiento: 1914 ______________________________

2. Camilo José Cela (España)

   premio Nobel: 1989 ______________________________

   nacimiento: 1916 ______________________________

3. Gabriel García Márquez (Colombia)

   premio Nobel: 1982 ______________________________

   nacimiento: 1928 ______________________________

4. Vicente Aleixandre (España)

   premio Nobel: 1977 ______________________________

   nacimiento: 1898 ______________________________

   muerte: 1984 ______________________________

5. Pablo Neruda (Chile)

   premio Nobel: 1971 ______________________________

   nacimiento: 1904 ______________________________

   muerte: 1973 ______________________________

E. ¡Qué desastre! A lo largo de los años ha habido huracanes originando en el Caribe que han hecho mucho daño. Aquí tiene Ud. una lista de algunos huracanes con su año y el número de muertos que causaron. Escriba los números en letras.

1. *Nombre del huracán: Celia*
   País, región o estado: Cuba, la Florida, Tejas

   Fecha: 30/VII–5/VIII/1970 ______________________________

   Causó (31) ______________________________ muertos.

2. *Nombre del huracán: Fifi*
   País, región o estado: Honduras

   Fecha: 19–20/IX/1974 ______________________________

   Causó (2.000) ______________________________ muertos.

3. *Nombre del huracán: Gilbert*
   País, región o estado: Caribe, Golfo de México

   Fecha: 10–17/IX/1988 ______________________________

   Causó (260) ______________________________ muertos.

4. *Nombre del huracán: Andrew*
   País, región o estado: la Florida, Luisiana
   Fecha: 24–26/VIII/1992 ______________________________
   Causó (14) ______________________________ muertos.

D *Telling time*

- All times begin with **Son las**, except for **Es la una** (*It's one o'clock*). To ask the time say, **¿Qué hora es?** In Spanish America **¿Qué horas son?** is very common.

  Son las tres. *It's three o'clock.*
  Son las tres y diez. *It's ten after three.*
  Son las tres y cuarto/y quince. *It's a quarter after three./It's three fifteen.*
  Son las tres y media/y treinta. *It's three thirty.*
  Son las cuatro menos veinte. *It's twenty to four.*
  Son las cuatro menos cuarto/menos quince. *It's a quarter to four.*

- An alternative system for expressing the times between the half hour and the following hour is very common in Spanish America. The verbs used are **faltar** and **ser**:

  Faltan/Son quince (minutos) para las cuatro. *It's a quarter to four.*
  Falta/Es un cuarto para las cuatro. *It's a quarter to four.*

- The equivalents of English A.M. and P.M. in Spanish are the phrases **de la mañana, de la tarde, de la noche** added to the expression of time. Spanish-Americans often use A.M. and P.M. as in English. For noon and midnight, people say **Son las doce del día, Son las doce de la noche** or **Es mediodía, Es medianoche.**

  Son las diez de la mañana. *It's 10 A.M.*
  Son las seis de la tarde. *It's 6 P.M.*
  Son las once y media de la noche. *It's 11:30 P.M.*

- To express time, Spanish uses the preposition **a**:

  A las ocho de la mañana. *At 8 A.M.*
  A veinte para las siete. *At twenty to seven.*

- In Spanish-speaking countries, a 24-hour clock is used for official purposes: train and plane schedules, show times. In the 24-hour clock, the minutes past the hour are counted from 1 to 59. **Cuarto** and **media** are replaced by **quince, treinta,** and **cuarenta y cinco**; and the phrases **de la mañana, de la tarde, de la noche** are not used.

  Mi avión sale a las **trece treinta.** *My plane leaves at one thirty P.M.*
  La película es a las **veinte cuarenta.** *The film is at 8:40 P.M.*

- The word **horas** often appears when using the 24-hour clock:

  El programa es a las dieciocho horas. *The program is at 6 P.M.*

Some useful expressions for talking about the time of day:

Son las seis en punto.	*It's six o'clock sharp.*
Es tarde./Es temprano.	*It's late./It's early.*
Se levanta tarde/temprano.	*He gets up late/early.*
Siento llegar tarde.	*I'm sorry to be late.*
Llego con anticipación.	*I'm early.*
Llego puntualmente.	*I'm on time.*
Mi reloj está adelantado/retrasado.	*My watch is fast/slow.*
Son las tres pasadas.	*It's after three, past three.*
ser madrugador(a)	*to be an early riser*
pegársele a uno las sábanas	*to sleep late, sleep in*

F. En el tren turístico. La Renfe, la sociedad nacional de trenes españoles, ofrece al público viajes turísticos en tren desde Madrid a los lugares históricos más importantes de España. Lea el programa de esta excursión de dos días a las tierras del Cid en Castilla la Vieja y conteste las preguntas con la hora oficial.

ren tierras del Cid.

Burgos. Tierra del Campeador. Punto de encuentro de Románico y Gótico. Punto de encuentro con el arte Medieval. Con el tren Tierras del Cid conócela a fondo. Recorre Covarrubias, Silos y La Yecla. Sal a su encuentro.

PROGRAMA

Sábado

07:30 h.- Recepción de viajeros en el punto de información de la estación de Madrid Chamartín.

08:00 h.- Salida hacia Burgos.

11:36 h.- Llegada a Burgos. Traslado en autocar a Covarrubias, visita a la Colegiata. Tiempo libre para almorzar.

16:00 h.- Salida en autocar para visitar Santo Domingo de Silos y la Yecla.

20:00 h.- Llegada a Burgos. Traslado al hotel. Tiempo libre.

21:30 h.- Saludo del Ayuntamiento en el antiguo Monasterio de San Juan. Vino, aperitivos y actuaciones folklóricas. Elección de la madrina del tren.

Domingo

09:30 h.- Desayuno en el hotel.

10:30 h.- Salida en autocar para visitar el Monasterio de las Huelgas. San Pedro de Cardeña (posibilidad de oír Misa) y Cartuja.

14:00 h.- Tiempo libre para el almuerzo.

16:30 h.- Concentración en la puerta de la Catedral para visitarla. Traslado en autocar a la estación de ferrocarril.

18:39 h.- Salida de la estación de Burgos hacia Madrid.

21:55 h.- Llegada a Madrid Chamartín. Fín de viaje.

MODELO ¿Cuándo es la salida en autocar a Santo Domingo de Silos?
→ El sábado a las dieciséis horas.

1. ¿Cuándo se reúnen los viajeros para empezar la excursión?
____
2. ¿Cuándo se llega a Burgos?
____
3. ¿Cuándo es el saludo del Ayuntamiento?
____
4. ¿Cuándo salen para visitar el Monasterio de las Huelgas?
____
5. ¿Cuándo es el almuerzo el domingo?
____
6. ¿Cuándo es la visita de la Catedral de Burgos?
____
7. ¿Cuándo sale el tren de Burgos a Madrid?
____

Nota cultural

- **Tierra del Cid Campeador.** Rodrigo Díaz nació en Vivar, a nueve kilómetros de Burgos, en 1026 y murió en 1099. Dado el título Cid (*señor*) por los musulmanes, fue el héroe de la Reconquista (los cristianos españoles lucharon por retomar la Península de los musulmanes). Fue un personaje semihistórico cuya fama aumentó a través de poemas como **El Cantar del Mío Cid,** escrito hacia 1180. Las hazañas (*deeds*) de este caballero castellano que luchó fielmente por su rey (Sancho II, luego su hermano Alfonso VI), marcan la historia de Castilla de finales del siglo XI.

- **Burgos,** capital de la provincia de Burgos, tiene la tercera catedral española por sus dimensiones. En este magnífico edificio gótico se encuentran los restos del Cid Campeador y de su esposa doña Jimena.

E *Arithmetic operations, fractions, percentages*

- The basic arithmetic operations are read as follows in Spanish:

$15 + 12 = 27$	quince **más** doce **son/es igual a** veintisiete
$40 - 24 = 16$	cuarenta **menos** veinticuatro **son/es igual a** dieciséis
$10 \times 15 = 150$	diez **por** quince **son/es igual a** ciento cincuenta
$120 \div 12 = 10$	ciento veinte **dividido por** doce **son/es igual a** diez

For division, the preposition **entre** is also used: **ciento veinte entre doce son diez.**

- Except for **un medio** (*one half*) and **un tercio** (*one third*), fractions have the same form as masculine ordinal numbers:

un cuarto *one-fourth*
tres quintos *three-fifths*

- Above one-tenth, the suffix **-avo** is added to the cardinal number to form the corresponding fraction: **un onceavo** (*one-eleventh*), **tres veinteavos** (*three-twentieths*).

  Note also **un centavo** or **un centésimo** (*one-hundredth*) and **un milésimo** (*one-thousandth*).

- Percentages in Spanish usually have an article (either **un** or **el**) before the figure:

Dan un veinte por ciento de descuento.	*They give a twenty percent discount.*
El diez por ciento de la población habla español.	*Ten percent of the population speaks Spanish.*

The words for mathematical operations are:

sumar *to add*	el quebrado *fraction*
restar *to subtract*	por ciento *percent*
multiplicar *to multiply*	el porcentaje *percentage*
dividir *to divide*	

G. Operaciones matemáticas. Ayude a un amigo hispano que no habla inglés a resolver estos problemas. Primero, escriba los problemas con números y luego resuélvalos.

1. ciento setenta y cuatro más ochenta y nueve son ______
2. seiscientos tres menos doscientos ochenta y uno son ______
3. cuarenta y nueve por cinco son ______
4. mil doscientos ochenta y cuatro dividido por cuatro son ______
5. tres cuartos de ochenta son ______
6. Juan ganó $15.000 en la lotería. Tiene que pagar un 30% de impuestos. ¿Cuánto tiene que pagar de impuestos? ______

Nota cultural

- **El álgebra** fue introducida en Europa hacia 950 por los árabes que la aprendieron de los griegos. El tratado de álgebra más antiguo fue escrito por el griego Diofante de Alejandría.

- **Álgebra** es una de las 4.000 palabras que entraron en el español del árabe a través de ocho siglos de dominación árabe en la Península. Por medio del español muchas de estas palabras han pasado a las otras lenguas europeas. Otras palabras traídas por los árabes en el campo de las matemáticas incluyen: **cero, cifra, cenit.**

H. Ejercicio oral. ¿Cuál es la fecha? Dos equipos tratan de ganar puntos identificando importantes acontecimientos en la historia, como por ejemplo: Colón descubre América: el doce de octubre de mil cuatrocientos noventa y dos; Pearl Harbor atacado por los japoneses: el siete de diciembre de mil novecientos cuarenta y uno, etcétera.

PART FOUR

Idiomatic Usage

CHAPTER 26

IDIOMS, EXPRESSIONS, & PROVERBS

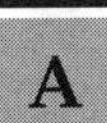

A Idioms and expressions with **tener**

tener ángel/mal ángel	*to be charming/lack charm*
tener buena/mala estrella	*to be lucky/unlucky*
tener calor/frío	*to be warm/cold*
tener corazón de piedra	*to be hard-hearted*
tener cuidado	*to be careful*
tener dolor de cabeza/estómago	*to have a headache, stomachache*
tener en la punta de la lengua	*to have on the tip of one's tongue*
tener éxito	*to be successful*
tener ganas de	*to feel like*
tener hambre/sed	*to be hungry/thirsty*
tener inconveniente	*to mind, object to*
tener la culpa de	*to be to blame for*
tener la palabra	*to have the floor*
tener la razón de su parte	*to be in the right*
tener líos	*to have difficulties*
tener los huesos molidos	*to be exhausted*
tener los nervios de punta	*to have one's nerves on edge*
tener lugar	*to take place*
tener madera para	*to be cut out for, made for*
tener mala cara	*to look bad*
tener malas pulgas	*to be short-tempered*
tener miedo de	*to be afraid of*
tener mundo	*to be sophisticated, know how to act in society*
tener ojo de buen cubero (*cooper*)	*to have a sure, accurate eye*
tener ojos de lince	*to have (sharp) eyes like a hawk* (literally, *lynx*)
tener pájaros en la cabeza	*to have bats in the belfry*
tener palabra	*to keep one's word*
tener por	*to consider someone to be*
tener prisa	*to be in a hurry*
tener que ver con	*to have to do with*
tener razón	*to be right*
tener sueño	*to be sleepy*
tener suerte	*to be lucky*
tener un disgusto	*to have a falling out*
tener vergüenza de	*to be ashamed of*
no tener arreglo	*not to be able to be helped*
no tener donde caerse muerto	*not to have a penny to one's name*
no tener nombre	*to be unspeakable*
no tener pelo de tonto	*to be nobody's fool*
no tener pelos en la lengua	*to be very outspoken*
no tener pies ni cabeza	*to not make any sense, have no rhyme or reason*

A. **Tener.** Complete cada oración con una expresión o un modismo con **tener** como reacción lógica a la escrita. Puede haber más de una expresión en algunos casos. Escriba las dos.

1. A Manolo le dieron un ascenso en la empresa y le dieron un aumento de sueldo también.

   Tuvo ______________________________.
2. Yo no comprendo nada de este libro.

   Para mí, el libro no tiene ______________________________.
3. El nombre del actor es …

   ¡Caramba! Lo tengo ______________________________.
4. Este niño es muy listo.

   ¿Verdad que no tiene ______________________________?
5. Pablo corrió tanto que ni puede levantarse por cansado.

   El chico tiene ______________________________.
6. Carmen ganó el premio gordo de la lotería.

   Esta señorita tiene ______________________________.
7. Rebeca siempre está molesta y se queja de todo.

   Ella tiene ______________________________.
8. El detective Sierra lo ve todo. No se le pierde nada.

   En efecto. Él tiene ______________________________.
9. Álvaro se ve mal y está nerviosísimo.

   El pobre chico tiene ________________ y tiene ________________.
10. Los padres de Gonzalito se sienten avergonzados porque su hijo siempre causa problemas en el colegio.

    Los señores tienen ________________ porque Gonzalito tiene muchos ________________ en el colegio.

B *Idioms and expressions with* ***tomar***

tomar algo a bien/a mal	*to take something well/badly*
tomar a broma/risa	*to take as a joke*
tomar a pecho	*to take to heart*
tomar aliento	*to catch one's breath*
tomar en serio	*to take seriously*
tomar la palabra	*to take the floor*
tomar partido por	*to side with*
tomar la delantera	*to get ahead of*
tomarle el pelo	*to pull someone's leg*
tomárselo con calma	*to take it easy*

B. Tomar. Escriba una paráfrasis de cada oración empleando una expresión con **tomar.**

1. Amparo lo aceptó tranquilamente.

___

2. Los García se pusieron tristes por la muerte del vecino.

___

3. Pedro se rió viendo las diablura de su hijo.

___

4. La profesora se enojó por lo que le dijo Marianela.

___

5. Paco apoyó a Juan Carlos en la discusión.

___

C *Idioms and expressions with* **estar**

está despejado/claro	*it's clear*
está nublado	*it's cloudy*
estar a sus anchas	*to be comfortable*
estar calado/mojado hasta los huesos	*to be soaked to the skin*
estar como el pez en el agua	*to be right at home*
estar con el alma en un hilo/en vilo	*to be in suspense*
estar de más/de sobra	*to be in excess*
estar en condiciones	*to be in good shape, be able (to do something)*
estar en la luna	*to have one's head in the clouds*
estar en las nubes	*to be in the clouds, daydreaming*
estar fuera de sí	*to be beside oneself emotionally (positive and negative)*
estar hecho polvo	*to get worn out*
estar hecho una fiera	*to get furious*
estar hecho una sopa	*to get soaked*
estar loco de atar/de remate	*to be completely crazy*
estar sin blanca	*to be flat broke*

C. Estar. Escriba una expresión con **estar** que sea sinónimo de la escrita.

1. cansarse ___
2. mojarse ___
3. no tener dinero ___
4. ponerse furioso ___
5. sentirse cómodo ___

D Idioms and expressions with **echar**

echar a perder	*to ruin, spoil*
echar chispas	*to be furious, get angry*
echar de menos	*to miss*
echar flores	*to flatter, sweet-talk*
echar la bronca a uno	*to give someone a dressing down*
echar la culpa	*to blame*
echarse a	*to start to*
echárselas de	*to fancy oneself as, boast of being*

D. ¿Qué le pasó a don Juan? Complete cada oración usando una de las expresiones con **echar.**

1. Lorenzo le dijo a Beti que la echaba ____________________ cuando ella estaba de vacaciones.
2. Al mismo tiempo, Lorenzo echaba ____________________ a Marisol y a Gloria.
3. Lorenzo ____________________ de ser don Juan.
4. Al volver, Beti se enteró de la situación y echó ____________________.
5. Beti le echó ____________________ a Lorenzo y rompió con él.

E Idioms and expressions with **dar**

dar a	*to face*
dar a luz un niño	*to give birth*
dar asco	*to disgust*
dar calabazas	*to jilt; to flunk*
dar carta blanca a uno	*to give someone a free hand, carte blanche*
dar cuerda a	*to wind*
dar con	*to find; run into*
dar de comer/beber	*to feed/give a drink to*
dar el golpe de gracia	*to finish someone off, give the coup de grâce*
dar gritos	*to shout*
dar guerra	*to cause, make trouble*
dar la hora	*to strike the hour*
dar la lata	*to make a nuisance of oneself*
dar las gracias	*to thank*
dar por sentado	*to take for granted; regard as settled*
dar rienda suelta a	*to give free rein to*
dar un abrazo	*to hug, embrace*
dar un paseo	*to take a walk, ride*

dar una vuelta	*to take a walk, ride*
dar vueltas a algo	*to think something over, thoroughly examine*
darse cuenta de	*to realize*
darse la mano	*to shake hands*
darse por vencido	*to give up*
darse prisa	*to hurry*

E. **¿Qué se dio en cada caso?** Complete cada oración usando una de las expresiones con **dar**.

1. Paquita era tan molesta y mal criada. Ella daba ______________________.
2. Los soldados dejaron de luchar. Se dieron ______________________.
3. Los soldados ultimaron a sus enemigos. Les dieron ______________________.
4. No deje que los chicos hagan esas cosas. No les dé ______________________.
5. Creo que ya tomamos la decisión. Di el asunto ______________________.

F *Idioms and expressions with* ***hacer***

hace + time expression + preterit	*ago*
hace buen/mal tiempo	*it's good/bad weather*
hace calor/frío	*it's warm/cold*
hace viento	*it's windy*
hacer caso	*to pay attention, heed*
hacer (buenas) migas	*to hit it off with someone*
hacer de las suyas	*to be up to one's old tricks*
hacer un papel	*to play a role*
hacer juego	*to match*
hacer la vista gorda	*to turn a blind eye, pretend not to notice*
hacer las paces	*to make peace*
hacer época	*to be sensational, attract public attention*
hacer pedazos (añicos)	*to break to pieces*
hacer su agosto	*to make a killing*
hacer un viaje	*to take a trip*
hacerse + profession, status, etc.	*to become*
hacerse daño	*to hurt oneself*
hacerse tarde	*to become late*
hacérsele agua la boca	*to make someone's mouth water*

F. **¿Qué quieren hacer?** Complete cada oración usando una de las expresiones con **hacer.**

1. dos amigos que se han peleado

   Quieren ______________________________.

2. una persona que estudia la Bolsa e invierte mucho dinero

 Quiere ______________________________.

3. una actriz que no ha trabajado en una película exitosa

 Quiere ______________________________.

4. unos padres que tienen vergüenza de las diabluras de sus hijos

 Quieren ______________________________.

5. un niñito travieso que ha tratado de portarse bien

 Quiere ______________________________.

G *Idioms and expressions with* ***ir, llevar,*** *and* ***quedar***

Ir

ir al grano	*to go straight to the point*
ir de juerga	*to be out on a spree*
ir sobre ruedas	*to run smoothly*
ir tirando	*to get by*

Llevar

llevar a cabo	*to carry out*
llevar la contraria	*to take an opposite point of view, contradict*
llevar leña al monte	*to carry coals to Newcastle*
llevarse como el perro y el gato	*to be always squabbling*
llevarse un chasco	*to be disappointed*

Quedar

quedar boquiabierto	*to be left agape in bewilderment*
quedarse con	*to keep*
quedarse con el día y la noche	*to be left penniless*
quedarse de una pieza	*to be dumbfounded*
quedar en	*to agree on*
quedarse sin blanca	*to be flat broke, to go broke*

G. Ir, llevar, quedar. Reescriba las oraciones con uno de los modismos de esta sección.

1. El proyecto está progresando sin problemas.

 El proyecto ______________________________.

2. Nos pusimos de acuerdo para vernos delante del cine.

 ______________________________ vernos delante del cine.

3. No me gusta ir a su casa. Siempre están discutiendo.
   No me gusta ir a su casa. ______________________.
4. Si viniste a ver a Micaela, vas a quedar sin satisfacción. Ella no está.
   Si viniste a ver a Micaela, vas a ______________________. Ella no está.
5. Es difícil hablar con Alfonso. Nunca está de acuerdo con nadie.
   Es difícil hablar con Alfonso. Siempre ______________________.
6. No sé si vamos a poder realizar este plan.
   No sé si vamos a poder ______________________ este plan.
7. Cuando me dijo eso, no pude hacer nada más que mirarlo en silencio.
   Cuando me dijo eso, ______________________.
8. El negocio del señor Ortega quebró y su familia quedó sin un centavo.
   El negocio del señor Ortega quebró y su familia ______________________.

H *Idioms and expressions with* ***meter*** *and* ***poner***

Meter

meter la pata	*to put one's foot in one's mouth*
meter las narices	*to snoop around*
meterse en donde no le llaman	*to meddle, snoop around*
meterse en la boca del lobo	*to enter the lion's den*
meterse en un callejón sin salida	*to get into a jam*

Poner

poner en ridículo	*to make look ridiculous*
poner las cartas sobre la mesa	*to put one's cards on the table*
poner los puntos sobre las íes	*to dot the i's and cross the t's*
poner a alguien por las nubes	*to heap praise on someone*
poner pleito	*to sue*
ponérsele a uno la carne de gallina	*to get goose pimples*
ponérsele los cabellos/los pelos de punta	*to have one's hair stand on end, be terrified*

H. Definiciones. Escriba al lado de cada definición la letra del modismo que le corresponda.

Definiciones

_____ 1. entrar en un lugar peligroso

_____ 2. llevar ante el juez, al tribunal

_____ 3. sentir mucho miedo

_____ 4. decir o hacer algo inapropiado y ofensivo

_____ 5. sentir pánico

_____ 6. buscarse un problema que no tiene solución

_____ 7. explicar las cosas para que no haya dudas

_____ 8. alabar a alguien con entusiasmo

Modismos

a. meterse en un callejón sin salida
b. meter la pata
c. poner en ridículo
d. meterse en la boca del lobo
e. poner pleito
f. ponérsele a uno la carne de gallina
g. poner por las nubes
h. poner las cartas sobre la mesa
i. ponérsele los cabellos, los pelos de punta
j. poner los puntos sobre las íes
k. meterse en donde no le llaman

I *Idioms and expressions with* ***ser***

ser de buena pasta	*to be a good guy, have a nice disposition*
ser de película	*to be sensational*
ser de poca monta	*to be of little value*
ser el colmo	*to be the limit*
ser harina de otro costal	*to be a horse of a different color*
ser el ojo derecho	*to be someone's pet*
ser la flor y nata	*to be the cream/best*
ser otro cantar	*to be a horse of a different color*
ser pan comido	*to be as easy as pie*
ser para chuparse los dedos	*to taste delicious*
ser todo oídos	*to be all ears*
ser un cero a la izquierda	*to be of no value, count for nothing (a person)*
ser un mirlo (*blackbird*) blanco	*to be an impossible dream*
ser una lata	*to be annoying*
ser una perla	*to be a jewel, treasure*
ser uña y carne	*to be close as can be*
no ser cosa del otro jueves	*to be nothing out of the ordinary*

I. **¿Cuál es?** Indique cuál de los modismos con **ser** significa lo mismo que la oración priincipal.

1. Ya has llegado al límite.
   a. Esto es pan comido.
   b. Esto es un mirlo blanco.
   c. Esto es el colmo.
2. Esta situación me fastidia mucho.
   a. Es una lata.
   b. Es de película.
   c. Es otro cantar.
3. Esas dos chicas son muy buenas amigas. Siempre están juntas.
   a. Son la flor y la nata.
   b. Son de buena pasta.
   c. Son uña y carne.
4. Lo que me dices ahora es algo totalmente distinto.
   a. Es una perla.
   b. Es harina de otro costal.
   c. Es de poca monta.
5. Este flan está riquísimo.
   a. Es todo oídos.
   b. Es para chuparse los dedos.
   c. Es un cero a la izquierda.

J *Otras expresiones verbales*

andar de boca en boca	*to be generally known*
andarse por las ramas	*to beat around the bush*
armarse un escándalo	*to cause a row*
buscar tres pies al gato	*to split hairs*
no caber en sí/su piel	*to be beside oneself with joy, anger, etc.; to be presumptuous*
caerse el alma a los pies	*to be down in the dumps*
consultar con la almohada	*to sleep on it*
decirle cuatro verdades	*to tell someone a thing or two*
no decir ni pío	*not to say a word*
dejar caer	*to drop*
dejar de + infinitive	*to stop (doing something)*
dejar plantado	*to stand up*
no dejar piedra por (sin) mover	*to leave no stone unturned*
dorar la píldora	*to sugarcoat something*
dormir a pierna suelta	*to sleep like a log*
dormir la mona	*to sleep off a hangover*
dormirse en/sobre los laureles	*to rest on one's laurels*
faltarle a uno un tornillo	*to have a screw loose*
hablar hasta por los codos	*to talk incessantly*
llamar al pan pan y al vino vino	*to call a spade a spade*
mandar a freír espárragos	*to tell someone to go jump in the lake/go fly a kite*
matar la gallina de los huevos de oro	*to kill the goose that lays the golden eggs*
matar dos pájaros de un tiro	*to kill two birds with one stone*

no importar un bledo/un comino/un pepino	*to not give a damn about*
pasar las de Caín	*to go through hell*
pedir peras al olmo	*to expect the impossible*
no pegar ojo en toda la noche	*to not sleep a wink all night*
quemarse las cejas	*to burn the midnight oil*
querer decir	*to mean*
no saber a qué carta quedarse	*to be unable to make up one's mind*
sacar/salir a luz	*to publish*
sacar en limpio/en claro	*to make clear*
salirse con la suya	*to get one's own way*
saltar a la vista	*to be obvious*
tocar en lo vivo	*to hurt deeply*
tragarse la píldora	*to be taken in, swallow a lie*
valer la pena	*to be worthwhile*
valer un mundo/un ojo de la cara/un Potosí	*to be worth a fortune*
venir de perlas	*to be just the thing, just right*
verlo todo color de rosa	*to see life through rose-tinted glasses*
verlo todo negro	*to be pessimistic*
no poder verlo ni en pintura	*to not be able to stand the sight of someone*
volver a las andadas	*to go back to one's old ways*
volver en sí	*to regain consciousness*

J. Sinónimos. Escoja en la columna B un sinónimo para cada modismo de la columna A.

A

_____ 1. llamar al pan pan y al vino vino
_____ 2. costar un ojo de la cara
_____ 3. dormir a pierna suelta
_____ 4. faltarle un tornillo
_____ 5. no decir ni pío
_____ 6. pedir peras al olmo
_____ 7. saltar a la vista
_____ 8. andarse por las ramas

B

a. ser evidente
b. buscar tres pies al gato
c. dormir profundamente
d. no abrir la boca
e. exigir lo imposible
f. llamar las cosas por su nombre
g. no ir al grano
h. valer un Potosí
i. no estar completamente bien de la cabeza
j. volver en sí

K. **Antónimos.** Escoja en la columna B un antónimo para cada modismo de la columna A.

	A		B
_____	1. andar de boca en boca	a.	comportarse mejor que antes
_____	2. no importarle un bledo	b.	no decir ni pío
_____	3. no pegar ojo	c.	tomar una decisión
_____	4. volver a las andadas	d.	caerse el alma a los pies
_____	5. dejar plantado	e.	preocuparse mucho
_____	6. no saber a qué carta quedarse	f.	ser muy amigo de uno
_____	7. no poder verlo ni en pintura	g.	ser una cosa ignorada de todos
_____	8. hablar hasta por los codos	h.	sacar en limpio
		i.	dormir a pierna suelta
		j.	acudir a la cita

K *Otros modismos*

¡A otro perro con ese hueso!	*Nonsense!, Don't give me that!* (literally, *to another dog with that bone*)
a pedir de boca	*perfectly, smoothly*
como el que más	*as well or better than anyone else*
contra viento y marea	*against all odds* (literally, *against wind and tide*)
dar gato por liebre	*to sell a pig in a poke, take someone in*
de buenas a primeras	*right off the bat*
de carne y hueso	*flesh and blood*
de categoría	*of importance*
de mal en peor	*from bad to worse*
de segunda mano	*second hand*
desde que el mundo es el mundo	*since the world began*
Dios mediante	*God willing*
el qué dirán	*what people say*
entre la espada y la pared	*between the devil and the deep blue sea* (la espada *sword*)
en un abrir y cerrar de ojos	*in the twinkling of an eye*
está chupado/tirado	*it's a piece of cake*
Hay gato encerrado	*There's something fishy*
Hay moros en la costa	*The coast isn't clear, careful.* (literally, *There are Moors on the coast.*)
Más vale cuatro ojos que dos.	*Two heads are better than one.*
¡Ojo!	*Be careful!*
peces gordos	*big shots, important people*
sin más ni más	*without further hesitation*
tocar madera	*to touch wood, to knock on wood*
todo el santo día	*the whole darn day*
Trato hecho.	*It's a deal.*

L. Sinónimos. Escoja en la columna B un sinónimo para cada modismo de la columna A.

A	B
_____ 1. está chupado	a. engañar
_____ 2. el qué dirán	b. existe una cosa que no vemos
_____ 3. dar gato por liebre	c. con mucha rapidez
_____ 4. hay gato encerrado	d. la opinión de los demás
_____ 5. de segunda mano	e. en seguida
_____ 6. en un abrir y cerrar de ojos	f. con gran esfuerzo
_____ 7. de categoría	g. es pan comido
_____ 8. de buenas a primeras	h. entre dos peligros
	i. usado, no nuevo
	j. de mucha importancia

L *Dichos y refranes (Sayings and proverbs)*

A caballo regalado no se le mira el colmillo.	*Don't look a gift horse in the mouth.* (colmillo *canine tooth*)
A lo hecho, pecho.	*It's no use crying over spilled milk.* (literally, *Chest out to what has been done.*)
Al que madruga, Dios le ayuda.	*The early bird catches the worm.* (madrugar *to get up early*)
Antes que te cases, mira lo que haces.	*Look before you leap.*
Aunque la mona se vista de seda, mona se queda.	*You can't make a silk purse out of a sow's ear.* (literally, *Although the she-monkey may dress in silk, she remains a monkey.*)
Cuando a Roma fueres/Allá donde fueres, haz como vieres.	*When in Rome, do as the Romans do.* (Fueres *and* vieres *are old future subjunctive forms.*)
Del dicho al hecho hay gran trecho.	*There's many a slip 'twixt the cup and the lip.* (el trecho *distance*)
De tal palo, tal astilla.	*A chip off the old block.* (el palo *stick;* la astilla *splinter*)
Desgraciado en el juego, afortunado en amores.	*Unlucky in cards, lucky in love.*
Dios los cría y ellos se juntan.	*Birds of a feather flock together.*
El infierno está lleno de buenos propósitos, y el cielo de buenas obras.	*The road to hell is paved with good intentions.*
El sapo a la sapa tiénela por muy guapa.	*Beauty is in the eye of the beholder.* (el sapo *toad;* la sapa *female toad;* tiénela = la tiene)
En tierra de ciegos, el tuerto es rey.	*In the land of the blind, the one-eyed is king.* (tuerto *one-eyed*)
En una hora no se ganó Zamora.	*Rome wasn't built in a day.*
Eso es el cuento de la lechera/Hacer las cuentas de la lechera.	*Don't count your chickens before they've hatched.*
Las paredes oyen.	*Walls have ears.*
Los dineros del sacristán, cantando se vienen y cantando se van.	*Easy come, easy go.* (el sacristán *church sexton*)
Más vale pájaro en mano que ciento volando.	*A bird in the hand is worth two in the bush.*

No es oro todo lo que reluce (brilla).	*All that glitters isn't gold.*
Obras son amores, que no buenas razones.	*Actions speak louder than words.* (razones *speech, talk*)
Ojos que no ven, corazón que no siente.	*Out of sight, out of mind.*
Poderoso caballero es don Dinero.	*Money talks.*
Quien mala cama hace, en ella se yace.	*You made your bed, now lie in it!* (yacer [*old*] *to lie down*)
Sobre gustos no hay nada escrito.	*Everyone to his own taste.*
Ver y creer.	*Seeing is believing.*

Nota cultural

- **Zamora** es una ciudad de León, región de España situada al oeste de Castilla. En la Edad Media, Zamora fue el teatro de muchas batallas entre musulmanes y cristianos y entre facciones de cristianos hasta que se impuso el dominio de los castellanos en 1072.
- **El cuento de la lechera** está incluido en una antología de la Edad Media, *El conde Lucanor*. En este cuento, una lechera (*dairymaid*) va al mercado llevando en la cabeza una jarra de leche para vender. Mientras camina, piensa en el dinero que le va a traer la venta de la leche. De repente se cae, y con ella la jarra. Con la jarra rota y la leche desparramada terminan sus sueños y las cuentas que sacaba con dinero que todavía no había ganado.

M. **¿Qué se diría?** Escoja el refrán apropiado para cada situación.

1. Uno nota que un muchacho se comporta exactamente como su padre.
   a. No es oro todo lo que reluce.
   b. De tal palo, tal astilla.
   c. Obras son amores, que no buenas razones.
2. Uno advierte a su compañero que deben ser discretos porque no se sabe quién escucha.
   a. Las paredes oyen.
   b. Ver y creer.
   c. Aunque la mona se vista de seda, mona se queda.
3. Uno quiere decirle a un amigo que hay que olvidar los errores del pasado.
   a. A lo hecho, pecho.
   b. Sobre gustos no hay nada escrito.
   c. Cuando a Roma fueres, haz como vieres.
4. Uno quiere advertirle a su amigo que debe actuar con prudencia en una situación complicada.
   a. Más vale pájaro en mano que ciento volando.
   b. El sapo a la sapa tiénela por muy guapa.
   c. Antes que te cases, mira lo que haces.
5. Un muchacho reprocha a su novia el no haberle escrito cuando estaba ella en el extranjero.
   a. Los dineros del sacristán cantando se vienen y cantando se van.
   b. Del dicho al hecho hay gran trecho.
   c. Ojos que no ven, corazón que no siente.

N. **¡El zoológico de expresiones!** Los siguientes proverbios y expresiones nombran a ciertos animales. Consulte las listas de proverbios y expresiones para completarlos con los nombres de los animales que faltan. Luego exprese la oración en inglés.

1. Aunque ____________________ se vista de seda, ____________________ se queda.

   ____

2. Más vale ____________________ en mano que ciento volando.

   ____

3. A otro ____________________ con ese hueso.

   ____

4. Que no le dé ____________________ por ____________________.

   ____

5. ____________________ por ____________________ tiénela por muy guapa.

   ____

6. Son los ____________________ gordos de la industria.

   ____

7. A ____________________ regalado no se le mira el colmillo.

   ____

8. Creo que hay ____________________ encerrado.

   ____

CHAPTER 27

WORD FORMATION & DIMINUTIVES

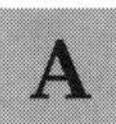

A Forming nouns from verbs

- Some nouns related to verbs consist of the verb stem + **-o** or **-a**:

aumentar *to increase*	➔	el aumento *increase*
ayudar *to help*	➔	la ayuda *help*
contar *to count*	➔	la cuenta *bill*
charlar *to chat*	➔	la charla *chat, talk*
dudar *to doubt*	➔	la duda *doubt*
encontrar *to meet*	➔	el encuentro *meeting, sports match*
espantar *to frighten*	➔	el espanto *fright, scare*
esperar *to wait*	➔	la espera *waiting*
fracasar *to fail*	➔	el fracaso *failure*
gastar *to spend*	➔	el gasto *expense*
practicar *to practice*	➔	la práctica *practice*
regresar *to return*	➔	el regreso *return*
volar *to fly*	➔	el vuelo *flight*

- Many nouns are formed from the past participle of verbs. These can also be seen as the verb stem + the suffixes **-ada** (for ***-ar*** verbs), **-ida** (for ***-er, -ir*** verbs):

bajar *to go down(stairs)*	➔	la bajada *way down; decline*
caer *to fall*	➔	la caída *fall*
comer *to eat*	➔	la comida *meal, food*
correr *to run*	➔	la corrida (de toros) *running (of bulls = bullfight)*
entrar *to enter*	➔	la entrada *entrance*
ir *to go*	➔	la ida *trip to somewhere, first leg of journey*
llegar *to arrive*	➔	la llegada *arrival*
mirar *to look (at)*	➔	la mirada *look, glance*
salir *to go out*	➔	la salida *exit*
subir *to go up*	➔	la subida *way up, rise*
volver *to go/come back*	➔	la vuelta *return, trip back*

- Many nouns are formed from **-ar** verbs with the suffix **-ción**. Most of these have English cognates ending in *-tion*:

admirar ➔ la admiración	organizar ➔ la organización
invitar ➔ la invitación	separar ➔ la separación

Note that not all English words ending in *-tion, -sion* have Spanish equivalents ending in **-ción, -sión**:

transportation ~ el transporte (**la transportación** is rare)

A. **¿Y el verbo original?** Escriba al lado de cada sustantivo el verbo de que se deriva.

1. la formación ______________________
2. la comprensión ______________________
3. la dominación ______________________
4. la preparación ______________________
5. la conversión ______________________
6. la decisión ______________________
7. la obligación ______________________
8. la complicación ______________________

- The suffixes **-ancia** and **-encia** are used to form nouns from verbs. Most of the nouns have English cognates:

  coincidir ➔ la coincidencia
  preferir ➔ la preferencia
  tolerar ➔ la tolerancia
  vigilar ➔ la vigilancia

  Note also **la estancia** (*stay*) from **estar**.

- The suffix **-miento** is widely used to form nouns from verbs. **-Ar** verbs have the vowel **a** before this suffix; both **-er** and **-ir** verbs have the vowel **i**:

  agotar *to exhaust* ➔ el agot**a**miento *exhaustion*
  entender *to understand* ➔ el entend**i**miento *understanding*

B. **El sustantivo que falta.** Complete la tabla siguiente con los sustantivos que faltan.

1. **comportarse** *to behave*	______________ *behavior*
2. **encarcelar** *to jail, imprison*	______________ *jailing*
3. **consentir** *to consent*	______________ *consent*
4. **mover** *to move*	______________ *movement*
5. **pensar** *to think*	______________ *thought*
6. **plantear** *to pose (a problem)*	______________ *posing*
7. **tratar** *to treat*	______________ *treatment*
8. **nombrar** *to nominate*	______________ *nomination*
9. **crecer** *to grow, increase*	______________ *growth*

B *Forming verbs from nouns*

- The suffix **-ear** is one of the most common ways to convert a noun into a verb. It can convey the impression of repeated movement or action of the noun:

  párpado *eyelid* ➔ parpadear *to blink*
  paso *step* ➔ pasear *to walk*

  Most of these verbs can then form a noun ending in **-eo**: **el parpadeo** *blinking,* **el paseo** *walk.*

C. Verbos nuevos. Adivine el significado de los verbos en negrita (*boldface*) partiendo de los sustantivos de los cuales se han formado.

1. el sabor *taste*

   Come lentamente y **saborea** estos platos. ______________________

2. la gota *drop (of liquid)*

   El agua **goteaba** del techo de la casa. ______________________

3. el golpe *blow, hit*

   El hombre **golpeaba** al perro cruelmente. ______________________

4. la tecla *key (on a keyboard)*

   La pianista **tecleaba** la sonata. ______________________

5. la hoja *leaf, sheet of paper*

   La bibliotecaria **hojeaba** las páginas del libro. ______________________

6. el zapato *shoe*

   Todos **zapateaban** al compás (*rhythm*) de la música. ______________________

7. la pata *paw; foot* (*slang*)

   Para jugar fútbol, hay que saber **patear**. ______________________

- Some nouns can be transformed into verbs by the prefix **en-** + infinitive ending **-ar**:

  la cadena *chain* ➔ encadenar *to chain*
  la máscara *mask* ➔ enmascarar *to mask*
  el veneno *poison* ➔ envenenar *to poison*

  Some of these verbs allow a new noun to be formed by adding **-miento:**

  el encadenamiento *chaining*
  el envenenamiento *poisoning*

D. Complete esta tabla de palabras relacionadas. Siga el modelo de **cadena—encadenar—encadenamiento; veneno—envenenar—envenenamiento.**

1. **Sp. la casilla** *Eng. mailbox, pigeonhole*	**Sp.** __________ *Eng. to pigeonhole*	**Sp. encasillamiento** *Eng. pigeonholing*
2. **Sp. la grasa** *Eng.* __________	**Sp. engrasar** *Eng.* __________	**Sp.** __________ *Eng. lubrication*
3. **Sp. la saña** *Eng. rage, fury*	**Sp.** __________ *Eng. to enrage, infuriate*	**Sp. ensañamiento** *Eng. raging, fury*
4. **Sp. la botella** *Eng. bottle*	**Sp.** __________ *Eng. to bottle (up)*	**Sp.** __________ *Eng. traffic jam*
5. **Sp. la pareja** *Eng. couple*	**Sp. emparejar** *Eng. to match, pair*	**Sp.** __________ *Eng. pairing, mating*
6. **Sp. la frente** *Eng. forehead, brow, face*	**Sp. enfrentar** *Eng. to face, confront*	**Sp.** __________ *Eng. clash, confrontation*

C *Forming verbs from adjectives*

- Certain adjectives can be transformed into verbs by the prefix **a-** + infinitive ending **-ar:**

fino *fine* ➔ afinar *to refine, tune*
llano *flat* ➔ allanar *to flatten, level*
liso *smooth* ➔ alisar *to smooth*
manso *tame* ➔ amansar *to tame, domesticate*

E. El detective del diccionario. Empareje los verbos de la columna A con su equivalente inglés de la columna B. Cada verbo deriva de un adjetivo que Ud. ya sabe.

A	B
_____ 1. acertar	a. assure
_____ 2. aclarar	b. lengthen
_____ 3. achicar	c. enlarge
_____ 4. aflojar	d. drive mad (with joy or delight)
_____ 5. agrandar	e. guess right, hit the mark
_____ 6. alargar	f. clarify
_____ 7. alocar	g. loosen
_____ 8. asegurar	h. reduce in size

- The suffix **-ecer** is added to the stem of some adjectives and nouns to create a new verb:

  oscuro ➔ oscurecer *to get dark*
  pálido ➔ palidecer *to grow pale*

  Like all **-ecer** verbs, the first-person singular and the present subjunctive have **-zc-** before the endings: Temo que **oscurezca** antes de que lleguemos. *I'm afraid it will get dark before we arrive.*

F. Acertijos (*riddles*) **léxicos.** Adivine qué significan estas palabras.

1. florecer ______
2. fortalecer ______
3. humedecer ______
4. robustecer ______
5. What household appliance is **la humedecedora**? ______

- Many adjectives can be made into verbs with the prefix **en-** (**em-** before **b** and **p**) and the suffix **-ecer**. Adjectives whose stems end in **c** change the **c** to **qu** before **-ecer**:

  triste ➔ entristecer *to sadden*
  pobre ➔ empobrecer *to impoverish*
  rico ➔ enriquecer *to enrich*

G. Formación de verbos. ¿Cuáles son los verbos que derivan de estos adjetivos?

1. duro ______
2. bello ______
3. flaco ______
4. noble ______
5. loco ______
6. negro ______
7. rojo ______
8. ronco (*hoarse*) ______
9. sordo ______

D *Suffixes added to nouns to form new nouns*

- The suffix **-ada** can have three different meanings:

  1. the full measure of the noun, the amount that the noun holds (**-ado** is used with some nouns)

     la cuchara *spoon* ➔ la cucharada *spoonful*
     la pala *shovel* ➔ la palada *shovelful*
     el puño *fist* ➔ el puñado *fistful*
     la boca *mouth* ➔ el bocado *mouthful;* (*also,* la bocanada *mouthful, swallow*)

2. a blow with the object designated by the noun

   el cuchillo *knife* ➔ la cuchillada *a slash made with a knife*
   el puñal *dagger* ➔ la puñalada *stab*
   la pata *foot, paw* ➔ la patada *kick*

3. an act typical of the object or person designated by the noun

   el animal *animal* ➔ una animalada *a stupid or gross thing to do*
   el payaso *clown* ➔ una payasada *clown-like action, action worthy of a clown*
   el muchacho *boy, kid* ➔ una muchachada *kid's prank*

- The suffix **-astro** is the equivalent of English *step-* with relatives:

  el hermanastro *stepbrother*

- The suffix **-azo**, like **-ada,** can signify a blow with the object designated by the noun. In Latin America, **-azo** can also be an augmentative suffix:

  la bala *bullet* ➔ el balazo *a shot, a bullet wound*
  el codo *elbow* ➔ el codazo *nudge, push with the elbow*
  los ojos *eyes* ➔ los ojazos *big eyes*

- The suffix **-era** designates the container for the object expressed by the noun. Some nouns use **-ero** as the suffix for this meaning:

  la sopa *soup* ➔ la sopera *soup bowl*
  la pimienta *pepper* ➔ el pimentero *pepper shaker*

- The suffix **-ero** has other important functions:

  1. the owner or person in charge

     la cárcel *jail* ➔ el carcelero *jailer*
     el molino *mill* ➔ el molinero *miller*

  2. the person who makes or sells the object denoted by the noun

     el libro *book* ➔ el librero *bookseller*
     el reloj *watch* ➔ el relojero *watchmaker*

  3. the person fond of whatever the noun designates

     el queso *cheese* ➔ quesero *fond of cheese, cheese-loving*
     el café *coffee* ➔ cafetero *fond of coffee, coffee-drinker, coffee-lover*

  The suffix **-ería**, derived from **-ero**, designates the corresponding store or place of business:

     la librería *bookstore*
     la relojería *watchmaker's store, watch store*

H. **¿Qué significa?** Escriba el significado de las siguientes palabras, analizando la raíz y el sufijo.

1. el pastelero ______________________________
2. la cucharada ______________________________
3. la sombrerería ______________________________
4. la cafetera ______________________________
5. la ensaladera ______________________________
6. el lapicero ______________________________
7. la bobada ______________________________

8. la barcada ______________________________

9. el portazo ______________________________

10. la hijastra ______________________________

11. el salero ______________________________

12. fiestero ______________________________

E *Diminutives and augmentatives*

- Diminutives are widely used in Spanish to add a note of smallness or endearment to the noun. The most common diminutive suffix is **-ito/-ita,** added to nouns and personal names. The following spelling changes occur when **-ito/-ita** is added: **c ➔ qu, g ➔ gu, z ➔ c**:

  la silla *chair* ➔ la sillita *small chair*
  el hermano *brother* ➔ el hermanito *little brother, younger brother*
  la cuchara *spoon* ➔ la cucharita *teaspoon*
  el gato *cat* ➔ el gatito *kitten*
  abuela *grandmother* ➔ abuelita *grandma*
  Paco ➔ Paquito
  Diego ➔ Dieguito
  Lorenza ➔ Lorencita

- The diminutive suffix **-ito/-ita** changes to **-cito/-cita** if the noun ends in **-n** or **-r**, or if the noun ends in **-e** and has more than one syllable:

  el pintor *painter* ➔ el pintorcito *painter, third-rate painter (often sarcastic)*
  la joven *young girl, teenage girl* ➔ la jovencita *young girl (endearing)*
  la madre *mother* ➔ la madrecita *dear mother*
  el puente *bridge* ➔ el puentecito *little bridge*

- Nouns of two syllables whose first syllable has **ie** or **ue** and which end in **-o** or **-a** drop the **-o** or **-a** and add **-ecito/-ecita** to form the diminutive. The same is true of one-syllable nouns ending in a consonant:

  la piedra *stone* ➔ la piedrecita *little stone*
  la fiesta *party* ➔ la fiestecita *little party*
  el cuerpo *body* ➔ el cuerpecito *little body (could be sarcastic)*
  la puerta *door* ➔ la puertecita *little door*
  la flor *flower* ➔ la florecita *little flower*

- Other diminutive endings are **-ico** (a regional variant of **-ito**), **-illo** (which can convey contempt as well as endearment), and **-uelo** (a diminutive ending that often conveys a note of contempt). These endings add **c** or **ec** (**z** or **ez** in the case of **-uelo**) the way **-ito** does:

  la cuesta *slope* ➔ la cuestecilla *slight slope*
  un abogado *lawyer* ➔ un abogadillo *third-rate lawyer*
  una república *republic* ➔ una republiquilla *a miserable government*
  la cosa *thing* ➔ la cosilla *insignificant thing*
  un rey *a king* ➔ un reyezuelo *a poor excuse for a king*
  un escritor *a writer* ➔ un escritorzuelo *a very bad writer*
  un muchacho *boy* ➔ un muchachuelo *small boy*

- Words with a diminutive suffix may take on an independent meaning:

  el zapato *shoe* ➔ la zapatilla *slipper*
  la mano *hand* ➔ la manecilla *hand of a watch or clock*
  la bolsa *bag* ➔ el bolsillo *pocket*

Nota cultural

- El diminutivo **-ico/-ica** se usa tanto en la república centroamericana de Costa Rica que se les ha apodado (*nicknamed*) a los costarricenses **«los ticos».**

- **Costa Rica** es una nación democrática cuya estabilidad presenta un contraste con el trágico desorden político y social del resto de Centroamérica. El ex-presidente de Costa Rica, Oscar Arias, que se esforzó incansablemente por resolver de una manera pacífica los conflictos de Nicaragua y El Salvador, recibió el premio Nobel de la Paz en 1987.

- The suffix **-ucho/-ucha** conveys the idea of ugliness:

  la casa *house* ➔ la casucha *hovel*
  el cuarto *room* ➔ el cuartucho *small, miserable, uncomfortable room*

- The most common augmentative suffix in Spanish is **-ón/-ona**:

  la mancha *stain* ➔ el manchón *big, dirty stain*
  la mujer *woman* ➔ la mujerona *big, hefty woman*
  la novela *novel* ➔ el novelón *long, boring novel*

  Note, however, that in **el ratón** (*mouse*) from **la rata** (*rat*) the suffix **-ón** functions as a diminutive.

- The suffix **-ón/-ona** can also be added to some verb stems to form adjectives meaning *given to doing the action of the verb*:

  contestar *to answer* ➔ contestón *given to answering back*
  llorar *to cry* ➔ llorón *crybaby, always crying*
  mirar *to look at* ➔ mirón *given to staring*
  preguntar *to ask* ➔ preguntón *inquisitive, given to asking too many questions*
  responder *to answer* ➔ respondón *fresh, insolent, given to answering back*
  burlarse *to make fun of* ➔ burlón *mocking, derisive*
  comer *to eat* ➔ comilón *big eater, glutton*
  dormir *to sleep* ➔ dormilón *sleepy-head*
  gritar *to shout, scream* ➔ gritón *loud-mouthed, always yelling*

- The suffix **-azo/-aza** is also augmentative, especially in Spanish America:

  el perro *dog* ➔ el perrazo *big dog*
  el éxito *success* ➔ el exitazo *great success, hit*

- The augmentative suffix **-ote/-ota** often adds a note of contempt to the idea of bigness:

  la palabra *word* ➔ la palabrota *bad word, dirty word*
  el animal *animal* ➔ el animalote *big animal; gross, ignorant person*

- As with diminutives, the addition of an augmentative suffix sometimes creates an independent word:

  soltero *unmarried* ➔ el solterón *old bachelor,* la solterona *old maid*
  la silla *chair* ➔ el sillón *armchair*
  la caja *box* ➔ el cajón *drawer; crate*

- Diminutive and augmentative suffixes can be added to adjectives and some adverbs. The suffixes vary in form as with nouns:

  pobre *poor* ➔ pobrecito/a *an unfortunate person*
  feo *ugly* ➔ feíto *somewhat ugly, a little ugly*
  viejo *old* ➔ viejito *rather old, getting on in years*
  flaco *thin* ➔ flacucho *skinny*
  inocente *innocent* ➔ inocentón *naive, gullible*
  guapo *good-looking* ➔ guapote *really good-looking*
  poco *little, not much* ➔ poquito *very little, rather little*
  ahora *now* ➔ ahorita *right now*
  tarde *late* ➔ tardecito *rather late, a little late*
  cerca *nearby* ➔ cerquita *really close, not at all far away*
  en seguida *right away* ➔ en seguidita *in just a moment*

I. Diminutivos. Escriba el diminutivo en **-ito/-ita** que corresponda a estas palabras.

1. la voz ______
2. la carta ______
3. el traje ______
4. el pez ______
5. el cuento ______
6. la pierna ______
7. el caballo ______
8. el bosque ______
9. el dolor ______
10. la cabeza ______
11. el lago ______
12. suave ______
13. el viento ______
14. el jugo ______
15. el carro ______
16. fuerte ______
17. chico ______
18. nuevo ______
19. fresco ______
20. la luz ______

CHAPTER 28

¡OJO! COMMON ERRORS & PITFALLS

A *Dejar* vs. *salir*

- **Dejar** and **salir** both mean *to leave*, but they are not interchangeable. **Dejar** is a transitive verb that means *to leave something or someone behind*:

—¿Dónde **dejaste las llaves** del coche?	*Where did you leave the car keys?*
—Creo que **las dejé** en la mesa del comedor.	*I think I left them on the dining room table.*
—¿Dónde **los puedo dejar**?	*Where can I leave you (off)?*
—**Déjeme a mí** delante del cine y **deje a mi marido** en la estación.	*Leave me in front of the movie theater and drop (= leave) my husband at the station.*

- **Salir** is an intransitive verb that means *to go out* or *leave*. The preposition **de** follows **salir** before the place being left:

—Nuestro tren **sale** a las tres y media.	*Our train leaves at three thirty.*
—En ese caso debemos **salir de casa** a las tres para no llegar tarde.	*In that case we should leave the house at three in order not to be late.*

Compare the following examples where **salir** and **dejar** contrast:

Salió de la casa a las cinco.	*He left the house at five o'oclock.*
Dejó la casa hecha un desastre.	*He left the house in a mess.*

- Note that **irse** and **marcharse** also mean *to leave* in the sense of *to go away*. They also require **de** before the name of the place. **Marcharse** may imply leaving forever or for a long period of time:

—**Me voy** de la oficina a las cinco.	*I'm leaving the office at five o'clock.*
—Ayer **te fuiste** a las cuatro, ¿verdad?	*Yesterday you left at four, didn't you?*
—**Se marchó** porque odiaba el trabajo aquí.	*He left because he hated the work here.*
—A ver si yo también **me marcho** pronto.	*Let's see if I (can) leave soon too.*

- **Dejar** + infinitive means *to let*. **Dejar** + **de** + infinitive means *to stop doing something*:

—¿Cuándo me **dejarás** salir, mamá?	*When will you let me go out, mom?*
—Cuando **deje de** llover.	*When it stops raining.*

- **Salir** + adjective or adverb means *to turn out*. An indirect object is often added:

Ese coche **te saldrá** muy caro.	*That car will turn out to be very expensive for you.*
Nos salió mal el proyecto.	*The project turned out badly for us.*
Los nuevos empleados **salieron** muy trabajadores.	*The new employees turned out to be very hard-working.*

A. **¿Cómo se dice?** Complete estas oraciones con la forma correcta de **salir, dejar, irse, marcharse**, según convenga.

1. No debemos ______________________ nada en el cuarto de hotel.
2. Si llueve, no quiero ______________________ a la calle. Prefiero esperar a que ______________________ de llover.
3. No ______________________ (*tú-imperative*) por favor. No me ______________________ solo aquí en el parque.
4. Ese sinvergüenza (*scoundrel*) ______________________ (*preterit*) del país y ______________________ a su mujer y a sus hijos sin un centavo.
5. Juan y yo ______________________ del correo y nos dirigimos al banco.
6. Oye, Carlitos, ______________________ de molestarme. Te dije que no podías ______________________ a jugar.
7. La fiesta de Francisca ______________________ estupenda. Yo lo pasé muy bien.
8. Casi todos los estudiantes ______________________ mal en el examen de física porque fue muy difícil.
9. Mis padres no me ______________________ manejar de noche.

B *Saber* vs. *conocer*

- **Saber** and **conocer** both mean *to know*. **Saber** is used for facts, information, or knowledge that can be stated:

—¿**Sabes** la dirección de Marta?	*Do you know Marta's address?*
—No, pero **sé** su número de teléfono.	*No, but I know her phone number.*

- **Conocer** means *to know a person, to be familiar with a place.* With places, **conocer** is often translated as *to have been* in English:

—¿**Conoces** a Pedro Gómez?	*Do you know Pedro Gómez?*
—No, pero **conozco** a su hermana.	*No, but I know his sister.*
—¿**Conocen** Uds. la universidad?	*Are you familiar with the university?*
—No, no la **conocemos**.	*No, we've never been there.*

- **Saber** + infinitive means *to know how to do something*:

—¿**Sabes** cocinar?	*Do you know how to cook?*
—**Sé** preparar algunas cosas sencillas.	*I know how to prepare some simple things.*

B. ***¿Saber* o *conocer?*** Indique cuál de las formas verbales dadas completa correctamente las oraciones.

1. Alfredo no ______________________ a nadie en esta ciudad. (sabe / conoce)
2. ¿No ______________________ Galicia? Entonces, tienen que ir. (saben / conocen)
3. ¿______________________ Ud. cuántos habitantes hay en Caracas? (Sabe / Conoce)

4. No ______________________ esta computadora. ¿Cómo funciona? (sé / conozco)
5. Mi abuela no ______________________ manejar. (sabe / conoce)

C *Oreja vs. oído*

- **Oreja** and **oído** both mean *ear*. **Oreja** refers to the outer ear; **oído** refers to the inner ear, thus the sense of hearing or the ear canal.

El peluquero me cortó **la oreja.**	*The hairdresser cut my ear.*
El bebé tiene una infección de **los oídos.**	*The baby has an ear infection.*

C. ¿Oyes? Complete las oraciones siguientes con **oreja** u **oído**, escogiendo entre las posibilidades dadas.

1. —¿Por qué llora tu hijo?
   —Creo que tiene dolor de ______________________. (orejas / oídos)
2. Después de la corrida de toros, le ofrecen ______________________ del toro al torero. (la oreja / el oído)
3. Tiene ______________________ para la música. (buena oreja / buen oído)
4. Le dio un golpe en ______________________. (la oreja / el oído)
5. Mi abuelo no oye bien. Es duro de ______________________. (oreja / oído)

Nota cultural

En **la corrida de toros,** si el torero torea bien según los jueces, le conceden una de las orejas del toro. Si torea sumamente bien, existe la posibilidad de que los jueces le premien con las dos orejas y el rabo (*tail*) del toro.

D *Meanings of* ***quedar***

- **Quedar** means to remain. One of its most frequent uses is to ask for the location of places:

—¿Dónde **queda** el estadio?	*Where's the stadium?*
—**Queda** lejos, cerca del aeropuerto.	*It's far away, near the airport.*

- When referring to people, **quedar** means *to remain, be in a certain emotional or physical state*:

quedar boquiabierto	*to be open-mouthed with astonishment*
quedar ciego, sordo, cojo	*to go blind, deaf, lame*
quedar en ridículo	*to look foolish*
quedar bien	*to come off well, make a good impression*
quedar mal	*to come off badly, make a bad impression*
hacer algo por quedar bien	*to do something to make a good impression*

- **Quedar** means *to have left*, often with an indirect object pronoun:

—¿Cuánto dinero **te queda**?	*How much money do you have left?*
—**Me quedan** mil pesos.	*I have a thousand pesos left.*
Quedan cinco kilómetros.	*There are five kilometers left (to go).*
Quedan seis estudiantes en la clase.	*There are six students left in the class.*
Quedan pocos días para las vacaciones.	*There aren't many days left until vacation.*
Me quedan tres páginas por escribir.	*I have three pages left to write.*

- **Quedarse** means *to stay, remain*:

quedarse en un hotel, en casa de sus amigos	*to stay at a hotel, at one's friends' house*

- **Quedarse con** means *to keep*; **quedarse sin** means *to run out of*:

Se quedó con mi libro de química.	*He kept my chemistry book.*
Me quedo con éste.	*I'll take this one. (in a store)*
Quédese Ud. con la vuelta.	*Keep the change.*
Me he quedado sin azúcar.	*I've run out of sugar.*
Lidia **se ha quedado sin** trabajo.	*Lidia has lost her job.*

Some expressions with **quedar(se)**:

No me queda más remedio.	*I have no choice, no alternative.*
Queda a tres kilómetros de aquí.	*It's three kilometers from here.*
Quedar con uno para ir al cine.	*To make a date with someone to go to the movies.*
Quedan en salir el domingo.	*They agree, arrange to go out on Sunday.*
¿En qué quedamos?	*What did we decide to do?*
No se queda con la cólera dentro.	*He can't hide his anger.*
No quise quedarme en menos.	*I refused to be outdone.*
Se quedó en nada.	*It came to nothing.*

D. Quedar. Exprese estas oraciones en español. En todas use el verbo **quedar(se)**.

1. We have two weeks left in Puerto Rico.

   ____

2. Keep the money. I don't need it. (*tú*)

   ____

3. I have run out of job opportunities. (*salidas*)

   ____

4. They stayed with a Mexican family.

   ____

5. You (*Uds.*) have three sentences left to translate.

   ____

6. He went deaf because of the explosion.

   ____

7. Where's the post office, please?

8. Paula and I agreed to go to the movies.

E *"To break" and "to tear"*

- The Spanish verb **romper** covers the meanings of English *to break* and *to tear*:

La ventana está rota.	*The window is broken.*
Mi camisa está rota./Tengo la camisa rota.	*My shirt is torn.*

- **Romperse** + article of clothing is often used with the meaning *to tear something*:

Cuidado, o te vas a romper el pantalón.	*Careful or you'll tear your pants.*

- *To be broken* in the sense of *to be out of order* is usually **estar descompuesto**. The verb is **descomponerse** and it may also appear with an indirect object pronoun (the unplanned occurrences construction): **descomponérsele a uno**:

El ascensor está descompuesto.	*The elevator is broken (out of order).*
Se descompuso el aire acondicionado.	*The air conditioner went on the blink.*
Se me descompuso el coche.	*My car broke down.*

Some expressions with **romper**:

romper con alguien *to break off with someone*
romper a llorar, romper en llanto *to burst out crying*
romper el fuego *to open fire*
romper las hostilidades *to start hostilities*
Quien rompe paga. *Actions have consequences.*
No te preocupes. No te vas a romper. *Don't worry. You're not so fragile.*

E. ¿Cómo se dice eso en español? Exprese las siguientes ideas en español.

1. Who tore my newspaper?

2. My chair is broken.

3. The radio is broken.

4. My coat is torn.

5. I hope the car doesn't break down on us.

6. We don't understand why she burst out crying.

7. Don't tear your jacket. (*tú*)

____

8. Elena broke off with her boyfriend.

____

9. The enemy opened fire.

____

10. Actions have consequences.

____

Nota de vocabulario

Note that **el radio** often refers to the radio as an appliance while **la radio** means radio as a medium of communication. Some speakers use **la radio** for both meanings.

F *"Wrong"*

- There is no one Spanish word that covers all the meanings of English *wrong*. When *wrong* means *morally* or *ethically wrong*, Spanish often uses **malo**:

Hiciste algo muy **malo**.	*You did something very wrong.*
¿Qué tiene eso de **malo**?	*What's wrong with that?*

- When *wrong* means *incorrect*, Spanish has several possibilities, not all interchangeable:

1. When said of people, Spanish uses **no tener razón**, **equivocarse,** or **estar equivocado**:

—Mónica dijo que la lámpara costaba cincuenta dólares.	*Monica said that the lamp cost fifty dollars.*
—**No tiene razón**. Cuesta cuarenta.	*She's wrong. It costs forty.*
—Quisiera hablar con el señor Lares.	*I'd like to speak with Mr. Lares.*
—Aquí no vive ningún señor Lares. Ud. ha marcado un número **equivocado**.	*There's no Mr. Lares (living) here. You've dialed the wrong number.*
—¿Aquí no vive la familia Laínez?	*Doesn't the Laínez family live here?*
—No. Ud. **se ha equivocado de casa**.	*No. You've come to the wrong house.*
—Creo que la respuesta es cinco y tres octavos.	*I think the answer is five and three eighths.*
—Ud. **está equivocado**. La respuesta es seis.	*You're wrong. The answer is six.*

2. When said of information, answers, etc., Spanish uses **incorrecto, inexacto, equivocado**, and **mal**.

La respuesta es incorrecta, inexacta.	*The answer is wrong.*
La receta está mal.	*The recipe is wrong.*
Mi reloj anda mal.	*My watch is wrong.*
Estos datos están equivocados.	*These data are wrong.*
Escribió Ud. mal mi dirección.	*You wrote my address wrong.*
Me comprendió Ud. mal.	*You didn't understand me correctly.*
El estudiante contestó mal.	*The student answered incorrectly.*

3. When *wrong* means *inopportune, unwanted* it is often translated as **no ... adecuado** or **no ... apropiado, impropio**:

No es el momento **adecuado/apropiado** para hablar de esas cosas. — *It's the wrong time to speak about those things.*

Decir algo **inoportuno** en español es *meter la pata.* — *To say the wrong thing in Spanish is* meter la pata.

4. When *wrong* expresses a result or outcome not desired or sought, it can have a variety of translations:

This is the wrong book. — *Éste no es el libro que hacía falta.*

This is the wrong train. — *Éste no es el tren que debíamos tomar./Nos hemos equivocado de tren.*

Your socks are wrong side out. — *Tienes los calcetines al revés.*

I'm in the wrong profession. — *Mi profesión no me conviene.*

He played a wrong note. — *Tocó una nota falsa.*

The chair is in the wrong place. — *La silla está mal colocada.*

You're driving on the wrong side of the road. — *Ud. maneja por el lado prohibido.*

5. When *wrong* means *amiss, to have something wrong*, the verb **pasar** is used:

—¿Qué te pasa, Luis?
—No me pasa nada.
What's wrong with you, Luis?
Nothing is wrong with me.

—¿Pasa algo aquí?
—No, profesora, no pasa nada.
Is something wrong here?
No, ma'am. Nothing is wrong.

—Le pasa algo a la computadora.
—Hay que llamar al técnico.
Something's wrong with the computer.
We have to call the repairman.

6. Note also the following expressions:

Distinguir entre el bien y el mal. — *To tell right from wrong.*

Entiéndeme bien. — *Don't get me wrong.*

Todo salió mal. — *Everything went wrong.*

Hiciste mal en prestarle el dinero. — *You were wrong to lend him the money.*

F. Está mal. Exprese estas oraciones en español.

1. I dialed the wrong number.

____

2. We took the wrong plane.

____

3. What's wrong with the tape recorder?

____

4. This is not the right time.

____

5. I read the title wrong.

____

6. Your gloves are wrong side out.

 ____

7. He's got the wrong job.

 ____

8. The definition is wrong.

 ____

9. I was wrong not to believe him.

 ____

10. You added wrong.

 ____

G *"To miss"*

- The verb *to miss* has several very different meanings in English, each of which is translated by a different Spanish verb. When *miss* means *to long for a person or thing*, Spanish uses **echar de menos** or, especially in Spanish America, **extrañar**:

—Echo de menos a mi familia.	*I miss my family.*
—Yo también extraño a mis padres.	*I also miss my parents.*

- Spanish uses the verb **perder** for *to miss a plane, train*, etc.:

—Date prisa. Vamos a perder el autobús.	*Hurry up. We're going to miss the bus.*
—Ya lo hemos perdido. Tomaremos el siguiente.	*We've already missed it. We'll take the next one.*

- Spanish uses the verb **perderse** for *to miss a show*, etc.:

—Me perdí la nueva película.	*I missed the new film.*
—Te has perdido algo muy bueno.	*You've missed something very good.*

Note that *to miss class* is usually **faltar a clase**.

- For *to miss the target, not to hit, to miss the mark*, etc. Spanish uses **errar el tiro** or **fallar (el blanco)**:

El ladrón disparó, pero falló el blanco.	*The thief shot, but missed.*
Es un método que nunca falla.	*It's a method that never misses, never fails.*

- *To be missing* can be expressed in two ways in Spanish, depending on the meaning:

Encontraron a los estudiantes desaparecidos.	*They found the missing students.*
Nos faltan tres cartas.	*We're missing three letters.*
Complete las oraciones con las palabras que faltan.	*Complete the sentences with the missing words.*

- Other uses of *to miss*:

You can't miss it.	No puedes dejar de encontrarlo.
I arrived late so I missed him.	Llegué tarde y no lo encontré.
Don't miss the museums when you're in Mexico.	No dejes de ir a los museos cuando estés en México.
I missed what you said.	No entendí lo que dijiste.

G. ¡A completar! Complete estas oraciones con una expresión adecuada que exprese la idea de *to miss.*

1. Anoche mi hermana no pudo salir. Por eso ______________________ la obra de teatro.
2. Si Alfonso ______________________ tantas veces a clase, va a salir muy mal en el curso.
3. Vamos rápido. No quiero ______________________ el avión.
4. El pillo (*hoodlum*) trató de romper la ventana con una piedra, pero ______________________.
5. Otra vez, por favor. Hay tanto ruido aquí que ______________________ lo que dijiste.
6. Con estas cintas, tienes que aprender inglés. Dicen que es un sistema que nunca ______________________.
7. —¿Todos los socios del club ya han llegado?
   —No, todavía ______________________ dos o tres.
8. Ojalá pudiera ver a mi novia. No sabes cuánto la ______________________.
9. Hubo muchos soldados ______________________ al terminar la guerra.

Examination

Section I

A. Present tense. Write the correct form of the verb in parentheses.

1. (Nosotros) ____________________ (ir) a un concierto.
2. Los Hernández ____________________ (venir) pasado mañana.
3. Yo ____________________ (saber) su dirección.
4. Paco ____________________ (dormir) ocho horas.
5. ¿Qué (tú) ____________________ (decir)?

B. Preterit. Write the correct form of the verb in parentheses.

1. Yo ____________________ (darse) cuenta de la situación.
2. ¿No ____________________ (querer) Ud. acompañarlos?
3. Miguel y yo ____________________ (trabajar) en la librería el sábado.
4. Uds. ____________________ (tener) una excelente idea.
5. Raquel no ____________________ (ser) muy responsable.

C. Imperfect. Write the correct form of the verb in parentheses.

1. ____________________ (Haber) unas flores exóticas en el parque.
2. ____________________ (Ser) las siete de la tarde.
3. Nosotros ____________________ (irse) de allí.
4. Yo ____________________ (ver) a Juan Carlos todos los días.
5. Uds. ____________________ (escribir) muchas cartas, ¿no?

D. Preterit and imperfect. Write the correct form of the verb in parentheses selecting either the preterit or the imperfect.

1. ____________________ (Hacer) muy buen tiempo cuando nosotros ____________________ (salir).
2. Cuando ellos ____________________ (volver), ____________________ (llover).
3. ¿Dónde (tú) ____________________ (estar) cuando yo te ____________________ (llamar)?

E. Verb + infinitive construction. Expand the following sentences by adding the verb or phrase in parentheses.

1. Comienzan el proyecto en febrero. (preferir)

   ____

2. Almuerzo con Felipe. (acabar de)

   ____

3. Cierras las ventanas. (deber)

   ____

4. Ella resuelve los problemas. (necesitar)

   ____

5. Consigues el puesto. (ir a)

   ____

F. Future. Write the correct form of the verb in parentheses in the future tense.

1. Ud. ______________ (hacer) un viaje.
2. Nosotros no ______________ (tener) tiempo.
3. Los chicos ______________ (venir) más tarde.
4. ¿Con quiénes ______________ (salir) Uds.?
5. Yo ______________ (querer) estudiar griego.

G. Conditional. Write the correct form of the verb in parentheses in the conditional.

1. Yo no ______________ (decir) eso.
2. Nadie ______________ (poder) entenderlo.
3. Pepe y yo ______________ (vivir) en Madrid.
4. Tú ______________ (ponerse) un smoking.
5. ¿Uds. nos las ______________ (traer)?

H. Present perfect. Write the correct form of the verb in parentheses in the present perfect (auxiliary *haber* + past participle).

1. Nosotros ______________ ______________ (ver) a Daniel.
2. El dependiente me lo ______________ ______________ (vender).
3. Los muchachos ______________ ______________ (romper) una ventana.
4. Vosotros nos las ______________ ______________ (devolver).
5. Yo se lo ______________ ______________ (prestar).

I. Present progressive. Write the correct form of the verb in parentheses in the present progressive.

1. Ramón y Alberto ______________ ______________ (jugar) béisbol.
2. Consuelo ______________ ______________ (poner) la mesa.
3. Nosotros ______________ ______________ (seguir) por esta calle.
4. Tú ______________ ______________ (servir) la cena.
5. Yo ______________ ______________ (leer) un libro de historia.

J. Present subjunctive. Write the correct form of the verb in parentheses in the present subjunctive.

1. Espero que ellos me ______________ (entender).
2. Prefieren que nosotros ______________ (encargarse) de los planes.
3. Le han pedido a Sara que no ______________ (quejarse) tanto.
4. Es posible que el avión ______________ (llegar) tarde.
5. Llegarán solos a menos que yo los ______________ (recoger).

K. Imperfect subjunctive. Write the correct form of the verb in parentheses in the imperfect subjunctive.

1. Les aconsejamos que ______________ (tener) paciencia.
2. Nos prestó la plata para que ______________ (poder) comprar el coche.
3. Era triste que Jaime no ______________ (reunirse) con nosotros.
4. No había casa que me ______________ (interesar).
5. Me gustaría que tú ______________ (asistir) a la conferencia.

L. Conditional sentences. Fill in the correct form of the verb in parentheses.

1. Yo estudiaría chino si ______________ (tener) mucho tiempo.
2. Si Uds. ______________ (venir) a la ciudad, nos visitarían, ¿verdad?
3. Si hace buen tiempo, Teresa ______________ (ir) al campo.
4. Si tú sales esta noche, nosotros ______________ (salir) contigo.
5. Ellas harían una tortilla si ______________ (haber) huevos.

M. Commands. Write the correct command form of the verb in parentheses.

1. estudiar (Uds.)
____
2. escribir (tú)
____
3. comer (Ud.)
____
4. venir (tú)
____
5. salir (Uds.)
____
6. decírmelo (Ud.)
____
7. divertirse (Uds.)
____
8. dárselas (tú)
____

Section II

A. Write the masculine or feminine form of the definite and indefinite articles for each of the following nouns.

	definite article	*indefinite article*	
1.	____________	____________	siglo
2.	____________	____________	vitrina
3.	____________	____________	sistema
4.	____________	____________	llave
5.	____________	____________	democracia
6.	____________	____________	mapa
7.	____________	____________	reunión
8.	____________	____________	cantidad
9.	____________	____________	mediodía
10.	____________	____________	cumpleaños
11.	____________	____________	nieve
12.	____________	____________	puente

B. Write the plural form for each of the following noun phrases.

1. el impresor ____________________
2. una voz ____________________
3. el agua ____________________
4. un andén ____________________
5. una habitación ____________________
6. el examen ____________________
7. el origen ____________________
8. un abrelatas ____________________
9. la amistad ____________________
10. la ley ____________________

C. Write the correct forms of the adjectives of nationality.

país	*masc. sing.*	*fem. sing.*	*masc. pl.*	*fem. pl.*
1. Argentina	________	________	________	________
2. España	________	________	________	________
3. Inglaterra	________	________	________	________
4. Canadá	________	________	________	________
5. Costa Rica	________	________	________	________
6. Alemania	________	________	________	________

D. Complete the following sentences with the correct form of the adjective in parentheses.

1. Beatriz y Marta son ____________________ (responsable) y ____________________ (encantador).
2. Pablo y Julia están ____________________ (ocupado) pero ____________________ (contento).
3. Daniel lleva unos pantalones ____________________ (marrón), una chaqueta ____________________ (azul), una camisa ____________________ (blanco), una corbata ____________________ (amarillo), medias ____________________ (marrón) y zapatos ____________________ (negro).

E. Complete the following sentences with the correct form of the shortened adjective.

1. El profesor Alba es un ____________________ (grande) historiador.
2. El quince de enero es el ____________________ (primero) día del ____________________ (segundo) semestre.
3. El flan es un ____________________ (bueno) postre.
4. Pepe nació el día de ____________________ (Santo) José.
5. Tengo ____________________ (alguno) lápices pero no tengo ____________________ (ninguno) bolígrafo.
6. Fue la ____________________ (tercero) vez que comimos en ese restaurante.

F. Write the correct plural form of the adjective.

1. ¡Qué tulipanes y rosas más ____________________ (hermoso)!
2. Hay ____________________ almacenes y tiendas (elegante) en esta calle.
3. Salamanca tiene colegios y una universidad ____________________ (antiguo).
4. ¿Visitaron tres regiones y provincias ____________________ (español)?

G. Write the correct form of the demonstrative adjective.

1. ____________________ (*Those*) chicos están en ____________________ (*this*) clase.
2. ____________________ (*That, over there*) señor es el gerente de ____________________ (*this*) almacén.
3. ____________________ (*These*) libros y revistas son de ____________________ (*those*) personas.
4. ____________________ (*Those, over there*) maletas no van a caber en ____________________ (*this*) armario.

H. Write a phrase consisting of the possessive adjective plus the noun, then write a phrase consisting of the long form of the possessive adjective after the noun.

1. la mochila (yo) ____________________ ____________________
2. los documentos (ella) ____________________ ____________________
3. el carro (nosotros) ____________________ ____________________
4. las fotos (tú) ____________________ ____________________
5. el dentista (Uds.) ____________________ ____________________
6. los guantes (Ud.) ____________________ ____________________

I. Personal pronouns. Write the correct subject pronoun next to the verb form. If there is more than one correct answer, write them all.

1. hice ______________________
2. das ______________________
3. erais ______________________
4. han vuelto ______________________
5. haremos ______________________
6. diría ______________________
7. tuvo ______________________
8. trajiste ______________________

J. Prepositional pronouns. Write the correct form of the prepositional pronoun that follows the preposition.

1. para ______________________ (yo)
2. de ______________________ (tú)
3. menos ______________________ (nosotros)
4. con ______________________ (yo)
5. en ______________________ (ellas)
6. por ______________________ (Ud.)
7. como ______________________ (él)
8. con ______________________ (tú)

K. Personal *a*. Complete the following sentences with the personal *a* if it is necessary.

1. Ayer conocí ______________________ ingeniero.
2. Esperemos ______________________ Tere aquí.
3. Jaime lleva ______________________ un gorro.
4. ¿No encontraste ______________________ los sobres?
5. Buscaban ______________________ jefe.

L. Direct object pronouns. Rewrite each of the following sentences changing the direct object noun to a pronoun. If there is more than one way to write the sentence, write it both ways.

1. Los Hernández hablan español.

____

2. Compré cuadernos.

____

3. Vamos a servir hamburguesas.

____

4. ¿No has visto a María?

____

5. Estás pidiendo sopa.

____

M. Indirect object pronouns. Rewrite each of the following sentences adding the indirect object pronoun. If there is more than one way to write the sentence, write it both ways.

1. Compramos flores. (a ella)

____

2. Dijo los motivos. (a mí)

____

3. Mandé la carta. (a vosotros)

____

4. Habían dado el paquete. (a ti)

____

5. Estamos enseñando las esculturas. (a ellos)

____

N. Indirect object pronoun with *gustar*, etc. Add the indirect object pronoun to each of the following sentences.

1. ____________________ (a ti) gustó la película.
2. ¿Cuántos exámenes ____________________ (a Ud.) quedan?
3. ____________________ (a mí) encantan las novelas policíacas.
4. ____________________ (a nosotros) sobra comida.
5. ____________________ (a ella) faltan cincuenta dólares.

O. Double object pronouns. Rewrite each sentence changing the direct object noun to a pronoun and making all necessary changes. If there is more than one possibility, write the sentence in both ways.

1. Les he hecho una ensalada.

 ____

2. Siguen trayéndome las revistas.

 ____

3. ¿Le pusiste el abrigo?

 ____

4. Nos dieron los disquetes.

 ____

5. Puede arreglarte el escritorio.

 ____

P. Prepositions. Select among *por, para, de,* and *en* to complete the following sentences.

1. Hay que estar de vuelta ______________ el quince de noviembre.
2. Aquella señora vestida ______________ rojo es mi tía.
3. Estas novelas fueron escritas ______________ Vargas Llosa.
4. Carmen López está ______________ vacaciones ______________ Puerto Rico.
5. Todos esos regalos son ______________ ti.

Q. Adverbs. Rewrite the following adjectives as adverbs.

1. hermoso ______________
2. fácil ______________
3. generoso ______________
4. diligente ______________
5. claro y abierto ______________

R. Negative words. Select *nada, nunca, nadie, ninguno,* or *tampoco* to complete each of the following sentences.

1. No hay ______________ en casa porque todos han salido.
2. No hemos visto a Elena ni a Roberto ______________.
3. No queda ______________ del dinero que Jorge retiró.
4. No me ha servido ______________ de los dos libros.
5. ______________ más volverán a ese hotel.

S. Numbers. Write out the following numbers as words.

1. 9.734.682 habitantes

   ____

2. 38 × 9 = 342

   ____

3. September 16, 1995

   ____

PART FIVE

Hispanic Culture

CHAPTER 29

LENGUA ESPAÑOLA

- La lengua española forma parte del grupo de lenguas románicas, las lenguas que derivan del latín. Otras lenguas de esta familia incluyen, en la Península Ibérica, el catalán y el portugués, y en el resto de Europa, el francés, el provenzal, el italiano y el rumano. Estos idiomas derivan no del latín clásico, el idioma literario que se estudia en la escuela, sino del latín hablado que fragmentó en un sinnúmero de dialectos locales al caer el Imperio Romano. Al formarse los estados nacionales, uno de los dialectos, por razones diferentes en cada país, llegó a desempeñar la función de idioma nacional.
- Los primeros romanos llegaron a España a finales del siglo III antes de Cristo y la conquista romana de la Península duró casi un siglo. Poco a poco la Península se romanizó, y los habitantes abandonaron los idiomas indígenas a favor del latín, lengua de la administración, del ejército y de las escuelas. Uno de los idiomas prerrománicos, el vascuence, sigue en uso hoy en día en el País Vasco. Subsisten algunos vocablos en el español de las lenguas prerrománicas: **cama, manteca, perro, vega** entre otros. El vascuence ha aportado más que los otros idiomas porque no desapareció, sino siguió como lengua hablada. Una gran parte de la onomástica española es de origen vasco: apellidos como **García**, **Ayala** y nombres como **Iñigo** y **Jimena**. Pero es el latín que triunfa en la Península, y es el latín que da la base estructural y léxica del español y de los otros idiomas que se hablan en la Península. Es un latín lleno de préstamos del griego. De origen griego son **escuela, cuerda, gobernar, bodega, menta, ancla, yeso, huérfano, idea** y muchos vocablos más. La caída del Imperio Romano ante la ola de invasiones germánicas lleva al establecimiento de un reino visigodo en España. Al latín hablado de España llegan palabras de origen germánico, como **guerra, robar, guardar, falda, ganas, rico** y **fresco**.
- La influencia extranjera que más caracteriza el español y que más lo distingue de las otras lenguas románicas es la del árabe. Con la conquista de la Península por los musulmanes a principios del siglo VIII, empieza una presencia árabe que durará ocho siglos, hasta la caída del reino de Granada en 1492. La Reconquista cristiana de la Península fue un proceso histórico que determinó la preeminencia del castellano sobre los otros dialectos peninsulares. En su origen un dialecto rudo e inculto de la zona montañosa al norte de Burgos en Castilla la Vieja, los que hablaban este dialecto castellano llegaron a desempeñar un papel importante en la Reconquista. Con ellos se difunde su dialecto, y el castellano llega a ser la lengua del centro y del sur de la Península, y el idioma de la corte española. Es el castellano y no los otros dialectos de la Península que los conquistadores llevan a América, y así el español se convierte en uno de los principales idiomas del mundo.
- El árabe ha aportado unas cuatro mil palabras al español que se agrupan en varias categorías, como la agricultura: **alcachofa, zanahoria, azúcar, algodón, berenjena, alberca**. En el campo comercial encontramos **tarifa, aduana**. Los árabes crearon ciudades y casas cómodas, como vemos en las palabras **arrabal, aldea, alcoba, zaguán, almohada, albañil, azulejo**. La administración árabe dio al español las palabras **alcalde** y **alguacil**. El nivel intelectual de la España árabe

sobrepasaba todo el resto de la Europa de la época, sobre todo en los tres primeros siglos de dominio moro. El vocabulario de las matemáticas de origen árabe—**algoritmo, cifra, cero, álgebra**—y el vocabulario de las ciencias de origen árabe—**alquimia, alambique, alcohol, jarabe, cenit, nadir**—demuestran sin duda alguna lo culta que era la España musulmana. Los musulmanes dejaron también muchos topónimos en la Península: **la Mancha, Guadalajara, Guadalquivir, Gibraltar, Calatayud**. Dos palabras características del español, **ojalá** y **tarea**, son también de origen árabe.

- La conquista de América trae conocimientos de muchas cosas, sobre todo de animales y plantas desconocidos en Europa. El español toma muchas palabras indígenas para expresarlos, y del español estos vocablos americanos pasan a las otras lenguas europeas: **tomate, chocolate, canoa, batata, caimán, tabaco, hamaca**. Estas palabras americanas se transmitieron durante el siglo XVI cuando España era el país más potente de Europa y cuando el dominio del español era esencial para cualquier hombre culto. Con la conquista de América, el castellano o el español se difunde por un territorio enorme. Puesto que la mayor parte de los conquistadores eran de Andalucía y de Extremadura, fue el español del sur de España que sirvió de base al español americano. En el suroeste de los Estados Unidos el vocabulario de la ganadería tiene muchas palabras de origen español: **lareat, lasso, vamoose, savvy, hoosegow, buckeroo, chaps**. Se ve la profunda influencia de los mexicanos que habitaban esta zona antes de que se incorporara a los Estados Unidos.
- Hoy día el español, enriquecido con palabras francesas, italianas e inglesas, es la lengua materna de más de 300.000.000 de personas. Oficial o co-oficial en 20 países, es el idioma extranjero más estudiado en los Estados Unidos y va aumentando también en Europa y en Japón. El español es el vehículo de una gran literatura internacional que pinta la vida de lugares tan diversos como la meseta castellana, la Pampa argentina o la selva tropical de Venezuela. También es la lengua de muchos escritores de fama universal, diez de los cuales han ganado el premio Nobel de literatura. Cientos de periódicos y revistas se publican en castellano no solamente en los países donde el español es oficial sino también dondequiera que haya grandes comunidades de hispanos, como en los Estados Unidos.
- En Hispanoamérica, sobre todo en México, Guatemala, Perú, Ecuador, Bolivia y Paraguay, hay millones de personas cuya lengua materna es un idioma indígena, pero el uso del español se difunde entre ellos, sobre todo cuando hay inmigración interna del campo a las ciudades. El español es uno de los idiomas oficiales de las Naciones Unidas y de la Unión Europea y se emplea en muchos congresos internacionales. En cuanto al número de hablantes, el español ocupa el cuarto lugar en el mundo, después del chino, del inglés y del hindustano.

A. Corrija las siguientes oraciones.

1. El griego es el elemento más importante en la formación del español.

   ____

2. El vascuence se habla en España a consecuencia de las invasiones germánicas.

   ____

3. El elemento extranjero más característico del español son las voces de origen francés.

   ____

4. El habla de Madrid es la base del español americano.

____

5. El español tiene poco uso en las relaciones internacionales.

____

B. Indique cuál de las posibilidades identifica correctamente las palabras dadas.

1. cama
   a. palabra de origen germánico
   b. palabra de origen prerromano
2. tomate
   a. préstamo inglés
   b. americanismo difundido por el español
3. los visigodos
   a. pueblo germánico que estableció un reino en España
   b. invasores árabes
4. alambique
   a. palabra de origen árabe
   b. palabra de origen griego
5. falda
   a. palabra de origen germánico
   b. palabra de origen vascuence
6. gobernar
   a. palabra de origen americano
   b. palabra de origen griego
7. la llegada de los romanos a España
   a. a finales del siglo III antes de Cristo
   b. a principios del siglo VIII
8. chocolate y tabaco
   a. palabras de origen vascuence
   b. palabras de origen americano
9. catalán, provenzal, rumano
   a. lenguas germánicas
   b. lenguas románicas
10. buckeroo y chaps
    a. influencia mexicana
    b. influencia guatemalteca

C. Escriba las palabras en inglés que derivan de estas palabras españolas.

1. vamos

____

2. lazo

____

3. sabe

____

CHAPTER 30

GEOGRAFÍA DE ESPAÑA

- España y Portugal forman la Península Ibérica, que es el tercer lugar europeo en área después de Rusia y Francia. España limita al norte con el mar Cantábrico (del Atlántico) y los Pirineos, montañas que la separan de Francia, al este y al sudeste con el Mediterráneo, al sudoeste con el Atlántico y al oeste con Portugal y el Atlántico. Al sur, el Estrecho de Gibraltar separa a España de África. Son de España las islas Baleares (Mallorca, Menorca, Ibiza) y las islas Canarias. Ceuta y Melilla, plazas de soberanía de Marruecos, son también territorio español. El centro de España tiene una extensa meseta. La Cordillera Central que va de nordeste a sudoeste—las Sierras de Guadarrama y de Gredos—, divide la meseta en dos submesetas. Al norte de la altiplanicie queda Castilla la Vieja y al sur Castilla la Nueva. La parte sudeste de Castilla la Nueva es La Mancha, una extensa y desnuda llanura. Al sur de la meseta se encuentran los montes de Toledo y más al sur, la Sierra Morena. Al norte del país se encuentran los Pirineos y al sur del país queda la Sierra Nevada, donde se encuentra el pico más alto de la Península, el Mulhacén (3.478 metros). España, aunque queda en la zona templada, tiene variedad climática por su relieve. Tiene tres tipos de clima: continental (casi todo el país), marítimo (el norte del país) y Mediterráneo (Andalucía).
- España tiene cinco grandes ríos, cuatro que desembocan en el Atlántico y uno, el Ebro, que desemboca en el Mediterráneo. El Ebro es de 927 kilómetros, el Duero, de 850 kilómetros, el Tajo, de 910 kilómetros, el Guadiana, de 820 kilómetros y el Guadalquivir, de 680 kilómetros.
- España (incluso las islas) tiene una población de 39.118.000 habitantes. El español es la lengua oficial. Otras lenguas habladas son el catalán, el gallego y el vasco. Un 90 por ciento de la población es católica romana. La capital es Madrid. Otras ciudades principales son Barcelona, Valencia y Sevilla. Los puertos principales son Barcelona, Valencia, Bilbao, Cartagena y Gijón.
- España es un país industrial y agrícola. Es uno de los países más importantes mundialmente en la producción de aceite de oliva y vinos. Unas regiones bien conocidas por sus vinos son Jerez, Málaga y La Rioja. Valencia se conoce por su cosecha de naranjas y arroz; Sevilla por naranjas y algodón; Granada por tabaco, caña de azúcar y remolachas; Murcia por los dátiles; el interior del país por los cereales como trigo y cebada. También se cultivan hortalizas como tomates y cebollas y habichuelas, maíz, patatas y castañas. La cría del ganado ovino, bovino y porcino es importante también. La costa atlántica es la zona pesquera principal de España. Se pescan sardinas, atún, merluza, bacalao y mariscos. España también tiene mucha industria: produce maquinaria, acero, coches, textiles, zapatos y comida procesada. España tiene minerales también: carbón, cobre, mercurio, plomo, uranio, hierro, cinc y manganeso.

Regiones y comunidades autónomas

- La administración de España comprende 50 provincias, 47 de ellas peninsulares y tres insulares (Baleares, Las Palmas, Santa Cruz de Tenerife). El país está dividido en 17 comunidades autónomas, definidas por la Constitución de 1978.

Son Galicia, Asturias, Cantabria, País Vasco, La Rioja, Navarra, Aragón, Cataluña, País Valenciano, Castilla-León, Castilla-La Mancha, Extremadura, Madrid, Murcia, Andalucía, Baleares y Canarias.

El norte—Galicia, Asturias, País Vasco (Provincias Vascongadas), Navarra

- **Galicia,** comunidad autónoma, queda al noroeste de la Península Ibérica, al norte de Portugal. El paisaje es verde y fértil porque la zona es muy húmeda. Hay muchos bosques. Los celtas se establecieron en esta región hacia el siglo VI a.C. A partir del siglo IX comenzaron las peregrinaciones a Santiago de Compostela. Los gallegos hablan gallego, una lengua románica derivada del latín. Las ciudades principales son La Coruña y Vigo. Vigo es el principal puerto trasatlántico de la Península. Es el primer puerto pesquero y uno de los centros industriales más importantes de España. Francisco Franco, que gobernó España de 1939 hasta su muerte en 1975, era de El Ferrol (del Caudillo), ciudad gallega. Galicia tiene muchas pequeñas aldeas que le dan un carácter rural y aislado. La comida se basa en pescados y mariscos como el pulpo, la merluza, los langostinos y los mejillones. El caldo gallego es un plato típico. En cuanto al folklore, el baile típico de la región es la muñeira y el instrumento típico es la gaita.
- **Asturias**, comunidad autónoma y provincia, es una región montañosa del norte de España. Sus ciudades principales son Oviedo, la capital económica, administrativa y cultural de la región, Gijón, un gran centro veraniego, y Avilés. Era reino independiente hasta que se unió con Castilla en 1037. Fue en Asturias, en Covadonga, que se inició la Reconquista. Los musulmanes conquistaron toda la Península. El rey visigodo don Pelayo se refugió con sus soldados leales en los Picos de Europa. Hacia 718 el emir Alcama mandó un ejército a matar a los rebeldes. Pelayo lo derrotó en Covadonga. Esta victoria animó a los cristianos a luchar para retomar el país. Asturias es el centro de la industria química, naval y mecánica tanto como de la producción de carbón y de hierro.
- **País Vasco (Provincias Vascongadas)**, comunidad autónoma, comprende Vizcaya, Álava y Guipúzcoa. El País Vasco, *Euskadi* en vascuence, queda al norte de España. La capital, centro administrativo y comercial, es Vitoria (Álava). San Sebastián (Guipúzcoa) es una ciudad industrial y un gran centro veraniego de fama internacional. Las industrias principales de la región incluyen la alimenticia, química, mecánica y la producción de maquinaria agrícola. Se juega pelota vasca contra un frontón (pared) y con cesta. Las famosas cuevas de Altamira con sus pinturas rupestres prehistóricas se encuentran en Santander, en la costa Cantábrica.
- **Navarra**, comunidad autónoma y provincia, linda con Francia en el norte de España. El antiguo reino de Navarra se extendía a ambos lados de los Pirineos. Perteneció desde el siglo X a los reyes de Aragón y a partir de 1134, fue regido por los príncipes franceses. Fernando el Católico incorporó a su corona la parte situada en la Península Ibérica en 1512. El norte de Navarra es montañoso y tiene muchos bosques. En el sur, que es llano, se cultivan cereales, uvas y aceitunas. Pamplona, capital de la comunidad, se conoce por la feria de San Fermín. La feria de los sanfermines, o encierro de toros, se celebra entre el seis y el catorce de julio.

El centro—Castilla

- **Castilla** es el nombre de las dos mesetas que ocupan el centro de la Península Ibérica. Están separadas por las Sierras de Gredos y Guadarrama. Castilla la Vieja queda al norte e incluye Santander, Burgos, La Rioja, Soria, Segovia, Ávila, Valladolid y Palencia. Castilla la Nueva queda al sur e incluye Madrid, Toledo,

Ciudad Real, Cuenca y Guadalajara. Es una región árida y seca con algunos valles frondosos. Se cultivan el trigo, el olivo y la vid. Castilla quedó definitivamente unida con el reino de León en 1230. El matrimonio de Isabel de Castilla con Fernando II de Aragón (1469) selló en 1479 la unión de Castilla y León con el reino de Aragón. Madrid, capital de España, se encuentra en Castilla la Nueva y es el centro de comunicaciones del país. Castilla dio el carácter, lengua y cultura nacionales a España. El castellano es la lengua oficial de España. **Castilla-León** es una comunidad autónoma. Esta región industrializada tiene hierro, carbón y ganadería. El turismo es importante. La ciudad de León se conoce por su catedral gótica que fue construida entre mediados del siglo XIII y fines del XIV. La ciudad de Segovia se destaca por su acueducto romano, de 28 metros de altura, su catedral y su alcázar. Toledo fue capital de la España visigoda y residencia de la Corte española hasta 1560. Se conoce por su catedral gótica, la iglesia de Santo Tomé y otras, la sinagoga del Tránsito, la casa de El Greco, etcétera.

- **Extremadura**, comunidad autónoma, es una región que limita al oeste con Portugal, al sur con Andalucía, al norte con Salamanca y al este con Castilla la Nueva. Incluye las provincias de Badajoz y Cáceres. La capital es Mérida. Es una región ganadera y agrícola donde se cultivan el trigo, olivo, hortalizas, tabaco, algodón y corcho. Extremadura significa "más allá del Duero". Durante la Reconquista los territorios que se encontraban al sur del Duero formaban la frontera cristiana. Casi todos los Conquistadores eran de Extremadura: Cortés, Pizarro, Núñez de Balboa, Hernando de Soto y Pedro de Valdivia. Había tradición guerrera y aventurera y también necesidad económica. Siempre había mucha emigración de Extremadura.

El sur—Andalucía

- **Andalucía**, comunidad autónoma desde 1982, es la región más extensa de España. El Guadalquivir pasa por aquí. Comprende ocho provincias: Huelva, Cádiz, Sevilla, Málaga, Almería, Granada, Jaén y Córdoba. Es una región fértil conocida por su viñedo (Jerez, Málaga, Montilla-Moriles) y otras cosechas. La Sierra Nevada y la Sierra Morena son importantes en la minería andaluza. La región fue llamada Bética por los romanos, es decir, la región del Betis, nombre antiguo del Guadalquivir. Fue colonizada por los fenicios, griegos, cartagineses y romanos. Los árabes invadieron España en el siglo VIII creando los reinos de Granada, Córdoba, Sevilla y Jaén. La rendición de Granada en 1492 puso fin a la dominación árabe. Andalucía es una región muy pintoresca, el país del flamenco, cante jondo, gazpacho, gitanos y mujeres vestidas de faralaes, peineta y mantilla. Ésta es la imagen que el mundo tiene de España: lo andaluz que se ha exportado al exterior. Sevilla, a orillas del Guadalquivir, es la capital de la comunidad. Tiene una magnífica catedral gótica, la Giralda, el Alcázar, el Archivo de Indias y la Biblioteca Colombina. Es célebre su Semana Santa y sus ferias de abril. Córdoba, también situada en el Guadalquivir, es una ciudad muy pintoresca. Se destacan la catedral, el Alcázar y el puente romano.

El este—Cataluña

- **Cataluña**, comunidad autónoma, es una región de gran actividad industrial y una agrícola muy rica. Sus riquezas naturales incluyen carbón, plomo y sal. Las industrias incluyen la metalurgia, industrias mecánicas, aviones, coches y textiles. El turismo es una importante fuente de ingresos. Barcelona es el puerto más grande de España. Cataluña siempre ha tenido fuertes sentimientos separatistas. Se habla catalán en Cataluña.
- **Valencia**, comunidad autónoma, se considera "la huerta de España" por ser una región agrícola muy rica. Las famosas naranjas valencianas se exportan al mundo

entero. El cultivo de arroz es muy importante. Los arrozales se encuentran en la Albufera, el lago salado a orillas del Mediterráneo. También se cultivan hortalizas. Se emplea un sistema de regadío iniciado por los romanos y perfeccionado por los musulmanes. Valencia es un gran centro industrial también. Hay industria naval, textil, química, metalúrgica, madera, etcétera. Valencia es la tercera ciudad española en población. La región atrae a muchos turistas, especialmente durante las célebres fallas que tienen lugar durante la semana del 12 al 19 de marzo.

- **Murcia**, provincia y comunidad autónoma, queda al sudeste de Valencia. Fue fundada por los árabes en 831. La capital, Murcia, está a orillas del río Segura, en medio de una fértil huerta. Su economía se basa en los dátiles, naranjas, limones y pimentón y en el comercio e industrias.
- **Aragón**, comunidad autónoma, queda al noreste del país. En 1137 Aragón se unió con Cataluña. En 1479 se unió Aragón con Castilla. La capital, Zaragoza, queda a orillas del Ebro. El baile típico de Aragón es la jota.

Posesiones extraterritoriales

- **Las islas Baleares**, comunidad autónoma y provincia, consisten en Mallorca, Menorca, Ibiza y otras islas menores. La capital es Palma de Mallorca. Las Baleares son un lugar turístico de fama mundial.
- **Las islas Canarias**, comunidad autónoma, consisten en siete islas grandes en el Atlántico. Quedan frente a la parte sur de Marruecos. Las dos provincias son Santa Cruz de Tenerife y Las Palmas.
- **Melilla** y **Ceuta** son plazas de soberanía que quedan en la costa de Marruecos. España consiguió Melilla en el siglo XV y Ceuta en el siglo XVII.

- **Madrid**, la capital más alta de Europa (646 metros), está situada en el centro de la Península. Aunque tuvo un desarrollo lento, es ahora una gran ciudad. Los árabes que invadieron España en el siglo VIII dieron el nombre Magerit a la ciudad. En 1083 Alfonso VI tomó la ciudad a los árabes. En 1477 los Reyes Católicos hicieron entrada solemne en Madrid. Felipe II nombró a Madrid capital de su reino en 1561 aunque no lo sería definitivamente hasta 1607. Los Borbones, especialmente Carlos III, embellecieron Madrid con monumentos. Hubo un levantamiento de los madrileños contra las tropas francesas el dos de mayo de 1808. Los franceses usaron armas contra los madrileños en un feroz combate, escena que fue pintada posteriormente por Francisco de Goya, pintor de la corte de Carlos III y Carlos IV. Goya captó la noche del dos de mayo y los fusilamientos del tres de mayo por los franceses en unos cuadros que se exhiben en el Museo del Prado de Madrid. El levantamiento de los madrileños dio ánimo a los otros españoles y así estalló la Guerra de la Independencia. Madrid es una ciudad moderna y sofisticada. La Gran Vía es una famosa avenida céntrica con muchos cines, espectáculos, hoteles, restaurantes, comercios, bancos y cafeterías. La calle Serrano tiene tiendas elegantes y caras. La capital se destaca en gastronomía, con cientos de restaurantes de cocina internacional, cafés al aire libre, bares y tascas. La Madrid vieja se encuentra alrededor de la Plaza Mayor, el centro arquitectónico de la Madrid de los Austrias. Se construyó en el reino de Felipe III (1619).

A. Empareje los lugares o los nombres geográficos de la columna A con su descripción de la columna B.

A

_____ 1. la Mancha

_____ 2. el Tajo

_____ 3. las Baleares

_____ 4. la Sierra de Guadarrama

_____ 5. el estrecho de Gibraltar

_____ 6. el Guadalquivir

_____ 7. la Sierra Nevada

_____ 8. el Cantábrico

_____ 9. las Canarias

_____ 10. los Pirineos

B

a. islas españolas en el Mediterráneo
b. islas españolas cerca de África
c. uno de los ríos más largos de España
d. separa a España de África
e. cordillera del sur de España
f. montañas que separan a España de Francia
g. España limita al norte con este mar
h. extensa llanura del centro de España
i. río que pasa por Sevilla y Córdoba
j. divide la meseta central en dos partes

B. Escoja la respuesta que complete correctamente la oración.

1. ____________________ es la tercera ciudad española en población.
   a. Valencia
   b. Salamanca

2. Bética es el nombre antiguo de ____________________.
   a. Aragón
   b. Andalucía

3. Barcelona está en el ____________________.
   a. Mediterráneo
   b. Cantábrico

4. *Euskadi* significa ____________________ en lengua ____________________.
   a. Cataluña/catalán
   b. País Vasco/vascuence

5. La Reconquista empezó en ____________________, en Asturias.
   a. Gijón
   b. Covadonga

6. La feria de ____________________ tiene lugar en Pamplona en julio.
   a. San Fermín
   b. San José

7. Madrid es la capital ____________________ de Europa.
   a. más alta
   b. más antigua

8. La costa ____________________ es la principal zona pesquera.
   a. mediterránea
   b. atlántica

9. El pico más alto de la Península es ____________________.
   a. el Mulhacén
   b. Ibiza

10. España tiene ______________________ millones de habitantes.
    a. 39
    b. 47

11. Las tres regiones más industrializadas y más ricas son Madrid, el País Vasco y ______________________.
    a. Galicia
    b. Cataluña

12. ______________________ limita al oeste con Portugal y al norte con Salamanca.
    a. León
    b. Extremadura

C. Empareje la región, provincia o comunidad autónoma de la columna A con su capital o ciudad importante de la columna B.

	A	B
_____	1. Valencia	a. Sevilla
_____	2. Extremadura	b. Burgos
_____	3. Vascongadas	c. Vigo
_____	4. Andalucía	d. Mérida
_____	5. Castilla la Vieja	e. Oviedo
_____	6. Aragón	f. Vitoria
_____	7. Navarra	g. Barcelona
_____	8. Galicia	h. Zaragoza
_____	9. Cataluña	i. Valencia
_____	10. Asturias	j. Pamplona

D. Escriba la palabra o la frase que falte.

1. Los musulmanes le dieron el nombre Magerit a la ciudad que actualmente se llama ______________________.
2. La ciudad gallega conocida por sus peregrinaciones a partir del siglo IX es ______________________.
3. El baile típico de Aragón es ______________________.
4. Se considera Valencia ______________________ por ser una región agrícola muy rica.
5. La dominación musulmana de la Península terminó con la derrota de los árabes en ______________________ en 1492.
6. En Galicia se toca ______________________ y se baila ______________________.
7. Cuando se casaron el rey Fernando II y la reina Isabel I se unieron los reinos de ______________________ y ______________________.
8. La casa de El Greco se encuentra en ______________________.

9. Cortés, Pizarro y otros conquistadores eran de ____________________.
10. Se encuentra un gran acueducto romano en ____________________.
11. ____________________ es la región más extensa de España.
12. Zaragoza queda a orillas del río ____________________.
13. Cante jondo, gazpacho y flamenco son elementos folklóricos de ____________________.
14. Córdoba queda a orillas del río ____________________.
15. Las tres islas más importantes de las Baleares son ____________________, ____________________ y(e) ____________________.

E. Cierto o falso. Indique si la oración es cierta o falsa. Si es falsa, corríjala.

1. Las islas Canarias se encuentran en el Mediterráneo.
   ____
2. La Albufera es un lago gallego.
   ____
3. La lengua oficial de España es el castellano.
   ____
4. La Plaza Mayor y el Museo del Prado son importantes lugares madrileños.
   ____
5. Francisco Franco nació en Barcelona.
   ____
6. San Sebastián y Gijón son grandes centros veraniegos.
   ____
7. Jerez y Málaga se conocen por sus vinos.
   ____
8. Vigo es el puerto más grande de España.
   ____
9. España tiene 17 comunidades autónomas.
   ____
10. Gredos y Guadarrama son los nombres de ríos españoles.
    ____
11. Las fallas de marzo tienen lugar en Sevilla.
    ____
12. Extremadura significa "más allá del Tajo".
    ____
13. La Península Ibérica es el segundo lugar europeo en área después de Rusia.
    ____

14. La zona pesquera principal de España es la costa mediterránea.

____

15. Casi toda España goza de un clima continental.

____

CHAPTER 31

HISTORIA DE ESPAÑA

- Los iberos y los tartesios vivían en las costas este y sur de España. Llegaron los fenicios y los griegos de Asia Menor y fundaron factorías comerciales en Gádir, hoy Cádiz. Los celtas, un pueblo centroeuropeo, cruzaron los Pirineos y entraron en España en dos migraciones grandes en los siglos IX y VII. Se establecieron en el oeste y en la meseta, al norte del Ebro y del Duero, donde se unieron con los iberos. El pueblo mixto se llamaban celtíberos.
- Los cartagineses dominaron el sudeste de España después de vencer a los griegos y a los tartesios. La toma de Sagunto (Valencia) por Aníbal desencadenó la segunda Guerra Púnica (218–201). Sagunto se conoce por su heroica resistencia al sitio. Roma venció a los cartagineses y comenzó la conquista con resistencia de parte del pueblo. En Numancia (cerca de Soria), por ejemplo, después de ocho meses de un asedio romano, los numantinos prefirieron quemar su ciudad y suicidarse que someterse. Las provincias españolas estaban totalmente bajo el control romano para el año 19 a.C. España se llamaba Iberia o Hispania. En el siglo I llegó el cristianismo a la Península. Llegó a ser una fuerza básica en la sociedad hispanorromana. Los romanos se quedaron en la Península unos seis siglos durante los cuales se formó la cultura española. Los romanos dieron la base de la lengua, las leyes y la estructura económica y social. Construyeron carreteras, acueductos, puentes y anfiteatros y fundaron grandes ciudades como Zaragoza, Mérida y Valencia. España era, por más de 400 años, parte de un imperio cosmopolita unido en sus leyes, su lengua y sus carreteras.
- En 405 dos tribus germánicas invadieron la Península. Los suevos establecieron un reino en el noroeste y los vándalos invadieron Andalucía, región nombrada por ellos. También invadieron los alanos y después los visigodos, que lograron crear una fuerte monarquía con su capital en Toledo. Unificaron la Península bajo Leovigildo (584–585).
- En la batalla de Guadalete en 711, los musulmanes entraron por el sur de África y vencieron al último rey visigodo, Rodrigo. Había muchos bereberes, sirios y persas y menos árabes, que representaban la aristocracia de la invasión. Los musulmanes lograron dominar España salvo unas regiones del norte.
- En 718 Pelayo, un noble visigodo, derrotó al ejército del moro Alcama en la batalla de Covadonga. Pelayo fue proclamado el primer rey de Asturias. Éste fue el primer episodio de la Reconquista de España, que duró ocho siglos hasta la caída del reino de Granada en 1492. Bajo la influencia musulmana, Al Ándalus o la España musulmana, era culta y avanzada en arte, arquitectura, el sistema de irrigación, etcétera.
- El rey cristiano de Castilla y León, Alfonso X "el Sabio" (1221–1284), reunió a cristianos, árabes y judíos para estudiar, traducir y enseñar. Estos eruditos de la corte dejaron importantes documentos sobre la España medieval. Alfonso subió al trono en 1252. Como historiador, dejó la *Crónica general de España*, como legislador, produjo *Las siete partidas*, como ensayista científico, creó tratados de astronomía y astrología. Sus actividades literarias incluían las *Cantigas de Santa María*, escritas en gallego, y los apólogos de *Calila e Dimna*.
- Los reinos cristianos trataron de unirse para reconquistar sus tierras. Rodrigo Díaz de Vivar, el Cid Campeador, nació cerca de Burgos en 1043 y murió en

Valencia en 1099. Luchó contra los moros venciéndoles en Valencia en 1094. Los moros le pusieron el título "Cid", que quiere decir "señor" en árabe. El Cid fue vasallo del rey Alfonso VI.

- Fernando II de Aragón (1452–1516) e Isabel I de Castilla (1451–1504) se casaron en 1469. Los dos reinos se unieron en 1479. Durante su reinado se organizó la Santa Hermandad en 1476 para proteger a la población rural de los bandoleros; se estableció la Inquisición en 1480 para descubrir y castigar a los herejes; se terminó la presencia de los musulmanes en la Península con la conquista de Granada en 1492; los judíos fueron expulsados de España en 1492; Navarra fue anexada en 1512; América fue descubierta por Colón en 1492, con el apoyo de los Reyes Católicos. Lo que ocurrió durante su reino fue la unificación de la España cristiana y una conformidad religiosa total.
- Carlos I de España, nieto de los Reyes Católicos, subió al trono español en 1516. Heredó los reinos habsburgos haciéndose emperador, Carlos V de Alemania, en 1519. Bajo su reinado, Hernán Cortés conquistó el Imperio Azteca en México en 1521, Francisco Pizarro conquistó el Imperio Inca en Perú (Cuzco) en 1533, Pedro de Mendoza conquistó el río de la Plata en 1534, Francisco Coronado descubrió el Gran Cañón del Colorado en 1535, Hernando de Soto tomó posesión de la Florida en 1539 y Pedro de Valdivia fundó Santiago de Chile en 1541. Carlos V abdicó a un monasterio español y dividió su imperio en 1556. Su hijo Felipe II heredó España, las tierras de Italia, los Países Bajos y las posesiones de América.
- Felipe II (1527–1598) quería ser campeón del catolicismo ante la Reforma y quería mantener la grandeza de España. España venció a los turcos en la batalla del estrecho de Lepanto (Grecia) en 1571. Para vengar la muerte de María Estuardo y destrozar a la reina Isabel I de Inglaterra, Felipe II envió la Armada Invencible contra Inglaterra en 1588. La batalla acabó con la marina española y con esta derrota empezó la decadencia del imperio español. Felipe II hizo construir un monasterio que era también palacio y mausoleo en el pueblo de San Lorenzo de El Escorial en 1563. El Escorial fue construido en recuerdo de la batalla de San Quintín (Francia), ciudad tomada por los españoles en 1557.
- España estaba agotada por las grandes guerras y los reyes Felipe III y Felipe IV eran incapaces de gobernar tantos territorios. España perdió Holanda en 1648. La dinastía de los borbones empezó con el reinado de Felipe V, rey francés (1700). (Carlos I, Felipe II, Felipe III y Felipe IV eran de la casa de Austria.) Por el Tratado de Utrecht (1713), España perdió todos sus dominios europeos, como Gibraltar.
- La Guerra de la Independencia contra Francia estalló en 1808 con un sublevamiento en Madrid que se extendió a todo el país. Napoleón había invadido España y colocado a su hermano José en el trono español. Hubo muchas batallas heroicas y para 1813 los franceses fueron derrotados.
- Fernando VII volvió al trono por segunda vez y gobernó como rey absoluto. Durante su reinado España perdió casi todos sus territorios de América. (Véase *Historia de Hispanoamérica*, las guerras de independencia).
- Al morir Fernando VII (1833), empezaron las guerras Carlistas por la sucesión al trono. Los carlistas tradicionalistas, es decir, los partidarios de Carlos, el hermano de Fernando, se opusieron a los liberales, los partidarios de Isabel II, hija del rey, que era menor de edad. Hubo tres guerras carlistas: 1833–1839, 1855–1860, 1872–1876. Los liberales ganaron esta última guerra civil.
- Durante la Primera República (1873), que duró 11 meses, hubo cuatro presidentes y un caos total. Alfonso XII, de la casa de Borbón, e hijo de Isabel II, volvió como rey en 1874. Murió en 1885. Durante la regencia de su esposa María Cristina, se acabó el resto del Imperio Español. Por el Tratado de París (1898) terminó la guerra entre Estados Unidos y España y España perdió a Cuba, Puerto Rico, Filipinas y Guam.
- Alfonso XIII, borbón, subió al trono en 1902. Hubo intrigas políticas, crisis, atentados, huelgas y sabotajes.

- En 1923, hubo un golpe de estado dirigido por Miguel Primo de Rivera, capitán general de Cataluña. Como jefe del Directorio Militar, Primo de Rivera restableció la autoridad, propuso un plan de obras públicas para construir carreteras, ferrocarriles y puertos y terminó la guerra de África (1925) que era un desastre para los españoles. Hubo oposición a Primo de Rivera entre los viejos partidos, políticos, intelectuales y compañías extranjeras afectadas por la creación del Monopolio de Petróleos.
- Se proclamó la Segunda República en 1931, que duró hasta 1936 cuando una coalición izquierdista, el Frente Popular, subió al poder.
- El general Francisco Franco, al frente del ejército de Canarias y Marruecos, se alzó contra el gobierno republicano. Así comenzó la Guerra Civil en 1936 y duró hasta 1939 cuando Franco venció a los republicanos y estableció una dictadura. Franco gobernó de 1939 hasta su muerte en 1975.
- España mantuvo una política de no beligerancia en la Segunda Guerra Mundial.
- La Ley de Sucesión de 1947 restableció el principio de la monarquía.
- En 1958 se concedió la independencia al protectorado de Marruecos, salvo a Ceuta y Melilla, plazas de soberanía.
- Hasta 1959 España tenía una política de aislamiento económico. Ese año el gobierno decidió europeizar su política económica. Durante los sesenta la economía española mejoró mucho por una política de liberalización y por los ingresos del turismo. Las inversiones extranjeras fueron muy importantes en la modernización de la economía.También hubo mucha emigración de obreros españoles a la Europa industrial. El dinero que mandaron a sus familiares en España ayudó a la economía. Hubo planes de desarrollo en 1964, 1969 y 1972.
- Durante los sesenta hubo un éxodo rural hacia las zonas industriales. Ciudades como Madrid y Barcelona registraron (y siguen registrando) un aumento demográfico mientras algunas provincias como Córdoba, Badajoz y Cáceres se iban despoblando. Las tres regiones más industrializadas, más ricas y más densamente pobladas de España son Madrid, Cataluña y el País Vasco. El turismo sigue siendo una importante fuente de ingresos. La hostelería está controlada por el gobierno español con su sistema de paradores u hoteles nacionales.
- Durante los ochenta hubo un boom expansionista. España hizo la transición a una economía de servicios e información. Sin embargo, en la España tradicional la agricultura domina todavía. En 1986 España firmó un acuerdo de ingreso en la Comunidad Económica Europea. Actualmente España es miembro de la Unión Europea. Estas naciones democráticas de la Unión—Francia, Bélgica, Italia, Alemania, Grecia, Portugal, Luxemburgo, Reino Unido, Irlanda, Dinamarca, Países Bajos y España—procuran integrar sus economías y desarrollar una unión política europea.
- En 1969 Franco nombró al príncipe Juan Carlos de Borbón, nieto de Alfonso XIII, a título de rey, sucesor en jefatura del Estado. Al subir Juan Carlos al trono en 1975, anunció sus própositos reformistas y su intención de integrarse en el mundo democrático occidental.
- En la España moderna, cada región tiene sus propias características culturales, económicas y políticas. Los habitantes de la región tienen lealtad a su región primero y después al concepto abstracto de España. El ejemplo más extremo de una feroz lealtad a región se ve en la campaña independentista y terrorista de los vascos.
- Hubo un intento de golpe de estado en 1981 impulsado por elementos anti-democráticos entre los militares. El golpe fue un fracaso, rechazado por el rey Juan Carlos, que defendió el derecho de los españoles a gobernarse democráticamente. En las elecciones de 1982, Felipe González, socialista, ganó como presidente y volvió a ser elegido en 1989 y 1993. Los españoles, hartos de los muchos problemas graves de los años de González—corrupción, inflación, desempleo, terrorismo de ETA (extremistas vascos)—votaron a José María Aznar, Presidente del Partido Popular, en las elecciones del 3 de marzo de 1996.

- El año '92 fue muy importante para España: los Juegos Olímpicos de Verano de la XXV Olimpiada tuvieron lugar en Barcelona; el Quinto Centenario del descubrimiento del Nuevo Mundo fue celebrado en Sevilla con la gran exposición internacional, EXPO '92; Madrid fue nombrada capital cultural de Europa para 1992.
- Aunque en este momento España está pasando por una etapa económica y políticamente difícil, no cabe la menor duda de que la evolución política y social de España es uno de los grandes acontecimientos políticos del siglo XX. El mundo ha visto la transformación de España de un régimen autoritario y centralizado a una democracia parlamentaria, liberal y pluralista. Y esta transformación ha sucedido sin guerra civil ni revolución. La descentralización ha devuelto el poder y responsabilidad a las regiones y comunidades autónomas y los españoles se han adaptado fácilmente a la democracia.

A. Empareje los sucesos históricos que se encuentran en la columna A con su fecha de la columna B.

	A	B
_____	1. matrimonio de Fernando de Aragón e Isabel de Castilla	a. 718
		b. 1492
_____	2. levantamiento de los españoles contra los franceses	c. 1469
_____	3. derrota de la Armada Invencible	d. 711
		e. 1898
_____	4. Juan Carlos de Borbón sube al trono a la muerte de Franco	f. 1588
_____	5. se termina la presencia musulmana con la conquista de Granada	g. 1936
		h. 1808
		i. 1975
_____	6. empieza la Guerra Civil Española	j. 1939
_____	7. los musulmanes vencen al rey visigodo Rodrigo en la batalla de Guadalete	
_____	8. Francisco Franco establece una dictadura al terminar la Guerra Civil	
_____	9. España pierde Cuba y Puerto Rico por el Tratado de París	
_____	10. se inicia la Reconquista	

B. Complete las oraciones con la respuesta correcta.

1. Rodrigo Díaz de Vivar fue ______________________.
   a. un rey visigodo
   b. el Cid Campeador
2. La Inquisición ______________________.
   a. castigó a los herejes
   b. protegió a los campesinos
3. Carlos I de España llegó a ser ______________________.
   a. Carlos V, emperador de Alemania
   b. Francisco Coronado
4. España venció a los turcos en la batalla de ______________________.
   a. Covadonga
   b. Lepanto

5. Los ____________________ dieron la base de la cultura española.
   a. musulmanes
   b. romanos
6. Al Ándalus fue ____________________.
   a. la España musulmana
   b. el rey moro vencido por Pelayo
7. *Las siete partidas* era una obra de leyes escrita por el rey ____________________.
   a. visigodo Rodrigo
   b. cristiano Alfonso X "el Sabio"
8. Hernán Cortés conquistó el imperio azteca y Francisco Pizarro conquistó el imperio inca bajo el reinado de ____________________.
   a. los Reyes Católicos
   b. Carlos V de Alemania
9. España perdió Gibraltar por el Tratado de ____________________.
   a. Utrecht
   b. París
10. El Rey Juan Carlos es de la casa de ____________________.
    a. Borbón
    b. Austria
11. Las Guerras Carlistas estallaron por ____________________.
    a. los territorios americanos
    b. la sucesión al trono
12. El golpe de estado de 1923 fue dirigido por ____________________.
    a. Miguel Primo de Rivera
    b. Felipe González

C. Cierto o falso. Indique si la oración es cierta o falsa. Si es falsa, corríjala.

1. Los iberos se unieron con los fenicios.

   ____

2. Roma controlaba todas las provincias españolas para el año 19 a.C.

   ____

3. Zaragoza, Valencia y Mérida fueron fundadas por los cartagineses.

   ____

4. Los suevos y los vándalos invadieron la Península en el siglo V.

   ____

5. La Reconquista comenzó con la derrota del rey moro por el rey visigodo Pelayo en la batalla de Covadonga.

   ____

6. Cristóbal Colón logró llegar al Nuevo Mundo con el apoyo de Alfonso X "el Sabio".

   ____

7. Los visigodos fueron expulsados de España en 1492.

____

8. La Segunda República española fue proclamada en 1931 y fue derribada en 1936.

____

9. El Quinto Centenario del descubrimiento del Nuevo Mundo se celebró en Barcelona.

____

10. Felipe II mandó la Armada Invencible contra Francia en 1588.

____

D. Escriba la palabra o la frase que falte.

1. _______________ restableció el principio de la monarquía española.
2. Las tres regiones más ricas y más industrializadas de España son _______________, _______________ y _______________.
3. Juan Carlos subió al trono español en el año _______________.
4. El edificio construido por Felipe II que le sirvió de monasterio, palacio y mausoleo fue _______________.
5. Los visigodos unificaron la Península y establecieron su capital en _______________.
6. La Reconquista de España comenzó en el siglo _______________ y terminó en el siglo _______________.
7. La Guerra de la Independencia contra Francia estalló en _______________ y continuó hasta _______________.
8. El cristianismo llegó a la Península en el siglo _______________.
9. Los tres grupos de eruditos responsables por la vida intelectual de la corte del rey Alfonso X "el Sabio" eran los _______________, los _______________ y los _______________.
10. La _______________ fue establecida en 1476 para proteger a la población rural de los bandoleros.

CHAPTER 32

LITERATURA DE ESPAÑA

EDAD MEDIA
Siglo XI

- Los orígenes de la literatura española remontan al siglo XI con la poesía mozárabe. Las jarchas son cancioncillas bilingües, es decir, romance primitivo con palabras árabes. Algunas jarchas son anónimas pero otras fueron compuestas por poetas árabes y judíos, como *la finida* o estribillo de composiciones más largas, las muwassahas, escritas en árabe. Tienen interés histórico y también literario. Las jarchas son la primera muestra de las literaturas romances, es decir, en las nuevas lenguas románicas que evolucionaron del latín.
- Desde el siglo XII se habló del mester de juglaría para describir un género de poesías épicas, anónimas y populares que los juglares (poetas ambulantes) recitaban de memoria. *El Cantar del Mio Cid* es la obra más importante del mester de juglaría. El mester de clerecía, en cambio, fue cultivado por clérigos o autores cultos y destinado a la lectura. *El Libro de Buen Amor* de Juan Ruiz, Arcipreste de Hita, es la obra más importante del mester de clerecía y la más importante de toda la poesía medieval española.

Siglo XII

- *El Cantar del Mio Cid*, escrito por un juglar o poeta anónimo, fue compuesto hacia 1140. Se cree que fue el juglar de Medinaceli (Soria) que lo compuso. Se considera la primera obra de la literatura española y el mejor ejemplo de la poesía épica española. Es una de las obras maestras de la literatura española y la literatura universal. Es uno de los cantares de gesta (de las *chansons de gestes* francesas), es decir, narración poética de hazañas importantes. *El Cantar del Mio Cid* narra las hazañas de El Cid Campeador, Rodrigo (Ruy) Díaz de Vivar, que nació cerca de Burgos en 1043 y murió en Valencia en 1099. El Cid sirvió a Alfonso VI, rey de León y Castilla, guerreando contra los moros y los cristianos. Al final de su vida El Cid defendió Valencia que había conquistado de los moros. Era casado con doña Jimena, parienta del rey Alfonso VI. El Cid, que significa "señor" en árabe, fue nombrado así por los musulmanes. Esta figura histórica llegó a mitificarse en las leyendas. Lo que se destaca de la épica es el hermoso relato de las hazañas y los conflictos familiares del Cid. El estilo poético del juglar es muy apropiado al tema de los valores humanos. Hay sobriedad, sentido dramático, emoción y espíritu en el cantar además de su obvio interés lingüístico.
- **Alfonso X "el Sabio"** (1221–1284), rey de Castilla y León, subió al trono en 1252. La literatura floreció durante su reinado. Él mismo escribió y recopiló prosa y verso y reunió en su corte a los cristianos, judíos y musulmanes más cultos del país para escribir y traducir textos. Estos documentos proporcionan mucha información sobre la Edad Media. Alfonso X, historiador, hizo escribir la *Crónica General o Estoria de España*. Fue iniciada por su orden y bajo su dirección y fue acabada en el reinado de Sancho IV. Alfonso X fue editor de *Las siete partidas* compuestas de 1256 a 1276. Es la colección de leyes más amplia de las varias que se hicieron bajo la dirección del rey y es la recopilación del derecho de la Edad Media más importante. Tiene valor jurídico y valor de ser documento de la vida

e ideas de su época. Tiene también valor lingüístico por presentar por primera vez una prosa escrita con esmero literario. Alfonso X escribió *Las Cantigas de Santa María*, colección poética de milagros y de alabanzas de la Virgen. El rey las escribió en gallego-portugués, lengua usada por los poetas castellanos de esa época.

- **Los libros de caballerías** empezaron a escribirse en el siglo XIV y gozaron de mucha fama hasta finales del XVI. Narraban las aventuras y episodios sobrenaturales de sus héroes con gran idealismo y un tono lírico. Al principio se usaban leyendas de origen bretón pero luego se añadió lo español en su carácter moral, didáctico y piadoso. Solía haber mezcla de lo real y lo fantástico, lo religioso y lo profano y lo occidental y lo oriental.
- **Don Juan Manuel** (1282–1348), sobrino del rey Alfonso X "el Sabio", es el prosista más importante de su época. Sus 14 obras son por la mayor parte de tipo didáctico-moral, con algún argumento narrativo. El *Libro de los ejemplos del conde Lucanor y de Patronio* es la obra principal de don Juan Manuel. Terminada en 1335, su primera parte es una colección de 51 ejemplos o cuentos en prosa. Esta obra se considera la más importante de la literatura española de la Edad Media.
- El mejor ejemplo de la poesía del siglo XIV es el *Libro de Buen Amor* de **Juan Ruiz, Arcipreste de Hita** (¿1283–1350?). La obra, compuesta entre 1330 y 1347, es una colección o cancionero de casi todos los motivos y formas de la poesía del siglo XIV. El tema central es la narración de unas aventuras amorosas. Se intercalan ejemplos e imitaciones de las fábulas francesas, trozos líricos religiosos y profanos, alegorías, sátiras, etcétera. Juan Ruiz emplea el humor y escribe con unidad de estilo.
- Las *Coplas* de **Jorge Manrique** (¿1440?–1479) se destacan como la mejor poesía lírica y elegíaca de la Edad Media. Manrique escribió estos poemas llenos de emoción y de finura, por la muerte de su padre, el maestre don Rodrigo.

ÉPOCA DE LOS REYES CATÓLICOS (1475–1516)

Poesía culta

- En la época de los Reyes Católicos, la poesía culta sigue las corrientes del siglo XV. Aunque en general el nivel de la poesía es superior, no hay poetas de gran importancia. Empieza el renacimiento de la poesía religiosa.

Poesía popular y tradicional

- Una de las más importantes creaciones de la literatura española es la poesía anónima de origen medieval, que es popular y tradicional. La poesía fue recitada y contada por el pueblo español y en todos los países de habla española y por los judíos de origen español que fueron expulsados de España en 1492.
- El *romance* es la forma más rica de esta poesía. Los romances derivan de las viejas *canciones de gesta,* fondo originario del romancero, que empezaron a fragmentarse a través de los siglos al ser recitadas por los juglares. Así nacieron los romances llamados *viejos*. El fenómeno empezó mucho antes de la época de los Reyes Católicos, pero es en esta época y en los años de transición entre la literatura medieval y la renacentista, cuando el romance llega a su plenitud y empieza a ser publicado y recogido. Los romances anónimos son los *históricos*, los más importantes, sobre héroes, hazañas y leyendas de la antigua tradición épica, como *El Cantar del Mio Cid*.
- En la época de los Reyes Católicos apareció el primero de los dramaturgos españoles. Aunque tenía una técnica medieval, demostraba un espíritu más renacentista. **Juan del Encina** (¿1469?–1529) usó muchos motivos renacentistas, religiosos y pastoriles. En esta época apareció la primera *Gramática castellana,* publicada en 1492. Su autor fue **Antonio de Nebrija** (1444–1522), el más famoso de los humanistas españoles del siglo XV. Su gramática es también la primera de

una lengua vulgar. En su prólogo a la gramática, dirigida a la reina Isabel, Nebrija escribió un maravilloso documento literario que demuestra el espíritu de su época.

- **Fernando de Rojas** (¿–1541?) fue un judío converso y autor de *La Celestina o Tragicomedia de Calisto y Melibea.* Publicada en Burgos en 1499, la obra inicia la gran literatura clásica española. Se destaca el valor humano de los personajes, el dramático ambiente de pasión, el estilo rico, su profunda concepción de la vida y el complejo de elementos artísticos que dan unidad a la obra. Este nuevo estilo de Rojas une la Edad Media y el Renacimiento, lo cómico y lo trágico, gente de clase baja tomada de la realidad y amantes ideales sacados de la tradición literaria, técnica narrativa de novela y acción dialogada del teatro, lenguaje popular y lenguaje literario. Rojas da vida a uno de los personajes universales de la literatura, la Celestina, que es alcahueta y bruja.
- **La novela de caballerías** *Amadís de Gaula* fue escrita hacia 1492 y publicada en 1508. Por su estilo y espíritu, es un libro del Renacimiento. Ésta es la obra que inicia la larga serie de libros de caballerías que llega hasta el *Quijote* de Cervantes. Aquí se describe el héroe Amadís y sus maravillosas y fantásticas aventuras, la exaltación del valor y del amor perfecto, la lealtad y la cortesía.

LA EDAD DE ORO (O EL SIGLO DE ORO): SIGLOS XVI Y XVII

- Es difícil fijar períodos exactos porque los movimientos literarios e históricos no corresponden a un siglo justo. Lo que separa esta época de la anterior es la creación de los grandes géneros modernos—novela, poesía lírica, teatro—y la aparición de los grandes autores clásicos. Los dos nombres grandes del período son **Cervantes** en la novela y la prosa y **Lope de Vega** en el teatro y la poesía lírica. Termina el período con la muerte de otro gran dramaturgo español, **Calderón de la Barca.**

Siglo XVI (Primera mitad)

- **Garcilaso de la Vega** (1503–1536) es el poeta más representativo del Renacimiento en España. Da expresión pura y perfecta a todos los metros y las formas de origen italiano adoptados por los poetas españoles. Sus temas, motivos y formas encuentran su expresión perfecta en sonetos, canciones, elegías y églogas.

Historia de Indias

La literatura de Indias o literatura escrita por los españoles sobre América empieza con las cartas que el descubridor **Cristóbal Colón** (1451–1506) escribió a los Reyes Católicos. (Véase *Literatura hispanoamericana.*)

- **Hernán Cortés** (1485–1547), conquistador de México, inicia un nuevo género de literatura histórica, el de los "cronistas de Indias". Cortés escribió cinco *Cartas de relación* al emperador Carlos V entre 1519 y 1526, contándole lo de sus hazañas. Son documentos históricos sin intención literaria.
- **Fray Bartolomé de las Casas** (1474–1566), sacerdote, misionero, colonizador y defensor de los indios, relata los abusos que, según él, caracterizan a la Conquista de América. Escribió denuncias del trato de los indios en su *Brevísima relación de la destrucción de las Indias.* El libro fue el origen principal de la "leyenda negra" de la Conquista.
- **Álvar Núñez Cabeza de Vaca** (¿1490–1564?) escribió los *Naufragios,* relato de su expedición a la Florida con Pánfilo de Narváez en 1527 y su marcha heroica hasta México.
- **Gonzalo Fernández de Oviedo** (1478–1557) cruzó el Atlántico doce veces y ocupó varios cargos en América. En 1526 publicó un *Sumario de la natural historia de las Indias,* lleno de descripciones de la naturaleza del nuevo continente.

- **Bernal Díaz del Castillo** (1495–1584), soldado de Cortés en la Conquista de México, escribió la *Historia verdadera de la conquista de la Nueva España*. La crónica es una historia vivida, un relato natural que demuestra mucha humanidad en juzgar a personas y sucesos. Con un estilo espontáneo que emplea la lengua hablada, Díaz del Castillo escribe sobre la importancia de todos los soldados en la empresa, no sólo la de Cortés.

Siglo XVI (Segunda mitad)

- **Alonso de Ercilla** (1533–1594) es el escritor más importante de la poesía épica durante este período. Ercilla, madrileño y de familia noble, se educó en la corte de Felipe II. Tomó parte en la Conquista de Chile, tema de su gran poema épico *La Araucana* (1569–1589).
- *Lazarillo de Tormes*, de autor anónimo, fue publicada en 1554. Esta obra inicia un género literario muy importante en la literatura española de la Edad de Oro—la novela picaresca. Es un relato autobiográfico de las aventuras de un pícaro, un joven sin familia y de condiciones humildes que sirve de criado a varios amos. El pícaro cambia de amo con frecuencia según las circunstancias. Es astuto y engaña a la gente para vivir. La obra es una excelente crítica satírica de la vida de la época y de las personas de las distintas clases sociales. Otras obras de este género se inspiran en su estilo natural y espontáneo y en la visión social sencilla que tiene el protagonista. A diferencia de otros protagonistas de la picaresca posteriores, éste no se pone ni amargo ni cínico a pesar de sus desengaños y desilusiones.

Ascética y mística

Hay algunos escritores místicos muy importantes que escriben durante la Edad de Oro. El místico es una persona que se dedica a Dios y describe sus experiencias íntimas de la vida espiritual de la unión del alma con Dios. El ascético es una persona que se dedica a los ejercicios espirituales de la vida cristiana para alcanzar la perfección.

- **Fray Luis de Granada** (1504–1580), místico y ascético, fue un gran prosista y orador elocuente. Escribió la *Guía de pecadores* (1556), colección de normas para alcanzar la vida eterna.
- **Santa Teresa de Jesús** (1515–1582), monja carmelita y reformadora de su Orden, nació en Ávila. Escribió con ardor sobre el amor divino. Escribió *Camino de perfección*. El misticismo español llegó a su máxima expresión humana con Santa Teresa.
- **Fray Luis de León** (1527–1591), agustino, nació en la provincia de Cuenca. Fue profesor en Salamanca. Sus poesías, *La perfecta casada* y otras obras demuestran su gran intelecto, su espíritu sereno y su tono lírico.
- **San Juan de la Cruz** (1542–1591), carmelita, nació en la provincia de Ávila. Escribió el *Cántico espiritual*, poesía lírica con un gran amor místico.

Miguel de Cervantes Saavedra (1547–1616) es el autor de *El ingenioso hidalgo don Quijote de la Mancha*, uno de los libros más leídos en todos los idiomas. Nació en Alcalá de Henares. Fue soldado en la batalla de Lepanto (1571) en la cual don Juan de Austria venció a los turcos. A Cervantes se le dio el apodo "el manco de Lepanto" por ser herido en la mano izquierda. Cervantes fue prisionero de los turcos en Argel y encarcelado varias veces por deudas y otros delitos. Tuvo una vida difícil. La primera parte del *Quijote* fue publicada en Madrid en 1605, la segunda parte en Madrid en 1615. La obra es una sátira de las novelas de caballerías. Cervantes narra la historia de un hidalgo de unos 50 años que se cree caballero andante. Don Quijote sale de su casa para resolver las injusticias del mundo y para tener aventuras en nombre de su señora Dulcinea, que es realmente una moza ordinaria. Don Quijote sale montado en su caballo Rocinante, acompañado de su escudero Sancho Panza. Además de ser una novela de episodios divertidos y cómicos, es una obra de profunda inteligencia de base filosófica y psicológica. Cervantes retrata a Don Quijote y a Sancho Panza como opuestos—idealismo y realismo—o como dos partes de una sola persona. Cervantes cultivó todos los géneros. Escribió novelas, poesías, obras de teatro y una colección de 12 novelas, las *Novelas ejemplares.*

- **Lope de Vega** (1562–1635), poeta y dramaturgo, nació en Madrid. Es fundador del teatro nacional y padre de la comedia moderna. Por el número de versos que escribió se le llamaba "Fénix de los ingenios" y según Cervantes, Lope fue un "monstruo de la naturaleza". Escribió más de 1.500 obras de teatro en verso. Se destacan sus obras *Fuenteovejuna* y *Peribáñez y el comendador de Ocaña, El caballero de Olmedo* y *El mejor alcalde, el rey.* Las obras son importantes por sus temas de historia y carácter nacional, el honor y la honra. Lope expresó sus teorías sobre el arte de escribir teatro en su *Arte nuevo de hacer comedias.*
- **Tirso de Molina** (¿1584?–1648) es el pseudónimo de Fray Gabriel Téllez, gran escritor y dramaturgo contemporáneo de Lope. Se destacan sus obras por su profundidad psicológica, la clara expresión de ideas teológicas y su gran sentido cómico. Tirso se conoce por un personaje que creó en su drama *El burlador de Sevilla y el convidado de piedra.* El infame don Juan llegó a ser un personaje universal.
- **Juan Ruiz de Alarcón** (¿1581?–1639) nació en México pero pasó la mayor parte de su vida en España. Sus obras no gozaron de mucha fama mientras vivió. Se considera creador del teatro de crítica de costumbres. Alarcón critica la mentira en *La verdad sospechosa,* quizás su mejor obra. Escribió *Las paredes oyen* contra la calumnia y *No hay mal que por bien no venga.*

Siglo XVII

- **Luis de Góngora y Argote** (1561–1627) nació en Córdoba. Es el poeta más importante del culteranismo y uno de los maestros más admirados de las nuevas generaciones de poetas. Cultivó el soneto, el romance y la letrilla. Su arte culmina en grandes poemas ultrabarrocos y complicados como la *Fábula de Polifemo y Galatea,* de inspiración de Ovidio, y *Las soledades,* uno de los textos mayores de la poesía española de todos los tiempos. Góngora dejó *Las soledades* sin terminar.
- **Francisco de Quevedo y Villegas** (1580–1645) nació en Madrid. Tuvo una vida activa en la corte e intervino en la política interior y exterior bajo Felipe III y Felipe IV. Combatió el culteranismo como representante del conceptismo. Escribió sonetos líricos y profundos y letrillas de carácter cínico y burlón. Llegó a la plenitud de su genio en la prosa de *Los sueños.* Escribe sobre la pesadilla de la locura humana en *Los sueños* y en sus fantasías morales como *La hora de todos.* Escribió una novela picaresca *Historia de la vida del Buscón llamado don Pablos* (1626). Es una obra satírica y cómica con una visión pesimista.
- **El Inca Garcilaso de la Vega** (1539–1616) nació en Perú de madre que era princesa incaica y padre que era de la familia de Garcilaso de la Vega y Jorge Manrique. Es símbolo encarnado del mestizaje que representa la Conquista. Vivió casi toda su vida en España. Su obra más conocida es *Comentarios reales que tratan del origen de los Incas* que fue publicada en Lisboa en 1609. Se ven los dos mundos del escritor, el español y el americano y su visión nostálgica del pasado incaico.
- **Pedro Calderón de la Barca** (1600–1681) y Lope de Vega son los dramaturgos más importantes del Siglo de Oro. Entre Lope y Calderón el teatro español llega a su plenitud. Las obras de Calderón son más intelectuales que las de Lope, que son más espontáneas. El arte de Calderón es más barroco y de mayor intensidad dramática. Dos dramas representativos de Calderón son *La vida es sueño* (1635), obra filosófico-religiosa sobre la predestinación y el libre albedrío, y *El alcalde de Zalamea.* En el primero, Calderón sugiere que el hombre está dotado del libre albedrío, que tiene que usar este don bien para poder ganar la eternidad, que

es lo único real. En el segundo, Calderón presenta un drama del honor, como se entendía en esa época. El protagonista, Pedro Crespo, es un hombre humilde, pero en defender su dignidad no se distingue del caballero noble.

SIGLOS XVIII Y XIX

El siglo XVIII es el menos importante artísticamente de la literatura española. Los escritores españoles reciben mucha influencia francesa durante estos años como se ve en el desarrollo del racionalismo y el espíritu crítico, el neoclasicismo y el enciclopedismo. La Ilustración es un movimiento europeo del siglo XVIII caracterizado por una gran confianza en la razón, por la crítica de las instituciones tradicionales y la difusión del saber. Al mismo tiempo aparecen nuevas formas de expresión literaria y artística en los estilos rococó, neoclásico y prerromántico. *La Real Academia Española de la Lengua* fue creada por el rey Felipe V en 1714 a imitación de la Academia Francesa. Sus objetivos eran la propiedad, elegancia y pureza de las voces del idioma castellano, enunciados en el lema: "limpia, fija y da esplendor".

El siglo XIX tiene dos movimientos literarios importantes: el romanticismo y el realismo. Los primeros años del siglo son de transición del neoclasicismo al prerromanticismo. El romanticismo creó una estética basada en un rechazo de la disciplina y reglas del clasicismo y del academicismo. El romanticismo incluye un intenso cultivo de la lírica, una valoración del paisaje, un gusto por las cosas de la Edad Media, un amor a lo folklórico y lo regional que da un renacimiento de lenguas como el catalán y el provenzal. El individuo y sus sentimientos se ponen encima de todo.

- **Ángel de Saavedra, Duque de Rivas** (1791–1865), poeta y dramaturgo cordobés, se considera el primero de los románticos españoles. Escribió obras de carácter neoclásico antes de 1834. Escribió los *Romances históricos* que cuentan leyendas y su drama *Don Álvaro o la fuerza del sino* (1835) inspiró a Giuseppe Verdi (1813–1901) a componer su ópera "La fuerza del sino".
- **Mariano José de Larra** (1809–1837) destaca por su obra romántica y por su personalidad. Demuestra un pesimismo romántico y un talento analítico en su prosa. Como escritor costumbrista criticó las costumbres y los prejuicios de los españoles de su época. Sus *Artículos de costumbres* son sátiras de costumbres. Usó unos pseudónimos como "Fígaro" y "El pobrecito hablador".
- **José de Espronceda** (1808–1842) nació en Badajoz. Es el poeta lírico más intenso de los poetas románticos. "El canto a Teresa" del poema "El diablo mundo" es una de las grandes poesías de amor de la literatura española. Escribió la leyenda lírica "El estudiante de Salamanca".
- **José Zorrilla** (1817–1893) nació en Valladolid. Escribió muchos dramas, leyendas y memorias de gran inspiración. Lo mejor de su obra es el teatro. "Don Juan Tenorio" es una obra típicamente romántica.
- **Gustavo Adolfo Bécquer** (1836–1870), poeta y escritor, nació en Sevilla. Aportó un acento emotivo e intimista al romanticismo con sus *Rimas*. Las poesías de las *Rimas* son íntimas, sentimentales y de un lirismo muy puro. Son recuerdos, ensueños y nostalgias. Bécquer es el último de los grandes románticos y el precursor del espíritu poético del siglo XX, por su sensibilidad y sentido íntimo.
- **Rosalía de Castro** (1837–1885), poetisa gallega, leyó los versos de Bécquer. (Y Bécquer leyó los versos de Castro.) Castro tiene un verdadero sentimiento lírico como Bécquer. Canta los temas eternos de amor, dolor, tiempo y muerte con una voz llena de emoción. Se ve lo regional en los poemas de Castro. Expresa lo gallego en una viva emoción de la naturaleza y de la tierra. Castro escribió los *Cantares gallegos* en gallego y *En las orillas del Sar* en español.
- **Fernán Caballero,** pseudónimo de Cecilia Böhl de Faber (1796–1877), inició la novela realista y costumbrista del siglo XIX en España. Se ve en esta primera novela, *La gaviota,* el interés de la autora en las costumbres y tradiciones de

Andalucía, su tierra adoptiva. Caballero escribió en una prosa sencilla y directa como la lengua hablada. No es la prosa artificial como la de la novela histórica del romanticismo. El padre de la novelista, Juan Nicolás Böhl de Faber, fue un hispanista alemán que se estableció en Andalucía.

- **Juan Valera** (1824–1905), diplomático y novelista, nació en Córdoba. Su estilo demuestra su gran cultura, una prosa castiza y su comprensión de la psicología. Su obra maestra es *Pepita Jiménez* (1874), un estudio psicológico de un joven seminarista que duda de su vocación religiosa al enamorarse de una viuda joven. Valera escribió otras novelas, cuentos y ensayos literarios.
- **Benito Pérez Galdós** (1843–1920), el escritor español más grande del siglo XIX, nació en Las Palmas de Gran Canaria. Hay varios críticos que opinan que Galdós es el mejor novelista después de Cervantes. Galdós escribió varias novelas, todas de tendencia realista y objetiva. Fue un gran observador y creó personajes y situaciones llenos de humanidad. Sus novelas de tema social incluyen: *Miau, Doña Perfecta, Fortunata y Jacinta, El amigo manso, Torquemada en la hoguera.* Sus *Episodios nacionales* son evocaciones históricas de la Guerra de la Independencia y otros temas. El teatro de tesis incluye *La de San Quintín, El abuelo* y *Electra.*
- **Emilia Pardo Bazán** (1852–1921), que nació en La Coruña, es la novelista de Galicia. Sus novelas más importantes son *Los pazos de Ulloa* y *La madre naturaleza.* La condesa de Pardo Bazán escribe obras realistas y naturalistas. El naturalismo se hereda de la literatura francesa. Esta escuela literaria del siglo XIX se opone al romanticismo. Su forma estética comprende la imitación de la naturaleza bajo todos sus aspectos, incluso lo feo. (El famoso novelista francés, Emilio Zola [1840–1902] desarrolló el naturalismo aplicando un método de análisis científico a los hechos humanos y sociales.)
- **Armando Palacio Valdés** (1853–1938) fue uno de los escritores más conocidos y populares. Escribió novelas de inspiración regional con tono optimista y humorístico, un humor a veces amargo. Escribió *La hermana de San Sulpicio* sobre Andalucía, *José* sobre Asturias y *Riverita* sobre la corrida de toros de Madrid.
- **Vicente Blasco Ibáñez** (1867–1927) es el novelista español de mayor éxito en su tiempo y de más fama fuera de España. Nacido en Valencia, Blasco Ibáñez escribió novelas sobre Valencia. *La barraca*, su obra maestra, pinta el ambiente valenciano con un fondo social. Su estilo es naturalista, con descripciones fuertes y ricas. Describe conflictos sociales o humanos con sentido dramático y enérgico. Escribió una novela sobre la Primera Guerra Mundial, *Los cuatro jinetes del Apocalipsis. Sangre y arena* es una novela de ambiente taurino (corrida de toros).

SIGLO XX

Alrededor de 1898 surge una literatura diferente de la anterior. Sale, en gran parte, de la Guerra de 1898 en que España perdió sus últimas posesiones en América a los Estados Unidos. Como resultado de la guerra, grupos de jóvenes intelectuales españoles se pusieron a examinar el estado espiritual, cultural e intelectual de España dentro del mundo moderno. Estos jóvenes pensadores se conocen como la **"Generación del '98".** Cultivan todos los géneros pero se dedican más que nada al ensayo y a la poesía lírica.

- **Francisco Giner de los Ríos** (1839–1915) fue el gran pedagogo y filósofo de fines del siglo XIX. Tuvo una influencia profunda en crear la sensibilidad y actitudes que predominaron en la literatura española después de 1898. Estaba a favor de la reforma de la enseñanza y fundó la Institución Libre de Enseñanza en Madrid.
- **Miguel de Unamuno** (1864–1936), novelista, filósofo y crítico de Bilbao, fue la figura más importante de su generación por su obra y por la fuerza de su personalidad. Unamuno expresó primero las ideas e inquietudes de su generación, la angustia de lo temporal y el interés por penetrar el alma española.

Tenía preocupación espiritual, curiosidad intelectual y visión. Fue rector de la Universidad de Salamanca. Unamuno cultivó todos los géneros. Escribió las novelas *Tres novelas ejemplares y un prólogo, Niebla, La tía Tula;* los ensayos *Del sentimiento trágico de la vida, En torno al casticismo, Vida de Don Quijote y Sancho;* poesía, artículos y cuentos.

- **Ramón María del Valle-Inclán** (1866–1936), uno de los mejores novelistas de la época, nació en Pontevedra. Su arte se centra en el estilo con su lenguaje rico. Es como una prosa modernista. La última fase de su arte es un expresionismo barroco. Se ve en los *Esperpentos* que elevan lo grotesco, lo feo y lo absurdo a categoría literaria. Sus grandes obras incluyen las *Sonatas—Sonata de otoño* (1902), *Sonata de estío* (1903), *Sonata de primavera* (1904) *y Sonata de invierno* (1905) y *Tirano Banderas,* novela que es sátira caricaturesca de las dictaduras hispanoamericanas. Valle-Inclán no menciona el país pero puede ser México porque el novelista hizo viajes a México. *Tirano Banderas,* como los *Esperpentos,* está construido a base de cuadros sueltos. Se nota una estilización impresionista del lenguaje popular, hasta vulgar.
- **Pío Baroja** (1872–1956) nació en San Sebastián y pinta el paisaje de las Vascongadas en algunas de sus novelas. Sus novelas, realistas y de tono personal, parecen ser de fragmentos e impresiones. Trata lo político en *El árbol de la ciencia* y *Camino de perfección* y las capas sociales humildes de Madrid en *La busca, Mala hierba* y *Aurora roja.*
- **José Martínez Ruiz** (Azorín) (1873–1967) es el crítico literario más importante de la generación. Escribió sobre los clásicos españoles en *La ruta de Don Quijote* y *Rivas y Larra* y sobre el pasado nacional y el paisaje en *Castilla.* Sus novelas como *La voluntad* son personales como confesiones.
- **Ramón Menéndez Pidal** (1869–1968), erudito y maestro de la escuela filológica española, nació en La Coruña. Escribió crítica literaria e historia e hizo edición e interpretación de textos. Es autor de estudios como *Los orígenes del español, La España del Cid, Poema de Mío Cid* y *El romancero español.*
- **Jacinto Benavente** (1866–1954), dramaturgo madrileño, ganó el Premio Nobel de Literatura de 1922. Escribió cerca de 200 obras incluso *Los intereses creados,* una comedia a la italiana, y *La malquerida,* una tragedia rural sobre el pueblo castellano. Su estilo incluye un diálogo hermoso y un fondo burlón que satiriza los defectos humanos.
- **Antonio Machado** (1875–1939), gran poeta sevillano, recibió influencias del modernismo y de la "Generación del '98". Sin embargo, encontró su propia voz poética que era sencilla, concentrada y auténtica. Su emoción profunda salía del recuerdo de una juventud melancólica. Los poemas demuestran un fuerte sentimiento hacia el paisaje castellano, los deseos de una España mejor y el amor noble. Se nota una angustia metafísica en los temas de la muerte, la busca de Dios y la relación entre el sueño y la realidad. Sus colecciones de poemas incluyen *Soledades* y *Campos de Castilla.* Machado fue profesor de francés en varios institutos y cultivó el teatro con su hermano Manuel.
- **Juan Ramón Jiménez** (1881–1958) recibió el Premio Nobel de Literatura de 1956. Escribió poesía y prosa de estilo modernista. Su estilo es puro, de emoción profunda y sentimiento refinado. Sus libros de poesías incluyen *Almas de violeta, Ninfeas, La soledad sonora* y *Animal de fondo. Platero y yo* es un libro en prosa que narra las andanzas del autor por Moguer a lomos de burro. Jiménez nació en Moguer (Huelva) y murió en Puerto Rico. Jiménez tuvo mucha influencia en los siguientes poetas.

Para el año de 1920, cuando las tendencias del '98 están en plenitud, se empieza a hablar de una literatura nueva o de "vanguardia" bajo la influencia de los "ismos" de la posguerra. Hay una rebelión en literatura contra todo lo precedente. Se cree que vale sólo la poesía lírica y se cultiva poco los otros géneros.

- **José Ortega y Gassett** (1883–1955), filósofo y ensayista, es el maestro de una generación de escritores en España e Hispanoamérica. Esta generación pone ideas nuevas frente a la "Generación del '98". Ve la necesidad de buscar la verdad objetiva. Ortega es creador de la filosofía de la razón vital. Se considera "espectador" ante el mundo, que es su "circunstancia". Medita con "amor intelectual" y habla del "perspectivismo" y de "la razón vital e histórica". Ortega fue catedrático de metafísica en la Universidad de Madrid. Escribió las *Meditaciones del Quijote, La rebelión de las masas, España invertebrada* y muchos otros libros de ensayos y de crítica.
- **Federico García Lorca** (1898–1936), gran poeta y dramaturgo granadino, murió al principio de la Guerra Civil Española. Sus obras influyeron mucho en el teatro español innovador. Escribió el *Romancero gitano* (1928), colección de poemas, y la trilogía de dramas *Bodas de sangre* (1933), *Yerma* (1934) y *La casa de Bernarda Alba* (1936). Usó temas folklóricos y tradicionales en su poesía. Sus obras de teatro tratan temas y costumbres españoles que Lorca eleva a nivel universal por los sentimientos y emociones humanos de sus personajes. Lorca forma parte de **la "Generación del '27".**
- **Rafael Alberti** (1902–), poeta de la "Generación del '27", escribió poesía popular y surrealista. Escribió *Marinero en tierra, Cal y canto* y otros libros de poesía.
- **Pedro Salinas** (1891–1951) escribió poesía lírica de mucha emoción—*Presagios, La voz a ti debida, Razón de amor.* Escribió el libro de crítica *Literatura española en el siglo XX.*
- **Jorge Guillén** (1893–1984), poeta de "poesía pura", nació en Valladolid. La "poesía pura" se sirve de lo abstracto y lo conceptual. Escribió *Cántico* (1928), *Final* (1981) y otros libros de poemas. Guillén estudió en España, Suiza y Alemania y fue catedrático de la Universidad de Murcia. Enseñó en universidades norteamericanas también.
- **Vicente Aleixandre** (1898–1984), poeta sevillano, ganó el Premio Nobel de Literatura en 1977. Las raíces de su poesía están en el modernismo, el romanticismo y el superrealismo. Escribió *La destrucción o el amor* (1934) y *Sombra del paraíso* (1944).
- **Alejandro Casona** (1900–1965) vivió en la Argentina después de la Guerra Civil Española y no volvió a presentar obras en España hasta 1962. Sus obras se destacan por su maestría técnica, profundo lirismo, el idealismo elevado y lo humorístico. Escribió *Los árboles mueren de pie, La dama del alba* y *Prohibido suicidarse en primavera* mientras estuvo en América. Escribió *Corona de amor y muerte* y *La sirena varada* cuando vivió en España.
- **Ramón Sender** (1902–1982) escribió varias novelas. Se considera *Réquiem por un campesino* su mejor novela. Escribió también *Mr. Witt en el Cantón* y *Crónica del alba.* Sender vivió en México y los Estados Unidos después de la Guerra Civil.

La generación literaria que se forma después de la Guerra Civil está preocupada por los problemas sociales y económicos de España.

- **Julián Marías** (1914–), filósofo y ensayista, fue discípulo de Ortega y Gassett. Escribió la *Historia de la filosofía* y la *Introducción a la filosofía.* Fue profesor en varias universidades norteamericanas.
- **Camilo José Cela** (1916–) nació en La Coruña. Ganó el Premio Nobel de Literatura en 1989. Cultivó la novela "tremendista", es decir, del realismo de la posguerra. Ganó fama en España y fuera del país con su primera novela, *La familia de Pascual Duarte* (1942). Este libro breve y dramático narra las memorias de un campesino extremeño que comete crímenes y acaba en el cadalso. Cela usa el humor que hace resaltar aún más las atrocidades que describe. Cela escribió las novelas *La colmena, Pabellón de reposo* y *San Camilo 1936.* Es conocido también por sus artículos y ensayos.
- **Antonio Buero Vallejo** (1916–), dramaturgo de Guadalajara, modernizó el teatro contemporáneo con sus obras. Escribió *Historia de una escalera*, que ganó el Premio

Lope de Vega, *Las meninas*, obra histórica, *En la ardiente oscuridad*, obra existencialista. Buero Vallejo pinta la realidad social en sus dramas.

- **Miguel Delibes** (1920–) nació en Valladolid. Escribe sobre la sociedad española en sus novelas. Escribió las novelas *El camino, Diario de un cazador* y *Las ratas*. Es cuentista, periodista y abogado también.
- **Carmen Laforet** (1921–) nació en Barcelona. Su novela *Nada* (1944) ganó el Premio Nadal pero causó un escándalo por su realismo nuevo y crudo. Laforet pintó la crisis espiritual de la posguerra con realismo, pero con ternura y emoción también. La novelista escribió las novelas *La isla y los demonios* y *La mujer nueva* además de unos libros de cuentos.
- **José Hierro** (1922–), poeta nacido en Madrid, escribió una poesía honda de la posguerra. Sus libros de poemas incluyen *Tierra sin nosotros* (1947), *Alegría, Quinta del 42* (1953), *Cuánto sé de mí* (1957).
- **Ana María Matute** (1926–) nació en Barcelona. Recibió muchos premios por sus novelas. Escribió *Primera memoria* (1960)—Premio Nadal, *Los hijos muertos*—Premio Nacional de Literatura (1959), *Pequeño teatro*—Premio Planeta, etcétera.
- **Alfonso Sastre** (1926–) da un mensaje social a sus obras de teatro. Escribió *La mordaza* (1954), *Escuadra hacia la muerte* (1953), *Oficio de tinieblas*. En su ensayo demuestra su afán de renovación en temas y técnica.
- **Juan Goytisolo** (1931–) nació en Barcelona. Sus novelas han sido traducidas a varios idiomas. Escribió *Juego de manos, Duelo en el paraíso, Fiesta, La resaca, Juan sin tierra*, etcétera.
- **Antonio Gala** (1937–) es conocido por sus obras de teatro de temas actuales como *Los verdes campos del Edén, Anillos para una dama* y *Petra Regalada*.
- **Juan Marsé** (1933–) escribió la novela *La oscura historia de la prima Montse*.
- **Juan José Millás** (1946–) ganó un premio con su primera novela *Cerbero son las sombras* y el Premio Nadal en 1990 con *La soledad era esto*.
- **Francisco Umbral** (1936–), novelista, escribió *Diario de un snob* y ganó el Premio Nadal con *Las ninfas* (1975).
- **Antonio Muñoz Molina** (1956–), novelista y periodista, escribió la novela *El invierno en Lisboa* (1987) que ganó el Premio Nacional de Literatura y el Premio de la Crítica.

A. Empareje el autor de la columna A con el título de su obra de la columna B.

A	B
_____ 1. Miguel de Cervantes	a. *Las siete partidas*
_____ 2. Pedro Calderón de la Barca	b. *las Coplas*
_____ 3. José Zorrilla	c. *La Araucana*
_____ 4. Antonio Buero Vallejo	d. *Los sueños*
_____ 5. Alfonso X "el Sabio"	e. *La vida es sueño*
_____ 6. Francisco de Quevedo	f. *La perfecta casada*
_____ 7. Jacinto Benavente	g. *Don Quijote*
_____ 8. Fray Luis de León	h. *La Celestina*
_____ 9. Jorge Manrique	i. *Historia de una escalera*
_____ 10. Alonso de Ercilla	j. *Las soledades*
_____ 11. Fernando de Rojas	k. *Los intereses creados*
_____ 12. Luis de Góngora	l. *Don Juan Tenorio*

B. Escoja el elemento que mejor identifique, defina o describa el tema propuesto.

1. *El Cantar del Mio Cid*
   a. el mester de juglaría
   b. compuesto en 1043
2. las jarchas
   a. poesía mozárabe
   b. mester de clerecía
3. *Gramática Castellana*
   a. el Arcipreste de Hita
   b. Antonio de Nebrija
4. San Juan de la Cruz
   a. cronista de Indias
   b. místico
5. el "Fénix de los Ingenios"
   a. Lope de Vega
   b. Juan Ruiz de Alarcón
6. *La Gaviota*
   a. primera novela realista y costumbrista del siglo XIX
   b. un libro de caballerías del siglo XIV
7. la "Generación del '98"
   a. Ramón Sender
   b. Miguel de Unamuno
8. las *Cantigas de Santa María*
   a. escritas en gallego-portugués
   b. escritas en castellano
9. el poeta más representativo del Renacimiento en España
   a. José de Espronceda
   b. Garcilaso de la Vega
10. la novela "tremendista"
    a. Camilo José Cela
    b. Francisco Umbral
11. Premio Nobel de Literatura de 1956
    a. Juan Ramón Jiménez
    b. Vicente Aleixandre
12. *La casa de Bernarda Alba*
    a. Benito Pérez Galdós
    b. Federico García Lorca

C. Empareje la obra de la sección B con su descripción de la sección A.

A

_____ 1. el pícaro tiene varios amos

_____ 2. colección de leyes de la Edad Media

_____ 3. Don Juan engaña a las mujeres

_____ 4. cancioncillas escritas en romance primitivo con palabras árabes

_____ 5. hidalgo y su escudero tienen muchas aventuras

_____ 6. el libre albedrío contra la predestinación del hombre

_____ 7. protagonista épico conquistó Valencia por su rey Alfonso VI

_____ 8. poemas sobre el paisaje castellano

_____ 9. un campesino de Extremadura castigado por sus crímenes

_____ 10. una tragedia sobre un pueblo de Castilla

B

a. las jarchas
b. *La vida es sueño*
c. *La malquerida*
d. *La familia de Pascual Duarte*
e. *El Cantar del Mio Cid*
f. *Lazarillo de Tormes*
g. *El burlador de Sevilla y el convidado de piedra*
h. *Las siete partidas*
i. *Campos de Castilla*
j. *Don Quijote*

D. Escriba la palabra o la frase que falta para completar las siguientes oraciones.

1. El filósofo y catedrático ____________________ escribió sobre el "perspectivismo" y "la razón vital e histórica".
2. El dramaturgo madrileño que ganó el Premio Nobel en 1922 es ____________________.
3. El gran filólogo español que escribió *Los orígenes del español* y *La España del Cid* es ____________________.
4. El Cid Campeador, Rodrigo Díaz de Vivar, nació cerca de ____________________ en ____________________ y murió en ____________________ en ____________________.
5. El ____________________, escrito por el Arcipreste de Hita, es el mejor ejemplo de la poesía del siglo XIV.
6. Los ____________________ ____________________ son anónimos y derivan de la antigua tradición épica, como *El Cantar del Mio Cid*.

7. *La Celestina*, publicada en 1499, une los estilos de
   ________________ y ________________.
8. El período histórico durante el cual escribieron los grandes autores clásicos de la literatura española y surgieron los géneros modernos se llama ________________.
9. Hernán Cortés, Fray Bartolomé de las Casas y Bernal Díaz del Castillo se llaman ________________ porque escribieron literatura sobre América.
10. *Lazarillo de Tormes* e *Historia de la vida del Buscón llamado don Pablos* son novelas ________________.
11. El misticismo español llegó a su apogeo con ________________, monja carmelita y reformadora de su Orden.
12. Miguel de Cervantes publicó la primera parte de ________________ en ________________ (*año*) y la segunda en ________________ (*año*).
13. El fundador del teatro español nacional y padre de la comedia moderna es ________________.
14. El personaje de don Juan fue creado por ________________.
15. *Las soledades*, poesías culteranas, fueron escritas por ________________.
16. Las ________________, poesías íntimas y nostálgicas, fueron escritas por ________________, el último de los grandes poetas románticos.
17. Francisco de Quevedo luchó contra el culteranismo con el ________________.
18. ________________ es el escritor español más importante del siglo XIX.
19. ________________ se considera la novelista de Galicia y ________________ se considera el de Valencia.
20. ________________, novela que satiriza las dictaduras hispanoamericanas, fue escrita por ________________.

CHAPTER 33

GEOGRAFÍA DE HISPANOAMÉRICA

Hispanoamérica, es decir, México, América Central, las Antillas y América del Sur, consiste en 19 países donde los habitantes tienen el español como lengua oficial.

- **México** o Estados Unidos Mexicanos. Las tres cuartas partes de México pertenecen geográficamente a América del Norte y el resto a América Central. México tiene límite con Estados Unidos al norte (el río Bravo o río Grande separa los dos países), con el golfo de México y el mar de las Antillas (el Caribe) al este, con Guatemala y Belice al sudeste y con el océano Pacífico al oeste. México tiene un área de 1.958.201 kilómetros cuadrados (incluyendo las islas que se mencionan a continuación), o sea, tres veces el tamaño de Tejas. México es como el puente entre los dos continentes americanos. Tiene cordilleras y montañas que se extienden hacia el istmo centroamericano. La actividad volcánica ha influido mucho en la formación del suelo mexicano. La Sierra Madre es el principal sistema de montañas. Se divide en la Sierra Madre Oriental y la Sierra Madre Occidental. Entre estas dos ramas se encuentra una inmensa altiplanicie, la Mesa Mexicana, que se extiende desde el centro de México hasta el interior de Estados Unidos. Hay importantes valles como los de México, Puebla y Toluca. Yucatán, una península que queda al este del país, es una zona baja y tropical. Hay gran varieded climática en México. Algunas islas importantes que forman parte del territorio mexicano son: Cozumel y Mujeres en el mar de las Antillas; Carmen y Puerto Real en el golfo de México; Ángel de la Guarda, Tiburón, San José, Espíritu Santo y Cerralvo en el golfo de California; las Tres Marías y el archipiélago de Revillagigedo en el Pacífico. La Ciudad de México, capital del Distrito Federal y de los Estados Unidos Mexicanos, queda en una meseta a 2.234 metros de altura. Allí es donde los aztecas tuvieron su capital de Tenochtitlán que fue conquistada por los españoles en 1521.

  Las ciudades principales de México son: Ciudad de México, Guadalajara, Monterrey, y los puertos de Veracruz, Tampico y Coatzacoalcos en el golfo de México y Mazatlán en el océano Pacífico. México tiene una población de algunos 92.380.000 habitantes. Ciudad de México tiene por lo menos 20 millones de habitantes.

  En cuanto a la economía de México, la riqueza se encuentra en la agricultura, la industria y la minería. Se cultivan el algodón, el café, el trigo, el maíz, la caña de azúcar, el arroz, el frijol, etcétera. Las industrias principales son el petróleo y el gas natural, el acero, los productos químicos, los textiles, la goma y el turismo. México se destaca por su producción de plata, plomo, oro y cinc. A pesar de sus enormes posibilidades económicas, México no ha logrado sus expectativas por razones mayormente políticas.

Centroamérica o **América Central** se extiende desde el istmo de Tehuantepec hasta el golfo de Darién. Es de 517.998 kilómetros cuadrados (sin contar las islas Antillas). Se conoce como una región de mucha actividad volcánica. En el istmo de Panamá se construyó un canal entre el océano Atlántico y el Pacífico. Hay otro istmo en Nicaragua. El archipiélago de las Antillas pertenece geográficamente a la América Central.

- **Guatemala** tiene una meseta central donde se encuentra la capital, Ciudad de Guatemala. El país tiene muchas montañas, lagos y volcanes. Las erupciones volcánicas y los terremotos han causado grandes desastres. Los puertos importantes son San José y Champerico en el océano Pacífico y Puerto Barrios en el Atlántico. Por su clima tan variado Guatemala produce diferentes productos agrícolas. Los principales para la exportación son el café y el plátano. También se cultivan el chicle, el tabaco, el algodón, el frijol, la caña de azúcar, el trigo, la cebada y la papa. Se producen maderas finas también. La civilización maya floreció en la región del Petén. Guatemala tiene una población de 9.784.000.
- **Honduras** tiene 500 millas de costa en el mar Caribe y 40 millas en el golfo de Fonseca (el océano Pacífico). Hay una cadena montañosa, una prolongación de los Andes Centroamericanos, que cruza Honduras del suroeste al sudeste. Por los diferentes niveles de su territorio, Honduras tiene un clima variado como los otros países centroamericanos. Honduras es un país agrícola con muchos valles y tierras fértiles donde se cultivan el plátano, que es la exportación principal, el café, el maíz, y el tabaco. Se producen también textiles y maderas finas. El país tiene oro, plata, cobre, plomo, cinc, etcétera. Las ciudades principales son Tegucigalpa, la capital, y San Pedro Sula. Honduras tiene una población de 4.949.000 personas.
- **El Salvador** es el país más pequeño de América Central. La superficie del país forma una meseta de 650 metros de altitud media. El Salvador tiene muchos ríos y 296 kilómetros de costa en el Pacífico. Es el único país centroamericano que no tiene costa en el Atlántico. La parte norte del país tiene muchos volcanes. El café es el producto principal de esta economía agrícola. También se producen algodón, maíz, azúcar, henequén y frutas tropicales. Son importantes también los bosques y la goma. San Salvador es la capital. El Salvador tiene una población de 5.574.000 habitantes. Muchos salvadoreños han emigrado a los Estados Unidos por razones políticas y económicas.
- **Nicaragua**, el país más grande de Centroamérica, tiene frontera con Honduras al norte, con Costa Rica al sur y limita con el Atlántico al este y con el Pacífico al oeste. Cada costa en el mar tiene más de 200 millas de largo. Hay dos cadenas de montañas, una cerca del Pacífico y otra que es una continuación de los Andes Centroamericanos. Hay un sistema de volcanes en la costa del Pacífico. Nicaragua es un país agrícola también. Los productos principales son el plátano, el algodón, la fruta, la yuca (la mandioca), el café, el azúcar, el maíz, el frijol, el arroz y el tabaco. En cuanto a la industria, el país tiene refinerías de petróleo, procesamiento de comida, productos químicos y textiles. Managua es la capital. Nicaragua tiene 3.878.000 habitantes.
- **Costa Rica** limita con Nicaragua al norte, con Panamá al sudeste, con el océano Atlántico al este y con el Pacífico al oeste. El país tiene una topografía variada con llanuras bajas y bosques al norte, una altiplanicie en el centro que es una fértil región agrícola y una cordillera al sur. Hay una cadena de volcanes en las llanuras. Costa Rica produce café (su exportación principal), plátanos, azúcar, cacao y algodón. Su industria incluye los muebles, procesamiento de comida, el aluminio, textiles y fertilizantes. Costa Rica tiene también oro, sal, hierro, etcétera. El ecoturismo ha ido cobrando importancia en los últimos años por la red de bosques nacionales. San José es la capital. Costa Rica tiene una población de 3.187.000 personas. A diferencia de los otros países centroamericanos, Costa Rica tiene una población que es casi en su totalidad de raza blanca (95%, con un grupo minoritario de mestizos). Costa Rica tiene una larga tradición democrática y es el único país de las Américas que no tiene ejército.
- **Panamá** queda en la parte más estrecha (de 50 a 200 kilómetros) del istmo de Centroamérica. Aquí se une América Central con América del Sur. Hay una cadena montañosa de los Andes Centroamericanos en la parte occidental del país. Hay grandes selvas en la parte oriental del país. Panamá limita al norte con el

mar Caribe o el Atlántico, al sur con el Pacífico, al este con Colombia y al oeste con Costa Rica. Una gran parte de la población de Panamá vive de las operaciones del Canal de Panamá. Debido a la densidad de la población en esa zona y la falta de comunicaciones, la agricultura no se ha desarrollado mucho. Por eso casi toda la comida se importaba. Pero ahora, la producción agrícola está creciendo. El producto principal de exportación es el plátano. Panamá produce también piña, cacao, maíz, coco y azúcar. Tiene refinerías de petróleo y banca internacional. La ciudad de Panamá es la capital. El país tiene 2.529.000 habitantes. Fernando de Lesseps, administrador y diplomático francés, intentó hacer construir un canal en el istmo. En 1903, Panamá declaró su independencia de Colombia y se firmó el acuerdo Hay-Bunau Varilla que creó la Zona del Canal. Panamá concedió a los Estados Unidos el uso y el control del Canal. En 1904, Estados Unidos empezó la construcción del canal, que quedó terminado en 1914. En 1978, se firmó un nuevo tratado que le entrega el Canal a Panamá para el año 2000. La prosperidad económica de Panamá, debida en gran parte a la Zona del Canal, ha favorecido su estabilidad política.

Las Antillas son un archipiélago que queda entre América del Norte y América del Sur en el mar Caribe. Las Antillas Mayores comprenden Cuba, Puerto Rico, Santo Domingo (la República Dominicana y Haití) y Jamaica. Las Antillas Menores incluyen las islas al este del mar Caribe como Granada, Guadalupe, Martinica, Trinidad, Tobago, etcétera.

- **Cuba** fue descubierta por Cristóbal Colón en su primer viaje en 1492. Las tres cuartas partes de la isla consisten en una llanura, con colinas suaves y valles fértiles. La Sierra Maestra en el este del país es la más alta de las tres cordilleras. La Habana es la capital y Santiago de Cuba y Camagüey son las otras ciudades principales. Cuba tiene una población de 10.846.000 habitantes. Los productos principales son el azúcar, con un 75 por ciento de todos los productos exportados, el tabaco, el arroz, el café y las frutas tropicales. La industria incluye el azúcar, el cemento y el procesamiento de comida. En 1952, Fulgencio Batista tomó el poder y estableció una dictadura en Cuba. Había mucha represión y corrupción en su gobierno hasta que Fidel Castro, guerrillero (un soldado de la guerrilla), lo venció en 1959, año en que Castro mismo tomó el poder. Castro hizo un programa de reforma agraria, económica y social sin restaurar las libertades de los cubanos. Hasta encarceló y asesinó a sus enemigos. Unos 700.000 cubanos se exiliaron de Cuba durante esos años. Castro nacionalizó las tierras, los bancos y las compañías internacionales sin compensar a sus dueños. La cosecha de caña de azúcar, el producto de exportación más importante, no rendía y la anterior Unión Soviética prestó apoyo a Cuba. Castro impuso la colectivación de las granjas, cooperativas, rígidos controles laborales y el racionamiento. Estados Unidos impuso un embargo a Cuba en 1962. Ese mismo año la Unión Soviética colocó misiles nucleares en Cuba, que fueron retirados finalmente por mandato del presidente Kennedy. Cuba siguió con el comunismo aún después que cayó la Unión Soviética. Por contar con la ayuda de la Unión Soviética, Cuba se encontró con grandes dificultades económicas al desaparecer su protector. Esta isla, que antes gozaba de una fama de paraíso tropical y que atraía por su magnífico paisaje y la vida nocturna de La Habana a turistas de todo el mundo, actualmente carece de comida. Muchos cubanos emigrarían de Cuba por razones políticas, económicas y sociales si pudieran entrar legalmente en Estados Unidos.
- **La República Dominicana** se encuentra en la isla de Santo Domingo, que fue nombrada La Española por Cristóbal Colón. La República Dominicana comparte la isla con Haití. La República Dominicana es montañosa y en general el clima es cálido. La economía se basa en la agricultura, principalmente el cultivo de la caña de azúcar. La caña se cosecha en el este del país. Los otros productos son el cacao, el café, el tabaco y el arroz. Hay refinerías de azúcar, cemento, productos

farmacéuticos y maderas. Santo Domingo es la capital. Es la ciudad más antigua de las ciudades americanas fundadas por los españoles y de allí salieron los conquistadores en sus expediciones a Cuba y Puerto Rico. Otra ciudad importante es Santiago de los Caballeros. La República Dominicana tiene una población de 7.515.000 habitantes. Muchos dominicanos emigran a los Estados Unidos por las malas condiciones económicas de su país.

- **Puerto Rico** es la isla que queda más al este de las Antillas Mayores. Esta isla rectangular es montañosa y tiene muchos ríos. Su clima es cálido y húmedo. Cristóbal Colón llegó a la isla en su segundo viaje en 1493. En 1917 se les concedió a los puertorriqueños la nacionalidad estadounidense. Puerto Rico es un Estado Libre Asociado a los Estados Unidos. Los puertorriqueños tienen los mismos derechos que tienen los ciudadanos estadounidenses salvo el derecho de votar en las elecciones nacionales. Viven según la Constitución y las leyes de Estados Unidos. A principios de 1993, el Gobernador de Puerto Rico declaró el inglés y el español las lenguas cooficiales de la isla. San Juan es la capital de Puerto Rico. Las otras ciudades más importantes son Ponce, en el Caribe, y Mayagüez, en la costa occidental. La isla tiene una población de 3.580.332 habitantes. Hay más de dos millones y medio de puertorriqueños que viven en Estados Unidos continental. Puerto Rico tiene cultivo de café, plátanos, piñas, tomates, caña de azúcar, tabaco, etcétera. La industria principal es la fabricación de productos farmacéuticos y químicos, maquinaria y metales, productos alimenticios, ropa y petróleo.

América del Sur consiste en mesetas, llanuras y montañas. Hay tres inmensas llanuras que se encuentran en el interior del continente y que se extienden hasta la costa del Atlántico: la del Amazonas, la Pampa, y el Chaco. En esa región quedan los valles de los ríos Orinoco, Paraná, Paraguay y Amazonas. La gran cordillera de los Andes, al oeste del continente, es la mayor cadena del mundo con una longitud de 7.500 kilómetros. La cumbre más alta de la cordillera y la más alta de América es la del Aconcagua, que tiene 6.959 metros. Queda en la Argentina. Entre las cadenas montañosas de los Andes se encuentran altiplanos y páramos. En la altiplanicie andina de Perú y Bolivia se encuentra el lago Titicaca, a 3.815 metros de altura. El lago, que pertenece a los dos países, es navegable para buques de vapor. El río Iguazú, que se encuentra al sur del Brasil, desemboca en el Paraná en el punto donde se juntan Argentina, Brasil y Paraguay. Tiene 1.320 kilómetros de longitud. Tiene 200 cataratas entre las cuales destaca el Salto Grande de Santa María que tiene 70 metros de altura. La línea ecuatorial pasa por Ecuador, Colombia y Brasil; los demás países sudamericanos quedan al sur del ecuador, salvo Venezuela, que queda al norte. Hay una gran variedad climática entre las regiones de los países sudamericanos. Las estaciones del año están al revés en el hemisferio sur comparadas con las del hemisferio norte. Casi todos los países de Sudamérica cuentan con la industria turística como parte importante de su economía.

- **La Argentina** es el segundo país sudamericano en área. Limita al norte con Brasil, Paraguay y Bolivia, al este con Brasil, Uruguay y el océano Atlántico, al oeste con Chile y al sur con el pasaje de Drake. Argentina posee una parte de la Antártida también. Argentina no pudo apoderarse de las islas Malvinas (Falklands), reclamadas por Argentina como parte de su territorio nacional, en una guerra con Inglaterra en 1982. En el oeste del país hay una región montañosa de los Andes. Por allí se encuentra la Puna, una árida meseta de 4.000 metros con cumbres elevadas. Hacia el sur en la provincia argentina de Mendoza se encuentra Aconcagua, la mayor cumbre del continente americano. La región de las llanuras incluye el Chaco, al norte y la Pampa, más al sur. La llanura mesopotámica queda entre los ríos Paraná y Uruguay. El río Iguazú, con su famosa catarata, el Salto Grande de Santa María, pasa por la Argentina. La región de las mesetas se extiende al sur, entre el mar argentino y los Andes Patagónicos. La Pampa es la gran llanura que queda entre el río Colorado al sur, la sierra de

Córdoba al oeste, el Paraná al este y el Gran Chaco al norte. Se extiende por casi toda la provincia de Buenos Aires. En la Pampa, una región fértil y húmeda y la llanura mesopotámica se cultivan cereales, maíz, uvas, azúcar, tabaco, arroz, lino, algodón, etcétera. La ganadería argentina es una de las más importantes del mundo. La pesca es también importante. El subsuelo de Argentina es rico en petróleo y hay yacimientos de carbón, hierro, plata, cinc, plomo, oro, estaño, uranio, etcétera. Los principales productos del país son los alimenticios, químicos, textiles, derivados del petróleo, maquinaria, automóviles, etcétera. Argentina tiene una población de 32.901.000 habitantes. Su capital, Buenos Aires, tiene 12.582.000 habitantes. Queda en la orilla derecha del río de la Plata. Otras ciudades importantes son Córdoba y Rosario, las dos al noroeste de la capital. Juan Díaz de Solís fue el primer español que llegó al río de la Plata (1516). Magallanes exploró las costas y descubrió el estrecho que hoy se llama el estrecho de Magallanes. Argentina tiene un 95 por ciento de habitantes de origen europeo, especialmente españoles e italianos. La inmigración en gran escala a Argentina de españoles, italianos y alemanes durante las décadas después de 1880 fomentó la modernización, industrialización, educación y prosperidad del país. Aunque Argentina es un país de relativa prosperidad dentro de las circunstancias sudamericanas, sus enormes posibilidades no se han realizado por los graves problemas políticos que han azotado al país.

- **Uruguay** linda con Argentina al oeste, con Brasil al norte, con el Atlántico al este y con el río de la Plata al sur. El país tiene mucha llanura donde se cultivan maíz, trigo, frutas, arroz, avena, etcétera. Las industrias principales son la cárnica, la textil, la producción de vinos, cemento y productos petroleros. Uruguay tiene una población de 3.121.000 habitantes entre los cuales predominan los de raza blanca de origen europeo (89%). La mayoría de éstos son de origen español e italiano. La capital de Uruguay es Montevideo.
- **Paraguay** y Bolivia son los dos países sudamericanos que no tienen puerto de mar. La República del Paraguay tiene frontera con Bolivia al norte, Argentina al sur, Brasil al este. El río Paraguay divide el país. Al este hay llanuras fértiles, colinas y prados. Al oeste está la llanura del Chaco. La agricultura y la ganadería son las fuentes de riqueza del país. También es importante la explotación de los bosques del Chaco por su madera. Se cultivan el maíz, el algodón, el frijol y el azúcar. Paraguay tiene una población de 4.929.000 habitantes. La capital es Asunción. El español y el guaraní son las lenguas cooficiales.
- **Bolivia** se declaró independiente de España en 1825 y se constituyó la República de Bolivia en homenaje a Simón Bolívar. "El Libertador" fue declarado Padre de la Patria y su primer presidente. Bolivia se encuentra en plena cordillera de los Andes. Linda con Chile y Perú al oeste, con Argentina y Paraguay al sur y con Brasil al este y al norte. La cordillera de los Andes se divide en dos cadenas, la occidental volcánica y la oriental (Real). Entre las dos cadenas queda el Altiplano donde está La Paz, la capital (no oficial) más alta del mundo (4.300 metros). Los llanos del Amazonas-Chaco quedan al este. El lago Titicaca, que queda en la frontera con Perú, es el lago más alto del mundo. Bolivia tiene una población de 7.323.000 habitantes. Como Perú, tiene muchos indios. En Bolivia hay un 30 por ciento de gente quechua y un 25 por ciento de gente aymara. El español, el quechua y el aymara son las lenguas oficiales. Sucre es la capital oficial pero La Paz es la sede del gobierno. Bolivia produce papas, azúcar, café, maíz, cacao y coca, que se vende para hacer cocaína. Ha habido problemas entre Estados Unidos y Bolivia por el cultivo de la coca y el narcotráfico.
- **Chile** limita al norte con Perú, al este con Bolivia y Argentina, al sur con el Polo Sur y al oeste con el Pacífico. La cordillera de los Andes queda al este del país. El desierto de Atacama, totalmente árido, queda al norte. Se encuentran las regiones agrícolas en la parte céntrica de Chile. A pesar de que menos de la mitad del país tiene tierra cultivable, la agricultura se ha desarrollado exitosamente.

Chile produce cereales, cebollas, frijoles, papas y frutas. La producción de los vinos es cada vez más importante. También produce cobre, nitratos, yodo (la mitad de la producción mundial), hierro, carbón, petróleo, oro, cobalto, cinc, mercurio, azufre, mármol, etcétera. Chile tiene una población de 13.528.000 habitantes. La capital es Santiago. Chile se independizó de España entre 1810 y 1818. Los héroes de la independencia fueron José de San Martín y Bernardo O'Higgins. Chile reclama una parte del territorio de la Antártida y comparte la Tierra del Fuego con Argentina. La Tierra del Fuego, que queda en la punta sur de Sudamérica, fue descubierta por Magallanes en 1520. Chile está disfrutando un período de gran crecimiento económico.

- **Perú** limita al norte con Colombia y Ecuador, al este con Brasil y Bolivia, al sur con Chile y al oeste con el Pacífico. Perú se divide en tres regiones naturales que van de norte a sur: 1) la costa árida, al oeste, 2) la montaña o selva, un inmenso llano forestal que cubre más de la mitad del país, 3) en medio de ambas regiones, la sierra constituida por la altiplanicie que dividen valles y los Andes. Los Andes ocupan un 27 por ciento del país. La mayoría de los peruanos pueden vivir en la costa gracias al sistema de riego. Aunque las tierras cultivables son escasas, la agricultura es la actividad fundamental del país. Se producen algodón, azúcar, café, maíz, cereales, cacao, coca, quina, etcétera. Perú produce también cobre, plata, plomo, cinc, hierro, petróleo, etcétera. Perú tiene una población de 22.767.000 habitantes. La capital es Lima. Otras ciudades importantes son Arequipa y Callao. El español y el quechua son las lenguas cooficiales; se habla el aymara también.
- **Ecuador** fue nombrado así por la línea ecuatorial que lo atraviesa. Limita al norte con Colombia, al este y al sur con Perú y al oeste con el Pacífico. Dos cadenas de los Andes cruzan el país de norte a sur, dividiéndolo en tres zonas: tierras cálidas y húmedas en la costa, altiplanicie entre las cadenas y tierras tropicales al este. Las islas Galápagos, donde viven tortugas gigantes, también pertenecen a Ecuador. Ecuador es el primer exportador de plátano en el mundo. También produce café, arroz, azúcar y maíz. Además tiene petróleo, cobre, hierro, plomo, plata, goma, maderas, etcétera. Ecuador es miembro de la Organización de Países Exportadores de Petróleo (OPEP). Ecuador tiene una población de 10.933.000 habitantes. El español es la lengua oficial aunque se habla mucho el quechua. La capital, Quito, queda a 2.827 metros de altura. Guayaquil, otra ciudad importante, queda en la costa del Pacífico.
- **Colombia** limita al norte con el Atlántico, al oeste con el Pacífico, al este con Venezuela y Brasil, al sur con Ecuador y Perú y al noroeste con Panamá. Hay tres cadenas de los Andes que van de norte a sur. Hay una región andina al oeste y tierras bajas al este. En el este corren los afluentes del río Orinoco y del Amazonas. El país es agrícola y minero. Se produce café (un 50% de sus exportaciones), arroz, maíz, azúcar, algodón, plátanos, etcétera. Hay también petróleo, gas natural, esmeraldas (un 90% de la producción mundial), oro, cobre, plomo, carbón, hierro, sal, goma, madera, textiles, cueros y productos químicos. Colombia tiene una población de 34.296.000 habitantes. La capital es Bogotá. Otras ciudades importantes son Medellín, Cali y Barranquilla.
- **Venezuela** limita al norte con el mar Caribe y el Atlántico, al este con Guyana, al sur con el Brasil y al oeste con Colombia. Venezuela tiene tres regiones bien definidas: una cadena de montañas, mesetas que ocupan casi la mitad del país y los llanos (una sabana) del Orinoco, situados entre las dos zonas anteriores. La región cultivada se encuentra en la zona montañosa del noroeste y en la costa. Se produce café, arroz, frutas, azúcar, etcétera. Venezuela es uno de los exportadores más importantes del petróleo y fue uno de los fundadores de la OPEP. También tiene hierro y oro y las industrias de acero, productos petroleros, textiles y papel. La capital es Caracas. La Guaira, que queda a 25 kilómetros de Caracas, sirve de puerto para la capital. Es el puerto más importante del país.

Otras ciudades importantes son Maracaibo (en el lago Maracaibo hay mucha explotación de petróleo), Barquisimeto y Valencia. Venezuela tiene una población de 20.675.000 habitantes.

A. Empareje los lugares de la columna A con los países o las descripciones de la columna B.

A	B
_____ 1. Maracaibo	a. desierto de Chile
_____ 2. Aconcagua	b. Colombia
_____ 3. La Paz	c. Honduras
_____ 4. Atacama	d. Venezuela
_____ 5. la Sierra Madre	e. Argentina
_____ 6. Bogotá	f. Costa Rica
_____ 7. la Pampa	g. Bolivia
_____ 8. San Juan	h. Ecuador
_____ 9. Tegucigalpa	i. México
_____ 10. Montevideo	j. Uruguay
_____ 11. Quito	k. Puerto Rico
_____ 12. San José	l. cumbre de los Andes

B. Escoja la respuesta correcta para cada oración.

1. El español, el quechua y el aymara son las lenguas oficiales de

   ____________________.
   a. Chile
   b. Paraguay
   c. Venezuela
   d. Bolivia

2. ____________________ es el primer exportador de plátanos en el mundo.
   a. Ecuador
   b. Argentina
   c. Uruguay
   d. Cuba

3. El río Bravo (o río Grande) separa dos países. Son ____________________ y

   ____________________.
   a. Argentina y Uruguay
   b. Estados Unidos y México
   c. Colombia y Panamá
   d. Chile y Perú

4. ____________________ fue nombrado en homenaje a Simón Bolívar, su primer

   presidente.
   a. Venezuela
   b. El Salvador
   c. Bolivia
   d. Ecuador

5. Una parte de la Antártida pertenece a ____________________.
   a. Colombia
   b. Chile
   c. México
   d. Panamá
6. Petén, donde floreció la civilización maya, se encuentra en ____________________.
   a. Guatemala
   b. Nicaragua
   c. La República Dominicana
   d. Perú
7. En el istmo de ____________________, hay un canal entre el Atlántico y el Pacífico.
   a. Nicaragua
   b. Tehuantepec
   c. Magallanes
   d. Panamá
8. En 1903, Panamá declaró su independencia de ____________________.
   a. Costa Rica
   b. Estados Unidos
   c. Colombia
   d. España

C. Empareje los lugares o las cosas de la columna A con los lugares de la columna B.

	A	B
_____	1. el lago Maracaibo	a. Buenos Aires
_____	2. Guadalajara	b. La Española
_____	3. acuerdo Hay-Bunau Varilla	c. Colombia
_____	4. Santo Domingo	d. la Argentina
_____	5. el río de la Plata	e. Puerto Rico
_____	6. Ponce	f. Venezuela
_____	7. las Antillas Mayores	g. el canal de Panamá
_____	8. el Iguazú	h. Paraguay
_____	9. Bogotá	i. México
_____	10. el guaraní	j. el mar Caribe

D. Subraye la cosa que no forme parte del grupo.

1. *capital*
   a. San José
   b. Managua
   c. Sucre
   d. Guayaquil

2. *puerto*
   a. La Habana
   b. Tampico
   c. Asunción
   d. La Guaira

3. *río*
   a. Córdoba
   b. Orinoco
   c. Iguazú
   d. Paraná

4. *llanura*
   a. el Chaco
   b. Aconcagua
   c. la Pampa
   d. la del Amazonas

5. *país con costa en el Atlántico*
   a. Chile
   b. la Argentina
   c. Colombia
   d. Venezuela

6. *país con costa en el Pacífico*
   a. Ecuador
   b. México
   c. Chile
   d. Uruguay

7. *país con puerto*
   a. México
   b. Panamá
   c. Bolivia
   d. Puerto Rico

8. *país con ejército*
   a. Honduras
   b. Costa Rica
   c. Uruguay
   d. Perú

9. *países que no comparten frontera*
   a. Panamá y Colombia
   b. Costa Rica y Venezuela
   c. Panamá y Venezuela
   d. Honduras y Ecuador

10. *países andinos*
    a. Chile
    b. la República Dominicana
    c. Colombia
    d. Perú

11. *el ecuador pasa por el país*
    a. Colombia
    b. Ecuador
    c. Uruguay
    d. Brasil

E. Escriba la respuesta correcta para completar cada oración.

1. La capital de Chile es ______________________.
2. El lago más alto del mundo es el ______________________.
3. Puerto Rico es un ______________________ a los Estados Unidos.
4. La Zona del Canal se encuentra en ______________________.
5. Petén, la antigua región maya, queda en ______________________.
6. Las Islas Galápagos son territorio de ______________________.
7. Las lenguas cooficiales de Paraguay son ______________________ y ______________________.
8. El puerto que queda cerca de Caracas se llama ______________________.
9. La cordillera de ______________________ es la más grande del mundo.
10. La gran llanura que se encuentra en la Argentina es ______________________.
11. Uno de los países fundadores de OPEP es ______________________.
12. La capital del único país comunista de Hispanoamérica es ______________________.
13. El país más grande de Centroamérica es ______________________.
14. Los dos países sudamericanos que no tienen puerto de mar son ______________________ y ______________________.
15. El país hispano de Norteamérica es ______________________.
16. La capital de ______________________, el país más pequeño de Centroamérica, es ______________________.
17. ______________________ y Haití se encuentran en la isla de ______________________.
18. Chile, Perú y Ecuador limitan al oeste con ______________________.

HISTORIA DE HISPANOAMÉRICA

CIVILIZACIONES Y CULTURAS INDÍGENAS PRECOLOMBINAS

- Había varios grupos de indios que vivían en el continente antes de la Conquista española. **Los araucanos**, llamados también **los mapuches,** vivían en una parte de Argentina antes de pasar al Chile central. Estos indios guerreros cultivaban el maíz y la papa y tenían ganado. Su educación era militar. **Los chibchas** (hacia 500 a.C.–1539 d.C.), llamados también **muiscas** o **moscas,** vivían en las altiplanicies de la Cordillera Oriental de Colombia. Se dedicaban a la agricultura y eran buenos artesanos. Su cultura era parecida a la incaica. Algunos investigadores consideran la cultura chibcha la cuarta más importante de la América precolombina. **Los nazcas**, contemporáneos de **los mochicas** (200–800 d.C.), eran como las otras culturas del Clásico Andino, es decir, se organizaron en estados teocráticos, no tenían mucho desarrollo urbano y se dedicaban al militarismo. Las "líneas de Nazca" son enormes diseños de animales estilizados grabados en la pampa. **Los guaraníes** eran buenos navegantes que hicieron migraciones desde el Paraguay hasta el Amazonas. La importancia de los guaraníes en la formación del pueblo paraguayo se demuestra por el hecho de que casi todos los paraguayos hablan español y guaraní y que las dos lenguas son cooficiales en el país. **Los caribes** venían de la cuenca del Orinoco y vivían en las Antillas en el siglo XV. Eran feroces guerreros que luchaban contra **los arawakos**. Éstos ocuparon las Antillas antes de los caribes y luego emigraron por el Amazonas hasta el Alto Paraguay y el Chaco argentino. Había tres civilizaciones indígenas precolombinas que eran más avanzadas que todas las demás: los mayas, los aztecas y los incas.
- **Los mayas**, que vivían en los bosques tropicales de Mesoamérica (en lo que hoy es el Yucatán, Guatemala, Honduras y Belice), tenían una civilización muy avanzada. Se destacaban en tres campos más bien intelectuales: la aritmética, el calendario y la escritura jeroglífica. Durante unos 2.600 años, estos indios desarrollaron una escritura jeroglífica compuesta por más de 700 signos que es en parte fonética y en parte ideográfica, la bóveda falsa en arquitectura, una escultura monumental de carácter religioso que asocia la estela y el altar (Tikal) y un sistema para medir el tiempo que parte de una fecha concreta. Los mayas construyeron los grandes centros ceremoniales y ciudades-estado como Tikal, Palenque, Copán y Bonampak. Los tres períodos de su civilización son: el Formativo, entre el siglo X a.C. y el siglo III d.C.; el Clásico, del siglo III al X d.C.; y el Posclásico, del siglo X a la Conquista. Las investigaciones de las últimas décadas han demostrado que los mayas no fueron un pueblo pacífico, como siempre se creía, sino una sociedad tan guerrera como las otras antiguas de América. Como parte de su religión, que era un instrumento político más que nada, los mayas tenían rituales que incluían el sacrificio humano y el autosacrificio.
- **Los aztecas** dominaban una gran parte de Mesoamérica cuando llegaron los conquistadores españoles a México en 1519. Tenían un vasto imperio que se extendía de la frontera norte del área al istmo de Tehuantepec y del Atlántico al Pacífico. El centro de su imperio era Tenochtitlán, una ciudad densamente

poblada del Valle de México. Hoy la Ciudad de México ocupa el lugar donde estaba Tenochtitlán. Los aztecas llegaron a dominar el Valle de México después que el imperio tolteca cayó a fines del siglo XII. Los mexicas, otro nombre de los aztecas, eran un grupo de lengua náhuatl originario de Aztlán, un lugar semimítico situado en el oeste de México. El militarismo de la sociedad azteca se reflejaba en la esfera religiosa. Los guerreros muertos en combate o en la piedra de los sacrificios iban al Paraíso Solar. Los sacerdotes abrían el pecho del cautivo con una navaja de piedra, sacaban el corazón y lo ofrecían al sol. Su escritura no era tan sofisticada como la de los mayas. Sí tenían un calendario y destacaron en todas las artes, especialmente en la escultura en piedra.

- **Los incas** tenían una cultura con dos rasgos muy importantes: el genio organizador y la estructura socio-política del Estado y el ayllu. Así pudieron crear un enorme imperio en menos de un siglo. El imperio tenía su centro en Cuzco y llegaba desde la frontera colombiano-ecuatoriana hasta el Chile central y de la costa pacífica a las selvas del Amazonas. Tenía entre 11 y 15 millones de habitantes. La verdadera historia de los incas (no según sus leyendas) comenzó con el reino de Pachacútec Inca Yupanqui (1438–1471). Los incas establecieron una unidad política, económica y social en los Andes centrales. La estructura social se basaba en el ayllu, un conjunto de familias que descendían del mismo antepasado. La organización política y económica era un sistema tiránico. Era un estado despótico, militarista y teocrático que explotaba económicamente a las comunidades campesinas. Para mantener su sistema, los líderes utilizaron métodos violentos en castigar a los ayllus rebeldes. Los incas adoraban a Inti, la divinidad solar. El culto al sol era la manifestación religiosa de la organización política imperial y se desarrolló con la expansión militar. Las ceremonias estaban relacionadas con las diferentes fases del ciclo agrícola. Se trataba de ofrendas, la muerte de llamas y el sacrificio de un niño o una virgen. Los incas no destacaron en las bellas artes. Su arquitectura sobresale más por su solidez y técnica que por la belleza de las formas. Los edificios de Cuzco, Pisac y Machu Picchu, sus ciudades principales, tenían un estilo sobrio y geométrico sin decoraciones, construidos para resistir los terremotos. La lengua de los incas, el quechua, es lengua cooficial de Perú y Bolivia y se habla también en Ecuador.

DESCUBRIMIENTO: EL ENCUENTRO DE EUROPA Y AMÉRICA

Cristóbal Colón (¿1451?–1506), célebre navegante, fue el primero de los grandes descubridores de América. Recibió la ayuda de los Reyes Católicos, Fernando e Isabel de España, facilitándole el viaje al Nuevo Mundo. En 1492, Colón firmó las Capitulaciones de Santa Fe, por las que la Corona española le reconocía los títulos de almirante del mar Océano, virrey y gobernador de las tierras que descubriera. Salió del puerto de Palos de Moguer, provincia de Huelva (España) el 3 de agosto de 1492 con tres carabelas y 120 hombres. El 12 de octubre vieron tierra, la isla de Guanahaní a la que Colón dio el nombre de San Salvador. Después llegó a Cuba y Haití, bautizada La Española. En el segundo viaje (1493), Colón reconoció las Antillas Menores, Puerto Rico y Jamaica; en el tercero (1498), descubrió la desembocadura del Orinoco y una parte de Venezuela; en el cuarto (1502), exploró las costas de Honduras, Nicaragua, Costa Rica y Panamá.

Exploración y conquista

La exploración y Conquista de Hispanoamérica por los españoles representa una de las mayores hazañas de la historia. De 1492 a 1657, fecha de la fundación de Caracas, los españoles lograron recorrer América del Sur, América Central y parte de América del Norte y dominar sus territorios y a sus miles de habitantes. Las dos fases del proceso incluyen la fase marítima, durante la cual los españoles exploraron las costas del continente y las islas del Caribe (hasta 1519); y la fase que se centró en la conquista del interior del continente (entre 1519 y 1535). Los Reyes Católicos rompieron el monopolio de Colón en 1498 permitiendo a cualquiera de sus súbditos explorar las nuevas tierras. Algunos de los principales conquistadores españoles que participaron en esta empresa colosal y única que cambió el mundo para siempre:

- **Juan Ponce de León** (¿1460?–1521) exploró Puerto Rico, fundó San Juan y fue el primer gobernador de la Isla (1509). Descubrió la Florida en 1513 y fue nombrado su adelantado, es decir, su autoridad política, militar y judicial.
- **Vasco Núñez de Balboa** (1475–1517) cruzó a pie el istmo de Panamá y llegó a las costas del océano Pacífico en 1513. Lo llamó Mar del Sur. Fue nombrado adelantado del Mar del Sur y Panamá.
- **Fernando de Magallanes** (¿1480?–1521), navegante portugués, quien al servicio de Castilla cruzó el océano y encontró el estrecho que hoy lleva su nombre (1520). Lo cruzó y cruzó el Pacífico alcanzando la isla de Cebú (Filipinas). Magallanes murió aquí a manos de los indígenas. Juan Sebastián Elcano tomó el mando de la expedición y volvió a Europa.
- **Hernán Cortés** (1485–1547) nació en Medellín (Extremadura) y estudió en Salamanca. Embarcó hacia las Indias y se estableció en La Española (1504). Luchó junto con Diego Velázquez en la conquista de Cuba (1511). Cortés encabezó la expedición de reconocimiento a México con 11 barcos, 500 soldados y 100 marineros (1518). Llegó a Cozumel y Tabasco y fundó la ciudad de Veracruz. Cortés se alió con los tlaxcaltecas, enemigos mortales de los aztecas, y así logró entrar en Tenochtitlán, capital del imperio azteca. Cortés tomó como prisionero a Moctezuma, emperador azteca, y logró la victoria definitiva sobre los aztecas en 1521. Fue nombrado gobernador y capitán general de la Nueva España por Carlos I. Administró hábilmente y organizó otras expediciones.
- **Francisco Pizarro** (¿1478?–1541) acompañó a Balboa en el descubrimiento del Mar del Sur. En 1524 y 1526 intentó la conquista del Perú pero fracasó. Luego, con el apoyo de Carlos I, Pizarro, sus hermanos y 180 soldados entraron en Perú (1531) y lo conquistaron. Pizarro logró entrar en Cuzco, la capital incaica (1533) y fundó la "Ciudad de los Reyes", la actual Lima en 1535.
- **Pedro de Valdivia** (¿1500?–1553) luchó en Venezuela y luego en Perú a las órdenes de Pizarro. Conquistó Chile y fundó Santiago (1541). Fue nombrado gobernador y capitán general de la nueva provincia. Murió a manos de los araucanos.
- **Álvar Núñez Cabeza de Vaca** (¿1500–1560?) hizo expedición a la Florida y una gira por el Misisipí y norte de México. Nombrado adelantado de la provincia del Río de la Plata, se quedó en Asunción en 1542. Exploró el Chaco. Narró sus aventuras en *Naufragios y comentarios.*
- **Francisco Vázquez de Coronado** (¿1510–1544?) estuvo en México como gobernador de Nueva Galicia. No tuvo suerte en su búsqueda de las siete ciudades de Cibola, una región mítica, pero sí descubrió el Cañón del Colorado (1540).

Las colonias

El período colonial duró unos tres siglos, hasta principios del siglo XIX. El rey español procuraba ejercer control sobre las colonias para evangelizar, es decir, convertir a los indios al catolicismo y explotar las riquezas de las colonias para la corona española. El rey, que era el dueño nominal del Nuevo Mundo, no podía hacerse cargo directamente de la empresa americana. Por eso, cedía sus derechos de conquista sobre un territorio especial a un señor a cambio de un porcentaje sobre los beneficios que se consiguieran. Se llamaba *el quinto real.* El contratante se comprometía a costear todos los gastos de la conquista. Al terminar la Conquista, el rey recuperó los poderes cedidos. Se establecieron ciertos órganos de gobierno metropolitanos como *la Casa de Contratación* (1503), que tenía una función económica. *El Consejo de Indias* (1517), máximo órgano del gobierno de Indias, realizó una tarea legislativa, es decir, adaptó o escribió leyes para el Nuevo Mundo. Las colonias estaban divididas en cuatro territorios administrativos, llamados *virreinatos* (el virrey desempeñaba las funciones del rey a quien representaba): (1) Nueva España, que comprendía México, América Central, las Antillas y parte de los Estados Unidos; (2) Perú, que comprendía Perú y Chile; (3) Nueva Granada, que comprendía Colombia, Venezuela, Ecuador y Panamá; (4) el Río de la Plata, que comprendía Argentina, Uruguay, Bolivia, Paraguay y parte de Brasil. Los que vivían en las colonias eran españoles, que gobernaban; criollos (de origen español pero nacidos en América), que vivían bien económicamente pero no gobernaban; mestizos (raza mixta de español e indio o negro), que no tenían ni dinero ni posición social ni derechos políticos; indios y esclavos negros.

Unos fenómenos de la colonia incluyen: (1) *el mestizaje*, la fusión de dos personas de diferentes razas; (2) los productos agrícolas de América (papa, maíz, frijol, pimiento, guayaba, etcétera) que se difundieron rápidamente en Europa; (3) la caída demográfica de los indios en la primera mitad del siglo XVI. Una razón por el descenso demográfico es la falta de defensas en los indios frente a las enfermedades llevadas por los europeos (sarampión, viruela, etcétera). No fue un genocidio calculado como han sugerido los partidarios de la *leyenda negra*, es decir, los críticos que le echan la culpa por todos los males a España. Si los españoles hubieran deseado la extinción de los indios, los misioneros y evangelizadores no les habrían enseñado a los indios la fe, la cultura y la lengua de España. Tampoco habrían tenido los conquistadores relaciones con las indias, asegurando así la continuación de la raza.

Los españoles llevaron al Nuevo Mundo su lengua, su cultura y sus ideas. En el siglo XVII la cultura adquirió rasgos americanos que se pueden ver en las obras del **Inca Garcilaso de la Vega** y **Sor Juana Inés de la Cruz** y en las artes y la arquitectura. El Barroco europeo adoptó los estilos precolombinos y la variada flora americana que llegó a ser el **Barroco americano** o **Ultrabarroco.** Las ciencias desarrollaron bien en América. **Fray Bernardino de Sahagún** creó el método antropológico. Hubo un esfuerzo notable de parte de las órdenes religiosas y las autoridades políticas en fundar colegios (para blancos e indios) y universidades. La universidad de México fue fundada en 1553, San Marcos de Lima en 1555, Cuzco en 1598, Buenos Aires en 1622, Bogotá en 1629.

La independencia

Las ideas más avanzadas y revolucionarias penetraban fácilmente en las colonias americanas gracias a los criollos ricos, la instrucción pública y las buenas comunicaciones que facilitaban la llegada de publicaciones y periódicos con toda regularidad. Hasta en las mismas colonias se publicaron muchos periódicos desde 1722. En México, **José Fernández de Lizardi** lanzó fuertes ataques contra la administración colonial en su periódico *El pensador mexicano.* Escribió el libro que se considera la primera novela hispanoamericana, *El periquillo sarniento,* que es una crítica de la sociedad mexicana. Las obras de los enciclopedistas y de los filósofos de la Ilustración circularon libremente. Las obras, que hablaban de la independencia y las libertades individuales, les llamaron la atención a los hispanoamericanos que a partir de 1750 más o menos expresaban insatisfacción con la injusticia política y social y las restricciones económicas impuestas por España. Las causas externas de la rebelión de las colonias son la influencia de la Guerra de la Independencia Norteamericana y la Revolución Francesa y la invasión de España por Napoleón. El proceso de separación entre España y sus colonias americanas se extiende desde 1808 hasta 1824.

Algunos de los principales líderes de la independencia:

- **Francisco Miranda** (1750–1816), general venezolano, fue un precursor importante de la emancipación hispanoamericana. Sirvió en el ejército español y participó en la Guerra de la Independencia Norteamericana (1780) y en la Revolución Francesa. Se unió a Simón Bolívar en Venezuela en 1810 y murió unos años después en una cárcel española.
- **Simón Bolívar** (1783–1830), general, estadista, escritor y orador venezolano, nació en Caracas. "El Libertador" es el hombre más importante en la guerra de la independencia de Sudamérica. Empezó a luchar en 1810, ganando la independencia de Colombia en 1819 con la victoria de Boyacá, la de Venezuela en 1821 con la victoria de Carabobo y la de Ecuador en 1822, con la victoria de Pichincha. Bolívar convocó el Congreso de Panamá en 1826 para organizar la solidaridad entre las naciones americanas. Bolívar fue el primer presidente de la República de la Gran Colombia que existió de 1822 a 1829. Viendo que se deshacía su sueño de una América unida, Bolívar murió desilusionado.
- **Antonio José de Sucre** (1795–1830), general y político venezolano, peleó al lado de Miranda y luego al lado de Bolívar. Liberó Ecuador en 1822 y Perú con la victoria de Ayacucho en 1824. Fue presidente de la República de Bolivia de 1826 a 1828. Murió asesinado.
- **José de San Martín** (1778–1850), general y estadista argentino, fue el libertador de Argentina (1816), Chile (1818) y Perú (1821). San Martín organizó el Ejército de los Andes con la ayuda de **Bernardo O'Higgins** (1778–1842), general y político chileno. Conoció a Francisco Miranda en Europa. Al volver a Chile, ingresó en el ejército. Luego pasó a Argentina donde colaboró con San Martín.
- **Miguel Hidalgo y Costilla** (1753–1811), sacerdote y patriota mexicano, se considera el padre de la independencia de México. Era párroco de Dolores (Guanajuato) cuando se hizo líder de un movimiento revolucionario de indios. Su famoso "Grito de Dolores" inició la Revolución Mexicana el 16 de septiembre de 1810. Ganó unas batallas. Murió fusilado. **José María Morelos** (1765–1815), sacerdote y patriota mexicano, se unió al movimiento de Hidalgo. Reunió en Chilpancingo el primer Congreso Nacional (1813). Murió fusilado.
- **Agustín de Iturbide** (1783–1824), general mexicano, luchó primero al lado de los españoles. En 1821 formuló el Plan de Iguala que propuso las tres garantías para los mexicanos: catolicismo, unión de españoles y criollos e independencia política dentro de una monarquía constitucional. En 1822, fue proclamado emperador, Agustín I, pero una revolución republicana encabezada por el general **Antonio López de Santa Anna** (1794–1876) le hizo abdicar. En 1824 México se constituyó en República Federal. Santa Anna fue presidente de la república, luchó en la guerra contra Estados Unidos y fue desterrado por **Benito Juárez** (1806–1872) por tratar de establecer una dictadura. Juárez fue presidente de la república y luchó contra la intervención francesa y el imperio de Maximiliano.
- **Carlos Manuel de Céspedes** (1819–1874), patriota, abogado y político cubano, que lanzó el grito de "¡Viva Cuba libre!" en 1868 para iniciar la lucha armada por la independencia. No fue hasta mediados del siglo XIX que Cuba comenzó su movimiento de independencia. **José Martí** (1853–1895), poeta y abogado cubano, fue desterrado a España por sus actividades revolucionarias (1871). Luego fue a México, Guatemala y regresó a Cuba (1878). Volvió a expatriarse a Venezuela (1881) y Nueva York donde fundó el Partido Revolucionario Cubano (1892). En la guerra entre Estados Unidos y España en 1898, Estados Unidos ocupó Cuba, Puerto Rico y las Filipinas. Cuba se constituyó en república en 1902. La Enmienda Platt, apéndice de la constitución de Cuba (1901), dio derecho a Estados Unidos a intervenir en la isla (se abrogó en 1934).

DESPUÉS DE LA INDEPENDENCIA: LA MODERNIZACIÓN

En el período de la pos-independencia las transformaciones deseadas no llegaron ni rápida ni fácilmente. Es que las estructuras básicas de la economía no habían sido cambiadas. Seguían las plantaciones, la ganadería y la minería y el sistema de la monoproducción. Surgió una competencia entre los países hispanoamericanos ahora que todos buscaban lugar en el mercado mundial. Los sectores más poderosos de la sociedad eran los terratenientes y los mineros. La exportación de la plata desde México y Perú fue muy importante hasta el fin de la época colonial. En la segunda mitad del siglo XIX, el ingreso de las naciones hispanoamericanas en el mercado internacional produjo el fenómeno de la especialización. Había países como Argentina, Uruguay, los valles centrales de Chile y el norte de México que dependían de la agricultura y la ganadería, es decir, la exportación de carne, lana o cereales. También había economías basadas en la plantación, como el café de Colombia y el azúcar de Cuba y la costa del Perú. A veces se desarrollaban bajo firmas extranjeras como la United Fruit Company en Centroamérica. Esta empresa tenía un monopolio sobre la producción del banano. En cuanto a la minería, los empresarios nacionales se encargaron del cobre en Chile. Esto impulsó el desarrollo de Santiago. La producción del salitre pasó a manos de los ingleses, luego a manos de los norteamericanos. En México y Venezuela, los yacimientos de petróleo estaban en manos de los ingleses, los holandeses y luego los norteamericanos a principios del siglo XX. Luego, fueron nacionalizados.

Después que los países ganaron su independencia, les tocó a los militares que habían luchado por la independencia normalizar y estabilizar la vida política, social y económica. Estos caudillos tomaban el poder tratando de parar la anarquía. En México, por ejemplo, el general Santa Anna se hizo presidente de su país. En la Argentina, el caudillo Juan Manuel de Rosas tomó el poder y gobernó desde Buenos Aires. Había planes de modernización que requerían la atracción de capitales e inmigrantes y el librecambio comercial con países extranjeros. Para los años 80 del siglo XIX, la oligarquía ganadera, de plantación y de minería ya tenía su proyecto político. Los caudillos no permitían la participación de las masas y explotaban las clases bajas como mano de obra. Los indios y los negros estaban marginados. La mayoría de la población no participaba en las elecciones.

Durante el siglo XIX surgieron dos partidos, los conservadores y los liberales, que adoptaron una postura diferente sobre la forma de organizar el estado. Los conservadores querían pocas transformaciones sociales y creían que la ideología liberal iba a fomentar anarquía y desorden porque destruía el orden tradicional y atacaba la Iglesia. Los liberales querían cambios fundamentales y lograron imponer por lo menos una parte de su programa. Abolieron el tributo indígena y el mayorazgo (la institución de la primogenitura, que aseguraba que los bienes pasaban al hijo mayor de la familia), impulsaron el fin de la esclavitud y destruyeron el sistema feudal de la Iglesia. Querían una separación entre la Iglesia y el Estado. Ambos partidos políticos, conservadores y liberales, veían las masas rurales con miedo, que ya puestas en movimiento por los caudillos, iban a reclamar la justicia social.

No fue hasta el siglo XX que entraron en la escena política los obreros y las clases medias. Había un progreso económico general y el ascenso de nuevas fuerzas sociales. Se formaron dos repúblicas nuevas, Cuba, como resultado de la derrota de España en 1898, y Panamá, que se independizó de Colombia en 1903. Surgieron dictadores que sustituían a los caudillos tradicionales. En México ocurrió la primera de las grandes revoluciones del siglo XX y llevó al derrocamiento de la dictadura de Porfirio Díaz. Juan Vicente Gómez fue dictador de Venezuela (1908–1935) y Augusto B. Leguía fue dictador de Perú (1919–1930). Un fenómeno político nuevo se vio con la presencia de un país extrarregional. Estados Unidos intervino en la política de la región para proteger sus intereses: en Cuba, Puerto Rico y el Canal de Panamá. Había mucha inmigración de Europa entre 1860 y 1914, cambiando enormemente la demografía del continente. La Gran Depresión de 1929 tuvo un gran impacto en los países latinos. En muchos países hubo golpes de estado militares que derribaron las presidencias liberales y crearon un vacío de poder.

Las ciudades crecían rápidamente a partir de los años treinta porque hubo un gran éxodo del campo a la ciudad donde la industrialización daba más posibilidades de empleo. La injusticia social seguía y las masas veían que no había posibilidad de reforma porque el gobierno representaba estructuras económicas y sociales que eran injustas. Reclamaban cambios radicales y por eso apoyaban a los líderes populistas como Juan Domingo Perón en la Argentina. Fidel Castro, que era guerrillero, tomó el poder en Cuba en 1959 derribando la dictadura de Batista con el apoyo de la población campesina. Estados Unidos apoyaba la dictadura de Batista en Cuba, Anastasio Somoza en Nicaragua y Rafael Trujillo en la República Dominicana. Durante los años sesenta, hubo movimientos revolucionarios en Nicaragua, Honduras, Guatemala y la República Dominicana. Durante los setenta, los hubo en El Salvador, Venezuela, Colombia, Perú y Bolivia. La pobreza e injusticia social daban ímpetu a la creación de una guerrilla urbana que reclamaba sus derechos. A pesar de las tentativas de reforma agraria, la gran mayoría de la población de Centroamérica vive en condiciones de pobreza y subdesarrollo. El nivel de urbanización sigue aumentando y hay una explosión demográfica. En 1920, había 94 millones de personas en América Latina; en 1984, había 390 millones. Se calcula que para el año 2000, habrá algunos 630 millones de personas, con más de la mitad concentrada en las ciudades. El aumento más grande de población se ve en América del Sur tropical y en América Central. Según el censo de 1992, hay 80 millones de habitantes en México y unos 20 millones en la capital.

La gente sigue llegando a las ciudades a montones y éstas no pueden proporcionarles los servicios más básicos de la infraestructura urbana como agua de llave, electricidad, alcantarillado, etcétera. Las clases pobres viven en construcciones improvisadas e irregulares de los barrios bajos; los ranchitos de Caracas, las callampas o poblaciones de Santiago, las villas miseria de Buenos Aires, los cantegriles de Montevideo o las barriadas de Lima, que llegan a llamarse pueblos jóvenes por su extensión. Otro problema que aflige estas sociedades, y que es realmente un problema mundial, es el narcotráfico. Colombia, Ecuador y Bolivia cultivan la hoja de coca para vender y Colombia tiene su cartel de Medellín que facilita la venta de las drogas en Estados Unidos y otros países.

Los gobiernos de los países latinoamericanos tienen que resolver todos estos problemas económicos, políticos y sociales que afligen su vida nacional: la inflación, el desempleo, el subempleo, la educación, la corrupción, la deuda externa, etcétera. El ascenso demográfico lo hace cada día más difícil. Pero si no encuentran soluciones puede haber masas de personas que reclamen justicia social y cambios radicales por vías revolucionarias. El fracaso del socialismo en Cuba y Nicaragua no quita la necesidad de reformas sociales que abran la sociedad hispanoamericana y que den la posibilidad de una vida mejor a las masas pobres. Lo que pasa con esos países afecta también a Estados Unidos que tiene bases e instalaciones militares en la región. América Central y el Caribe, especialmente, tienen mucha importancia estratégica y una gran reserva de materias primas. Aunque hasta ahora el modelo desarrollista de una comunidad de países latinoamericanos no ha logrado sus objetivos, es importante que estos países sigan hablándose y compartiendo sus ideas. Y tienen que empezar a tomar medidas concretas para fomentar el desarrollo y fortalecer la democracia.

A. Empareje las figuras históricas con las hazañas que se encuentran a continuación.

A

_____ 1. Vasco Núñez de Balboa

_____ 2. Francisco Pizarro

_____ 3. Simón Bolívar

_____ 4. Cristóbal Colón

_____ 5. Miguel Hidalgo y Costilla

_____ 6. José Martí

_____ 7. Hernán Cortés

_____ 8. Francisco Miranda

_____ 9. Fernando de Magallanes

_____ 10. José de San Martín

B

a. Conquistó a los aztecas.
b. Ganó la independencia de Colombia, Venezuela y Ecuador.
c. Fundó el Partido Revolucionario Cubano.
d. Cruzó el istmo de Panamá y descubrió el Pacífico.
e. Fue el libertador de Argentina, Chile y Perú.
f. Participó en la Guerra de la Independencia Norteamericana y la Revolución Francesa.
g. Fue el primer gran descubridor.
h. Lanzó el "Grito de Dolores" que inició la Revolución Mexicana.
i. Llevó a cabo la conquista del Perú.
j. Encontró el estrecho que hoy lleva su nombre.

B. Cierto o falso. Indique si cada oración es cierta o falsa. Si es falsa, corríjala.

1. Los aztecas también se llamaban mexicas.

____

2. Tikal y Palenque eran grandes centros ceremoniales incaicos.

____

3. La lengua de los aztecas era el aymara.

____

4. La civilización de los mayas existió del siglo X a.C. hasta la Conquista.

____

5. Los incas desarrollaron la bóveda falsa usada en la arquitectura.

____

6. Los caribes y los arawakos eran enemigos.

____

7. El imperio tolteca existió después del azteca.

____

8. El imperio incaico tenía su centro en Cuzco.

____

9. Los incas y los aztecas adoraban al dios del sol.

____

10. La hazaña española de explorar y conquistar consistía en entrar en el continente primero y luego explorar las costas y las islas del Caribe.

____

C. Identifique las siguientes descripciones escogiendo la palabra o la frase correcta de la lista que sigue a continuación.

1. persona de origen español nacida en América ______________
2. conjunto familiar de la civilización incaica ______________
3. centro ceremonial y ciudad-estado de los mayas ______________
4. ciudad fundada por Fernando Pizarro en 1535 ______________
5. importante ciudad del imperio incaico ______________
6. persona que representaba autoridad política, militar y judicial durante la colonia ______________
7. centro del imperio azteca ______________
8. órgano del gobierno de América que adaptó y escribió leyes para las colonias ______________
9. indios que ayudaban a Cortés en la conquista del imperio azteca ______________
10. lengua de los incas ______________
11. dinero dado al rey español a cambio de los derechos de conquista sobre un territorio de América ______________
12. lugar semimítico del México occidental de donde vinieron los aztecas ______________
13. emperador azteca tomado preso por Cortés ______________
14. persona de raza mixta, blanca e india o negra ______________

a. Machu Picchu
b. quechua
c. el Consejo de Indias
d. Moctezuma
e. criollo
f. Tenochtitlán
g. la "Ciudad de los Reyes"
h. mestizo
i. Aztlán
j. ayllu
k. el quinto real
l. adelantado
m. tlaxcaltecas
n. Copán

D. Complete cada oración escribiendo la palabra o la frase que falta.

1. Las colonias estaban divididas en cuatro territorios administrativos que se llamaban ____________________.
2. El estilo europeo de arte y arquitectura que adoptó los estilos americanos produjo el estilo llamado ____________________.
3. ____________________ atacó la administración colonial mexicana en su periódico ____________________.
4. Hernán Cortés conquistó el imperio azteca en el año ____________________.
5. La Universidad de ____________________ fue fundada en 1553.
6. En 1540, ____________________ no encontró Cibola, la ciudad mítica que buscaba, sino ____________________.
7. Perú se independizó de España con la batalla de ____________________ en 1824.
8. Simón Bolívar convocó ____________________ en 1826 para unificar las naciones americanas.

E. Escoja la respuesta correcta para completar la oración.

1. ____________________ fue un caudillo argentino.
   a. Antonio López de Santa Anna
   b. Juan Manuel de Rosas
2. La economía de Colombia dependía de la exportación ____________________.
   a. del café
   b. de la lana
3. La primera de las grandes revoluciones del siglo XX ocurrió en ____________________.
   a. Cuba
   b. México
4. Dos minerales importantes en la economía chilena eran ____________________.
   a. el hierro/el mercurio
   b. el cobre/el salitre
5. Los ____________________ querían mantener el orden tradicional y los ____________________ querían transformar la sociedad.
   a. conservadores/liberales
   b. liberales/conservadores
6. Porfirio Díaz, Juan Vicente Gómez y Augusto B. Leguía eran ____________________.
   a. mineros
   b. dictadores

7. A principios del siglo XX, los ingleses, los holandeses y los norteamericanos controlaban la producción del petróleo en ____________ y ____________.
   a. México/Venezuela
   b. Argentina/Uruguay
8. ____________ tomó el poder en Cuba en 1959 derribando la dictadura de ____________.
   a. Fidel Castro/Fulgencio Batista
   b. Daniel Ortega/Anastasio Somoza
9. El país hispanoamericano con más problemas demográficos es ____________.
   a. Chile
   b. México
10. La marginalidad se refiere a la gente que vive en ____________.
   a. miseria en los barrios bajos urbanos
   b. casas en las afueras de las ciudades
11. El conjunto de cosas básicas que se necesitan para vivir como el agua de llave y la electricidad se llama ____________.
   a. mayorazgo
   b. infraestructura
12. Unos problemas graves de los países de la América Latina son ____________ y ____________.
   a. el éxodo de las personas al campo/el exceso de exportaciones
   b. la explosión demográfica/la deuda externa

CHAPTER 35

LITERATURA DE HISPANOAMÉRICA

LAS LITERATURAS INDÍGENAS

Había tres civilizaciones indígenas precolombinas de América en las cuales florecieron culturas avanzadas: la civilización maya, que incluye hoy Guatemala, Honduras y el Yucatán; la civilización azteca, que comprende la región central y sur de México; y la civilización incaica, que incluye la región de los Andes del Perú, Ecuador y Bolivia. Estas civilizaciones produjeron muchas obras espléndidas, como pirámides, templos, cerámica y pinturas. Lo que sabemos de *literatura indígena* viene a través de transcripciones al alfabeto latino hechas por los españoles o por un indígena educado. Así nos llegó El Libro del Consejo o *Popol Vuh,* una recopilación de las creencias sobre los orígenes del universo y recuerdos históricos y legendarios de la cultura maya. El *Popol Vuh* fue escrito entre 1554 y 1558, probablemente por un indígena educado por españoles. El libro es una transcripción del quiché a la escritura latina.

El primer Renacimiento (1492–1556) es la época del descubrimiento, exploración, conquista y colonización del Nuevo Mundo bajo los Reyes Católicos y Carlos V. Los orígenes de la literatura hispanoamericana se encuentran en las crónicas escritas durante esta época, es decir, los relatos y narraciones de los españoles que fueron soldados o misioneros en el Nuevo Mundo a finales del siglo XV y hasta mediados del siglo XVI. Describieron en sus crónicas de las Indias la realidad del Nuevo Mundo y los acontecimientos de la Conquista.

- **Cristóbal Colón** (¿1451?–1506), famoso navegante que obtuvo la ayuda de los Reyes Católicos la cual hizo posible sus viajes al Nuevo Mundo. Fue el primer cronista que escribió sobre el Nuevo Mundo en su diario de viaje.
- **Fray Bartolomé de las Casas** (1474–1566), religioso andaluz que fue a Santo Domingo para evangelizar a los indios. Defendió a éstos del trabajo forzado al que fueron sometidos por los conquistadores. Escribió la *Historia de las Indias.*
- **Hernán Cortés** (1485–1547) mandó cinco cartas a Carlos V entre 1519 y 1526 en las cuales expresó su amor a las tierras conquistadas de la Nueva España (México) y su deseo de estar enterrado en esas tierras. Fue el primer soldado que entendió y comentó la grandeza de una civilización indígena, la azteca.
- **Bernal Díaz del Castillo** (1495–1584), soldado de Cortés, escribió sobre el valor y dignidad de Cortés, los ideales de gloria de la conquista de México, el cristianismo, la lealtad al rey, la codicia y otras cosas en su *Historia verdadera de la conquista de la Nueva España.* Escribe como representante de los conquistadores, *nosotros* en vez de *yo,* añadiendo a la idea de un héroe de la Conquista la idea de grupo.

La época de la colonización bajo Felipe II se considera el período del segundo Renacimiento y Contrarreforma (1556–1598).

- **El Inca Garcilaso de la Vega** (1539–1616) nació en Perú, hijo mestizo de un capitán español y una princesa incaica. El Inca fue a España cuando tenía veintiún años y nunca más volvió a Perú. Su gran obra, los *Comentarios reales,* demuestra su conciencia de sus dos mundos, el europeo y el indio. Esta obra es importante como literatura y como crónica.

- **Alonso de Ercilla y Zúñiga** (1534–1594), soldado del rey Felipe II, llegó al Nuevo Mundo a los veintiún años. Escribió el primer poema épico de América, *La Araucana,* en el cual narra sus experiencias en las guerras entre los conquistadores españoles y los indios araucanos de Chile. Se destaca esta crónica por su visión estética y por la conciencia que tiene el poeta del proceso creador. Fue la primera obra de gran calidad poética que trató el tema de América.

El período de los últimos reyes Austrias—Felipe III, Felipe IV y Carlos II—va del Renacimiento al Barroco (1598–1701).

- **Sor Juana Inés de la Cruz** (México, 1648–1695) es la voz más importante de la poesía lírica americana de la época colonial. La monja, a quien se le llama *La décima musa,* escribió poesías, obras de teatro y prosa. Toda la corte de México y la Iglesia sabían que Sor Juana era muy inteligente. La monja escribió la *Respuesta a Sor Filotea de la Cruz* (1691), un brillante ensayo autobiográfico en el cual cuenta su temprano interés en el estudio, su curiosidad intelectual y las desventajas de ser mujer. Otros elementos autobiográficos se encuentran en sus poemas como el *Primero sueño.* Parece que Sor Juana nunca encontró paz interior y tenía una sed de saber que no se podía satisfacer. En el *Primero sueño* se reúnen elementos barrocos con un estilo muy personal. La poeta puede huir del mundo y del amor escondiéndose en la soledad y el mundo hermético del barroco. Sor Juana creyó que el mundo era irreal; que la vida interior era lo real. Escribió sonetos, romances, décimas, redondillas y villancicos. En muchos de éstos captó el alma popular de México.

Durante la época de las Guerras de Independencia predomina el neoclasicismo y llegan las primeras noticias del romanticismo inglés (1808–1824).

- **Andrés Bello** (Venezuela, 1781–1865) fue escritor, poeta, político, abogado, filólogo. Nació en Caracas y murió en Santiago de Chile. Trabajó con Bolívar en Londres en 1810, y en 1829 se fue a Chile donde ayudó a fundar la universidad de Chile (1843). Fue rector de la universidad y redactó el *Código Civil* de Chile (1855). Era un erudito que conoció a fondo los clásicos latinos. Bello es mejor conocido por su *Gramática castellana* que hasta hoy día se considera una de las mejores.
- **José Joaquín Fernández de Lizardi** (México, 1776–1827) escribió la primera novela hispanoamericana, *El Periquillo Sarniento* (1816). Es una novela picaresca: descripción realista, hasta sórdida, narración en primera persona, aventuras del héroe (o anti-héroe) con diferentes amos, sermones para dar lecciones. Fernández de Lizardi, conocido con el seudónimo de "el Pensador Mexicano", logra retratar la sociedad mexicana poco antes de la Independencia.
- **Simón Bolívar** (Venezuela, 1783–1830), el gran general y estadista que fue el padre de la independencia americana, escribió cartas, ensayos y proclamas que demuestran su inteligencia y su enorme visión. Escribió *Mi delirio en el Chimborazo* (1824), la *Carta de Jamaica* (1815), en la cual habla del futuro y de la independencia de las colonias, etcétera. Se le llama "El Libertador".

Durante la época de la separación de las colonias en naciones hay anarquía y caudillismo. Los escritores de este período se sirven del romanticismo, del realismo y del costumbrismo para describir las situaciones políticas (1825–1860). En la época de organización política emerge la segunda generación romántica. Se ve una fuerte actitud intelectual y crítica (1860–1880).

- **José María Heredia y Heredia** (Cuba, 1803–1839), uno de los primeros románticos hispanoamericanos, vivió exiliado en Estados Unidos y México. En sus poemas más famosos, *El Niágara* y *En el teocalli de Cholula,* escribe con gran emoción y voz lírica sobre la naturaleza americana. Demuestra una gran sensibilidad romántica ante el espectáculo de las cataratas del Niágara y las ruinas aztecas.

- **Esteban Echeverría** (Argentina, 1805–1851) nació en Buenos Aires. Fue el más importante de los escritores que introdujeron el romanticismo francés en la Argentina. Vivió cuatro años en París donde observó la síntesis del romanticismo y el liberalismo que se producía. Fue desterrado por el tirano argentino Juan Manuel de Rosas. La obra maestra de Echeverría, *El matadero,* es un cuadro de costumbres realista, o cuento, escrito con la intención política de mostrar la horrible muchedumbre que apoyaba a Rosas.
- **Domingo Faustino Sarmiento** (Argentina, 1811–1888) fue político, escritor y pedagogo. Durante el gobierno de Rosas, Sarmiento se exilió en Chile. Fue presidente de la Argentina de 1868 a 1874. Su obra maestra, *Civilización y barbarie: Vida de Juan Facundo Quiroga* (1845), es un libro de historia, política y sociología que trata los problemas de las ciudades como civilización en contraste con la pampa como un mar de barbarie, el caudillismo y la dictadura.
- **José Mármol** (Argentina, 1817–1871), escritor y político, fue encarcelado y desterrado por el tirano Rosas. Es famoso por su novela política y autobiográfica *Amalia*, en la cual describe cómo era la vida en Buenos Aires durante los años de Rosas.
- **Gertrudis Gómez de Avellaneda** (Cuba, 1814–1873) escribió poesía, dramas y novelas. Nació en Cuba y vivió en España donde publicó y tuvo éxito. Sus poesías cantan del amor, Dios y una nostalgia por Cuba. Su novela *Sab* trata el tema de la esclavitud y describe la realidad cubana.
- **Rafael Pombo** (Colombia, 1833–1912) es representante del romanticismo colombiano. Alcanzó su plenitud poética mientras vivía en Estados Unidos. Tuvo amistad con Longfellow e hizo traducciones de escritores clásicos y modernos. Escribió *Preludio de primavera.*
- **Jorge Isaacs** (Colombia, 1837–1895) es conocido por su novela romántica muy leída en Hispanoamérica *María* (1867). La novela trata de la idealización del amor puro y la muerte. Se destacan el costumbrismo (color local) y el americanismo en la descripción del paisaje.
- **José Hernández** (Argentina, 1834–1886), poeta romántico, es el máximo representante de la poesía gauchesca. Escribió su épica del gaucho *Martín Fierro* (1872, "la Ida"; 1879, "la Vuelta") en la cual el payador (campesino que improvisa canciones *payas* que se cantan con guitarra) canta sus experiencias. Hernández escribió su épica gauchesca para demostrarle al público culto que este género tenía valor y para darles a los gauchos lecciones morales que mejoraran su condición.
- **Ricardo Palma** (Perú, 1833–1919). Este escritor, historiador y crítico fue el representante más importante del romanticismo peruano y del costumbrismo hispanoamericano. Entre 1872 y 1906 publicó sus célebres *Tradiciones peruanas,* que son una mezcla de cuadro de costumbres, novela histórica, leyenda y cuento. Presentan elementos históricos, geográficos, sociológicos y psicológicos desde la época de los incas hasta la vida contemporánea. Palma usó crónicas, historias, vidas de santos, libros de viajes y la palabra oral para pintar especialmente la sociedad virreinal de la Lima del siglo XVIII.
- **José Enrique Rodó** (Uruguay, 1871–1917) fue escritor, humanista y el mejor prosista del modernismo. Es el pensador que mejor reconcilió la literatura modernista con el espiritualismo. Es famoso por su obra *Ariel* (1900), un ensayo sobre la democracia, el idealismo y la moralidad, y por su obra maestra *Los motivos de Proteo.*
- **Florencio Sánchez** (Uruguay, 1875–1910) fue el dramaturgo más importante de la época. Sus obras son representativas del realismo en el drama hispanoamericano. Uno de sus temas principales fue la vida en el campo con los conflictos entre los criollos y los inmigrantes europeos o entre la tradición y el progreso. *Barranca abajo* es su obra maestra; *M'hijo el dotor* y *La gringa* son importantes también.

Es una época de capitalismo, prosperidad, inmigración, desarrollo técnico y mayor estabilidad política. Sigue una época de industrialización y de capitalismo internacional. España pierde sus últimas posesiones en América. Se apegan en los círculos literarios de América las novedades europeas como el naturalismo. Surge la primera generación de *modernistas*, poetas que intentan renovar la lengua poética. El modernismo predomina, especialmente en poesía (1880–1910).

- **José Martí** (Cuba, 1853–1895), poeta, escritor, abogado y político, es el escritor más importante de la época y uno de los primeros poetas en introducir el modernismo. Vivió y murió como héroe, luchando siempre por la independencia de su patria. Fue encarcelado y desterrado a España. Luego fue a Venezuela y a Nueva York, donde fundó el Partido Revolucionario Cubano (1892). Sus libros de poemas incluyen *Ismalillo* (1882), *Versos libres* y *Versos sencillos* (1891). Martí fue un poeta romántico y modernista, muy personal en su tono, original en sugerir imágenes para ideas abstractas.
- **Manuel Gutiérrez Nájera** (México, 1859–1895) fue el primer modernista mexicano y una influencia importante en la transición de la poesía romántica a la modernista. Su poesía se destaca por las imágenes, la elegancia y el refinamiento. Sus temas incluyen el amor imposible, la tristeza, el misterio y la muerte. Escribió las poesías *Tristissima Nox, Pax Animae, Ondas muertas,* etcétera. También escribió los *Cuentos frágiles* (1883), y los *Cuentos color de humo,* críticas, crónicas de viajes, etcétera. Usó el seudónimo de "Duque Job".
- **José Asunción Silva** (Colombia, 1865–1896) fue el último de los poetas románticos americanos y el primero de los simbolistas. Recibió influencias europeas cuando fue a París y Londres. Su poesía se caracteriza por el tono lírico e íntimo, el misterio, la melancolía. Sus *Nocturnos* son sus obras más importantes por su alta expresión lírica.
- **Rubén Darío** (Nicaragua, 1867–1916) es la figura más importante del modernismo. Sus innovaciones en métrica y ritmo y el refinamiento de su expresión transformaron la poesía en español no sólo en Hispanoamérica sino también en España. Sus obras más importantes son *Cantos de vida y esperanza* (1905), *Prosas profanas* (1896) y *Azul* (1888).
- **Julián del Casal** (Cuba, 1863–1893) escribió poesía romántica y modernista. Publicó dos libros de poesías, *Hojas al viento* y *Nieve.* Su poesía es amarga y nostálgica. Escribió prosa también.
- **Leopoldo Lugones** (Argentina, 1874–1938) fue el principal poeta modernista de la Argentina. Sus obras poéticas demuestran un gran dominio del lenguaje y un ritmo musical. Escribió el *Lunario sentimental* (1909), *Odas seculares* (1910), *El libro fiel* (1912), etcétera.
- **Santos Chocano** (Perú, 1875–1934) fue el modernista más importante del Perú. Chocano, a diferencia de casi todos los modernistas hispanoamericanos, se dedicó a cantar lo que se ve en América: la naturaleza, la historia, las leyendas, los indios, la acción política. Demuestra un lirismo entusiasta en cantar a su patria. Fue revolucionario y protector de los indios. Escribió *Alma América* y *¡Fiat, Lux!*
- **Guillermo Valencia** (Colombia, 1873–1943), poeta modernista, político y orador, escribió *Ritos* (1898).
- **Amado Nervo** (México, 1870–1919), poeta modernista y diplomático, es autor de *Serenidad* (1914), *Elevación* (1917), *La amada inmóvil, El estanque de los lotos,* entre otras obras.

Al terminar la Primera Guerra Mundial en 1918, algunos poetas hispanoamericanos se dedicaron a tendencias postmodernistas. Había experimentos con el expresionismo, el creacionismo, el dadaísmo, etcétera. Otros poetas hispano-americanos, como Jorge Luis Borges, se unieron con sus colegas españoles para formular un nuevo programa estético. Esta literatura de vanguardia se llamaba *ultraísmo.* Fue una síntesis de las tendencias nuevas, integrando lo hispanoamericano, lo europeo y lo hispánico. Otro movimiento importante en Hispanoamérica fue el surrealismo, pero más con conciencia política que con subconciencia automática (Pablo Neruda, César Vallejo). Otros movimientos que tenían sus aficionados en las generaciones de escritores hispanoamericanos incluyen el existencialismo, el marxismo, el idealismo, el estructuralismo, etcétera. En la prosa seguía el realismo (Azuela), el naturalismo y la estética de técnicas impresionistas (Gallegos, Rivera, Güiraldes, Guzmán, Barrios, Bombal). También se cultiva la novela indigenista (Alegría, Icaza), la psicológica (Sábato, Bullrich) y las novelas de tendencias europeas como el expresionismo. Se veían influencias técnicas y temáticas de Europa como el desafío a la civilización, el super-intelectualismo, los monólogos interiores, los desplazamientos en el tiempo, el flujo de conciencia, etcétera. Hubo muchos experimentos en las novelas de Asturias, Carpentier y Mallea. Éstos siguieron los temas americanos de Quiroga, Gallegos, Azuela, Rivera y Güiraldes pero añadieron una imaginación de vanguardia, de 1918 a 1939. La siguiente generación de narradores experimentaron aún más que los anteriores: Rulfo, Cortázar, Sábato, Onetti, Lezama Lima. Después de la Segunda Guerra Mundial predomina la idea de lo absurdo de la vida en la novela o antinovela. En cuanto a la técnica se ven múltiples perspectivas, fluir de conciencia, acciones simultáneas, retrospectivas, etcétera. Cambió el lugar de acción del campo a la ciudad y de la sociedad agraria a la industrial. Se describían las luchas de clases sociales en su ambiente urbano (Benedetti, Mallea). Algunos escritores se valían del tema de los orígenes indígenas y del realismo mágico (Fuentes, García Márquez, Paz). Unos escritores de las últimas décadas han llegado a tener una fama internacional.

Poesía

- **Vicente Palés Matos** (Puerto Rico, 1903–1963) escribió poesía "negra" o "afroantillana". Escribió sobre el folklore negro usando palabras, sonidos musicales, ritmos y sensaciones sacados de esa cultura. Se nota en su poesía un tono irónico. Su primer libro de poemas negros fue *Tuntún de pasa y grifería* (1937).
- **Nicolás Guillén** (Cuba, 1902–1989) fue el mejor representante de la poesía negra como poesía política de combate, es decir, el poeta denuncia las condiciones en que vivían los cubanos de raza africana. Escribió *Motivos del son* y *Sóngoro cosongo* (1931).
- **Gabriela Mistral** (Chile, 1889–1957) recibió el primer Premio Nobel de Literatura en América (1945). Fue maestra de escuela y diplomática. Escribió poesías de un humanismo apasionado y de una fuerza emocional y lírica. Prefiere el tema del amor: a Dios, a la naturaleza, a los niños. Escribió *Desolación* (1922), *Ternura* (1924), *Tala* (1938).
- **Alfonsina Storni** (Argentina, 1892–1938) nació en Suiza. Fue maestra, periodista y feminista. Escribió poemas del amor siempre malogrado, amargo y desdeñoso. Escribió *El dulce daño* (1918) y *Ocre* (1925).
- **César Vallejo** (Perú, 1892–1938) escribió *Los heraldos negros* (1918) y *Trilce* (1922). Es autor de poemas de tristeza, sufrimiento, amargura, emoción y compasión. Vallejo vivió con los recuerdos de su pobreza, su orfandad, la cárcel y la injusticia social y política. Se expatrió del Perú después de *Trilce* y no volvió jamás a su patria.
- **Vicente Huidobro** (Chile, 1893–1948) fundó el creacionismo en la poesía. Se ven muchos neologismos e imágenes nuevas de este movimiento de vanguardia en *Altazor* (1931) y *Ver y palpar* (1941).
- **Juana de Ibarbourou** (Uruguay, 1895–1979) escribió poesía llena de amor y gozo de vivir. Cantó con voz clara y pura. Usó mucho colorido y palabras, metáforas e imágenes de lo vegetal y lo animal, como flor, fruta, gacela. Escribió *Las lenguas*

de diamante (1919), *Raíz salvaje* (1920) y otros libros de poesía. Se le llama "Juana de América".

- **Pablo Neruda** (Chile, 1904–1973) es uno de los poetas más importantes de la poesía hispana. Ganó el Premio Nobel de Literatura en 1971. Escribió varios libros de poesía, algunos de los cuales son: *Veinte poemas de amor y una canción desesperada* (1924), *Residencia en la tierra* (dos tomos, 1925–1935), *Tercera residencia* (1947), *Canto general* (1950), *Odas elementales* (1954–1959). Los libros demuestran las varias etapas de su evolución poética que comienza en el modernismo y termina en una poesía política y didáctica. Esta última etapa corresponde a su adhesión al partido comunista. Tuvo que expatriarse por su comunismo. Antes fue diplomático en España, México y Asia.
- **José Lezama Lima** (Cuba, 1912–1974) se dedicó al estudio de la literatura y ayudó a formar la futura generación de poetas con sus ideas innovadoras. Escribió libros de poesía y ensayos que eran muy eruditos. Ganó fama con su novela *Paradiso* (1966) en la cual describe una clase social de cierta época histórica.
- **Octavio Paz** (México, 1914) ganó el Premio Nobel de Literatura en 1990. El célebre escritor mexicano pertenece a la generación literaria mexicana de *Taller* (1938–1940). Paz pasó por el surrealismo, el marxismo, el idealismo, el existencialismo, el simbolismo, el budismo, el estructuralismo, etcétera, pero no se ha quedado en ninguno de estos ismos. Ha creado una poesía original, muy lírica, de brillantes imágenes. Paz tiene profunda conciencia del Yo y del pueblo mexicano y del hombre universal. Presenta los grandes conflictos y contradicciones de la época: soledad y comunión, esperanza y desesperanza, cultura occidental y cultura oriental. Paz explicó su teoría de la poesía en *El arco y la lira* (1956). Sus libros de poesía incluyen *Raíz del hombre, Libertad bajo palabra, Piedra de sol,* etcétera. Los libros de ensayos incluyen *El laberinto de la soledad* y *Las peras del olmo.* Paz ha vivido en Estados Unidos, Francia y Suiza y fue diplomático de México en la India.
- **Julia de Burgos** (Puerto Rico, 1914–1953) demuestra mucha emoción y dolor de una pasión no satisfecha en su poesía. Escribe sobre temas metafísicos, la belleza del amor, la naturaleza y escenas de América. Escribió el *Poema en veinte surcos.*
- **Nicanor Parra** (Chile, 1914) escribió una poesía popularista, de la sociedad de masas. Empezó escribiendo romances populares y pintorescos como en su *Cancionero sin nombre* (1937). Luego experimentó con sus "antipoemas" que mezclaban la poesía tradicional con el superrealismo. Su antología *Obra gruesa* (1969) incluye críticas, crónicas, conversaciones y obras sarcásticas y de humor.
- **Rosario Ferré** (Puerto Rico, 1938) escribe poesía, cuentos cortos y crítica literaria en los cuales se destacan el simbolismo y el feminismo. Sus libros incluyen *Papeles de Pandora* (1976), *Sitio a Eros* (1980), *Fábulas de la garza desangrada* (1982), colección de poemas sobre las mujeres, y *Maldito amor* (1986), su primera novela. Las mujeres tienen un papel importante en esta novela que trata del estado político de Puerto Rico. Ferré sacó su doctorado en la Universidad de Maryland y fue editora de una revista literaria (1970–1974) que introdujo la crítica feminista en la literatura hispánica.

Teatro

- **Rodolfo Usigli** (México, 1905–1979) escribió sátiras políticas y sociales y dramas históricos y políticos. *El gesticulador* (1937), "pieza para demagogos", trata del tema de la hipocresía social en México. Un profesor de historia se hace pasar por un general de la Revolución Mexicana, asesinado misteriosamente. Puede interpretarse también como el problema universal de la verdad y la mentira en la conciencia humana. *Corona de sombra* (1943) trata el tema histórico de Maximiliano y Carlota y la locura de ésta.

- **Francisco Arriví** (Puerto Rico, 1915) escribió obras de temas de vida nacional, empleando recursos nuevos. Escribió *El diablo se humaniza* (1941) y *Club de solteros* (1953).
- **Carlos Solórzano** (Guatemala, 1922) es un importante dramaturgo y crítico de teatro que, a pesar de ser guatemalteco de nacimiento, se considera una figura de la literatura mexicana. El tema más tratado por Solórzano es el de la libertad y cómo se logra o se pierde según la rebeldía. Escribió *Las manos de Dios* (1956) y *Los fantoches* (1958).
- **Sebastián Salazar Bondy** (Perú, 1924–1965) escribió ensayos y poesía pero es mejor conocido por su teatro. Escribe obras que demuestran sus preocupaciones por los problemas humanos y las condiciones sociales. *Ifigenia en el mercado* es un cuadro de costumbres y *El rabdomante* es un drama poético en un acto.
- **Emilio Carballido** (México, 1925) es quizás el dramaturgo más importante de su generación. Escribe sobre la clase media de provincias, lo absurdo de la vida, etcétera. Entre sus mejores obras figuran *Rosalba y los llaveros, La danza que sueña la tortuga* y *El día que se soltaron los leones.*
- **Osvaldo Dragún** (Argentina, 1929) es un dramaturgo de temas serios. *La peste viene de Melos* (1954) es una obra antiimperialista. *Túpac Amaru* es una tragedia histórica sobre el inca peruano que se sublevó contra la autoridad española. Es obra universal sobre la dignidad humana.
- **Jorge Díaz** (Chile, 1930) escribe obras que tratan lo absurdo de la vida. Usa la comedia o tragicomedia y la falta de lógica en *El cepillo de dientes* (1966) y *La ergástula.*

Narrativa

- **Mariano Azuela** (México, 1873–1952) fue un novelista realista que escribió novelas que tratan la Revolución Mexicana (1910) y sus consecuencias. Su obra maestra, *Los de abajo* (1916), salió de sus experiencias como médico en el ejército. Azuela es un revolucionario desilusionado que se dedica a pintar la Revolución con una gran fuerza realista.
- **Horacio Quiroga** (Uruguay, 1878–1937) fue el gran narrador de los temas raros. Se destacan sus cuentos cortos por su expresión, su descripción de la naturaleza americana y su originalidad. Se nota la influencia de Poe en sus cuentos. Escribió *Cuentos de amor, de locura y de muerte* (1917), *Cuentos de la selva* (1918), entre otras obras.
- **Rómulo Gallegos** (Venezuela, 1884–1969) se considera uno de los novelistas hispanoamericanos más importantes. Escribió novelas y cuentos que describen la realidad venezolana. Su obra maestra que le valió una fama universal es *Doña Bárbara* (1929). Gallegos emplea un estilo realista tradicional del siglo XIX para describir el paisaje de la llanura venezolana y la lucha entre las fuerzas de la civilización y la barbarie. Gallegos fue elegido presidente de Venezuela en 1947.
- **Eduardo Barrios** (Chile, 1884–1963) escribió novelas de análisis psicológico, como *El niño que enloqueció de amor* (1915) o el famoso *El hermano asno* (1922). Esta novela, escrita en primera persona con la forma de un diario, describe unos casos psicológicos raros. Barrios penetra en las almas de los personajes y describe la vida chilena también en *Tamarugal* (1944) y *Gran señor y rajadiablos* (1948), que presenta un panorama social e histórico del campo chileno.
- **Ricardo Güiraldes** (Argentina, 1886–1927) es conocido por su obra maestra *Don Segundo Sombra* (1926) que trata la vida de los gauchos. Usa un estilo impresionista.
- **Martín Luis Guzmán** (México, 1887–1976), novelista, se conoce por su obra *El águila y la serpiente* (1928) que es realmente un conjunto de relatos. Estas historias salen de las experiencias que tuvo Guzmán en la Revolución Mexicana.
- **José Eustasio Rivera** (Colombia, 1888–1928) es conocido por su novela *La vorágine* (1924) que tiene lugar en los llanos del Orinoco y una región del

Amazonas. Los temas de la novela son la soberanía de Colombia, amenazada por invasiones; los colombianos como prisioneros de la selva; la psicología complicada de la persona obsesionada por su fracaso.

- **Teresa de la Parra** (Venezuela, 1891–1936) escribió *Ifigenia: Diario de una señorita que escribió porque se fastidiaba* (1924) que cuenta la injusta situación de la mujer criolla. En su segunda y última novela, *Las memorias de Mamá Blanca* (1929), la novelista describe su infancia feliz en una hacienda de caña de azúcar cerca de Caracas. Pinta la clase aristocrática y la vieja sociedad que se deshacen. Escribe con amor, nostalgia, ternura, simpatía y sensibilidad. Su prosa es muy subjetiva, llena de impresiones y metáforas.
- **Jorge Luis Borges** (Argentina, 1899–1986), cuentista, ensayista y poeta, se considera uno de los mayores escritores de nuestro tiempo. Es uno de los fundadores del ultraísmo. Sus obras demuestran su gran imaginación creadora, su brillante uso de la metáfora, su profundo conocimiento de la cultura y la literatura universales, su enorme habilidad lingüística y su rigor lógico. Es conocido por sus cuentos más que nada. Sus antologías de cuentos incluyen la *Historia universal de la infamia* (1935), *Ficciones* (1944) y *El aleph* (1949).
- **Miguel Ángel Asturias** (Guatemala, 1899–1974), novelista y poeta, ganó el Premio Nobel de Literatura en 1967. El lenguaje que emplea Asturias es poético. Escribió las *Leyendas de Guatemala* (1930) con su visión mágica de los mayas. Hizo estudios antropológicos sobre la civilización de los mayas en París. Es famoso por sus novelas. Aunque Asturias no menciona el país en *El señor Presidente* (1946), su obra maestra, se sabe que escribe sobre la tiranía del dictador guatemalteco Estrada Cabrera. Como novela de crítica política y social, puede referirse a cualquier país hispanoamericano. Otras novelas de Asturias incluyen *Hombres de maíz* (1949) y la trilogía de *Viento fuerte* (1950), *El Papa verde* (1954) y *Los ojos de los enterrados* (1960).
- **Eduardo Mallea** (Argentina, 1903) escribió una novela autobiográfica, *Historia de una pasión argentina*, en 1935. Demuestra su angustia con su circunstancia argentina. Los cuentos de *La ciudad junto al río inmóvil* (1936) presentan personajes conscientes de su soledad y desesperación en Buenos Aires. *Fiesta en noviembre* (1938) es la primera novela de Mallea que emplea diálogos en contrapunto; antes, todo era monólogo. En *Todo verdor perecerá* (1941) y las novelas que siguen, los personajes buscan lo que significa ser mujer u hombre en la situación argentina.
- **Alejo Carpentier** (Cuba, 1904–1980) fue músico, escritor y poeta cuyas obras demuestran su profundo conocimiento de la historia, la música, la antropología y el folklore. Conoce a fondo la realidad de su país y de América. Escribió sobre la historia afrocubana en *Ecué-Yamba-O* (1931), sobre la historia y sociedad de Haití en *El reino de este mundo* (1949). *Los pasos perdidos* (1953), novela muy lograda, contrasta la vida en las ciudades modernas y la vida de la selva. Esta novela tiene magia, visión, fantasía, descripciones líricas de la naturaleza (la selva venezolana) y música indígena. Escribió también *La guerra del tiempo* (1958), *El siglo de las luces* (1962), etcétera.
- **Jorge Icaza** (Ecuador, 1906–1978) es conocido por su novela indigenista *Huasipungo* (1934) que interesa más por ser documento político y sociológico que por ser literatura. Icaza defiende al indio de su amo que le quita su "huasipungo", palabra quechua que significa parcela (de tierra). Describe la avaricia del amo, la violencia contra los indios, las costumbres primitivas y la miseria.
- **Ciro Alegría** (Perú, 1909–1967) escribió novelas indigenistas de contenido social y humano. Su estilo es realista, de prosa sencilla pero poderosa. Alegría demuestra su simpatía por los indios y los humildes en general en *La serpiente de oro* (1935), *Los perros hambrientos* (1939) y *El mundo es ancho y ajeno* (1941). Esta última trata de los sufrimientos de una comunidad de indios peruanos entre 1910 y 1928.
- **Juan Carlos Onetti** (Uruguay, 1909) escribió *La vida breve* (1950), *Juntacadáveres* (1969) y *Dejemos hablar al viento* (1980). El novelista tiene una visión pesimista

de la vida. La acción de sus novelas y cuentos transcurre en una región imaginaria, en una ciudad rioplatense donde los personajes acaban neuróticos, viciosos y vencidos.

- **María Luisa Bombal** (Chile, 1910–1980) escribe una prosa subjetiva, impresionista y poética. Sus novelas tienen lugar en una región mágica en donde las cosas desvanecen. Se ve lo humano entrelazado con lo sobrehumano en *La útlima niebla* (1934) y *La amortajada* (1941).
- **Ernesto Sábato** (Argentina, 1911) ha escrito novelas de tipo intelectual, psicológico y metafísico. Sus personajes tienen angustias y problemas metafísicos. Sábato escribió *El túnel* (1948) y *Sobre héroes y tumbas* (1961).
- **Silvina Bullrich** (Argentina, 1915) cultivó la novela psicológica con un tono poético. Se nota un ambiente de misterio en *La tercera versión* (1944). Pinta las clases sociales en *Los burgueses* (1964). También escribió *Mañana digo basta* y *Los monstruos sagrados* (1971).
- **Julio Cortázar** (Argentina, 1916–1984) nació en Bruselas. Se destaca por sus cuentos y novelas y también por la enorme influencia que tuvo en el arte narrativo en general. Experimentó mucho con formas lingüísticas y narrativas. Trata los temas de la realidad y la fantasía, lo absurdo de la vida, lo monstruoso, lo bestial, el destino humano. Escribió libros de cuentos como *Las armas secretas* y novelas como *Los premios* (1961) y *Rayuela* (1963), novela experimental.
- **Juan Rulfo** (México, 1918–1986) fue novelista y cuentista que escribió sobre la vida dura, el dolor, el sufrimiento y la muerte de los campesinos mexicanos. En su libro de cuentos *El llano en llamas* (1953), Rulfo refleja lo cruel y lo estéril de la tierra en sus personajes y sus temas de crimen, inocencia, muerte. La vida exterior (de los paisajes) y la vida interior (de los personajes) se reflejan la una a la otra. Esta realidad interiorizada que se ve en el cuento "Luvina", se profundiza y se intensifica en la novela *Pedro Páramo* (1955). Aquí en el pueblo de Comala todo es sobrenatural; hay fantasmas, murmullos, ecos, ánimas en pena.
- **Juan José Arreola** (México, 1918) es célebre por sus cuentos cortos. Cultivó el cuento fantástico, los juegos intelectuales y las paradojas en el *Confabulario total* (1962). Escribió obras sarcásticas en *Palindroma* (1971). En la novela *La feria* (1963) Arreola narra la desorganización social de un pueblo mexicano en viñetas satíricas.
- **René Marqués** (Puerto Rico, 1919–1978) es conocido por sus cuentos cortos aunque escribió obras de teatro importantes. Marqués se preocupa por las cuestiones políticas de la soberanía de Puerto Rico como en su novela *La víspera del hombre* (1959). Trata los temas del tiempo, la angustia, el miedo, la libertad, lo absurdo de la vida y la muerte en su antología de cuentos *Otro día nuestro* (1955). *La carreta* (1952), una obra de teatro, presenta una familia puertorriqueña que se desarraiga del campo para mudarse a San Juan y luego a Nueva York.
- **Mario Benedetti** (Uruguay, 1920) escribió cuentos y novelas que penetran el alma y la psicología de las personas que viven en las ciudades. Escribió una antología *Cuentos completos* (1970) y las novelas *La tregua* (1960) y *Gracias por el fuego* (1965).
- **Augusto Monterroso** (Guatemala, 1921) es el cuentista más importante del grupo "Acento". Las piezas de *Obras completas y otros cuentos* (1959) son breves, satíricas, sorprendentes y de estilo sencillo. Escribió *La oveja negra y demás fábulas* (1969) y *Movimiento perpetuo* (1972). Estos cuentos tienen ironía, imaginación, alusiones cultas, duplicaciones, etcétera.
- **José Donoso** (Chile, 1925) hace crítica social empleando el tema de las clases sociales y la descomposición de la sociedad en sus novelas *Coronación* (1957), *Este domingo* (1966), *El lugar sin límites* (1967), *El obsceno pájaro de la noche* (1970), etcétera.
- **Rosario Castellanos** (México, 1925–1974) escribió narrativa, poesía y teatro que demuestran una voz sincera y seria que confiesa su soledad y sus amores y tristezas y canta la tierra y el pueblo mexicanos. Escribió el libro de cuentos *Álbum de familia* (1971). En su novela *Balún Canán* (1955) Castellanos describe la

vida provinciana de Chiapas a través de los ojos de una niña y otros personajes. Se ven sus prejuicios, supersticiones y la injusticia contra los indios. En *El oficio de tinieblas* (1962) la novelista narra el triunfo del indio mexicano en su lucha social.

- **Gabriel García Márquez** (Colombia, 1928) recibió el Premio Nobel de Literatura en 1982. Su novela más famosa es *Cien años de soledad* (1967), obra que cuenta la historia de una familia (los Buendía) de Macondo (un lugar ficticio que representa Colombia y toda América). La vida pintada es real, mágica, fantástica y grotesca. Todo se entrelaza en el espacio y en el tiempo. García Márquez es un buen narrador. También escribió *La hojarasca* (1955), *El coronel no tiene quien le escriba* (1961), *Los cuentos de la Mamá Grande,* etcétera.
- **Carlos Fuentes** (México, 1928) goza de una fama mundial por sus novelas. Ha experimentado con nuevas técnicas a lo largo de los años. Se ve su preocupación por la historia y la cultura mexicanas y por los temas universales y la psicología humana. *La región más transparente* (1958) tiene como protagonista la ciudad de México, que se enfoca a través de las distintas clases sociales. Fuentes presenta lo indígena y lo criollo y su tema frecuente de la traición a la Revolución Mexicana. La traición a la Revolución y la descomposición de la sociedad mexicana son temas de otra novela muy lograda, *La muerte de Artemio Cruz* (1962). Otras novelas de Fuentes: *Aura* (1962), *Zona sagrada* (1966), *Terra nostra* (1975), etcétera.
- **Guillermo Cabrera Infante** (Cuba, 1929) tuvo gran éxito con *Tres tristes tigres* (1967), novela que tiene lugar en la época de Batista. Cabrera Infante juega mucho con el lenguaje, el tiempo y el punto de vista. El novelista usa la fragmentación, dialectos, escenas simultáneas y otros recursos innovadores. También escribió *La Habana para un infante difunto, Cuerpos divinos,* etcétera.
- **Manuel Puig** (Argentina, 1932–1990) escribe novelas como su autobiografía novelada *La traición de Rita Hayworth* (1968), en la cual un chico de un pueblo de la Pampa se refugia en el mundo del cine. Otras novelas tratan las clases sociales, la sociedad argentina y los problemas psicológicos: *Boquitas pintadas* (1969), *Buenos Aires Affair* (1973) en la cual hace una parodia de los gustos de las masas, *El beso de la mujer araña* (1976), etcétera.
- **Elena Poniatowska** (México, 1933), nació en París, hija de un conde polaco y de una mexicana de la clase alta social, escribe novelas y cultiva el género que mezcla literatura y periodismo. Esta combinación de ficción y no-ficción se ve en *La noche de Tlatelolco: Testimonios de historia oral* (1971) que cuenta las manifestaciones políticas de 1968 en la plaza de las Tres Culturas. Su novela *Hasta no verte, Jesús mío* (1969) narra la historia de la vida de una soldadera (una mujer que seguía a los soldados con comida y otras cosas durante la Revolución Mexicana). *Querido Diego, te abraza Quiela* (1978) es una novela que cuenta la desesperanza de una de las queridas de Diego Rivera después que el pintor mexicano la dejó y volvió a México. *Flor de lis* (1988) es una novela autobiográfica.
- **Mario Vargas Llosa** (Perú, 1936) es novelista, crítico, periodista, analista político y erudito literario de renombre internacional. Ha experimentado con temas y técnicas desde su primera novela *La ciudad y los perros* (1963). La ciudad es Lima y los perros son los cadetes de un colegio militar. Vargas Llosa demuestra lo vulgar y lo despreciable de esa vida, de esa gente, y por extensión, de la naturaleza humana. Usa técnicas del montaje y múltiples perspectivas en *La casa verde* (1966). *Conversación en la catedral* (1969) es una novela política que trata de los años de un vil presidente peruano. Entre sus otras novelas figuran *La guerra del fin del mundo* (1981), *Historia de Mayta* (1984), *¿Quién mató a Palomino Molero?* (1986) y *El hablador* (1987). Vargas Llosa, nacionalizado español, ha sido elegido recientemente miembro de la Real Academia de la Lengua. Fue candidato a presidente del Perú en 1992.
- **Cristina Peri Rossi** (Uruguay, 1941) se exilió en 1972 y ahora es ciudadana española. *Viviendo* (1963) es su primer libro de cuentos cortos. Usando muchas imágenes y una sensibilidad erótica, la cuentista narra las costumbres sociales,

la tradición literaria y las estructuras políticas. Como novelista postmodernista Peri Rossi describe un mundo vacío, en proceso de desintegración en *Los museos abandonados* (1968) y *El libro de mis primos* (1969).

- **Isabel Allende** (Chile, 1942) nació en Perú y se crió en Chile. Su familia se exilió de Chile por el golpe de estado militar en 1973. Vivió en Caracas por muchos años y ahora vive en California. Trabajó de periodista y escribió su primera novela en 1981, *La casa de los espíritus*. Esta obra le trajo una fama internacional. También escribió *De amor y de sombra* (1984), *Eva Luna* (1987), *Cuentos de Eva Luna* (1990), *El plan infinito* (1991), su primera novela que tiene lugar en Estados Unidos. En su última obra, *Paula* (1994), Allende narra la trágica experiencia personal de la muerte de su hija Paula.

A. Escoja la respuesta que termine correctamente cada oración.

1. El español que defendió a los indios del trabajo forzado fue __________.
   a. Bernal Díaz del Castillo
   b. Fray Bartolomé de las Casas
   c. Jorge Icaza
   d. Hernán Cortés

2. Una poesía gauchesca argentina muy conocida se titula __________.
   a. *Ricardo Güiraldes*
   b. *Julián del Casal*
   c. *José Hernández*
   d. *Martín Fierro*

3. El novelista colombiano que recibió el Premio Nobel de Literatura en 1982 fue __________.
   a. José Asunción Silva
   b. José Eustasio Rivera
   c. Gabriel García Márquez
   d. Miguel Ángel Asturias

4. Se le llama "Juana de América" a __________.
   a. Juana de Ibarbourou
   b. Julia de Burgos
   c. Juan Rulfo
   d. Sor Juana Inés de la Cruz

5. *El Periquillo Sarniento* fue __________.
   a. un movimiento literario del siglo XIX
   b. la primera poesía modernista
   c. la primera novela hispanoamericana
   d. la primera crónica de Indias

6. El poeta nicaragüense que encabezó el movimiento modernista de Hispanoamérica fue __________.
   a. José Enrique Rodó
   b. Leopoldo Lugones
   c. Vicente Palés Matos
   d. Rubén Darío

7. __________ describió la Revolución Mexicana en sus novelas.
   a. Mariano Azuela
   b. José Donoso
   c. Ciro Alegría
   d. Rómulo Gallegos

8. __________ fue el autor de la *Historia verdadera de la conquista de la Nueva España.*
   a. Hernán Cortés
   b. Bernal Díaz del Castillo
   c. Alonso de Ercilla y Zúñiga
   d. Juan José Arreola

9. __________ escribió una *Gramática castellana.*
   a. Simón Bolívar
   b. Andrés Bello
   c. Guillermo Cabrera Infante
   d. Jorge Luis Borges

10. El novelista Mario Vargas Llosa fue candidato a presidente de __________.
    a. Colombia
    b. Argentina
    c. Perú
    d. Chile

11. El *Primero Sueño* fue escrito por la poetisa barroca __________.
    a. Teresa de la Parra
    b. Alfonsina Storni
    c. Gertrudis Gómez de Avellaneda
    d. Sor Juana Inés de la Cruz

12. __________ recibió el primer Premio Nobel de Literatura en América en __________.
    a. Gabriela Mistral/1945
    b. Octavio Paz/1990
    c. Miguel Ángel Asturias/1967
    d. Pablo Neruda/1971

B. Empareje los escritores de la columna A con las obras de la columna B.

	A	B
_____	1. Carlos Fuentes	a. *Cuentos de amor, de locura y de muerte*
_____	2. El Inca Garcilaso de la Vega	b. *La Araucana*
_____	3. Rómulo Gallegos	c. *Sóngoro Cosongo*
_____	4. Alonso de Ercilla	d. *El matadero*
_____	5. Alejo Carpentier	e. *Comentarios reales*
_____	6. Isabel Allende	f. *Residencia en la tierra*
_____	7. Nicolás Guillén	g. *La muerte de Artemio Cruz*
_____	8. Pablo Neruda	h. *Los pasos perdidos*
_____	9. Ernesto Sábato	i. *El túnel*
_____	10. Rosario Ferré	j. *Doña Bárbara*
_____	11. Esteban Echeverría	k. *Fábulas de la garza desangrada*
_____	12. Horacio Quiroga	l. *Cuentos de Eva Luna*

C. Identifique las siguientes cosas escogiendo la respuesta correcta.

1. gran cuentista argentino
   a. Jorge Luis Borges
   b. Augusto Monterroso
2. poesía afroantillana
   a. René Marqués
   b. Vicente Palés Matos
3. *Libertad bajo palabra* y *Piedra de sol*
   a. obras de teatro de Rodolfo Usigli
   b. antologías de poesía de Octavio Paz
4. crónica sobre la conquista de México
   a. Bernal Díaz del Castillo
   b. Cristóbal Colón
5. Premio Nobel de Literatura 1967
   a. Carlos Fuentes
   b. Miguel Ángel Asturias
6. escritor, político y filósofo
   a. Andrés Bello
   b. Ricardo Palma
7. Gabriel García Márquez
   a. nació en Ecuador
   b. *Cien años de soledad*
8. Simón Bolívar
   a. el Libertador
   b. el Pensador Mexicano
9. se le llama *la décima musa*
   a. Sor Juana Inés de la Cruz
   b. María Luisa Bombal
10. influencia de Poe en sus cuentos
    a. José Enrique Rodó
    b. Horacio Quiroga
11. la barbarie de la llanura venezolana
    a. *La vorágine*
    b. *Doña Bárbara*
12. la Revolución Mexicana
    a. *Los de abajo*
    b. *El mundo es ancho y ajeno*

D. Empareje el tema de la obra de la columna A con el título de la obra de la columna B.

A	B
_____ 1. historia de los Buendía de Macondo	a. *La vorágine*
_____ 2. la vida de los gauchos en la Pampa	b. *El mundo es ancho y ajeno*
_____ 3. ánimas en pena y murmullos en Comala	c. *Cien años de soledad*
_____ 4. la traición a la Revolución Mexicana	d. *Don Segundo Sombra*
_____ 5. los llanos del Orinoco y la selva del Amazonas	e. *La muerte de Artemio Cruz*
_____ 6. los cadetes de un colegio militar limeño	f. *El señor presidente*
_____ 7. la tiranía de un dictador centroamericano	g. *La ciudad y los perros*
_____ 8. el sufrimiento de los indios peruanos	h. *Pedro Páramo*

E. Complete las siguientes oraciones escribiendo la información que falta.

1. *La ciudad y los perros* es la primera novela escrita por ______________________.
2. Una novela de Carlos Fuentes, ______________________, tiene como protagonista la ciudad de México.
3. *El gesticulador* y *Corona de sombra* son obras de teatro escritas por ______________________.
4. ______________________ fue el primer poeta modernista mexicano.
5. ______________________ luchó por la independencia de su patria formando un partido político mientras vivía en Nueva York.
6. Desterrado por el tirano argentino Rosas, Echeverría escribió ______________________, un cuento que pinta lo terrible del régimen del dictador.
7. La obra más importante de ______________________, el dramaturgo uruguayo, se titula *Barranca abajo.*
8. Ricardo Palma creó las ______________________, que son una mezcla de cuadro de costumbres, novela histórica, leyenda y cuento.
9. ______________________ escribió *Los pasos perdidos* sobre el contraste entre la vida urbana y la selva venezolana.
10. Julio Cortázar escribió una novela experimental titulada ______________________.

Verb Charts

Regular Verbs

-ar verbs

cantar *to sing*	
indicative mood	
PRESENT	canto, cantas, canta, cantamos, cantáis, cantan
IMPERFECT	cantaba, cantabas, cantaba, cantábamos, cantabais, cantaban
PRETERIT	canté, cantaste, cantó, cantamos, cantasteis, cantaron
FUTURE	cantaré, cantarás, cantará, cantaremos, cantaréis, cantarán
CONDITIONAL	cantaría, cantarías, cantaría, cantaríamos, cantaríais, cantarían
PRESENT PERFECT	he cantado, has cantado, ha cantado, hemos cantado, habéis cantado, han cantado
PLUPERFECT	había cantado, habías cantado, había cantado, habíamos cantado, habíais cantado, habían cantado
PRETERIT PERFECT	hube cantado, hubiste cantado, hubo cantado, hubimos cantado, hubisteis cantado, hubieron cantado
FUTURE PERFECT	habré cantado, habrás cantado, habrá cantado, habremos cantado, habréis cantado, habrán cantado
CONDITIONAL PERFECT	habría cantado, habrías cantado, habría cantado, habríamos cantado, habríais cantado, habrían cantado
subjunctive mood	
PRESENT	cante, cantes, cante, cantemos, cantéis, canten
IMPERFECT	cantara, cantaras, cantara, cantáramos, cantarais, cantaran
	cantase, cantases, cantase, cantásemos, cantaseis, cantasen
PRESENT PERFECT	haya cantado, hayas cantado, haya cantado, hayamos cantado, hayáis cantado, hayan cantado
PLUPERFECT	hubiera/hubiese cantado, hubieras/hubieses cantado, hubiera/hubiese cantado, hubiéramos/hubiésemos cantado, hubierais/hubieseis cantado, hubieran/hubiesen cantado
imperative mood	canta/no cantes (tú), cante (Ud.), cantemos (nosotros), cantad/no cantéis (vosotros), canten (Uds.)

-er verbs

comer *to eat*	
indicative mood	
PRESENT	como, comes, come, comemos, coméis, comen
IMPERFECT	comía, comías, comía, comíamos, comíais, comían
PRETERIT	comí, comiste, comió, comimos, comisteis, comieron
FUTURE	comeré, comerás, comerá, comeremos, comeréis, comerán
CONDITIONAL	comería, comerías, comería, comeríamos, comeríais, comerían
PRESENT PERFECT	he comido, has comido, ha comido, hemos comido, habéis comido, han comido
PLUPERFECT	había comido, habías comido, había comido, habíamos comido, habíais comido, habían comido
PRETERIT PERFECT	hube comido, hubiste comido, hubo comido, hubimos comido, hubisteis comido, hubieron comido
FUTURE PERFECT	habré comido, habrás comido, habrá comido, habremos comido, habréis comido, habrán comido
CONDITIONAL PERFECT	habría comido, habrías comido, habría comido, habríamos comido, habríais comido, habrían comido
subjunctive mood	
PRESENT	coma, comas, coma, comamos, comáis, coman
IMPERFECT	comiera, comieras, comiera, comiéramos, comierais, comieran
	comiese, comieses, comiese, comiésemos, comieseis, comiesen
PRESENT PERFECT	haya comido, hayas comido, haya comido, hayamos comido, hayáis comido, hayan comido
PLUPERFECT	hubiera/hubiese comido, hubieras/hubieses comido, hubiera/hubiese comido, hubiéramos/hubiésemos comido, hubierais/hubieseis comido, hubieran/hubiesen comido
imperative mood	
	come/no comas (tú), coma (Ud.), comamos (nosotros), comed/no comáis (vosotros), coman (Uds.)

-ir verbs

vivir *to live*	
indicative mood	
PRESENT	vivo, vives, vive, vivimos, vivís, viven
IMPERFECT	vivía, vivías, vivía, vivíamos, vivíais, vivían
PRETERIT	viví, viviste, vivió, vivimos, vivisteis, vivieron
FUTURE	viviré, vivirás, vivirá, viviremos, viviréis, vivirán
CONDITIONAL	viviría, vivirías, viviría, viviríamos, viviríais, vivirían
PRESENT PERFECT	he vivido, has vivido, ha vivido, hemos vivido, habéis vivido, han vivido
PLUPERFECT	había vivido, habías vivido, había vivido, habíamos vivido, habíais vivido, habían vivido
PRETERIT PERFECT	hube vivido, hubiste vivido, hubo vivido, hubimos vivido, hubisteis vivido, hubieron vivido
FUTURE PERFECT	habré vivido, habrás vivido, habrá vivido, habremos vivido, habréis vivido, habrán vivido
CONDITIONAL PERFECT	habría vivido, habrías vivido, habría vivido, habríamos vivido, habríais vivido, habrían vivido
subjunctive mood	
PRESENT	viva, vivas, viva, vivamos, viváis, vivan
IMPERFECT	viviera, vivieras, viviera, viviéramos, vivierais, vivieran
	viviese, vivieses, viviese, viviésemos, vivieseis, viviesen
PRESENT PERFECT	haya vivido, hayas vivido, haya vivido, hayamos vivido, hayáis vivido, hayan vivido
PLUPERFECT	hubiera/hubiese vivido, hubieras/hubieses vivido, hubiera/hubiese vivido, hubiéramos/hubiésemos vivido, hubierais/hubieseis vivido, hubieran/hubiesen vivido
imperative mood	vive/no vivas (tú), viva (Ud.), vivamos (nosotros), vivid/no viváis (vosotros), vivan (Uds.)

Verbs with Changes in the Vowel of the Stem

pensar (e > ie) *to think*	
PRESENT INDICATIVE	pi**e**nso, pi**e**nsas, pi**e**nsa, pensamos, pensáis, pi**e**nsan
PRESENT SUBJUNCTIVE	pi**e**nse, pi**e**nses, pi**e**nse, pensemos, penséis, pi**e**nsen
IMPERATIVE	———, pi**e**nsa, pi**e**nse, pensemos, pensad, pi**e**nsen
Other tenses and forms present no changes in the vowel of the stem	

entender (e > ie) *to understand*	
PRESENT INDICATIVE	enti**e**ndo, enti**e**ndes, enti**e**nde, entendemos, entendéis, enti**e**nden
PRESENT SUBJUNCTIVE	enti**e**nda, enti**e**ndas, enti**e**nda, entendamos, entendáis, enti**e**ndan
IMPERATIVE	———, enti**e**nde, enti**e**nda, entendamos, entended, enti**e**ndan
Other tenses and forms present no changes in the vowel of the stem	

recordar (o > ue) *to remember*	
PRESENT INDICATIVE	rec**ue**rdo, rec**ue**rdas, rec**ue**rda, recordamos, recordáis, rec**ue**rdan
PRESENT SUBJUNCTIVE	rec**ue**rde, rec**ue**rdes, rec**ue**rde, recordemos, recordéis, rec**ue**rden
IMPERATIVE	———, recuerda, recuerde, recordemos, recordad, recuerden
Other tenses and forms present no changes in the vowel of the stem	

volver (o > ue) *to return*	
PRESENT INDICATIVE	v**ue**lvo, v**ue**lves, v**ue**lve, volvemos, volvéis, v**ue**lven
PRESENT SUBJUNCTIVE	v**ue**lva, v**ue**lvas, v**ue**lva, volvamos, volváis, v**ue**lvan
IMPERATIVE	———, v**ue**lve, v**ue**lva, volvamos, volved, v**ue**lvan
Other tenses and forms present no changes in the vowel of the stem	

Stem-changing **-ir** verbs have three types of possible changes in the vowel of the stem **e > ie, e > i, o > ue**. In addition to the expected changes in the present subjunctive and imperative, verbs having the change **e > ie** and **e > i** have **i** as the stem vowel and verbs having the change **o > ue** have **u** as the stem vowel in the following forms:

a. the **nosotros** and **vosotros** forms of the present subjunctive
b. the **nosotros** command and the negative **vosotros** commands
c. the third-person singular and third-person plural forms of the preterit
d. all persons of the imperfect subjunctive (both **-ra** and **-se** forms)
e. the present participle

Sample Conjugations

sentir (e > ie) ***to feel, regret***	
PRESENT INDICATIVE	siento, sientes, siente, sentimos, sentís, sienten
PRESENT SUBJUNCTIVE	sienta, sientas, sienta, sintamos, sintáis, sientan
IMPERATIVE	——, siente, sienta, sintamos, sentid, sientan
PRETERIT	sentí, sentiste, sintió, sentimos, sentisteis, sintieron
IMPERFECT SUBJUNCTIVE	sintiera, sintieras, sintiera, sintiéramos, sintierais, sintieran
	sintiese, sintieses, sintiese, sintiésemos, sintieseis, sintiesen
PRESENT PARTICIPLE	sintiendo
Other tenses and forms present no changes in the vowel of the stem	

pedir (e > i) ***to ask for***	
PRESENT INDICATIVE	pido, pides, pide, pedimos, pedís, piden
PRESENT SUBJUNCTIVE	pida, pidas, pida, pidamos, pidáis, pidan
IMPERATIVE	——, pide, pida, pidamos, pedid, pidan
PRETERIT	pedí, pediste, pidió, pedimos, pedisteis, pidieron
IMPERFECT SUBJUNCTIVE	pidiera, pidieras, pidiera, pidiéramos, pidierais, pidieran
	pidiese, pidieses, pidiese, pidiésemos, pidieseis, pidiesen
PRESENT PARTICIPLE	pidiendo
Other tenses and forms present no changes in the vowel of the stem	

dormir (o > ue) *to sleep*	
PRESENT INDICATIVE	d**ue**rmo, d**ue**rmes, d**ue**rme, dormimos, dormís, d**ue**rmen
PRESENT SUBJUNCTIVE	d**ue**rma, d**ue**rmas, d**ue**rma, d**u**rmamos, d**u**rmáis, d**ue**rman
IMPERATIVE	———, d**ue**rme, d**ue**rma, d**u**rmamos, dormid, d**ue**rman
PRETERIT	dormí, dormiste, d**u**rmió, dormimos, dormisteis, d**u**rmieron
IMPERFECT SUBJUNCTIVE	d**u**rmiera, d**u**rmieras, d**u**rmiera, d**u**rmiéramos, d**u**rmierais, d**u**rmieran
	d**u**rmiese, d**u**rmieses, d**u**rmiese, d**u**rmiésemos, d**u**rmieseis, d**u**rmiesen
PRESENT PARTICIPLE	d**u**rmiendo
Other tenses and forms present no changes in the vowel of the stem	

Verbs with Spelling Changes

1. Verbs ending in **-car** (**c** > **qu** before **e**)
   The change occurs in the first-person singular of the preterit, in all persons of the present subjunctive, and in imperative forms derived from the present subjunctive.

tocar *to touch, play an instrument*	
PRETERIT	to**qué**, tocaste, tocó, tocamos, tocasteis, tocaron
PRESENT SUBJUNCTIVE	to**que**, to**que**s, to**que**, to**que**mos, to**qué**is, to**que**n

2. Verbs ending in **-gar** (**c** > **gu** before **e**)
   The change occurs in the first-person singular of the preterit, in all persons of the present subjunctive, and in imperative forms derived from the present subjunctive.

llegar *to arrive*	
PRETERIT	lle**gué**, llegaste, llegó, llegamos, llegasteis, llegaron
PRESENT SUBJUNCTIVE	lle**gue**, lle**gue**s, lle**gue**, lle**gue**mos, lle**gué**is, lle**gue**n

3. Verbs ending in **-zar** (**z** > **c** before **e**)
The change occurs in the first-person singular of the preterit, in all persons of the present subjunctive, and in imperative forms derived from the present subjunctive.

cruzar *to cross*	
PRETERIT	cru**c**é, cruzaste, cruzó, cruzamos, cruzasteis, cruzaron
PRESENT SUBJUNCTIVE	cru**c**e, cru**c**es, cru**c**e, cru**c**emos, cru**c**éis, cru**c**en

4. Verbs ending in **-ger** and **-gir** (**g** > **j** before **a** and **o**)
The change occurs in the first-person singular of the present indicative, in all persons of the present subjunctive, and in imperative forms derived from the present subjunctive.

recoger *to pick up*	
PRESENT INDICATIVE	reco**j**o, recoges, recoge, recogemos, recogéis, recogen
PRESENT SUBJUNCTIVE	reco**j**a, reco**j**as, reco**j**a, reco**j**amos, reco**j**áis, reco**j**an

exigir *to demand*	
PRESENT INDICATIVE	exi**j**o, exiges, exige, exigimos, exigís, exigen
PRESENT SUBJUNCTIVE	exi**j**a, exi**j**as, exi**j**a, exi**j**amos, exi**j**áis, exi**j**an

5. Verbs ending in **-guir** (**gu** > **g** before **a** and **o**)
The change occurs in the first-person singular of the present indicative, in all persons of the present subjunctive, and in imperative forms derived from the present subjunctive.

seguir *to follow*	
PRESENT INDICATIVE	si**g**o, sigues, sigue, seguimos, seguís, siguen
PRESENT SUBJUNCTIVE	si**g**a, si**g**as, si**g**a, si**g**amos, si**g**áis, si**g**an

6. Verbs ending in a consonant + **-cer, -cir** (**c** > **z** before **a** and **o**)
The change occurs in the first-person singular of the present indicative, in all persons of the present subjunctive, and in imperative forms derived from the present subjunctive.

convencer *to convince*	
PRESENT INDICATIVE	conven**z**o, convences, convence, convencemos, convencéis, convencen
PRESENT SUBJUNCTIVE	conven**z**a, conven**z**as, conven**z**a, conven**z**amos, conven**z**áis, conven**z**an

7. **-Er** verbs having stems ending in a vowel
*These verbs change the **i** of the preterit endings **-ió** and **-ieron** and the **i** of the present participle ending **-iendo** to **y**. The **y** appears in all persons of the imperfect subjunctive. These verbs also add written accents to the endings of the second-person singular and the first- and second-persons plural of the preterit.*

creer *to believe*	
PRETERIT	creí, creíste, creyó, creímos, creísteis, creyeron
IMPERFECT SUBJUNCTIVE	creyera (creyese), creyeras, creyera, creyéramos, creyerais, creyeran
PRESENT PARTICIPLE	creyendo

Irregular Verbs

1. Verbs ending in a vowel + **-cer** or **-cir**
*These verbs change the final **c** of the stem to **-zc-** before **a** and **o**. The **-zc-** appears in the first-person singular of the present indicative, in all persons of the present subjunctive, and in imperative forms derived from the present subjunctive.*

conocer *to know*	
PRESENT INDICATIVE	cono**zc**o, conoces, conoce, conocemos, conocéis, conocen
PRESENT SUBJUNCTIVE	cono**zc**a, cono**zc**as, cono**zc**a, cono**zc**amos, cono**zc**áis, cono**zc**an

2. Verbs ending in **-uir** (not including those ending in **-guir**)
*These verbs add **y** before a vowel other than **i** and change the unaccented **i** between vowels to **y**. The **y** appears in all singular forms and the third-person plural of the present, in the third-persons singular and plural of the preterit, in all persons of the present and imperfect subjunctive, and in all imperative forms except the affirmative **vosotros** command.*

construir *to build*	
PRESENT INDICATIVE	constru**y**o, constru**y**es, constru**y**e, construimos, construís, constru**y**en
PRETERIT	construí, construiste, constru**y**ó, construimos, construisteis, constru**y**eron
IMPERATIVE	constru**y**e, constru**y**a, constru**y**amos, construid, constru**y**an
PRESENT SUBJUNCTIVE	constru**y**a, constru**y**as, constru**y**a, constru**y**amos, constru**y**áis, constru**y**an
IMPERFECT SUBJUNCTIVE	constru**y**era (constru**y**ese), constru**y**eras, constru**y**era, constru**y**éramos, constru**y**erais, constru**y**eran

Other Irregular Verbs

andar *to walk*	
PRETERIT	anduve, anduviste, anduvo, anduvimos, anduvisteis, anduvieron
IMPERFECT SUBJUNCTIVE	anduviera (anduviese), anduvieras, anduviera, anduviéramos, anduvierais, anduvieran

caer *to fall*	
PRESENT INDICATIVE	caigo, caes, cae, caemos, caéis, caen
PRETERIT	caí, caíste, cayó, caímos, caísteis, cayeron
IMPERATIVE	cae (no caigas), caiga, caigamos, caed (no caigáis), caigan
PRESENT SUBJUNCTIVE	caiga, caigas, caiga, caigamos, caigáis, caigan
IMPERFECT SUBJUNCTIVE	cayera (cayese), cayeras, cayera, cayéramos, cayerais, cayeran
PRESENT PARTICIPLE	cayendo
PAST PARTICIPLE	caído

dar *to give*	
PRESENT INDICATIVE	doy, das, da, damos, dais, dan
PRETERIT	di, diste, dio, dimos, disteis, dieron
IMPERATIVE	da (no des), dé, demos, dad (no deis), den
PRESENT SUBJUNCTIVE	dé, des, dé, demos, deis, den
IMPERFECT SUBJUNCTIVE	diera (diese), dieras, diera, diéramos, dierais, dieran
PAST PARTICIPLE	dado

decir *to say, tell*	
PRESENT INDICATIVE	digo, dices, dice, decimos, decís, dicen
PRETERIT	dije, dijiste, dijo, dijimos, dijisteis, dijeron
FUTURE	diré, dirás, dirá, diremos, diréis, dirán
CONDITIONAL	diría, dirías, diría, diríamos, diríais, dirían
IMPERATIVE	di (no digas), diga, digamos, decid (no digáis), digan
PRESENT SUBJUNCTIVE	diga, digas, diga, digamos, digáis, digan
IMPERFECT SUBJUNCTIVE	dijera (dijese), dijeras, dijera, dijéramos, dijerais, dijeran
PRESENT PARTICIPLE	diciendo
PAST PARTICIPLE	dicho

estar *to be*

PRESENT INDICATIVE	estoy, estás, está, estamos, estáis, están
PRETERIT	estuve, estuviste, estuvo, estuvimos, estuvisteis, estuvieron
IMPERATIVE	está (no estés), esté, estemos, estad (no estéis), estén
PRESENT SUBJUNCTIVE	esté, estés, esté, estemos, estéis, estén
IMPERFECT SUBJUNCTIVE	estuviera (estuviese), estuvieras, estuviera, estuviéramos, estuvierais, estuvieran

haber *to have (auxiliary verb)*

PRESENT INDICATIVE	he, has, ha, hemos, habéis, han
PRETERIT	hube, hubiste, hubo, hubimos, hubisteis, hubieron
FUTURE	habré, habrás, habrá, habremos, habréis, habrán
CONDITIONAL	habría, habrías, habría, habríamos, habríais, habrían
PRESENT SUBJUNCTIVE	haya, hayas, haya, hayamos, hayáis, hayan
IMPERFECT SUBJUNCTIVE	hubiera (hubiese), hubieras, hubiera, hubiéramos, hubierais, hubieran

hacer *to do, to make*

PRESENT INDICATIVE	hago, haces, hace, hacemos, hacéis, hacen
PRETERIT	hice, hiciste, hizo, hicimos, hiciste, hicieron
FUTURE	haré, harás, hará, haremos, haréis, harán
CONDITIONAL	haría, harías, haría, haríamos, haríais, harían
IMPERATIVE	haz (no hagas), haga, hagamos, haced (no hagáis), hagan
PRESENT SUBJUNCTIVE	haga, hagas, haga, hagamos, hagáis, hagan
IMPERFECT SUBJUNCTIVE	hiciera (hiciese), hicieras, hiciera, hiciéramos, hicierais, hicieran
PAST PARTICIPLE	hecho

ir *to go*

PRESENT INDICATIVE	voy, vas, va, vamos, vais, van
PRETERIT	fui, fuiste, fue, fuimos, fuisteis, fueron
IMPERATIVE	ve (no vayas), vaya, vamos/(no) vayamos, id (no vayáis), vayan
PRESENT SUBJUNCTIVE	vaya, vayas, vaya, vayamos, vayáis, vayan
IMPERFECT SUBJUNCTIVE	fuera (fuese), fueras, fuera, fuéramos, fuerais, fueran
PRESENT PARTICIPLE	yendo

oír *to hear*	
PRESENT INDICATIVE	oigo, oyes, oye, oímos, oís, oyen
PRETERIT	oí, oíste, oyó, oímos, oísteis, oyeron
IMPERATIVE	oye (no oigas), oiga, oigamos, oíd (no oigáis), oigan
PRESENT SUBJUNCTIVE	oiga, oigas, oiga, oigamos, oigáis, oigan
IMPERFECT SUBJUNCTIVE	oyera (oyese), oyeras, oyera, oyéramos, oyerais, oyeran
PRESENT PARTICIPLE	oyendo
PAST PARTICIPLE	oído

poder *to be able, can*	
PRESENT INDICATIVE	puedo, puedes, puede, podemos, podéis, pueden
PRETERIT	pude, pudiste, pudo, pudimos, pudisteis, pudieron
FUTURE	podré, podrás, podrá, podremos, podréis, podrán
CONDITIONAL	podría, podrías, podría, podríamos, podríais, podrían
IMPERATIVE	puede, pueda, podamos, poded, puedan
PRESENT SUBJUNCTIVE	pueda, puedas, pueda, podamos, podáis, puedan
IMPERFECT SUBJUNCTIVE	pudiera (pudiese), pudieras, pudiera, pudiéramos, pudierais, pudieran
PRESENT PARTICIPLE	pudiendo

poner *to put*	
PRESENT INDICATIVE	pongo, pones, pone, ponemos, ponéis, ponen
PRETERIT	puse, pusiste, puso, pusimos, pusisteis, pusieron
FUTURE	pondré, pondrás, pondrá, pondremos, pondréis, pondrán
CONDITIONAL	pondría, pondrías, pondría, pondríamos, pondríais, pondrían
IMPERATIVE	pon (no pongas), ponga, pongamos, poned (no pongáis), pongan
PRESENT SUBJUNCTIVE	ponga, pongas, ponga, pongamos, pongáis, pongan
IMPERFECT SUBJUNCTIVE	pusiera (pusiese), pusieras, pusiera, pusiéramos, pusierais, pusieran
PAST PARTICIPLE	puesto

producir *to produce*

PRESENT INDICATIVE	produzco, produces, produce, producimos, producís, producen
PRETERIT	produje, produjiste, produjo, produjimos, produjisteis, produjeron
IMPERATIVE	produce (no produzcas), produzca, produzcamos, producid (no produzcáis), produzcan
PRESENT SUBJUNCTIVE	produzca, produzcas, produzca, produzcamos, produzcáis, produzcan
IMPERFECT SUBJUNCTIVE	produjera (produjese), produjeras, produjera, produjéramos, produjerais, produjeran

querer *to want*

PRESENT INDICATIVE	quiero, quieres, quiere, queremos, queréis, quieren
PRETERIT	quise, quisiste, quiso, quisimos, quisisteis, quisieron
FUTURE	querré, querrás, querrá, querremos, querréis, querrán
CONDITIONAL	querría, querrías, querría, querríamos, querríais, querrían
IMPERATIVE	quiere (no quieras), quiera, queramos, quered (no queráis), quieran
PRESENT SUBJUNCTIVE	quiera, quieras, quiera, queramos, queráis, quieran
IMPERFECT SUBJUNCTIVE	quisiera (quisiese), quisieras, quisiera, quisiéramos, quisierais, quisieran

saber *to know*

PRESENT INDICATIVE	sé, sabes, sabe, sabemos, sabéis, saben
PRETERIT	supe, supiste, supo, supimos, supisteis, supieron
FUTURE	sabré, sabrás, sabrá, sabremos, sabréis, sabrán
CONDITIONAL	sabría, sabrías, sabría, sabríamos, sabríais, sabrían
IMPERATIVE	sabe (no sepas), sepa, sepamos, sabed (no sepáis), sepan
PRESENT SUBJUNCTIVE	sepa, sepas, sepa, sepamos, sepáis, sepan
IMPERFECT SUBJUNCTIVE	supiera (supiese), supieras, supiera, supiéramos, supierais, supieran

salir *to go out*

PRESENT INDICATIVE	salgo, sales, sale, salimos, salís, salen
FUTURE	saldré, saldrás, saldrá, saldremos, saldréis, saldrán
CONDITIONAL	saldría, saldrías, saldría, saldríamos, saldríais, saldrían
IMPERATIVE	sal (no salgas), salga, salgamos, salid (no salgáis), salgan
PRESENT SUBJUNCTIVE	salga, salgas, salga, salgamos, salgáis, salgan

ser *to be*

PRESENT INDICATIVE	soy, eres, es, somos, sois, son
PRETERIT	fui, fuiste, fue, fuimos, fuisteis, fueron
FUTURE	seré, serás, será, seremos, seréis, serán
CONDITIONAL	sería, serías, sería, seríamos, seríais, serían
IMPERATIVE	sé (no seas), sea, seamos, sed (no seáis), sean
PRESENT SUBJUNCTIVE	sea, seas, sea, seamos, seáis, sean
IMPERFECT SUBJUNCTIVE	fuera (fuese), fueras, fuera, fuéramos, fuerais, fueran

tener *to have*

PRESENT INDICATIVE	tengo, tienes, tiene, tenemos, tenéis, tienen
PRETERIT	tuve, tuviste, tuvo, tuvimos, tuvisteis, tuvieron
FUTURE	tendré, tendrás, tendrá, tendremos, tendréis, tendrán
CONDITIONAL	tendría, tendrías, tendría, tendríamos, tendríais, tendrían
IMPERATIVE	ten (no tengas), tenga, tengamos, tened (no tengáis), tengan
PRESENT SUBJUNCTIVE	tenga, tengas, tenga, tengamos, tengáis, tengan
IMPERFECT SUBJUNCTIVE	tuviera (tuviese), tuvieras, tuviera, tuviéramos, tuvierais, tuvieran

traer *to bring*

PRESENT INDICATIVE	traigo, traes, trae, traemos, traéis, traen
PRETERIT	traje, trajiste, trajo, trajimos, trajisteis, trajeron
IMPERATIVE	trae (no traigas), traiga, traigamos, traed (no traigáis), traigan
PRESENT SUBJUNCTIVE	traiga, traigas, traiga, traigamos, traigáis, traigan
IMPERFECT SUBJUNCTIVE	trajera (trajese), trajeras, trajera, trajéramos, trajerais, trajeran
PRESENT PARTICIPLE	trayendo
PAST PARTICIPLE	traído

valer *to be worth*

PRESENT INDICATIVE	valgo, vales, vale, valemos, valéis, valen
FUTURE	valdré, valdrás, valdrá, valdremos, valdréis, valdrán
CONDITIONAL	valdría, valdrías, valdría, valdríamos, valdríais, valdrían
IMPERATIVE	vale (no valgas), valga, valgamos, valed (no valgáis), valgan
PRESENT SUBJUNCTIVE	valga, valgas, valga, valgamos, valgáis, valgan

venir *to come*

PRESENT INDICATIVE	vengo, vienes, viene, venimos, venís, vienen
PRETERIT	vine, viniste, vino, vinimos, vinisteis, vinieron
FUTURE	vendré, vendrás, vendrá, vendremos, vendréis, vendrán
CONDITIONAL	vendría, vendrías, vendría, vendríamos, vendríais, vendrían
IMPERATIVE	ven (no vengas), venga, vengamos, venid (no vengáis), vengan
PRESENT SUBJUNCTIVE	venga, vengas, venga, vengamos, vengáis, vengan
IMPERFECT SUBJUNCTIVE	viniera (viniese), vinieras, viniera, viniéramos, vinierais, vinieran
PRESENT PARTICIPLE	viniendo

ver *to see*

PRESENT INDICATIVE	veo, ves, ve, vemos, veis, ven
PRETERIT	vi, viste, vio, vimos, visteis, vieron
IMPERFECT INDICATIVE	veía, veías, veía, veíamos, veíais, veían
IMPERATIVE	ve (no veas), vea, veamos, ved (no veáis), vean
PRESENT SUBJUNCTIVE	vea, veas, vea, veamos, veáis, vean
IMPERFECT SUBJUNCTIVE	viera (viese), vieras, viera, viéramos, vierais, vieran
PAST PARTICIPLE	visto

Vocabulary List

This vocabulary list contains all words used in the exercises and the cultural chapters. It does not contain basic vocabulary covered in first-year Spanish nor does it include the words introduced in the **Estructuras en acción** sections. Verb irregularities are indicated in abbreviated fashion. Thus (**c** > **z/a, o**) means that **c** changes to **z** before **a** and **o**. Verbs marked *irreg.* should be looked up in the verb charts.

Note: In accordance with the latest spelling reforms of the Spanish Real Academia de la Lengua this vocabulary list does not treat **ch** *and* **ll** *as separate letters of the alphabet.*

a caballo on horseback
a causa de because of
(a)delante in front
a doble espacio double-spaced
a escondidas stealthily, behind someone's back
a espaldas de uno behind someone's back
a fin de que in order that
a finales de toward the end of
a fondo thoroughly
a fuego lento low heat, slowly
(a)fuera de outside of
a la americana, a lo americano American-style
a la derecha, a mano derecha on the right
a la española Spanish-style
a la izquierda, a mano izquierda on the left
a la medianoche at midnight
a la mesa at the table
a la salida de at the edge of, when leaving
a lo largo de along
a mediados de around the middle of (+ *month*)
a menos que unless
a menudo often
a mi juicio, a mi parecer in my opinion
a pesar de in spite of
a pie on foot
a principios de toward the beginning of
a regañadientes reluctantly
a través de through
a veces sometimes
a(l) mediodía at noon
abajo down, downstairs
abdicar (**c** > **qu/e**) to abdicate, abandon the throne
abierto open
el **abono** subscription
abrazar to hug, embrace
el **abrazo** hug
el **abrelatas** can opener
la **abreviatura** abbreviation
el **abrigo** overcoat
abril April
abrir to open
abrocharse los cordones to tie one's shoelaces
abstracto abstract
la **abuela** grandmother
el **abuelo** grandfather
los **abuelos** grandparents
aburrido: estar aburrido to be bored; **ser aburrido** to be boring
el **aburrimiento** boredom
aburrir to bore someone
aburrirse to get, be bored
acabar con to destroy
acabar de to have just done something
acabársele a alguien to run out of
acampar to camp
el **accidente** accident
la **acción** share of stocks
el **aceite** oil
el **aceite de oliva** olive oil
la **aceituna** olive
aceptar to accept
acerca de about (concerning)
acercar (**c** > **qu/e**) to bring something closer, over
acercarse to approach
acercarse a (+ *inf.*) to approach
el **acero** steel
acertar (**e** > **ie**) to be on target, guess right
achicar to reduce in size
aclarar to clarify
el/la **acomodador(a)** usher
acompañar to go with, accompany
aconsejar to advise
el **acontecimiento** event
acordarse (**o** > **ue**) **(de)** to remember
acostado lying down, in bed
acostar(se) (**o** > **ue**) to put to bed, go to bed
acostumbrarse a (+ *inf.*) to be accustomed to
la **actitud** attitude
la **actividad** activity
el **acto** act
el **actor** actor
la **actriz** actress
actualmente at present
actuar (**actúo**) to act
el **acueducto** aqueduct
adecuado adequate, correct
adelantado fast (*clock*)
el **adelanto** progress
adelgazar (**z** > **c/e**) to get thin
la **adhesión** membership
adjetival adjectival
el **adjetivo** adjective
¿adónde? where? (to what place?)
adorar to worship; adore
la **aduana** customs
el **aduanero** customs officer
adverbial adverbial
el **adverbio** adverb
advertir (**e** > **ie**) to notify, warn
el **aeropuerto** airport
el **afán** eagerness
afeitarse to shave
la **afición** hobby, avocation
el **aficionado** fan (*supporter*)
aficionado/a a la ópera opera fan
afinar to refine, tune
afligir (**g** > **j/a, o**) to afflict
aflojar to loosen
africano African
afroantillano pertaining to Caribbean blacks
las **afueras** suburbs
la **agenda (de entrevistas)** appointment book
agosto August
agotado exhausted

agradar to please
agradecer (-zc-) to thank
agrandar to enlarge
agrario rural, agricultural
agregar (g > gu/e) to add
agrícola agricultural
agruparse to be grouped
el **agua** water (*fem.*)
el **agua mineral** mineral water
el **aguacate** avocado
aguantar to stand
el/un **águila** eagle (*fem.*)
la **ahijada** goddaughter
el **ahijado** godson
los **ahijados** godchildren
ahogarse (g > gu/e) to drown
ahora mismo right now
ahorita right now
ahorrar to save
el **aire acondicionado** air conditioning
el **ajedrez** chess
el **ajetreo** hustle and bustle
el **ajo** garlic
al aire libre outdoors
al fondo in back, at the bottom
al lado next door, next to it
al lado de next to
el **alambique** still
alargar (g > gu/e) to lengthen
el **albañil** bricklayer
el **albedrío**: **libre albedrío** free will
la **alberca** pool
la **alcachofa** artichoke
la **alcahueta** go-between, procurer
el **alcalde** mayor
alcanzar (z > c/e) to reach, overtake
el **alcázar** citadel, fortress
la **alcoba** bedroom
la **aldea** village
alegrar to make someone happy
alegrarse to be glad, happy
alejar to move something away
alejarse (de) to move away from
el **alfabeto** alphabet
el **alfiler** pin
la **alfombra** carpet
algo something
algo de (+ *noun*) a little
algo: **algo así** something like that
algo: **Algo es algo. Más vale algo que nada.** Something is better than nothing.
algo: **De algo lo conozco.** I know you from somewhere.
algo: **tener algo que ver con** to have something to do with
algo: **Ya es algo.** That's something at least./It's a start.
algo: **¡Por algo será!** There must be a reason.
el **algodón** cotton
el **alguacil** marshall
alguien someone, somebody
alguna vez sometime
algunas veces sometimes
alguno some
el **alicate** pliers
alimenticio food (*adj.*)
alisar to smooth
allanar to flatten, level
allí arriba up there
el/un **alma** soul (*fem.*)
el **almacén** department store; warehouse
la **almendra** almond
el **almendro** almond tree
la **almohada** pillow
almorzar (o > ue; z > c/e) to eat lunch
el **almuerzo** lunch
alocar (c > qu/e) to drive mad (*with joy or delight*)
alquilar to rent
alrededor de around
los **alrededores** surroundings
la **altiplanicie** high plateau
el **altiplano** plain high in the mountains
la **altitud** height, altitude
alto high, tall; loudly
alto de estatura tall
la **alubia** bean
el **aluminio** aluminum
alzarse (z > c/e) contra to rise up against
el **ama de casa** housewife (*fem.*)
amable kind
amansar to tame, domesticate
amargo bitter
la **amargura** bitterness
amarillo yellow
amarrarse los cordones to tie one's shoelaces
el **ambiente** environment
amenazar to threaten
amenazar con to threaten to
la **amistad** friendship
el **amo** master
el **amor** love
ampliar to broaden
el **analista** analyst
la **anarquía** anarchy
ancho de espaldas broad-shouldered
el **ancla** anchor
el **andamio** scaffold
las **andanzas** wanderings
andar a gatas to crawl on all fours
andino Andean, of the Andes
el **anfiteatro** amphitheater
el **anfitrión** host
la **anfitriona** hostess
el **ángel** angel
la **angustia** anguish
el **anillo** ring
el **ánima en pena** soul in purgatory
el **animal** animal
la **animalada** stupid or gross thing to do
animar to cheer someone up, encourage someone
animarse to cheer up, take heart, feel like doing something
anoche last night
anónimo anonymous
antártico Antarctic (*adj.*)
los **anteojos** eyeglasses
anterior a before, preceding
anteriormente formerly
antes before (*adv.*)
antes (de) que before (*conj.*)
anticipación: **con anticipación** early
antiguo old; former
antillano West Indian

las **Antillas** West Indies, Antilles
antipático unpleasant
anunciar to announce
el **anuncio** ad
añadir to add
apagar to put out, extinguish, shut off, turn off
apagar el fuego to put out the fire
apagar las luces to put out the light
apañárselas to manage, get by
el **aparato** machine, appliance
aparecer (-zc-) to appear
apasionado passionate
apegarse to catch on
apenas hardly
el **apéndice** appendix, addendum
el **aplauso** applause
apodar to nickname
el **apodo** nickname
apoderarse (de) to take possession (of)
aportar to contribute
el **apóstol** apostle
apoyar to support (*morally, politically*)
aprender to learn
aprender a (+ *inf.*) to learn to
aprender de memoria to memorize
apresurarse de to hurry
apretar (e > ie) to be tight, squeeze
aprobar (o > ue) to pass (*course, test, etc.*)
aprovechar algo to take advantage of something
aprovecharse (de) to take advantage (of)
aproximadamente approximately
apuntarse to sign up
apuntarse a/para to register, sign up for
apunte: **tomar apuntes** to take notes
los **apuntes** notes
aquí abajo down here
aquí cerca near here
el/la **árabe** Arab
la **araña** spider
el **árbitro** umpire
el **árbol** tree
el **arbusto** bush
el/un **arca** ark (*fem.*)
el **archipiélago** archipelago, chain of islands
el **archivo** file, repository
el **arco de triunfo** triumphal arch
ardiente burning, fiery
el/un **área** area (*fem.*)
la **arepa** (Venezuela) white corn bread
la **argamasa** mortar
el/un **arma** arm, weapon (*fem.*)
la **armadura** suit of armor
el **armario** closet
el **armiño** ermine
el/un **arpa** harp (*fem.*)
la **arqueóloga** archeologist (*fem.*)
la **arqueología** archeology
arqueológico archeological
el **arqueólogo** archeologist
la **arquitecta** architect (*fem.*)
el **arquitecto** architect
la **arquitectura** architecture
el **arrabal** neighborhood
arrancar (c > qu/e) to pull/root out; start up (vehicle)
arrebatarle algo a alguien to snatch, grab something from someone
arreglar to arrange, straighten up; to fix
arreglarse to get ready, spruced up
arreglárselas to manage, get by
arrepentirse de (e > ie) to regret, repent
arriba up, upstairs
arrogante arrogant
el **arroz** rice
el **arrozal** rice paddy
el **arte** art (*masc.*); plural: **las artes**
el **artesano** craftsman
la **artesanía** handicrafts
ártico Arctic
el **asalto** attack
asar to roast
el **ascensor** elevator
el **asedio** seige
asegurar to assure
aserruchar to saw
asesinar to murder
asiático Asian, Asiatic
el **asiento** seat
el **asilo de ancianos** old age home
asistir a to attend
asociado associated
asomarse to lean out
la **aspiradora** vacuum cleaner
asumir to assume
asustar to frighten
asustarse to get scared
atacar (c > qu/e) to attack
el **ataque** attack
atardecer to fall (said of the evening): **al atardecer** at the end of the day
atarse los cordones to tie one's shoelaces
el **atentado** assassination attempt
el **aterrizaje** landing
aterrizar (z > c/e) to land
el/la **atleta** athlete
la **atracción** attraction
atractivo attractive
atraer (*conjugated like* ***traer***) to attract
atrapar to catch
atrás in back
atrasarse to get delayed
atravesar (e > ie) to cross
atreverse a (+ *inf.*) to dare to
atribuir (-uyo) to attribute
el **atún** tuna
aumentar to increase
el **aumento** increase
aún still, yet
aunque although
los **auriculares** earphones
ausentarse to be away, be absent
australiano Australian
autobiográfico autobiographical
la **autopista** superhighway
la **autoridad** authority
el **autosacrificio** self-sacrifice, self-immolation
la **avaricia** avarice
el **ave** (*fem.*) bird
la **avena** oats
avergonzarse de (z > c/e; o > üe) to be ashamed of
las **averías** breakdowns
averiguar to find out
la **ayuda** help

	ayudar to help
el	**ayuntamiento** city hall
el	**azafrán** saffron
	azteca Aztec
el	**azufre** sulphur
	azul blue
el	**azulejo** tile
	azul marino navy blue
el	**bacalao** cod
	bahamiano Bahamian
	bailar to dance
el	**bailarín** dancer
la	**bailarina** dancer
el	**baile de etiqueta** dress ball
el	**baile de gala** prom
la	**bajada** way down; decline
	bajar to go down(stairs); lower, turn down
	bajo softly
	bajo under
el	**balazo** a shot, a bullet wound
el	**balcón** balcony
	balear from the Balearic Islands
el	**balneario** beach resort
el	**baloncesto** basketball
el	**banco** bank
la	**bandeja** tray
el	**bandolero** bandit
la	**banquera** banker (*fem.*)
el	**banquero** banker
	bañarse to take a bath
el	**baño** bathroom
la	**barbarie** barbarism
el	**barco** boat
la	**barraca** hut, shack
	barrer to sweep
el	**barrio** neighborhood
	barroco Baroque
la	**base** basis: **a base de** on the basis of
la	**basura** garbage
la	**batalla** battle
	batir to beat
	bautizar to baptize
el	**baúl** trunk (car)
el	**bebé** baby
	beber to drink
la	**bebida** drink
la	**beca** scholarship
el	**béisbol** baseball
	belga Belgian (*masc. & fem.*)
la	**bella durmiente** Sleeping Beauty
las	**bellas artes** fine arts
la	**berenjena** eggplant
	besar to kiss
el	**beso** kiss
la	**bibliografía** bibliography
la	**biblioteca** library
la	**bicicleta** bicycle
el	**bien** good (*noun*)
	bien educado well brought up
los	**bienes** goods
el	**billete de avión** plane ticket
el	**billete de ida y vuelta** round-trip ticket
el	**billón** a trillion
la	**biografía** biography
	biográfico biographical
la	**biología** biology
la	**bisabuela** great-grandmother
el	**bisabuelo** great-grandfather
los	**bisabuelos** great-grandparents
el	**bizcocho** cake
	blanco white: **en blanco** blank
la	**blusa** blouse
la	**boca** mouth
el	**bocadillo** snack, small sandwich
el	**bocado** mouthful
la	**bola** ball
el	**boleto** ticket
el	**bolígrafo** ballpoint pen
la	**Bolsa** Stock Market, Stock Exchange
la	**bolsa de viaje** travel bag
la	**bomba de aire** air pump
el	**bombero** fireman
el	**bombón** (*pl.* **los bombones**) candy
	borbón Bourbon
	bordeado de árboles tree-lined
	borrar to erase
el	**bosque** woods
	bostezar (z > c/e) to yawn
la	**bota** boot
	botánico botanical
el	**botones** bellhop
la	**bóveda** arch
	bovino pertaining to cattle
	brasileño Brazilian
	bravo angry
	brillante brilliant
	brillar to shine
	brindar por to toast in someone's honor
la	**broma** joke
la	**bruja** witch
	bucear to go scuba diving
	buena gente nice (person/people)
la	**bufanda** scarf
la	**buhardilla** attic
el	**buque** boat
	burlarse de to laugh at, make fun of
	burlón(-ona) mocking, derisive
	buscar (c > qu/e) to look for
la	**búsqueda** search
el	**buzón** mailbox
el	**caballero** horseman, knight
el	**caballero andante** knight errant
el	**caballo** horse
	caber (yo quepo) (*irreg.*) to fit
la	**cabina telefónica** phone booth
la	**cacerola** saucepan
el	**cadalso** gallows
la	**cadena** chain
	caer (caigo) to fall
	caer: Me cae mal. I don't like him/her.
	caerle mal a uno to disagree with someone (*said of food*)
	caerse to fall down
	caérsele a alguien to drop
	café (*adj.*) brown
el	**café** coffee; café
	cafetero coffee-loving
la	**caída** fall

el **caimán** alligator
la **caja** box
la **cajera** cashier (*fem.*)
el **cajero** cashier
el **cajón** drawer, crate
la **cal** lime (mineral)
el **calambre** cramp
los **calcetines** socks (*Spain*)
la **calculadora** calculator
calcular to figure, to compute
el **cálculo** calculus
el **caldo** broth, soup
el **calendario** calendar
el **calendario trepado** tear-off calendar
calentar (**e** > **ie**) to heat
la **calidad** quality
cálido warm
callarse to keep quiet
calmar to calm someone down
calmarse to calm down
el **calor** heat: **Hace calor.** It's warm.
caluroso warm (*weather*)
la **cama** bed
el **cámara** cameraman
la **cámara** camera
la **camarera** chambermaid; waitress
el **camarero** waiter
el **camarón** shrimp
cambiar to change
el **cambio** change; exchange
el **cambio de ideas** discussion, exchange of ideas
caminar to walk
la **camisa** shirt
la **camiseta** T-shirt
el **campamento** camp
la **campaña** campaign
el **campeón** champion
la **campeona** champion (*fem.*)
el **campesino** peasant
el **campo** country(side); field
la **caña** sugar cane
canadiense Canadian
canario from the Canary Islands
la **cancha** court, playing field
el **candidato** candidate
cansado tired
el **cansancio** fatigue
cansar to tire someone out
cansarse to get tired
el/la **cantante** singer
cantar to sing
la **cantidad** amount, quantity
cantidades great amounts, an awful lot
la **capa** cape
la **capa social** social stratum
el **capital** money
la **capital** capital (city)
el **capitalismo** capitalism
el **capitán** captain
captar to capture
la **cara** face
la **carabela** sailing vessel
la **característica** characteristic
el **carbón** coal
la **carcajada** peal of laughter: **reírse a carcajadas** to burst out laughing
la **cárcel** jail
el **carcelero** jailer
carecer (**-zc-**) **de** to lack
el **cargamento** load, shipment
cargar (**g** > **gu/e**) to load; **cargar la batería** to charge the battery
el **cargo** position, official post
caricaturesco that caricatures
la **caridad** charity
el **carnaval** carnival (*pre-Lenten celebration*)
la **carne** meat
la **carne de res** beef
la **carnicería** butcher shop
cárnico meat (*adj.*); meat-packing
la **carpintería** carpentry
el **carpintero** carpenter
la **carrera** course of study; race
la **carretera** highway
el **carro** car (*Am.*)
la **carta** letter; menu
el **cartaginés** Carthaginian
la **cartera** wallet; purse
la **casa de campo** country house
la **casa editora** publishing house
casarse (con) to get married (to)
la **cáscara** shell, peel
el **casco** inner part of a city
la **castaña** chestnut
castaño brown (hair, eyes)
el **castaño** chestnut tree
castigar to punish
el **castillo** castle
castizo linguistically pure, well-written
la **casucha** hovel
la **catarata** waterfall
la **catedral** cathedral
el **caucho** rubber
el **caudillismo** strong-man regime
el **cautivo** captive
la **cebada** barley
la **cebolla** onion
ceder to yield
celebrar to celebrate
célebre famous
los **celos** jealousy; **tener celos** to be jealous
el **celta** Celt
el **cemento** cement
la **cena** dinner, supper
cenar to have dinner
el **cenit** high point, zenith
la **ceniza** ash
el **censo** census
el **centenario** hundredth anniversary
centrarse to be concentrated
céntrico central
el **centro** center, middle; downtown
el **centro comercial** shopping center
cepillar(se) to brush
la **cerámica** ceramics
cerca nearby
cerca de near; about (approximately)
el **cerdo** pig
la **cereza** cherry
el **cerezo** cherry tree
cerrado closed
cerrar (**e** > **ie**) to close

la **certidumbre** certainty
la **cerveza** beer
el **césped** lawn
la **cesta** basket
la **chachapa** Venezuelan soft tortilla
el **chalet** country cottage
el **champiñón** mushroom
el **champú** shampoo
el/la **chantajista** blackmailer
la **chaqueta** jacket
la **charada** charades
la **charla** chat, talk
charlar to chat
el **charol** patent leather
el **cheque** check
el **cheque de viajero** traveler's check
chino Chinese
el **chisme** piece of gossip
el **chorizo** sausage
ciego del ojo izquierdo blind in one's left eye
el **cielo** sky; heaven
la **ciencia-ficción** science fiction
las **ciencias** science
científico scientific
cierto certain; true
el **cigarrillo** cigarette
los **cimientos** foundation
el **cinc** zinc
el **cine** movies
cínico cynical
la **cinta** tape
el **cinturón** belt
el **círculo** circle, club
el **cirujano** surgeon
la **cita** date, appointment
la **ciudad** city
la **civilización** civilization
claro clear; light (*of colors*)
claro que of course (+ *verb*)
clásico Classical
la **cláusula** clause
el **clavel** carnation
el **clérigo** cleric, clergyman
el **clima** climate
el **cobalto** cobalt
cobrar to charge; to cash
cobrar más importancia to take on greater importance
el **cobre** copper
cocer (**c** > **z/a, o; o** > **ue**) to cook
el **coche todo terreno** jeep
cocido cooked
el **cociente intelectual** IQ
cocinar to cook
el **codazo** nudge, push with the elbow
el **código** code
el **código civil** civil law code
el **codo** elbow
coger (**g** > **j/a, o**) to grab, catch
coincidir con to coincide with
conjugar (**g** > **gu/e**) to conjugate
colaborar to work together
el **colchón** mattress
la **colección** collection
coleccionar to collect
el **colegio** school
colgar (**o** > **ue; g** > **gu/e**) to hang; fail a student
la **colina** hill
el **collar** necklace
colocar (**c** > **qu/e**) to put, place
la **colonia** colony
el **coloquio** panel discussion
el **colorido** color, coloration
la **comedia** comedy
comentar to comment, write about
comenzar (**z** > **c/e; e** > **ie**) to begin
comer to eat
comer fuerte to eat heartily
el **comercio** commerce, trade; store
comerse de envidia to be eaten up with envy
la **cometa** kite
cometer to commit
cómico funny
la **comida** food, meal; lunch (*Spain*)
comilón big eater, glutton
la **cómoda** chest of drawers
¿cómo? how?
cómodo comfortable
la **compañera de clase** classmate (*fem.*)
el **compañero de clase** classmate
compartir to share
la **competencia** competition: **hacer competencia** to compete
competente competent
el **complemento** complement, object
completar to complete
componer (*conjugated like* ***poner***) to compose
componérselas to manage, get by
la **composición** composition
la **compra** purchase: **ir de compras** to go shopping
comprar to buy
comprarle algo a uno to buy something from someone
comprender to understand; to include
comprobar (**o** > **ue**) to check
comprometerse to get engaged
el **compromiso** engagement
la **computadora** computer (*Sp. Am.*)
la **Comunidad Autónoma** administrative division of Spain
con tal (de) que provided that, as long as
concebir (**e** > **i**) to conceive
la **conciencia** awareness
el **concierto** concert
concluir (**-uyo**) to conclude
concurrido busy, much frequented
el **conde** count
condimentar to season
los **condimentos** spices, seasoning
conducir (**-zc-; -duje**) to drive
la **conducta** conduct
confeccionar to manufacture
la **conferencia** lecture
confesar (**e** > **ie**) to confess
confiar (en) (**confío**) to rely (on), confide (in)
conforme in agreement
el **congreso** conference
conífero coniferous
la **conjetura** conjecture
conmemorar to commemorate
conmover (**o** > **ue**) to move (*emotionally*)
conocer (**-zc**) to know

conocido famous
la **conquista** conquest
el **conquistador** conqueror
conseguir (**e > i**) (**consigo**) to get
consentir en (**e > ie**) to consent, agree to
conservar to preserve
el **conservatorio** conservatory
consistir en to consist of
constituirse (**-uyo**) to be formed
la **construcción** construction, building
construir (**-uyo**) to build
el **contacto** contact
la **contaminación** pollution
contaminado polluted
contar (**o > ue**) to count, tell
contar con (**o > ue**) to rely on
contener (*conjugated like* ***tener***) to contain
contento happy, content
la **contestadora** answering machine
contestar to answer
contestón given to answering back
la **continuación** continuation: **a continuación** below (*on a page*)
continuar (**continúo**) to continue
contraer (*conjugated like* ***traer***) to contract
el **contrapunto** counterpoint
la **Contrarreforma** the Counter-Reformation
contratar to hire
el **contratante** contracting party (*Lat. Am. hist.*)
contribuir (**-uyo**) to contribute
controlar la inflación to control inflation
convencer (**c > z/a, o**) to convince
el **convenio** agreement
convenirle a alguien (*conjugated like* ***venir***) to suit someone, be good for someone
convertir (**e > ie**) to convert
convertirse en (**e > ie**) to change into, become
copiar to copy
el **corazón** heart
la **corbata** necktie
el **corcho** cork
el **cordero** lamb
la **cordillera** mountain range
Corinto Corinth
el **coro** chorus, choir
la **corona** crown
correcto correct
corregir (**e > i**) (**corrijo**) to correct
el **correo** mail; post office
el **correo electrónico** e-mail
correr to run; to move (an object)
correrse to move over, make room for
la **correspondencia** mail
la **corrida (de toros)** running (of bulls=bullfight)
corriente current
el **cortacésped** lawnmower
cortar to cut
cortarse el pelo to get a haircut
la **corte** court
cortés courteous
cosechar to harvest
cosmopolita cosmopolitan
las **cosquillas** tickling
costar (**o > ue**) to cost; **costar un ojo de la cara** to cost an arm and a leg
costear to bear the cost of
la **costumbre** custom
el **costumbrismo** literary movement built around the description of local customs and manners
la **costura** sewing: **de alta costura** *haute couture*
el **creacionismo** creationism (*literary movement*)
creador creative
el **creador** creator
crecer (**-zc-**) to grow
el **crecimiento** growth
la **creencia** belief
la **cría** raising
el **criado** servant
criarse to grow up, be raised
el **crimen** crime
el **criollo** person born in the New World
la **crisis** crisis
el **cristal** glass
el **cristal de ventana** windowpane
el **cristiano** Christian
la **crónica** chronicle
el **cronista** chronicler
el **crucigrama** crossword puzzle
cruzar (**z > c/e**) to cross
el **cuaderno de trabajo** workbook
cuadrado square
el **cuadro** picture, painting
el **cuadro de costumbres** description of local customs
¿cuál?, ¿cuáles? which one(s)?
la **cualidad** quality, virtue, strong point
cualquier cosa anything at all
cualquier(a) any
¿cuándo? when?
¿cuánto? how much?; **¿cuántos?** how many?
cuarto fourth
el **cuarto de baño** the bathroom
cubierto overcast
el **cubierto** place setting
cubrir to cover
la **cucharada** spoonful
la **cuchillada** slash made with a knife
la **cuenca** river basin
la **cuenta** (bank) account; bill
la **cuenta corriente** checking account
cuenta: **darse cuenta de** to realize
el/la **cuentista** short story writer
el **cuento** short story
el **cuento de hadas** fairy tale
el **cuero** leather
la **cuestión** question, matter
la **cueva** cave
el **cuidado** care: **con cuidado** carefully; **tener cuidado** to be careful
cuidadoso careful
cuidar de/a to take care of
la **culpa** blame, fault; **echar la culpa** to blame
cultivar to grow (*trans.*)
culto educated
la **cumbre** peak, summit
la **cumpleañera** birthday girl
la **cuñada** sister-in-law
el **cuñado** brother-in-law
los **cuñados** brother- and sister-in-law
el **cura** priest
la **curiosidad** curiosity
cursar to take courses, to take (a course)
cuyo whose (*relative pronoun*)

las **damas** checkers
el **daño** damage, harm
daño: hacer daño to hurt
daño: hacerse daño to hurt oneself
dar de comer to feed
dar gato por liebre to put something over on someone
dar gritos to shout
dar un paseo to take a walk
los **dardos** darts
darse cuenta (de) to realize
darse prisa to hurry
el **dátil** date (*fruit*)
de alguna manera, de algún modo somehow, in some way
de día during the day
de ninguna manera, de ningún modo in no way
de noche during the night
de veras really
deber ought, must, to be supposed to
debido a due to
la **década** decade
la **decadencia** decadence, decay
el **decano** dean
decidir to decide
decidirse a to make up one's mind
la **décima** ten-line stanza (*type of poetry*)
décimo tenth
decir (*irreg.*) to say, tell
el **decorado** scenery
el **decreto** decree
dedicarse a (**c** > **qu/e**) to devote oneself (to)
el **dedo** finger
¿de dónde? from where?
defender (**e** > **ie**) to defend
la **defensa** defense
definitivamente definitively
dejar to let, leave
dejar caer to drop
dejar de to stop
dejar en paz to leave alone
delante de in front of
delgado thin
el **delirio** delirium, delusion
el **demagogo** demagogue, rabble-rouser
la **democracia** democracy
democrático democratic
demostrar (o > **ue)** to show
la **densidad** density
el/la **dentista** dentist
dentro inside
dentro de inside of, within
denunciar to denounce
depender de to depend on
dependiente dependent
el/la **dependiente** salesclerk in a store
el **deporte** sport
deportivo sport (*adj.*)
el **depósito de artículos perdidos** lost and found
¿de quién?, ¿de quiénes? whose?
la **derecha** right side: **a la derecha** to the right
derecho straight ahead
el **derecho** right (*privilege*)
derrotar to defeat
derrumbar to knock down, make collapse
desabrocharse los cordones to untie one's shoelaces
desamarrarse los cordones to untie one's shoelaces
desaparecer (**yo desaparezco**) to disappear
desarraigarse to be uprooted
desarrollar to develop
el **desarrollo** development
el **desastre** disaster
desatarse los cordones to untie one's shoelaces
descapotable convertible (*car*)
descender (**e** > **ie**) to go down
descolgado off the hook (*of the phone*)
descolgar (**o** > **ue**) to pick up the phone
descompuesto out of order
descongelar to defrost
desconocer (**-zc-**) not to know, be ignorant of
describir to describe
la **descripción** description
el **descubridor** discoverer
el **descubrimiento** discovery
el **descuento** discount
descuidado careless
desde since, from; **desde aquí** from here; **desde hace** since
¿desde cuándo? since when?
desdeñoso disdainful
desear to want
desembarcar (**c** > **qu/e**) to disembark
la **desembocadura** mouth of a river
desembocar en (**c** > **qu/e**) to flow out into (*of a river*)
desempeñar to carry out, perform
desencadenar to unchain, unleash; cause
desenchufar los aparatos eléctricos to unplug the appliances
desenredar to unravel, untangle
desenvolver (**o** > **ue**) to unroll
la **desgana** reluctance, weakness, faintness
el **desgraciado** unlucky
deshacer (*conjugated like* ***hacer***) to undo
desilusionado disillusioned, disappointed
la **desinencia** ending (*grammar*)
desleal disloyal
deslizarse to slip
desmayarse to faint
desnudo naked, nude, bare
desolado desolate
el **desorden** mess
desparramar to spill
despedir (**e** > **i**) to fire
despedirse (de) (**e** > **i**) to say good-bye
despegar (**g** > **gu/e**) to take off
el **despegue** take-off
despejado clear
despertar (**e** > **ie**) to wake someone up
despertarse (**e** > **ie**) to wake up
el **desplazamiento** movement, change of location
despreciable contemptible
destacarse (**c** > **qu/e**) to stand out
destapar to uncork
desterrar (**e** > **ie**) to exile
el **destinatario** addressee
los **destrozos** destruction
destruir (**-uyo**) to destroy
el **desván** attic
desvanecer (**-zc-**) to disappear
la **desventaja** disadvantage
el **detective** detective

detener (*conjugated like* ***tener***) to stop, bring to a halt; detain
detenerse (*conjugated like* ***tener***) to stop, come to a halt
detrás de in back of
la **deuda** debt
devolver (o > ue) to return, give back
el **Día de la Raza** Columbus Day
el **Día de los Enamorados** Valentine's Day
el **Día de los Inocentes** April Fool's Day
el **Día de Reyes** Three Kings' Day (*Jan. 6*)
el **día feriado** holiday, day off
el **diablo** devil
las **diabluras** mischief
el **diálogo** dialogue
el **diamante** diamond
diario daily
el **diario** diary; daily newspaper
dibujar to draw
el **dibujo** drawing
el **diccionario** dictionary
diciembre December
el **dictador** dictator
la **dictadura** dictatorship
didáctico didactic, instructional
la **dieta** diet: **a dieta** on a diet
la **diferencia** difference; **a diferencia de** in contrast to
diferenciar to differentiate
difícil difficult
difundir to spread
la **dignidad** dignity
digno de confianza trustworthy
la **dinastía** dynasty
el **dineral** fortune, huge sum of money
el **diplomático** diplomat
la **dirección** address
el **director** director
la **directora** director (*fem.*)
dirigir (g > j/a, o) to direct, conduct
el **disco compacto** compact disc
la **discoteca** discotheque
disculpa: **pedir disculpas** to apologize
disculparse (con) to apologize (to)
discutir to discuss, argue
la **diseñadora** designer
diseñar to design
el **disfraz** disguise
disfrazarse (z > c/e) (de) to disguise oneself (as)
disfrutar de to enjoy
disimular to hide the fact that, to conceal
disponer (*conjugated like* ***poner***) to dispose
disponerse a (+ *inf.*) to get ready to
distinguido distinguished
distinguir (gu > g/a, o) to distinguish
distraer (*conjugated like* ***traer***) to distract
distribuir (-uyo) to distribute
la **diversión** fun, amusement
divertir (e > ie) to amuse
divertirse (e > ie) to have a good time
dividir to divide
divorciarse to divorce
doblar to turn (change direction)
el **doceavo** twelfth
el **documental** documentary
el **documento** document
el **dólar** dollar
doler (o > ue) to hurt, ache
dominar un idioma to speak a language well
el **domingo** Sunday
el **Domingo de Resurrección** Easter Sunday
dominical Sunday (*adj.*)
el **dominio** mastery; domination, rule
el **dominó** dominoes
el **don** gift
el **don de gentes** charm, getting on well with people
¿dónde? where? (at what place?)
dorado gilded
dorar to brown
dormir (o > ue) to sleep
dormirse (o > ue) to fall asleep
dormirse en los laureles to rest on one's laurels
el **dormitorio** bedroom
dotado de having the gift of
el **dramaturgo** playwright
el **dramón** sob story
la **droguería** drugstore
ducharse to take a shower
la **duda** doubt
dudar to doubt
dudar en to hesitate over
dudoso doubtful
la **dueña** owner; chaperone
el **dueño** owner
dulce sweet
el **dulce de leche** custard dessert
el **duque** duke
durante during
durar to last
el **durazno** peach

echar to throw
echar la soga tras el caldero to throw good money after bad
echar(se) a (+ *inf.*) to begin to
echarse to lie down
echarse agua de colonia to put on cologne
echárselas de (+ *adj., noun*) to boast of being
el/la **economista** economist
el **ecoturismo** environmental tourism
la **edad** age
la **Edad Media** Middle Ages
el **edificio** building
eficaz efficient
ejecutar to execute
el **ejemplo** example; **por ejemplo** for example
ejercer (c > z/a, o) to exercise, exert, wield
el **ejercicio** exercise
el **ejército** army
los **electrodomésticos** household appliances
elegir (g > j/a, o; e > i) to choose, elect
embarcar(se) (c > qu/e) to embark, go on board
embellecer (-zc-) to beautify
el **embotellamiento** traffic jam
embotellar to bottle up
emergir (g > j/a, o) to emerge
emigrar to emigrate
el **emparejamiento** mating, pairing
empeñarse (en) to insist (on), persist (in)
empezar (e > ie; z > c/e) to begin
el **empleado** employee

emplear to use
el **empleo** job
empobrecer to impoverish
la **empresa** firm, company; undertaking
el **empresario** businessman
empujar to push
en broma not seriously, as a joke
en caso de que in case (*conj.*)
en cuanto a as for, as regards, in the area of
en lo alto up, up there, up high
en punto sharp (*said of clock time*)
en seguida right away
en un dos por tres in a jiffy
en/por algún lado / sitio / lugar somewhere
en/por alguna parte somewhere
en/por ningún lado / sitio / lugar nowhere
en/por ninguna parte nowhere
enamorado (de) in love (with)
enamorarse (de) to fall in love (with)
el **enano** dwarf
encabezar (**z** > **c/e**) to be at the head of; to head
el **encadenamiento** chaining
encadenar to chain
encantador charming, delightful
encantarle a alguien to love something
encarcelar to jail
encargar (**g** > **gu/e**) to put in charge, entrust, to order
encargarse de (**g** > **gu/e**) to take charge of
encasillar to pigeonhole
encender (**e** > **ie**) to light
encerar el piso to wax the floor
encerrar (**e** > **ie**) to lock in, contain
el **encierro de toros** running of the bulls
encima de on, upon, on top
encoger (**g** > **j/a, o**) to shrink: **encogerse de hombros** to shrug one's shoulders
encontrar (**o** > **ue**) to find
encontrarse (**o** > **ue**) to be located
la **encrucijada** crossroad
el **encuentro** meeting, sports match
la **encuesta** survey
enero January
enfadar to make (someone) angry
enfadarse to get angry
enfermar to make someone sick
enfermarse to get sick
la **enfermedad** sickness, illness
enfermo sick
enfocar (**c** > **qu/e**) to focus
el **enfrentamiento** clash, confrontation
enfurecerse (**-zc-**) to get furious
engañoso deceitful
engordar to get fat
engrasar to grease, lubricate
el **enjambre** swarm (*of bees, etc.*)
enloquecer (**-zc-**) to go crazy
enmascarar to mask
enmudecer (**-zc-**) to become mute
enojar to make (someone) angry
enojarse to get angry
enorgullecerse (**-zc-**) to become haughty
enriquecer to enrich
enriquecerse (**-zc-**) to become rich
la **ensalada** salad
ensañar to infuriate
ensayar to rehearse
el/la **ensayista** essayist
el **ensayo** essay
enseñar to teach; show
ensordecer (**-zc-**) to go deaf
entender (**e** > **ie**) to understand
enterarse (de) to find out (about)
enterrar (**e** > **ie**) to bury
la **entrada** entrance; ticket (*to sports event or show*)
la **entrada de datos** data input
entrar to go/come in, enter
entre between, among
entregar (**g** > **gu/e**) to hand in/over
entrelazado intertwined
el **entrenador** trainer, coach
entristecer (**-zc-**) to sadden
entusiasmado thrilled
entusiasmar to excite, thrill, stir
entusiasmarse to get excited, feel thrilled
entusiasta enthusiastic
envejecer (**-zc-**) to grow old
el **envenenamiento** poisoning
envenenar to poison
enviar (**envío**) to send
el **envío** shipment
envolver (**o** > **ue**) to wrap up
épico epic
la **época** era, epoch
el **equipaje** luggage
el **equipaje de mano** hand luggage
el **equipo** team
el **equivalente** equivalent
equivaler a to be the equivalent of
equivocarse (**c** > **qu/e**) to be mistaken
el **erudito** learned man
la **escala** scale
la **escalera** staircase
la **escalera mecánica** escalator
el **escalofrío** chill
escampar, despejar to clear up
escapar to escape
escaparse (de) to escape, run (from)
escaparse por un pelo to have a narrow escape, to escape by the skin of one's teeth
escaso rare, few, scarce
escayolado in a plaster cast
la **escena** stage
la **escenografía** staging
la **esclavitud** slavery
escoger (**g** > **j/a, o**) to choose
esconder(se) to hide
esconderle algo a alguien to hide something from someone
el **escondite** hide-and-seek
escribir to write: **escribir a lápiz** to write in pencil
el **escritor** writer
la **escritora** writer (*fem.*)
la **escritura** writing
la **escuadra** squad
escuchar algo/a alguien to listen to something/to someone
el **escudero** squire
la **escuela secundaria** secondary school
el **escultor** sculptor
la **escultora** sculptor (*fem.*)
la **escultura** sculpture

esforzarse por (**o > ue; z > c/e**) to strive to, try hard to
el **esfuerzo** effort
el **esmalte de uñas** nailpolish
la **esmeralda** emerald
el **esmoquin** tuxedo
el **espacio** space
español (**española**) Spanish
espantar to frighten
el **espanto** fright, scare
los **espárragos** asparagus
el **espacio en blanco** blank
el/la **especialista** specialist
especialmente especially
la **especie** species
el **espectáculo** spectacle
el **espejo** mirror
la **espera** waiting
la **esperanza** hope
esperar to wait, hope, expect
el **espía** spy
espiar (**espío**) to spy
el **espionaje** spying, espionage
espolvorear to sprinkle
esquiar (**esquío**) to ski
la **esquina** street corner, outside corner
la **estabilidad** stability
establecer (**yo establezco**) to establish
la **estación** station; resort
estacionar to park
el/la **estadista** statesman, stateswoman
la **estadística** statistic
el **estado** state
el **estado civil** marital status
estadounidense U.S. (*adj.*)
estafar to cheat, swindle
estallar to break out, burst
la **estancia** stay, visit
el **estante** shelf
la **estantería** bookcase
estar a punto de (+ *inf.*) to be about to
estar conforme to be in agreement
estar de acuerdo (con) to be in agreement (with)
estar de vacaciones to be on vacation
estar de vuelta to be back
estar para (+ *inf.*) to be about to
estar por (+ *inf.*) to be inclined to, be in favor of
estatal state (*adj.*)
la **estatua** statue
la **estatuilla** figurine
la **estela** stele, column
estético aesthetic
estilizado stylized
el **estilo** style
estrecho narrow
el **estrecho** strait
el **estribillo** refrain
estudiar to study
el **estudio** study
la **etapa** step, stage
la **etiqueta** label
europeo European
evangelizar (**z > c/e**) to Christianize, spread the Gospel
evaporar to evaporate
evidente evident

exagerar to exaggerate
el **examen** exam, test
exasperar to exasperate, make (someone) lose his/her patience
exasperarse to get exasperated, lose one's patience
la **excavación** excavation
excelente excellent
excepto except
la **excursión** tour, trip, excursion
exigirle (**g > j/a, o**) **algo a alguien** to demand something of someone
exiliar to exile
las **existencias** stock
el **exitazo** great success, hit
el **éxito** success: **tener éxito** to be successful
el **éxodo** exodus; mass emigration
expatriarse to leave one's country, become an expatriate
la **expectativa** expectation
la **experiencia** experience
experimentar to experience, experiment
la **explicación** explanation
explicar (**c > qu/e**) to explain
el **explorador** explorer
explorar to explore
explotar to exploit
la **exportación** export
la **exposición** exhibit
la **expresión** expression
expulsar to expel
extenderse (**e > ie**) to stretch, extend
extenso big, broad, extensive
extinguir (**gu > g/a, o**) to extinguish
extrañar to surprise; miss
extranjero foreign; **en el extranjero** abroad
extremadamente extremely

la **fábrica** factory
fabricar (**c > qu/e**) to make, manufacture
fácil easy
la **factoría** trading post
la **facultad** school or department of a university
la **facultad de medicina** the medical school
la **faja** cummerbund
las **fallas** floats; festival in Valencia, Spain
faltar to be absent; be missing
faltarle a alguien to be missing something, not to have something
la **fama** fame, reputation
familiar family (*adj.*)
los **familiares** relatives
famoso famous
el **fanfarrón** braggart
el **fantasma** ghost
los **faralaes** frills on a dress (*especially of the gypsy dresses used in festivals in southern Spain*)
la **faringitis** pharyngitis
el **faro** headlight
fascinarle a alguien to be fascinated
la **fe** faith: **de buena/mala fe** in good/bad faith
febrero February
la **fecha** date
la **felicidad** happiness
felicitar to congratulate
feliz happy

el **fenicio** Phoenician
el **fenómeno** phenomenon
las **ferias** fair, carnival
feroz ferocious, fierce
el **ferrocarril** railroad
el **festival** festival
fiarse (de) (**fío**) to trust
fiel faithful
el **fiestero** party-lover
la **figura** figure
figurar to appear, be represented
figurarse to imagine
fijar to set, fix, define
fijarse en to notice
la **fila** row
el **fildeo** fielding
filipino Filipino
filmar to film
el **filólogo** philologist
el **fin de semana** weekend
el **final** end
la **finca** farm
fingir (**g** > **j/a, o**) to pretend
la **finura** refinement
firmar to sign
flacucho skinny
el **flamenco** typical dance of southern Spain
el **flan** custard dessert
la **flauta** flute
el **flechazo** love at first sight
la **flor** flower
el **florero** vase
el **flujo** flowing
fomentar to promote
el **fondo** background
la **fonética** phonetics
el **fontanero** plumber (*Spain*)
la **forma** form, shape
la **formación** education, training
formular to formulate, phrase
el **formulario** form (*to fill out*)
forrado (de) lined (with)
la **fortaleza** fortress
forzar una entrada to break in
la **foto** photo
fotocopiar to make photocopies
la **fotografía** photograph
fracasar to fail
el **fracaso** failure
el **fraile** monk
el **frasco** small bottle
la **frase** phrase, sentence
la **fraternidad** brotherhood
frecuentar to go frequently to a place
fregar (**g** > **gu/e**) **las cacerolas** to scour the pans
freído past participle **freír** (**frito** more commonly used)
freír to fry
frenar to brake
frenético frenzied
los **frenos** brakes
el **frente** front (*weather, military*)
la **frente** forehead
frente: **en frente de** opposite
fresco cool; fresh
el **frijol** bean, kidney bean
el **frío** cold: **Hace frío.** It's cold.
frito past participle **freír**; **estar frito** to be all washed up, done for
frondoso verdant, green, rich in vegetation
la **frontera** border
el **frontón** court
el **fuego** fire
la **fuente** serving dish; fountain
fuerte strong; loudly
el **fuerte** fort
fumar to smoke
la **fundación** founding
el **fundador** founder
fundamental fundamental
el **fusil** gun, rifle
el **fusilamiento** shooting, execution by firing squad
fusilar to execute by firing squad
el **fútbol** soccer
el **fútbol americano** American football

la **gacela** gazelle
las **gafas** eyeglasses
la **gaita** bagpipe
la **galería** gallery
la **galleta** cookie; cracker
la **gana**: **no me da la gana** I don't feel like it
la **ganadería** cattle-raising
ganadero pertaining to cattle-raising
ganar to earn, win
ganarle algo a uno to win something from someone
ganarse la vida to earn one's living
las **ganas** desire, eagerness; **tener ganas de** to be eager to
el **garaje** garage
el **gas** carbonation
la **gasolinera** gas station
gastar to spend, waste
el **gasto** expense
el **gato** cat; jack (*car*)
gauchesco having to do with the Argentine **gauchos**
el **gaucho** Argentine cowboy
la **gaveta** drawer
los **gemelos** twins; binoculars; cuff links
gemir (**e** > **i**) to groan
generalmente generally
el **género** literary genre
generoso generous
genial very clever
el **genocidio** genocide
la **gente** people
geométrico geometric
el **gerente** manager
gimnasia: **hacer gimnasia** to do gymnastics
la **gira** tour, excursion
el **glaseado** icing
el **globo** balloon
gobernar (**e** > **ie**) to govern
el **gobierno** government
el **golfo** gulf
el **golpe** blow, hit
el **golpe de estado** coup d'état
la **goma** rubber; rubber band
la **goma de borrar** eraser
gordo fat
el **gorro** cap
el **gorro de cocinero** cook's hat

la **gota** drop (*of liquid*)
gotear to drip
gótico Gothic
gozar de (**z** > **c/e**) to enjoy
el **gozo** joy, enjoyment
grabar to record; carve
gracioso witty
graduarse (**gradúo**) to graduate
el **gráfico** graph
granadino from Granada
la **grandeza** greatness
granizar (**z** > **c/e**) to hail
la **granja** farm
la **grapa** staple
la **grapadora** stapler
Grecia Greece
griego Greek
la **gringa** immigrant girl (*Arg.*)
gritar to shout, scream
grito: **poner el grito en el cielo** to scream bloody murder
gritón loud-mouthed
grueso thick, heavy
gruñir to grunt
el **guacamole** Mexican avocado salad
los **guantes** gloves
guapo good-looking
guapote really good-looking
guardar to keep; put away
guardia: **de guardia** open 24 hours
la **guerra** war
guerrear to wage war
guerrero war-like
el **guía** guide
la **guía** guide (*fem.*), guidebook
guiar (**guío**) to guide
el **guión** script
el **guisado** stew
el **guisante** pea
el **guiso** stew

el/un **haba** bean (*fem.*)
la **habichuela** kidney bean
habérselas con to be up against, face, have to deal with
hábil clever
el/un **habla** speech; language (*fem.*): **de habla hispana** Spanish-speaking
hablador(a) talkative
hablar to speak
hablar en serio to be serious, mean what one says
hace (+ *time expression* + *present*) for (+ *time expression*)
hacer (*irreg.*) to make, do
hacer cola to stand in line
hacer diabluras to make mischief
hacer ejercicio to exercise
hacer el papel de to play the role of
hacer la cama to make the bed
hacer la compra to do the shopping
hacer la reservación to book
hacer las maletas to pack
hacer payasadas to clown around
hacer preguntas to ask questions
hacer saber to let someone know
hacer un inventario to take inventory
hacer un viaje to take a trip
hacer una pregunta to ask a question
hacerle caso a uno to pay attention to someone
hacerle falta a alguien to need something
hacerse (*irreg.*) to become
hacerse el desentendido to pretend not to understand
hacerse el dormido/la dormida to pretend to be asleep
hacerse el sordo/la sorda to turn a deaf ear
hacerse el tonto/la tonta to play dumb
hacerse tarde to get late
el **hacha** hatchet
hacia toward
hacia abajo downward
hacia adelante toward the front
hacia allá toward that place far away
hacia arriba upward
hacia atrás backward; toward the rear
la **hacienda** ranch, plantation
el **hada** (*fem.*) fairy
el **halcón** falcon
el **hambre** hunger
la **hamburguesa** hamburger
la **harina** flour
hasta until
hasta allí up to there
hasta pronto see you soon
la **hazaña** deed
el **hecho** act, deed, fact
hecho a mano made by hand
la **heladería** ice cream store
helar (**e** > **ie**) to freeze
el **henequén** hemp
heredar to inherit
el **hereje** heretic
el **herido** wounded person
el **hermanastro** stepbrother
el **hermanito** little brother
hermético hermetic, closed
el **héroe** hero
la **herramienta** tool
hervir (**e** > **ie**) to boil
el **hidalgo** nobleman
el **hielo** ice
la **hierba** grass: **mala hierba** weeds
el **hierro** iron
hincapié: **hacer hincapié en** to emphasize
hindú Hindu, Indian
el **hipermercado** large supermarket and discount store
la **hipocresía** hypocrisy
hirviendo boiling
la **historia** history, story
el **historiador** historian
el **historial** curriculum vitae; résumé
histórico historical
la **historieta** comic book
la **hoja** leaf, sheet of paper
la **hojarasca** dry leaves
holgazán(a) lazy bones
el **hombro** shoulder
hondo deep
honesto honest
honrado honorable
la **hora oficial** twenty-four hour clock
el **horario** schedule

el **horario corrido** workday without traditional lunch break
el **horario de trabajo** work schedule
la **hormiga** ant
el **hormiguero** anthill
la **hortaliza** garden vegetable
la **huelga** strike
el **huérfano** orphan
la **huerta** orchard
el **hueso de la alegría** funny bone
el **huésped** guest (*in hotel*)
el **huevo** egg
huir (-uyo) to flee
el/la **humanista** humanist
húmedo damp
humilde humble
el **humor** humor; mood; **estar/ponerse de buen/mal humor** to be/get into a good/bad mood
el **huracán** hurricane
el **huso horario** time zone

el **ibero** Iberian (*pre-Roman inhabitant of Spain*)
la **ida** trip to somewhere, first leg of journey
ideográfico pertaining to picture writing
el **ideograma** ideogram, pictorial character
el **idioma** language
la **iglesia** church
igual que just like
la **Ilustración** Enlightenment
la **imagen** image
imaginar(se) to imagine
impedir (e > ie) to prevent
el **imperio** empire
el **impermeable** raincoat
impersonal impersonal
imponer (*conjugated like* ***poner***) to impose
la **importancia** importance
importarle a alguien to care about something, to mind
la **imprenta** printing press
impresionado impressed
impresionante impressive
impresionar to impress, make an impression
impresionista Impressionist
impulsar to impel, push
incaico pertaining to the Incas
incansable tireless
el **incendio** destructive fire
inclinarse to bend over
incluir (-uyo) to include
independiente independent
independizarse (z > c/e) to become independent
indianista presenting the life of the Indians
indicar (c > qu/e) to indicate
indígena indigenous, Indian
indigenista Indianist, indigenist
indocumentado illegal, not having the necessary official papers
la **industria** industry
industrial industrial
la **infancia** childhood
el **infinitivo** infinitive
influir (-uyo) to influence
la **informática** computer science
el **informe** report
la **infusión de manzanilla** chamomile tea
la **ingeniera** engineer (*fem.*)
la **ingeniería** engineering
el **ingeniero** engineer
inglés (inglesa) English
ingresar to enter (*hospital, army*)
iniciar to introduce; begin
la **injusticia** injustice
inmenso immense
la **inmigración** immigration
innovador(a) innovative
inocentón naive
inolvidable unforgettable
la **inquietud** anxiety, restlessness
el **insecto** insect
insistir (en) to insist (on)
instalar to install
instalarse to move in
la **institución** institution
el **instituto** high school; institute
el **instrumento** instrument
insular located on an island
intelectual intellectual
inteligente intelligent
intenso intense
intentar to attempt, try to
el **intercambio** exchange
el **interés** interest
el **interesado** person interested
interesar to interest
interesarse en/por to be interested in
el **interior** inland, the interior
internacional international
el/la **intérprete** interpreter
interrumpir to interrupt
íntimo intimate
la **intriga** intrigue
la **introducción** introduction
introducir (-zc-, -duje) to introduce
el **introductor** initiator
intuir (-uyo) to intuit, feel
inútil useless
la **inversión** investment
invertir (e > ie) to invest
la **investigación** research
investigar (g > gu/e) to investigate, research
el **invierno** winter
invitar (a) (+ *inf.*) to invite (to)
ir (*irreg.*) to go
ir de camping to go camping
iraní Iranian
irlandés (irlandesa) Irish
irreal unreal
irse (*irreg.*) to go away
la **isla** island
israelí Israeli
el **istmo** isthmus
italiano Italian

jactarse de to boast about
el **jaguar** jaguar
el **jai alai** jai alai
jamás never
jamás: **jamás de los jamases** never ever
japonés (japonesa) Japanese

el **jarabe** syrup
la **jarcha** early Spanish couplet written in Arabic letters
el **jardín** garden
el **jarro** pitcher
los **jeans** jeans
el **jefe** boss
el **jerez** sherry
el **jeroglífico** hieroglyphic
el **jonrón** home run
el/la **joven** young man/woman
la **joyería** jewelry store
jubilarse to retire
judicial judicial
judío Jewish
el **juego** set
el **jueves** Thursday; **No es cosa del otro jueves.** It's nothing special.
el **juez** judge
el **jugador** player
jugar (u > ue) to play
el **juglar** minstrel, wandering poet/performer of the Middle Ages
el **jugo** juice
el **juguete** toy
julio July
junio June
junto a close to, right next to
la **juventud** youth

el **laberinto** maze, labyrinth
el **laboratorio** laboratory
el **laboratorio de lenguas** language lab
el **lado** side: **al lado** next door; **al lado de** next to
ladrar to bark
el **ladrón** thief, robber
el **lago** lake
la **lana** wool
el **langostino** prawn
lanzar (z > c/e) to throw
la **lástima** pity, shame
lástima: **estar hecho una lástima** to be a sorry sight
lastimar to hurt someone
lastimarse to get hurt
el **lavado** wash
la **lavandera** laundress
la **lavandería** laundry
el **lavaplatos** dishwasher
lavar to wash
lavar la ropa to do the laundry
lavarse to wash up
lavarse la cabeza to wash one's hair
lavarse los dientes to brush one's teeth
el **lazo** tie, bond
la **lección** lesson
la **lechera** dairymaid
leer to read
la **legumbre** vegetable
lejos far off
lejos de far from
el **lema** motto
la **lengua** tongue; language
lento slow
el **león** lion
la **leona** lioness
levantado up (*out of bed*)
el **levantamiento** uprising
levantar to raise; to get someone out of bed
levantar la mano to raise one's hand
levantar to lift
levantarse to get up, rise
la **ley** law
la **leyenda** legend
la **libertad** liberty
el **libre mercado** free market
la **librería** bookstore
el **librero** bookseller
la **libreta de apuntes** notepad
el **libro de consulta** reference book
el **libro de texto** textbook
el **liceo** high school
el/la **líder** leader
limarse las uñas to file one's nails
limitar to limit; border
el **limón** lemon
la **limonada** lemonade
la **limosina** limousine
el **limpiacristales** window cleaner
limpiar to clean
limpiarse los dientes to brush one's teeth
la **limpieza** cleaning
lindar con to border
lindo pretty, nice
la **línea** line
la **línea ecuatorial** equator
el **lino** flax
la **linterna** flashlight
el **lío** trouble, bad situation
lírico lyric
el **lirismo** lyricism
la **lista** list
listo: **estar listo** to be ready
listo: **ser listo** to be smart
literario literary
la **literatura** literature
el **litoral** coastline
llamar to call
llamar a la puerta to knock at the door
llamar la atención to attract one's attention, be noteworthy
llamativo attractive; showy
el **llano** plain, plateau
la **llanura** plain
la **llave** key
la **llegada** arrival
llegar to arrive
llegar a (+ *inf.*) to get to, succeed in
llegar a ser to become
llenar to fill, fill out
llenar el tanque del coche to fill the tank
llevar to carry, wear; take somebody somewhere
llevar a (+ *inf.*) to lead to
llevarse bien/mal con to get along well/badly with
llorar to cry
llorón always crying
llover (o > ue) to rain: **llover a cántaros** to rain cats and dogs
la **lluvia** rain
loco crazy
logrado well-done
lograr to manage to, be successful in

el **lomo** back of an animal; **a lomos de burro** riding a donkey
la **lotería** lottery; lotto
luchar (por) to struggle (for)
la **lucha de clases** class struggle
lucir (**-zc-**) to shine, show off
luego then, afterwards
el **lugar** place; **tener lugar** to take place
el **lugar histórico** historic site
el **lugar turístico** tourist attraction
el **lunes** Monday
el **luto** mourning; **de luto** in mourning

la **madera** wood
la **madrina** godmother
madrugador early riser
madrugar (**g** > **gu/e**) to get up early
la **magia** magic
magnífico magnificent
el **maíz** corn
majestuoso majestic
el **mal** evil (*noun*)
la **mala lengua** vicious tongue
malcriado spoiled
el **malecón** jetty
la **maleta** suitcase
el **maletín** small suitcase
mallorquín Mayorcan
malogrado ill-fated
el **manantial** spring (*of water*)
la **mancha** stain, spot
manco missing or having lost the use of an arm
mandar to order; send
el **mandato** command, order
el **mando** lead, direction
manejar to drive
la **manera** way, manner
la **mano** hand; **mano de obra** labor, labor force
la **manta** blanket, poncho
la **manteca** lard
el **mantel** tablecloth
mantener (*conjugated like* ***tener***) to maintain
la **mantilla** Spanish shawl
la **manzana** apple
el **manzano** apple tree
el **mañana** tomorrow
el **mapa** map
maquillarse to put makeup on
maquillarse la cara to put makeup on
la **máquina de lavar** the washing machine
la **maquinilla de afeitar** electric razor
el **mar** sea
el **maratón** marathon
la **maravilla** wonder
marcar (**c** > **qu/e**) to dial, mark
marear to make dizzy
marearse to get, feel dizzy
la **mariposa** butterfly
los **mariscos** shellfish
marítimo sea-going, maritime
el **mármol** marble
marroquí Moroccan
el **martes** Tuesday
el/la **mártir** martyr
marzo March

mascar to chew; **mascar chicle** to chew gum
la **máscara** mask
masticar to chew
matar to kill
materno: **lengua materna** mother tongue
la **matrícula** tuition
matricularse to register
maullar to meow
el **maullido** meowing
máximo maximum, highest
mayo May
la **mayonesa** mayonnaise
la **mayor parte (de)** most (of)
el **mecánico** mechanic
la **mecedora** rocking chair
mecer (**mezo; c** > **z/a, o**) to rock, swing (*a child*)
la **medianoche** midnight
las **medias** socks (*Sp. Am.*); stockings (*Spain*)
el **médico** doctor
la **médico; médica** doctor (*fem.*)
medio half; average
el **mediodía** noon
los **medios** means
medir (**e** > **i**) to measure
la **mejilla** cheek
el **mejillón** mussel
mejorar to improve
la **melancolía** sadness
la **memoria** memory
menos except
menos mal fortunately
el **mensaje** message
la **menta** mint
mentir (**e** > **ie**) to lie
mentiroso lying, fibbing
el **mercado** market
la **mercancía** merchandise
merecer (**-zc-**) to deserve
el **mercurio** mercury
la **merienda** afternoon snack; picnic
la **merluza** hake
el **mes** month
la **meseta** tableland, plain
mesopotámico between two rivers
mestizo of mixed Spanish and Indian blood
metafísico metaphysical
la **metáfora** metaphor
meteorológico weather (*adj.*)
meter to put inside, to insert
meterse a (+ *inf.*) to start to
meterse en to get involved in
el **metro** meter
el **metro** subway
la **mezquita** mosque
el **miembro** member
el **miércoles** Wednesday
miércoles de Ceniza Ash Wednesday
la **miga** crumb
mil millones a billion
la **milla** mile
la **mina** mine
minero mining (*adj.*)
minoritario minority (*adj.*)
la **mirada** look, glance
mirar algo/a alguien to look at something/at someone

mirón given to staring
la **Misa del Gallo** Midnight Mass
el **misionero** missionary
mismo himself
el **misterio** mystery
la **mochila** backpack
la **moda** fashion
el/la **modelo** model
modernizar (z > c/e) to modernize
moderno modern
modificar to modify, change
el **modismo** idiom
el **modisto** dressmaker
mojar to wet
mojarse to get wet
moler (o > ue) to grind
molestar to annoy, bother
molestarse to get annoyed
molesto annoying
el **molinero** miller
el **molino** mill
la **moneda** coin
la **monja** nun
el **mono** monkey
el **monólogo interior** internal monologue
el **monopolio** monopoly
la **montaña** mountain
la **montaña rusa** roller coaster
montar to set up, establish, launch
montar a caballo to go horseback riding
montar en bicicleta to ride a bike
el **monte** mountain
la **montura** frame (*eyeglasses*)
el **monumento** monument
morado purple
moreno dark-haired
morirse de sueño/risa to be dying of sleepiness/laughter
el **moro** Moor
el **mosaico** mosaic
el **mosquito** mosquito
el **mostrador** counter (*store*)
mostrar (o > ue) to show
el **motivo** motive, reason; motif, theme
la **moto** motorcyle
la **motocicleta** motorcycle
mover (o > ue) to move (*put in motion*)
moverse (o > ue) to move, stir, budge
la **moza** waitress; servant girl
el **mozo** waiter
la **muchachada** kid's prank
muchas veces often
la **muchedumbre** crowd
mucho antes a long time before
mudarse to move (*change residence*)
el **mueble** piece of furniture
los **muebles** furniture
la **mujer** woman
la **muleta** crutch
múltiple multiple
multiplicar to multiply
la **multitud** crowd, multitude
mundial world (*adj.*)
el **mundo** world
el **mural** mural
el/la **muralista** mural painter
la **muralla** fortification wall
el **murmullo** murmur
el **museo** museum
el **músico** musician
el **musulmán** Moslem

nacer (-zc-) to be born
el **nacimiento** birth
la **nación** nation
nacional national
la **nacionalidad** nationality
nacionalista nationalistic
nada nothing
nada de (+ *noun*) no, not any at all
nada: **antes de (que) nada** first of all
nada: **casi nada** hardly
nada: **como si nada** as if it were nothing at all
nada: **de nada, por nada** you're welcome
nada: **dentro de nada** in a moment
nada: **más que nada** more than anything
nada: **nada de eso** nothing of the sort
nada: **nada de extraordinario** nothing unusual
nada: **nada de nada** nothing at all
nada: **nada más** that's all
nada: **no por nada** for good reason
nada: **no servir para nada** to be useless
nada: **no tener nada de** (+ *noun*) to have no ____ at all
nada: **no tener nada de particular** to have nothing special about
nada: **por nada del mundo** for nothing in the world
nada: **quedarse en nada** to come to nothing
nada: **tener en nada** to think very little of; take no notice of
nadar to swim
nadie nobody
nadie: **ser un don nadie** to be a nobody
el **nadir** nadir, low point
el **nailon** nylon
la **naranja** orange
el **naranjo** orange tree
el **narcotráfico** drug trade
la **nariz** nose
el **narrador** narrator
narrar to narrate, recount
la **natalidad** birthrate
la **naturaleza** nature
el **naturalismo** naturalism (realism)
la **navaja** blade, knife
el **navegante** navigator
necesitar to need
negar (e > ie; g > gu/e) to deny
negarse a (+ *inf.*) **(e > ie)** to refuse to
la **negativa** negative reply
negro black
el **neoclasicismo** neoclassicism
neoclásico neoclassical
el **neologismo** new word, invented word
nervioso nervous
nevar (e > ie) to snow
ni hablar, ni modo nothing doing
ni, ni siquiera not even
ni ... ni neither ... nor
la **niebla** fog
la **nieta** granddaughter

el **nieto** grandson
los **nietos** grandchildren
la **nieve** snow
la **niñez** childhood
ninguno no; not one, none
el **nitrato** saltpeter
el **nivel** level
el **nivel de vida** standard of living
la **Nochebuena** Christmas Eve
la **Nochevieja** New Year's Eve
nombrar to name
el **nombre** name
nominal: **cláusula nominal** noun clause
el **noroeste** northwest
norteamericano American, from the U.S.
la **nostalgia** nostalgia
la **nota** grade, mark (*school*)
notar to notice
las **noticias** news
la **novedad** novelty
la **novela** novel
noveno ninth
el **noveno piso** ninth floor
la **novia** girlfriend
el **noviazgo** engagement, courtship
noviembre November
el **novio** groom, fiancé
los **novios** bride and groom
nublado cloudy
nuclear nuclear
el **número de teléfono** telephone number
nunca más never again
nunca, jamás never
nunca: **casi nunca** hardly ever
nunca: **el cuento de nunca acabar** the never-ending story
nunca: **nunca jamás** never ever
nunca: **nunca más** never again, no more
nunca: **¡Hasta nunca!** Good-bye forever!

o or
o … o either … or
obedecer (-zc-) to obey
obligar a (+ *inf.*) to force, compel to
la **obra** work (*literary or artistic*)
la **obra de teatro** play
la **obra maestra** masterpiece
las **obras públicas** public works
el **obrero** worker
observar to observe
el **observatorio** observatory
obsesionado obsessed
obtener (*conjugated like* ***tener***) to get
el **océano** ocean
octavo eighth
octubre October
ocultarle algo a alguien to hide something from someone
ocupado busy
ocupar to occupy, take up
ocuparse de to take care of
ocurrir to happen, occur
ocurrírsele a alguien to dawn on, get the idea of
odiar to hate
el **oeste** west
ofender to insult
ofenderse to get offended, insulted; feel hurt
la **oferta** offer
la **ofrenda** offering (*religious*)
la **oficina** office
el **oficio** trade, profession
ofrecer (-zc-) to offer
el **oído** inner ear
oír (*irreg.*) to hear
oler (o > hue) to smell
el **olivo** olive tree
el **olmo** elm tree
oloroso fragrant
olvidarse (de) to forget
olvidársele a alguien to forget
el **onceavo** eleventh
la **onomástica** system of personal names
la **ópera** opera
oponerse a (*conjugated like* ***poner***) to oppose, be against
la **oración** sentence; prayer
el **orador** orator
el **orden** order, orderliness: **poner en orden** to straighten up, put away
la **orden** order, command: **por orden de** by order of
el **ordenador** computer (*Spain*)
ordenar to clean up; order
ordeñar to milk
la **oreja** outer ear
la **orfandad** condition of being an orphan
oriental Eastern
el **origen** origen, background
la **orilla** shore: **a orillas de** on the shores of
el **oro** gold
la **orquesta** orchestra
el/la **ortodoncista** orthodontist
el **oso** bear
el **otoño** fall, autumn
otra vez again
ovino pertaining to sheep
el **oyente** auditor, listener

el **padrino** godfather
los **padrinos** godparents
la **paella** Spanish dish of rice and seafood
pagado: **estar muy pagado de sí mismo** to have a high opinion of oneself
pagar (g > gu/e) to pay
la **página** page
el **país** country
el **paisaje** landscape
la **paja** straw
la **pala** shovel; bat, paddle (*in jai-alai*)
palabra: **libertad bajo palabra** parole
las **palabras cruzadas** crossword puzzle
la **palabrota** dirty word
el **palacio** palace
la **palada** shovelful
palidecer (-zc-) to turn pale
la **palomilla** gang, group of friends
las **palomitas de maíz** popcorn
palpar to touch
el **panda** panda bear
la **pandilla** gang
el **pantalón vaquero** jeans

los **pantalones** pants
el **panteón** cemetery
la **papa** potato (*Am.*)
el **papel de escribir** stationery
la **papelería** stationery store
el **paquete** package
para con toward, with regards to
para entonces by that time
para otra vez for another (later) occasion
para que so that
¿para qué? for what purpose?
para siempre forever
para variar just for a change
el **parabrisas** windshield
el **parachoques** bumper
la **parada** stop (*bus, etc.*)
la **paradoja** paradox
el **parador** government-owned hotel (*Spain*)
el **paraguas** umbrella
el **paraíso** paradise; highest balcony in the theater
el **páramo** wasteland
parar to stop
el **pararrayos** lightning rod
pararse to stand up (*especially Span. Am.*)
la **parcela** plot of ground
parecer (-zc-) to seem
parecerse a (-zc-) to resemble
parecido a similar to
la **parodia** parody
parpadear to blink
el **parpadeo** blinking
el **párpado** eyelid
el **parque de atracciones** amusement park
parte: **una gran parte de** a large part of
particular private
el **partidario** supporter
el **partido** game, match
partir to leave
partir: **a partir de** starting with, from X on
pasado mañana day after tomorrow
pasar to spend (time), pass
pasar a ser to become
pasar la aspiradora to run the vacuum
pasar lista to take attendance
pasar por to pass by, to pick up (*someone*)
la **Pascua** Easter
pasear to walk around; take for a walk
pasearse to stroll
el **paseo** boulevard; walk
el **paso** step
paso a paso step by step
Pasó el examen por los pelos. He barely got through the exam.
el **pastel** pastry, pie
la **pastelería** pastry shop
el **pastelero** pastry chef
la **pata** paw; foot (*slang*)
la **patada** kick
la **patata** potato (*Spain*)
patinar to skate
el **patio** patio
la **patria** homeland
el **patrimonio** patrimony, heritage
patrocinado por sponsored by
la **patrona** patron saint (*fem.*)
la **payasada** clownish prank
el **payaso** clown
payo country, rural
la **paz** peace
el **peatón** pedestrian
el **pedagogo** educator
el **pedazo** piece
pedir (e > i) to ask for something
pedir prestado to borrow
el **pegamento** glue
pegar (g > gu/e) to stick; beat
pegársele a uno las sábanas to sleep late, sleep in
peinar to comb someone's hair
peinarse to comb one's hair
la **peineta** Spanish comb
pelar to peel
los **peldaños del éxito** ladder of success
pelearse (por) to fight (over)
la **película** film
el **peligro** danger
peligroso dangerous
la **pelota** ball
la **peluquería** beauty salon, barber shop
la **pena** shame, pity
el **pendiente** earring
el **pensador** thinker
la **pera** pear
el **peral** pear tree
perder (e > ie) to lose
perderse (e > ie) to get lost; to miss (*a show, movie, etc.*)
perdérsele a alguien to lose
la **peregrinación** pilgrimage
la **pereza** laziness
perfeccionar to improve
perfectamente: **estar perfectamente** to be in very good health
perfecto perfect
el **periódico** newspaper
el **periodismo** journalism
el/la **periodista** journalist
el **período** period (*time*)
la **perla** pearl
permanecer (-zc-) to remain
perpetuo perpetual
el **perrito** puppy
el **perro** dog
el **perro caliente** hot dog
perseguir (e > i) (persigo) to pursue
la **persona** person
el **personaje** character (*in a book, play*)
perspicaz perceptive
persuadir to persuade
pertenecer (-zc-) to belong
la **pesa** weight (*for lifting*)
la **pesadilla** nightmare
pesado heavy; boring, annoying
el **pésame** sympathy, condolence call: **dar el pésame** to pay a condolence call
la **pesca** fishing
el **pescado** fish
pescar (c > qu/e) to fish, catch
el **peso** monetary unit of several Latin American countries
pesquero fishing (*adj.*)
el **petróleo** oil
petrolero oil (*adj.*)

el **pez** fish
el **piano** piano
la **picadura** bite
picar (**c** > **qu/e**) to chop
el **pícaro** rascal, rootless young man (*hero of Spanish literary genre, the Picaresque novel*)
el **pico** peak
el **pie** foot
la **piedra** stone
la **piel** skin
la **pieza de repuesto** spare part
la **pila** battery (*flashlight*)
el **pimentero** pepper shaker
el **pimentón** green pepper
la **pimienta** pepper
la **pimienta picante** hot pepper
la **piña** pineapple
la **pinacoteca** painting gallery
la **piñata** paper-mâché or ceramic party figure full of sweets
el **pincel** paintbrush
el **pinchazo** blowout
pintar to paint
pintarse to put makeup on
pintarse los labios to put lipstick on
el **pintor** painter
la **pintora** painter (*fem.*)
pintoresco picturesque
la **pintura** painting
la **pirámide** pyramid
el **pirata** pirate
los **Pirineos** Pyrenees
pisar to step, step on
el **piso** floor
la **pista** track, trail
la **pista de baile** dance floor
la **placa** license plate
el **plan** plan
planear to plan
el **planeta** planet
la **planilla de retiro** withdrawal form, slip
la **planta** plant
la **planta baja** ground floor
la **plata** silver; money
el **plátano** banana
la **platería** silver shop
el **plato** dish, plate
la **playa** beach
la **plaza de toros** bullring
la **plenitud** height of literary production
el **plomo** lead
el **pluscuamperfecto** pluperfect
el/la **plusmarquista** record holder
pobre poor, unfortunate
la **pocilga** pigsty
el **poder** power
poderoso powerful
el **poema** poem
la **poesía** poetry
polaco Polish
el **policía** policeman
la **policía** policewoman; police force
el **poliéster** polyester
polinesio Polynesian
el **político** politician
el **pollo** chicken

poner (*irreg.*) to put
poner al horno to put in the oven
poner el grito en el cielo to kick up a fuss
poner en orden to straighten up
poner la mesa to set the table
poner por las nubes to praise to the skies
ponerse (*irreg.*) to become
ponerse (+ *article of clothing*) to put on
ponerse a (+ *inf.*) to begin to
ponerse de acuerdo to come to an agreement
ponerse de pie to stand up (*esp. Spain*)
por acá/ahí/allá/aquí around here/there/there/here
por ahora for now
por algún sitio/lado somewhere
por añadidura in addition
por aquel entonces at that time
por casualidad by chance
por ciento percent
por cierto certainly
por completo completely
por consecuencia consequently
por consiguiente consequently
por culpa de the fault of
por dentro y por fuera inside and outside
por desgracia unfortunately
por ejemplo for example
por esa época around that time
por escrito in writing
por eso therefore, that's why
por excelencia par excellence
por favor please
por fin finally
por las buenas o por las malas whether one likes it or not
por lo común usually
por lo demás furthermore
por lo general generally
por lo menos at least
por lo mismo for that very reason
por lo pronto for the time being
por lo que a mí me toca as far as I'm concerned
por lo tanto therefore
por lo visto apparently
por los cuatro costados on both sides
por medio de by means of (*a synonym of* ***mediante***)
por mi parte as far as I'm concerned
por motivo de on account of
por ningún sitio/lado nowhere, not anywhere
por poco almost
por primera vez for the first time
¿por qué? why?
por si acaso just in case
por si las moscas just in case
por su cuenta on one's own
por su parte as far as one is concerned
por supuesto of course
por último finally
por un lado, por otro on the one hand, on the other
la **porcelana** porcelain, china
el **porcentaje** percentage
porcino pertaining to pigs, swine
portarse to behave
portarse bien/mal to behave well/badly
el **porte** size, build
portugués (**portuguesa**) Portuguese

pos: **en pos de** after, in pursuit of
poseer to possess
la **posesión** possession
la **posguerra** post-war period
la **postal** postcard
posteriormente subsequently
el **postre** dessert
el **potencial** conditional tense
el **potencial compuesto** conditional perfect
potente powerful
la **práctica** practice
practicar (**c** > **qu/e**) to practice
el **prado** meadow
el **precio** price
preciso necessary
el **precursor** forerunner
predominar to predominate
preferir (**e** > **ie**) to prefer
la **pregunta** question
preguntarle a alguien to ask someone
preguntón(-ona) inquisitive
el **prejuicio** prejudice
el **premio** prize: **el premio gordo** jackpot
prender to turn on
la **prensa** press
preocupado worried
preocupar to worry someone
preocuparse to worry
preparar to prepare
prepararse to get ready
los **preparativos** preparations
prerrománico pre-Roman
la **presencia** presence
presentar to present, introduce
el **presente** present, present tense
presidencial president's, presidential
el **presidente** president
el **préstamo** loan
prestar apoyo to lend support
presumido conceited
presumir de to boast about
la **prima** female cousin
la **primavera** spring (*season*)
la **primavera**: **las quince primaveras** party for fifteen-year-old girls
primero first
primitivo primitive
el **primo** male cousin
los **primos** cousins
principal main, principal
el **príncipe** prince
prisa: **darse prisa** to hurry up
privado private
privatizar to privatize
la **probabilidad** probability
probar (**o** > **ue**) to try, taste
probarse (**o** > **ue**) to try on
el **problema** problem
el **procesamiento** processing
el **proceso** process
procurar (+ *inf.*) to try to
producir (**-zc-**) to produce
el **producto para la limpieza** cleaning product
el **producto químico** chemical
profundo deep
el **programa** playbill, program
el **programador** programmer
la **programadora** programmer (*fem.*)
prohibir to forbid, prohibit
prometer (+ *inf.*) to promise to
pronunciar to pronounce
la **propiedad** property
la **propina** tip
proponer (*conjugated like* ***poner***) to propose, suggest
la **prosa** prose
proseguir (**e** > **i; gu** > **g/a, o**) to proceed
el **prosista** prose writer
la **prosperidad** prosperity
el/la **protagonista** main character
proteger (**g** > **j/a, o**) to protect
el **provecho** benefit
la **provincia** province
provinciano provincial, of the provinces
próximo next
la **proyección** screening
el **proyecto** project
psíquico mental
publicar (**c** > **qu/e**) to publish
público public (*adj.*)
el **público** public
el **pueblo** the people
el **puente** bridge
el **puerto** port
el **puesto** job
la **pulgada** inch
el **pulpo** octopus
el **punto de vista** point of view
punto: **en punto** sharp (*of time*)
el **puñado** fistful
la **puñalada** stab
el **puño** fist
puro pure

¿qué? what?
el **quebrado** fraction
la **quebradura** fracture, break
quebrar (**e** > **ie**) to break
quebrarse (**e** > **ie**) (+ *part of the body*) to break
quedar bien to come off well, make a good impression
quedar boquiabierto to be open-mouthed with astonishment
quedar ciego, sordo, cojo to go blind, deaf, lame
quedar en to agree to
quedar en ridículo to look foolish
quedar mal to come off badly, make a bad impression
quedar to remain, be left
quedarle a alguien to have something left
quedarse to remain, stay
quedarse con to keep, hold onto
quedársele a alguien to leave something behind
quejarse de to complain about
quemar to burn
quemar(se) to burn
quesero fond of cheese
el **quiché** Mayan language
¿quién?, ¿quiénes? who? (*subject*); **¿a quién?, ¿a quiénes?** whom? (*object*)
la **quina** quinine
quinto fifth

quitarle algo a alguien to take something away from someone
quitarse (+ *article of clothing*) to take off
quizá(s) perhaps, maybe

el **racionamiento** rationing
radical in the stem (*grammar*)
la **radio** radio
la **rama** branch
el **ramillete** bouquet
rápido fast (*adj. and adv.*)
raro strange
el **rascacielos** skyscraper
el **rasgo** characteristic, trait
rayado scratched
la **razón** reason
reaccionar to react
real real; royal
realista realistic
realizar (**z** > **c/e**) to carry out, fulfill
realmente really
la **rebanada** slice
la **rebeldía** rebellion
el **recado** message
recaudar to collect (*money*)
la **recepción** check-in desk
la **receta** recipe; prescription
rechazar (**z** > **c/e**) to reject
rechoncho plump, chubby
recibir to receive
recién recently, just
reclamar to demand
recoger (**g** > **j/a, o**) to gather, pick up
recomendar (**e** > **ie**) to recommend
reconocer (**-zc-**) to recognize
reconquistar to reconquer
la **recopilación** compiling
recordar (**o** > **ue**) to remember
recordarle (**o** > **ue**) **a alguien** to remind someone
recorrer to travel through
recostarse (**o** > **ue**) to lie down
el **rector** university president
el **recuerdo** souvenir; remembrance; memory
recuperar to recover
el **recurso** device (*literary*)
la **red** net; network
la **redacción** editorial office (*newspaper*)
redactar to draw up, write, compose
la **redondilla** quatrain
reducir (**-zc-**, **-duje**) to reduce
reemplazar (**z** > **c/e**) to replace
referirse (**a**) (**e** > **ie**) to refer (to)
el **refinamiento** refinement
la **refinería** refinery
reformar to fix up, renovate
el **refrán** proverb
el **refresco** soft drink
el **regadío** irrigation
regar (**e** > **ie; g** > **gu/e**) to water
la **regata** boat race
regatear to dribble
el **regazo** lap
el **régimen** regime; diet: **a régimen** on a diet
regir (**g** > **j/a, o**) to rule
registrarse to check in
regresar to return, come/go back
el **regreso** return
rehogar (**g** > **gu/e**) (*Spain*) to brown
la **reina** queen
reinar to rule, reign
el **reino** kingdom
reír(se) (de) (**e** > **i**: **río**) to laugh (at)
el **relámpago** lightning
relampaguear to lighten
el **relato** narration, tale
el **relieve** surface variation
religioso religious
el **religioso** monk
relleno stuffed (*food*)
el **reloj** watch, clock
la **relojería** watchmaker's store, watch store
el **relojero** watchmaker
la **remolacha** beet
remover (**o** > **ue**) to stir
renacentista of the Renaissance
el **Renacimiento** Renaissance
el **renacimiento** rebirth
rendir (**e** > **i**) to surrender
el **renombre** fame
la **renovación** remodeling
renovar (**o** > **ue**) to renew
renunciar a (+ *inf.*) to renounce
reñir (**e** > **i**) scold
reparar to repair, fix
repasar to review
el **repertorio** repertoire
repetir (**e** > **ie**) to repeat; have a second helping
reponerse (*conjugated like* ***poner***) to get well
el **reportero** reporter
el **representante** representative
el **reptil** reptile
el **requisito** requirement
resaltar: **hacer resaltar** to bring out
el **rescate** ransom
la **reserva** reserve
resfriarse (**resfrío**) to catch cold
resolver (**o** > **ue**) to solve
respecto a about (concerning)
respirar to breathe
respondón insolent, given to answering back
responsable responsible, reliable
la **respuesta** answer
restar to subtract
la **restauración** restoration
restaurar to restore
el **resto** the rest, remainder
el **resultado** result
el **resumen** summary
retener (*conjugated like* ***tener***) to retain
retirar to withdraw
retomar to retake
retrasado slow (*clock*)
retratar to paint, draw the portrait of, depict
el **retrato** portrait
retumbar to thunder
la **reunión** meeting, get together
reunir (**reúno**) to join, gather, collect
reunirse to get together
revés: **al revés** backwards
el **rey** king
los **reyes** king and queen

rezar (**z** > **c/e**) to pray
Ricitos de Oro Goldilocks
el **riego** irrigation
el **río** river
la **riqueza** wealth
el **ritmo** rhythm
el **rizo** curl
robarle algo a alguien to steal something from someone
el **rodaje** filming
rodar (**o** > **ue**) to film
rogar (**o** > **ue; g** > **gu/e**) to beg, ask
el **romance** ballad (*poetic genre of Spanish literature*)
el **romancero** collection of ballads
el **romántico** Romantic
el **rompecabezas** puzzle
romper to break; tear
romper con to break off a relationship with
romperse (+ *article of clothing*) to tear; (+ *part of the body*) to break
rompérsele a alguien to break
roncar (**c** > **qu/e**) to snore
ronco hoarse
el **ronquido** snore
la **ropa** clothing
ropero pertaining to clothing
el **rotulador** felt-tip pen
el **rubí** ruby
el **ruido** noise
rupestre: **pintura rupestre** cave painting
ruso Russian

el **sábado** Saturday
saber (*irreg.*) to know
el **saber** knowledge
el **sabor** taste
saborear to savor
el **sabotaje** sabotage
sabroso tasty
el **sacacorchos** corkscrew
sacar (**c** > **qu/e**) to take out
sacar fotos to take pictures
sacarle algo a alguien to get something out of someone
el **sacerdote** priest
el **saco** jacket
el **saco (la bolsa) de dormir** sleeping bag
sacudir el polvo to dust
sagaz wise
sagrado sacred
la **sal** salt
la **sala** living room; room, auditorium
la **salchicha** sausage
la **salida** exit
la **salida de datos** data output
salir (*irreg.*) to go out
salirle mal a uno to turn out badly for someone
salirse con la suya to get one's own way
el **salón de actos** assembly hall, auditorium
salpimentar to season
la **salsa** sauce, dressing
saltar to jump
saltar a la vista to be obvious
saludar to greet
salvar to save
el **salvavidas** lifeguard; life preserver
salvo except
el **sancochado** Peruvian stew
el **sancocho** Venezuelan stew
las **sandalias** sandals
el **sánscrito** Sanskrit
Santiago Saint James
el **santo** saint; Saint's day
el **santoral** calendar of Saints' days
el **sapo** toad
el **sarampión** measles
la **sartén** frying pan (*also: **el sartén***)
el **secador** hair dryer
secar (**c** > **qu/e**) to dry
seco dry
secreto secret (*adj.*)
la **sed** thirst
la **seda** silk
seguir (**e** > **i; gu** > **g/a, o**) to follow, continue
seguir (+ *present participle*) to keep on doing something
según according to
segundo second
la **seguridad** security
seguro: **estar seguro** to be sure; **ser seguro** to be safe
el **sello** postage stamp
la **selva** jungle
la **Semana Santa** Holy Week
el **semestre** semester
semimítico partially mythical
el **senador** senator
la **señal** sign, roadsign
la **sencillez** simplicity
sencillo simple
la **sensibilidad** sensitivity
sentar(se) (**e** > **ie**) to seat, sit down
el **sentido de humor** sense of humor
sentir(se) (**e** > **ie**) to regret, feel
separarse to separate
septiembre September
séptimo seventh
el **sepulcro** tomb, grave
la **serie** series
serio serious
la **serpiente** snake
servir (**e** > **ie**) to serve; **servir de** to function as, serve as
el **seudónimo** pseudonym
sexto sixth
siempre always; **es lo de siempre** it's the same old story; **para siempre** forever
la **sierra** mountains, mountain range
la **siesta** nap
el **significado** meaning
siguiente following
el **silenciador** muffler
el **sillón** armchair
simpático nice, pleasant
simple simple
sin without
sin que without (*conj.*)
la **sinagoga** synagogue
sincero sincere
el **sindicato** union
la **sinfonía** symphony

la **sinfónica** symphony orchestra
sinfónico symphonic
el **sinnúmero** large amount
sino but (*after a negative*)
la **síntesis** synthesis
el **sistema** system
el **sitio** site, location
situado located
el **smoking** tuxedo (*also spelled* ***el esmoquin***)
la **soberanía** sovereignty
sobrar to be more than enough
sobrarle a alguien to have more than enough of something
sobre on, above, about
el **sobre** envelope
sobrehumano superhuman
sobresaltado startled
la **sobriedad** sobriety, restraint, moderation
sobrio sober
la **sociedad** society
el **socio** partner; club member; **hacerse socio de un club** to join a club
el **sol** sun; **hace sol** it's sunny
el **soldado** soldier
la **soledad** loneliness
solemne solemn
soler (**o** > **ue**) (+ *inf.*) to usually do something
solicitarle algo a alguien to ask, request something of someone
sollozar to sob
soltero single (*not married*)
el **solterón** old bachelor
la **solterona** old maid
solucionar to solve
la **sombra** shadow
el **sombrero** hat; **sombrero de copa** top hat
someter to submit, subject
someterse to submit, yield
el **soneto** sonnet
el **sonido** sound
sonreír(se) (**e** > **ie**) to smile
soñado dreamed of, ideal, perfect
soñar con (**o** > **ue**) to dream of, about
la **sopa** soup: **estar hecho una sopa** to be soaking wet
la **sopera** soup bowl
soplar to blow
soportar to stand
sórdido sordid, seamy
sorprendente surprising
sorprender to surprise
sorprenderse to be surprised
el **sorteo** drawing (*lottery*)
la **subconciencia** subconscious
el **súbdito** subject (*of a king, etc.*)
sube el telón the curtain goes up
la **subida** way up, rise
subir to go up; raise; (*trans.*) to take up
el **subjuntivo** subjunctive
sublevarse contra to rise up in revolt against
subordinado subordinate, dependent
subsistir to subsist, continue alive
el **subsuelo** subsoil
el **suburbio** suburb
suceder to happen
el **suceso** event
la **sucursal** branch (*of a business*)
sudamericano South American
el **sudoeste** southwest
la **suegra** mother-in-law
el **suegro** father-in-law
el **sueldo** salary
el **suelo** floor
suelto loose, disconnected
el **sueño** dream; sleep; sleepiness
la **suerte** luck
el **suéter** sweater
el **sufrimiento** suffering
sufrir to suffer
sugerir (**e** > **ie**) to suggest
suicidarse to commit suicide
los **sujetalibros** bookends
los **sujetapapeles** paper clips
el **sujeto** subject
sumamente extremely
sumar to add
la **superficie** surface
suponer (*conjugated like* ***poner***) to suppose
el **sur** south
surgir (**g** > **j/a, o**) to arise
suspenderle algo a alguien to revoke, cancel something of someone's
el **sustantivo** noun
sustituir (**-uyo**) to substitute
el **susto** fright, scare
susurrar to whisper
el **susurro** whispering

la **tabla** chart
tacaño stingy
el **taco** writing pad (*also,* ***el bloc de papel***)
el **tacón** heel (*of shoe*)
tal para cual two of a kind
el **tamaño** size
también also
tampoco neither, not either
tan pronto como as soon as
el **tanque de gasolina** gas tank
tapar to cover
las **tapas** hors d'oeuvres
la **taquilla** box office
tardar to be late; delay in, be long in
tardar en llegar to take long to arrive
la **tarea** assignment, task, homework
la **tarjeta (de crédito)** (credit) card
la **tasca** pub
el **taxi** taxi
el **teatro** theater
la **tecla** key (*on a keyboard*)
el **técnico** manager
la **teja** tile
tejano Texan
la **tela** cloth
la **telaraña** cobweb, spiderweb
las **telecomunicaciones** telecommunications
la **telenovela** TV serial, soap opera
el/la **televidente** TV viewer
la **televisión** television
el **televisor** TV set
el **tema** subject
temer to fear
la **temperatura** temperature

la **tempestad** storm
templado mild
el **templo** temple
temporal pertaining to time; temporary
temprano early
tener (*irreg.*) to have
tener personalidad to have personality or character
tener que ver con to have to do with
tener razón to be right
tenérsela jurada a alguien to have it in for someone
el **teniente** lieutenant
el **tenis** tennis
el/la **tenista** tennis player
el **tenor** tenor
teocrático theocratic
la **tercera edad** old age
tercero third
el **terciopelo** velvet
terco stubborn
terminar to finish, end
terminar de to stop
la **ternera** veal
la **ternura** tenderness
la **terraza** terrace
el **terremoto** earthquake
el **territorio** territory
el **terror** terror
la **tesis** thesis
el/la **testigo** witness
textil textile
el **texto** text
la **tía** aunt
el **tiempo**: **¿Qué tiempo hace?** What's the weather like?
el **tiempo** time
tiempo completo full-time
tiempo parcial part-time
tiempo: **¿cuánto tiempo hace que ...?** for how long?
tiempo: **hace buen/mal tiempo** the weather's good/bad
la **tienda** store
la **tienda de campaña** tent
el/la **tigre** tiger (also, ***tigresa***)
las **tijeras** scissors
las **tinieblas** darkness
la **tintorería** dry cleaner's
el **tío** uncle
los **tíos** aunt and uncle
típico typical
el **tiple** 12-string guitar typical of Colombia
la **tira cómica** comic strip
el **tirano** tyrant
tirar to throw
tirarse to jump, throw oneself; to lie down
la **tirita** strip
los **titulares** headlines
titularse to be entitled, have the title of
el **título** university degree
la **toalla** towel
el **tobillo** ankle
el **tocadiscos** record player
tocar (**c** > **qu/e**) to touch; play a musical instrument; **tocar a la puerta** to knock at the door; **tocar el timbre** to ring the bell
tocarle a uno to be someone's turn
todavía still
todavía no not yet
tomar to take, drink
tomar apuntes to take notes
tomarle el pelo a uno to kid someone
el **tomate** tomato
el **tono** tone
tonto silly, stupid
la **topografía** topography, land surface
la **toponimia** place names
torcer (**o** > **ue; c** > **z/a, o**) to twist
torcerse el tobillo to twist one's ankle
el **torero** bullfighter
la **tormenta** storm
tormentoso stormy
el **toro** bull
torpe awkward
la **torre** tower
la **torta** cake
la **tortilla** omelette (*Spain*); flat corn bread (*Mex.*)
la **tortuga** turtle
toser to cough
tostado toasted
el **total** total
trabajador(a) hard-working
trabajar to work; **trabajar por cuatro** to work like a slave
el **trabajo forzado** forced labor
la **tradición** tradition
tradicionalmente traditionally
traducir (**-zc-; -duje**) to translate
traer (*irreg.*) to bring
tragar (**g** > **gu/e**) to swallow
el **trago** swallow; (*alcoholic*) drink
la **traición** betrayal
traído por los pelos farfetched
el **traje** suit
el **traje de baño** bathing suit
el **trámite** procedure
tranquilizar (**z** > **c/e**) to calm someone down, reassure
tranquilizar(se) to calm down
la **transcripción** transcription
transcurrir to occur, happen, take place
transformarse en to change into, become
transitado trafficked
el **tránsito** traffic
el **transporte** transportation
el **tranvía** streetcar
el **trapo** cleaning rag
trasladar to transfer, move
trasnochar to stay up very late
el **tratado** treaty; treatise
tratar to treat; deal with, cover
tratar de to try to
tratarse de to concern, be a question of
la **tregua** truce
tremendo terrible
trepar to climb
el **tres en raya** tic-tac-toe
la **tribuna** seats
el **tribunal de exámenes** board of examiners
el **trigo** wheat
la **trilogía** trilogy
triste sad
triunfal triumphant
la **trompeta** trumpet
el **trompeta** trumpet player

tronar (**o** > **ue**) to thunder
tropezar (**e** > **ie; z** > **c/e**) to trip, stumble
trotar to jog
el **trozo** piece; excerpt
el **trueno** thunderclap
el **tubo** tube
el **tulipán** tulip
tumbarse to lie down, stretch out
el **turismo** tourism: **hacer turismo** to go sightseeing
el/la **turista** tourist
turístico of interest to tourists

el **umbral** threshold
único only
la **unidad** unity
unido united, close
unirse a to join up with
uno a uno one by one
la **urbanización** residential development
usar to use, wear
útil useful

la **vaca** cow
las **vacaciones** vacation
vacilar en to hesitate over
vacío empty
valer (*irreg.*) to be worth
la **valla** hurdle
el **valle** valley
el **valor** value; bravery
la **vanguardia** vanguard
la **vanidad** vanity, conceit
el **vapor** steam
variado varied
variar (**varío**) to vary
varios several
vasco Basque
el **vasco**, el **vascuence** Basque language
la **vega** plain
el **veinteavo** twentieth
el **velero** sailboat
vencer (**c** > **z/a, o**) to win, beat, conquer, overcome
la **venda** bandage
el **vendaje** dressing
vender to sell
el **veneno** poison
venezolano Venezuelan
vengar (**g** > **gu/e**) to avenge
venir (*irreg.*) to come
la **ventaja** advantage
la **ventana** window
la **ventanilla** car window; teller's window (station)
ver: **No los puedo ver.** I can't stand them.
veraniego summer (*adj.*)
el **verano** summer
el **verbo** verb
la **vereda** path
vérselas con to explain oneself to
el **vestíbulo** vestibule, lobby
el **vestido** dress
vestir(se) (**e** > **ie**) to dress
la **vez** time, occasion
la **vez**: **a veces** sometimes
la **vez**: **dos veces** twice
viajar to travel
el **viaje** trip: el **viaje de negocios** business trip
el **viajero** traveler
el **vicio** vice
vicioso depraved
la **víctima** victim
la **vid** vine
la **vida nocturna** night life
viejo old
el **viento** wind: **hace viento** it's windy
el **viernes** Friday
el **villancico** Christmas carol
el **viñedo** vineyard
la **viñeta** vignette
vinícola (*masc. and fem.*) wine-producing
el **vino** wine
el **vino de mesa** table wine
el **violín** violin
el/la **violonchelista** cellist
el **violonchelo** cello
la **viruela** smallpox
virreinal of the viceroyalty, pertaining to colonial Spanish America
el **virrey** viceroy
la **visa** visa
la **visita** visit
visitar to visit
la **víspera** day before, evening before
vivir to live
vivo: **estar vivo** to be alive; **ser vivo** to be quick, sharp
el **volante** steering wheel
volar (**o** > **ue**) to fly
el **volcán** volcano
volcánico volcanic
volcar (**o** > **ue; c** > **qu/e**) to knock over
el **vólibol** volleyball
volver a (+ *inf.*) (**o** > **ue**) to do (something) again
volverse to become
la **vorágine** vortex
la **voz**: **en voz alta** aloud; **en voz baja** in a low voice, softly
el **vuelo** flight
la **vuelta** turn; return trip: **a la vuelta de la esquina** around the corner

ya no no longer
el **yacimiento** deposit (*of oil, etc.*)
el **yacu-chupe** Peruvian soup
la **yema** egg
el **yodo** iodine
la **yuca** manioc root, cassava

la **zanahoria** carrot
la **zapatería** shoe store
la **zapatilla** slipper
los **zapatos** shoes
zapatos de tacón alto high-heeled shoes
zapatos de tenis tennis shoes
la **zona** zone, area, neighborhood
el **zoológico** zoo

INDEX

Acknowledgments

The publisher wishes to thank the following for permission to reproduce their material:

page 17: "Don Planchón" (*Cambio 16*, Madrid, España; 26 septiembre 1994, No. 1.192, pág. 42).

page 29: Consorcio Transportes, Madrid (España).

page 50: "Tiempos difíciles" (*Cambio 16*, Madrid, España; 23 enero 1995, No. 1.209, pág. 100). "Los jueves, la química del éxito" (*Cambio 16*, Madrid, España; 6 marzo 1995, No. 1.215).

page 67: "¿Dónde está mi violín?" (*Cambio 16*, Madrid, España; 23 enero 1995, No. 1.209, págs. 80-82).

page 87: "Piedra santa" (photo from *Spain 1993*, Ministerio del Portavoz del Gobierno, page 99).

page 101: "Matrimonio—Sí quiero pero menos" (*Cambio 16*, Madrid, España; 20 marzo 1995, No. 1.217, págs. 18, 22).

page 125: "México se asfixia" (*Semana*, Bogotá, Colombia; abril 4-11 de 1995, Edición No. 674, pág. 93).

page 134: "Cursos y conferencias" (*Los Andes*, Mendoza, Argentina; lunes, 3 de abril 1995, pág. 12; año CXIII, no. 38.095). "Universidades" (*Los Andes*, Mendoza, Argentina; lunes, 3 de abril 1995, pág, 8; año CXIII, No. 38.095).

page 149: "La crisis no perdona: Portugal espera menos turistas españoles" (*ABC*, Madrid, España; sábado, 8/IV/95, pág. 72).

page 161: "¡Basta ya de perder . . . !" (*El País*, Madrid, España; martes, 18 de abril de 1995).

pages 196-197: "Exámenes: La prueba final" (*Cambio 16*, Madrid, España; 22 mayo 1995, No. 1,226, págs. 62, 64-65).

page 207: "Costa Cruceros" (*El País*, Madrid, España; miércoles, 7 de junio de 1995, pág. 54). "Tele ABC" (*ABC*, Madrid, España; jueves, 15/VI/95, pág. 22). "SEAT" (*El País*, Madrid, España; miércoles, 7 de junio de 1995, pág. 45). "Olivetti" (*El País*, Madrid, España; miércoles, 7 de junio de 1995, pág. 7). "Paradores" (*ABC*, Madrid, España; jueves, 15/VI/95, pág. 61).

page 225: "No permitas . . . " (*ABC*, Madrid, España; jueves, 15/VI/95, pág. 102). "Bellsouth . . . " (*El Mercurio*, Santiago de Chile; lunes, 3 de abril de 1995, C-3). "Acer . . . " (*Excelsior*, México, D.F.; lunes, 3 de abril de 1995, pág. 18-A). "American Language . . . " (*El diario /La prensa*, Nueva York, domingo, 9 de abril de 1995, pág 9).

page 261: "Veladas literarias" (*ABC*, Madrid, España; domingo, 2/VII/95, pág. 68).

page 292: "El tiempo" (*ABC*, Madrid, España; 2/VII/95, pág. 66. *El País*, Madrid, España; domingo, 2 de julio de 1995, pág. 36).

page 337: "Con una casa . . . " (*ABC*, Madrid, España; sábado, 15/VII/95, pág. 41).

page 381: "Un agente . . . " (*ABC*, Madrid, España; viernes, 21/VII/95, pág. 11).

page 409: "Tierra Santa" (*Excelsior*, México, D.F.)

page 419: "Tren tierras del Cid" (*Pasa a la historia*; RENFE, Trenes turísticos).

Notas

Notas

Notas

Notas